AND BOOK TRAINING PACKAGE AVAILABLE

D1825439

ExamSim

Experience accurate, simulated exams on your own computer with interactive ExamSim software. This computer-based test engine offers knowledge-based and scenario-based questions modeled after the real exam questions and exam review tools that show you where you went wrong and why. ExamSim also allows you to mark questions for further review and provides a score report that shows your overall performance on the exam.

Knowledge-based questions present challenging material in a multiple-choice format. Answer treatments not only explain why the correct options are right, they also tell you why the incorrect answers are wrong.

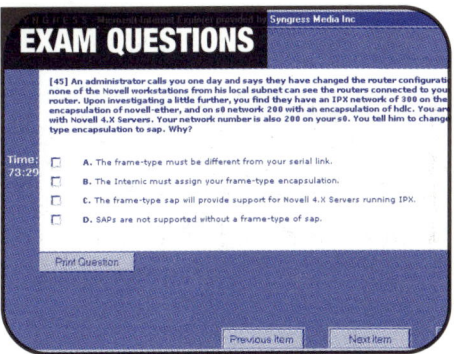

Scenario-based questions challenge your ability to analyze and address complex, real-world case studies.

Additional CD-ROM Features

- Complete hyperlinked **e-book** for easy information access and self-paced study

System Requirements:

A PC running Microsoft® Internet Explorer version 5 or higher

The **Score Report** provides an overall assessment of your exam performance as well as performance history.

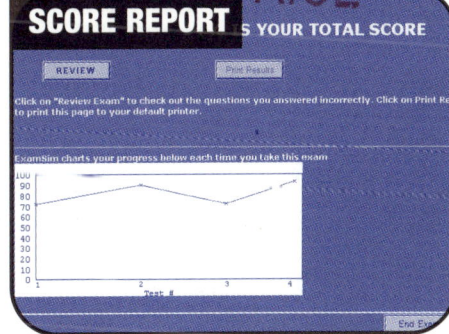

MCSE Supporting and Maintaining a Windows NT® Server 4.0 Network Study Guide

(Exam 70-244)

MCSE Supporting and
Maintaining a Windows NT®
Server 4.0 Network
Study Guide

(Exam 70-244)

Syngress Media, Inc.

Osborne McGraw-Hill

New York   Chicago   San Francisco   Lisbon   London   Madrid
Mexico City   Milan   New Delhi   San Juan   Seoul   Singapore   Sydney   Toronto

Osborne/**McGraw-Hill**
2600 Tenth Street
Berkeley, California 94710
U.S.A.

To arrange bulk purchase discounts for sales promotions, premiums, or fund-raisers, please contact Osborne/**McGraw-Hill** at the above address. For information on translations or book distributors outside the U.S.A., please see the International Contact Information page immediately following the index of this book.

MCSE Supporting and Maintaining a Microsoft Windows NT® Server 4.0 Network Study Guide (Exam 70-244)

1234567890 DOC DOC 01987654321

Book p/n 0-07-219163-5 and CD p/n 0-07-219162-7
parts of ISBN 0-07-219161-9

Publisher Brandon A. Nordin	**Editorial Management** Syngress Media, Inc.	**Indexer** Valerie Robbins
Vice President and Associate Publisher Scott Rogers	**Technical Editor** James Truscott	**Computer Designers** Carie Abrew George Charbak Elizabeth Jang
Acquisitions Editor Nancy Maragioglio	**Technical Reviewer** Ryan Neil Sokolowski	**Illustrators** Michael Mueller
Project Editor Patty Mon	**Copy Editor** Michael McGee	Alex Putney Beth Young
Acquisitions Coordinator Jessica Wilson	**Proofreader** Stefany Otis	**Series Design** Roberta Steele

This book was published with Corel VENTURA™ Publisher.

FOREWORD

From Global Knowledge

At Global Knowledge we strive to support the multiplicity of learning styles required by our students to achieve success as technical professionals. In this series of books, it is our intention to offer the reader a valuable tool for successful completion of the Supporting and Maintaining a Microsoft Windows NT Server 4.0 Network Certification Exam.

As the world's largest IT training company, Global Knowledge is uniquely positioned to offer these books. The expertise gained each year from providing instructor-led training to hundreds of thousands of students worldwide has been captured in book form to enhance your learning experience. We hope that the quality of these books demonstrates our commitment to your lifelong learning success. Whether you choose to learn through the written word, computer-based training, Web delivery, or instructor-led training, Global Knowledge is committed to providing you the very best in each of those categories. For those of you who know Global Knowledge, or those of you who have just found us for the first time, our goal is to be your lifelong competency partner.

Thank you for the opportunity to serve you. We look forward to serving your needs again in the future.

Warmest regards,

Duncan Anderson
President and Chief Executive Officer, Global Knowledge

The Global Knowledge Advantage

Global Knowledge has a global delivery system for its products and services. The company has 28 subsidiaries, and offers its programs through a total of 60+ locations. No other vendor can provide consistent services across a geographic area this large. Global Knowledge is the largest independent information technology education provider, offering programs on a variety of platforms. This enables our multi-platform and multi-national customers to obtain all of their programs from a single vendor. The company has developed the unique Competus™ Framework software tool and methodology which can quickly reconfigure courseware to the proficiency level of a student on an interactive basis. Combined with self-paced and on-line programs, this technology can reduce the time required for training by prescribing content in only the deficient skills areas. The company has fully automated every aspect of the education process, from registration and follow-up, to "just-in-time" production of courseware. Global Knowledge Network through its Enterprise Services Consultancy, can customize programs and products to suit the needs of an individual customer.

Global Knowledge Classroom Education Programs

The backbone of our delivery options is classroom-based education. Our modern, well-equipped facilities staffed with the finest instructors offer programs in a wide variety of information technology topics, many of which lead to professional certifications.

Custom Learning Solutions

This delivery option has been created for companies and governments that value customized learning solutions. For them, our consultancy-based approach of developing targeted education solutions is most effective at helping them meet specific objectives.

Self-Paced and Multimedia Products

This delivery option offers self-paced program titles in interactive CD-ROM, videotape and audio tape programs. In addition, we offer custom development of interactive multimedia courseware to customers and partners. Call us at 1-888-427-4228.

Electronic Delivery of Training

Our network-based training service delivers efficient competency-based, interactive training via the World Wide Web and organizational intranets. This leading-edge delivery option provides a custom learning path and "just-in-time" training for maximum convenience to students.

ARG

American Research Group (ARG), a wholly-owned subsidiary of Global Knowledge, one of the largest worldwide training partners of Cisco Systems, offers a wide range of internetworking, LAN/WAN, Bay Networks, FORE Systems, IBM, and UNIX courses. ARG offers hands on network training in both instructor-led classes and self-paced PC-based training.

Global Knowledge Courses Available

Network Fundamentals

- Understanding Computer Networks
- Telecommunications Fundamentals I
- Telecommunications Fundamentals II
- Understanding Networking Fundamentals
- Implementing Computer Telephony Integration
- Introduction to Voice Over IP
- Introduction to Wide Area Networking
- Cabling Voice and Data Networks
- Introduction to LAN/WAN protocols
- Virtual Private Networks
- ATM Essentials

Network Security & Management

- Troubleshooting TCP/IP Networks
- Network Management
- Network Troubleshooting
- IP Address Management
- Network Security Administration
- Web Security
- Implementing UNIX Security
- Managing Cisco Network Security
- Windows NT 4.0 Security

IT Professional Skills

- Project Management for IT Professionals
- Advanced Project Management for IT Professionals
- Survival Skills for the New IT Manager
- Making IT Teams Work

LAN/WAN Internetworking

- Frame Relay Internetworking
- Implementing T1/T3 Services
- Understanding Digital Subscriber Line (xDSL)
- Internetworking with Routers and Switches
- Advanced Routing and Switching
- Multi-Layer Switching and Wire-Speed Routing
- Internetworking with TCP/IP
- ATM Internetworking
- OSPF Design and Configuration
- Border Gateway Protocol (BGP) Configuration

Authorized Vendor Training

Cisco Systems

- Introduction to Cisco Router Configuration
- Advanced Cisco Router Configuration
- Installation and Maintenance of Cisco Routers
- Cisco Internetwork Troubleshooting
- Cisco Internetwork Design
- Cisco Routers and LAN Switches
- Catalyst 5000 Series Configuration
- Cisco LAN Switch Configuration
- Managing Cisco Switched Internetworks
- Configuring, Monitoring, and Troubleshooting Dial-Up Services
- Cisco AS5200 Installation and Configuration
- Cisco Campus ATM Solutions

Bay Networks

- Bay Networks Accelerated Router Configuration
- Bay Networks Advanced IP Routing
- Bay Networks Hub Connectivity
- Bay Networks Accelar 1xxx Installation and Basic Configuration
- Bay Networks Centillion Switching

FORE Systems

- FORE ATM Enterprise Core Products
- FORE ATM Enterprise Edge Products
- FORE ATM Theory
- FORE LAN Certification

Operating Systems & Programming

Microsoft

- Introduction to Windows NT
- Microsoft Networking Essentials
- Windows NT 4.0 Workstation
- Windows NT 4.0 Server
- Advanced Windows NT 4.0 Server
- Windows NT Networking with TCP/IP
- Introduction to Microsoft Web Tools
- Windows NT Troubleshooting
- Windows Registry Configuration

UNIX

- UNIX Level I
- UNIX Level II
- Essentials of UNIX and NT Integration

Programming

- Introduction to JavaScript
- Java Programming
- PERL Programming
- Advanced PERL with CGI for the Web

Web Site Management & Development

- Building a Web Site
- Web Site Management and Performance
- Web Development Fundamentals

High Speed Networking

- Essentials of Wide Area Networking
- Integrating ISDN
- Fiber Optic Network Design
- Fiber Optic Network Installation
- Migrating to High Performance Ethernet

DIGITAL UNIX

- UNIX Utilities and Commands
- DIGITAL UNIX v4.0 System Administration
- DIGITAL UNIX v4.0 (TCP/IP) Network Management
- AdvFS, LSM, and RAID Configuration and Management
- DIGITAL UNIX TruCluster Software Configuration and Management
- UNIX Shell Programming Featuring Kornshell
- DIGITAL UNIX v4.0 Security Management
- DIGITAL UNIX v4.0 Performance Management
- DIGITAL UNIX v4.0 Intervals Overview

DIGITAL OpenVMS

- OpenVMS Skills for Users
- OpenVMS System and Network Node Management I
- OpenVMS System and Network Node Management II
- OpenVMS System and Network Node Management III
- OpenVMS System and Network Node Operations
- OpenVMS for Programmers
- OpenVMS System Troubleshooting for Systems Managers
- Configuring and Managing Complex VMScluster Systems
- Utilizing OpenVMS Features from C
- OpenVMS Performance Management
- Managing DEC TCP/IP Services for OpenVMS
- Programming in C

Hardware Courses

- AlphaServer 1000/1000A Installation, Configuration and Maintenance
- AlphaServer 2100 Server Maintenance
- AlphaServer 4100, Troubleshooting Techniques and Problem Solving

About Syngress Media

Syngress Media creates books and software for Information Technology professionals seeking skill enhancement and career advancement. Its products are designed to comply with vendor and industry standard course curricula, and are optimized for certification exam preparation. You can contact Syngress via the Web at www.syngress.com.

Contributors

Michael Cross (MCSE, MCPS, MCP+I, CNA) is the network administrator, Internet specialist, and a programmer for the Niagara Regional Police Service. In addition to administering their network, programming, and providing support to a user base of over 800 civilian and uniform users, he is Webmaster of their Web site at www.nrps.com.

Michael also owns KnightWare, a company that provides consulting, programming, networking, Web page design, computer training, and various other services. He has served as an instructor for private colleges and technical schools in London and Ontario, Canada. He has been a freelance writer for several years and has been published over two dozen times in numerous books and anthologies.

George D. Hoffman (MCSE, MCT) resides in Stoneham, MA with his wife Ann-Marie, a native of Dublin, Ireland. After graduating from Boston College, George served as a navy officer and subsequently operated his own advertising and marketing business before "joining the crowd and moving to the world of computers." In addition to teaching applications and Microsoft technical classes in the United States, he has taught and consulted extensively in Ireland. In his spare time, while not preparing for the next Microsoft exam, George enjoys woodworking and golf, much more successful at the former than the latter.

M. Troy Hudson (MCSE, MCT, MCP+I, Master CNE, Master CNI) has been working in the IT industry for over 10 years. He has worked for 7 years as a technical support engineer for WordPerfect and Novell and began teaching in 1996. Troy has been teaching Microsoft and Novell networking full-time since 1997 and has added to his knowledge through owning his own consulting company, TekEASE, Inc.

Troy has been involved in technical certifications since 1994 when he helped write the first WordPerfect certification exam and became certified in products like WP Office, GroupWise, and NetWare. He holds a CNE in NetWare 3x, 4x, IntraNetWare, 5x, GW4, and GW5. He has a Master CNE in Messaging. He has his MCSE in both Windows NT and Windows 2000. Troy is widowed and spends much of his time with his four boys.

Feridun Kadir (MCP, MCP+I, MCSE, MCT) is a freelance IT consultant and trainer who has worked in the IT field since 1988. He remembers selling a TRS-80 home PC with 4Kilobytes RAM (yes kilobytes!) in the early 1980s for over $1000. His early IT experience was with UNIX systems and local area networks. In more recent years he has worked with Microsoft products. Having discovered that he liked giving presentations, he became an MCT and regularly teaches Microsoft technical courses including Windows NT4.0, Windows 2000, TCP/IP, and SQL Server 7.0 Administration. Feridun also provides IT consulting services to all types of businesses. Feridun lives with his wife Liz and son Jake in Stansted, Essex in England.

Hal Kurz (CCNA, MCSE 2000, MCSE NT 4.0, MCT) is Director of Education for FastTrain II, a Microsoft Solution Provider in Miami, FL (www.fasttrain.com). Hal is also owner of Innovative Technology Consultants and Company, Inc., a computer consulting firm located in Miami, FL (www.itccinc.com). He graduated from the University of Florida with a Bachelor of Science in Engineering.

Hal's early networking experience began with a Vax 3100 running VMS and a DEC Alpha 255/300 also running VMS. Soon after, Hal began working with Windows NT; he prepared for Microsoft Certification through self-study. He lives in Miami with his wife Tricia and three children Alexa, Andrew, and Alivia. *Thanks Tricia and kids for all of your patience through countless hours of study and projects.*

Nathan McAfee (MCP+I, MCSE, MCT, A+, I-Net+, CIW) entered the IT world in 1982 programming BASIC on an Apple II. He has run a consulting and technical instruction company since 1991 working with clients such as EDS, NovaQuest, BrightStar, and Sarcom. Nathan currently is a presales systems engineer for Microsoft, based in Redmond, WA where he works on OEM market readiness for Windows XP.

Chris Rima (M.S., MCSE+I, MCT) is the Technical Programs Administrator for the Southern Arizona Campus of the University of Phoenix, the nation's largest private university. Chris administers a Microsoft Authorized Academic Training

Partner (AATP) program and teaches Windows NT, Windows 2000, A+, and Network+ courses. As a member of the University's MCSE steering committee, he develops MCSE teaching materials and provides overall program guidance. Chris is a master-certified instructor for Microsoft's New Employee Support Training (NEST), Windows 95/98, and FrontPage 98 support curriculums.

Chris formerly worked at Microsoft and Keane Inc. in Tucson, AZ, where he started a Microsoft Certified Technical Education Center (CTEC).

Susan Snedaker (MCSE, MCP, MCT, MBA) has been involved with information systems technology for over 10 years. She is currently President and CEO of Virtual Team (www.virtualteam.com), a consulting firm working with high-tech startups.

During her career, Susan has worked for both hardware and software vendors. Prior to founding Virtual Team, Susan worked for a software startup firm as Vice President of Client Services. She has also worked for Microsoft, Honeywell, and Keane in key executive and technical roles.

Jada Brock-Soldavini (MCSE) is a Senior Network Services Administrator for the State of Georgia. With over 7 years in the IT field, Jada has a very diverse background. Her experience includes a number of years building and supporting desktop clients and network servers as well as network administration and architecture development in both Windows NT/2000 and Exchange 5.5/2000 and Cisco Technologies. Previously, she worked as a consultant for a business ISP firm in Atlanta primarily with Linux, Unix, and Apache Web Servers. She is also the founder of a nonprofit organization that distributes information for women who would like to join the technical industry.

Jada graduated from Massey Business College in Atlanta, GA with an AS in Computer Information Systems and holds a membership with the Network Professional Association and the IEEE Society. Jada lives in the suburbs of Atlanta, GA with her husband Michael and two children Alyssa and Daniel. She is currently working on her CCNP certification. She is a published author who enjoys writing technical articles and technical books in her spare time.

Technical Editor

James Truscott (MCSE, MCP+I, Network+) is an instructor in the MCSE program at Eastfield College and the Dallas County Community College District. He is also Senior Instructor for the Cowell Corporation and is teaching the Windows 2000 track for CLC Corporation in Dallas, TX. He is the Webmaster for Cowell Corporation in Richardson, TX and does consulting services for several Dallas-based businesses.

His passion for computers started back in the 1960s when he was a programmer for Bell Telephone. One of his current projects includes developing Web sites for his students.

Technical Reviewer

Ryan Neil Sokolowski (MCSE 2000 & NT, CCNA, CCDA, CNE, CNA, VCE) is currently Systems Analyst for the Microsoft Secure Extranet Team at Microsoft headquarters in Redmond, WA. He has been involved with Windows 2000 from its earliest stages, including being a participant in the Microsoft-sponsored Rapid Deployment Program (RDP). Ryan is a participant in the Internet Engineering Task Force (IETF) and a member of the Institute of Electrical and Electronics Engineers (IEEE), the SANS Institute and the Association of Windows NT Systems Professionals. With a true love of technology and a strong background in design, architecture, implementation, engineering, and consulting services, Ryan's specialties include network operating systems, directory services, and Cisco networking environments. This is his third title with Syngress Publishing, with previous topics covering the Cisco CCDA exam and the Windows 2000 Server MCSE exam. Ryan dedicates all that he does to his parents.

ACKNOWLEDGMENTS

We would like to thank the following people:

- Richard Kristof of Global Knowledge for championing the series and providing us access to some great people and information.
- All the incredibly hard-working folks at Osborne/McGraw-Hill: Brandon Nordin, Scott Rogers, Timothy Green, Gareth Hancock, and Jessica Wilson.

CONTENTS AT A GLANCE

CONTENTS

This book's primary objective is to help you prepare for the MCSE 2000 Supporting and Maintaining a Microsoft Windows NT Server 4.0 Network exam under the Windows 2000 certification track. As the Microsoft program continues to transition from Windows NT 4.0, it will become increasingly important that current and aspiring IT professionals have multiple resources available to assist them in increasing their knowledge and building their skills.

At the time of publication, all the exam objectives have been posted on the Microsoft Web site and the beta exam process has been completed. Microsoft has announced its commitment to measuring real-world skills. This book is designed with that premise in mind; its authors have practical experience in the field, using the NT 4.0 and Windows 2000 operating systems in hands-on situations.

Because the focus of the exams is on application and understanding, as opposed to memorization of facts, no book by itself can fully prepare you to obtain a passing score. It is essential that you work with the software to enhance your proficiency. Toward that end, this book includes many practical step-by-step exercises in each chapter that are designed to give you hands-on practice as well as guide you in truly learning Supporting and Maintaining a Microsoft Windows NT Network, not just learning *about* it.

In This Book

This book is organized around the actual structure of the 70-244 exam administered at Sylvan Prometric and VUE Testing Centers. Microsoft has let us know all the topics we need to cover for the exam. We've followed their list carefully, so you can be assured you're not missing anything. Each chapter covers a major aspect of the exam, with an emphasis on the "why" as well as the "how to" of working with and supporting NT as a network administrator or engineer.

In Every Chapter

We've created a set of chapter components that call your attention to important items, reinforce important points, and provide helpful exam-taking hints. Take a look at what you'll find in the chapters:

- Each chapter begins with the **Certification Objectives**—what you need to know in order to pass the section on the exam dealing with the chapter topic.

The Certification Objective headings identify the objectives within the chapter, so you'll always know an objective when you see it!

■ **Certification Exercises** are interspersed throughout the chapters. These are step-by-step exercises. They help you master skills that are likely to be an area of focus on the exam. Don't just read through the exercises; they are hands-on procedures that you should be comfortable completing. Learning by doing is an effective way to increase your competency with the language and concepts presented.

CertCam 1-1

■ The **CertCam** icon that appears in many of the exercises indicates that the exercise is presented in .avi format on the accompanying CD-ROM. These .avi clips walk you step-by-step through various system configurations and are narrated by George D. Hoffman.

■ **From the Classroom** sidebars describe the issues that come up most often in ewthe training classroom setting. These sidebars give you a valuable perspective into certification- and product-related topics. They point out common mistakes and address questions that have arisen from classroom discussions.

■ **Scenario & Solution** sections lay out specific scenario questions and solutions in a quick and easy-to-read format.

SCENARIO & SOLUTION

I have set up a trust relationship between two domains, but it doesn't seem to work. On one domain, I specified the other as the Trusted Domain. I then went to the PDC in the Trusted Domain and set the other domain as the Trusting Domain. What have I done wrong?	Nothing. If the Trusted Domain relationship is set before the Trusting Domain relationship, the trust relationship won't take effect immediately. By doing it in this order, it may take as long as 15 minutes before the trust relationship takes effect.
Which is the best model to use for a network?	The model you should use will depend on your needs. If your company has less than 40,000 users, then the single domain model or single master domain model will be useful. If your company has (or expects to have) more than this number of users, then the multiple master domain or complete trust models will be useful. Other elements that will go into your decision are outlined earlier in this chapter.
I want to access a NetWare server from my Windows NT Server, but I'm unable to install CSNW. Why?	Client Services for NetWare is only available with Windows NT 4.0 Workstation. It doesn't come with Windows NT Server.

■ The **Certification Summary** is a succinct review of the chapter and a re-statement of salient points regarding the exam.

■ The **Two-Minute Drill** at the end of every chapter is a checklist of the main points of the chapter. It can be used for last-minute review.

■ The **Self Test** offers questions similar to those found on the certification exam. The answers to these questions, as well as explanations of the answers, can be found at the end of the particular chapter. By taking the Self Test after completing each chapter, you'll reinforce what you've learned from that chapter, while becoming familiar with the structure of the exam questions.

■ The **Lab Question** at the end of the Self Test section offers a unique and challenging question format that requires the reader to understand multiple chapter concepts to answer correctly. These questions are more complex and more comprehensive than the other questions, as they test your ability to take all the knowledge you have gained from reading the chapter and apply it to complicated, real-world situations. These questions are aimed to be more difficult than what you will find on the exam. If you can answer these questions, you have proven that you know the subject!

Some Pointers

Once you've finished reading this book, set aside some time to do a thorough review. You might want to return to the book several times and make use of all the methods it offers for reviewing the material:

1. *Re-read all the Two-Minute Drills,* or have someone quiz you. You also can use the drills as a way to do a quick cram before the exam.

2. *Review all the Scenario & Solution sections* for quick problem solving.

3. *Re-take the Self Tests.* Taking the tests right after you've read the chapter is a good idea, because it helps reinforce what you've just learned. However, it's an even better idea to go back later and do all the questions in the book in one sitting. Pretend you're taking the exam. (For this reason, you should mark your answers on a separate piece of paper when you go through the questions the first time.)

4. *Complete the exercises.* Did you do the exercises when you read through each chapter? If not, do them! These exercises are designed to cover exam topics, and there's no better way to get to know this material than by practicing.

5. *Check out the Web site.* Global Knowledge invites you to become an active member of the Access Global Web site. This site is an online mall and an information repository that you'll find invaluable. You can access many types of products to assist you in your preparation for the exams, and you'll be able to participate in forums, on-line discussions, and threaded discussions. No other book brings you unlimited access to such a resource. You'll find more information about this site in Appendix B.

The CD-ROM Resource

This book comes with a CD-ROM that includes test preparation software and provides you with another method for studying. You will find more information on the testing software in Appendix A.

INTRODUCTION

MCSE Certification

This book is designed to help you pass the MCSE 2000 Supporting and Maintaining a Microsoft Windows NT Server 4.0 Network. We wrote this book to give you a complete and incisive review of all the important topics that are targeted for the exam. The information contained in Table FM-1 will provide you with the required foundation of knowledge that will not only allow you to succeed in passing the 70-244 exam, but will also make you a better Microsoft Certified Systems Engineer.

The nature of the Information Technology industry is changing rapidly, and the requirements and specifications for certification can change just as quickly without notice. Microsoft expects you to regularly visit their Web site at **http://www .87microsoft.com/mcp/certstep/mcse.htm** to get the most up-to-date information on the entire MCSE program.

TABLE FM I   Windows Certification Track

Core Exams		
Candidates Who Have Not Already Passed Windows NT 4.0 Exams All 4 of the Following Core Exams Required:	OR	**Candidates Who Have Passed 3 Windows NT 4.0 Exams (Exams 70-067, 70-068, and 70-073)** **Instead of the 4 Core Exams on Left, You May Take:**
Exam 70-210: Installing, Configuring, and Administering Microsoft® Windows® 2000 Professional		**Exam 70-240:** Microsoft® Windows® 2000 Accelerated Exam for MCPs Certified on Microsoft® Windows NT® 4.0 The Accelerated Exam will be available until December 31, 2001. It covers the core competencies of exams **70-210, 70-215, 70-216,** and **70-217.**

| TABLE FM-I | Windows Certification Track *(continued)* |

Core Exams
Exam 70-215: Installing, Configuring, and Administering Microsoft® Windows® 2000 Server
Exam 70-216: Implementing and Administering a Microsoft® Windows® 2000 Network Infrastructure
Exam 70-217: Implementing and Administering a Microsoft® Windows® 2000 Directory Services Infrastructure
PLUS—All Candidates—1 of the Following Core Exams Required:
*Exam 70-219: Designing a Microsoft® Windows® 2000 Directory Services Infrastructure
*Exam 70-220: Designing Security for a Microsoft® Windows® 2000 Network
*Exam 70-221: Designing a Microsoft® Windows® 2000 Network Infrastructure
PLUS—All Candidates—2 Elective Exams Required: For a full listing of elective exams that apply, please see www.microsoft.com/trainingandservices
* Note that some of the Windows 2000 Core Exams can be used as elective exams as well. An exam that is used to meet the design requirement cannot also count as an elective. Each exam can only be counted once in the Windows 2000 Certification.

Let's look at two scenarios. The first applies to the person who has already taken the Windows NT 4.0 Server (70-067), Windows NT 4.0 Workstation (70-073), and Windows NT 4.0 Server in the Enterprise (70-068) exams. The second scenario covers the situation of the person who has not completed those Windows NT 4.0 exams and would like to concentrate ONLY on Windows 2000.

In the first scenario, you have the option of taking all four Windows 2000 Core Exams, or you can take the Windows 2000 Accelerated Exam for MCPs if you have already passed exams 70-067, 70-068, and 70-073. (Note that you must have passed those specific exams to qualify for the Accelerated Exam; if you have fulfilled your NT 4.0 MCSE requirements by passing the Windows 95 or Windows 98 Exam as your client operating system option, and did not take the NT Workstation Exam, you don't qualify. Please note that as of this writing the Accelerated Exam is scheduled to be retired on December 31, 2001.)

After completing the Core requirements, either by passing the four Core Exams or the one Accelerated Exam, you must pass a "design" exam. The design exams include Designing a Microsoft Windows 2000 Directory Services Infrastructure (70-219), Designing Security for Microsoft Windows 2000 Network (70-220), and Designing a Microsoft Windows 2000 Network Infrastructure (70-221). One design exam is REQUIRED.

You also must pass two exams from the list of electives. However, you cannot use the design exam that you took as an elective. Each exam can only count once toward certification. This includes any of the MCSE electives that are current when the Windows 2000 exams are released. The 70-244 exam counts towards one of your Windows 2000 elective exams. In summary, you would take a total of at least two more exams, the upgrade exam and the design exam. Any additional exams would be dependent on which electives the candidate may have already completed.

In the second scenario, if you have not completed, and do not plan to complete the Core Windows NT 4.0 exams, you must pass the four Core Windows 2000 exams, one design exam, and two elective exams. Again, no exam can be counted twice. In this case, you must pass a total of seven exams to obtain the Windows 2000 MCSE certification.

How to Take a Microsoft Certification Exam

If you are new to Microsoft certification, we have some good news and some bad news. The good news, of course, is that Microsoft certification is one of the most valuable credentials you can earn. It sets you apart from the crowd, and marks you as a valuable asset to your employer. You will gain the respect of your peers, and Microsoft certification can have a wonderful effect on your income.

The bad news is that Microsoft certification tests are not easy. You may think you will read through some study material, memorize a few facts, and pass the Microsoft examinations. After all, these certification exams are just computer-based, multiple-choice tests, so they must be easy. If you believe this, you are wrong. Unlike many "multiple guess" tests you have been exposed to in school, the questions on Microsoft certification examinations go beyond simple factual knowledge.

The purpose of this introduction is to teach you how to take a Microsoft certification examination. To be successful, you need to know something about the purpose and structure of these tests. We will also look at the latest innovations in Microsoft testing. Using *simulations* and *adaptive testing*, Microsoft is enhancing both the validity and security of the certification process. These factors have some important effects on how you should prepare for an exam, as well as your approach to each question during the test.

We will begin by looking at the purpose, focus, and structure of Microsoft certification tests, and examine the effect these factors have on the kinds of questions you will face on your certification exams. We will define the structure of examination questions and investigate some common formats. Next, we will present a strategy for answering these questions. Finally, we will give some specific guidelines on what you should do on the day of your test.

Why Vendor Certification?

The Microsoft Certified Professional program, like the certification programs from Lotus, Novell, Oracle, and other software vendors, is maintained for the ultimate purpose of increasing the corporation's profits. A successful vendor certification program accomplishes this goal by helping to create a pool of experts in a company's software, and by "branding" these experts so that companies using the software can identify them.

We know that vendor certification has become increasingly popular in the last few years because it helps employers find qualified workers, and because it helps software vendors like Microsoft sell their products. But why vendor certification rather than a more traditional approach like a college degree in computer science? A college education is a broadening and enriching experience, but a degree in computer science does not prepare students for most jobs in the IT industry.

A common truism in our business states, "If you are out of the IT industry for three years and want to return, you have to start over." The problem, of course, is *timeliness*; if a first-year student learns about a specific computer program, it probably will no longer be in wide use when he or she graduates. Although some colleges are trying to integrate Microsoft certification into their curriculum, the problem is not really a flaw in higher education, but a characteristic of the IT industry. Computer software is changing so rapidly that a four-year college just can't keep up.

A marked characteristic of the Microsoft certification program is an emphasis on performing specific job tasks rather than merely gathering knowledge. It may come as a shock, but most potential employers do not care how much you know about the theory of operating systems, networking, or database design. As one IT manager put it, "I don't really care what my employees know about the theory of our network. We don't need someone to sit at a desk and think about it. We need people who can actually do something to make it work better."

You should not think that this attitude is some kind of anti-intellectual revolt against "book learning." Knowledge is a necessary prerequisite, but it is not enough. More than one company has hired a computer science graduate as a network administrator, only to learn that the new employee has no idea how to add users, assign permissions, or perform the other day-to-day tasks necessary to maintain a network. This brings us to the second major characteristic of Microsoft certification that affects the questions you must be prepared to answer. In addition to timeliness, Microsoft certification is also job task oriented.

The timeliness of Microsoft's certification program is obvious, and is inherent in the fact that you will be tested on current versions of software in wide use today. The job task orientation of Microsoft certification is almost as obvious, but testing real-world job skills using a computer-based test is not easy.

Computerized Testing

Considering the popularity of Microsoft Certification, and the fact that certification candidates are spread around the world, the only practical way to administer tests for the certification program is through Sylvan Prometric or Vue testing centers, which operate internationally. Sylvan Prometric and Vue provide proctor testing services for Microsoft, Oracle, Novell, Lotus, and the A+ computer technician certification. Although the IT industry accounts for much of Sylvan's revenue, the company provides services for a number of other businesses and organizations, such as FAA pre-flight pilot tests. Historically, several hundred questions were developed for a new Microsoft Certification exam. The Windows 2000 MCSE exam pool contains hundreds of new questions. Microsoft is aware that many new MCSE candidates have been able to access information on test questions via the Internet or other resources. The company is very concerned about maintaining the MCSE as a "premium" certification. The significant increase in the number of test questions, together with stronger enforcement of the NDA (Non-disclosure agreement) helps ensure that a higher standard for certification is attained.

Microsoft treats the test-building process very seriously. Test questions are first reviewed by a number of subject matter experts for technical accuracy and then are presented in a beta test. Taking the beta test may require several hours, due to the large number of questions. After a few weeks, Microsoft Certification uses the statistical feedback from Sylvan to check the performance of the beta questions. The beta test group for the Windows 2000 certification series included MCTs, MCSEs, and members of Microsoft's rapid deployment partners groups. Because the exams have been normalized based on this population, you can be sure that the passing scores will be difficult to achieve without detailed product knowledge.

Questions are discarded if most test takers get them right (too easy) or wrong (too difficult), and a number of other statistical measures are taken of each question. Although the scope of our discussion precludes a rigorous treatment of question analysis, you should be aware that Microsoft and other vendors spend a great deal of time and effort making sure their exam questions are valid.

The questions that survive statistical analysis form the pool of questions for the final certification exam.

Test Structure

The questions in a Microsoft form test will not be equally weighted. Essentially different questions are given a value based on the level of difficulty. You will get more credit for getting a difficult question correct, than if you got an easy one correct. Because the questions are weighted differently, and because the exams use the adapter method of testing, your score will not bear any relationship to how many questions you answered correctly.

Microsoft has implemented *adaptive* testing. When an adaptive test begins, the candidate is first given a level three question. If it is answered correctly, a question from the next higher level is presented, and an incorrect response results in a question from the next lower level. When 15 to 20 questions have been answered in this manner, the scoring algorithm is able to predict, with a high degree of statistical certainty, whether the candidate would pass or fail if all the questions in the form were answered. When the required degree of certainty is attained, the test ends and the candidate receives a pass/fail grade.

Adaptive testing has some definite advantages for everyone involved in the certification process. Adaptive tests allow Sylvan Prometric or Vue to deliver more tests with the same resources, as certification candidates often are in and out in 30 minutes or less. For candidates, the "fatigue factor" is reduced due to the shortened testing time. For Microsoft, adaptive testing means that fewer test questions are exposed to each candidate, and this can enhance the security, and therefore the overall validity, of certification tests.

One possible problem you may have with adaptive testing is that you are not allowed to mark and revisit questions. Since the adaptive algorithm is interactive, and all questions but the first are selected on the basis of your response to the previous question, it is not possible to skip a particular question or change an answer.

Question Types

Computerized test questions can be presented in a number of ways. Some of the possible formats are used on Microsoft Certification exams and some are not.

True/False

We are all familiar with True/False questions, but because of the inherent 50 percent chance of guessing the correct answer, you will not see questions of this type on Microsoft Certification exams.

Multiple Choice

The majority of Microsoft Certification questions are in the multiple-choice format, with either a single correct answer or multiple correct answers. One interesting variation on multiple-choice questions with multiple correct answers is whether or not the candidate is told how many answers are correct.

EXAMPLE:

Which two files can be altered to configure the MS-DOS environment? (Choose two.)

Or

Which files can be altered to configure the MS-DOS environment? (Choose all that apply.)

You may see both variations on Microsoft Certification exams, but the trend seems to be toward the first type, where candidates are told explicitly how many answers are correct. Questions of the "choose all that apply" variety are more difficult and can be merely confusing.

Graphical Questions

One or more graphical elements are sometimes used as exhibits to help present or clarify an exam question. These elements may take the form of a network diagram, pictures of networking components, or screen shots from the software on which you are being tested. It is often easier to present the concepts required for a complex performance-based scenario with a graphic than with words.

Test questions known as *hotspots* actually incorporate graphics as part of the answer. These questions ask the certification candidate to click on a location or graphical element to answer the question. For example, you might be shown the diagram of a network and asked to click on an appropriate location for a router. The answer is correct if the candidate clicks within the *hotspot* that defines the correct location.

Free Response Questions

Another kind of question you sometimes see on Microsoft Certification exams requires a *free response* or type-in answer. An example of this type of question might present a TCP/IP network scenario and ask the candidate to calculate and enter the correct subnet mask in dotted decimal notation.

Simulation Questions

Simulation questions provide a method for Microsoft to test how familiar the test taker is with the actual product interface and the candidate's ability to quickly implement a task using the interface. These questions will present an actual Windows 2000 interface that you must work with to solve a problem or implement a solution. If you are familiar with the product, you will be able to answer these questions quickly, and they will be the easiest questions on the exam. However, if you are not accustomed to working with Windows 2000, these questions will be difficult for you to answer. This is why actual hands-on practice with Windows 2000 is so important!

Knowledge-Based and Performance-Based Questions

Microsoft Certification develops a blueprint for each Microsoft Certification exam with input from subject matter experts. This blueprint defines the content areas and objectives for each test, and each test question is created to test a specific objective. The basic information from the examination blueprint can be found on Microsoft's Web site in the Exam Prep Guide for each test.

Psychometricians (psychologists who specialize in designing and analyzing tests) categorize test questions as knowledge-based or performance-based. As the names imply, knowledge-based questions are designed to test knowledge, while performance-based questions are designed to test performance.

Some objectives demand a knowledge-based question. For example, objectives that use verbs like *list* and *identify* tend to test only what you know, not what you can do.

EXAMPLE:

Objective: Identify the MS-DOS configuration files.

Which two files can be altered to configure the MS-DOS environment? (Choose two.)

A. COMMAND.COM

B. AUTOEXEC.BAT

C. IO.SYS

D. CONFIG.SYS
Correct answers: B, D.

Other objectives use action verbs like *install, configure,* and *troubleshoot* to define job tasks. These objectives can often be tested with either a knowledge-based question or a performance-based question.

EXAMPLE:

Objective: Configure an MS-DOS installation appropriately using the PATH statement in AUTOEXEX.BAT.

Knowledge-based question:

What is the correct syntax to set a path to the D: directory in AUTOEXEC.BAT?

A. SET PATH EQUAL TO D:

B. PATH D:

C. SETPATH D:

D. D:EQUALS PATH
Correct answer: B.

Performance-based question:

Your company uses several DOS accounting applications that access a group of common utility programs. What is the best strategy for configuring the computers in the accounting department so that the accounting applications will always be able to access the utility programs?

A. Store all the utilities on a single floppy disk and make a copy of the disk for each computer in the accounting department.

B. Copy all the utilities to a directory on the C: drive of each computer in the accounting department and add a PATH statement pointing to this directory in the AUTOEXEC.BAT files.

C. Copy all the utilities to all application directories on each computer in the accounting department.

D. Place all the utilities in the C: directory on each computer, because the C: directory is automatically included in the PATH statement when AUTOEXEC.BAT is executed.

Correct answer: B.

Even in this simple example, the superiority of the performance-based question is obvious. Whereas the knowledge-based question asks for a single fact, the performance-based question presents a real-life situation and requires that you make a decision based on this scenario. Thus, performance-based questions give more bang (validity) for the test author's buck (individual question).

Testing Job Performance

We have said that Microsoft Certification focuses on timeliness and the ability to perform job tasks. We have also introduced the concept of performance-based questions, but even performance-based multiple-choice questions do not really measure performance. Another strategy is needed to test job skills.

Given unlimited resources, it is not difficult to test job skills. In an ideal world, Microsoft would fly MCP candidates to Redmond, place them in a controlled environment with a team of experts, and ask them to plan, install, maintain, and troubleshoot a Windows network. In a few days at most, the experts could reach a valid decision as to whether each candidate should or should not be granted MCDBA or MCSE status. Needless to say, this is not likely to happen.

Closer to reality, another way to test performance is by using the actual software and creating a testing program to present tasks and automatically grade a candidate's performance when the tasks are completed. This *cooperative* approach would be practical in some testing situations, but the same test that is presented to MCP candidates in Boston must also be available in Bahrain and Botswana. The most workable solution for measuring performance in today's testing environment is a *simulation* program. When the program is launched during a test, the candidate sees a simulation of the actual software that looks, and behaves, just like the real thing. When the testing software presents a task, the simulation program is launched and the candidate performs the required task. The testing software then grades the candidate's performance on the required task and moves to the next question. Microsoft has introduced simulation questions on the certification exam for Internet Information Server 4.0. Simulation questions provide many advantages over other testing methodologies, and simulations are expected to become increasingly important in the Microsoft Certification program. For example, studies have shown that there is a very high correlation between the ability to perform simulated tasks on a computer-based test and the ability to perform the actual job tasks. Thus, simulations enhance the validity of the certification process.

Another truly wonderful benefit of simulations is in the area of test security. It is just not possible to cheat on a simulation question. In fact, you will be told exactly what tasks you are expected to perform on the test. How can a certification candidate cheat? By learning to perform the tasks? What a concept!

Study Strategies

There are appropriate ways to study for the different types of questions you will see on a Microsoft Certification exam.

Knowledge-Based Questions

Knowledge-based questions require that you memorize facts. There are hundreds of facts inherent in every content area of every Microsoft Certification exam. There are several keys to memorizing facts:

- **Repetition**   The more times your brain is exposed to a fact, the more likely you are to remember it.

- **Association**   Connecting facts within a logical framework makes them easier to remember.

- **Motor Association**   It is often easier to remember something if you write it down or perform some other physical act, like clicking on a practice test answer.

We have said that the emphasis of Microsoft Certification is job performance, and that there are very few knowledge-based questions on Microsoft Certification exams. Why should you waste a lot of time learning filenames, IP address formulas, and other minutiae? Read on.

Performance-Based Questions

Most of the questions you will face on a Microsoft Certification exam are performance-based scenario questions. We have discussed the superiority of these questions over simple knowledge-based questions, but you should remember that the job task orientation of Microsoft Certification extends the knowledge you need to pass the exams; it does not replace this knowledge. Therefore, the first step in preparing for scenario questions is to absorb as many facts relating to the exam content areas as you can. In other words, go back to the previous section and follow the steps to prepare for an exam composed of knowledge-based questions.

The second step is to familiarize yourself with the format of the questions you are likely to see on the exam. You can do this by answering the questions in this study guide, by using Microsoft assessment tests, or by using practice tests on the included CD-ROM. The day of your test is not the time to be surprised by the construction of Microsoft exam questions.

At best, performance-based scenario questions really do test certification candidates at a higher cognitive level than knowledge-based questions. At worst, these questions can test your reading comprehension and test-taking ability rather than your ability to use Microsoft products. Be sure to get in the habit of reading the question carefully to determine what is being asked.

The third step in preparing for Microsoft scenario questions is to adopt the following attitude: Multiple-choice questions aren't really performance-based. It is all a cruel lie. These scenario questions are just knowledge-based questions with a story wrapped around them.

To answer a scenario question, you have to sift through the story to the underlying facts of the situation and apply your knowledge to determine the correct answer. This may sound silly at first, but the process we go through in solving real-life problems is quite similar. The key concept is that every scenario question (and every real-life problem) has a fact at its center, and if we can identify that fact, we can answer the question.

Simulations

Simulation questions really do measure your ability to perform job tasks. You must be able to perform the specified tasks. There are two ways to prepare for simulation questions:

1. Get experience with the actual software. If you have the resources, this is a great way to prepare for simulation questions.

2. Use official Microsoft practice tests. Practice tests are available that provide practice with the same simulation engine used on Microsoft Certification exams. This approach has the added advantage of grading your efforts.

Signing Up

Signing up to take a Microsoft Certification exam is easy. Sylvan Prometric or Vue operators in each country can schedule tests at any testing center. There are, however, a few things you should know:

1. If you call Sylvan Prometric or Vue during a busy time, get a cup of coffee first, because you may be in for a long wait. The exam providers do an excellent job, but everyone in the world seems to want to sign up for a test on Monday morning.

2. You will need your social security number or some other unique identifier to sign up for a test, so have it at hand.

3. Pay for your test by credit card if at all possible. This makes things easier, and you can even schedule tests for the same day you call, if space is available at your local testing center.

4. Know the number and title of the test you want to take before you call. This is not essential, and the Sylvan operators will help you if they can. Having this information in advance, however, speeds up and improves the accuracy of the registration process.

Taking the Test

Teachers have always told you not to try to cram for exams because it does no good. If you are faced with a knowledge-based test requiring only that you regurgitate facts, cramming can mean the difference between passing and failing. This is not the case, however, with Microsoft Certification exams. If you don't know it the night before, don't bother to stay up and cram.

Instead, create a schedule and stick to it. Plan your study time carefully, and do not schedule your test until you think you are ready to succeed. Follow these guidelines on the day of your exam:

1. Get a good night's sleep. The scenario questions you will face on a Microsoft Certification exam require a clear head.

2. Remember to take two forms of identification—at least one with a picture. A driver's license with your picture and social security or credit card is acceptable.

3. Leave home in time to arrive at your testing center a few minutes early. It is not a good idea to feel rushed as you begin your exam.

4. Do not spend too much time on any one question. You cannot mark and revisit questions on an adaptive test, so you must do your best on each question as you go.

5. If you do not know the answer to a question, try to eliminate the obviously wrong answers and guess from the rest. If you can eliminate two out of four options, you have a 50 percent chance of guessing the correct answer.

6. For scenario questions, follow the steps we outlined earlier. Read the question carefully and try to identify the facts at the center of the story.

Finally, we would advise anyone attempting to earn Microsoft MCDBA and MCSE certification to adopt a philosophical attitude. The Windows 2000 MCSE will be the most difficult MCSE ever to be offered. The questions are at a higher cognitive level than seen on all previous MCSE exams. Therefore, even if you are the kind of person who never fails a test, you are likely to fail at least one Windows 2000 certification test somewhere along the way. Do not get discouraged. Microsoft wants to ensure the value of your certification. Moreover, it will attempt to so by keeping the standard as high as possible. If Microsoft Certification were easy to obtain, more people would have it, and it would not be so respected and so valuable to your future in the IT industry.

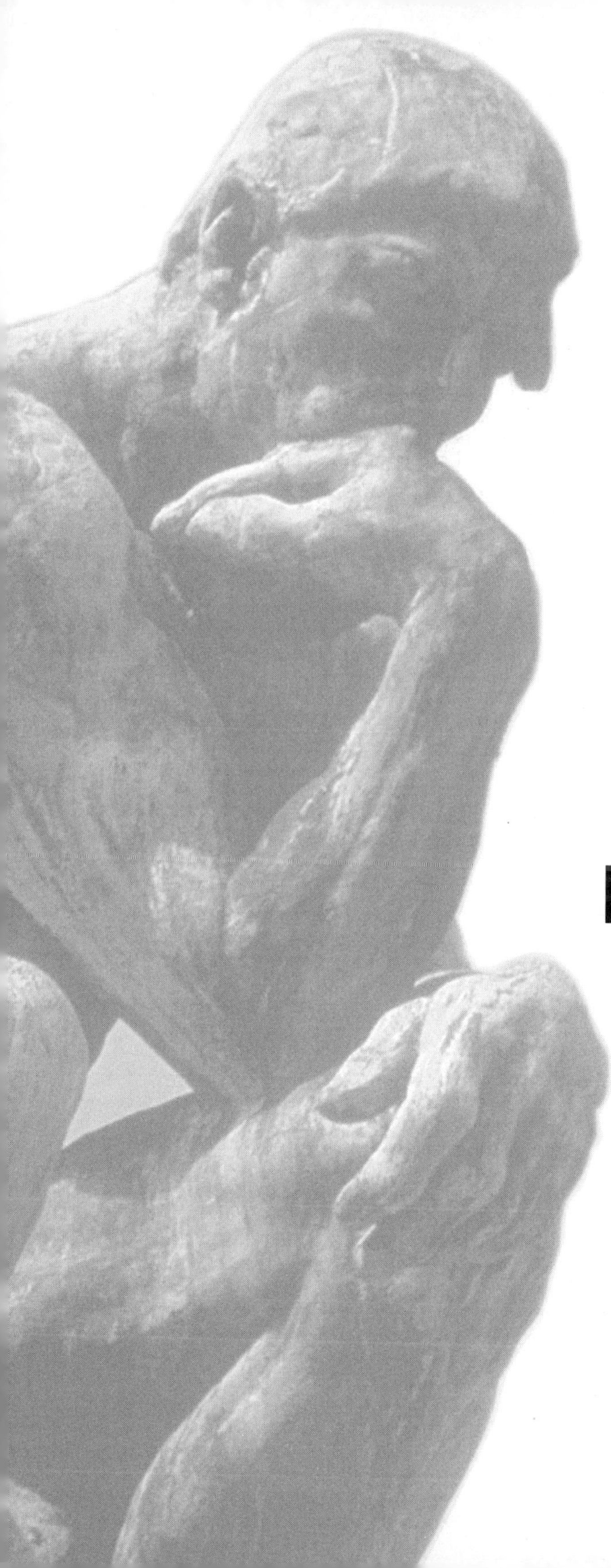

MCSE

MICROSOFT CERTIFIED SYSTEMS ENGINEER

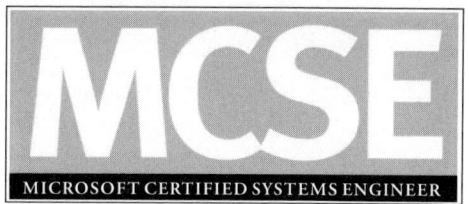

1

Introduction to Supporting and Maintaining a Microsoft Windows NT Server 4.0 Network

CERTIFICATION OBJECTIVES

1.01	What Is "Supporting and Maintaining a Microsoft Windows NT Server 4.0 Network"?
1.02	Overview of Exam 70-244
1.03	What We'll Cover in This Book
1.04	Windows NT Server Terminology
✓	Two-Minute Drill
Q&A	Self Test

W elcome to Supporting and Maintaining a Microsoft Windows NT Server 4.0 Network. This Microsoft Exam, 70-244, is part of the new Windows 2000 curriculum. Although corporations are migrating to Windows 2000, there are still many Windows NT 4.0–based networks playing critical roles in companies around the world. In many cases, companies have a blend of Windows 2000 and Windows NT networks that must seamlessly integrate and interoperate. As a result, this Windows NT Server 4.0 exam was established to ensure today's IT professionals have a strong understanding of Microsoft Windows NT Server 4.0–based technologies and how they work in a large, networked enterprise.

Many IT professionals have sought to increase their skills through the Microsoft certification program. As of December 31, 2001, individuals must pass the new Windows 2000 curriculum to attain or maintain their Microsoft Certified Systems Engineer (MCSE) certification. Many MCSEs who took the Windows NT Server 4.0 track have had to update their skills to include all of the new features of Windows 2000. At the same time, there are many IT professionals who began with the Windows 2000 courses and must now learn Windows NT Server 4.0 in order to work effectively in a mixed networking environment. This course is focused on Windows NT Server 4.0, although some comparisons between Windows NT and Windows 2000 are made to help map your knowledge between the operating systems.

For a variety of reasons, companies run different operating systems. Desktop users often work with Windows 95, Windows 98, Windows NT Workstation 4.0, and other third-party operating systems. On the server side, companies run Unix, Linux, Sun, as well as Windows NT Server 4.0 and Windows 2000 Server. As a result, today's network environment is typically a mix of operating systems on servers, desktops, and an array of mobile units. Users interact with the network from their desks, their laptops and other mobile devices, and from computers in remote locations. This intricate framework of networking and interoperability will only continue to gain complexity as the capabilities of technology increase at an accelerating pace. The need to understand a broad scope of technologies is important to success as an IT professional.

In the next nine chapters, we'll introduce you to the operating system features you need to understand to effectively manage a Windows NT Server 4.0–based network. Where relevant, we'll point out the differences between NT 4.0 and Windows 2000 so you'll be able to understand the underlying similarities and differences. This will help you build a solid foundation necessary for the exam, and for the job.

In this chapter, we'll take a look at what is involved with supporting and maintaining a Windows NT Server 4.0 network. We'll also review what's on the Microsoft Exam 70-244 and what skills are measured. From there, we'll step through what is covered in this book so you'll have a clear understanding of how the book is organized and what information you can expect to find. Finally, we'll learn some of the terminology related to the Windows NT 4.0 operating system to help you understand the material in-depth.

When you've finished this book and thoroughly understand the material, you'll be armed with the knowledge needed to successfully pass the exam. More importantly, you'll be ready to apply your knowledge on the job, and successfully support and maintain a Microsoft Windows NT Server 4.0 network. Let's get started.

CERTIFICATION OBJECTIVE 1.01

What Is "Supporting and Maintaining a Microsoft Windows NT Server 4.0 Network"?

Supporting and maintaining any network requires an understanding of general networking, operating systems, and troubleshooting principles. Supporting and maintaining a Windows NT Server 4.0–based network requires an additional understanding of features specific to this operating system. Managing the computer's resources, including memory, processors, disk and network subsystems, and the services and applications running on the server are all important components. In addition, Windows NT Server 4.0 has features significantly different than Windows 2000. While this book does not specifically compare each Windows NT and Windows 2000 feature, you will learn about some of the more relevant differences as you read each chapter. Let's take a brief look at what supporting and maintaining a Windows NT Server 4.0 network entails.

Server Hardware

How much RAM is needed to optimize a file and print server? What's the best disk configuration for fault tolerance on a database server? Server hardware can be maintained and optimized through a variety of methods. From adding more memory to implementing fault-tolerant disk subsystems, each subsystem must be optimized according to the load placed on it. Servers running in small organizations or with few services and applications on them will require fewer resources than servers in large organizations or with many services and applications on them. Establishing baselines and monitoring hardware resources is an important element in network administration. In Windows NT, there are different choices than in Windows 2000. Understanding Windows NT features is important when working in a mixed environment.

Operating System

If the hardware resources on a server are inadequate to handle the job, tuning the operating system will yield only minimal improvements. However, once there are adequate hardware resources in place, the operating system itself can be the source of problems, if not properly maintained. If problems do occur, it's important to have an established procedure for recovering and restoring the system. These techniques, in many cases, are distinctly different than with Windows 2000 servers. The files needed to restore the system and the methods of restoring system files, registry keys, and disk partitions to enable the system to run properly are fundamental skills needed when working with Windows NT Server 4.0. There are also key differences between Windows 2000 and Windows NT with regard to service packs and hotfixes that you must understand in order to effectively maintain Windows NT servers.

Access to Resources

One of the major differences between Windows NT and Windows 2000 is the way domains and users are managed. As a result, it's important to understand exactly how to configure and troubleshoot trusts, manage account and system policies and manage users. All of these elements contribute to a secure network environment. In Windows NT, domains can have implicit and explicit trust arrangements. These trusts then determine user access and other rights to resources.

Windows 2000 introduced the concept of organizational units as a way to more efficiently manage users and resources. This feature is not available in Windows NT. As a result, it's important to have a clear understanding of the similarities and differences between these two operating systems. It's also vitally important to learn how to manage users and access to resources in a Windows NT 4.0 environment. Although some of the fundamentals are the same between the two operating systems, configuring user accounts, user profiles and logon scripts, as well as managing groups, are all accomplished in distinctly different ways.

Security

In today's Internet-enabled computing environments, security has risen to the top of concerns for corporations worldwide. Windows 2000 has implemented some very advanced security features not present in Windows NT. Familiarity with a Windows 2000 network environment does not automatically provide you with adequate information about the security features in Windows NT. Being able to effectively analyze and configure security in a Windows NT 4.0 environment will ensure your network is safe whether it's part of a larger Windows 2000 configuration or not.

The operating system and user environments can be configured using the Security Configuration Manager in Windows NT 4.0. This allows the network administrator to manage a variety of security configuration options for the entire network. Using the built-in auditing and monitoring tools, a network administrator can establish a process for maintaining a secure network environment.

Access to resources can present additional security risks. Although using the Internet as a business tool is now very common, moving data to and from the Internet has many potential security risks. Being very familiar with the many ways security is managed in Windows NT 4.0 and how this differs from Windows 2000 is absolutely essential in today's computing environment.

Some of the security features in Windows NT 4.0 will be recognizable to those already familiar with Windows 2000. Other features are unique to Windows NT 4.0 and require special attention.

The goal of supporting and maintaining a Windows NT Server 4.0–based network is to provide the fastest, easiest access to resources for users on the network while maintaining a secure environment. Effectively managing the various elements— hardware, operating system, services, resource access and control, and security—are all part of supporting and maintaining a Windows NT Server 4.0 network. Understanding the similarities and differences between Windows 2000 and Windows NT 4.0 will help you effectively manage networks in a mixed environment, or evaluate the desirability of migrating your current Windows NT Server–based network to Windows 2000.

SCENARIO & SOLUTION

Why does Microsoft Exam 70-244 exist?	Although many companies have migrated to Windows 2000, scores of companies are still using Windows NT Server 4.0–based networks.
What are four critical server hardware components?	Processor, memory, disk, and network subsystems.
What must be present for an operating system to start?	Boot information for the disk and system files for the operating system.
Organizational units are native to which operating system?	Windows 2000, not Windows NT.
How can operating system and user environments be configured in Windows NT?	Using the Security Configuration Manager in Windows NT 4.0.

CERTIFICATION OBJECTIVE 1.02

Overview of Exam 70-244

The Microsoft Exam 70-244 is part of the new Windows 2000 series. Although many companies have migrated to Windows 2000, there are still many Windows NT Server 4.0–based networks deployed throughout the world. As an Information Technology professional, it is important to know how both Windows 2000 and Windows NT Server 4.0 should be deployed, maintained, and repaired. This exam, 70-244, tests your understanding of Windows NT Server 4.0.

Audience Profile

Anyone pursuing a Windows 2000 certification should consider this course. In addition, candidates for this exam are typically in medium to large companies with networks that use Windows NT Server 4.0 as the primary operating system.

Typically, you should have a minimum of one year's experience implementing and administering Windows NT Server 4.0 environments. Managing a network with these characteristics is most common for those likely to pursue certification via Exam 70-244:

- The company has one to fifty physical locations.
- The company has two hundred to twenty six thousand users.
- Network services include file and print, database, messaging, proxy or firewall, dial-in, desktop, and Web hosting.
- Branch offices and individual users need different kinds of connectivity.
- Different desktop, user, and server operating systems may be deployed, including Windows 2000 Professional, Windows NT Workstation 4.0, Windows 9x and third-party operating systems like Unix and Linux.

Skills Measured

We'll briefly look at the skills measured by the exam. Since this book is geared toward teaching you the material needed to successfully manage Windows NT Server 4.0 networks and pass the Microsoft Exam 70-244, the material in this book tracks with the exam requirements published by Microsoft. The exam measures your ability to manage and support networks using Windows NT Server 4.0. The exams may include adaptive testing technology and simulations as well. The exam tests your understanding of Windows NT Server 4.0 features as well as your understanding of how these features interact in a network environment. The exam, like many Microsoft exams, will also require an understanding of how networks support the corporate business. For example, network security can be configured so it is virtually impossible to compromise. That level of security often costs far more than most corporations are willing, or able, to spend on a computer network. Learning to balance user needs with corporate requirements and network functionality is not only needed to successfully navigate the exam, but is essential for success as a network administrator in today's market.

Here's an overview of what you can expect on the Windows NT Server 4.0 exam.

Although we review the exam requirements in sections, the actual exam is not divided into sections. You'll receive a specific number of questions relating to each of these sections, but they will not be identified as being from a particular area. If you've never taken an MCP exam before, make sure you review information in this book and on the Microsoft Web site regarding the format of MCP exams. Most often, you'll encounter exams that are adaptive, which means that the next test question you receive will be determined by whether or not you answer the current question correctly. Thus, your exam can be shorter or longer than others taking the same exam. Don't be concerned about the number of questions you get—focus on answering each question correctly based on your understanding of the material and your careful reading of the question. Remember, adaptive-style exams do not let you go back to a previous question, so make sure you take adequate time on each question before proceeding. Finally, if you're not sure, take a guess based on your first instinct. Your initial response is often correct and second-guessing yourself usually results in a lower score.

Maintaining, Troubleshooting, and Optimizing Servers

This section of the exam tests your ability to optimize, configure, manage, and troubleshoot hardware. It also covers the use of service packs and hotfixes in keeping your server operating system current.

You'll need to know:

- How to recover from hardware failures.
- Different types of hardware, including processors, memory, hard disks, RAID controllers, and network adapters.
- How to configure and troubleshoot fault-tolerant disks and disk subsystems.
- How to upgrade a server to multiple processors.
- How to troubleshoot and resolve hardware problems.

As part of any good network maintenance plan, you should establish a regular, defined backup procedure. This is part of the exam, and topics such as how to back up and restore data, how to select data for backup, how to schedule backups, and what type of backup to perform are covered.

The ability to restore the system, from backups or other means, is a critical ability on the job and is tested in this exam. Your understanding of which files are needed to boot and run the operating system, as well as how to recover from a severe failure such as single or multiple disk drive failures will be tested.

The last skill checked in this section of the exam is how to troubleshoot and optimize server performance. Some of what you'll be tested on is:

■ How to troubleshoot performance problems using the built-in Windows NT Server tools (Task Manager, Event Viewer, and Performance Monitor).

■ How to move, size, or add new paging files.

■ How to allocate server hardware to match the requirements of the applications and services running on the server, including Web services, file and print services, messaging and database applications, and proxy services.

■ How to modify backup domain controller (BDC) placement to optimize network traffic, application response, fault tolerance, and user logon.

exam
ⓦatch

You're likely to see several questions related to restoring the operating system. Make sure you understand the various ways you can recover from a severe disk error and what files are needed to do so. If possible, perform these recoveries in a lab to see exactly how to perform these procedures. You can be sure you'll see one or two questions on the exam related to recovery.

Configuring and Troubleshooting Users and Groups

Networks exist to provide authorized users access to resources. Therefore, a large part of managing a Windows NT Server network is related to users and groups. It follows, then, that the exam would cover this material in-depth as well.

You'll need to understand how to configure and troubleshoot trust relationships between domains. This is different in Windows NT than in Windows 2000, so you'll need to clearly understand the Windows NT framework. You'll be tested on cross-domain resource access as well as one-way and two-way trust arrangements.

Also at the domain level, you'll need to understand account policies. These include setting policies for password uniqueness, password length, password age, and account lockout. All of these apply across the domain and are set for all users.

Groups are collections of users that have the same requirements for resource access, such as members of the Print Operators group or the Backup Operators group. You'll need to understand how to configure and troubleshoot groups. You should understand group membership guidelines, default groups, global groups and local groups.

exam
ⓦatch

Keep this rule in mind. Put users into global groups and global groups into local groups. To many people, this sounds like it's backwards, which can be a good way to remember it. Any question on the exam that has you putting local groups into global groups, or individual users into local groups, is wrong. Use this to eliminate wrong answers immediately. Windows 2000 provides another group type, the universal group. Universal groups are used to consolidate groups that span domains. Users should still be added to global groups, but in Windows 2000, global groups can be placed within groups having universal scope. Using this strategy, any membership changes in the groups having global scope do not affect the groups with universal scope. Changes to groups with universal scope must be replicated across the entire forest. Therefore, changes to universal groups should be infrequent. The universal group is not available in Windows NT Server.

You'll also be tested on configuring and troubleshooting user accounts, user profiles, and logon scripts. You'll need to know how to:

- Create and rename user accounts, including accounts and deleted accounts.
- Configure and troubleshoot user profiles, including roaming, mandatory, and local user profiles.
- Configure and troubleshoot user accounts, including how to disable accounts, restrict user logon, and set dial-in permissions.
- Troubleshoot logon scripts, including script location, user account configuration, and replication of the shared NETLOGON folder.

Also in this section of the exam, you'll be tested on your knowledge of system policies. You'll need to have a solid understanding of client computer operating systems, file locations and names, and how local security and system policies interact. Understanding of user-specific system policies and computer policies will also be tested.

Roaming, mandatory, and local user profiles can be confusing when you first learn about them. Make sure you spend time understanding the details of each type of profile, how it's implemented and what the symptoms are when it's not working correctly. You're almost guaranteed to see several questions related to user profiles on the exam.

Analyzing, Configuring, and Monitoring Security

Security is a significant concern in today's corporations. Your understanding of how security is implemented and managed in Windows NT Server will be thoroughly tested on the exam.

The first topic in this section is how to analyze and configure the operating system environment and the user environment using the Security Configuration Manager. Using the Security Configuration Manager, you should know how to:

■ Apply the appropriate security template based on the role of the server.

■ Analyze the current environment.

■ Customize existing security templates to meet organizational security needs.

Implementing auditing and monitoring security is also tested on Microsoft Exam 70-244. To secure your network, you should know how to configure an Audit policy, how to enable auditing on various objects, such as files, shares, and printers, and how to analyze resulting audit logs.

Sometimes newer network administrators get overzealous in their auditing efforts once they discover how useful the data can be for monitoring security. However, you can also audit too many meaningless events and get quickly inundated with irrelevant data. Make sure your auditing policy makes sense for your company's environment and the level of security necessary to provide a reasonable level of safety.

Finally, you should understand some of the advanced security features in Windows NT Server 4.0 including implementing the syskey utility, configuring Server Message Block (SMB) signing, and enforcing usage of the appropriate version of Windows NT LAN Manager (NTLM).

Configuring, Managing, and Troubleshooting Access to Resources

In Windows NT Server, access to resources is granted based on permissions. Therefore, it's critical to understand how permissions are set, granted, and are combined to form a secure computing environment. In this section, you'll be tested on configuring, managing, and troubleshooting resource access.

You're practically guaranteed to get several questions testing your understanding of configuring and troubleshooting permissions. Considerations include combined NTFS and share permissions, printer permissions, and default permissions. You'll also need to understand how permissions are applied when a user is a member of several groups with different permissions as well as how the Deny permission is used. Windows 2000 has two features related to permissions not found in Windows NT Server. The Block Policy Inheritance and the No Override features allow the network administrator to determine whether or not a set of permissions can be inherited or blocked from being overridden as they are applied in the forest, domain, and organizational unit.

One very common resource users access are network printers. You'll be tested on how to configure, manage, and troubleshoot printers and print devices. The components you'll need to know include installing and updating printer drivers, troubleshooting connectivity issues, how to form and troubleshoot printer pools, and how to manage print queues, Print Spooler, and TCP/IP printing. You're likely to get one or more printing-related questions on the exam.

exam Watch

Printing in a networked environment is another area in which you're likely to see several exam questions. Your knowledge of printer pools and managing print queues will almost certainly be tested. Understanding how drivers are managed is also another area often tested. For instance, you should know that you have to update the driver on the print server and that you must provide a driver for each operating system (Windows 95, Windows 98, Windows NT) supported.

You should understand how the HTTP, HTTPS, and FTP protocols are implemented and used in this environment. Windows 2000 includes a new Internet Printing Protocol (IPP) that allows users to print directly to a URL over an intranet or the Internet. In addition, Windows 2000 Server automatically generates print-job information in HTML format, so users can view it in their browsers. This is another feature new to Windows 2000 not found in Windows NT Server 4.0.

Finally, you may encounter a question on how to install, configure, and troubleshoot file-based resource access using Distributed file system (Dfs) on multiple servers.

Configuring, Managing, Troubleshooting, and Optimizing Network Services

Network services covers a lot of territory, and your understanding of these topics will likely be thoroughly tested on the exam. Many of the concepts in this section apply to a wide array of networks, so you may already have a baseline understanding of these concepts. Be sure to thoroughly review this material and understand how these features are implemented in Windows NT Server specifically.

Topics related to top-level network connectivity include:

- **Name resolution servers**   What they do and how they work.

- **Default gateways**   How to configure and troubleshoot issues related to default gateways.

- **Automatic Private IP Addressing (APIPA)**   How to implement and troubleshoot APIPA.

- **IPConfig**   How to use this IP utility.

- **DHCP**   How to implement automatic IP address assignments using DHCP.

Web services are implemented in Windows NT Server using Internet Information Server, or IIS. The areas you should be familiar with include hosting multiple Web sites, performance tuning, and how to use Windows Load Balancing Service (WLBS).

Your skills in name resolution will also be tested on the exam. You should know how to monitor, maintain, and troubleshoot NetBIOS name resolution, host name resolution, IP address resolution, and the Computer Browser service.

Remote Access Service (RAS) is also covered in this section. Understand Remote Access Service (RAS) and Routing and Remote Access Service (RRAS). Know how to back up and restore RRAS configuration, Internet Authentication Service (IAS), and virtual private network access.

on the
Öob

Remote access has traditionally been heavily tested on Microsoft exams because remote users have become more and more prevalent. With the growing popularity of mobile devices, remote access issues have become more complex and more critical to the organization. Thoroughly understanding all the ins and outs of remote access in a Windows NT environment will help ensure you provide high levels of security and resource availability for your users.

The last topic covered by Microsoft Exam 70-244 is network performance. You should understand how to use the built-in tools to monitor, troubleshoot, and optimize network performance. Your familiarity with Event Viewer, Performance Monitor, and Network Monitor will be tested.

exam
ⓦatch

Performance tuning has been a favorite topic on many Microsoft exams. Understanding Performance Monitor and Network Monitor is critical to doing well on the exam. You're likely to see one or more questions that will require you decide which are the best objects or counters to use in Performance Monitor, or how to set filters in Network Monitor to assess specific problems.

SCENARIO & SOLUTION

How would you give permissions to a user to access files in the Human Resources group?	Add the user to a global group. Add the global group to the local group.
What three tools could you use to troubleshoot performance problems?	Task Manager, Event Viewer, and Performance Monitor.
What are three types of name resolution used in Windows NT?	NetBIOS name resolution, host name resolution, and IP address resolution.
What feature of Windows NT manages IP addressing?	DHCP, or Dynamic Host Configuration Protocol, is used to manage IP addresses, including automatic IP address assignment. (Not to be confused with APIPA.)

CERTIFICATION OBJECTIVE 1.03

What We'll Cover in This Book

This book tracks closely with the objectives of Exam 70-244. Each chapter is designed to help you understand key concepts and master the information needed to have a firm foundation of knowledge about Windows NT Server 4.0. In this section, we'll look at what you can expect to learn in each chapter.

FROM THE CLASSROOM

Windows NT Server 4.0 and Windows 2000

Windows NT Server 4.0 used to be taught in two courses, because there's a lot to cover in a complex operating system. Windows 2000 is now taught in a number of different courses because of the added functionality and complexity of the operating system. Students come into the classroom with a variety of backgrounds and skill levels. Some have already studied Windows NT or Windows 2000, while others are new to information technology and Microsoft operating systems. Regardless of your background and skill set, make sure you thoroughly understand the fundamentals before setting out to pass this Microsoft exam. If you have a good foundation in hardware, disk management,

networking, connectivity, and security, the concepts and ideas in Windows NT and Windows 2000 will be much easier to absorb and retain. This book guides you through many of the fundamental concepts so as to build a solid foundation for Windows NT Server knowledge. If at any point a concept is unclear, stop and review the material. In the classroom, I'm an expert at spotting those glazed over eyes students have when they don't understand. In this book, we use the Two-Minute Drill and the questions at the end of each chapter to test comprehension. Don't skip over these important learning tools. You'll be glad you reviewed them when it comes time for your Microsoft exam.

—*Susan Snedaker, MCSE, MCT, MBA*

Maintaining, Troubleshooting, and Optimizing Server Hardware: Chapter 2

We begin the course content with concepts regarding maintaining, troubleshooting, and optimizing server hardware. The various subsystems, including processor, memory, disk, and network components will be discussed.

Processors come in basically two types: Intel x86-based processors and RISC-based processors. Systems can have one or more processors if the hardware and software support this configuration. Processor capacity is closely tied to memory availability, both cache and random access memory (RAM). Memory requirements for systems vary according to both their use (the applications and services on the server) and their load (the number of users accessing those resources). There is a wide range of memory types on the market today and this chapter briefly reviews the different types, their characteristics, and uses.

Disk subsystems is another area where many hardware choices exist today. Disk controller types are reviewed, and disk drives, throughput, and access times are discussed. Software and hardware solutions for fault tolerance, including mirror sets, stripe sets, and stripe sets with parity are also reviewed. Network services provided through the network adapter and protocols used can impact overall system performance. Optimizing performance using hardware solutions is discussed in-depth.

Finally, as part of the hardware on a network, backup hardware must exist. While this typically takes the form of a high speed, high capacity tape backup unit, other media can be used. Chapter 2 reviews the planning and management of a backup process that will ensure data integrity, safety, and availability in almost any circumstance.

Maintaining, Troubleshooting, and Optimizing the Operating System: Chapter 3

Maintaining an operating system in today's environment means being able to keep the network up and running efficiently, keeping network resources secure, and being able to seamlessly interoperate with different systems, including other operating systems, other devices, and the Internet.

Chapter 3 takes an in-depth look at the operating system with a special focus given to recovering from system failures. Hardware failures do occur and are most likely to occur in the systems that have moving parts—in other words, disk drives of all kinds. Thus, knowing how to recover from disk failure is an absolutely critical skill for a network administrator to have. Chapter 3 covers the files needed to boot the operating system, the tools available to boot the system in the event of a disk failure, and the tools that can be used to troubleshoot and repair operating system problems.

Optimizing server performance is an ongoing task of a network administrator. Determining how servers are used, as well as what users will connect to server resources, is important in determining how to optimize the server. Adding or removing services, applications, or hardware components can have an impact on server performance. Chapter 3 introduces three important tools for monitoring server performance— Task Manager, Event Viewer, and Performance Monitor. Each is discussed at length so you'll have a solid understanding of how they're used to identify potential performance problems.

Chapter 3 concludes with a comparison of Windows NT Server 4.0 and Windows 2000 service packs. The application of service packs in Windows NT Server 4.0 differs from Windows 2000 in two significant ways. Understanding these differences, as well as how to manage service packs and hotfixes on your Windows NT Server 4.0–based system, is clearly explained in this chapter.

on the Job

It's important to emphasize that being able to recover from various hardware and software failures is a mission-critical skill for a network administrator. Users rarely appreciate how well a network runs until it crashes. Downtime becomes very stressful because users are clamoring for server resources, and managers are demanding an estimated repair time. Such moments are the worst possible times to learn how to restore an operating system. Regardless of the configuration of your network, take time to periodically review your servers to ensure you have all the tools and resources needed to restore your operating system should there be a severe failure. Create a test lab so you can actually walk through all the steps to make sure you perform the restore under pressure. The material in this book will give you guidelines and best practices. It's up to you to create a well thought-out plan for recovery when failure does occur, and for putting your knowledge to the test before it's needed on the job.

Configuring and Troubleshooting Trusts, Account Policies, and System Policies: Chapter 4

Managing domains, including trusts and policies, is one area that is significantly different in Windows NT Server 4.0 than in Windows 2000. Whether or not you are familiar with the Windows 2000 model, you'll need a clear understanding of the Windows NT–based model to pass this exam. Chapter 4 focuses on concepts needed to manage the network at the enterprise level.

In Windows NT Server 4.0 networks, security is implemented via domains. However, domains must often provide access to other domains in order for users to use resources across the enterprise. As a result, understanding how to establish and maintain trust relationships is a mission-critical element of managing a Windows NT Server 4.0–based domain at the enterprise level. Interoperability with Novell's NetWare operating system is discussed via the Gateway Services for NetWare (GSNW) and Client Services for NetWare (CSNW) features in Windows NT Server 4.0. You'll learn how NWLink, Microsoft's implementation of IPX/SPX, is used in each case.

In Chapter 4, we also learn about account policies, implemented at the enterprise level. Three key account policies implemented at the top level of the organization are password length, password uniqueness, and password age. These are set globally and should be determined according to the needs of the organization. Chapter 4 teaches you the implications of different choices and how to evaluate your company's needs. Account lockout is a feature in Windows NT Server 4.0 that is substantially different in Windows 2000. This chapter will explain how the feature works and what the key differences are between Windows NT Server 4.0 and Windows 2000.

Chapter 4 also discusses system policies. How to implement policies, where policy files are stored, and how to troubleshoot system policy issues is discussed in detail here. User-specific system policies, computer policies, and group policies are covered to help you understand policies in a Windows NT Server 4.0–based environment.

Configuring and Troubleshooting User Accounts, Profiles, and Logon Scripts: Chapter 5

A network exists to provide greater access to resources for authorized users. Managing user accounts, profiles, and logon scripts is at the heart of the network from a user perspective. It's important to keep in mind that although the job of network administrator encompasses many facets—from security to optimizing performance—the primary responsibility is to provide authorized users with access to the resources they need, when they need them.

Chapter 5 discusses user accounts: how to create them, copy them, delete them, and deactivate them. Using templates, you can quickly create new accounts (something you'll learn in Chapter 5). We'll also look at user profiles and how to create, manage, and troubleshoot them. You'll learn about uses for roaming profiles, mandatory profiles, and local profiles, and how to identify and resolve problems in these areas. You'll also learn how to manage security via user accounts, including restricting or setting login hours or dial-in permissions. Logon scripts, which control computer behavior based on user logon, are also discussed.

We conclude Chapter 5 with information on how groups work and how they should be managed in Windows NT Server 4.0. Although Windows 2000 contains a variety of new features related to managing groups of users, it's vital to understand how groups work in Windows NT, chiefly because the two are significantly different. Default, global, local, and universal groups assist in network management, and, as such, are tested in-depth on the exam.

Analyzing, Configuring, and Monitoring Security: Chapter 6

Without strong security measures in place, any network today will be compromised at some point. As we mentioned earlier, the primary purpose of the network is to provide *authorized* users with access to resources to support the business functions of the company. The key here is that users must be legitimate users, accessing resources to which they have permissions and rights. Ensuring the safety and integrity of the data on the network is a fundamental element of security, and is the focus of Chapter 6.

We begin with understanding how the Security Configuration Manager is used to configure and manage security in the operating system and user environments. We'll review using security templates based on server configuration and requirements, and we'll also take a look at how templates can be used or modified to meet the various security needs of today's corporations.

Chapter 6 continues with an in-depth look at auditing and how to configure auditing policies. Various system objects can be audited to monitor access and usage of resources. Audit logs provide detailed information that can be reviewed, analyzed, and then used as the foundation of security monitoring across the network. Chapter 6 concludes with a discussion of advanced security options including, Server Message Blocks (SMB).

Configuring, Managing, and Troubleshooting Access to Resources: Chapter 7

Access to resources is a key element of security. However, in this section we'll look not at specific users and their permissions, but overall use of permissions to access resources, as well as installing and troubleshooting file-based resource access.

In the Windows NT Server 4.0–based network environment, NTFS and share permissions are used alone and in combination. Chapter 7 walks you through how these permissions interact, and what the results are for users. The various permissions for printers, including the ability to manage the print queue are also discussed. Default permissions must be clearly understood in order to effectively manage security across the domain. Another important aspect of access discussed in Chapter 7 is the effect of group membership. When users belong to different groups, their effective permissions will be determined by the combined permissions assigned to all the groups. While this may sound confusing, Chapter 7 explains exactly how this works.

Finally, Chapter 7 will teach you about Distributed file system (Dfs) and how file-based resources are accessed. The Distributed file system (Dfs) for Windows NT Server is a network server component that makes it easier for you to find and manage data on your network. Chapter 7 walks you though how Dfs is implemented, and how files can span multiple file servers to better manage enterprise data and storage resources.

Configuring and Troubleshooting Printing, Internet, and Intranet Access to Resources and Internet Protocols: Chapter 8

Although computer networks once had the laudable goal of creating a paperless office, the truth is that companies are using more paper than ever. With the surge in data available across the organization, more people need access to printer resources. Configuring and managing print resources has a big impact on the user's experience. Having to run three flights down to grab a printout of confidential financial data is not a viable setup. Users connect both locally and remotely and need access to a variety of print resources. Locating and managing printers to meet the diverse needs of the organization is part of managing a network.

In Chapter 8, we explore the intricate details of managing network printers, including how drivers are installed and managed, and how to create and manage printer pools. We'll learn how to manage print queues by understanding the queuing process as well as how the spooler works. We'll also learn about using TCP/IP in the printing environment.

Chapter 8 concludes with information on external (Internet) and internal (intranet) access to printer resources including how to configure and troubleshoot access to these resources with the HTTP, HTTPS, and FTP protocols.

Configuring, Managing, Troubleshooting, and Optimizing Network Services: Chapter 9

Network services includes network connectivity and performance, as well as name resolution. Chapter 9 begins by discussing connectivity issues. Name resolution services and default gateways are the methods used in Windows NT to locate and connect to services not on the local host. Issues surrounding IP addressing are also examined in this chapter. Private IP addressing, the IPConfig utility, and the use of DHCP to dynamically assign IP addresses are all discussed at length.

Chapter 9 continues with a look at name resolution services. Resources on a network are located using NetBIOS, host names, and browser services. You'll learn about how these work in Windows NT Server. Chapter 9 concludes with a review of the tools available for monitoring and optimizing performance. Event Viewer and Performance Monitor, discussed in Chapter 3, are revisited here. In addition, Chapter 9 discusses Network Monitor, which allows you to examine network traffic to and from the server at the packet-level. It also allows you to capture network traffic so you can analyze it later, making it easier to solve network problems.

Configuring and Troubleshooting IIS Web Servers, RAS, and Performance Tuning: Chapter 10

In the Windows NT Server 4.0–based network, Web services are implemented through Internet Information Server (IIS). These services include Web-based protocols such as HTTP and FTP as well as Web management tools. Many users connect to the network remotely, making Remote Access Server (RAS) an important element for connectivity. Monitoring the load on resource and tuning the system for optimal performance is important for companies that have Web and remote services.

Our final chapter in this book teaches you about Internet Information Server (IIS), what it does, how to configure it, and how to troubleshoot it. Chapter 10 discusses hosting multiple Web sites using IIS and how to tune performance in this setting. In Microsoft's Windows Load Balancing Service (WLBS), two or more servers work together to service the network traffic from the Internet.

SCENARIO & SOLUTION

What two factors influence how much memory a system should have?	Memory requirements for systems vary according to both their use (the applications and services on the server) and their load (the number of users accessing those resources).
What Windows NT Server 4.0 feature allows you to create new user accounts from other user accounts?	The Copy feature allows you to copy an account to create a new one with the same rights and permissions. You can also create and use a template for setting up user accounts.
If you wanted to ensure that files in the Human Resource department's payroll folder were only accessible by Human Resource personnel, what could you implement in Windows NT?	Auditing access of those files or of the entire folder, and then logging the results to an audit log would help monitor those files for unauthorized access or attempts at unauthorized access.
How can you monitor packet-level network traffic in Windows NT?	By using Network Monitor, a built-in Windows NT Server 4.0 tool, you can monitor and examine network traffic down to the packet level.

Chapter 10 concludes with Remote Access Service (RAS). In Windows NT Server, remote access services are provided through direct-dial connections and virtual private networking (VPN) based on the Point-to-Point Tunneling Protocol (PPTP). Providing and securing remote access using RAS, VPN, and PPTP are reviewed.

After completing the reading, exercises, and Q&As in each chapter, you should feel confident in your knowledge of Windows NT Server 4.0. You will have the information you need to successfully pass the exam and to effectively manage an NT Server–based network on the job.

CERTIFICATION OBJECTIVE 1.04

Windows NT Server Terminology

Before we head off into Chapter 2, let's review some terminology you'll find throughout this book. It's organized by sections: Access, Server Hardware, Networking, and Security. The terminology is alphabetic within each section.

Access

- **Access Control List (ACL)** The part of a security descriptor that allows or disallows access to the object based on permissions the owner of the object has set.

- **Access token (or security token)** An object that uniquely identifies the user who has logged on to the network.

- **Account lockout** A security feature that locks a user account if the number of failed logon attempts exceeds those specified in the account lockout policy. Locked accounts cannot log on to the network.

- **Account policy** The account policy controls the way passwords work on all user accounts in a domain or on an individual computer. The policy defines minimum length of password, frequency of password change, and reuse of old passwords.

- **Administrator privilege** One of three privilege levels you can assign to a Windows NT user account. Guest and User are the other two privilege levels available.

- **Auditing** Auditing tracks the activities of users by recording selected events in the security log.

- **Audit policy** The audit policy defines the types of security events that will be logged for servers of a domain, or for an individual computer.

- **Authentication** The process of validating the identity of a user for the purpose of accessing network resources.

- **Global group** A group that can be used in its own domain and in trusting domains that contain only user accounts from its own domain. Global groups can be added to local groups.

- **Guest privilege** One of three privilege levels you can assign to a Windows NT user account. Administrator and User are the other two levels available.

- **Local group** For a Windows NT Server, a group that can be granted permissions only for the domain controllers in its own domain. Can contain user accounts and global groups from its own domain, and from trusted domains.

■ **Local user profiles**   Profiles that are automatically created the first time a user logs on to a computer running Windows NT.

■ **Logon script**   A file that runs automatically each time a user logs on. It can establish various environment settings for the logon session.

■ **Mandatory user profile**   A profile downloaded to the user's desktop at each logon. It cannot be changed by the user.

■ **Roaming user profile**   A user profile that is enabled by an administrator when creating a path to a profile on a server. Whenever the user logs on, the path to the profile is established, allowing the user to have the same computing environment, regardless of the physical location of logon.

■ **System default profile**   The user profile that is loaded when Windows NT is running but no user is logged on.

■ **System policy**   A policy created using the System Policy Editor to control the user work environment.

■ **User default profile**   The user profile that is loaded by a server when a user's specific profile cannot be loaded.

■ **User privilege**   One of three privilege levels you can assign to a Windows NT user account. Administrator and Guest are the other two privilege levels available.

Server Hardware

■ **Backup types**   The Windows NT Backup program can create backups in the following formats: copy, daily, differential, incremental, and normal.

■ **Boot partition**   The volume that contains the Windows NT operating system and supporting files. The boot partition can be the same as the system partition (but does not have to be the same).

■ **Cache**   Memory that stores frequently accessed random access memory (RAM) locations and the addresses of where this data is stored.

■ **Copy backup**   Copies all selected files, but does not mark files as having been backed up.

■ **Daily backup**   Copies all selected files that have been modified the day of the backup.

■ **Device driver** A program designed to enable a specific hardware device to communicate with the operating system.

■ **Differential backup** Copies those files created or changed since the last normal or incremental backup.

■ **Fault tolerance** The ability of a disk subsystem to recover from various errors. In Windows NT, this is provided by the FtDisk.sys driver and is implemented via mirror and stripe sets.

■ **File allocation table (FAT)** A list maintained by some operating systems to track segments of the disk. Both FAT and NTFS are supported in Windows NT.

■ **Hard page fault** A fault that occurs when a program needs data that is neither in its working set in the main memory nor anywhere else in physical memory, and yet data must be retrieved from the disk.

■ **Incremental backup** Copies only those files created or changed since the last normal or incremental backup.

■ **Master boot record (MBR)** The MBR is an area on the hard disk. It contains the partition table for the disk and a small amount of executable code to begin the boot process.

■ **Mirror set** For the selected disk, an identical copy of the data is written to a second disk called a shadow disk, providing fault tolerance.

■ **Normal backup** Copies all selected files and marks each as having been backed up.

■ **NT File System (NTFS)** A file system supported only in Windows NT that allows for greater management and control of file resources. All files are treated as objects with user-defined and system-defined attributes.

■ **Page fault** A page fault occurs in the processor when a process refers to a virtual page in memory that is not in its working set in main memory.

■ **Redundant Array of Inexpensive Disks (RAID)** A method of using disk drives in an array to provide fault tolerance and performance improvements. Windows NT supports three levels of RAID: 0, 1, and 5.

■ **Shadow disk** The second disk in a mirror set that contains an exact copy of data on the primary disk, providing fault tolerance.

■ **Stripe set** A method of writing data across several physical disk drives to improve access times.

- **Stripe set with parity**   A method of writing data across several physical disk drives using parity. Parity is an algorithm used to regenerate data if any of the other data is lost.

- **System partition**   The location of the hardware-specific files needed to load Windows NT.

Networking

- **Computer Browser**   Maintains a current list of computers and provides the list to applications when requested.

- **Default gateway**   The intermediate device on the network that has knowledge of other networks. Packets destined for remote networks are passed through the default gateway.

- **Distributed file system (Dfs)**   A network server component that allows files to span multiple file servers in order to better manage enterprise data and storage resources.

- **DNS name servers**   The servers containing information about a portion of the DNS database, providing name resolution across the Internet

- **Domain**   A collection of computers that share a common directory database.

- **Domain Name System (DNS)**   The service that provides domain name resolution for TCP/IP hosts..

- **Dynamic Host Configuration Protocol (DHCP)**   A protocol used to automatically assign IP addresses to computers on a network.

- **File Transfer Protocol (FTP)**   Supports transferring files between local and remote computers. FTP is implemented as part of the Internet Information Service (IIS) in Windows NT.

- **Gateway**   Translates different protocols for heterogeneous networks. Translates transport protocols or data formats.

- **Gateway Services for NetWare (GSNW)**   A service in Windows NT that allows Windows-based clients to access resources on a NetWare server through the gateway.

- **Hypertext Markup Language (HTML)**   A markup language using ASCII text files with embedded codes denoting formatting and hypertext links.

- **Hypertext Transfer Protocol (HTTP)**   The protocol by which clients and servers communicate on the World Wide Web (WWW). It is an application level protocol.

- **Internet Information Server (IIS)**   A file and application server that supports multiple Internet-related protocols including HTML and HTTP.

- **Internet Protocol (IP)**   The messenger protocol that is part of the TCP/IP suite of protocols, responsible for addressing and sending TCP packets over the network.

- **Internet service provider (ISP)**   A company or institution that provides Internet access to remote users via dial-up or leased lines.

- **Intranet**   A TCP/IP network using Internet technology that is typically internal to a company and not connected directly to the Internet.

- **IP address**   An address used to identify each device on a network and to specify routing information. Each IP address on a network must be unique.

- **IP router**   A component connected to two or more physical TCP/IP networks that can deliver IP packets between networks.

- **IPX/SPX**   A set of transport protocols used by Novell NetWare networks. Windows NT implements this protocol using NWLink.

- **Member server**   A computer running Windows NT Server that is not a PDC or BDC. Also called a stand-alone server.

- **NetBEUI**   A network protocol used in small networks. NetBEUI cannot be routed.

- **One-way Trust**   One domain (the trusting domain) "trusts" a second domain (the trusted domain) and allows the second (trusted) domain's users to access its resources.

- **Open Systems Interconnection model (OSI)**   Each layer of the TCP/IP model corresponds to one or more layers in the International Standards Organization (ISO) seven-layer OSI model. TCP/IP layers are Application, Transport, Internet, and Network Interface. The OSI layers are Application, Presentation, Session, Transport, Network, Data Link, and Physical.

- **Owner**   Every file and directory on an NTFS volume has an owner. By default, the owner is the one who creates the object and can control access through setting permissions.

- **PING** A command used to verify connections to one or more remote hosts (computers).

- **Printing pool** Two or more identical print devices associated with one printer.

- **Print spooler** A set of dynamic link libraries (DLLs) that receive, process, schedule, and distribute documents for printing.

- **Remote Access Service (RAS)** A service that provides remote network access to file and print services, e-mail, scheduling, and other network-based tasks.

- **Server Message Block (SMB)** A file-sharing protocol that allows access to files on remote computer systems.

- **Simple Mail Transfer Protocol (SMTP)** Part of the TCP/IP suite of protocols that controls the exchange of e-mail.

- **Simple Network Management Protocol (SNMP)** A protocol used to get and set status information about computers (hosts) on a TCP/IP network.

- **Subnet** A portion of a network that shares a network address with other parts of the network, but has a distinct subnet number.

- **Transmission Control Protocol/Internet Protocol (TCP/IP)** A suite of networking protocols that allow communication across interconnected networks.

- **Virtual private network (VPN)** A virtual network created using the Point-to-Point Tunneling Protocol (PPTP) that provides for secure network connectivity from a remote location.

- **Windows Internet Name Service (WINS)** A name resolution service that translates Windows computer names to IP addresses. A WINS server manages these services.

Security

- **Backup Domain Controller (BDC)** In a Windows NT Server domain, a server that receives a copy of the domain's directory database. The database is synchronized periodically and BDCs can authenticate users during the logon process.

■ **Built-in groups**   Default groups provided with Windows NT Server that have been granted a set of commonly used rights and capabilities for a particular group of users.

■ **Directory database**   The database of security information containing user account names, passwords, and security settings. Also called the Security Accounts Manager (SAM).

■ **Encryption**   The process of making data indecipherable to protect it from unauthorized access and viewing.

■ **Firewall**   A system that protects the boundary between two or more networks, and keeps intruders out of private networks.

■ **One-way Trust**   One domain "trusts" the domain controllers in a second domain to properly authenticate users to provide access to resources. The second domain does not "trust" the first domain, therefore it does not allow users from the first domain access to resources.

■ **Password uniqueness**   The requirement that when users change passwords, they use new, unique passwords for a period of time defined in the domain's policies.

■ **Point-to-Point Tunneling Protocol (PPTP)**   A secure networking technology that supports multiprotocol virtual private networks (VPNs).

■ **Primary Domain Controller (PDC)**   In a Windows NT Server domain, a server that authenticates domain logons and maintains the directory database for a domain. This database is replicated to BDCs.

■ **Public key cryptography**   A method of securing data between servers.

■ **Secure Sockets Layer (SSL)**   A protocol used to provide secure data communications through data encryption and decryption. It utilizes public key cryptography and bulk data encryption.

■ **Security Accounts Manager (SAM)**   A directory database that stores user account names, passwords, and security settings.

■ **Security identifier (SID)**   A unique name used to identify a logged-on user.

■ **Security policy**   In Windows NT Server, security policies consist of Account, User Rights, Audit, and Trust Relationship policies. They are managed via User Manager For Domains.

- **Trust relationship** A link between two or more domains enabling users from one domain to access resources on another domain.

- **Two-way Trust** A relationship between two domains in which the users of each domain are allowed access to resources on the other domain.

- **User Manager For Domains** A Windows NT Server tool used to manage security for the domain, including user accounts, groups, and security policies.

We've covered a lot of ground in this section. Although we reviewed a lot of terminology, chances are you were already familiar with some of it. As you read through the rest of the book, you'll become more familiar with these concepts and terms.

CERTIFICATION SUMMARY

In this chapter, we've taken a brief look at the road ahead. We started by understanding a bit about a Windows NT Server 4.0 network and the components of such a network. Next, we looked at the requirements for Microsoft Exam 70-244. We

SCENARIO & SOLUTION

What does the operating system check before allowing a user to read a file?	The Access Control List (ACL) is used to determine whether a user has sufficient permissions to access an object, like a file.
What feature in Windows NT translates the Windows name to an IP address for a computer?	WINS, or Windows Internet Name Service, is a name resolution service used to translate Windows computer names to IP addresses.
What database is used to manage user security for Windows NT?	Security Accounts Manager (SAM) is a directory database that stores user account names, passwords, and security settings.
What type of trust relationship allows users of one domain to access resources in a second domain, but does not allow users in the second domain access to resources in the first domain?	A one-way trust relationship.

reviewed not only the target audience for the test, but the topics covered on the exam. Although we looked at the topics by related segments, we learned that the real exam will not deliver questions by segment. Finally, we looked in more detail at what you can expect from each chapter. Having a roadmap of the course ahead, you should now be prepared to learn about Windows NT Server 4.0 and pass Microsoft Exam 70-244 with flying colors.

Windows NT Server 4.0 has many similarities with Windows 2000. It also has features that are unique to the operating system and completely different than Windows 2000. With so many installations of Windows NT Server 4.0 still implemented in corporations around the world, a successful network administrator will need to understand Windows NT–based networking alone, and as part of a larger Windows 2000 solution.

 **TWO-MINUTE DRILL**

What Is "Supporting and Maintaining a Microsoft Windows NT Server 4.0 Network"?

❑ Microsoft Exam 70-244, Supporting and Maintaining a Microsoft Windows NT Server 4.0 Network, is part of the new Windows 2000 curriculum.

❑ There are thousands of installations of Windows NT Server 4.0 worldwide, which require specialized knowledge of the operating system's unique features.

❑ Windows 2000 and Windows NT share many similar features, but they also have many unique features and characteristics that a network professional should be familiar with.

❑ Supporting and maintaining a Windows NT Server 4.0 network requires knowledge of hardware, operating system, networking and connectivity, managing users and resource access, and security.

Overview of Exam 70-244

❑ The exam is geared toward individuals who have one or more years' experience in the IT profession, and who manage a medium to large Windows NT network.

❑ The exam covers optimizing and tuning the server, including hardware, operating system, and subsystem performance (disk, network).

❑ The exam requires in-depth knowledge of managing access to resources, including auditing, user accounts, system policies, profiles, and groups.

❑ Security, network services, and managing Internet-related functions are also critical knowledge areas.

What We'll Cover in This Book

❑ Optimizing server hardware typically includes reviewing processors, memory, disk, and network subsystems.

❑ Restoring the operating system is a mission-critical task. Determining the operating system failure and the most efficient method for recovery is important when managing a large network.

❑ Enterprise-wide activities include establishing trusts, defining and establishing account policies, and defining and establishing system policies.

❑ Users can be managed via User Manager For Domains. Users and groups are given permission to access resources within the domain.

❑ Security includes managing user access through logon hours, logon scripts, user profiles, and auditing.

❑ Access to resources includes printer and other network resources, both local and remote.

❑ Remote Access Service, or RAS, is an increasingly important element in today's networking environment. Remote access is via direct dial-in or via the Internet using virtual private networks (VPNs) and the Point-to-Point Tunneling Protocol (PPTP).

❑ Internet services are implemented via Internet Information Service (IIS) and provide the capability to manage Web sites, balance Web site loads, and manage Internet protocols like HTTP, HTTPS, and FTP.

Windows NT Server Terminology

❑ Many of the Windows NT Server 4.0 terms are similar to terms and concepts used in general networking and in Windows 2000.

❑ Terms related to access are authentication, account policy, and user profiles.

❑ Terms related to hardware and optimization are cache, master boot record (MBR), boot partition, and system partition.

❑ Networking concepts covered in the terminology section include TCP/IP and related utilities, IPX/SPX and NWLink, as well as Internet-related protocols, including HTTP, HTTPS, and FTP.

❑ Encryption, Secure Sockets Layer, Security Policy and Trusts are all elements of security implemented in Windows NT.

SELF TEST

The following questions will help you measure your understanding of the material presented in this chapter. Read all the choices carefully, as there may be more than one correct answer. Choose all correct answers for each question.

What Is "Supporting and Maintaining a Microsoft Windows NT Server 4.0 Network"?

1. Why is the Microsoft Exam 70-244 part of the new Windows 2000 curriculum?

    A. Most companies have completely migrated to Windows 2000.

    B. Windows 2000 and Windows NT Server 4.0 contain very similar features.

    C. Many companies still interoperate with Novell NetWare, so understanding Windows NT Server 4.0 is essential.

    D. Many companies run both Windows 2000 and Windows NT.

2. Which of the following, when added to a system, is likely to yield the best performance increase on a Windows NT server?

    A. Memory

    B. Disk drives

    C. Network bandwidth

    D. Disk controller

3. When restoring an operating system, which elements are most critical? (Choose all that apply.)

    A. Locating and restoring operating system files

    B. Locating and restoring disk partition information

    C. Locating and restoring network protocol binding order

    D. Locating and restoring operating system registry keys

4. Which statement about service packs is true?

    A. Windows 2000 service packs can be applied to Windows NT machines, but Windows NT service packs cannot be applied to Windows 2000 machines.

    B. Windows 2000 and Windows NT service packs are applied in exactly the same way and have exactly the same features.

    C. Windows 2000 and Windows NT service packs are applied in the same way, but have different features.

    D. Windows 2000 and Windows NT service packs are interchangeable.

5. What is one method of managing the user security environment in a Windows NT environment?

   A. Using the Security Configuration Manager

   B. Using organizational units

   C. Using domains

   D. Using workgroups

Overview of Exam 70-244

6. Which is not a feature of the target audience for Exam 70-244?

   A. The company has one to fifty physical locations.

   B. The company has two hundred to twenty six thousand users.

   C. Network services include file and print, database, messaging, proxy or firewall, dial-in, desktop, and Web hosting.

   D. Branch offices and individual users need the same kinds of connectivity.

7. Which activity is likely to provide long-term data integrity to the network?

   A. Performing daily backups and storing tapes off site

   B. Doing monthly performance monitoring

   C. Creating baseline metrics for specific hardware functions

   D. Implementing auditing on all events

8. At the enterprise level, what are account policies used for? (Choose all that apply.)

   A. Account policies specify which users can have accounts in the domain.

   B. Account policies specify password uniqueness requirements.

   C. Account policies specify which password length can be applied to each group type.

   D. Account policies specify account lockout characteristics.

9. What areas in Windows NT Server 4.0 IIS are tested on the exam? (Choose all that apply.)

   A. Hosting multiple Web sites

   B. Performance tuning

   C. Using Windows Load Balancing Service (WLBS)

   D. Managing top-level domain names

10. Which tools can be used to monitor network performance?

   A. Event Viewer, Performance Monitor, and the Security Configuration Manager

   B. Event Viewer, Performance Monitor, and Network Monitor

   C. Event Viewer, PING, and Network Monitor

   D. Paging File, Performance Monitor, and Network Monitor

What We'll Cover in This Book

11. Which of these features would improve the processing of threads from various applications?

   A. Adding an Alpha processor to an x86-based system

   B. Adding a second x86-based processor to a system

   C. Physically connecting three servers and enabling clustering

   D. Adding additional RAM

12. What feature is included in Windows NT Server 4.0 that provides interoperability with Novell Networks? (Choose all that apply.)

   A. Gateway Services for NetWare (GSNW)

   B. Client Services for NetWare (CSNW)

   C. IPX/SPX

   D. NWLink

13. What types of groups are found, by default, in Windows NT Server 4.0?

   A. Default and global groups

   B. Default, global, local, and universal groups

   C. Default, global, and local groups

   D. Global, local, and universal groups

   E. Default, global, and universal groups

14. Which is true of a Distributed file system?

   A. Files are distributed according to file type.

   B. Backups are configured to back up only specific files across the enterprise.

   C. Files can span multiple file servers.

   D. Files can span multiple domains.

15. How is RAS implemented in Windows NT Server 4.0? (Choose all that apply.)

A. Through direct dial-in connections

B. Through virtual private networks (VPNs)

C. By way of Point-to-Point Tunneling Protocol (PPTP)

D. By way of Server Message Blocks (SMB)

Windows NT Server Terminology

16. Which definition best describes authentication?

A. The process of validating the identity of a user for the purpose of accessing network resources.

B. The process of validating the telephone number of a dial-in user.

C. The process of validating the identity of users accessing a secure object.

D. The process of validating the identity of a user for the purpose of joining built-in user groups.

17. Which type of profile establishes a consistent user environment that cannot be changed by the user?

A. A roaming profile

B. A roaming personal profile

C. A roaming mandatory profile

D. A local personal profile

18. Which partition on a disk drive contains the operating system files on a Windows NT Server 4.0–based server?

A. System

B. Boot

C. Extended

D. Volume set

19. If you wanted to implement a software fault tolerance solution in Windows NT Server 4.0, which of the following could you use? (Choose all that apply.)

A. Level 0

B. Level 1

C. Level 2

D. Level 3

E. Level 5

20. If you were to implement security on your Web site, what protocol would you want to avoid using for normal file transfer?

A. FTP

B. Gopher

C. SSL

D. PPTP

SELF TEST ANSWERS

What Is "Supporting and Maintaining a Microsoft Windows NT Server 4.0 Network"?

1. ☑ **D.** Most companies are still running a combination of Windows 2000 and Windows NT. Understanding how to manage a Windows NT network is still an important aspect of network administration in a Windows environment.

   ☒ **A** is incorrect because many companies have migrated to Windows 2000, but other companies are still planning on using Windows NT Server 4.0 for a number of reasons. **B** is incorrect because Windows 2000 and Windows NT have very different features. As a result, just knowing Windows 2000 will not give you sufficient knowledge to successfully administer a Windows NT network. **C** is incorrect because although many companies use Novell's NetWare operating system, both Windows 2000 and Windows NT will interoperate with NetWare.

2. ☑ **A.** Adding more memory generally improves performance of any system. Memory is used to store information awaiting processing or that which is the result of processing. If physical memory is in short supply, data will be written to the disk drive, which always slows response time down.

   ☒ **B** is incorrect. Disk drives may be the bottleneck if you don't have sufficient disk space. However, the biggest performance boost will come from adding memory. **C** is incorrect. Network bandwidth generally shouldn't be "added to a system." In many cases, the network connection is fast enough but the system becomes bogged down in processing the various requests. **D** is not correct. Adding a disk controller can improve throughput to the disk drives. However, adding memory will generally provide a more noticeable performance boost.

3. ☑ **A, B,** and **D.** Operating system files are critical for the operating system to properly start and run. Disk partition information is important because the system will attempt to find the system and boot partitions in order to locate needed system files. If partition information cannot be found, the system may not be able to locate needed files for booting the operating system. Finally, the registry is the database of information about the configuration and status of the computer. If this file is corrupt or missing, the system will not operate correctly. Thus, repairing the registry, if needed, is a critical component to restoring a system to full functionality.

   ☒ **C** is incorrect because the protocol binding order may speed up certain network-based functions, but is not a critical element in restoring a system.

4. ☑ **C.** Windows 2000 and Windows NT service packs can be applied in the same ways. However, Windows 2000 service packs have additional features. Windows NT service packs must be reapplied when the system configuration changes, which is not true in Windows 2000.
   ☒ **A** is incorrect because you cannot apply service packs from a different operating system to either Windows 2000 or Windows NT. **B** is incorrect because while they are applied in the same way, they have different features. **D** is incorrect because service packs are not interchangeable between operating systems. They are written specifically for the operating system to which they must be applied.

5. ☑ **A.** The Security Configuration Manager is a tool in Windows NT used to configure security for operating system and user environments.
   ☒ **B** is incorrect because organizational units (OUs) are found in Windows 2000, not Windows NT. **C** is incorrect because domains are used, in part, for user security, but are also employed to manage resources. So, this is not the best answer. **D** is incorrect because workgroups can be used to manage users, but it is not the best answer in terms of managing user security.

Overview of Exam 70-244

6. ☑ **D.** The IT professional managing an NT network would likely deal with branch offices and individual users that need different kinds of connectivity.
   ☒ **A, B,** and **C** are incorrect. Each of these statements reflects features of a network that would typically be managed by someone in the target audience for this exam.

7. ☑ **A.** Performing daily backups and storing the tapes off site is the best way to ensure the long-term integrity of your system's data.
   ☒ **B** is incorrect because monitoring should be an ongoing process. Although monthly checks of certain key performance metrics may be warranted, this is not the best way to ensure the long-term integrity of your network's data. **C** is incorrect because creating baselines for processor, memory, and other hardware components is certainly part of "best practices," but is not specifically the best way to ensure the integrity of the data. **D** is incorrect because auditing on all events will likely bog down your server and provide far too much detail to be of use. Choosing which objects and events to audit based on the needs of your organization is a better strategy.

8. ☑ **B** and **D.** Account policies are used for setting policies for password uniqueness, password length, password age, and account lockout. All of these apply across the domain and are set for all users.

☒ A is incorrect because account policies do not specify which users can have accounts in the domain. This may be set by network policies or trust relationships with other domains. C is incorrect because account policies, such as password length, are set for all users, not specific sets of users, such as groups.

9. ☑ **A, B,** and **C.** Hosting multiple Web sites on a Windows NT Server, tuning the performance of the Web site(s) and using the Windows Load Balancing Service (WLBS) are all topics you should be familiar with for the exam.
☒ **D** is incorrect because top-level domain names are the .com, .net, .gov, .mil, or .org extensions for domain names. These are handled by an external organization whose purpose is to manage top-level domains for the entire Internet. Top-level domains are not managed by individual organizations.

10. ☑ **B.** Event Viewer allows you to view various system events and look at the details of those events. Performance Monitor allows you to select objects and counters that will help determine the performance of each object. Network Monitor allows you to view network traffic and analyze it.
☒ **A** is incorrect because Event Viewer and Performance Monitor are used, but the Security Configuration Manager is used for configuring operating system and user security environments. **C** is incorrect because although the PING utility can help you troubleshoot network connectivity issues, it generally isn't helpful in monitoring and optimizing network performance. Because of this, it is not the best answer available. **D** is incorrect. The paging file can impact overall system performance but is not specifically used to tune network performance.

What We'll Cover in This Book

11. ☑ **B.** Adding a second processor can improve the server's ability to process threads from different applications. This lowers the queue time and improves overall performance.
☒ **A** is incorrect because you cannot add an Alpha processor (RISC-based) to an x86-based system. **C** is incorrect because although this would improve throughput, the feature is only available in Windows 2000. **D** is incorrect because additional RAM often improves system performance, but will not improve the processor's throughput. RAM is used to store the results of processing or to store data that requires processing. Cache is used by a processor, and additional processor cache may improve processor performance in some cases.

12. ☑ **A, B,** and **C.** Gateway Services for NetWare provides a gateway for NT users to access Novell resources. Client Services for NetWare is used to allow direct connections to file and

printer resources running Novell's NetWare operating system. NWLink is Microsoft's implementation of IPX/SPX and is the protocol used either by the server or the client to communicate with a Novell network.

☒ **D** is incorrect because Novell uses the IPX/SPX suite of protocols rather than TCP/IP. However, this is not a feature in Windows NT.

13. ☑ **C.** The three types of groups found in Windows NT by default are default, global, and local groups.

☒ **A** is incorrect because the list is incomplete. It should include local groups as well. **B, D,** and **E** are incorrect. Universal groups are new to Windows 2000 and are not found in Windows NT.

14. ☑ **C.** Dfs can be implemented in Windows NT Server. Files can span multiple file servers to better manage enterprise data and storage resources.

☒ **A** is incorrect because there is no system in Windows NT Server to distribute files according to file type. When viewing files and folders, you can specify a file type, but this is not the definition of Dfs. **B** is incorrect because backups can be configured to back up sets of files, but this is not inherent to Dfs. **D** is incorrect because files can span multiple file servers in the same domain.

15. ☑ **A, B,** and **C.** In Windows NT Server, remote access services are provided through direct-dial connections and virtual private networks (VPNs) based on Point-to-Point Tunneling Protocol (PPTP). This provides for two different types of connections based on the security needs of the individual and the organization.

☒ **D** is incorrect because Server Message Blocks are an advanced security feature of Windows NT Server, but is not related to RAS. Server Message Blocks is a protocol used to pass information between networked computers.

Windows NT Server Terminology

16. ☑ **A.** Authentication is specifically the process of validating the identity of a user in order to provide that user with access to network resources.

☒ **B** is incorrect because the callback feature of RAS allows the system to call a user back at a specific phone number for security purposes. This is not the process of authentication. **C** is incorrect because although access to secure objects is one of the results of authentication, authentication is more specifically defined as authenticating the user to access all network resources. **D** is incorrect because users can be added to built-in user groups for the purposes of providing various rights and permissions to those users. However, this is not the process of authentication.

17. ☑ **C.** A roaming mandatory profile is a user profile that is enabled by an administrator creating a path to a profile on a server. Whenever the user logs on, the path to the profile is established, requiring the user to have the same computing environment regardless of the physical location of logon. The settings cannot be altered by the user, hence the use of the term mandatory.

☒ **A** is incorrect because a roaming profile can be a personal profile, which the user can modify. A roaming profile can also be a mandatory profile, which a user cannot modify. There are essentially three profile types in Windows NT Server: local personal, roaming personal, and roaming mandatory. **B** is incorrect because a roaming personal profile allows the user to modify settings, but provides a consistent user environment regardless of logon location. **D** is incorrect because a local personal profile is a profile available only on the user's machine.

18. ☑ **B.** The boot partition is the volume that contains the Windows NT operating system and supporting files. The boot partition can be the same as the system partition (but does not have to be the same).

☒ **A** is incorrect because the system partition contains files that allow the system to boot and locate the operating system in the boot partition. **C** is incorrect because an extended partition is a nonbootable portion of a drive that can be subdivided into logical drivers. There can be only one extended partition per drive. **D** is incorrect because a volume set is a volume that uses the unused disk space on several drives to create a single unit. It is formatted like a single hard disk drive. It can have a drive letter assigned to it even though it spans several drives.

19. ☑ **A, B, and E.** If you implement fault tolerance via the Windows NT Server 4.0 operating system, you could implement Level 0, 1, and 5 only. Level 0 is a stripe set, Level 1 is a mirror set, and Level 5 is a stripe set with parity.

☒ **C and D** are incorrect solutions.

20. ☑ **C.** Secure Sockets Layer (SSL) is a protocol used to provide secure data communications through data encryption and decryption. It utilizes public key cryptography and bulk data encryption. However, it requires a significant amount of processing time to encrypt and decrypt data, so normal file transfer would take much longer and require more processor time than without SSL.

☒ **A** is incorrect because FTP, or File Transfer Protocol, is used specifically for transferring files via the Internet. **B** is incorrect because Gopher is another method of transferring files that predates the existence of the World Wide Web. It is used to display files in hierarchical order for viewing or access. **D** is incorrect because PPTP, or Point-to-Point Tunneling Protocol, is used to secure a virtual private network (VPN) connection and can be used for file transfer when connected to the network remotely.

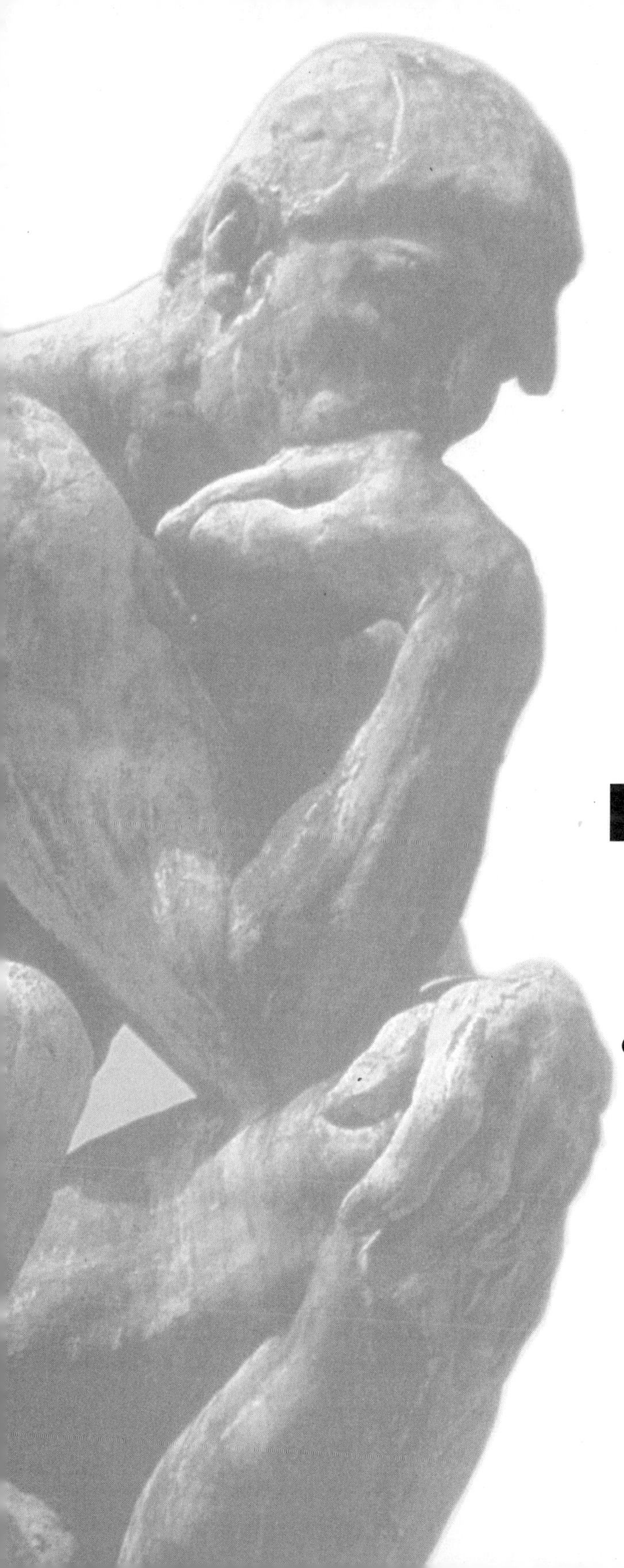

MCSE

MICROSOFT CERTIFIED SYSTEMS ENGINEER

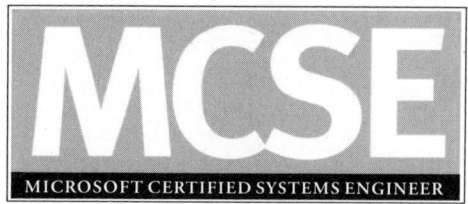

2

Maintaining, Troubleshooting, and Optimizing Server Hardware

CERTIFICATION OBJECTIVES

T he reliability of any network begins with the dependability of each of the hardware components in the network. Servers form the backbone of the network and provide many different services to users including hosting applications, storing data, and providing a wide array of network services such as logon, security, and network communications.

Microsoft Windows NT 4.0 Server contains a number of tools for optimizing, configuring, maintaining, and troubleshooting the server hardware. In this chapter, we'll look at these tools and learn how to work with hardware and software resources to provide a well-balanced approach to keeping the network hardware running at peak performance. In addition, we'll take a close look at data backups, the part backups play in maintaining a network, as well as how to recover from a hardware failure using backups.

Today's network computing environment leaves little room for downtime. Managing hardware resources efficiently and effectively is the key to providing a network that helps users accomplish their jobs more effectively. This chapter will look at how this can be accomplished by working effectively with hardware resources.

CERTIFICATION OBJECTIVE 2.01

Optimizing, Configuring, Maintaining, and Troubleshooting Hardware

Within Microsoft Windows NT 4.0 Server, there are a number of tools and techniques that help a network administrator manage servers. To begin, let's review how to recover from hardware failures involving processors, RAM, and disk drives.

Recovering from Hardware Failures

As reliable as computer hardware has become, components will still fail from time to time. Failures can be placed in two categories: preventable and unpreventable. Preventable failures include servers affected by power spikes because no surge protection was in place, or a processor that overheats due to a location hotter than the manufacturer's recommendations. These types of failures are generally preventable. The cost of avoiding these kinds of failures is typically far lower than the cost of recovering from them, so adequate preventive measures should be taken. Other failures simply occur: processors, RAM, or disk drives fail to function with no apparent external cause. Sometimes a known manufacturing defect is identified and the component is replaced or repaired before failure. In most cases, however, a component simply fails. In such cases, a clear recovery plan will minimize network disruption and speed up recovery dramatically.

Clearly, planning can resolve both preventable and unpreventable failures. A solid maintenance plan should include power protection, control of environmental factors, as well as other strategies designed to eliminate preventable failures. Planning also provides a way to manage unforeseen failures. Each company must assess its risk as well as the cost of various recovery plans in order to develop an organized method of recuperating from these failures. For instance, some companies cannot afford *any* downtime and will run several redundant servers. Others, on a more modest budget, may elect to simply keep spare disks, memory, and peripherals handy and deal with a component failure on a case-by-case basis. Regardless of the amount of redundancy your firm requires, planning for recovery will minimize downtime and disruption to users.

Finally, all hardware that is currently running in a Windows NT 4.0 environment must meet the specifications of the Hardware Compatibility List (HCL). This is a list of tested hardware components that will work with Windows NT 4.0. While other components not listed in the HCL may work, they have not been tested and may not work reliably. Therefore, it is wise to ensure all hardware incorporated into a Windows NT 4.0 computer system is listed in the HCL. This also includes any and all replacement hardware installed as a result of the failures discussed next.

Processors

The processor is the heart of the computer. Processor failure typically disables the machine completely. In such cases, replacing the processor is the only recovery method. Most companies opt to replace the entire motherboard, including the processor chip, rather than just replacing the processor. The reasons for this are:

- The processor chip must be matched to the characteristics of the motherboard. Mismatching these critical components can cause various strange and intermittent errors.

- It is often more cost-effective to replace the entire board rather than just the processor.

In cases where a company has a large number of similar machines, keeping several replacement processor chips handy can make sense.

When a processor chip fails, two possible problems arise. In the first case, the processor fails, the machine halts, and all activity on the computer ceases. In this case, data is typically not lost. Replacing the processor chip (and possibly the motherboard) and then restarting the computer typically resolves the problem. In some cases, the processor failure can be a bit more subtle. Although less likely, processor failure can sometimes corrupt data. In general, processor failure rates are typically low.

Once the hardware failure is repaired, care should be taken to review the integrity of the data stored on that server prior to bringing it back online. This will ensure data accuracy and reduce the likelihood of further problems.

RAM

Random access memory, or RAM, is the main memory used in the computer. RAM is where short-term memory activities occur, such as storing a file that is being edited, or storing the pointers for managing memory itself.

RAM failure is fairly easy to diagnose and correct, being that memory failures often generate errors that point to specific locations within memory. The infamous Windows NT 4.0 "blue screen" often occurs when memory fails (although this is not the only cause of the blue screen). Since RAM comes in segments, or banks, each bank can be tested for errors using any one of a number of off-the-shelf utility programs. Whenever a computer is booted or restarted, RAM is tested. Therefore, memory failures often appear when a computer is started or restarted.

Once the specific location in memory is identified, the suspect bank of RAM can be replaced. Running the same memory diagnostics will determine whether or not there were multiple errors in RAM. Sometimes "false errors" are detected as a result of one failure. Thus, using common troubleshooting techniques and replacing only one component at a time will ensure that only the failing memory bank is replaced. Replacing a bank of RAM is a fairly straightforward task and there is no associated data loss. Each motherboard holds banks of RAM. In some cases, the banks must be installed in pairs. RAM has different specifications and therefore replacement RAM should be exactly matched. The slots in the motherboard will dictate what type of RAM can be used, but RAM also has chip speeds that range from approximately 6ns to 10ns. Having RAM with mismatched speeds can create additional, intermittent memory problems. For more information, you should check the motherboard manufacturer's specifications prior to installing new RAM.

Spare RAM should always be kept on hand. Since different computers use different configurations of RAM (including speed, capacity, and the use of parity), spares for each memory type used in the organization is a good investment.

Hard Disks

In any computer, the components with moving parts are the most likely to fail. Therefore, it is reasonable to assume you may experience a hard disk failure long before you experience a processor failure simply because a hard drive has moving parts. The disk platters spin, and the heads move in and out to read and write data on the platters. The distance from the heads to the platter is a fraction of the width of a human hair. The platters spin at thousands of revolutions per minute. There's not much room for error inside a disk drive. Still, they have become increasingly reliable and relatively inexpensive.

Recovering from a disk failure is perhaps the most difficult recovery to perform. Data may or may not have been lost as the drive failed. In addition, because there is a single point of failure (unless fault-tolerant configurations are used), the computer will cease operating until the drive is restored.

Recovering from a failed disk may involve reformatting the drive and restoring drive data. In more extreme cases, the drive is completely unrecoverable and a new one must be installed. Afterward, it may have to be low-level and high-level formatted. Today, in most instances, the drive simply requires formatting for the particular operating system used (high-level formatting). In such an event, the drive is replaced and formatted for use in Windows NT 4.0. Files stored on this drive are replaced using the most recent (or most reliable) backup. Once files are restored, the system can be brought back online. We'll review backups, and restoring systems using backups, later in this chapter.

RAID Controllers

Redundant Array of Inexpensive Disks, or RAID, is a group of disks that work as a unit. These RAID disks, composed typically of three to five disks in an array, work together to provide more storage, more redundancy, and in some cases, more throughput for the server and its users. RAID provides the redundancy necessary to recover from a single disk failure. RAID can be implemented as both a hardware or software solution. Windows NT 4.0 provides two software solutions using RAID: mirror sets and stripe sets. Most experts agree it is preferable to implement a hardware RAID solution for faster performance and enhanced functionality.

Some hardware vendors make RAID arrays that allow you to replace the disk while the subsystem is powered up and running. This is called "hot swapping." In other cases, the array must be powered down before a disk can be replaced. RAID is not designed to recover from multiple drive failures. In such cases, the failed drives must be replaced and the volume (stripe set with parity, for instance) must be re-created from backups.

In a hardware implementation, the RAID controller handles the creation and regeneration of redundant information for the array. This data is automatically used if a single disk fails. Many companies use a single controller to manage the RAID arrays. However, a single RAID controller creates a single point of failure that could potentially disable the entire server. If the controller that manages several disks fails, no communications from the disks to the processor can occur, and the system will be unable to continue working. Thus, the entire server becomes disabled. To prevent this, some companies elect to install multiple RAID controllers. This eliminates the single point of failure and makes a complete outage unlikely.

To replace a controller, the board must meet the same specifications as the failed board. Typically, the RAID array is a complete "hardware solution" from a particular vendor. While nonvendor-supplied parts may work, it is important to review all the product's specifications to ensure replacement parts are identical. Some RAID controllers come with additional drivers and software used to manage the array. Once the board is replaced, the associated drivers and vendor-supplied software should be installed. The procedure for replacing a RAID disk will depend on whether or not the drive can be hot-swapped. If it can, the failed drive is simply removed, and an identical, new drive is installed. The system will automatically prepare the new drive, then transfer the necessary information to the drive to make it a functional part of the array. Otherwise, the RAID array must be powered down prior to installing a new drive. For more detailed instructions, the manufacturer's specifications and instructions should be followed.

Windows NT 4.0 provides for software management of two types of RAID arrays. Using the Disk Administrator, you can create mirror sets and stripe sets with parity. We'll discuss this in more detail later in this chapter.

Network Adapters

The Network Adapter is often called the Network Interface Card, or NIC. This board manages all communications from the server to the network and all network communications to the server. Loss of functionality in this board will cause the server to be unable to send and receive information to and from the network. This tends to cause the server to appear to be "offline" to users and other resources. Unless the malfunction is severe, failure of the NIC will not disrupt data on the server, but will make communicating with it difficult or impossible.

Most networks today use Ethernet as their networking standard. IBM developed a proprietary token ring network configuration that was popular for some time. Others use ATM, FDDI, or other networking topologies. However, Ethernet is by far the most popular standard used today. The throughput for standard Ethernet is 10MB, and 100MB for fast Ethernet. The network card, as well as routers, switches, and cabling, must all support fast Ethernet for the network to have the higher throughput rate.

Recovering from a network adapter failure is a relatively simple task, assuming the failure can be pinpointed to the NIC. Following the diagnosis, the board must be replaced with a similar board. If the adapter is listed in the Hardware Compatibility List for Windows NT, it should work after being installed. Drivers and other software provided by the manufacturer may be required.

Motherboard Types

Motherboards are the main component in computers. They hold the processor (discussed previously) as well as a whole host of other chips. These boards have many functions built into them, including parallel and serial ports, USB ports, memory, cache, power management, and BIOS (Basic Input/Output System). These functions all reside on the motherboard and the failure of any of these subsystems could require replacement of the motherboard. While some of these boards can be repaired, they generally cannot be repaired in the field.

There are a number of different motherboards on the market today. The varieties are endless, but the classifications are generally based on the types of buses on the motherboard. Currently, bus types used are as follows: PCI, ISA, EISA, MCA, and VESA. Each type will be discussed briefly in the following sections. Keep in mind that the type of motherboard dictates the type of adapters that can be installed in the computer. For instance, if you have a motherboard that only uses the ISA and PCI bus types, you cannot use an MCA adapter in that computer. Each bus uses a different type of connector, so plugging in the wrong type of board is difficult, if not impossible.

Peripheral Component Interconnect   The Peripheral Component Interconnect, or PCI, is a bus type found in most computers today. Motherboards typically have ISA expansion bus slots (see the next listing) as well as PCI bus slots.

The PCI bus is a 64-bit bus, but it is often implemented as a 32-bit bus. It runs at a clock speed of 33MHz or 66MHz. This is a fairly fast bus type and many peripheral controllers utilize the PCI bus for faster throughput. At 33MHz using a 32-bit bus, the throughput on the PCI bus is 133 Mbps. PCI has become increasingly popular, making it the *de facto* standard today.

Industry Standard Architecture   The Industry Standard Architecture, or ISA, bus is found in virtually all computers. It is based on older IBM XT computer architecture, and today is being replaced by the PCI bus. Nevertheless, many computer systems still use the ISA bus for slower peripherals that do not require the fast throughput the PCI bus provides. In 1993, Microsoft and Intel introduced the Plug-and-Play ISA. This enabled all configuration data to be automatically configured by the operating system, or manipulated via software, rather than having to physically set switches and jumpers on the board.

Extended Industry Standard Architecture   The Extended Industry Standard Architecture (EISA) bus is an updated version of the ISA bus, originally designed for use with the 80386, 80486, and Pentium processors. EISA buses, like PCI buses, are 32-bits wide and support multiprocessing.

   The EISA bus was designed by a consortium of nine companies to compete with IBM's proprietary MCA bus design (described next). Both are 32-bit and provide multiprocessing capabilities. EISA, however, is backward-compatible and can accommodate the older ISA adapters. MCA, on the other hand, is not backward-compatible. EISA and PCI provide very similar capabilities, and in recent years, PCI has become far more popular than EISA.

Micro Channel Architecture   Micro Channel Architecture (MCA) was designed by IBM to replace the older AT bus. It competed with the EISA bus, but was a proprietary architecture. For a variety of reasons, it never became popular in the industry and is now seen only in older machines.

Video Electronics Standards Association   The Video Electronics Standards Association, or VESA, is a consortium of video adapter and monitor manufacturers that developed various standards for video in computer systems. The VESA Local Bus, or VL-Bus, was used to deliver higher performance for video components. It was popular in 486-based computers. It has since been replaced by the use of PCI adapters in most Pentium-based (and higher) systems.

Memory

There are several different types of memory used in computers. These include: RAM, ROM, PROM, EPROM, and EEPROM. Each will be discussed briefly in the following sections.

Random Access Memory   Random access memory (RAM) is considered the main memory of the computer, and can both read and write information. Most RAM is *volatile*, meaning that all data stored in RAM is lost when the computer is powered down or rebooted.

There are many variations of RAM on the market today. For instance, DRAM is dynamic random access memory. VRAM is video RAM and differs from RAM in that two devices can access it simultaneously. It is often used on video accelerator cards. WRAM is Windows RAM and provides even better video performance than VRAM. MDRAM, meanwhile, is multibank DRAM, developed by MoSys, and is faster than DRAM because it utilizes its own internal bus and can be configured in smaller increments.

Read-Only Memory   Read-only memory (ROM) typically resides on the motherboard and is used to execute instructions necessary to boot the computer. Some peripheral controllers also contain ROM. When a particular set of computer instructions must be executed consistently, ROM is often used to store those instructions. These chips are hardwired to perform the same instructions repeatedly and cannot be modified in any way.

Programmable Read-Only Memory   A programmable read-only memory (PROM) chip can be programmed with particular data. It is similar, in concept, to a writeable CD-ROM. It is a blank that is formatted in a particular way. Once the blank is recorded (or programmed, in the case of PROM), it cannot be erased or rewritten. In other words, once the data is programmed onto a PROM chip, it is permanent.

Erasable Programmable Read-Only Memory   An erasable programmable read-only memory (EPROM) chip is one that can both be programmed and erased. To erase an EPROM, it must be exposed to ultraviolet light. Therefore, it cannot be erased while residing in the computer, but must be purposefully erased using special equipment.

Electronically Erasable Programmable Read-Only Memory

Electronically erasable programmable read-only memory (EEPROM) is a programmable memory chip that can be erased by exposing it to an electrical charge. Typically, these chips are placed in a machine that can reprogram them using electricity rather than ultraviolet light.

As you can see, there are numerous variations on the types of memory available today. They fall primarily into two categories: random access memory, used for temporary storage by the processor, system, or peripherals; and read-only memory used to store instructions that must always be available and executed in exactly the same manner each time.

Configuring and Troubleshooting Fault-Tolerant Disks and Disk Subsystems

Microsoft Windows NT 4.0 Server provides capabilities to manage fault-tolerant disks and disk subsystems. In Windows NT 4.0, fault-tolerant disks and subsystems are implemented using Redundant Array of Inexpensive Disks, or RAID. RAID can be implemented via software using features built into Windows NT 4.0. However, experts agree that implementing RAID using a hardware solution, rather than relying upon Windows NT 4.0 software is a far superior choice. Hardware solutions provide significantly improved performance. This improved performance is the

SCENARIO & SOLUTION

What is the only type of architecture that is not backward-compatible?	IBM's Micro Channel Architecture (MCA).
How does EPROM differ from ROM?	EPROM can be programmed and erased. Both are read-only memory.
Which two bus architecture types are most similar?	PCI and EISA. They both are 32-bit and have faster throughput. PCI, however, has become more popular in recent years.
What is the minimum number of disks required to implement a RAID solution?	Two for mirror sets; three for stripe sets (with parity).
Which type of memory is considered volatile?	Random access memory.

result of the ability to utilize hardware specifically designed to manage certain activities, such as parity, for the disk subsystem. Reliance on a software solution is acceptable but not optimal.

RAID was originally defined in 1988 using Levels 1 through 5. Since then, RAID Level 0 and RAID Level 6 have been added. There is also a proprietary RAID Level 7 and, in time, other variations will undoubtedly be created. Only RAID Level 0, 1, and 5 are supported by Windows NT 4.0, therefore only those levels will be discussed here.

RAID Level 0 is a stripe set without parity. This provides faster throughput and improved disk subsystem performance, but provides no fault tolerance. Because of this, it was not originally included in RAID definitions.

RAID Level 1 is the mirror set. This does not improve disk subsystem throughput, but it does provide the first level of fault tolerance. In a mirror set, one disk is the primary partition, while the second disk is the shadow partition. All data written to the first disk is also written to the second disk. If either disk fails, it is transparent to the user because the remaining disk is an exact copy of the failed disk. Disk duplexing is a mirror set, with each disk attached to a separate controller. With two disks and two controllers, there is no single point of failure. If any one component fails, it is completely recoverable by the remaining components.

RAID Level 5 is a stripe set with parity. This configuration improves disk subsystem performance and provides a high level of fault tolerance. Mirror sets, stripe sets, and stripe sets with parity will be discussed further in this chapter since they are the three Windows NT 4.0–based software RAID solutions. Stripe sets without parity, providing no fault tolerance, are typically not widely implemented. Stripe sets are supported in Windows NT because:

- The same information for formatting and storing disk and Registry data is required for stripe sets and stripe sets with parity.

- Stripe sets form the foundation for stripe sets with parity.

- Stripe sets, while lacking fault tolerance capabilities, can improve I/O performance of the disk subsystem.

Overview and Configuration

In this section, we'll examine mirror sets and stripe sets with parity in some detail. We'll review the basics of each of these systems and discuss how to configure them.

Mirror Sets A mirror set provides an identical "twin" for a selected drive partition. All data written to a mirror set is written to both partitions. This means that data storage capacity is cut in half. Since data is written to two partitions when a write request occurs, system performance can be significantly reduced. To mitigate this, many mirror set implementations include the use of two disk controllers. This allows the write function to occur simultaneously on each disk because each is controlled independently. This configuration is often called disk duplexing. You can mirror any partition, including the system or boot partition.

A mirror set requires only two disks and provides Level 1 fault tolerance, while needing less memory and providing the best overall performance. It does not degrade performance when there is a subsystem failure, but it does have a significantly higher cost per megabyte of storage since each piece of data is written to two locations (for a 50 percent utilization). It is an excellent solution where high data reliability and availability is a requirement, and performance is not a significant issue.

on the **job**

If you use mirror sets with the system or boot partition, you should create and test a Windows NT startup floppy disk. In the case of RISC-based computers, you need to create an alternate boot selection to be able to use the Windows NT startup floppy. The startup floppy must be able to access the alternate boot information in order to recover from a failure that impacts the boot partition on the primary drive.

Mirror Set Configuration To configure a mirror set, you must have two disk drives, and the original partition you want to mirror must already exist. On the second disk, you must have an area of unpartitioned disk space at least as large as the original partition. The second disk's partition is called the *shadow* partition because its data shadows the original partition. If the area on the second disk is larger, the unused space can be used to create an additional partition as long as there are fewer than four partitions on the disk.

on the **job**

In some cases, the size of the shadow partition is slightly larger than the original partition. This occurs when the geometry of the two disks differs. Using identical disks will prevent this situation, but it should be of no concern if the two partitions vary slightly in size when using different disk drives.

EXERCISE 2-1

Enable a Mirror Set on Your System

1. Using Disk Administrator, select the partition you want to duplicate.

2. Press the CTRL key and click the area of unpartitioned space on another disk that you want to use as the shadow partition.

3. Click on the Fault Tolerance menu and select Establish Mirror. Disk Administrator will create an equal-sized partition in the unpartitioned space on the second drive to create the mirror set. It will also assign a drive letter to the mirror set.

4. On the Partition menu, click Commit Changes Now.

5. Select Yes in the Commit Changes dialog box to complete the creation of the mirror set.

6. A Confirm Change/Restart dialog box is displayed. Select Yes in this dialog as well. You will be reminded to update your emergency repair disk (which you can do using Rdisk.exe). Finally, you are prompted to shut down and restart the computer. Click OK (the only option).

7. After the system restarts, open Disk Administrator. The status bar will show Mirror Set #N [INITIALIZING]. The drive letter, volume label, and the size of the mirror set will appear in red text. This indicates the system is in the process of creating the mirror set in the background.

exam
ⓦatch

In the Disk Administrator display, information about the partition is not updated automatically. If you click on a partition, information for that volume updates. You can use the event log to assess when generation of the shadow partition is complete. You may see questions relating to making changes that aren't reflected in the Disk Administrator.

Stripe Sets   Stripe sets are made up of strips of data written on several different disk drives. At least two disks are required to create a stripe set and the set can contain as many as 32 disks in all. Data is written in 64K segments. Data is written sequentially across the disks. Figure 2-1 shows conceptually how data is written across four disks.

FIGURE 2-1

A four-disk
stripe set

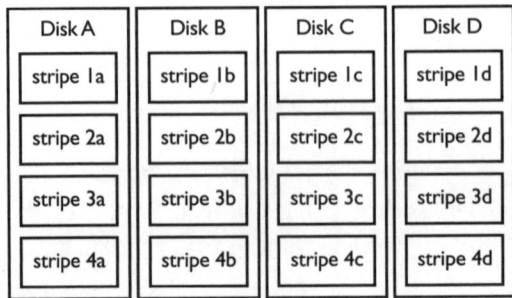

Using this example, data is written first to Disk A on stripe 1a, then on Disk B on stripe 1b, and so forth, until it reaches the last drive (in this case, Disk D). Subsequent data is then written to Disk A on stripe 2a, and so on.

Stripe sets do not contain any redundant data. As such, they do not provide fault tolerance. What they do offer, however, is faster throughput. Rather than waiting for a single disk drive to access information from one location, a stripe set can access data on multiple disks simultaneously. This multiple read-and-write capability can improve performance significantly.

These kinds of stripe sets are best used in certain types of environments, such as those concerning:

- Rapid access to data, such as large databases

- Storing program images, DLLs, or run-time libraries

- Asynchronous data collection from external sources at high transfer rates

- Multiple applications requiring access to the same data

Similarly, there are situations for which stripe sets are not appropriate, such as those involving:

- Programs that use small, sequential blocks of data. For this type of application, a single disk provides a more efficient use of resources.

- Programs that make random synchronous requests for small amounts of data. 16-bit single-threaded programs fit into this category.

Stripe sets can be quite useful for improving I/O performance in a variety of settings. In most cases, companies use stripe sets with parity to combine acceptable performance with strong fault tolerance. In fact, stripe sets form the foundation of stripe sets with parity, our very next section.

Stripe Sets with Parity   The stripe set with parity combines the advantages of a stripe set with enhanced fault tolerance over a mirror set. A stripe set with parity uses one of the stripes for parity. For example, using the Four-Disk Stripe Set scenario shown earlier, parity might be written on Stripe 1a, 2b, 3c, and 4d. If any disk in the set were to fail, the parity information stored on the other three disks could be used to re-create and regenerate the data on the fourth disk. Figure 2-2 shows a four-disk stripe set with parity.

Generating parity data requires additional overhead, which is why implementing a hardware RAID Level 5 solution is preferred. Parity information must be generated for each write command. Thus, a very active server could be tied up generating parity rather than attending to other processing requests. Using hardware components, parity can be generated for the drives without involving the main computer processor. This frees up the processor and greatly enhances performance.

Stripe Set Configuration   The first step is to confirm that all the disk hardware is on the Windows NT Hardware Compatibility List (HCL). If any equipment is not listed, it may not work well with the operating system and components. If possible, use identical disks. Although this is not a requirement, it simplifies management of the disk subsystem.

on the

Ü o b

Regardless of whether you implement RAID configurations or use multiple stand-alone disk configurations, always have spare disk drives and controllers on hand. When one of these components fails, it will disable an entire system. Sometimes the computer on which these components fail is a mission-critical server, and the entire network can become impaired or completely disabled. Eliminating single points of failure should be a top priority. The cost of spare drives and controllers is low compared with the cost of downtime as well as the lost productivity of end users. Using similar types of disks and controllers for all computers also helps lower the cost of spare stock, and decreases downtime when failures do occur.

Once you've determined that your hardware is listed in the HCL and that you have adequate spare parts, you're ready to proceed with the configuration. To create a stripe set with parity, you must have at least three drives with unpartitioned areas. Even if a partition is not completely full, you cannot use an unused portion of an existing partition. As with a mirror set, the unused space left over can be used for other partitions.

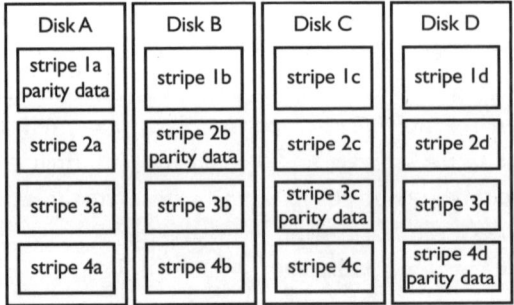

FIGURE 2-2

A four-disk stripe
set with parity

exam
ⓦatch

Keep in mind that you can use mirroring or stripe sets with just two drives, but stripe sets with parity require a minimum of three drives. Knowing this will help steer you toward the right solution on the exam.

If you don't have enough unpartitioned space, but do have adequate unused space, you can create unpartitioned disk areas by using the following four steps:

1. Back up the data on the existing partition.

2. Delete the partition.

3. Create a new, smaller partition, leaving part of the disk unpartitioned.

4. Restore the data to the new, smaller partition.

Once you have adequate space, you can create a stripe set. The following steps will create a stripe set with parity on your Windows NT 4.0–based server. These tasks are accomplished through the Disk Administrator interface.

EXERCISE 2-2

Creating a Stripe Set with Parity

1. Select areas of unpartitioned space on each disk drive to be included in the set. You must have at least three disks in the set and you cannot exceed 32 disks in a set.

2. Select the first partition on the first disk. Then Press CTRL and select additional unpartitioned areas on other disks.

3. On the Fault Tolerance menu, click Create Stripe Set with Parity. The Disk Administrator will display the minimum and maximum sizes for the stripe set with parity. The default size is equal to the maximum size allowed for the unpartitioned areas selected.

   The size you select is the total disk space that will be used, not the size of each partition. For example, if four 500MB partitions are selected, Disk Administrator will display 2000MB (2GB) for the maximum size. 1500MB will be used for data and 500MB will be used for parity information. If you wish to use less than the maximum size available, employ the following formula:

   Data size = Total size − (Total size / number of disks)

4. In the Create Stripe Set with Parity dialog box, type the size of the *set* you want to create and click OK. The Disk Administrator will divide the total size you specified by the number of disks, and create equal-sized unformatted primary partitions on each drive. It will assign a *single* drive letter to the collection of unpartitioned areas to create the stripe set with parity. The Disk Administrator will then display the stripe set with parity as new unformatted space.

5. On the Partition menu, click Commit Changes Now. When prompted to save the disk configuration changes, click Yes.

6. The system will notify you that you must restart your computer in order for the configuration changes to be written to the Registry and take effect. Click Yes in the dialog box.

7. The system will notify you the disks were updated successfully. This dialog box will also prompt you to update your emergency repair disk.

8. You are prompted to restart your computer so the changes can take effect. The only option is OK. All open applications will automatically close and the system will restart.

9. When the restart is complete, open the Disk Administrator. On the Tools menu, click Format. You can choose either FAT or NTFS as the file system for the stripe set with parity. When you have entered all the information in the Format dialog box, click Start. The stripe set with parity will begin initializing. The Disk Administrator will display the message Stripe Set with Parity #N [INITIALIZING] on the status bar in red. When complete, the stripe set with parity is ready for use.

exam

Watch

*The smallest partition will determine the maximum partition size used on each disk. For example, if you have four partitions of the following sizes: 500MB, 800MB, 650MB, and 900MB, each partition in the set will be 500MB. Keep this in mind on the exam when calculating total disk spaced used. The calculation is the smallest partition size * the number of disks.*

Fault-Tolerant Disks and Disk Subsystem Troubleshooting

The general areas of failure, in the order of likelihood of occurrence are: single disk drive, controller(s), multiple disk drives, and software. As mentioned earlier, moving parts are more likely to fail than parts that simply contain electronics. All parts, however, are susceptible to problems such as static discharge, power surges, power outages, or other environmental irregularities.

Single Disk Failure   The most likely problem to occur is a single disk failure. When a single disk fails in a mirror set, the other disk is used automatically. Thus, the failure is transparent to the user. However, the system no longer has fault-tolerance capabilities. The failed drive must be replaced and the mirror set must be re-created. The process of error detection and recovery for mirror sets and stripe sets with parity are very similar and will be discussed together in a moment.

In a stripe set with parity, a single disk failure will also be transparent to the user. The primary difference, however, is that the data can be recovered using the parity information. If you're using a hardware solution that allows for "hot swapping" (replacing the failed drive with an identical drive), the system will automatically recover the information and continue functioning. However, the software implementation found in Windows NT 4.0 Server requires additional steps.

In either case, a failed volume will generate an error message indicating an "orphaned" volume. The FtDisk (fault-tolerant driver) can determine that a disk has been orphaned and will direct all subsequent *reads* and *writes* to the other disk(s) in the set. A drive can only become orphaned during a *write*. The error message that will be generated when a disk becomes orphaned is a System Process – FT Orphaning dialog box stating: "A disk that is part of a fault-tolerant volume can no longer be accessed." In the event log, a severe error will be logged, indicating that steps must be taken to resolve the problem quickly.

The first step is to ensure important data has been recently backed up. If not, back up important data immediately. Use a new tape for backup since you may need your current backups for recovery. Next, replace the failed disk. This typically entails shutting down the server or RAID tower (if "hot swapping" is not a feature of the disk subsystem) and replacing the drive. Next, begin recovery of the mirror or stripe set with parity as soon as possible. Since Microsoft Windows NT 4.0 Server supports the software implementation of mirror sets and stripe sets with parity, we'll discuss recovery from this perspective. Use the manufacturer's instructions for recovery when using a hardware-based fault-tolerance solution.

If the system cannot locate a partition in a mirror set or stripe set with parity during initialization, it logs a severe error in the event log, marks the partition as an orphan, and uses the remaining portion(s) of the mirror set or stripe set with parity. The system continues to function by using the fault-tolerant features. In the Disk Administrator, if a volume has failed, you'll see a message in the status bar: <Volume> #N [RECOVERABLE], where <Volume> is either the mirror set or the stripe set with parity.

Recovering a Mirror Set   The method of recovering from a failure in a mirror set will depend both on which partition failed and on whether or not the failed partition contains the system or boot information. If the system or boot partition is involved, you will have to use the Windows NT startup floppy disk to start from the shadow partition, or reconfigure the shadow disk as the primary disk. To recover from a mirror set failure, you must first break the mirror set, then reconstruct it.

EXERCISE 2-3

Breaking a Mirror Set

1. In the Disk Administrator, select the mirror set you want to break.

2. On the Fault Tolerance menu, select Break Mirror.

3. In the Confirm dialog box, select Yes.

The remaining disk inherits the drive letter from the mirror set. The orphaned partition is given the next available drive letter or whatever available drive letter you assign to it. You can now shut down the system and replace the failed disk. It is recommended that you replace the drive with a similar drive, which must be the same size or larger if you intend to re-create the mirror set.

If the failed disk contained the system partition, you'll need to reconfigure the system partition on the mirror set. If any of the files that Windows NT installs on the system partition are missing or corrupt, you will be unable to start the computer. That's when having an updated Windows NT startup floppy comes in handy. You can restore any of the files listed in Table 2-1 by using the Repair process and the emergency repair disk. However, if you have updated the Windows NT startup floppy, you can boot from that instead.

If you're using a RISC-based system, you will need the Osloader.exe file in the \Os\Winnt40 folder instead of the NTLDR file. The Hal.dll file on a RISC-based system resides in the \Os\Winnt40 folder along with the *.pal files (Alpha-based computers).

To utilize the Windows NT startup floppy disk to restore system files, use the following steps:

1. Start the computer with the Windows NT startup floppy disk.

2. Replace individual files or replace all files by copying them from the Windows NT startup floppy disk to the corresponding location on your system partition.

To reconstruct the mirror set:

1. Perform a low-level format of the new disk on the same controller that will be used with the new disk. This eliminates the possibility of translation problems later. If the failed disk was the shadow disk, use the same SCSI ID as the failed disk. If the failed disk was the original disk, you might want to swap the SCSI ID so the shadow disk becomes SCSI ID 0.

TABLE 2-1	Files Needed for x86-based System	Folder Location
Files Required on Windows NT System Partition (x86-based System)	NTLDR	root
	Boot.ini	root
	Bootsect.DOS	root
	Ntdetect.com	root
	Ntbootdd.sys (SCSI only)	root
	Hal.dll	boot partition

2. Restart the system.

3. Re-create the mirror set by using the steps outlined earlier for creating a mirror set. This requires that you restart the system again, once the mirror set is created.

4. After the mirror set is initialized, update your system information and your Windows NT startup floppy.

Recovering a Stripe Set with Parity   When a member of a stripe set with parity is orphaned, you can reconstruct the data from the other members of the set. When you start the computer, the FtDisk program reads the information from the stripes on the other member disks, reconstructs the data of the missing members, and writes it to a new member.

on the **Job**

If the computer running the stripe set with parity fails, you can move the set to another computer and modify the Registry on the new computer. This action might be warranted if the data on the set was urgently needed before the computer could be repaired. To do this, you would have to build the Registry key HKEY_LOCAL_MACHINES\SYSTEM\DISK by using the FtEdit program.

EXERCISE 2-4

Reconstructing a Stripe Set with Parity

1. Replace the failed drive with a similar or identical drive that has an unpartitioned size at least as large as the other members of the stripe set's partitions.

2. Open the Disk Administrator and select the recoverable stripe set with parity.

3. Select an area of unpartitioned space of the same size (or larger) as the partition on the failed disk. If the failure was a result of a power loss or a bad cable on a single device, you can regenerate data within the orphaned member of the original stripe set with parity once the hardware is repaired.

4. On the Fault Tolerance menu, choose the Regenerate command. The unpartitioned section will be initialized and the data will be regenerated to that drive based on the data on the remaining drives.

5. Quit the Disk Administrator and restart the computer.

6. The regeneration occurs in the background. During this process, if you open the Disk Administrator, Stripe set with parity #N [INITIALIZING] will show up in the status bar.

7. You may receive an error when attempting to regenerate data. The message is:

```
The drive cannot be locked for exclusive use…
```

This occurs if the Disk Administrator does not have exclusive access to the stripe set with parity. This happens if the page file or some other system service (like Microsoft Systems Management Server, for example) is accessing the disk. Temporarily shutting down services that access the disk, and relocating the paging file until regeneration is complete will avoid this problem.

exam
ⓦatch

You may see a question about where a page file should be placed when using fault tolerance in Windows NT 4.0. Place the page file on a mirror set, not a stripe set with parity. Placing a page file on a stripe set with parity will degrade performance significantly.

Multiple Disk Failure   Multiple disk failures are rare except in cases where environmental factors are involved, such as power problems or heating/cooling issues. Using multiple controllers will help minimize risk. If you are using mirror sets, and have each drive attached to a separate controller, you reduce the risk of losing the ability to communicate with both drives due to a single controller failure.

Neither a mirror set nor a stripe set with parity is designed to be able to recover from multiple drive failures. In this case, you would have to break up the set (if possible), replace the failed drives, and restore the data from backup. Later in this chapter, we'll go over backups, as well as restoring systems using backups.

Upgrading a Server from a Single Processor to Multiple Processors

Before you start, make sure you have a complete, working backup of the system files and the Registry. Also, ensure you have a current emergency repair disk (ERD) handy. To create an updated ERD, run Rdisk.exe from a command prompt, then select Update

SCENARIO & SOLUTION

Which levels of RAID are supported by the Windows NT operating system?	Levels 0, 1, and 5.
Which levels of RAID can be implemented on an NT Server?	All levels of RAID can be implemented if using a hardware solution.
If you wanted to ensure your system files were part of a fault-tolerant solution, which RAID implementation would make the most sense?	A mirror set is the best way to provide fault tolerance for system files.
If you have four disks and performance is the most important requirement, what solution might you implement?	Stripe sets without parity provide fast throughput but no fault tolerance.

Repair Info. Some computers require a different Hal.dll file, so be sure to read the computer (or motherboard) manufacturer's instructions for specific information.

FROM THE CLASSROOM

The Importance of Experimenting with Multiple Disks, Disk Subsystems, and RAID Systems

Most students do not get the opportunity to experiment with multiple disks, disk subsystems, or RAID systems at home since most home computers have only one disk drive. In the classroom, we spend time working on several computers with multiple disk drives so students become quite comfortable with managing disks. This is especially true with mirror sets and stripe sets with parity. By working with various configurations, including those using multiple drives and controllers, students learn how to use the Disk Administrator to create disk solutions that will be used on the job. Most companies today have a lab that can be used to test various configurations prior to live implementation. If you've never used the Disk Administrator on more than one drive, make sure you practice these configurations in a lab environment before trying them on a live system. There's no substitute for hands-on experience.

—*Susan T. Snedaker,*
MCSE, MCP, MCT

Windows NT 4.0 Server can be upgraded to include support for multiprocessors. The motherboard must support multiprocessors and you must install the exact same type of processor as the original. Processors have a variety of differences, such as step settings, on-chip cache, and speed, all of which impact the system. Failure to use identical processors may prompt anomalous behavior throughout the entire system, including halts, blue screens, and other strange behavior.

To upgrade to multiprocessors, follow the manufacturer's instructions for installing additional processors. Once installed, use the Uptomp.exe file found in the Windows NT Resource Kit under Resource Tools Kit Help, Performance and System Monitoring Tools. Check to make sure your computer model is included in the tool and the associated HAL files. If not, ensure the latest service packs are installed on your system, or check the Microsoft Web site for HAL and Uptomp.exe updates.

Run the Uptomp.exe file. When it has completed, a dialog box will indicate the update was successful, the system must be restarted for changes to take place, and you should run Rdisk after the restart to update the saved configuration. It is very important to click the Update Repair Info option in Rdisk before clicking Create Repair Disk. If you do not have the Windows NT 4.0 Server Resource Kit, you can manually update the system using Microsoft Knowledge Base article Q156358. However, if you plan on running Windows NT 4.0 Server for any period of time, the Resource Kit is a wise investment.

If the computer you are updating is running Microsoft Proxy 2.0 Server, and you are changing to or from single or multiple processors, you must replace the Ipfltdrv.sys driver located at %systemroot%\system32\drivers. The single-processor version is a 36K file located on the Proxy 2.0 CD-ROM in the Msproxy\I386\Routing\Up folder. The multiple-processor version is a 34K file located on the Proxy 2.0 CD-ROM in the Msproxy\I386\Routing folder.

Troubleshooting Problems with Hardware

In this section, we'll review basic troubleshooting theory and discuss the various tools and techniques that can be used to diagnose problems with mirror sets and stripe sets. We'll also discuss how to recover from these types of problems.

Troubleshooting system problems should be a methodical process. The "shotgun" approach to troubleshooting can create more problems than it resolves. This approach usually involves the random replacement of hardware or reloading of software, based on nothing more than guesswork. A methodical approach should involve these basic steps:

1. **Isolate the problem.** Can you identify when or where the problem occurs? Is there a specific error message or system message? What are the symptoms of the problem? Have diagnostics or utilities been used? If so, what devices or systems appear suspect?

2. **Identify what works and what doesn't.** Isolating what is working from what is not working will help track down the problem. Also, determine whether the suspected device or subsystem has ever worked before. Finally, determine what, if anything, has been changed recently. Typically, whatever component was last changed is the most likely suspect.

3. **Define an action plan.** After assessing the problem, defining an action plan should be the next step before taking action. The action plan should indicate which symptoms have been observed, which diagnostics or utilities have been run, what the results have been, and what order of troubleshooting will occur. This plan need not be a formal plan. Rather, it may simply consist of a list of troubleshooting steps recommended to resolve the issue. This will prevent confusion as to what the next steps should be while in the midst of troubleshooting.

4. **Keep a maintenance log.** Whether it be a physical log book in the server room or an electronic document stored on the network, a maintenance log can be an invaluable tool in the realm of problem solving. The log provides insight into what was done, what troubleshooting steps were taken, what the results were, as well as other relevant data such as diagnostic results. This data should be used to establish a baseline for performance so that variations from that baseline can be identified and corrected. A log can also be extremely helpful in resolving intermittent problems, as we'll discuss next.

These troubleshooting steps should be used for every problem encountered to minimize recovery time and maximize troubleshooting efficiency.

Another valuable approach to hardware troubleshooting is to continuously divide the problem in half. For instance, if you're having trouble logging on to the network from one computer, you don't initially know if the problem is the computer's network connectivity or a problem with your logon. By trying to log on to another computer, you can immediately determine whether the problem is isolated to the first computer or to your logon. While this example is rather simplistic, it illustrates how to divide the problem in half. If you keep working in a logical manner to divide the problem in half, you will isolate the problem fairly quickly. Intermittent problems, however, pose another dilemma.

Solving intermittent hardware problems is perhaps one of the most challenging aspects of maintaining hardware. Problems that seem to randomly come and go can be difficult to pinpoint. In addition to using the steps listed previously, it is critical to keep a log of the failures and to begin trying to identify patterns. To identify patterns, the following questions should be answered:

- Does the problem occur at a specific time of day?
- Does the problem occur on a specific day of the week?
- Does the problem only occur on a specific computer or server?
- Does the problem only occur with a specific logon account?
- Does the problem occur at a specific time related to computer activities (startup, restart, backups, viewing logs, starting a particular service or application, and so on)?
- Is the problem related to the room's heating/cooling?
- Is the problem related to power?
- Does the problem occur at night or on weekends?
- Could this problem have been caused intentionally?
- What was the last thing that was changed on the network or system before the intermittent failure began occurring?

Occasionally, it can be time- and cost-effective to swap out suspected hardware and monitor the results. When a failure is intermittent and disruptive, it can be helpful to replace the suspected part, after walking through the steps just outlined and answering the questions posed earlier. It is critical to keep track of what was replaced and what the results were. Replacing only one part at a time will help avoid the "shotgun" approach and is critical to solving the problem. Parts that have been taken out should be marked as suspect, and you should allow sufficient time for the problem to re-appear. If it does not re-appear, mark the removed part to indicate the failure, and dispose of it according to your company's guidelines. If the problem does reappear, replace the original part before replacing anything else. This will help avoid introducing a new symptom into the scenario, thereby causing more confusion and delays.

Microsoft Windows NT Server 4.0 has two tools that can be useful in diagnosing hardware problems, in addition to the event viewer and log files. The Windows NT Hardware Detection Tool, NTHQ, is an MS-DOS–based program. It can be used to view the hardware that the operating system detects. The Windows NT Diagnostic Administrative Tool enables you to view information about the hardware connected to your computer and identify device drivers and services that should start when you start the computer.

The Windows NT Hardware Detection Tool, or NTHQ, is located on the Windows NT Server product CD.

EXERCISE 2-5

CertCam 2-5

Running the Windows NT Hardware Detection Tool

1. Insert a blank 3.5-inch floppy in the floppy drive on the server.

2. Run Makedisk.bat from the \Support\Hqtool on the Windows NT Server CD.

3. Leave the floppy disk inserted and restart your system.

4. When the system comes back up, you will be running NTHQ.

The file Readme.txt on the floppy disk contains information about the NTHQ tool. There are three primary ways NTHQ can help:

- Print hardware information, save it to a file, and keep the report and file with other configuration information about your computer. This report can be used when planning changes to the configuration.

- If you are having trouble installing Windows NT, you can start NTHQ from the floppy disk and use it for troubleshooting. See the NTHQ help file (Readme.txt) for more detailed information.

- If you cannot start Windows NT, or have installed new hardware that cannot be accessed, NTHQ can be used to troubleshoot the problem. NTHQ lets you view hardware it detects, so you can determine if there is any hardware present that is not being detected.

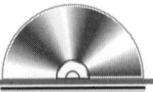

EXERCISE 2-6

CertCam 2-6

Running Windows NT Diagnostics

1. Click Start, select Programs, then choose Administrative Tools (Common).

2. Double-click Windows NT Diagnostics.

3. A dialog box opens that has nine tabs: Version, System, Display, Drives, Memory, Services, Resources, Environment, and Network. Each tab is described briefly in the following:

   ■ **Version** shows operating system and hardware information, including the number and type of processors present.

   ■ **System** displays more details about the computer, including type of processor and the Hardware Abstraction Layer (HAL).

   ■ **Display** contains information about the video display (monitor) and device driver.

   ■ **Drives** holds information regarding the disks connected to the system, the partitions, logical drives, and network shares.

   ■ **Memory** shows information about the physical memory and the page file.

   ■ **Services** displays the status of all services and devices on the system. It provides more information than the Services and Devices option in the Control Panel.

   ■ **Resources** provides information about IRQs, DMA channels, memory addresses, and I/O ports.

   ■ **Environment** displays system and user environment settings.

   ■ **Network** displays user and network information.

Troubleshooting hardware in the Windows NT environment is usually fairly straightforward. The tools, logs, and other operating system capabilities provide a wide variety of methods of viewing and diagnosing system problems. There are also many third-party software applications specifically written to diagnose hardware problems. Finally, many hardware manufacturers ship specific utilities to diagnose problems relating to their hardware. With all these tools at one's disposal, the task of troubleshooting and repairing hardware is greatly simplified. While problems sometimes stump even the experts, using the right tools and troubleshooting methodologies will usually yield fast, consistent results, not to mention lower the mean repair time.

CERTIFICATION OBJECTIVE 2.02

Backing Up and Restoring Hardware

Backing up and restoring hardware is a mission-critical activity. No matter how much fault tolerance or redundancy is built into your system, the reality is that hardware fails. It is important to understand that the role of the IT department is to provide network, server, and application availability to users. Users depend on the data stored on the system. Without a solid backup and recovery plan, the network is vulnerable. In this section, we'll review backing up and restoring hardware. Disk configuration and recovery was discussed earlier and will not be repeated here. Nevertheless, it is a critical component of recovery.

As general guidelines, there are several things you can do to make recovery a bit easier:

1. Develop plans and procedures for recovering from failures *before* you experience one.

2. Create and test floppy disks that enable you to restart your computer after a failure.

3. Maintain hardware configuration information for each computer, especially disk configuration information.

4. Maintain software configuration information, including the version of the operating system, service packs applied, and any hotfixes installed.

In addition, Windows NT Server 4.0 has several utilities available related to backing up and restoring hardware and system functionality. Table 2-2 describes each briefly.

The Windows NT Backup utility, Ntbackup, does not include functionality for scheduling unattended backups. However, you can use the Schedule service with the

TABLE 2-2	Utility	Purpose	Usage
Windows NT Backup and Restore Utilities	AT	Run Windows NT backup at a scheduled time	Backup
	Cacls	Display and modify Access Control Lists (ACLs) for NTFS files and folders	File System
	Compact	Display and change compression of NTFS files and folders	File System
	Convert	Convert volume from FAT to NTFS	File System
	Expand	Expand files that are compressed	File System
	DiskMap	Display information about the disk and the contents of the Partition Table	Disk
	DiskProbe	Low-level disk editor	Disk
	DiskSave	Save and restore Master Boot Record and Partition Boot Sector	Disk
	FtEdit	Recover stripe sets, stripe sets with parity, and volume sets	Disk

command-line capabilities of Ntbackup to set up unattended backups. You can also use a third-party backup utility program to provide a more robust backup solution.

When creating a backup plan, the first consideration is what data to back up. In some organizations, user data is stored on servers. In other organizations, user data is stored on local computers. Users do not typically do a good job of backing up their critical data. Many organizations point user data to centralized user folders so critical data is backed up regularly by IT staff. Other organizations point only certain critical application data to a centralized location and allow other data to reside on the user's local hard drive. It is important to minimize disruption to users and maintain a high level of data integrity at the same time.

If user data is stored on servers, the data can be backed up on a regular basis. This is the most optimal solution but requires large amounts of server storage. Providing user folders is another option, which allows users to choose where to store data. If it should be backed up, the user can choose to store it in their folder on the server. This is also a viable option.

The most common medium for backups is magnetic tape. Currently, the most common tape types are quarter-inch cartridges (QICs), digital audio tapes (DATs), and 8-mm cassettes. Most high-capacity tape drives use a SCSI controller. For more information about supported tape drives, consult with the Windows NT Server Hardware Compatibility List (HCL). Since technology changes rapidly, you should research the characteristics of each type of tape drive. When selecting a drive, consider the speed, reliability, capacity, and media cost of each. The tape subsystem should have error detection and correction built in. The selected drive should have more than enough capacity to back up an entire drive on your largest server. With large-capacity drives, a jukebox style tape subsystem can be an effective solution.

Backup Types

There are basically five different types of backups: normal (full), copy, incremental, differential, and daily. Typically, network administrators use full, incremental, and differential.

- **Normal**   A normal backup copies all selected files and marks each as having been backed up. With normal, or full, backups, system restores can be finished quickly because the files on the tape are current and complete.

- **Copy**   A copy backup copies all selected files but does not mark them as having been backed up. This is useful if you want to back up files between regular backup intervals, because it does not interfere with regularly scheduled backup operations.

- **Incremental**   An incremental backup copies only those files created or changed since the last normal or incremental backup. Many network administrators use a combination of normal and incremental backups. However, if a full restore is required, you must start with your last normal backup and work through each of the incremental backups to fully restore the system.

- **Differential**   A differential backup copies only those files created or changed since the last normal or incremental backup. It does not mark the files as having been backed up. If you use normal and differential backups, restoring requires only the last normal tape and the last differential tape.

- **Daily**   A daily backup copies all selected files modified the day the daily backup is performed. These files are not marked as having been backed up.

There is no one right way to devise a backup plan. It is safe to say that a normal or full backup takes the most time to back up and the least time to recover. An incremental backup takes the least time to back up, but the most time to recover.

The differential model falls right in between. Finding the right mix between time to back up and time to recover will depend on the variables of your network and company requirements.

Frequency of Backup

You'll want to schedule your backups for times when the fewest users are on the system. For most companies, this is usually in the early morning hours—typically between midnight and 6 A.M.

The frequency of the backups is driven primarily by the rate of data change. Many companies make full backups once per week and incremental or differential backups each night. In addition, they may make monthly copies and archive copies. If files on a particular server rarely change, weekly or monthly backups may be sufficient to protect the data. In other cases, where data changes rapidly, such as e-mail or critical database files, backups should be performed daily.

Regardless of the backup schedule, you should always have a set of tapes on hand and a set of tapes offsite. If the building catches fire, for example, the onsite set of tapes may be destroyed or rendered unusable. Some companies will store sets of weekly tapes offsite and rotate those tapes every three to four weeks. Whatever your configuration, ensure there is more than one backup set preserved, preferably offsite, at any given time. Keep in mind that tapes (and tape drives) have been known to fail during the restore procedure.

Verifying Backups

Having tape backups is very important, but verifying them is equally important. Tape drives, like disk drives, have many moving parts and are subject to failure. A verify operation compares the files on the disk to the files that have been written to the tape. It is similar to the restore procedure except that the files on the tape are not written to the disk. Most tape backup programs include this feature. It takes about as long to verify as it does to perform the backup, so make sure there's adequate time for this task. Best practices dictate performing a verify operation on every backup. Otherwise, you cannot be sure the backup is reliable. If a file changes between backup and verify, the verify procedure will fail.

Once you have verified the backup, the tapes should be stored. As mentioned earlier, tapes should be stored offsite in a secure location. They will last longer in cool, humidity-controlled locations.

Accurate backup records should be kept to ensure that tape backups of each server can be quickly and accurately identified. Tapes should be labeled and a backup log kept. Labels should contain the date, type of backup, and information regarding the contents. Indicating the type of backup is critical. If you are using full and incremental backups, you will need to know which tape contains the full backup and which contain incremental backups. You'll need this in order to restore the system using the tapes in the correct order.

The Windows NT Backup Program

The Windows NT Backup program is located in the Administrative Tools folder. It can also be run from the command line using Ntbackup. You can use the program to back up and restore local and remote files on both NTFS and FAT partitions. You can also select files for backing up or restoring according to volume, directory, or individual filename. In addition, the program allows you to perform normal, copy, incremental, differential, and daily backup operations as well as verifications of the backup. If necessary, it can create a batch file to automate the repeated backups of drives. When restoring, the Windows NT Backup program allows you to control the destination drive and directory for data.

When you start Windows NT, it automatically checks for a tape drive and initializes the hardware each time you open Backup. The tape drive must be attached to the computer where the Backup program is running. Keep in mind that the tape drive must be powered on prior to starting Windows NT, otherwise the associated drivers may not be properly loaded.

Performing the Backup

Before running the Windows NT Backup program, each computer's disk to be backed up must be established as a logical drive on the computer to which the tape unit is attached. If using a batch file, incorporate the logical drive connections in this file.

Each time you start the program, it scans for new or additional tape drives. You can have multiple tape drives attached to the system, but you can only select one at a time.

You can specify which files to back up—all files or selected files. If you connect to another network drive using Backup, choose Refresh from the Window menu to update the Drives window and view the additional network drive.

Certain files, by default, are not backed up by the Backup program. These include files you do not have permission to read, paging files, Registry files on remote computers, and files exclusively locked by application software. Windows NT itself locks two types of files: event logs and Registry files. However, the Backup program will back up these files on the local system as part of the operating system.

Restoring Data

Just as policies outlining backup procedures are important, so too are policies outlining restoration procedures. Practicing the restore procedure ahead of time with a spare drive or computer will help you become proficient in restoring data. When a real need to restore data occurs, you'll be more confident that critical files will be available and that needed data will not be overwritten or lost.

In restoring data, begin by assessing the backup plan you used. If you used incremental or differential backups, you must first restore to the last good normal backup. If you used an incremental approach, then each incremental tape starting with the earliest, must be used to restore the system. If you used differential backups, you should use the most recent differential tape after restoring the last normal backup.

Choosing What to Restore

You can restore the current tape, one or more backup sets, or just individual files. The process is the reverse of the backup procedure. You select the data from the tapes you want to restore and select the drive and destination folder(s) for restored data.

Certain files are not automatically restored. This includes files on the tape that are older than the files on the destination drive and files to be restored to a directory for which you do not have adequate permissions. In order to avoid problems, you should have backup and restore rights if you (or someone in your department) is responsible for backups. The Backup Operators group has these permissions and anyone responsible for backing up or restoring data should be a member of this group.

EXERCISE 2-7

Setting Restore Options

1. Using Administrative Tools, select the Backup program.

2. Choose one or more tapes, backup sets, or files.

3. On the Operations menu, select the Restore command.

4. In the Restore Information dialog box, review the tape-specific information provided to ensure the tape or set is the correct one.

5. Select the drive and destination for the restore.

6. Check the Verify After Restore check box to compare files after the restore to ensure data integrity.

7. Determine whether to Restore Local Registry and Restore File Permissions. Check each box accordingly.

8. Click OK to begin the restore.

Two check boxes mentioned in the exercise are important to review. First, you can choose to Restore Local Registry. You will need to restart the computer for these new settings to take place. Remember that you cannot restore *remote* Registry files. Also keep in mind that if you are going to restore the Registry for a new computer or a new disk drive in a computer, you must first install the Windows NT operating system and restore a full backup tape of your hard drive.

Second, the Restore File Permissions check box allows you to restore file permissions on an NTFS volume. Otherwise, the files inherit the permissions information of the folder in which they are restored. You should not restore file permissions if:

- You are transferring files to a computer outside the original domain.

- You are restoring files to a computer that has not been completely restored following the corruption of the operating system.

Performing system and network backup and restore procedures is not complex, but it is critical to the integrity of the network data. These two tasks are among the most important tasks network administrators perform. By creating a clear backup plan, by backing up important data in an organized and methodical manner, and by verifying the backed up data, you will have excellent data integrity. By practicing the restore procedures in the lab and by having a restore procedure outlined in advance, you'll ensure that recovery from failures will be fast and effective.

SCENARIO & SOLUTION

What are the advantages of server-only backups?	Fewer tape drives needed Less media to manage Less expensive than backing up each workstation along with each server
What are the advantages of local workstation backups?	Faster to back up than the server Quicker file recovery
What are the disadvantages of server-only backups?	Registries and event logs of remote computers are not backed up Backups and restores are slower due to network throughput limitations Backups and restores require far more planning Recovery is a more complex process
What are the disadvantages of local workstation backups?	Each workstation requires its own tape drive Users must remember to back up data or rotate tape media for scheduled backups

exam
ⓦatch

Most of the questions in Windows NT Server 4.0 exams do not specifically cover backups and restores. However, occasional questions will involve strategies for backing up critical network data such as database servers. Another possible question type will deal with restoring files and how permissions behave in this situation. Understanding backup and recovery strategies, the pros and cons of various strategies, how recovery affects the Registry on local and remote computers, and how recovery impacts file permissions are all areas you should be familiar with.

CERTIFICATION SUMMARY

As we've seen throughout this chapter, hardware maintenance is a mission-critical function of any IT department. Hardware will fail at some point. We know hardware with moving parts, such as disk drives and tape drives, are more prone to failure than stationary parts, such as RAM and video boards. Still, any component in a computer can fail causing disruption in computer and network services. Being prepared for these outages will make a significant difference in the amount of downtime the network experiences.

Repairing, configuring, and troubleshooting hardware requires a methodical approach. Understanding the various components and what typical failures look like will help you more quickly diagnose and repair hardware issues.

In the first section of this chapter, we looked at many different hardware components and reviewed the function of each. We also reviewed fault tolerance built into Windows NT Server 4.0, including mirror sets and stripe sets with parity. We reviewed how to configure these fault-tolerant volumes and how to recover should one or more hard disk drives fail.

In the second section of this chapter, we reviewed data backups and restores. We saw that a methodical approach to planning backups and recoveries will go a long way toward ensuring the integrity of critical network data. We reviewed the pros and cons of each backup strategy and learned how to use the Windows NT Backup program.

TWO-MINUTE DRILL

Optimizing, Configuring, Maintaining and Troubleshooting Hardware

❏ Planning is critical for configuring, maintaining, and troubleshooting hardware.

❏ Processors and RAM are the core components in the system.

❏ Hard disks, with moving parts, are the most likely components to fail.

❏ Redundant Array of Inexpensive Disks, or RAID, is a fault-tolerant solution that can be implemented using Windows NT Server 4.0 software or third-party hardware.

❏ Network adapters typically use Ethernet in today's computing environment.

❏ The most common motherboard type in use today is the PCI board.

❏ There are many different kinds of memory. The most common memory type is random access memory (RAM).

❏ Windows NT Server 4.0 supports RAID Levels 0, 1, and 5 only.

❏ RAID has Levels 0 through 7 currently defined.

❏ A mirror set requires two disk drives and one controller. Adding a second controller is called disk duplexing and removes the single point of failure.

❏ A stripe set with parity requires at least three disk drives and one or more controllers.

❏ A stripe set without parity provides faster performance but no fault tolerance.

❏ A stripe set with parity can withstand a single disk failure.

❏ Windows NT Server 4.0 supports multiple processors. The Uptomp.exe utility is used to upgrade from single to multiple processors.

❏ Troubleshooting hardware problems involves four distinct steps: isolating the problem, identifying what works, defining an action plan, and keeping a log.

Backing Up and Restoring Hardware

❏ A backup plan should take into consideration the location of servers, the type of data on servers and local workstations, the time to back up, and the cost of backup media.

❏ Always keep an updated set of Windows NT 4.0 floppies for use when restarting your system in the event of a failure.

❏ Server-only backups are more efficient, but risk the loss of user data stored on local workstations.

❏ Backup types include normal (full), copy, incremental, differential, and daily.

❏ Backups should always be verified to ensure the data on the tapes can be read and used for restores in the event of future hardware failures.

❏ The restore function should be tested with tapes on a lab system (not live) to ensure the procedure is understood and that critical data is being preserved.

❏ Remote registries and event logs cannot be backed up or restored remotely.

❏ If file permissions are not restored, the files will inherit the permissions in the target folder.

SELF TEST

The following questions will help you measure your understanding of the material presented in this chapter. Read all the choices carefully, as there may be more than one correct answer. Choose all correct answers for each question.

Optimizing, Configuring, Maintaining, and Troubleshooting Hardware

1. A new help desk technician is overheard commenting that the system he just repaired isn't working properly. It appears to have memory problems but the diagnostics run without error. What is the most likely cause of the problem?

   A. The system BIOS is not set correctly.

   B. The hard drive is probably bad.

   C. The new RAM does not match the remaining, original RAM.

   D. The new RAM uses parity.

2. You've decided to create a mirror set so you can have a copy of your system files available in the event of a disk failure. Your original partition is 200MB. Your second disk drive has an unpartitioned area of 650MB. The drive has four other partitions on it. Which statement is true?

   A. You cannot create a mirror set using the space on the second drive because it has four other partitions on it.

   B. You cannot create a mirror set using the second drive because it is not the same size as the original disk.

   C. A mirror set cannot use an unpartitioned area greater than 600MB on a shadow disk.

   D. You cannot use a mirror set for system files.

3. Which statement about mirror sets is true?

   A. If you are using a drive larger than 100MB, you must enable translation.

   B. You should not use a mirror set if your system partition exceeds 1GB.

   C. If you are using a drive larger than 1GB, you cannot place operating system files on this partition.

   D. You should not use a mirror set if your disk drive manufacturer does not support it.

4. You are implementing a stripe set with your system's five disk drives. You do not have a budget for purchasing any additional hardware. Your manager has told you that performance is

absolutely critical and fault tolerance is important. What solution would you recommend to meet these criteria?

A. Implement disk duplexing

B. Implement a stripe set with parity and make frequent backups

C. Implement a mirror set

D. Implement a stripe set without parity and make frequent backups

5. You have six drives you want to use for a stripe set with parity. The drives have the following unpartitioned areas:

Disk 1	800MB
Disk 2	950MB
Disk 3	450MB
Disk 4	575MB
Disk 5	900MB
Disk 6	425MB

What is the maximum data size for this stripe set with parity?

A. 425MB

B. 2125MB

C. 2550MB

D. 4100MB

E. 3414MB

6. Where can you find the status of initialization for a mirror set or stripe set with parity?

A. In the display, which is updated by the Disk Administrator during initialization

B. In the display, which the Disk Administrator updates by default every five minutes

C. In the event log

D. In the Network Monitor

7. When does a fault-tolerant disk become orphaned? (Choose the best answer.)

A. During the read operation

B. During a write operation

C. During a read or a write operation

D. After a mirror set or stripe set with parity is selected and before it gets formatted

8. If a drive that was part of a stripe set with parity were to fail, what message would you see?

    A. Severe error in the event log

    B. Recoverable error in the event log

    C. Disk error in the event log

    D. No error would be logged, because the error is recoverable

9. You are working on upgrading a user's PC. The upgrade includes adding more memory and a network adapter card. The computer has an Intel Pentium processor and 16MB of RAM. What issues must you consider before adding the hardware? (Choose all that apply.)

    A. Determine how many available slots there are for additional RAM.

    B. Determine how many open EISA slots the motherboard has available for network adapters.

    C. Determine whether or not the paging file is sized to utilize the additional RAM.

    D. Determine what type of bus the motherboard uses and ensure the network adapter board utilizes the same bus type.

10. Your system uses a stripe set with parity. The set consists of five drives in an external redundant array. The fault tolerance is implemented as a sophisticated hardware solution. You notice an error message on the server display that says: "A disk that is part of a fault-tolerant volume can no longer be accessed." What steps must you take to repair this problem?

    A. Remove the failed drive. Replace it with an identical drive. Do nothing more.

    B. Power down the server. Remove the failed hard drive, replace it with an identical unit. Restart the server. Format the drive and re-create the stripe set with parity.

    C. Using the Disk Administrator, break the stripe set with parity. Then power down the external array, remove the failed disk and replace it with an identical unit. Power the external array back up, reboot the server, and re-create the stripe set with parity.

    D. Using FtEdit.exe, edit the parameters of the stripe set to exclude the partition on the failed disk. Remove the failed unit, replace it with an identical disk drive, and use FtEdit.exe again to create a replacement stripe on the new disk.

Backing Up and Restoring Hardware

11. You are attempting to perform your weekly system backup, but the backup program indicates no tape drive is found. It was working last week. What is the most likely problem? (Choose the best answer.)

A. The tape drive is broken.

B. The tape drive drivers are not current.

C. The system Registry is corrupt.

D. The tape drive was not powered on when the system was booted.

12. After a backup has completed successfully, you realize you forgot to set the program to run the verify operation. You head off for a break just as your colleague comes in. When you return, you run the verify operation, but it fails. What could be wrong?

A. Believing your backup was complete, your colleague changed some files while you were on your break.

B. The backup operation failed but you left on break before the message appeared.

C. The verify operation failed because too much time elapsed between the backup and the verify.

D. The tape went bad, causing the verify operation to fail.

13. What are the five types of backups?

A. Normal, Incremental, Differential, Daily, and Weekly

B. Normal, Incremental, Differential, Copy, and Daily

C. Full, Incremental, Differential, Daily, and Weekly

D. Full, Normal, Incremental, Differential, and Daily

14. You receive an unusual number of complaints from users about errors on files in a folder called \Public\UsersAll on an NTFS-formatted network drive. You are concerned the data is either corrupt or the drive is about to fail. You notify users that you will restore the folder and the data in the folder that night and the problem should be resolved the next day. However, the next day, you receive a rash of e-mails and phone calls from users who are now completely unable to access the data in the \Public\UsersAll folder. What is the most likely cause of this problem?

A. You did not select the Restore File Permissions check box, so the restored files inherited default disk permissions.

B. You did not select the Restore File Permissions check box, so the files inherited folder permissions.

C. You selected the Restore File Permissions check box, so the files kept their original permissions.

D. You selected the Restore File Permissions check box, so the file permissions were set through local policies.

15. Which utility is used to save and restore the master boot record (MBR) and the Partition Boot Sector (PBS)?

A. DiskMap

B. DiskProbe

C. DiskSave

D. FtEdit

16. After a hard drive failed on a remote computer, you ran a restore operation from a good backup tape. However, there appear to be irregularities with the Registry on that computer. What is the best method for resolving this problem?

A. Restore the Registry for the remote computer using the Windows NT Backup program.

B. Back up the Registry for the remote computer using the Windows NT Backup program, then restore the Registry using the AT utility.

C. Restart the remote computer to implement the changes to the Registry that occurred during the restore operation.

D. Use the emergency repair disk for the remote computer to restore Registry settings.

17. Users store critical files in several locations. There are three servers on which users can store important files. In addition, users store critical files on their local workstations. Which backup plan best addresses these factors?

A. Performing server and workstation backups each week. Performing incremental backups on the servers only.

B. Performing normal server and workstation backups each week. Performing differential backups on the servers and having each user perform incremental backups daily.

C. Creating folders for each user on the server(s). Setting each user's home directory to be the server folder for that user. Performing normal backups on those servers weekly and incremental backups daily.

D. Performing normal backups on each server and each workstation weekly.

18. Which is not a commonly used magnetic tape type for backing up and restoring computer data?

A. QIC

B. 16-mm

C. DAT

D. 8-mm

19. Adam, your backup operator, called in sick. One of your new network assistants, Chris, offered to run the backups. The next day, you decide to review the backup log and notice that Chris attempted a restore that failed. You call Chris into your office and ask what happened. Chris says he tried to run the backups but not all the files copied over. He decided to try a restore and found it also failed. What is the most likely cause of the problem?

A. Chris did not have backup and restore permissions so certain files were not copied over. Chris should not have run a restore operation.

B. Chris did not have backup and restore permissions, so certain files were copied but not listed in the catalog. Chris misunderstood this symptom and erroneously attempted a restore.

C. Chris did have backup and restore permissions since they are assigned to the Everyone group automatically. The files that appeared to be missing were hidden system files. The backup and restore actually completed successfully.

D. Chris logged on as a network administrator rather than as the Account Operator. Thus, the file listing was incomplete. Chris should have logged off and logged back on as an Account Operator.

20. How can the Windows NT Server 4.0 Backup utility be scheduled to perform backups automatically? (Choose the best answer.)

A. By using the scheduling function in Windows NT Server 4.0 in the command prompt.

B. By using the built-in scheduling function in Windows NT Server 4.0 with a batch file using the AT command.

C. By using the scheduling function in Windows NT Server 4.0 with a third-party program to create a batch file.

D. The Windows NT Server 4.0 Backup program cannot be automatically set to perform backups.

LAB QUESTION

You manage a small network. On one server, you have three hard drives. You have implemented a mirror set and a stripe set with parity in the following configuration:

Disk 0

5GB primary mirror partition

5GB stripe set with parity partition

5GB other

Disk 1

5GB shadow partition

5GB stripe set with parity

Disk 2

5GB stripe set with parity

5GB other

In this morning's meeting, your boss mentioned that the network had been running exceptionally well lately, but that average time to recovery after a failure was a problem. You were tasked with improving recovery time and developing a detailed plan for doing so. When you arrive back at your desk, you receive an alert that Disk 0 has failed.

Answer the following questions:

1.   How much data was contained in the mirror set? (capacity, in GB)

2.   What was the total data size of the stripe set with parity? (capacity, in GB)

3.   What symptoms are you likely to see when Disk 0 fails?

4.   What steps must you take to recover from this failure in the least amount of time?

SELF TEST ANSWERS

Optimizing, Configuring, Maintaining, and Troubleshooting Hardware

1. ☑ **C.** The new RAM likely does not match the original RAM. Factors such as speed, capacity, and the use of parity can cause a mismatch in the memory and cause strange problems. When tested, each bank of memory appears to be working correctly.

   ☒ **A, B,** and **D** are incorrect. The system BIOS would not likely be impacted by replacing memory. The hard drive will not cause memory-type errors. The last thing replaced should be the first thing to check when repairing hardware. The new RAM may use parity but this will only cause problems if the old RAM does not while still being used in the system.

2. ☑ **A.** If the second drive has four or more partitions on it, you cannot use it for a mirror set, regardless of the amount of unpartitioned space on the drive.

   ☒ **B, C,** and **D** are incorrect. The size of the unpartitioned area on the second drive must be at least as large as the partition on the original disk. There are no other size limitations. A mirror set can be used for system files and is preferred to stripe sets with parity.

3. ☑ **B.** You should not use a mirror set if your system partition exceeds 1GB. Exceeding 1GB requires enabling translation, and this can cause problems for system partitions.

   ☒ **A, C,** and **D** are incorrect. A drive must have translation enabled if it exceeds 1GB, not 100MB. You can place operating system files on a drive larger than 1GB. A manufacturer does not need to support mirroring. This is a function of Windows NT Server 4.0 and can be implemented with two identical drives.

4. ☑ **D.** A stripe set without parity provides the best performance but does not provide fault tolerance. Therefore, it will be important to back up the stripe set frequently to ensure the system has some level of ability to recover from a hardware or disk failure.

   ☒ **A, B,** and **C** are incorrect. Disk duplexing, involving a mirror set with each disk drive attached to its own controller, actually does provide both fast performance and fault tolerance. However, the question stated that you wanted to implement a stripe set. A stripe set with parity slows down performance because each write command requires the calculation and writing of parity data. A mirror set does not meet the requirements of the question.

5. ☑ **B.** The formula for determining total data size is: *total size – (total size / number of disks)*. Therefore, the calculation would be as follows:
   The total size for this set is 425MB × 6 = 2550MB.
   2550MB – (2550MB / 6) = 2550MB – 425MB = 2125MB
   Therefore, the maximum data size is 2125MB. The other 425MB will be used for parity.

☒   A, C, D, and E are incorrect. A is the maximum stripe size for the set. C is the total size of the set before subtracting out the parity stripe. D is the total of all the disks, without accounting for the fact that the smallest size available to the set will determine the maximum size used on each drive. E is the calculation result if you forget to take the maximum size into account.

6.   ☑   C. Disk Administrator does not update the display, so using the event log is the best way to monitor the status of the initialization process.
☒   A, B, and D are incorrect. Disk Administrator does not dynamically update the display, and Network Monitor is not useful for monitoring disk initialization activities.

7.   ☑   B. A fault-tolerant disk can only become orphaned during the write process since a read does not affect the data on the system.
☒   A is incorrect because although a volume may not be read, the data can be extrapolated due to the implementation of fault tolerance. Therefore, a disk cannot become orphaned during a read. C is incorrect because a disk can only become orphaned during a write process. D is incorrect because a disk does not become orphaned during the creation of a fault-tolerant volume.

8.   ☑   A. During system initialization, if a drive that is part of a fault-tolerant system fails, it is orphaned and a severe error is entered in the event log. The system will continue to run normally, relying upon the built-in fault-tolerant features.
☒   B is incorrect because while the system can be recovered, the event log will have a severe error recorded. If you view the status of the disks in the Disk Administrator, you will notice a message in the status bar stating: <Volume> #N: [RECOVERABLE]. This means the system will continue to run normally until you are able to replace the failed drive. C is incorrect because the error type is a severe error although it is related to the disk subsystem. D is incorrect because although the problem is recoverable, a severe error is generated indicating that recovery must take place to restore the system to full functionality again. Once one disk has failed, a second disk failure will likely be unrecoverable.

9.   ☑   A and D. Most motherboards have two or four slots for RAM. If there are no available slots, you must remove the old RAM and replace it with higher capacity RAM. If there are slots available, you must match the additional RAM with the original RAM to ensure they will work together. Also, if the motherboard only uses ISA slots, for example, and your network adapter board uses the PCI bus, you will not be able to plug the network adapter board into the motherboard.
☒   B and C are not correct. While you do want to ensure there is an available slot open for the network adapter board, it may not be (and is not likely to be) an EISA bus type. The sizing of the paging file is not impacted by the amount of RAM in a machine.

10.   ☑   A. The fault-tolerant capabilities of a sophisticated RAID solution include the ability to recover from a single disk failure and the ability to hot swap. Removing the failed drive and

replacing it with an identical one should be all the steps needed to recover from this error. Once the new drive is installed, the system will automatically re-create the data from the "lost" drive on the new drive by using the parity information from the stripe set.

☒ **B, C,** and **D** are incorrect. If you are using an external RAID, there is no need to power down the server. You do not need to re-create the stripe set as the parity information will be used to re-create the data automatically. If only a single unit fails, you do not need to remove the stripe set. FtEdit.exe can be used to repair a stripe set with parity if information in the Registry regarding the stripe set with parity is missing or corrupt. However, you would not use FtEdit to exclude the failed partition. This occurs automatically when the unit fails.

Backing Up and Restoring Hardware

11. ☑ **D.** The tape drive will not be recognized by the operating system if it is not powered on when the system is booted.

☒ **A, B,** and **C** are incorrect. Although the tape drive could be broken, it is unlikely it broke between the last backup and this one with no other activity or indicators. This could be the problem, but it is not the most likely cause. If the tape backup worked during the last normal backup, it is unlikely the issue concerns the drivers, unless you recently changed them. The system Registry, as well, would probably not be the culprit. Although the Registry can become corrupt, the most likely cause would still be **D.**

12. ☑ **A.** Your colleague most likely changed a few files while you were on break. Typically, a verify operation should be run right after the backup operation completes. This ensures the backup is good and prevents users from changing files between the backup and the verify. In this case, it is likely your colleague inadvertently changed files that were backed up. When the verify operation was run, the system noticed a difference between the data recorded on the tapes and the data on the disk drive, causing the verify operation to fail.

☒ **B, C,** and **D** are incorrect. The backup operation indicated it had completed successfully. An error would not occur after that point to indicate a failure of the backup. While there is no set limit to the time between a backup and a verify, they are typically performed in immediate succession to avoid files changing between the backup and the verify operations. It is possible the tape could go bad after successfully performing a backup, but in this scenario, changed data is the more likely culprit.

13. ☑ **B.** The five types are normal, which is a full backup; incremental, which copies only changed data since the last full backup and flags the data as backed up; differential, which copies only changed data since the last full backup but does not flag the data as being backed up; Copy, which copies all selected files but does not flag the data as being backed up; and

Daily, which copies all selected files modified the day the daily backup is performed and does not mark the files as having been backed up.

☒   **A, C,** and **D** are incorrect. A weekly backup is not a legitimate type of backup but may be used to indicate the frequency of normal backups. Full and normal are used synonymously, and the list given in answer **D** does not include the Copy option.

14. ☑   **B.** Files will inherit the folder permissions if you do not renew file permissions during the restore.

   ☒   **A, C,** and **D** are incorrect. If you do not choose to restore file permissions, the files will inherit the permissions of the folder into which they are restored. If you restore the files to a FAT partition, the permissions will be lost altogether.

15. ☑   **C.** DiskSave is used to save and restore the master boot record (MBR) and the Partition Boot Sector (PBS). The DiskSave utility is an MS-DOS utility (it cannot be run from the command prompt) used to restore these two binary files for a disk drive. You should save these files to your Windows NT startup floppy or your MS-DOS bootable floppy in the event the computer fails to start due to problems with the MBR or PBS.

   ☒   **A, B,** and **D** are incorrect. DiskMap is used to display information about the disk and the contents of the partition table. DiskProbe is a low-level disk editor. FtEdit is used to recover stripe sets, stripe sets with parity, and volume sets.

16. ☑   **D.** The Windows NT Backup program will not back up or restore the Registry of a remote computer. Therefore, the Registry must be restored using the emergency repair disk (ERD). Any time changes are made to a computer, the ERD should be updated so changes to the Registry are saved for possible restores.

   ☒   **A, B,** and **C** are incorrect. The Windows NT Backup program will not back up the Registry on a remote computer. The AT utility is used for scheduling automatic backups, not for restoring the Registry files. No changes are made to the Registry during the restore operation when using the Windows NT Backup utility.

17. ☑   **C.** While it is not as convenient for users, critical data that is not stored centrally is not likely to be backed up regularly. Having the home directory point to a network server is a good solution to saving user's data automatically. Should a local workstation fail, the data will not be lost.

   ☒   **A, B,** and **D** are incorrect. Performing weekly backups on the workstations would require a large number of tape drives and tapes. It may be a viable solution in companies where critical data is stored on every computer, but in most cases it is impractical. There would be no reason to perform incremental backups on the servers and differential backups on the workstations. Both still demand a large number of tapes and tape drives. Performing normal (full) backups on servers weekly with no interim backups (such as incremental or differential) puts the network at extreme risk. If the backup is performed at midnight on Saturdays and the system fails the next Friday at noon, six days' worth of data could potentially be lost.

18. ☑ **B.** 16-mm is not a commonly used tape type for backing up and restoring computer data.
☒ **A, C,** and **D** are incorrect. QIC, or Quarter Inch Cartridge, is a tape type often used. DAT, or digital audio tape, is another tape type commonly used. Finally, 8-mm tapes are frequently used for computer backups.

19. ☑ **A.** Chris apparently did not have adequate permissions to run the backup operation. If someone other than a backup operator attempts to run a backup, the person must have Read permissions for all selected files or they will not be backed up. The user should be added to the Backup Operators group to perform backups and restores.
☒ **B, C,** and **D** are incorrect. If the person attempting the backup does not have Read permissions, the backup will not copy those files. There is no function that allows files to be copied but not listed as copied. Backup and restore permissions are not automatically assigned to the Everyone group by default. Users can be added to the Backup Operators group. This group has the right to log on locally, shut down the system, and back up and restore files and directories on servers and domain controllers. Adam was a member of this group, but it is likely Chris was not. Regardless of whether Chris logged on as a network admin or as himself, he did not have adequate permissions to run the backups. The Account Operator group can manage accounts, log on locally, and shut down the system, but it does not have permission to back up and restore files and directories.

20. ☑ **B.** By combining the AT command with a batch file, you can create an automatic backup that is performed per your scheduling requirements. The AT command has various command line options that can be used to customize the backup schedule to some degree.
☒ **A, C,** and **D** are incorrect. The automation of the backup schedule does not occur in the command prompt but by using the AT command in a batch file. You can create a batch file using a simple text-editing program such as Notepad. No third-party program is required to create a batch file. You may use a third-party backup program that includes scheduling capabilities. The last answer is tricky. The Windows NT 4.0 Backup program, itself, cannot be set to run automatically. Using the scheduler function in Windows NT and a batch file using the AT command, you can create an automated backup schedule. Thus, while technically correct, this is not the best answer.

LAB ANSWER

1. The mirror set data size was 5GB. Although it contained two disks, each with 5GB partitions, the capacity for data was 5GB since all data was replicated on Disk 1.

2. The total amount of space dedicated to data on the stripe set with parity was 10GB. The total set was 15GB, but one stripe (5GB) was used for parity information.

3. The following symptoms are likely to be seen when Disk 0 fails:

   a. A server error will be entered in the event log.

   b. When the system attempts to write to Disk 0, a system message will be displayed, stating: "A disk that is part of a fault-tolerant volume can no longer be accessed."

   c. The Disk Administrator will indicate a [RECOVERABLE] status message.

   d. The write operation will be successful. If the data was intended for the mirror set, the data will be written to the shadow partition. If the data was intended for the stripe set with parity, the data will be written to another available partition.

4. The following steps must be taken to resolve this problem:

   a. Break the mirror set.

   b. The Boot indicator flag should be set in the System ID field of the system partition. If you have not previously done this on the shadow partition, you can do so in the Disk Administrator once you've broken the set.

   c. Shut down the computer.

   d. Remove the old, original disk drive (Disk 0).

   e. Replace with the same or similar disk with at least 10GB of available unused partition. Ideally, you should use an identical drive.

   f. Restart the computer, booting from the former shadow disk (Disk 1).

   g. The shadow disk will become the primary partition. If this disk is a SCSI disk, swap the SCSI ID so the former shadow disk will become SCSI ID 0.

   h. Re-create the mirror set first. Using the Disk Administrator I Fault Tolerance menu, choose Establish Mirror. Applying the same steps used to create the mirror set initially, create a new mirror set now.

   i. Choose Commit Changes Now to initialize the creation of the mirror set.

   j. The computer will reboot and initialization of the mirror set will begin.

k. In the Disk Administrator, the status will indicate [INITIALIZING].

l. When it is complete, use the Disk Administrator to regenerate the RAID stripe set with parity. In the Disk Administrator, choose Regenerate from the Fault Tolerance menu.

m. Choose Commit Changes Now to initialize the regeneration of the RAID set.

n. In the Disk Administrator, the status will indicate "Stripe set with parity #n [INITIALIZING]."

o. Update your emergency repair disk.

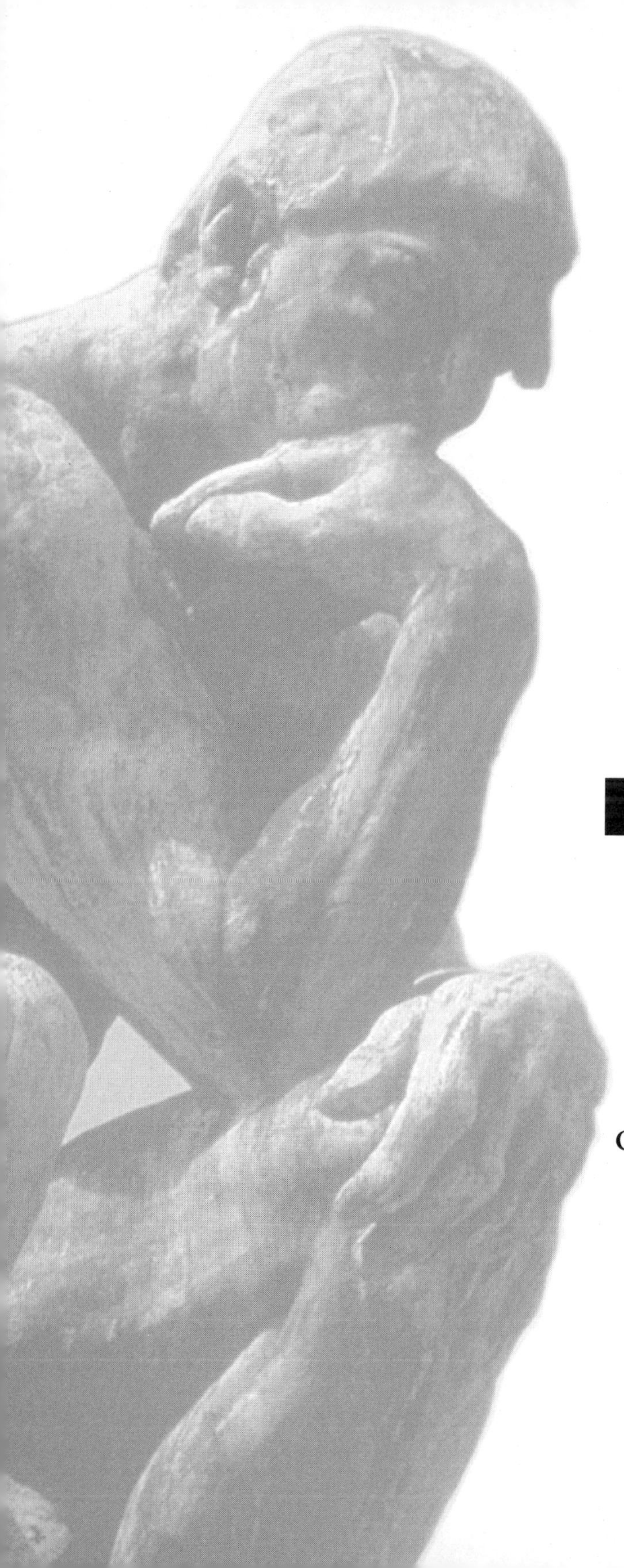

MCSE

MICROSOFT CERTIFIED SYSTEMS ENGINEER

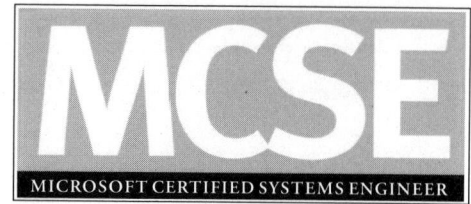

3

Maintaining, Troubleshooting, and Optimizing the Operating System

CERTIFICATION OBJECTIVES

I n the previous chapter, we discussed maintaining and restoring hardware. In this chapter we'll continue to discuss recovery issues, but we'll focus on the operating system. We'll look at system files and how to recover to a previous operating system environment. We'll also cover troubleshooting, optimizing the server, and how to deploy service packs and hotfixes to keep Windows NT Server 4.0 systems up and running with the latest revisions in place.

CERTIFICATION OBJECTIVE 3.01

Recovering System Files, and Reestablishing the Previous OS Environment

Recovering system files and restoring previous operating systems is a critical task that must be accomplished after catastrophic failures, particularly disk drive failures. In this section, we'll look at which files are needed to start a system and how to recover from a loss of those files on a disk drive or disk subsystem.

Backing Up the Registry

The Registry contains internal configuration information that is needed by Windows NT to function. It is critical to have up-to-date copies of the Registry. If you have a backup device on the computer, you can include the Registry in your normal backups. You must select this option in the Windows NT Backup program, which is discussed in detail in Chapter 2.

After any changes in the configuration of the system, it is important you use the Repair Disk program, Rdisk.exe, to update files in the *%systemroot%\Repair* folder. You should also create a new emergency repair disk for the system at that time. For safety, it's always a good idea to make a second copy of the ERD and store it offsite with your backup tapes.

You can use the Windows NT Registry Editor, Regedt32.exe, to save and restore selected Registry keys. The Windows NT Resource Kit also contains two utilities, Regback.exe and Regrest.exe, which can be used to back up and restore the Registry.

Saving the SYSTEM Key

One of the most important keys in the Registry is HKEY_LOCAL_MACHINE\ SYSTEM, which contains configuration information used by the operating system during startup. Although this key is stored on the emergency repair disk (ERD), there are times you may want to restore this key from another disk.

You can save the SYSTEM key by using the Disk Administrator or the Windows NT Registry Editor, Regedt32.exe. The main difference is that the Disk Administrator always saves the key to a floppy disk. Using Regedt32.exe, you can save the key to any disk location you choose.

EXERCISE 3-1

CertCam 3-1

Using the Disk Administrator to Save the SYSTEM Key

1. Open the Disk Administrator.

2. Choose the Partition menu and select Configuration.

3. On the Configuration menu, select Save. A message will be displayed describing what will be saved, and its location.

4. Insert a floppy disk with at least 512K free space. Use the Windows NT startup floppy, if possible.

5. Click OK to save the data to the floppy disk.

EXERCISE 3-2

CertCam 3-2

Using the Registry Editor to Save the SYSTEM Key

1. Click Start, select Run, then type **Regedt32.exe**.

2. Click the HKEY_LOCAL_MACHINE\SYSTEM key.

3. On the Registry menu, select Save Key.

4. Enter the path where you want to save the key.

As you can see, saving the Registry, or a key in the Registry, is a fairly simple, but important, process. Later in this chapter, we'll learn how to restore this key.

Saving the DISK Subkey

Anytime you make changes to your disk subsystem, you should consider backing up your entire Registry, or the DISK subkey at the very least. This subkey contains information about currently defined drive letters, volume sets, mirror sets, stripe sets (with and without parity), as well as CD-ROM and drive mappings.

Having a backup of just this key is helpful when you want to restore Registry settings related to the disk subsystem, but do not want to restore the entire SYSTEM key or Registry file. For instance, if a computer fails and you want to move an entire mirror set or stripe set to another computer, you can use just the DISK subkey. If information about your disk setup has become corrupted, or if you need to replace hardware, you may also have use for a DISK subkey backup.

To back up the DISK subkey, run Regedt32.exe. Click the HKEY_LOCAL_ MACHINE\SYSTEM\DISK subkey. Then, select Save Key from the Registry menu. Enter the path where you want to save the subkey.

Creating an Emergency Repair Disk

During the installation of Windows NT, Setup forms the Registry information from *%systemroot%\System32\Config*. For recovery, Setup also creates a *%systemroot%\ Repair* folder that contains a number of files needed to recover from various failures. The files are listed in Table 3-1. Note that compressed filenames end with the underscore (_) character.

During installation, you will be prompted to create an emergency repair disk. You should select Yes. The files are copied from *%systemroot%\Repair* to the floppy disk. This allows you to use the ERD later to repair a corrupt Partition Boot Sector.

When you run Rdisk.exe, you can update repair information. This updates information in the *%systemroot%\Repair\Software* and the *%systemroot%\sRepair\ System* files with information in the %systemroot%\System32\Config. To update this information, click the Update Repair Info button from Rdisk.exe.

| TABLE 3-1 | Files Placed in the %systemroot%\Repair Folder During Setup |

Filename	Contents
Autoexec.nt	Used to initialize the MS-DOS environment.
Config.nt	Used to initialize the MS-DOS environment.
Default._	Registry key HKEY_USERS\DEFAULT, in compressed format.
Ntuser.da_	Compressed version of %systemroot%\Profiles\Default user\Ntuser.dat.
Sam._	Compressed version of the Registry key HKEY_LOCAL_MACHINE\SAM.
Security._	Compressed version of the Registry key HKEY_LOCAL_MACHINE\SECURITY.
Setup.log	Log of which files were installed. This is a read-only, hidden, System file.
Software._	Compressed version of the Registry key HKEY_LOCAL_MACHINE\SOFTWARE.

If you run Rdisk.exe from the command prompt with the \s switch, it will update all files in the *%systemroot%\Repair* folder. If you run the Repair Disk program from Windows NT Explorer or My Computer, it will not update the Default, Sam, and Security files.

exam
ⓦatch

It's important to understand how to use the Rdisk.exe utility for the exam. In particular, you should know that the information from %systemroot%\Repair is copied to the emergency repair disk. The %systemroot% is the location of the Windows NT operating system files, typically C:\WINNT. If you changed the target folder when installing Windows NT, the name of the %systemroot% folder will be different. On an exam, you might be given a named path such as C:\WINNT rather than %systemroot%.

Backing Up the Master Boot Record and Partition Boot Sector

You should back up the master boot record (MBR) on a disk every time you change partition information for primary or extended partitions. This way, if something happens to the MBR, you can attempt to recover it before having to completely re-create the drive. The Partition Boot Sector (PBS) should be backed up when you format a volume, install Windows NT on the volume, or convert a volume from the FAT file system to the NTFS file system.

In Chapter 2, we briefly reviewed two programs that can be used to restore the MBR or the PBS. The Windows NT–based program, DiskProbe, or the MS-DOS–based program DiskSave can both be used to back up these disk sectors. At the very minimum, you should have a copy of the MBR and the PBS for any volume used to initialize your system(s). Other drives, though important, will not prevent your system from initializing, and are therefore not as critical.

Backing up all data stored on hard disks on your systems is also very important. This is covered at length in Chapter 2 and will not be reviewed here.

Understanding ARC Pathnames

Advanced RISC Computing (ARC) is a naming convention used in Windows NT to identify the location of a file or a program on a device such as a hard drive or a floppy disk. In order to create paths to use to start the computer from an alternate location, such as a shadow drive after a primary drive fails, you will need to understand ARC pathname conventions.

For x86-based computers, such as an Intel Pentium II–based computer, the ARC path in the Boot.ini file appears in one of two formats.

- multi(W)disk(X)rdisk(Y)partition(Z)\ *%systemroot%*
- scsi(W)disk(X)rdisk(Y)partition(Z)\ *%systemroot%*

For RISC-based computers, you use ARC pathnames to show the location of:

- The folder containing Osloader.exe and Hal.dll
- The full path to Osloader.exe
- The path to the boot partition
- Devices detected by firmware such as keyboards or video devices

multi(W)disk(X)rdisk(Y)partition(Z)

This ARC path naming convention is used on x86-based computers. In Windows NT 4.0, it is used to indicate that it should rely on the system BIOS to load system files. That means the NTLDR, the boot loader in x86-based computers, will use the BIOS to find and load Ntoskrnl.exe and other files in order to get the system up and running.

This naming convention is often referred to simply as multi(). In this scheme, the letters W, X, Y, and Z are each used in the following manner:

- **W** is the ordinal number of the controller and should always be 0.

- **X** is not used for multi() and is always 0.

- **Y** is the ordinal number for the disk on the controller and is always 0 or 1 for disks attached to the primary controller. The range is 0 through 3 for dual-channel EIDE controllers.

- **Z** is the partition number. These numbers start at 1, as opposed to all other entries, which begin counting at 0. All partitions receive a number except for extended partitions (type 5) and unused partitions (type 0).

For configurations using IDE and EIDE disk controllers, the multi() syntax works for up to four disks on the primary and secondary channels of a dual-channel controller. In a SCSI-only configuration, the multi() works for the first two disks on the first SCSI controller. The first SCSI controller is simply the controller whose BIOS loads first. If the computer has both IDE and SCSI disks, the multi() syntax works only for the IDE disks on the first controller.

scsi(W)disk(X)rdisk(Y)partition(Z)

The scsi() syntax is used for both RISC-based and x86-based computers to indicate that the operating systems needs to load a SCSI device driver to access the boot partition.

On an x86-based system, the device driver is Ntbootdd.sys. It is a copy of the disk controller driver in use. On a RISC-based computer, the driver is built into the firmware, so no file is required.

The W, X, Y, and Z definitions for scsi() are as follows:

- **W** is the ordinal number of the controller as identified by Ntbootdd.sys.

- **X** is the SCSI ID of the target disk.

- **Y** is the SCSI logical unit number (LUN) of the disk that contains the boot partition. Y is almost always 0.

- **Z** is the partition number. As with multi(), all partitions receive numbers except for extended partitions (type 5) and unused partitions (type 0). These numbers, like multi(), always begin numbering with 1 rather than 0.

Now that we've reviewed ARC pathnames, let's look at an example. You have an Intel Pentium III computer with one IDE controller that has two 10GB hard drives attached. Each drive is a single partition. Based on this, the ARC pathname that would be in the Boot.ini file is:

```
Multi(0)disk(0)rdisk(0)partition(1)\Winnt
```

If those two drives were attached to a SCSI controller using ID0 and ID4, what would the ARC pathname look like?

```
Scsi(0)disk(0)rdisk(0)partition(1)
```

exam
ⓦatch

You will likely get at least one question that requires that you discern the difference between the multi() and the scsi() syntax or that requires you fully understand ARC path naming conventions. The most likely question will ask you the right ARC pathname given a set of criteria. Be sure to understand ARC pathnames both for the exam and for recovering from disk failures on the job.

Restoring Disk Information

If you backed up the Registry, master boot records, and Partition Boot Sectors, as recommended throughout this chapter, recovering from most disk and startup problems without reinstalling the operating system is much more likely. In this section, we'll review how to use floppy disks and other tools to restart and restore your system.

Windows NT Startup Floppy Disk

The Windows NT startup floppy disk allows you to start your system when it is unable to start using the information on the hard disk. If you are able to start your system using the Windows NT startup floppy, but not using the hard disk, you can begin narrowing down the cause of the problem. This symptom might indicate that there are problems with the system partition, the Partition Boot Sector information, or that the files on the system partition are missing or corrupt.

Files to Copy x86-based Computer   If using an x86-based system, the following are files you should have on the floppy:

- NTLDR
- Boot.ini
- Ntdetect.com
- Bootsect.dos
- Ntbootdd.sys

Files to Copy for a RISC-based Computer   If using a RISC-based system, the following are files you should have on the floppy:

- Osloader.exe
- Hal.dll
- *.pal (AXP-based computers only)

Once you have created the Windows NT startup floppy, you should create a path to it.

EXERCISE 3-3

Creating a Path to the Windows NT Startup Floppy

1. Start the computer. The Boot menu will be displayed.
2. On the Boot menu, select the Supplementary menu.
3. On the Supplementary menu, select Setup The System.
4. On the Setup menu, select Manage Boot Selection Menu.
5. On the Boot Selections menu, select Add A Boot Selection.
6. After entering the required information, you will be back at the Boot Selections menu. Select Setup Menu.
7. On the Setup menu, select Supplementary menu and choose Save Changes.

By modifying the Boot menu ahead of time, you'll be able to boot from the Windows NT startup floppy if you run into problems later.

Emergency Repair Disk

If you are unable to start your system normally, the next step typically is to try "Last Known Good Configuration" in the Startup menu. However, if your system files, Registry, or Partition Boot Sector are corrupt, you will still be unable to boot your system. In this case, the next step would be to use the Repair process in Windows NT setup to restore your system.

To repair the operating system, Setup needs either the information stored in *%systemroot%\Repair* or the emergency repair disk. Keep in mind that not all disk problems can be resolved using the ERD. The information on the ERD must match the current operating system exactly. You should *never* use an ERD from another system. By now, it should be clear that creating and maintaining a current ERD for each installation of Windows NT is mission-critical for recovery.

EXERCISE 3-4

Using the Emergency Repair Disk

1. Start the computer using the Windows NT Setup disk 1. When prompted, insert disk 2, then select the option to Repair by pressing the R key. The Setup program will display these options:

   [X] Inspect Registry files

   [X] Inspect startup environment

   [X] Verify Windows NT system files

   [X] Inspect boot sector

   Continue (perform selected tasks)

2. Clear the X from any tasks you do not want to perform. Select Continue (perform selected tasks).

3. You will be prompted to insert disk 3. After disk 3, you will be prompted to insert the emergency repair disk.

4. Once the system has completed repairing the files, a message will display indicating Setup has completed repairs and that the computer must be restarted.

5. Restart the computer normally.

exam
ⓦatch

On the Windows NT Server exam, you're likely to get one or more questions on booting a server that has system or boot partition problems. Make sure you thoroughly understand the use of the emergency repair disk. This disk is not used to boot the system. You must use the Setup disks or your Windows NT Startup floppy to boot the system before you can repair problems.

Inspect Registry Files

You can repair Registry keys in Windows NT by using the Windows NT Setup program's Repair process. Using Setup disks, the first menu option is Inspect Registry Files. If you select this option, the system will display a list of Registry files that can be restored. Keep in mind that restoring keys can result in permanent loss of critical information, so be sure to have a solid recovery plan in place before attempting this.

The options for restoring Registry keys are:

- ■ [ ] SYSTEM (System Configuration)
- ■ [ ] SOFTWARE (Software Information)
- ■ [ ] DEFAULT (Default User Profile)
- ■ [ ] NTUSER.DAT (New User Profile)
- ■ [ ] SECURITY (Security Policy) and SAM (User Accounts Database)
- ■ Continue (perform selected tasks)

To select various tasks, enter an X between the brackets, then select Continue (perform selected tasks). Once you've restored Registry keys, be sure to update your emergency repair disk using the Rdisk.exe command.

Inspect Startup Environment

The second option in the Repair menu is the Inspect Startup Environment option. This verifies the Windows NT files in the system partition are the right ones. If any of the needed files are missing or corrupt, this option replaces them from the Windows NT installation CD.

Verify Windows NT System Files

This third Repair option uses a checksum to verify each file in the installation is a good file and matches the version needed by the operating system. The Setup.log file is used to compare installed files with actual files and their checksums. This process also looks for needed boot files, such as NTLDR and Ntoskrnl.exe. If a file is determined to be missing or is the wrong version, the system will identify the file and prompt you to replace it.

Inspect Boot Sector (x86-based Computers)

The last option in the Repair menu is the Inspect Boot Sector option. This is only used on x86-based computers. This option verifies the Partition Boot Sector information on the system partition still references the NTLDR. If it does not, it will copy it from the emergency repair disk. The Repair process can only replace the PBS for the system partition of the first disk or on the startup disk.

FROM THE CLASSROOM

Restoring Operating Systems

When working with students on restoring the operating system, we always work through each of these scenarios on a broken computer. You don't want the first time you try to restore a system to be when you're under pressure on the job. While it can be confusing at first, if you take time to work through the various scenarios and methods of restoring a system, you'll find that it all comes together. Essentially, the operating system needs certain files to start and run. If those files are missing or if the system cannot find them, you need to fix the problem. That always entails finding a way to boot the system, determine the nature of the problem, and replace or restore files. Practice this in a lab or on a test system before facing this situation on the job and you'll do well on the exam and on the job.

—*Susan T. Snedaker, MCSE, MCT, MBA*

Restoring Registry Information

There are three methods you can use to restore the Registry in Windows NT Server 4.0.

1. Employ the Repair process in Windows NT Setup using the emergency repair disk.

2. Restore the Registry from your backup media if you selected that option in Windows NT Backup or from the Regback.exe command.

3. Restore just the SYSTEM or DISK key using the procedures described next.

Restoring the SYSTEM Key

If you have not created an emergency repair disk, if it is not up-to-date, or if it has been misplaced, you can restore the SYSTEM Registry key using the Disk Administrator.

EXERCISE 3-5

CertCam 3-5

Restoring the SYSTEM Key from the Disk Administrator

1. In the Disk Administrator, on the Partition menu, select Configuration.

2. On the Configuration menu, select Restore.

3. Insert the floppy disk containing saved configuration information.

4. Click OK. Your system will be restarted automatically.

Restoring the DISK Subkey

You can restore the DISK subkey using the Windows NT Registry Editor, Regedt32.exe.

EXERCISE 3-6

Restoring the DISK Subkey from the Registry Editor

1. Run Regedt32.exe.

2. Select the Registry key HKEY_LOCAL_MACHINE\SYSTEM\DISK.

3. On the Registry menu, select Restore.

4. Enter the filename or path to the file.

5. Click OK.

on the Job

If you're restoring the DISK subkey on a remote computer (which, as you'll recall, cannot be done using the Backup program), the C drive designation in the list refers to the remote computer's C drive. Don't confuse this with the local C drive. Although restoring the DISK subkey on a remote computer is not an often-used procedure, you should practice it in your lab environment in the event you need to move a stripe set from one computer to another. This is the most common use of this procedure.

Replacing the Master Boot Record and Partition Boot Sector

There may be times you'll need to replace either the master boot record (MBR) or the Partition Boot Sector (PBS). You should use extreme caution when doing either of these procedures as data can be permanently lost if the disk is improperly configured.

Most of the time, the easiest way to repair the master boot record (MBR) on a computer is to use an MS-DOS bootable floppy and run the Fdisk.exe program. You should not run Fdisk if you're using a third-party translation program, or if you're using a program (dual-boot or third-party partitioning programs in particular) that writes information in the area between the code and the Partition Table. If you are not sure, do not use Fdisk. You should also refrain from using Fdisk if the drive is part of a volume set such as a mirror set or stripe set with parity. When Windows NT creates a volume set, it overwrites the MBR with additional information. Using Fdisk will destroy this information and make the volume sets unusable.

To replace the MBR, start the computer using the MS-DOS bootable floppy. At the A:\ prompt, type **fdisk /mbr**. This replaces the MBR without altering the Partition Table.

To replace the Partition Boot Sector, you can use DiskProbe or DiskSave (discussed earlier and in Chapter 2), if you have saved this information. On NTFS volumes, the file system writes a copy of the PBS at the end of the volume. You can use DiskProbe to locate and copy this sector to the beginning of the volume. Once you have replaced this information, you should be able to boot the drive into Windows NT.

Restoring Windows NT Files on the System Partition

Earlier, we discussed the files needed on the system partition. If any of these files becomes corrupt or is missing, Windows NT will not start. To restore these files, start your computer using the Windows NT startup floppy. Determine any missing or corrupt files and copy them from the startup floppy to the system partition on the drive. The files are listed in Table 3-2 for both x86-based computers and RISC-based computers.

TABLE 3-2   Files Required on the System Partition

X86-based Files	Folder	RISC-based Files	Folder
NTLDR	root	Osloader.exe	\Os\Winnt40
Boot.ini	root	no equivalent	
Bootsect.dos	root	no equivalent	
Ntdetect.com	root	no equivalent	
Ntbootdd.sys (SCSI drives only)	root	no equivalent	
Hal.dll in boot partition		Hal.dll	\Os\Winnt40
No equivalent		*.pal (Alpha-based computers)	\Os\Winnt40

SCENARIO & SOLUTION

What is the best way to back up a remote Registry?	Using Regback.exe.
The Ntbootdd.sys is a copy of what file?	The SCSI device driver.
Where will you find the ARC pathname(s) listed?	Boot.ini
Why would you modify an ARC pathname?	If the bootable drive was no longer available and you wanted to boot from another drive.
Which Windows NT tools can be used to inspect and repair the Partition Boot Sector?	Emergency repair disk or DiskProbe.

In this section, we've discussed system files and recovering the operating system in-depth. By now, you should understand the importance of updating the emergency repair disk, the uses of the Windows NT startup floppy, and various methods of restoring the operating system when files are corrupt or missing.

CERTIFICATION OBJECTIVE 3.02

Troubleshooting and Optimizing Server Performance

Troubleshooting and optimizing Windows NT Server performance should be part of an ongoing process to ensure the network servers are working at peak efficiency. Changes to the servers, such as additional services or applications being run, can impact the server, creating bottlenecks and problems that impact end users.

There are essentially four resource areas that should be monitored and tuned for peak performance. These are memory, processor, disk subsystem, and network subsystem. In this section, we'll review the tools Windows NT provides for troubleshooting performance problems and look at some best practices for optimizing the servers.

Subsystem Monitoring

Memory, processors, disk subsystems, and network subsystems form the backbone of all server operations. In this section, we'll briefly review the different elements of each subsystem. In subsequent sections, we'll look at the following Windows NT tools: Task Manager, Event Viewer, and Performance Manager. System optimization includes these steps:

1. Creating a baseline of current use.

2. Monitoring use over time.

3. Analyzing data to find and resolve abnormalities in the system use.

4. Determining expected response times for specific numbers of users and system use.

5. Determining how the system should be used.

Keep these steps in mind as we review the various subsystems and Windows NT tools for optimizing system performance. When monitoring system resources, it is important to monitor each resource individually as well as the system as a whole. An application or service may run fine when it's the only thing running. Once a system is under its customary load, it may perform quite differently.

Memory

RAM is discussed in more detail later in this chapter. However, memory bottlenecks are fairly common. It's relatively easy and inexpensive to increase RAM and resolve or avoid potential bottlenecks. Both RAM and cache should be monitored.

Processors

The type and number of processors will impact system performance. For instance, the Digital Alpha XP processor is far superior to the Intel 80486 processor. Using the latest processor (Alpha- or Intel-based) will improve performance. Adding additional processors if the processor and motherboard support multiple processors will also enhance performance. Windows NT supports symmetric multiprocessing. This is when processing is shared across the processors. This is done automatically in Windows NT when more than one CPU is present, but can be manually tuned for specific application requirements.

TABLE 3-3	Controller Type	Throughput (in MB Per Second)
Differences Between Controller Types	IDE	2.5
	Standard SCSI	3
	SCSI-2	5
	Fast SCSI-2	10
	PCI	40

Disk Subsystems

There are a number of factors that will impact performance of the disk subsystem, including:

- **Type and number of disk controllers**   Types and numbers of controllers will affect system throughput. Installing multiple controllers can result in greater responsiveness. Table 3-3 shows the significant differences between controller types.

- **Busmaster controllers**   A busmaster controller has an on-board processor that handles all interrupts until data is ready to be passed to the CPU for processing. This helps manage processor queues by limiting interruptions for data.

- **Caching**   Caching is the storage of frequently used or recently used data in a special memory location. If a disk controller has the ability to cache, it will store data retrieved from the disk. In the event the CPU requests that data again, it will be faster retrieving it from cache than from the disk. Therefore, more disk cache is better and improves disk subsystem performance significantly.

- **Controllers supporting RAID**   Hardware implementations of RAID offer more superior performance than software implementations of RAID. By implementing disk striping or disk striping with parity via a hardware solution, throughput can be significantly enhanced. Improvements in performance can vary up to about 20 percent faster with hardware RAID.

- **Type of disk activity**   Some applications require many read and writes. These applications are considered "disk-bound." Implementing the fastest disk subsystem would provide the best performance in this case.

■ **Type of drives implemented**   Disk drives all have a metric called disk access time. This is calculated based on the average amount of time it takes for a particular head on the disk to reach a specific sector after other random reads. In other words, regardless of where the heads are at any given moment, it takes on average x amount of time for a particular head to read a particular sector. This access time is measured in milliseconds (ms). For solid system performance, all drives on the system should have access times in the low teens or lower. Remember, the lower the number, the faster the drive.

Network Subsystems

The network subsystem contains many components, each of which can impact overall system performance. Each component is discussed briefly in the following:

■ **Network adapter type**   There are three common network adapter types available, though only two are in common use. The 8-bit network adapter had a transfer rate up to about 400 Kbps and is not generally used anymore. The 16-bit network adapter has a transfer rate of about 800 Kbps and is still commonly used. The latest is the 32-bit network adapter with transfer rates up to 1.2 Mbps. Avoid using programmed I/O (PIO) adapters as they require CPU cycles to move data from the network adapter to RAM.

■ **Multiple network adapters**   Installing multiple network adapters can improve subsystem performance because the processor can hand requests to multiple controllers for simultaneous processing. If your network uses multiple protocols, limiting each controller to a single protocol can also help manage throughput. It's also a common practice to place all server-based traffic on a single controller.

■ **Number of users**   The overall number of users concurrently connected to a server increases the amount of work the server is actively performing. However, you must also actively monitor inactive connections as well. Each connection, whether or not it is active, requires cycle time from the processor. When a server has a large number of active and inactive connections, response time will suffer.

■ **Protocols**   Keep in mind that the more protocols in use, the more processing required. Using the fewest protocols possible will increase performance. Most protocols have similar performance speeds, so protocols should be selected based on the amount of traffic generated for any given function.

■ **Network services in use**   Every service you run on a server adds to the system overhead. It increases the load on the CPU(s) and on memory. Examples of services that may not need to be running on a particular server are: Services for Macintosh, WINS, DHCP, and RAS. Stop any services that are not needed to enhance system performance.

■ **Applications in use**   Applications, like services, require additional work from the processors and memory. In addition, they can require services from the disk and network subsystems. Advanced planning will help determine where applications should be installed and what resources will be required for them to run efficiently. Applications, such as Internet Services, Microsoft SQL Server, or Microsoft Systems Management Server, all require additional resources and often involve the networking subsystem to a large extent. Monitoring the effect of these applications on server and network performance is an important aspect of server optimization.

■ **Directory services**   Directory services (in the domain model and structure) can affect network capacity and performance. Factors include number of users, number of BDCs, and the proximity of BDCs to the PDC. For instance, the number of simultaneous logon requests will impact network and server performance. BDCs can assist with user logons but each must be synchronized. The more BDCs used, the more network traffic is generated via synchronizations activities. Finally, if the BDCs must be synchronized via slower WAN links, network traffic on that link can be taken up almost entirely by synchronization. Consider using scheduling to limit the amount of bandwidth consumed or the time at which synchronization occurs.

Troubleshooting Performance Problems

There are three primary tools used for troubleshooting performance problems in Windows NT Server 4.0. There are many third-party products that can be used to monitor, troubleshoot, and optimize server performance as well. First, we'll learn about bottlenecks, utilization, and queues. Then, we'll look at Task Manager, Event Viewer, and Performance Monitor to understand how these Windows NT tools can be used to troubleshoot and tune your system.

Bottlenecks, Utilization, and Queues

A bottleneck is a condition that limits one part of the system from performing optimally. The device with the lowest capacity or speed will generally become a bottleneck if demand is high enough. The primary indicator of a bottleneck is consistently high utilization for one or more system resources and low rates of utilization on related resources.

Reduced user response time is often a good indicator of a bottleneck, which, by definition, is determined by the number of requests for service, the arrival pattern of those requests, and the amount of time requested. When these factors are random, queues develop. A queue is simply a waiting line for service. According to queuing theory, if the arrival pattern of requests and the duration of the requests are unpredictable, a device that is 66 percent utilized will develop a queue of two items. Thus, a utilization rate well below 90 percent can still be a bottleneck.

System Objects   Windows NT views active components on the system as objects with certain characteristics. System object counts are important because each object takes up space in the nonpaged memory area. As you'll recall, nonpaged memory is system memory that is not written out to the disk. Too many system threads or processes can degrade performance across the board, resulting in a bottleneck in the processor or memory. You can track objects in Task Manager and Performance Monitor, as discussed in the following sections.

System Processes   Processes include both user applications and Windows NT services. These can become bottlenecks as well. When investigating processor, disk, or memory use, chart use by process. Start then stop a process to see how it impacts resources and your system. Both Task Manager and Performance Monitor show counts of running processes. Task Manager is best for short term monitoring. Performance Monitor includes more detailed counters and allows you to log data over time in different formats.

Task Manager

Task Manager allows you to monitor active processes and applications. You can start and stop processes and applications as well as make changes such as altering the base priority class of a process. Task Manager gets its data from the same functions as Performance Monitor (described later). It receives this information directly and cannot create a log file or monitor remote computers. Nevertheless, it is a very useful tool for checking basic counters and monitoring the local computer, or for short-term monitoring activities.

Task Manager can be started several ways. You can select Start, then Run and type in **Taskmgr.exe**. Alternatively, you can press CTRL-ALT-DEL and click Task Manager. You can press CTRL-ALT-ESC to bring up Task Manager, or right-click on the Task Bar then click Task Manager. Task Manager has three tabs: Applications, Processes, and Performance. The Applications tab allows you to view running applications and end them or switch to them. The Processes tab allows you to view processes running on the system. It is on this tab that you can change the base priority class of a process. Lastly, the Performance tab is used to monitor CPU and memory usage on the system.

Task Manager Processes   Task Manager contains many different data elements related to each process. Table 3-4 briefly describes each process measure.

TABLE 3-4	Process Measurements in Task Manager

Process Measure	Description
Image Name	Name of the process.
Process Identifier (PID)	Numerical ID assigned to the process while it is running.
CPU Usage	Percentage of time the threads of the process used the processor since the last update.
CPU Time	Total processor time used by the process since it was started, in seconds.
Memory Usage	Amount of main memory used by the process, in kilobytes.
Memory Usage Delta	Change in memory use since the last update, in kilobytes.
Page Faults	Number of times data had to be retrieved from disk for this process, because it was not found in memory. This is a cumulative value since the process was started.
Page Faults Delta	Change in the number of page faults since last update.
Virtual Memory Size	Size of the process's share of the paging file, in kilobytes.
Paged Pool	Amount of paged pool used by the process, in kilobytes.
Nonpaged Pool	Amount of nonpaged pool (system memory) used by the process, in kilobytes.
Base Priority	Base priority of the process, which is used to determine the order in which threads of a process are scheduled.
Handle Count	Number of object handles in the process's object table.
Thread Count	Number of threads running per process.

To add an element to the display in Task Manager, click the View menu and choose Select Columns.

This list of processes is refreshed in Task Manager periodically. A process can be ended by right-clicking the process and selecting End Process from the context menu, or by selecting the process and clicking the End Process button in the lower-right corner of the Task Manager dialog box.

Task Manager Base Priority Class   Other than ending tasks or viewing system resource usage, Task Manager can be useful for changing the base priority class of a process. While the base priority class is usually set in the application code, you can modify it in Task Manager. This change lasts as long as the process does. Once the process is restarted, it will revert to its original base priority class.

To change the base priority class, open Task Manager and select the Processes tab. Select the process you wish to change and right-click it. Select Set Priority from the context menu. Then, select the priority you want: Realtime, High, Normal, or Low. A bullet point indicates the process's current priority.

on the job

Changing the base priority class to Realtime can destabilize your system. If a process is very active and is set to Realtime, it can essentially lock out all other processes and prevent them from running on the system. This includes system essential processes and services. Unless you have a good reason for setting a process to Realtime, you should avoid using this setting.

You can also use the Processes tab in Task Manager to distribute processes across multiple processors, if you have more than one CPU. Normally, Windows NT will automatically distribute thread processing across multiple processors using *soft affinity*. Typically, a thread will always run on the processor it ran on last in order to take advantage of processor cache. You can, however, redirect the processing to one or more CPUs in your system. To select processors for a process, right-click the process name in the Task Manager Processes tab. Click Set Affinity and select one or more processors from the list. Click OK to complete this task.

Task Manager Performance   The Performance tab of Task Manager, as shown in Figure 3-1, is used to monitor CPU and memory usage. This provides a snapshot of system resources and can be useful in identifying system bottlenecks.

In the Totals section, Handles is the number of object handles in the tables of all processes. Threads is the number of threads running, including one Idle thread per processor. Processes is the number of active processes, including the Idle process.

The Task
Manager
Performance tab

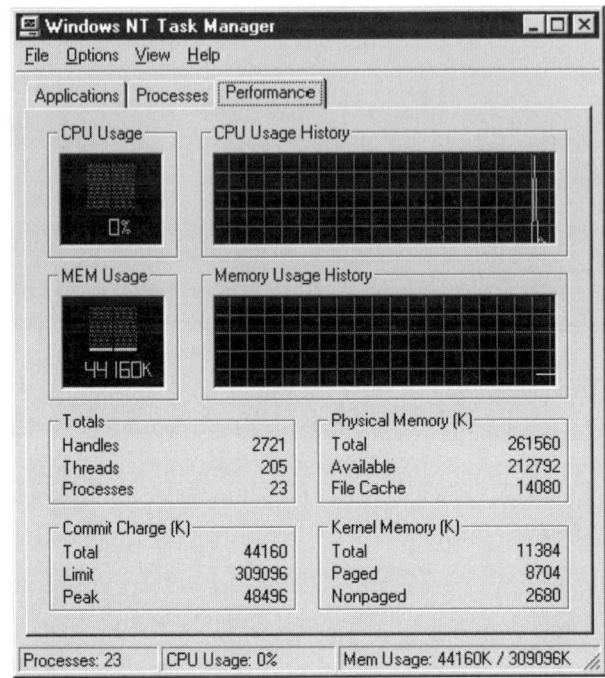

In the Physical Memory (K) section, total and available memory are shown. This is one area to check if you suspect memory problems. The Commit Charge (K) is the size of virtual memory in use by all processes. Kernel Memory (K) refers to the memory available to the operating system components running in highly privileged kernel mode.

Event Viewer

Event Viewer is accessed via Administrative Tools. There are essentially three logs available via Event Viewer: system, security, and application. You can also use Event Viewer to view logs on other computers.

In Event Viewer, you can:

- View descriptions and additional details of an event source.
- Sort events in ascending or descending data order.
- Filter events to view only events matching certain criteria.
- Search for events based on event descriptions or criteria.

Logging begins automatically when you start the computer. Logging stops when the log file becomes full and cannot overwrite itself. This occurs if the first event is not old enough to be overwritten, or if you have set the log for manual clearing. You can set the log size and storage period from the Log menu by using the Log Settings menu option.

The Event Viewer can be used to help predict and identify sources of problems. If log warnings show a disk has to make multiple attempts to read or write to a particular sector, you may be seeing early indications of a likely sector or disk failure. Problems with applications will show up in the application log, and these events can be viewed when troubleshooting application crashes. Details of events can be obtained by double-clicking the event.

Performance Monitor

Performance Monitor is the third tool provided in Windows NT that can be used to monitor, troubleshoot, and optimize the system. Performance Monitor can be initiated at the command line by typing **Perfmon.exe**. It can also be started selecting Performance Monitor in Administrative Tools.

When using Performance Monitor, you select object counters to monitor and customize the view using Chart, Log, Report, or Alert. Unlike Task Manager, you can save these counter and option settings to a file. You can save settings for one or more views as a group called a workspace. Each view has a different file extension as shown in Table 3-5.

Performance Monitor measures various objects in your computer. Each object represents a thread or process, section of memory, or physical device. It collects information on the usage and demand of each object. Table 3-6 shows objects that are always present when running Windows NT Server. Other objects only appear when the application or process is running.

TABLE 3-5	**View**	**File Extension**
File Extensions for Performance Monitor Views	Alert	.pma
	Chart	.pmc
	Log	.pml
	Report	.pmr
	Workspace	.pmw

	Object	Descrption
TABLE 3-6 Performance Monitor Objects in Windows NT Server	Cache	File system cache that holds recently used data
	Logical Disk	Disk partitions and logical views of disk space
	Memory	Random access memory
	Objects	System software objects
	Paging File	File used to back up virtual memory allocations
	Physical Disk	Hardware disk unit
	Process	Software object for program that is running
	Processor	Hardware unit that executes code
	Redirector	Diverts file request to network servers
	System	Counters that apply to all system hardware and software
	Thread	Part of a process

This list of Performance Monitor objects is helpful in developing a strategy for troubleshooting or optimizing performance. Begin by logging Logical Disk, Memory, Process, Processor, System, and Thread objects. Run the log for several days at an Update Interval of about 60 seconds. Charting the results will give you a good look at the status of your system.

The counter used most often is the Processor: % Processor Time counter. Each object has a default counter, which is highlighted when you select an object. These default counters are the most useful counters, and using the default settings across the board should provide excellent information for you.

Table 3-7 shows some of the most useful counters and what they measure. These can be used to form a solid baseline when you're becoming familiar with Performance Monitor.

It's also a good idea to include counters for your network services. These counters will depend on which network protocol(s) are being used and whether the computer is a client, server, or both. The Network Interface: Bytes Total/sec is a good overview counter for TCPIP/SNMP. If the computer is primarily a server, use Server: Bytes Total/sec to monitor network activity.

Setting Alerts   If you use the Alert command on the Options menu, you can choose the alert interval and alert method. The options include switching to the Alert view, logging the event in the Event Viewer Application log, and sending a network alert message to yourself or someone else. In order to send a network alert

TABLE 3-7   Objects and Counters for Baseline Measurements

Object	Default Counter	Use
Cache	Data Map Hits %	This measures how often requested data is found in cache. Every time data is not found in cache, it must go to memory or disk for information. A low hit rate could indicate insufficient memory.
Logical Disk	Avg. Disk Queue Length	This measures the activity of each logical partition on a disk. An Avg. Disk Queue Length of 1.0 indicates the disk was busy for the entire sample period. Sustained high values, over time, may indicate a disk bottleneck.
Memory	Pages/Sec	This measures the number of pages between main memory and the disk drive in each second. If this counter, over time, is consistently high, it may indicate a memory shortage. Sustained paging degrades performance.
Physical Disk	Avg. Disk Queue Length	This measures activity of the entire disk subsystem and is useful for measuring activity for disk sets and multiple volumes.
Processor	% Processor Time	This measures the demand for the processor and the efficiency with which the processor handles demand.

message, the Messenger Service must already be running, and the net name must already be defined on the recipient's computer. For details on how to run this, you can type **net start messager/?** or **net name/?** at the command prompt.

As you can see, Performance Monitor has many objects and counters that can be used to monitor and optimize network performance. Certain default counters provide solid information about performance and potential bottlenecks. With practice, you can become familiar with the extensive features of Performance Monitor and develop a monitoring and optimization routine that meets the needs of your organization.

Moving, Sizing, and Adding New Paging Files

The first step in managing memory is to review paging. If a memory problem is suspected, you can use three counters in Performance Monitor to help in troubleshooting the issue. Memory: Page Faults/sec, Memory: Pages Input/sec, and Memory: Page Reads/sec all indicate how often processes must go beyond their current memory set to find needed information. This includes paging—how often paging is required from the disk and how many pages are moved with each disk transfer. Comparing Page Faults/sec to Pages Input/sec will give you an idea of how many soft to hard page faults are occurring. Soft page faults (Page Faults/sec) do not actively degrade system performance. Subtracting these from Pages Input/sec will give you an idea of how many hard page faults are occurring over time. If this becomes higher than your baseline readings, you may have a memory bottleneck. In the following, we'll discuss various ways to resolve this issue.

The paging file, Pagefile.sys, will expand when there is little excess memory. This file is a block of disk space reserved by the operating system to back up physical memory (RAM). When a process requires more memory, the Virtual Memory Manager (VMM) will write a portion of RAM to disk to free up space for the process. As demand increases, VMM will increase the paging file until it runs out of disk space, or until it hits a preset limit.

Multiple Disk Location

One method of improving performance is to create additional paging files. By default, Windows NT Server 4.0 creates one paging file on the physical drive where the operating system is installed. You can create additional paging files, one on each logical disk partition in your configuration. Figure 3-2 shows the screens that you'll

FIGURE 3-2

Viewing or modifying Virtual Memory settings

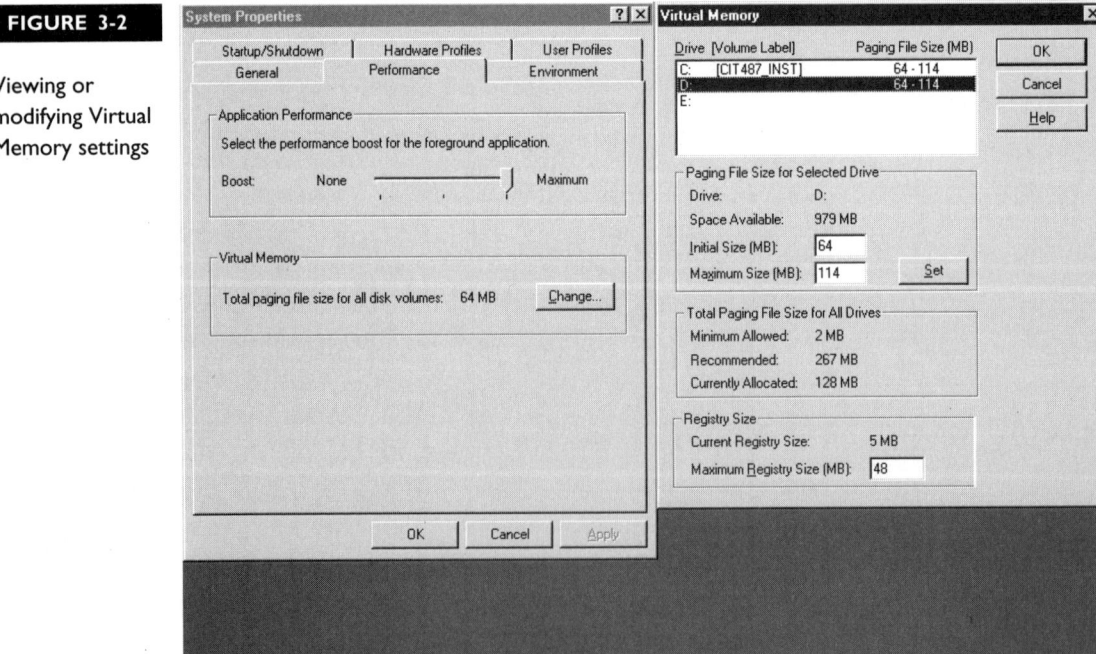

use to view or modify the paging file in the following exercise. It also shows a paging file that is located on two different disk volumes.

Now, using the steps in the following exercise, you can view or modify the settings on your server.

EXERCISE 3-7

CertCam 3-7

Examining Default Pagefile.sys Settings

1. Open the Control Panel and choose System.

2. In System, select the Performance tab.

3. The Virtual Memory dialog box shows the current size of paging files and lets you add new files or change the size of existing ones.

4. To change a value, select Change to display the Virtual Memory window.

5. Click Set to accept changes.

Having a paging file on multiple physical disks will provide greater throughput when pages are written to or read from disk. Keep in mind that you should avoid having your paging file on a stripe set with parity. Calculating parity for a page file is unnecessary and can slow system performance.

RAM and Page File Size

In the case of RAM, more is always better. The default page file size is physical memory plus 12MB. You can increase performance by increasing physical RAM in your server and by increasing the maximum size of the paging file. If you're experiencing frequent soft page faults, you probably want to increase both your RAM and the size of your paging file.

To increase performance, the paging file should be moved from the system partition to another partition. Also, keep in mind that your disk subsystem can appear to be the bottleneck when, in fact, the system needs more RAM. If you suspect a disk bottleneck, check your page faults and the size of the paging file to determine if this might be the underlying cause.

<table>
<tr><td colspan="2">SCENARIO & SOLUTION</td></tr>
</table>

If an object counter exceeded a certain threshold, what feature in Windows NT could be used to notify you?	The Alert function could be used to notify you of a critical condition.
Why would you create a paging file on two different disk drives?	To improve performance when paging to or from disk.
What object counter, if at a level of 1.0 over a sustained period of time, indicates a possible disk subsystem bottleneck?	Logical Disk: Avg. Disk Queue Length.
If you wanted to save a number of different views of your objects and counters, what could you use?	You could create a workspace.

The paged pool size is a very important Windows NT resource to monitor, because the paged pool is limited to a maximum size of 192MB. However, the paged pool shares a common address space with the nonpaged pool. Together, the sum of these two pools may never exceed 256MB. If the paged or nonpaged pool limits are exceeded because of memory leaks or faulty applications, a server may perform a crashdump or perform erratically.

Allocating Server Hardware Based on Application Requirements

Server hardware must be allocated based on the requirements of all applications residing on that server. Keep in mind that many applications, such as Microsoft Office, are installed on the local machine and do not require server resources (except in certain configurations). However, other applications are meant to be run only on servers. As such, they have certain requirements for system resources in order to run at optimum efficiency. Examples of such applications are Microsoft SQL Server, Lotus Domino, or Customer Relationship Management (CRM) and Enterprise Resource Planning (ERP) applications. In this section, we'll look at Web services, file and print services, messaging and database applications and proxy services as examples of server-based applications that require resource allocation.

Web Services

Web services are provided in Windows NT 4.0 Server via Internet Information Server (IIS). Web services provide the HTTP, FTP, and Gopher protocols. Enabling these three protocols requires about 400K of RAM. However, it is the traffic the server must handle as a result of implementing these protocols that is of primary concern. A server with light Web services use may also be employed as a file and print server or a database server. However, many companies find it useful to deploy IIS on a server dedicated to Web services to ensure fast response times and throughput.

Security features related to Web services can impact server performance. Creating a set of baseline performance metrics for the server, prior to implementing Web services, will help in monitoring the impact of various security features. Some of the most likely areas to be impacted are:

Processor Activity and Processor Queue   SSL protocol, authentication, and encryption schemes are just three security features that can impact processor utilization. If queues increase as a result of implementing various security features, your processor is not handling the demand. In such cases, upgrading the processor or increasing the number of processors will address this bottleneck.

Physical Memory Used   Storing and retrieving security information is likely to drive up the use of physical memory. The SSL protocol uses long keys, 40 bits to 1024 bits, for encrypting and decrypting messages. This places demand on physical memory. Increasing RAM will help ensure this does not become a bottleneck with Web services.

Network Activity   Perhaps the most likely place for system degradation to occur is in the network area. SSL can cause increased latency. Latency is defined as the amount of time to complete a task. For instance, downloading a file from a Web server using the SSL protocol can be up to 100 times *slower* than downloading that file without SSL.

You can use Performance Monitor objects and counters to monitor the performance of the server both before and after implementing Web services and security. You can also run a Microsoft tool called the Microsoft Web Capacity Analysis Toolkit (WCAT) alone or in conjunction with other Microsoft tools, such as Performance Monitor and Internet Information Service logging.

File and Print Services

File and print services are an inherent part of Windows NT 4.0 Server. Part of file services is the option to use the DOS-based FAT file system or the NT-based NTFS file system. NTFS provides for greater file security and management and in many cases can improve disk throughput. Print services on a typical server require minimal resources, unless a server is a dedicated print server. Sixteen megabytes of RAM is adequate for x86-based print servers controlling a small number of print devices. Managing larger numbers of printers or managing many large documents will require more memory. Disk space requirements are minimal, except where many documents (or large documents) are likely to be printed.

Using Windows NT 4.0 Server for both file and print sharing, file operations have priority. Printing transactions will never slow access to files. File operations have negligible impact on printers attached directly to the server; parallel and serial ports are always the greater bottleneck. A dedicated print server may be necessary only if the server is to manage many heavily used printers.

Messaging and Database Applications

Messaging and database applications include enterprise e-mail systems like Microsoft Exchange Server and enterprise database applications such as Microsoft SQL Server. Each of these requires a significant amount of server resources. Unless your organization is fairly small and the server has adequate computer power, you should consider running only one of these on a server. For instance, you may choose to have a server be a file server and Microsoft SQL Server, but only if the demand for each is fairly low. In many cases, running Exchange or SQL on dedicated servers will yield the best results.

Messaging applications will cause performance degradation if there is high traffic. Indications will be processor activity and queue, physical memory, disk drive performance, and network activity. As discussed throughout this chapter, determining baseline metrics prior to implementing messaging will provide a method of monitoring performance.

Database applications can be small, custom-built applications based on Microsoft Access (and other, similar types of database applications), or they can be large, enterprise applications based on Microsoft SQL Server (or other, comparable enterprise database applications). If the database is small and there are not frequent changes to it, there may be a negligible effect on server performance. In contrast, running SQL Server on a Windows NT 4.0–based Server, with many users and changes, can create significant system demands. The most noticeable changes will be disk performance and activity, processor activity, and physical memory. While the network portion may become the bottleneck if too many users are attempting to access the database(s), it is more likely the server will become bogged down with disk I/O. Using stripe sets or stripe sets with parity can greatly enhance the performance, unless the database writes data in certain patterns. Small, sequential writes are not well suited to stripe sets with parity.

Proxy Services

Proxy Services are part of an Internet security solution often employed in Windows NT 4.0. Proxy Services help maintain an efficient, reliable, and cost-efficient Internet connection. The location and anticipated number of users will determine how many Proxy Servers you'll need. Microsoft recommends the following configuration for server hardware on Intel-based systems:

- 1 to 300 clients: Pentium 133 with 2GB of cache and 32MB of RAM

- 300 to 2,000 clients: Pentium 166 with 2 to 4GB of cache and 64MB of RAM

- 2,000 to 3,500 clients: Pentium 200 with 8 to 16GB of cache and 256MB of RAM

It is important you assess your company's specific needs when determining hardware and configuration requirements. Most companies today will use a minimum of Pentium 200 with 64MB of RAM for any Windows-based server. In addition, practical experience dictates always having a minimum of 64MB of RAM on any Windows NT–based systems.

SCENARIO & SOLUTION

If you implement Web services, what addition to your server would likely provide the most benefit?	More powerful processor or additional processors.
What resources are most impacted by downloading a file using SSL?	Processor, physical memory, and network. The processor must encrypt and decrypt, while additional information passes over the network when using SSL.
Under what circumstances will print operations take precedence over file operations?	File operations are always given first priority. Print operations will never supercede file operations.

Modifying BDC Placement

In a Microsoft Windows NT 4.0–based network, you will have one Primary Domain Controller (PDC) and one or more Backup Domain Controllers (BDCs). Backup Domain Controllers serve two primary purposes. The first is as a backup for the Primary Domain Controller. The second is to authenticate users based on security information replicated to it from the PDC. Reviewing the placement of the BDCs is part of a thorough performance enhancement plan.

BDCs receive replication of security data from the PDC. This replication can take place automatically or it can be manually scheduled. If all users are located in one location, BDC placement is essentially based on the number of users. For every 2000 users, there should be one BDC. So, a network of 4005 users should, hypothetically, have at least three BDCs.

- BDC1: Users 1 – 2000
- BDC2: Users 2001 – 4000
- BDC3: Users 4001 – 4005

If an inadequate number of BDCs are online for the current number of users, logons will be slow. The bottleneck can appear in any number of places, but the most likely bottlenecks will be in the processor. Adding BDCs will reduce the processor load and greatly enhance the speed of user logon. Since user perception of network performance is often based upon the logon experience, it is important to ensure speedy logon for users at all locations. All user logons must be authenticated. If users are geographically dispersed, authentication will occur in one of two ways. Logon authentication can occur across the WAN to a BDC located at the "main" site. Authentication traffic can also be managed by a local BDC. If logon authentication always travels across the WAN, the WAN link will be bogged down authenticating users and user logon may be unacceptably slow. If a BDC is placed locally, authentication information must be replicated to the BDC from time to time. In this case, the WAN link can be bogged down by replication traffic.

The recommended solution is to place an adequate number of BDCs at each geographical location. Schedule replication traffic to occur during slow WAN usage times, often in the early hours of the morning when most companies have the least number of users logging on. Ensure the processor can handle the demand and add BDCs as needed.

exam
ⓦatch

You may find questions on the Windows NT exam related to how many BDCs are needed in a network. Your answer should reflect the guidelines discussed previously. You'll also need to consider whether or not the scenario involves a WAN link. If so, your answer should take into consideration both user logon needs and replication schedules.

on the
ⓙob

Replication to BDCs can take a surprising amount of network resources. When planning the location of your BDCs, make sure you've taken into consideration the disbursement of your users. For instance, if you have 50 users at one location, 1400 users at another location, and 500 users at another location, you are still under the 2000 user limit, but may want to consider having at least three BDCs to service each of the user locations. This will enhance user logons and network responsiveness.

CERTIFICATION OBJECTIVE 3.03

Deploying Service Packs and Hotfixes

Microsoft releases service packs as problems or issues are discovered. As with any complex operating system, unanticipated problems, such as incompatibility with popular applications, can occur. Problems deemed necessary to correct prior to the next full release of the operating system are addressed through service packs.

Windows 2000 service packs include several enhancements not found in the Windows NT 4.0 service packs. For instance, Windows 2000 service packs have the following features that earlier versions lacked.

- Integrated Installation makes it easier to apply and update service packs. Customers can create an integrated installation of the Windows 2000 operating system and SP1 on a network distribution share or CD.

- SP1 eliminates the need to reinstall the service pack after installing new system components or devices.

- Support for the overlaying of service packs enables customers to update their installation process and upgrade existing machines from a central location.

In this section, we'll review some of the basics of Windows NT 4.0 Server service packs.

As of June 2001, the latest service pack for Windows NT 4.0 Server was Service Pack 6a (located on the Microsoft Web site. Each service pack includes instructions explaining what the service pack fixes, and what previous service pack level is required. For instance, you can install Service Pack 6a over Service Pack 4. Service Pack 6a addresses problems with Lotus Notes and Winsock.

EXERCISE 3-8

CertCam 3-8

Determine the Service Pack Level on Current System

To determine what service pack is currently installed on your system, run the Winver.exe program.

1. Click Start.

2. Choose Run.

3. Type **Winver** in the Run: box, then click OK.

4. This will bring up the About Windows NT dialog box. You will see information resembling the following. (If a service pack has not been revised, the dialog will not show the last line.)

Microsoft(R) Windows NT (R)
Version 4.0 (Build 1381: Service Pack 6)
Copyright (C) 1981-1996 Microsoft Corp
Revised Service Pack 6a

Service packs sometimes address operating system problems that impact performance. Often, security problems or weaknesses are addressed similarly. It is recommended you keep your systems up-to-date with all released service packs.

If you install new system services or components, you must reinstall the service pack. The service pack will only install updates to existing files. Thus, if a new component is added, the service pack must be reapplied in order to ensure updating of these new components as well. As mentioned earlier, Windows 2000 does not require you to reinstall service packs after adding new services or components.

Service packs are typically installed using the Update Installation type. Windows 2000 contains an additional feature for installation called the Integrated Installation, which allows you to simultaneously install Windows 2000 and the service pack. This feature is not present in Windows NT 4.0. The Combination Installation type, which, as its name implies, is a combination of the Update and Integrated installation types, is also available only in Windows 2000.

Hotfixes, also called Quick Fix Engineering (QFE), are fixes for mission-critical problems that are discovered with the operating system. These kinds of problems typically cause severe errors or downtime and significantly disrupt network operations. Once a QFE has been released, it is incorporated into the next service pack release. If the QFE is not an issue that impacts your system, you can generally wait for the release of the service pack.

When you receive a hotfix from Microsoft Quick Fix Engineering, you have two primary options to implement these fixes.

Option One

Run the Hotfix.exe program, which is always included in the fix package you receive from Microsoft. Hotfix.exe checks the version of the service pack you are currently using and installs the hotfix automatically if the service pack version is older than the provided hotfix and the language is the same. If your service pack version is newer than the hotfix, the installation will not work, and the following error message may be displayed:

Hotfix Setup has detected that the Service Pack version of the system installed is newer than the update you are applying to it.

The Setup program is always interrupted if the language version of the installed fix does not match the system's language. If there is no version conflict, Hotfix.exe installs the fixed file(s) without any user intervention. Hotfix.exe always reads the Hotfix.ini file and registers the fix under the HKLM\Software\Microsoft\Windows NT\CurrentVersion\Hotfix Registry key.

The Registry entries differ from version to version of the Hotfix.ini file, because there is no common rule about what entries must be stated in the Registry key, as these are for informational purposes only. The Installed key is the only key always included under the hotfix entries, which is set to 1 when the fix is installed on your computer. The Hofix.ini file should never be edited.

Option Two

Hfx.exe may also be included with a hotfix received from Microsoft. It is probably the easiest way of managing hotfixes on your system. When you start the program, a menu is displayed that enables you to administer all fixes installed on your computer. The menu is only displayed if you have previously installed all your fixes with the Hfx.exe or Hotfix.exe program. If you are installing a new hotfix, point to the path of the Hotfix.ini file, and then click OK. The hotfix is then installed on your computer.

With Hfx.exe, you can install new hotfixes, delete old ones, or view the hotfixes installed on your computer. Sometime fixes installed using older versions of Hotfix.exe or Hfx.exe are not visible when running Hfx.exe. If you are unsure about which fixes are installed on your system, you can check the Registry under HKEY_ LOCAL_ MACHINE\Software\Microsoft\Windows NT\CurrentVersion\Hotfix and look at the Installed key.

exam
Watch

It is unlikely you'll see a question that directly tests your knowledge of service packs and hotfixes. You may, however, see questions or scenarios that test that knowledge indirectly. Questions may test whether or not you understand the difference between the installation options in Windows NT and those in Windows 2000.

SCENARIO & SOLUTION

You have five Windows NT Servers and you don't know which service packs are installed. What should you do?	Start Winver.exe at the Run prompt on each server.
You recently learned Microsoft had supplied a QFE for your system. What is the next step you should take?	Back up your critical system data and apply the QFE using Hfx.exe.
If all you needed was to view the fixes installed on your system, what's the easiest way to do it?	Run Hfx.exe. Viewing the Registry key would also yield this information if you were not sure the Hfx.exe listing was complete.

CERTIFICATION SUMMARY

In this chapter, we learned how to recover system files and restore the operating system. We studied various methods of saving and restoring the Registry along with critical keys inside the Registry. We also looked at tuning server performance. The three primary tools in Windows NT are Task Manager, Event Viewer, and Performance Monitor. These provide the network administrator with a number of tools that can be used to optimize server performance. We reviewed the important objects and counters utilized in Performance Monitor to establish baseline server performance and to review potential problems and bottlenecks. Finally, we reviewed the management of paging files, the placement of BDCs, and the installation of service packs and hotfixes.

✓ TWO-MINUTE DRILL

Recovering System Files and Reestablishing the Previous OS Environment

❑ Backing up the Registry can be accomplished using the Windows NT Backup utility for local computers only.

❑ Use Rdisk.exe to update files in the *%systemroot%\Repair* folder after any configuration changes.

❑ Portions of the Registry, including the SYSTEM key and the DISK subkey can be saved and restored individually, if needed.

❑ The Regedt32.exe program allows you to save the SYSTEM key to any disk location. Saving the SYSTEM key from the Disk Administrator allows you to save the key to the floppy drive only.

❑ During Setup, Registry information is formed from *%systemroot%\System32\Config*. For recovery, Setup also creates the *%systemroot%\Repair* folder.

❑ The emergency repair disk (ERD) should be updated after any significant server change.

❑ ARC pathnames provided in the boot.ini file are used to identify the location of the boot partition.

❑ multi(W)disk(X)rdisk(Y)partition(Z) is the naming convention used when system BIOS must be loaded onto system files, typically for IDE and EIDE controllers.

❑ scsi(W)disk(X)rdisk(Y)partition(Z) is the naming convention used when the system needs to load a SCSI driver to access the boot partition.

Troubleshooting and Optimizing Server Performance

❑ Optimizing server performance begins with creating a set of baseline metrics against which future performance can be compared.

❑ Three common bottleneck areas are memory, processor, and disk. The network can be a source of bottlenecks in some cases.

❑ Task Manager, Event Viewer, and Performance Monitor are three tools provided in Windows NT to help monitor and optimize performance.

❑ Use Task Manager to view applications, processes, and performance.

❑ Base class priority can be temporarily changed in Task Manager.

❑ Event Viewer has three different logs: system, security, and application. Event Viewer can be used to view logs on other computers.

❑ Performance Monitor contains objects and counters. Selecting default counters on processor, memory, cache, and disk will provide a good starting point for baseline metrics.

❑ Performance Monitor provides Chart, Log, Report, or Alert views, all of which can be saved to disk.

❑ The default setting for the paging file, pagefile.sys is RAM + 12MB.

❑ Determining the use of the server will help in optimizing performance. Various services require more memory, disk space, processor time, or network throughput.

❑ Adding BDCs to remote locations will reduce authentication traffic over the WAN.

❑ Replication for BDCs over a WAN can be scheduled for times when WAN traffic is lowest.

Deploying Service Packs and Hotfixes

❑ Windows NT service packs must be reapplied when new components or devices are installed.

❑ Windows 2000 service packs eliminate the need to reapply service packs after installing new system components or devices.

❑ Windows 2000 service packs have an Integrated Installation feature that allows the operating system and the service pack to be installed at the same time.

❑ Use Winver.exe to determine the level of service packs that have been applied to a system.

❑ Use Hotfix.exe or Hfx.exe to manage hotfixes on the system.

SELF TEST

The following questions will help you measure your understanding of the material presented in this chapter. Read all of the choices carefully, as there may be more than one correct answer. Choose all correct answers for each question.

Recovering System Files and Reestablishing the Previous OS Environment

1. You have four servers running a variety of applications and services. The servers have the following names: Jupiter, Mars, Venus, and Pluto. Pluto has a stripe set with parity as well as a mirror set. Jupiter has one disk drive that is near capacity. Mars and Venus each have two disk drives that are mirrored and duplexed. Pluto fails. It appears you will be unable to get replacement hardware for Pluto for at least two weeks due to a shortage of a particular component. Pluto was heavily used and users are complaining about needing access to the data. What can you do? (Choose the best answer.)

   A. Buy another server to replace Pluto. When parts come in for Pluto, repair it and use it as a spare.

   B. Move the stripe set with parity to Jupiter and restore the DISK subkey from Pluto to Jupiter.

   C. Back up Pluto's Registry remotely using the Windows NT Backup program and restore the Registry to Venus or Mars.

   D. Wait for the replacement parts since moving the data would involve too much work and create an unstable environment on the network.

2. What is the default folder used by Setup for emergency recovery?

   A. %systemroot%\System32\Config

   B. %systemroot%\Winnt

   C. %systemroot%\Repair

   D. %systemroot%

3. You have a server with the following configuration: a single Pentium 600MHz processor with 256MB of RAM; one IDE controller running two disk drives that are mirrored and which contain the system partition; and one SCSI controller running four disk drives that are a four-disk stripe set with parity. The primary partition of the mirror set fails. What is the proper ARC pathname that should be located in the Boot.ini file to enable you to boot from the shadow partition?

A. scsi(0)disk(0)rdisk(1)partition(1)

B. scsi(0)disk(0)rdisk(0)partition(1)

C. multi(0)disk(0)rdisk(0)partition(1)\Winnt

D. multi(0)disk(0)rdisk(0)partition(2)\Winnt

4. Based on the scenario in Question 3, what step would you have to take to make the shadow partition bootable in the event of a failure of the primary partition? (Choose all that apply.)

A. Ensure the Boot.ini file had the proper ARC pathname

B. Break the mirror set

C. Ensure the boot partition is still accessible via the shadow partition

D. Use DiskProbe to set the Boot Indicator flag

5. Your system is having intermittent problems booting up. You want to inspect the boot sector. What is the best way to accomplish this?

A. Use a third-party disk utility

B. Use the Windows NT emergency repair disk

C. Use the Windows NT Setup disks

D. Use the Windows NT Disk Administrator

6. Windows NT Server 4.0 requires several files in order to successfully start the operating system. Which of these files is not required to start an x86-based computer?

A. Osloader.exe

B. Ntbootdd.sys

C. Hal.dll

D. NTLDR

7. You attempt to boot your Windows NT 4.0–based server. The server is a Pentium P800 with 128MB of RAM and one 10GB IDE hard disk drive. You are unable to boot the server from the drive. You want to use the emergency repair disk, but recall that you never created that floppy after your Windows NT operating system was properly installed. What should you do next?

A. Use an ERD from another, identical system.

B. Try to boot from your Windows NT Setup floppies and choose the Repair option.

C. Copy the NTLDR file to the hard drive's primary partition, then boot normally.

D. Repair the disk drive using the Rdisk.exe command.

Troubleshooting and Optimizing Server Performance

8. You're considering upgrading your disk subsystems on three different servers. Server One currently has two IDE controllers, each managing one disk drive. Server Two has one PCI controller running two disks. Server Three has one Fast SCSI-2 controller with three drives attached. Assuming the drives all have identical speeds and access times, which server likely has the fastest disk throughput?

   A. Server One.

   B. Server Two.

   C. Server Three.

   D. Servers Two and Three are essentially identical in throughput.

   E. Need more information.

9. An application considered "disk-bound" has what characteristics?

   A. The application cannot be run on certain disks because of the size of its executable files.

   B. The application cannot be run on certain types of disks because of the way it reads and writes to disk.

   C. The application performs many reads and writes.

   D. The application performs very few reads and writes, but writes in large blocks when it does write to disk.

10. You manage a small Windows-based network. You have five servers performing various functions. Your network uses TCP/IP and IPX/SPX. You install a second network adapter in two of the servers. However, after installing these adapters, you notice performance is significantly slower. What could you check that might improve performance immediately? (Choose all that apply.)

   A. Limit each controller to a single protocol

   B. Place all server-based traffic on a single controller

   C. Configure each controller to handle multiple protocols

   D. Change the binding order of protocols on each adapter

11. Your system's performance has degraded somewhat over time. You never established baseline metrics for the systems. Now, you want to figure out where the problems are occurring. What method of troubleshooting would yield useful information about system processes?

   A. Chart use of memory over time

B. Chart use of processor by threads

C. Chart use of memory, processor, and disk by process

D. Chart use of disk by paging file

12. One of your junior network administrators shows up at your office door with a terrified look on his face. He explains that he crashed a server and doesn't know what to do. After ascertaining that he changed the base class priority of a very active application to *Realtime,* the system crashed. What would you suggest he do?

A. Reboot the system

B. Find the emergency repair disk and the application's installation disk

C. Boot the system using the Windows NT Startup floppy, then reinstall the application

D. Boot the system using the Windows NT Setup floppies, then set the application's base class priority to *Normal* using Task Manager

13. What would a consistently high measurement of the Memory object's Pages/Sec counter indicate?

A. Insufficient disk space

B. A memory shortage

C. Slow memory performance

D. An application that is using too much system memory

14. Certain users have complained that system response time is slow. They are all connecting to a particular server to run queries of various databases on the server. What counter would you check first? (Choose the best answer.)

A. Cache: Data Map Hits %

B. Logical Disk: Avg. Disk Queue Length

C. Network Interface: Bytes Total/Sec

D. Processor: % Processor Time

15. What determines the size of the paging file, pagefile.sys? (Choose all that apply.)

A. Lack of disk space

B. RAM plus 12MB

C. Virtual Memory Manager

D. System performance

16. Your company has merged with another company located in another state. You've been asked to oversee the integration of network services. All of the new company's employees have usernames and logon credentials on your network. However, you've heard complaints that their logons are slow. What could you do to improve the situation? (Choose all that apply.)

    A. Add RAM to your BDC at the home office

    B. Place a BDC at the new office

    C. Add another BDC to the home office and to the new office

    D. Set replication for midnight

Deploying Service Packs and Hotfixes

17. Which service pack installation method provided in Windows NT allows you to install the operating system and the service pack at the same time?

    A. Integrated installation

    B. Update installation

    C. Combination installation

    D. These must still be done as separate tasks

18. You have just accepted a job as a network administrator for a company. You have been tasked with maintaining the ten NT Servers onsite. You've been told that the servers were not well maintained in the past and that each server should be thoroughly inspected. How could you determine if service packs were up-to-date on each machine?

    A. Right-click System properties in the Control Panel

    B. Run the Winver.exe program

    C. Use Administrative Tools

    D. Right-click the desktop and select Properties

19. While inspecting the servers mentioned in Question 18, you determine that Microsoft released a QFE that appears to apply directly to your situation. Because of the critical nature of the QFE, you decide to install the QFE immediately. What will happen if the service pack is newer than the QFE you are trying to install?

    A. The system will halt and log a severe error.

    B. The QFE will be installed anyway.

    C. The QFE will not install.

    D. The QFE will read the Hotfix.ini file to determine what service packs are installed on the system.

20. You decide to use the Hfx.exe to manage the hotfixes on your system. You've never used it before, but you understand that when you run Hfx.exe, a pop-up menu should be displayed. When you run Hfx.exe, no pop-up menu is displayed. What would cause this problem? (Choose the best answer.)

A. If you don't use Hfx.exe to install your fixes with the Hfx.exe or Hotfix.exe program, it will not display the pop-up menu.

B. If the hotfixes were applied before new services or components were installed, the pop-up menu will not be displayed.

C. The wrong Installed key was updated in HKEY_LOCAL_MACHINE\Software\Microsoft\ Windows NT\ CurrentVersion\Hotfix.

D. You must apply all service packs before using Hfx.exe.

LAB QUESTION

You have just been hired as the IT Manager for a small high-tech startup company. They are counting on you to implement their entire network infrastructure, and you have been given a budget that accommodates the purchase of hardware and software. However, the company already has five servers running Windows NT 4.0 Server. They do not have the budget to upgrade to Windows 2000 at this time, though they expect to be able to do this with the next round of funding. They've asked you to set up these servers to meet the needs of the company, to optimize the network resources, and to make any recommendations for changes you feel might be appropriate.

The servers have the following names: Blake, Poe, Ginsburg, Dickinson, and Donegan. Each server has a Pentium III 800MHz processor with 128MB of RAM. The disk configuration of each server is shown in Table 3-8.

TABLE 3-8	Server	Controller Type	Disk Drives	Capacity
Disk Configurations for Lab Question	Blake	Fast SCSI-2	Four	1GB each
	Poe	PCI	One	10GB
	Ginsburg	PCI	Two	4GB each
	Dickinson	Fast SCSI-2	Four	2.4GB each
	Donegan	2 PCI	Four	10GB each

The network will have a maximum of 100 users. About half of the users work intensively with a database application. Another 25 or so are developers that require 100 percent network uptime in order to work efficiently. These developers use two servers for testing and debugging code as well as other development-related activities. The remaining users constitute various administrative support personnel that require access to a financial application and word processing software.

Based on this information, create a plan for implementing a network structure that will meet the needs of this organization. Also, list the types of baseline measurements you will create and which areas you will monitor for performance.

SELF TEST ANSWERS

Recovering System Files and Reestablishing the Previous OS Environment

1. ☑ **B.** The stripe set with parity can be moved to another server (in this case, Jupiter) by restoring the DISK subkey from Pluto to Jupiter. While this does involve some risk, you are likely to get the data back online faster than if you await the arrival of parts.

☒ **A** is incorrect because although one option would be to replace the server, this might be a very expensive option. Depending on your future network needs, this might be viable, but given the information presented, this is not the best answer. **C** is incorrect because you cannot use the Windows NT Backup program to back up a remote Registry. **D** is incorrect because waiting for replacement parts may be the least risky option, but users have indicated they need access to the information on the stripe set attached to Pluto. Therefore, this is not the best answer.

2. ☑ **C.** The default folder used by Setup is %systemroot%\Repair.

☒ **A** is incorrect because during the installation of Windows NT, Setup forms the Registry information from %systemroot%\System32\Config. For recovery, however, the Setup program uses the %systemroot%\Repair folder. **B** is incorrect because the convention %systemroot% is used to indicate the location of the operating system. In most systems, this is Winnt, unless you manually changed the location of the operating system during installation. Therefore, %systemroot%\Winnt would be redundant. In addition, this is not where Setup stores emergency recover information. **D** is incorrect because the emergency recovery information is not stored at the root.

3. ☑ **D.** The shadow partition on the IDE drive would be identified by the ARC pathname multi(0)disk(0)rdisk(0)partition(2)\Winnt. This indicates the second partition, which unlike other ARC pathname features, begins numbering at 1 instead of at 0.

☒ **A** and **B** are incorrect because the system partition is located on the primary partition (the first IDE drive) as well as the shadow partition. Therefore, the proper ARC pathname would have to use the multi() naming convention. **C** is incorrect because the first partition is the drive that has failed. The partition numbering scheme begins with 1, therefore, the shadow partition would be identified as partition(2).

4. ☑ **A, B, and D.** As in Question 3, the Boot.ini file must have an ARC pathname that correctly identifies the location of the system files in order to properly boot the machine. In addition, if you are attempting to boot off the shadow drive, you must break the mirror set and set the Boot Indicator flag on the shadow drive. The Disk Administrator does not set the Boot

Indicator flag on the shadow partition when a mirror set is created. Once this flag is set, the shadow partition can be used to boot the system. Since the Disk Administrator does not set this flag, you can manually set it using the DiskProbe program.

☒   **C** is incorrect because although the boot partition is needed to complete the system boot process, the first partition the operating system requires is the system partition. Unless the ARC pathname to the shadow drive is correct and the Boot Indicator flag is set, the operating system cannot locate the system partition. Once it locates the system partition, it will find pointers to the boot partition, whether or not the boot partition is in the same partition as the system partition.

5. ☑   **C.** To inspect the boot sector, you can use the Windows NT Setup disks. After inserting disk 2, select the Repair option by pressing the R key. A menu of four options will be displayed. The fourth option, Inspect Boot Sector, can be selected by placing an X in the box to the left of the menu option and then selecting Continue.

   ☒   **A** is incorrect because although you could use a third-party disk utility, the best way to accomplish this task is by using the Windows NT Setup disks. **B** is incorrect because the emergency repair disk contains information used to restore the operating system (including the Partition Boot Sector) but does not contain an option to allow you to *inspect* the boot sector. This option is accessed via the Windows NT Setup disks. The ERD is used once the system has been booted using the Setup disks. **D** is incorrect because the Disk Administrator program is used to administer various aspects of the disk subsystem, but does not allow you to inspect the boot sector.

6. ☑   **A.** The Osloader.exe file is used to start RISC-based computers. Its x86-based equivalent is the NTLDR file.

   ☒   **B** is incorrect because the Ntbootdd.sys file is used when an x86-based system needs to load SCSI drivers. **C** is incorrect because the Hal.dll file is used for both x86 and RISC-based computers. **D** is incorrect because the NTLDR file is used by x86-based computers to load the operating system.

7. ☑   **B.** If you cannot boot your system normally, you should try using the Windows NT Setup floppies. After inserting disk 2, you will be given various options to inspect Registry files, the startup environment, system files, or the boot sector. If the disk is still accessible, you may be able to access the %systemroot%\Repair folder to return the system to its prior state.

   ☒   **A** is incorrect because although you may think an emergency repair disk from an identical system will work, it should not be attempted. There are subtle differences from one system to another, even those that are "identical." This is not an acceptable solution and should not be attempted. **C** is incorrect because you have no way of copying the NTLDR file to the hard drive's primary partition until you boot the system. In addition, there is no information to indicate the NTLDR file is the problem. Repairing suspected problems without performing logical troubleshooting steps will likely either not fix the problem or make the problem worse. **D** is incorrect because the Rdisk.exe command can be used to repair various disk-related problems. However, as with answer **C**, you must still first be able to boot the system in order to repair problems.

Troubleshooting and Optimizing Server Performance

8. ☑ **B.** Server Two, using a PCI disk controller, likely has the fastest throughput. PCI's typical throughput is approximately 40 Mbps.

☒ **A** is incorrect because an IDE controller has throughput of about 2.5MB per second, making this likely the slowest server. **C** is incorrect. Server Three, using Fast SCSI-2 controllers would have average throughput of about 10 Mbps. **D** is incorrect. Server Two, as stated, is about 40 Mbps compared to Server Three at about 10 Mbps. **E** is incorrect because all drives have identical speeds and access times. The disk controllers have the most influence over the throughput of the disk subsystem.

9. ☑ **C.** An application is considered "disk-bound" when it performs many reads and writes. This means the speed, performance, and responsiveness of the application is limited, or *bound*, by the performance and throughput of the disk drive.

☒ **A** is incorrect because although an application with large executable files may have performance problems in some cases, this is not what the term disk-bound means. **B** is incorrect because applications can run on any type of disk drive. The read and write characteristics of an application may dictate whether or not it is suitable to working with mirror sets, stripe sets, or stripe sets with parity. However, the type of drive or controller is not a factor. **D** is incorrect because this is not the definition of disk-bound applications. This is a factor that should be considered when implementing various disk solutions such as stripe sets or mirror sets.

10. ☑ **A and B.** On a network using multiple protocols, limiting each controller to a single (or fewer) protocols can increase performance. The fewer protocols a controller has to manage, the faster it can service the protocols for which it is configured. Placing all server-based traffic on a single controller is another method of potentially improving performance quickly.

☒ **C** is incorrect because the fewer protocols a controller has to handle, the faster it can manage traffic from each protocol. **D** is incorrect because changing the binding order of protocols can speed up certain processes, but it is not the best answer.

11. ☑ C. If you chart use of memory, processor, and disk by process, you can start then stop a process to see how it impacts system resources.

    ☒ A is incorrect because charting the use of memory over time will give you an overall idea of how memory is being utilized. However, if you wanted fast information about how system processes impact your system, this is not the best answer. B is incorrect because a service or application may have many different threads. Consequently, this will not yield the most helpful information with regard to system processes. D is incorrect because system memory is never paged out to disk. Therefore, this will not yield helpful information as to potential problems with system processes.

12. ☑ A. When the base class priority for an application is manually reset, it is effective only for that session. Thus, after the computer crashed, the priority would be automatically reset when rebooted.

    ☒ B is incorrect because there should be no need to repair the system or reinstall the application. C is incorrect because the system will boot normally and there is no need to reinstall the application. D is incorrect because the system can be booted normally and the base class priority will be automatically reset to its default setting upon reboot.

13. ☑ B. This counter measures the number of pages between main memory and the disk drive each second. Sustained paging degrades performance, because needed information is not immediately available in memory and must be paged from the disk drive. Storing information in memory, rather than going to the disk drive, provides the fastest response and throughput.

    ☒ A is incorrect because the disk subsystem will always be slower than physical memory. Therefore, the counters are not pointing to a slow disk subsystem, but rather to an insufficient amount of physical memory. C is incorrect because the Pages/Sec counter of the memory object indicate how often needed information is paged to or from the disk. Therefore, the speed of memory is not in question, the capacity of total memory is. D is incorrect because system memory is never paged to the disk, so the Memory: Pages/Sec counter would not be relevant.

14. ☑ D. Processor: % Processor Time measures the total demand for processor time. This gauges the efficiency with which the processor handles demand. If this counter is consistently high, it could be a result of slow system response time.

    ☒ A is incorrect because the Cache object's Data Map Hits % counter measures how often requested data was found in cache. A low hit rate would indicate insufficient memory. This can be helpful, but is not the most likely cause of slow overall system performance in this case. B is incorrect because the Avg. Disk Queue Length counter is used to measure activity of each logical partition on a disk. Sustained high values over time may indicate a disk bottleneck. This could be the cause, but you should not begin tuning your disk subsystem until you've checked the two most likely culprits: processor and memory. **C** is incorrect because the network interface could be the problem, especially since users are complaining of slow response time to a particular server, however, the first place to check is memory and processor. If these appear to be ok, then the network and disk subsystems would be the next suspects.

15. ☑ **A** and **B**. As demand increases, the paging file will expand until it either runs out of disk space or it hits a predefined size limit. This size can be set in the Performance tab of System properties. The default size of the paging file is RAM plus 12MB, but it can be changed.
☒ **C** is incorrect because Virtual Memory Manager manages the paging file, but does not determine the size of the file. **D** is incorrect because system performance can be impacted by the size of the paging file, but does not determine its size.

16. ☑ **B** and **D**. The likely problem with user logon is that their authentication takes place across the WAN. To alleviate this problem, you could add a BDC to the new office so user authentication can be done locally. By setting replication for midnight, the replication traffic will occur when the least amount of traffic is on the system. This will ensure the data on the remote BDC is current and will help speed up the remote logon process.
☒ **A** is incorrect because adding RAM to the local BDC may increase performance of that BDC, but the bottleneck in this case is the WAN link. **C** is incorrect because there is no indication at this time that another BDC is required at the home office. Typically, another BDC should be added for each new 2000 users or when remote locations are authenticating across a WAN.

Deploying Service Packs and Hotfixes

17. ☑ **D**. In Windows NT, the operating system installation and service pack installation must be done separately.
☒ **A** is incorrect because the Windows 2000 service packs have an added feature called Integrated installation. This feature allows you to integrate the installation of Windows 2000 and the service pack (currently SP1) on a network distribution share or CD. **B** is incorrect because update installation is the current method of installing a service pack in Windows NT. This does not, however, install the operating system, only the service pack. **C** is incorrect because the combination installation type is also a feature unique to Windows 2000. It is a combination of the Update and Integrated installation types, and is not available in Windows NT.

18. ☑ **B.** The Winver.exe program will show the version and build of Windows NT. It will also list any service packs that have been applied.

    ☒ **A** is incorrect because you can access System properties from the Control Panel, but the version and service pack revisions will not be listed there. **C** is incorrect because Administrative Tools provides a wide range of tools you can use to administer your system, but you cannot determine service pack levels from this. **D** is incorrect because right-clicking the desktop and choosing Properties will allow you to set the properties of the display.

19. ☑ **C.** The QFE will not install. Typically, a service pack that is released after a QFE will incorporate that QFE. There is no need to reinstall the QFE and it may cause problems to do so. Therefore, a QFE that is older than the installed service pack will not install and a system message will be generated indicating this.

    ☒ **A** is incorrect because the system will not generate a severe error but it will generate the following message: "Hotfix Setup has detected that the Service Pack version of the system installed is newer than the update you are applying to it." **B** is incorrect because the QFE will not be installed because doing so could cause problems. A service pack incorporates many different fixes, patches and updates that have been tested together. To reapply an older QFE could cause problems that were resolved by the service pack. **D** is incorrect because the first step in the Hotfix.exe program execution is to check the service pack version. If it finds the service pack version is lower than the QFE, it will then read the Hotfix.ini file and register the fix under the HKEY_LOCAL_MACHINE\Software\Microsoft\Windows NT\Current Version\Hotfix Registry key.

20. ☑ **A.** If you do not use either the Hfx.exe or Hotfix.exe program to install QFEs, the pop-up menu will not be displayed. You can check the Registry under HKEY_LOCAL_ MACHINE\ Software\Microsoft\Windows NT\CurrentVersion\Hotfix to look at the Installed key to determine which hotfixes have been applied.

    ☒ **B** is incorrect because in Windows NT, if you add services or components after you have applied a service pack, you must reapply the service pack. However, this would not be the cause of the pop-up menu not being displayed. **C** is incorrect because there is only one Installed key in the HKEY_LOCAL_MACHINE\Software\Microsoft\Windows NT\CurrentVersion\Hotfix. The information in the Installed key could potentially become corrupt or missing and cause this problem. **D** is incorrect because using Hotfix.exe to install hotfixes will automatically check for required service packs. If the service pack version is newer than the hotfix you are attempting to install, you will receive a system message indicating this. You do not need to install the hotfix, then, since the hotfix is included in the newer service pack.

LAB ANSWER

As with many planning exercises, there can be several correct answers. The key is that your answer contains some of the chief components of tuning and optimization. If your answer differs substantially from the one that follows, check your assumptions against best practices to ensure you understand the underlying concepts.

In this example, the network has five servers for about 100 people. That seems like a lot of servers until you realize two of the servers are needed exclusively by the developers. That leaves three servers to meet the needs of the database group and the administrative group. The administrative group has fairly "light" computing needs compared to the others.

Based on this information, we can assign tasks to various servers as shown in Table 3-9.

This is one possible configuration. While the PDC might normally not be used as anything but a PDC in a network, combining it with the light usage of a small group of users will make better use of the server hardware on hand. Setting up the database servers as BDCs will provide necessary redundancy. The developers' servers are not set up as BDCs since it is likely those servers may be rebooted, restarted, or rebuilt from time to time based on the changing needs of the developers.

The disk configuration for these various servers can now be developed. The configuration in Table 3-10 is one possible way to provide the best performance for each group.

Now that servers and disk configuration have been planned, the next step would be to set the servers up, create emergency repair disks for each server, test the configuration and server, then begin to establish performance baselines. Using the preceding configuration information, the following baseline measurements shown in Table 3-11 would likely establish a meaningful baseline.

Now, let's look at the servers and the most likely causes of performance problems. Based on this, you might add additional counters for the objects discussed.

Poe, the PDC and admin server, should be monitored for processor usage and memory usage. If the server were to get bogged down, it will likely do so at the processor. The disk subsystem is fast and the network activity is not likely to be the source of a bottleneck, though these should be monitored from time to time.

	Group	Function	Server	Disk Capacity
TABLE 3-9 Tasks Assigned to Various Servers	Admin	PDC	Poe	10GB
	Database	BDC	Blake	4GB
	Database	BDC	Donegan	40GB
	Developers	Server	Ginsburg	8GB
	Developers	Server	Dickinson	9.6GB

TABLE 3-10		Configuration to Provide the Best Performance for Each Group	
Server	**Disk Capacitzy**	**Configuration**	**Comments**
Blake	Four 1GB drives	Drive 1 and 2: Mirror set with system partition and boot partition. Drive 2, 3, and 4: Stripe set with parity.	Blake has a Fast SCSI-2 controller. The throughput is about 10 Mbps. This should be adequate for database work and for BDC services. Mirroring the system and boot partitions provides fault tolerance and the stripe set with parity provides performance and fault tolerance.
Poe	One 10GB drive	Drive 1: Two partitions.	This server is used as a PDC and by the admin staff. The PCI controller has throughput of 40 Mbps. There is no fault tolerance on this system.
Ginsburg	Two 4GB drives	Drives 1 and 2: Drives 1 and 2 are mirrored. Drives 1 and 2 also have other partitions in addition to the mirror set.	This server is used by the developers. The mirror set provides some fault tolerance, but not the best performance. The other partitions can be used and configured to meet the needs of the developer staff.
Dickinson	Four 2.4GB drives	Drives 1 and 2 are mirrored. Drives 1 through 4 also have other partitions in addition to the mirror set.	This server is also used by developers. Again, the small mirror set provides fault tolerance for system files. The other four drives have partitions the developers can configure to meet their particular needs.
Donegan	Four 10GB drives on two controllers	Drive 1 and Drive 3 (each on separate controllers) form a mirror set. Drives 1 through 4 also have a stripe set with parity.	This server has the role of BDC (along with Blake), and is the server of the database group. With its four 10GB drives, it provides sufficient capacity for a large database application. Each PCI controller (40 Mbps throughput) controls two drives. The mirror set and disk duplexing provide significant fault tolerance. The stripe set with parity provides an excellent balance between performance and fault tolerance.

Blake and Donegan, the database servers are also BDCs. The most likely source of slowdown for these servers is processor or memory. The BDCs provide logon authentication services. However, since each BDC can handle up to 2000 users, the likelihood of a slowdown due to BDC functions on this small network is low. Nevertheless, with intensive database activities, the processor will have to work hard to handle requests. If memory is insufficient, it could be paged frequently to and from disk causing performance degradation. The disk subsystem on these two servers consists of a Fast SCSI-2 controller and 2 PCI controllers. The throughput on the 2 PCI controllers each handling two drives should be sufficient. The Fast SCSI-2 controller is managing four 1GB drives. It is possible this will become the source of a bottleneck. If possible, place the more disk-intensive tasks on Donegan to avoid this.

Ginsburg and Dickinson, the developer servers, do not serve as BDCs due to the flexibility needed by the developers in working with their servers. Depending on the nature of the work done by the developers, it is probable the processor and memory will be the likely causes of bottlenecks. As code is tested or debugged, the processor may be tied up. Demands on memory to process these activities could also impact performance.

After establishing baselines and measuring performance, additional views or workspaces can be created for each server, reflecting the different demands on each server. The measurements of every server should be compared to baseline objects and counters on a regular basis to ensure performance is not slowly degrading over time.

TABLE 3-11 Baseline Measurements

Object	Default Counter	Use
Cache	Data Map Hits %	This measures how often requested data is found in cache. Every time data is not found in cache, it must go to memory or disk for information. A low hit rate could indicate insufficient memory.
Logical Disk	Avg. Disk Queue Length	This measures the activity of each logical partition on a disk. An Avg. Disk Queue Length of 1.0 indicates the disk was busy for the entire sample period. Sustained high values, over time, may indicate a disk bottleneck.
Memory	Pages/Sec	This measures the number of pages between main memory and the disk drive each second. If this counter, over time, is consistently high, it may indicate a memory shortage. Sustained paging degrades performance.
Physical Disk	Avg. Disk Queue Length	This measures the activity of the entire disk subsystem and is useful for determining activity for disk sets and multiple volumes.
Processor	% Processor Time	This measures the demand for the processor and the efficiency with which the processor handles demand.

Finally, the recommendations you might make would be:

1. Have a dedicated PDC

2. Have a dedicated BDC

3. Add another disk drive to Poe to be able to implement some sort of fault tolerance on the system

4. Upgrade Blake to add disk throughput and capacity for the database group

5. Add more memory to Blake, Donegan (database servers) and Ginsburg, and Dickinson (developer servers)

As you can see, there are a number of things to consider when planning and optimizing your new network. If your answers varied significantly from these, check to ensure you understand the answers provided in this lab and review the areas where there were significant differences.

MICROSOFT CERTIFIED SYSTEMS ENGINEER

4

Configuring and Troubleshooting Trusts, Account Policies, and System Policies

CERTIFICATION OBJECTIVES

C ontrol is always an issue when being a network administrator. You need to ensure users have enough access to do the work they need, but not so much that they can cause problems for themselves and others. The need of users to access features and data in Windows NT without compromising security and ease-of-use is the major thread of this chapter.

In Chapter 4, we will discuss trust relationships, account policies, and system policies. Trust relationships are used to connect two or more domains, so users can access resources in other domains. Account policies are used to control security settings, and specifically deal with issues involving passwords. Finally, system policies are used to control the environment and actions of users. By understanding how these elements work, and the issues surrounding their operation, you will be able to configure and troubleshoot their various components as necessary.

CERTIFICATION OBJECTIVE 4.01

Configuring and Troubleshooting Trust Relationships

When networks first started, computers were arranged in workgroups that allowed the machines to communicate with one another. The problem with this was that every time a user wanted to access resources on another machine, a username and password had to be provided for every shared directory or resource. To make administration and usage of the network easier, domains became a common, popular step-up from workgroups.

Windows NT domain networks are based upon the concept of a single username and password allowing access to its resources. A domain is a logical grouping of users and computers that share a single database of security permissions. This database dictates what users are able to access, and provides centralized administration of user accounts. By logging onto the domain, users can access printers, files, folders, and other resources permitted for use.

However, a domain acts as an administrative barrier on a network. Users who have a valid user account in one domain are blocked from using resources in other domains. You could compare being a member of a domain to being a citizen of a country. While a citizen of the United States can utilize resources like Social Security, they cannot access similar resources in neighboring countries (for instance, Social Insurance in Canada). The exception would be someone who had dual-citizenship. In terms of networking, the equivalent of this concept would be a person with a valid user account in both domains. Unfortunately, each person with multiple accounts proportionally increases administration of the network. The administrator would need to create an account in each domain, make each person a member of specific groups, set permissions for them, and so on. To decrease the amount of work, and keep with Microsoft's philosophy of a single logon to access resources, trust relationships were invented to allow a single user account to access resources in multiple domains.

Trust relationships are used to extend domains by providing a secure communication link between them. With a trust relationship, a domain can accept user accounts created in a different domain, and allow these users to access local resources. Basically, the relationship acts as a road between two kingdoms, allowing citizens of one country to travel to another and use whatever resources the administrator deems accessible. For example, let's say a user has an account in a domain called ROME and needs to access a database located in a domain called CARTHAGE. Although the user doesn't have an account in the CARTHAGE domain, a trust relationship can be implemented to allow resource sharing. With the trust relationship, the domains are combined into a single administrative unit, providing centralized administration, and allowing the user to log on once to access resources in multiple domains.

Trusted and Trusting Domains

In a trust relationship, there are two kinds of domains: a trusting domain and a trusted domain. The trusting domain allows users from another domain to use its resources. The trusted domain contains user accounts that allow users to log on and then use the resources in this domain, as well as other trusting domains. This relationship is shown in Figure 4-1.

Trust relationships are comprised of trusted and trusting domains

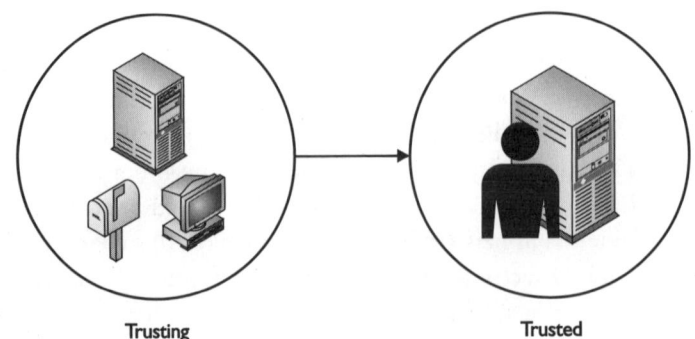

Trusting   Trusted

In looking at this figure, you will notice an arrow pointing from the trusting domain to the trusted domain. This is used to depict the trust relationship. All illustrations of a trust relationship have the arrow pointing from the trusting domain to the trusted domain in this manner.

Trust relationships are always one-way. Although a relationship exists between two domains, the trusting domain will allow access to the trusted domain, but the trusted domain may not allow access to the trusting domain. To give an example, let's say a domain called ROME trusts a domain called CARTHAGE. This means

FROM THE CLASSROOM

The Trusted and Trusting Domain

Students often have trouble remembering which is the trusted domain, which is the trusting domain, and the role each plays in a trust relationship. The trusted domain contains the accounts. This is where the user logs on to the domain. The trusting domain contains the resources that users wish to use.

The best way to remember this is a play on words: TrustEd and TrustThing. Think of a

user named Ed having an account in one domain, and wanting access to various resources (or things) in another domain. With a trust relationship, the domain with Ed's account would be Trusted (Trust Ed), while the domain containing the things he needs to access would be Trusting (Trust Thing).

—Michael Cross, MCSE, MCPS, MCP+I, CNA

that CARTHAGE has access to resources in the ROME domain, but because the trust is one way, ROME doesn't have access to resources in the CARTHAGE domain. For the two domains to trust one another, and for each to have access to one another's resources, two one-way trusts must be created.

Trust relationships on Windows NT networks are also nontransitive, meaning that a trust between two domains doesn't extend to other domains. In other words, my domain may trust yours, and your domain may trust someone else, but that doesn't mean that my domain trusts this third party. Because trust relationships are nontransitive, the connection between the domains doesn't allow all the domains to access one another's resources. Trust relationships only extend between two (and only two) domains.

To illustrate how trust relationships are nontransitive, refer to Figure 4-2. In Figure 4-2, trust relationships exist between domains in three different locations. We can see that the domain in Keystone City trusts the Gotham domain. This allows Gotham users access to the resources in the Keystone City domain. We can also see that Metropolis trusts the Keystone City domain, but doesn't have a trust relationship with Gotham. Because trust relationships in NT are nontransitive,

FIGURE 4-2

Trust
relationships are
nontransitive

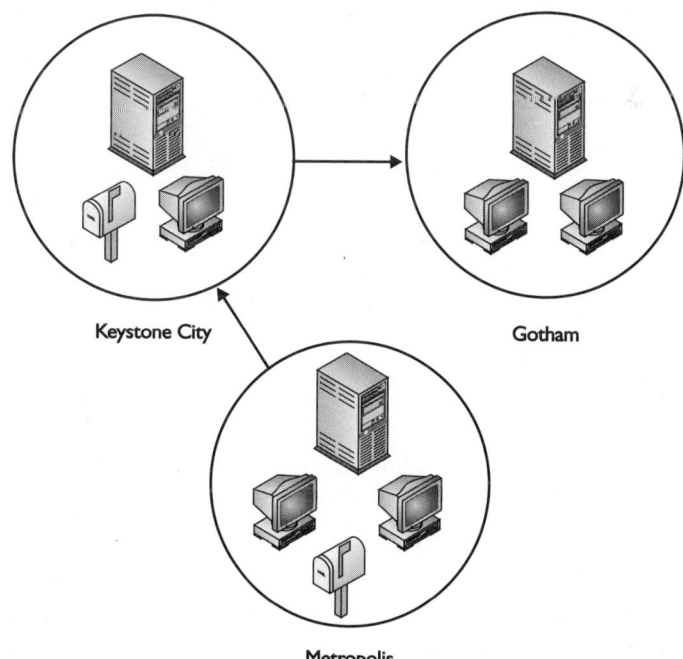

Keystone City   Gotham

Metropolis

Gotham will be able to access resources in Keystone City, but won't be able to access resources in Metropolis. The nontransitive nature of the trust relationship keeps the data in Metropolis safe. Gotham will only be able to access its resources if a third trust relationship is established between Gotham and Metropolis.

exam
ⓦatch

Windows NT trusts are different from Windows 2000 trusts. In Windows NT, trusts are one-way and nontransitive. Windows 2000 trusts, on the other hand, are two-way and transitive. Don't confuse the way trusts are established when taking the exam.

Domain Models

To understand domains and trusts, it is important to look at the different models available. These models show how your network will be structured, and how trust relationships may be used to combine domains together. There are four different domain models to choose from:

- Single domain model
- Single master domain model
- Multiple master domain model
- Complete trust model

Choosing the correct model for your network is an important part of planning Windows NT domains. It can be difficult changing from one model to another after the network structure is established, so it is important you choose a model that suits the needs of your enterprise. As we'll see in the sections that follow, each model has distinct advantages and disadvantages.

The Single Domain Model

A single domain model doesn't use trust relationships, but is the foundation on which all other models are built. As shown in Figure 4-3, the trusts are unnecessary because all the resources are located in one domain. All users, groups, and computers reside in this domain, thereby removing the need to manage trusts.

In addition to users, groups, and workstations, the domain may consist of a number of different components. A Primary Domain Controller (PDC) is required

FIGURE 4-3

A single domain
model

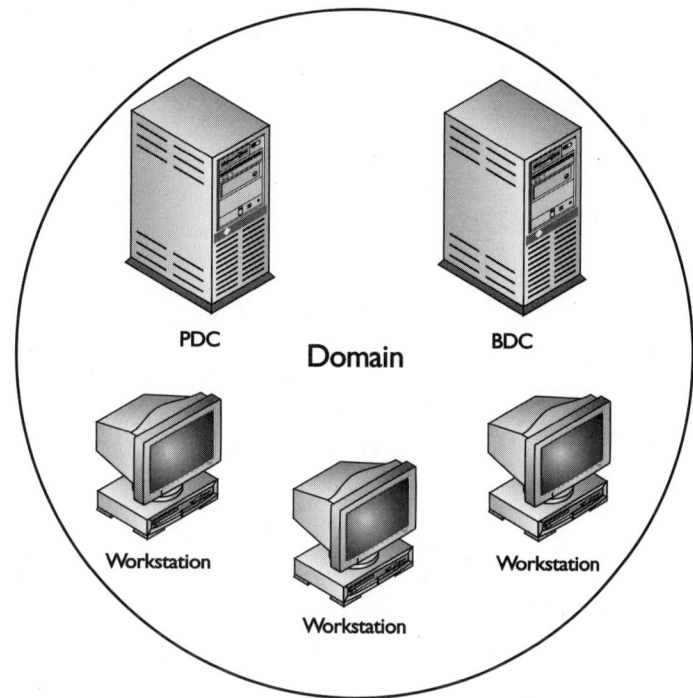

to authenticate users and holds the master copy of the database used to store user
and computer accounts as well as security information. The domain may also
have an optional number of Backup Domain Controllers (BDCs). The BDC is used
to authenticate users if the PDC doesn't respond. The PDC replicates security
information to any BDCs in the domain for this purpose. In addition to these, the
domain may also have an optional number of member servers, which serve resources
(i.e., files, applications, and so on) to clients on the network.

Many companies commonly use this single domain model because it is easy to
implement, and provides centralized management of user accounts and resources.
However, it may be unwise to use this on larger enterprise networks with a large user
base. A domain can support a maximum of 40,000 accounts, so this model can only
be used in enterprises with less than 40,000 accounts. Even if total users don't exceed
this number, the network may experience poor performance if too many users or
groups are accessing the PDC or other servers.

The Single Master Domain Model

Unlike the single master domain model, other models allow you to group users and resources into organizational units. As shown in Figure 4-4, this model consists of one domain containing the user accounts, and one or more other domains containing resources. The single domain containing user accounts is referred to as the "master domain" or "account domain," while those containing resources are called "resource domains."

As the arrows in this figure show, the resource domains are trusting, while the master domain is trusted. This means the master domain has access to the resource domains, allowing the master domain to act as an administrative unit for accounts. Because all other domains trust the master domain, they recognize all of the users and groups in this domain. This allows users to log on to the master domain, and then access resources in the resource domains.

Medium-sized companies often use this model, because it provides centralized administration of accounts and decentralized resource management. The master domain centralizes accounts, allowing the administrator to add, delete, and modify users and groups. Each resource domain can be a department of the company, or geographical location. This allows the resource domains to be administered locally, and manage its own resources.

on the
① o b

Larger enterprises may be unable to use the single master domain model. Because all user accounts are stored in a single domain, this means it has the same limitations as the single domain model. Your network must have fewer than 40,000 accounts, or this model cannot be used.

While Windows NT has a limitation of 40,000 accounts, Windows 2000 does not. This is because of changes to the way account information is managed. In Windows 2000, the Active Directory is used. It supports millions of objects, so you can use millions of user accounts in a domain.

When this model is used, local and global groups are used. Local groups are groups that reside in the local accounts database of Windows NT/2000 servers and workstations, and allow you to control the access that members of these groups have to that machine. A local group can contain either user accounts or global groups. Global groups are group accounts maintained by a PDC, and contain members from that particular domain. Global groups are important to the single master domain model because they are the only group that can cross a trust relationship, from one domain to another.

FIGURE 4-4

A single master
domain model

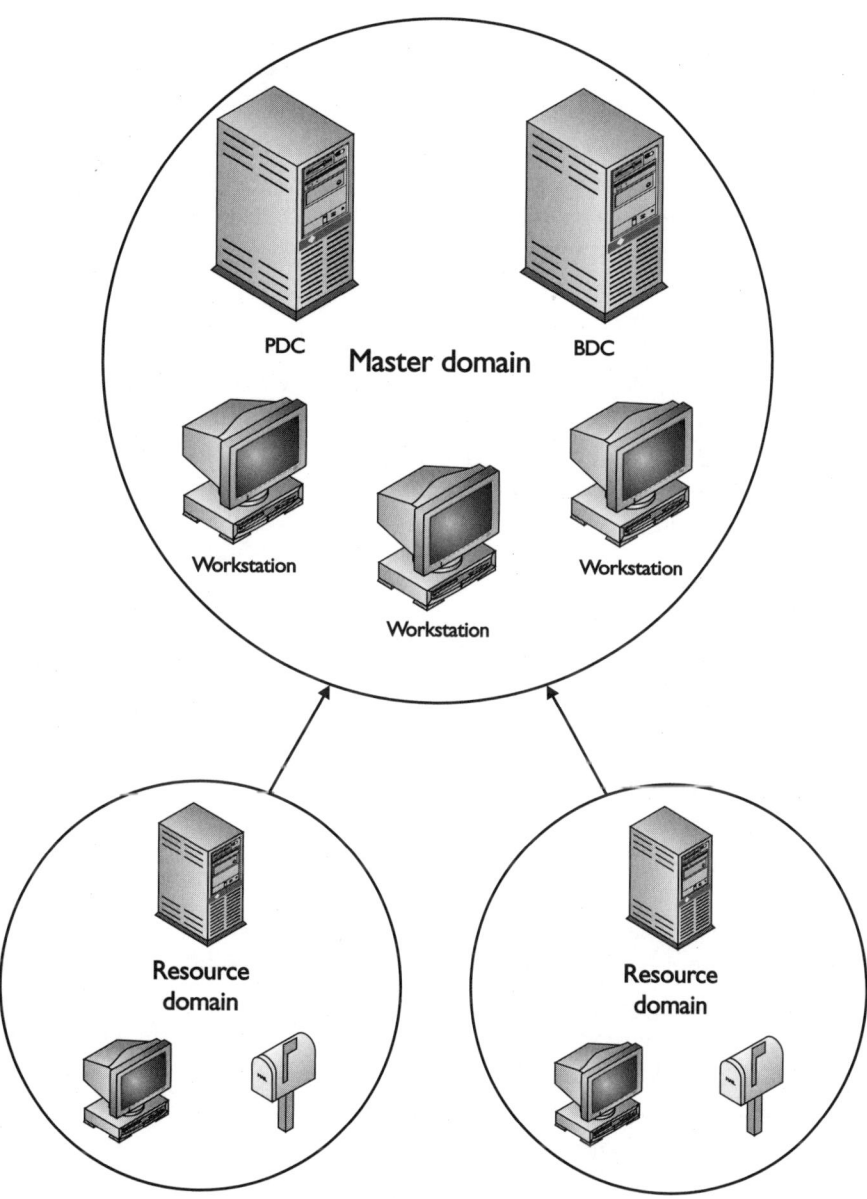

Global groups and local groups allow you to control access to resources. You can
add users to a global group in the master domain, and then add this group to a local

group on a server in a resource domain. To illustrate this, let's say you have a SQL Server in a resource domain, which only certain users should have access to. To control access, you create a global group in the master domain called SQLUsers. You then add any user accounts that need to access the SQL Server to this group. On the SQL Server, a local group is created that has permissions allowing users to access the database, and perform necessary tasks. The global group is then added to the local group. When a new user needs access to the SQL Server, you only need to add the users to the global group. This simplifies administration, because management of accounts is centralized.

exam
ⓦatch

Unlike Windows 2000, Windows NT does not support universal groups. Universal groups allow you to set access permissions for users, regardless of which domain they are a part of in the enterprise network. This means that when you add users to a universal group, it doesn't matter where in the network they are. If the Windows 2000 network is running in native mode, a universal group can be used anywhere in the same forest.

The Multiple Master Domain Model

Unlike the previous two models, the multiple master domain model can be used on networks with more than 40,000 accounts. In this model, accounts are distributed among two or more master domains, which allows you to increase the number of accounts available for use on your network, making this a good model for use in larger companies.

As shown in Figure 4-5, the master domains are connected to one another with two-way trusts. Because a trust relationship in Windows NT can only be one-way, two one-way trust relationships are established between the domains to create the two-way trust. Each of the resource domains in this model has a one-way trust with each of the master domains, allowing access to the various resources available in these domains.

A common method of designing a multiple master domain model is to create master domains in a location where the company's IT staff resides. This may be the headquarters of the network. Resource domains are then created based on geographical locations, departments, or resources. For example, you might create one resource domain for each branch office or department in the company, allowing you to group resources logically. This allows departments to have administrators who control their own resources, while allowing the network administrator to control which user accounts have access to the various resource domains.

FIGURE 4-5

A multiple master
domain model

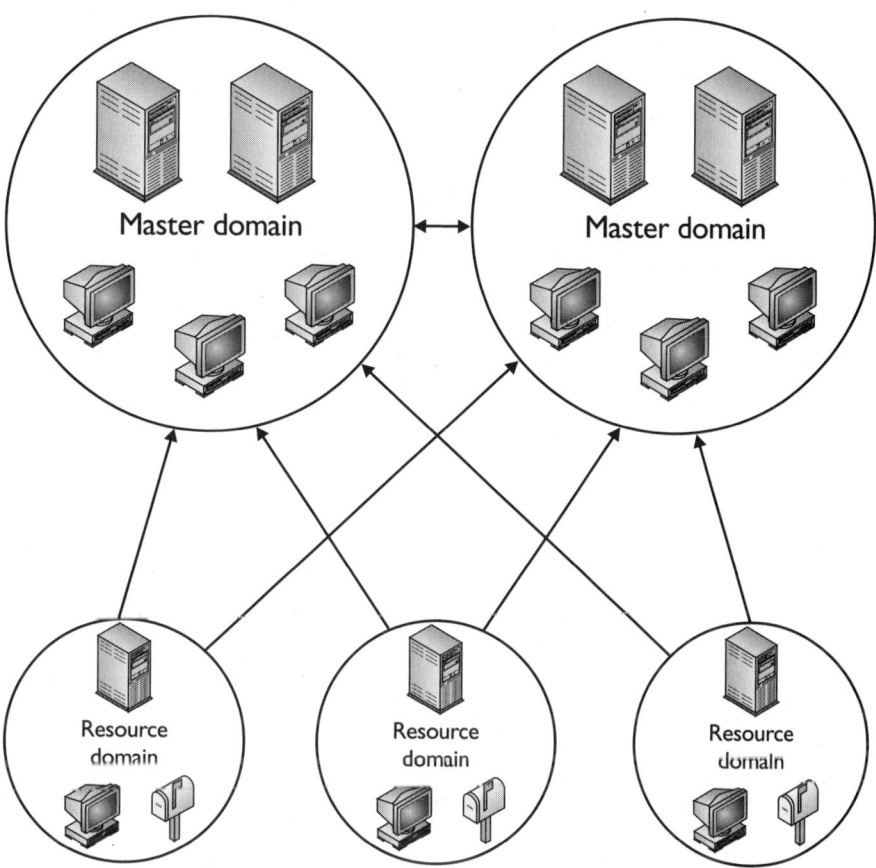

In developing a network that uses the multiple master domain model, trusts will
be created to allow users to log on to the domain containing their account, and then
to access resources in other domains. To determine the number of trusts required by
your network, the following formula can be used:

```
M×(M-1)+(R×M)
```

In this formula, *M* is the number of master domains, while *R* is the number of
resource domains. To explain this further, let's look at the multiple master domain
depicted in Figure 4-5. In this figure, there are two master domains, and three
resource domains. This would make the following equation:

```
2×(2-1)+(3×2)
```

This would equal 2×1+6, which equals 8. When comparing this to the number of trust relationships shown in Figure 4-5, you can see that this accurately shows the same number of trusts.

Just as trusts become more complicated with this model, so do groups. In the single master domain model, we saw that global groups and local groups are used to control access to resources in the resource domains. Because multiple master domains are used with this model, global groups need to be duplicated. In each master domain, you will need to create the same global group. These global groups are then added to local groups on servers in the resource domains.

Complete Trust Model

Like the multiple master domain model, the complete trust model is highly scalable. As such, it is useful for companies with a large (or growing) number of users. User accounts are distributed across multiple domains, allowing you to go beyond the 40,000 accounts limitation of a single domain. However, the difference between this model and the previous two we've discussed is that no resource domains are used. Instead, the complete trust model is more like the single domain model, with two-way trust relationships between each of the single domains. In this model, user accounts and resources are distributed across each domain.

As shown in Figure 4-6, each of the domains in this model has a trust relationship with one another. The trust relationship is two-way, with each domain having two one-way trust relationships with each of the other domains. This allows users in each domain to use resources in other domains.

The problem with this model is that it isn't useful for companies with a centralized Information Technology department, where one network administrator controls user access. With this model, each domain trusts every other domain, and has the ability to manage users and groups. As such, each domain must have faith that other domains will put the proper users into the proper groups, and not create security vulnerabilities by giving users more access than necessary.

Because two one-way trusts are required between every domain, the number of trust relationships required by this model can become quite complex. The following formula can be used to determine the number of trusts required in a complete trust model:

```
n×(n-1)
```

In this formula, n is the number of domains. If we were to use this formula with the number of domains shown in Figure 4-6 (which has four domains), we would

FIGURE 4-6

A complete
trust model

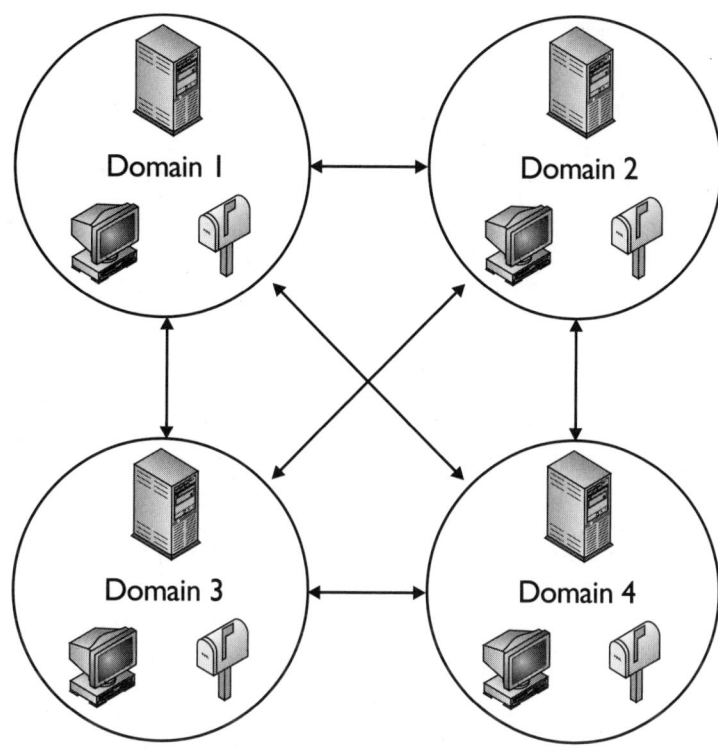

see that this formula would become 4×(4-1) or 4×3. This means that a network with four domains using the complete trust model would require 12 trust relationships.

Creating a Trust Relationship

As we'll see in this section, creating a trust relationship is a two-part process. Each domain needs to specify whether they are a Trusted or a Trusting Domain. An administrator in one domain must specify on an NT Server that another domain is a Trusted Domain. Then, the administrator in the other domain must specify that the first domain is a Trusting Domain. Once this is done, a trust relationship is established.

Although creating a trust relationship between two domains is relatively simple, certain requirements must be met before it can be done. First, an administrator account must be used to set up either side of the trust relationship. This is the only account that can be used to set up the trust. Next, the PDCs in each domain must be able to communicate with one another. This means they must use the same protocol to establish a connection, and must be free of any other sessions. This is because the system account will be used to establish the connection between the PDCs, and if they are already communicating with a different account, the session to create the trust will fail. Finally, each domain in the trust will require a unique SID. Since user accounts are authenticated based on the account's SID, any problems with the SID will cause errors in the trust relationship. For this reason, you cannot copy NT Server from one server to another without changing the SID. By cloning the machines in this manner, each will have identical SIDs and will be unable to properly authenticate accounts.

To set up a trust relationship, User Manager For Domains is used on each PDC in each domain involved in the trust relationship. Once this program is opened, you then need to open the Policies menu, and click Trust Relationships. This will display the Trust Relationships dialog box, shown in Figure 4-7. In this dialog box, there are two sections:

- Trusted Domains, which is completed by the trusting domain. This section is where you specify which domains are trusted by your domain.

- Trusting Domains, which is completed by the trusted domain. This section is where you specify the domains that trust your domain.

To complete either of these sections, you click the Add button beside the section you wish to complete. This will display another dialog box, where you enter the name of the domain and a password (Figure 4-7).

FIGURE 4-7

The Trust
Relationships
dialog box

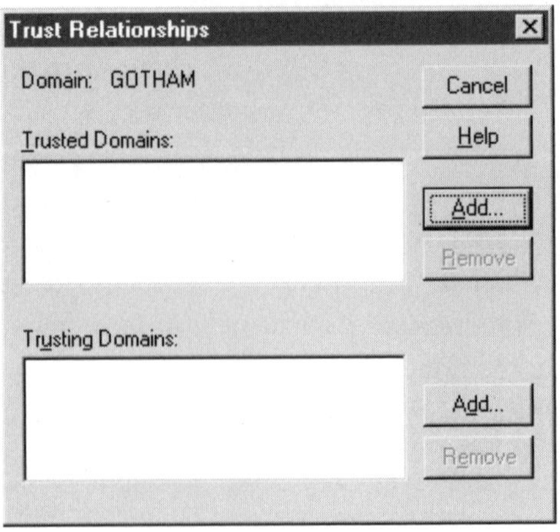

Although it is unimportant as to the order in which the relationship is established, Microsoft recommends that the administrator of the trusted domain (i.e., the master domain) begin the process. This administrator should add the name of the trusting domain in the Trusting Domains section on the PDC of that domain. Once this is done, the administrator of the trusting domain (i.e., the resource domain) should then add the trusted domain to the Trusted Domains section on the PDC in his or her domain. By doing it in this order, the trust relationship will be established immediately.

If you wish to create a two-way trust, as is needed in networks using the complete trust model or where multiple master domains need a two-way trust, you will need to create two one-way trusts. To explain this, let's say we have two domains called DomainA and DomainB. On DomainA, you would specify DomainB as the Trusting Domain. On DomainB, you would specify DomainA as the Trusting Domain. Once this is done, you would then establish relationships for the Trusted Domains. On DomainA, you would specify DomainB as the Trusted Domain. On DomainB, you would specify DomainA as the Trusted Domain. Once done, the two-way trust would be established, and take effect immediately.

EXERCISE 4-1

CertCam 4-1

Creating Trust Relationships

1. On a PDC in the domain that will become a Trusted Domain, click the Windows Start menu. Under Programs, select Administrative Tools (Common), then click User Manager For Domains.

2. Once User Manager For Domains opens, click the Policies menu and then click the item called Trust Relationships.

3. When the Trust Relationships dialog box appears, look for the section labeled Trusting Domains. Click the Add button beside this section.

4. When a second dialog box appears, enter the name of the Trusting Domain. You may specify a password by entering one and then reentering it in the field below to verify it. Click OK.

5. On the PDC in the domain that will become a Trusting Domain, follow the steps in Step 1 of this exercise to open User Manager For Domains. Once this is open, repeat Step 2 of this exercise to display the Trust Relationships dialog box.

6. When the Trust Relationships dialog box appears, look for the section labeled Trusted Domains. Click the Add button beside this section.

7. When a second dialog box appears, enter the name of the Trusted Domain. If the Trusted Domain has specified a password, enter this password in the field below it. Click OK.

Common Problems with Trust Relationships

Although establishing trust relationships is relatively simple, problems can result. In such cases, you will need to troubleshoot the situation, determine what the problem is, and deal with it accordingly. Although some problems may be more involved than others, there are a few that are commonly experienced with trusts.

If you are trying to establish a trust relationship, and find you cannot, you should ensure that you're using the administrator account. This is the only account that can be used to set up a trust relationship. You should also ensure that the PDC in each domain is running. If they are not, then the PDC you're setting the trust on will not be able to connect to the PDC in the other domain involved in the relationship. If both PDCs are working, then you should verify that the PDCs in each domain can resolve each other's names. If DNS, WINS, or other name resolution methods aren't working, then the two PDCs will be unable to find one another on the network.

When discussing how to create a trust relationship, it was mentioned that it is better to initiate the relationship by establishing the Trusting Domain first. On the PDC in the Trusted Domain, you should set the name of the Trusting Domain. Once this is done, you should then set the name of the Trusted Domain on the PDC in the Trusting Domain. By doing so, this will establish the relationship immediately. If it is done in the reverse order, then it may take as long as 15 minutes before the trust relationship takes effect. This delay may make you think you have incorrectly created the trust, when in fact it is merely taking time for the two PDCs to communicate with one another.

Another common problem occurs when the trusts are set up in the wrong direction. In other words, the master domain is set as a trusting domain and a resource domain is set as a trusted domain. If this occurs, then users will be unable to access resources in the domain where those resources reside. To fix this problem, you need to break the current trust, and re-create it properly.

In some cases, trusts may be broken. This may occur when a domain is renamed, the NETLOGON service has failed or stopped, a network cable has been damaged, or other events have occurred that prevent a connection between the two domains. If a trust relationship is broken, then it will need to be reestablished by re-creating the trust.

Cross-Domain Resource Access

In larger corporations, it is common to see more than one operating system being used on a network. As Microsoft's largest competition (and the longest running leader) in network operating systems is Novell NetWare, it is no surprise that Microsoft included support for Novell clients and servers. This support comes in the form of Client Services for NetWare, as well as Gateway Services for NetWare.

Client Services for NetWare (CSNW) allows clients to access NetWare servers directly, without the need of passing requests through a gateway. CSNW is a redirector, which is a program that takes client requests and redirects them. When a client request is made from a Microsoft network, CSNW will translate the request into commands that the NetWare server will understand. This is important, because the two network operating systems use different commands, and without a program like CSNW, the Microsoft Network client would be unable to request services and resources from the NetWare server. Because only clients use it, CSNW is strictly available on Windows NT 4.0 Workstations.

Gateway Services for NetWare (GSNW) runs on a Windows NT 4.0 Server, and allows the server and clients using this server to access resources on NetWare servers. Because users access the NetWare server through an NT Server, clients don't require CSNW to access the NetWare network. Commands are sent to the Windows NT Server running GSNW, which translates the commands, and passes them to the NetWare server using a single account. In this way, GSNW works as a middleman between the Microsoft network and the NetWare network.

When Windows NT 4.0 was released, the default protocol used by NetWare was Internetwork Packet Exchange/Sequenced Packet Exchange (IPX/SPX). Although current versions of NetWare use TCP/IP as the default protocol, to use CSNW or GSNW, you will need to install the Microsoft implementation of IPX/SPX. This protocol is called NWLink, and must be installed on machines running CSNW or GSNW. If it is not, then it will be automatically installed when you load either of these services.

SCENARIO & SOLUTION

I have set up a trust relationship between two domains, but it doesn't seem to work. On one domain, I specified the other as the Trusted Domain. I then went to the PDC in the Trusted Domain and set the other domain as the Trusting Domain. What have I done wrong?	Nothing. If the Trusted Domain relationship is set before the Trusting Domain relationship, the trust relationship won't take effect immediately. By doing it in this order, it may take as long as 15 minutes before the trust relationship takes effect.
Which is the best model to use for a network?	The model you should use will depend on your needs. If your company has less than 40,000 accounts, then the single domain model or single master domain model will be useful. If your company has (or expects to have) more than this number of users, then the multiple master domain or complete trust models will be useful. Other elements that will go into your decision are outlined earlier in this chapter.
I want to access a NetWare server from my Windows NT Server, but I'm unable to install CSNW. Why?	Client Services for NetWare is only available with Windows NT 4.0 Workstation. It doesn't come with Windows NT Server.

CERTIFICATION OBJECTIVE 4.02

Configuring and Troubleshooting Account Policy

Network security is an important aspect of running any kind of network. This not only involves creating, modifying, and deleting accounts, but ensuring that users don't create security vulnerabilities through their actions. After all your efforts in creating a secure environment, you don't want someone hacking an account with an easy to guess password, or having users exchange usernames and passwords with one another.

Account policy allows you to control universal security settings, and addresses issues dealing with passwords. A good account policy will force a user to change their password regularly, have a unique password of a certain length, and determine what will occur when a user tries to guess passwords and repeatedly enters the wrong password. This enhances the security of your network, because it lowers the chances of unauthorized users accessing the accounts of other people.

on the
Job

A common security problem in any networked environment is when users exchange usernames and passwords with one another. For example, one user may be going on vacation or may transfer temporarily to another department. During this time, a temp or another full-time employee will take over this user's duties. Rather than contacting the network administrator to have this replacement's account changed to the necessary security level, one user will give the other user his or her password. Not only does this remove accountability for the replacement's actions (while using another person's account), but, when the person returns to their original duties, the replacement will still have that person's valid username and password. This will allow the replacement to continue accessing data and services, which they would otherwise be unable to do. To deal with this problem, account policies can be set to force regular password changes, to prevent users from having other people's passwords for very long.

Setting account policies is done through the User Manager For Domains tool. To open this tool, click the User Manager For Domains item that's found in the Programs | Administrative Tools (Common) folder on the Windows Start menu. Once User Manager For Domains has started, open the Policies menu and click the Accounts item. This will display the dialog box shown in Figure 4-8.

FIGURE 4-8

The Account
Policy dialog box

Account Policy

Domain: GOTHAM   [OK] [Cancel] [Help]

Password Restrictions

Maximum Password Age
- Password Never Expires
- Expires In 42 Days

Minimum Password Age
- Allow Changes Immediately
- Allow Changes In ___ Days

Minimum Password Length
- Permit Blank Password
- At Least ___ Characters

Password Uniqueness
- Do Not Keep Password History
- Remember ___ Passwords

- No account lockout
- Account lockout

Lockout after ___ bad logon attempts

Reset count after ___ minutes

Lockout Duration
- Forever (until admin unlocks)
- Duration ___ minutes

☐ Forcibly disconnect remote users from server when logon hours expire
☐ Users must log on in order to change password

As you can see by this dialog box, the options available are broken into different segments. At the top of the dialog box, you are shown the domain name that the account policy will apply to. This is for information purposes only, and can't be modified. Below this are settings that deal with Password Restrictions. This controls the length, age, and uniqueness of passwords, as well as the settings that deal with account lockout. Each of these will be discussed in sections to follow.

At the bottom of the screen are two check boxes. The Forcibly Disconnect Remote Users From Server When Logon Hours Expire check box relates to the hours that users are allowed to log on. If checked, then users are forced to log off when their timeframe reaches its end. However, this option only applies to users who are working on Windows NT machines.

The other check box is the Users Must Log On In Order To Change Password box. If checked, then users are forced to log on to the network in order to change their passwords. If a user has an expired password, then they will need to contact the network administrator to make the change for them.

Password Uniqueness

A problem with forcing password changes is that users will often reuse passwords. Most users have a few passwords that they use for everything. They use the same few passwords for network access, logging on the Internet, e-mail accounts, bank machines or even memberships at video stores. Because they use the same stable of passwords, someone who knows one or two of them can keep trying a user's account until that user reuses the password. For example, they may have two or three children, and use each of their names for a password. If you can guess the right child's name, you have access to their files.

Because this is a well-known problem in terms of users, password uniqueness allows you to specify how many passwords a user must choose before reusing an old password. The Password Uniqueness section of the Account Policy dialog box has two options that allow you to control how many passwords Windows NT will remember before allowing a user to reuse old passwords.

The Do Not Keep Password History option is the default setting. When this is selected, Windows NT allows users to reuse old passwords. It turns off the password uniqueness feature on your server.

The Remember Passwords option allows you to set how many passwords Windows NT will remember. When this is selected, the default limit will display five passwords. However, you can specify between 1–24 passwords to be stored in the password history.

exam
Watch

Windows NT Password Uniqueness is similar (although somewhat different to Windows 2000). In Windows 2000, you can adjust the setting to low, medium, or high security. With low security, Windows 2000 will remember the last 1–8 passwords. Medium security will remember the last 9–16 passwords, while high security will remember the last 17–24 passwords. As the administrator, you can set exactly how many passwords will be remembered.

Password Length

The Minimum Password Length option allows you to set the minimum number of characters a password must contain. By setting this option, you can prevent users from using short passwords that will be easy to guess. This will make it harder for hackers to obtain the passwords of user accounts, and ensure simple passwords aren't being used on your network.

on the
Job

Short passwords are easy to guess. You should require at least six to eight characters for the minimum password length. Anything less than this, and it will be significantly easier for hackers to guess a password, and much more difficult for those to remember a password that they see a user type in.

If the Permit Blank Password option is set, then users will be able to use blank passwords. In other words, all the person will need to do is enter their username and then click OK to log on. This can be dangerous if the user account has significant access to your system or has access to sensitive data. All a hacker would need to do is get the username to log on to that account.

If the At Least…Characters option is set, then you can specify the minimum number of characters a user can have in their password. You can set the value in this field to 1–14 characters. The reason you can set a maximum of 14 characters as the minimum password length is that Windows NT passwords cannot be longer than 14 characters.

exam
ⓦatch

Don't confuse the password length in Windows NT with the password length in Windows 2000 or other operating systems. Windows NT is limited to passwords that are 14 characters or less. In Windows 2000, passwords can be up to 128 characters in length. In Windows 95 and Windows 98, users are limited to passwords up to 14 characters in length.

Password Age

There are two segments in the Password Restrictions section that deal with password age. The first is the Maximum Password Age. This allows you to set the maximum amount of time a user can retain the same password without being forced to change it. In other words, the user can keep that password for the number of days you specify before being forced to change it. By default, the Expires In…Days field is set to 42 days. However, you can change this value to 1–999 days, depending on what you feel is an adequate amount of time. If you don't want a time limit set on the amount of time a user can utilize a password, then select the Password Never Expires option.

The other segment in the Password Restrictions section that deals with password age is the Minimum Password Age. This allows you to set the minimum amount of time a user can utilize a password before they are able to change it. This is important, because a common problem is that some users will change their password, then change it back to their old password. This has the same effect as if they'd never changed their password to begin with. By specifying the number of days a user must wait, users will be unable to immediately return to their old password. As with the Maximum Password Age setting, you can set this to a value of 1–999 days. If you don't want to set a time limit, select the Allow Changes Immediately option.

Account Lockout

The two main tools of hackers are time and patience. Account lockout is used to prevent hackers from repeatedly trying to guess user passwords. If this isn't set, a hacker could try password after password until getting it right, and gaining access to the user account. Once configured, the account lockout settings will prevent anyone from using the account for a specified period of time.

There are several settings on the Account Policy dialog box that can be configured for account lockout. The first of these is the No Account Lockout option. This disables the account lockout settings, so a user can enter incorrect passwords indefinitely, without repercussions. The next option is Account Lockout which specifies you want to use the other settings discussed in this section.

The Lockout After … Bad Logon Attempts setting allows you to specify the number of failed logon attempts that can be made before the account is locked out. This means that if a user enters a bad password a specific number of times, the account will be disabled. When account lockout is set, the default number of bad logon attempts will be set to five.

The Reset Count After setting allows you to specify the number of minutes the system will wait after a bad set of logon attempts before resetting the count. If this option wasn't available, a user could be locked out after making a number of bad logons over a period of hours, months, days, and so on. Once the account lockout option has been selected, the value for this setting is 30 minutes, by default. After this period expires, the count of bad logons is reset. If the user reaches the number of bad logons before this period of time has passed, and the count isn't reset, then the account will remain locked out until an administrator releases it.

The Lockout Duration segment of the account lockout section determines how long a user account will be locked out before the system releases it. There are two options here. The first is Forever (Until Admin Unlocks) which specifies that the system cannot unlock the account. If this is set, the administrator will need to release the account. The second option is the Duration that an account will be locked out, until the system unlocks it. If this is set, you configure the number of minutes the account will remain locked out. By default, the value of this is 30 minutes. Once this period of time passes, the account is reset, and the user can then continue making attempts logging onto the network.

SCENARIO & SOLUTION

How long should I set the minimum password length to?	You can set it to 1–14 characters in Windows NT, but it is best to set it to somewhere in-between (such as 7 characters). The longer and more complex the password, the more difficult it will be to guess.
Isn't it better to set the lockout duration to Forever (Until Admin Unlocks) to keep users from repeatedly trying to hack an account?	Although this will allow you to control and monitor which user accounts are experiencing problems, it may result in a number of help desk calls from users who are misspelling their passwords. It is better to ask users to tell you whenever their account locks them out for apparently no reason. Setting auditing on accounts can also help in monitoring these accounts.

CertCam 4-2

EXERCISE 4-2

Setting Account Policies

1. Open the User Manager For Domains. From the Windows Start menu, select Programs and then Administrative Tools (Common), then click User Manager For Domains.

2. Once User Manager For Domains has started, click the Policies menu, then click the item labeled Accounts. The Account Policies dialog box will appear.

3. Set the Maximum Password Age to 30 days, so users must change their password every 30 days.

4. Set the Minimum Password Age to 7 days to keep users from immediately changing the password back to the original password.

5. Under Minimum Password Length, select the At Least...Characters option and type 7, so that passwords must be at least 6 characters in length.

6. Select the Account Lockout option, then set the Lockout After...Bad Logon Attempts to 5. This will keep users from repeatedly entering passwords more than 5 times.

7. Select the Duration...Minutes option, and set it to 45 minutes.

8. Click OK to confirm these changes to account policy.

CERTIFICATION OBJECTIVE 4.03

Configuring and Troubleshooting System Policies

Windows NT configuration settings are stored in a hierarchical database of keys, hives and values called the Registry. Because the Registry can be complex and confusing to modify directly, Windows NT provides a number of methods to interact with the Registry using GUI tools and policies. To restrict users from making such modifications, and enable administrators to control their environment and actions, system policies are used.

System policies are rules and restrictions placed on computers and users. These rules determine what a user can do when he or she sits at a computer or logs on to the network. When a system policy is modified, you are accessing Registry settings that control a variety of system features and components. While we'll discuss the various elements you can control later in this chapter, these include:

- Network settings, logons, and access

- Specifying which programs and options are available through the Control Panel

- Customizing the user desktop

System policies are created and modified through a GUI interface called the System Policy Editor. This tool exposes Registry settings, allowing you to enable, disable, and set specific settings. In doing so, this will affect how the user will be able to interact with the computer, network, and available resources.

exam
ⓦatch
System Policy Editor can be started by clicking on the System Policy Editor item under Programs | Administrative Tools (Common) on the Windows Start menu. The executable for this program is POLEDIT.EXE, and entering POLEDIT from the Run command can also start it. On the exam, and in the real world, you may find that this tool is called either System Policy Editor or Poledit. The two names are interchangeable.

As shown in Figure 4-9, System Policy Editor breaks these Registry settings into two areas. One applies to the local user, while the other applies to the local computer. When settings in either of these are changed, the settings will overwrite those in the current user and local machine areas of the Registry. User policy settings allow you to control the environment of the user who is currently logged on. Changes here will modify the HKEY_CURRENT_USER subtree of the Registry. Local computer settings are used to configure the computer. Changes to this will modify the HKEY_LOCAL_MACHINE subtree of the Registry.

The System Policy Editor has two modes: Registry and Policy File. In Registry mode, the Registry of the local computer or a remote computer can be modified. In this mode, when many changes are made, they will take effect immediately. However, in some cases, you will need to reboot the computer before they take

FIGURE 4-9

The System
Policy Editor

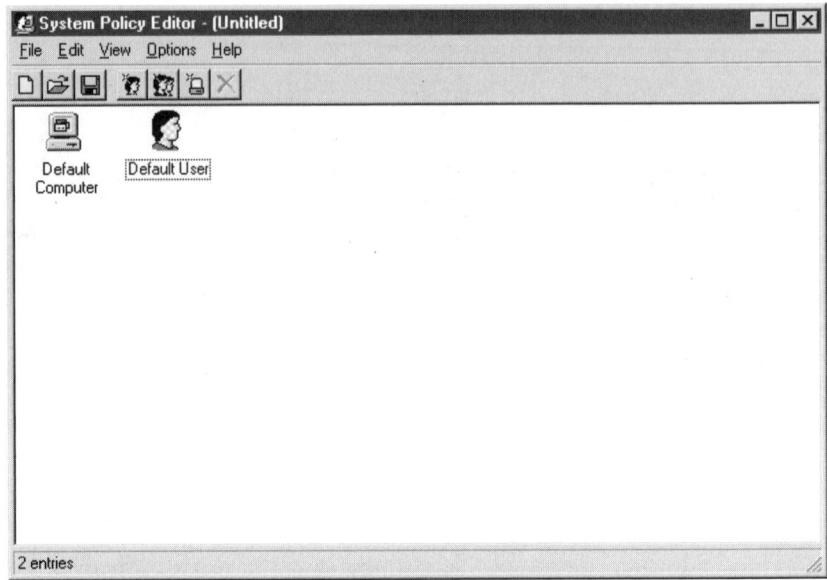

effect. In Policy File mode, settings are saved to a separate file. When this is used, changes will not take effect until the user logs on, and the policy is downloaded.

The ability to save to both the Registry and separate files is important to creating system policies. This is because system policies can apply to an entire domain, or to a single user, computer, or group. System policies must be saved to a file called NTConfig.pol on the Primary Domain Controller. When users log on to the domain, these settings are then applied to them. If, however, certain users or groups need to have specific settings, then you can create separate policy files for them, which can then be applied at logon. This provides greater control over what users will be able to do, and how their environment will appear.

on the
job

System policies are commonly used to lock down workstations on networks and prevent users from changing settings. For example, your company may want their company logo to appear as a background on each computer, to provide a more professional appearance. To prevent users from changing the background, the display may be restricted, keeping them from changing this to another image. While this is a more cosmetic example of the abilities of a system policy, you can also control other settings, keeping users from modifying them and creating problems for themselves.

Client Computer Operating System

System policies are used to modify Registry settings, but it is important to realize that the Registry isn't used by all operating systems. Although NT networks will support clients using other operating systems, such as Apple Macintosh, system policies won't apply to such machines because there is no Windows Registry to modify. Even when Microsoft operating systems that use a Registry are involved, certain issues must be considered before system policies are used on your network.

Windows NT and Windows 9x operating systems both have a Registry, but they don't use the same type of Registry. Differences between the two come in the form of different settings unique to each. This prevents you from being able to use the same policies for both Windows NT and 9x machines.

To deal with this problem, you will need to create different policies for machines running Windows 9x and those running Windows NT on your network. These can be created using template files installed with the System Policy Editor. The templates are installed when the System Policy Editor is installed with Windows NT, and allow you to change settings that will be applied to the Registry, while breaking them down into various categories that are easier to work with. The template files consist of:

- WINNT.ADM
- WINDOWS.ADM
- COMMON.ADM

The WINNT.ADM file is used to modify settings specific to Windows NT. These settings only exist in the Windows NT operating system and directory structure. Therefore, policies created for other operating systems using this template will not function.

WINDOWS.ADM contains settings that are specific to Windows 9x Registry structures. Just as WINNT.ADM can't be used for policies dealing with Windows 9x computers, WINDOWS.ADM cannot be used to set policies for Windows NT computers.

COMMON.ADM is used for both Windows NT and 9x operating systems. This System Policy template file contains settings common to both Windows NT and Windows 9x Registry structures. However, it should not be considered something that should be used instead of WINDOWS.ADM or WINNT.ADM, as it isn't a replacement to the other two templates. The settings contained in this template aren't found in either of the other templates.

File Locations and Names

In using system policies, it is important to understand the different files used and where they are located. As mentioned, system policies can be saved as files. When the user logs on to the system, Windows NT looks for the policy files in a specific location, then merges the settings into the Registry. For this to work however, the files must be stored in the correct location.

To create system policies for domains, you will need to create the policy and save it to a file called NTConfig.pol. This is the policy file that will apply to Windows NT clients on your network, and can be created using the WINNT.ADM and COMMON.ADM system policy templates. The NTConfig.pol file will need to be saved in the \System32\Repl\Import\Scripts folder in the root directory of Windows NT, on the boot partition of the Primary Domain Controller. This directory can also be accessed by the share name *PDC_servername*\Netlogon$. When users log on to their Windows NT machine, it will look for the NTConfig.pol file in this directory, and then apply those settings contained in it.

Windows NT will always look for the NTConfig.pol file in the Netlogon$ directory. On a network using a single domain, this directory is located on the PDC for that domain. However, if trusts are used to connect two or more domains, then confusion may result as to which PDC containing the file will be used. In all cases, the system policy will be taken from the domain containing the user's account. In other words, if a user logs on to a computer located in DOMAIN1, and his or her account is in DOMAIN2, then the NTConfig.pol file located on the DOMAIN2 PDC will be used. It doesn't matter which domain the computer is in, only which domain the user account is located.

As mentioned earlier, system policies for Windows NT are incompatible with Windows 9x machines. You can't run Windows system policy files on computers running Windows 9x, or policies created for Windows 9x on Windows NT machines. As such, Windows 9x system policies need to be created with the WINDOWS.ADM and COMMON.ADM templates, and saved as a file called CONFIG.POL. The CONFIG.POL file will need to be saved to the Netlogon$ shared directory on the PDC. This is the same directory that the NTConfig.pol file is stored.

Windows 9x machines will always look in the Netlogon$ directory, unless load balancing has been enabled. This can be selected in the Network | System Policy Update | Remote Update | Load Balancing setting in the System Policy Editor. If this has been selected, the client will take its system policy from whatever server authenticates it.

Interaction Between Local Security Policy and System Policies

System policies can be created on the local computer or stored on a PDC, which contains settings for all computers logging on to the domain. Because multiple policies may be used, this means that more than one policy's settings may be applied to the Registry. The policies that may be applied are:

■ NTConfig.pol, which is the system policy file that applies to all computers logging in to the domain.

■ User Policy, which applies to specific users.

■ Group Policy, which applies to groups of users.

■ Computer Policy, which applies to specific computers.

■ Default User Policy, which is applied when no user policy is present for the user account being used to log on.

■ Default Computer Policy, which is applied when no computer policy is present for the computer being logged on to.

When implementing policies on your network, you can make a single policy or enact all of those just mentioned. If multiple policies are used, then different settings in the policies are merged. In other words, settings for a user or group may be merged with those meant for all users in the current domain.

Because multiple policies may be applied, Windows NT must apply them in a specific order. If they weren't applied in a specific order, those meant for default users would overwrite an individual user's policy or domain-wide settings. This possibility requires Windows NT to check for policies and load them in a particular sequence.

When a user logs on to a domain computer, Windows NT will check whether a user profile exists for that user. If it does, then it will be loaded. Windows NT will then check the NETLOGON shared network directory (Netlogon$) to see if there is a file called NTConfig.pol. This file contains the settings meant for all users in the domain. If the NTConfig.pol file exists and defines system policy for the user, these settings are merged into the current user portion of the Registry.

exam
ⓦatch

The NTConfig.pol file contains system policies for users of the domain. This is the domain containing the user account of the user logging on to the computer. If a trust exists between domains, then the NTConfig.pol file in the domain containing the user account is used.

Because it is easier to create groups and add users to them, group policies are often used instead of user policies. If a user policy hasn't been created for a user logging on to the computer, but group policies are being used, then the policy settings for the groups the user belongs to are merged into the current user portion of the Registry. The group policies are only applied if the user doesn't have an individual user policy.

In some cases, users logging on to the computer may not have a user policy and aren't members of any groups with group policies. In such cases, the Default User policy is used. The settings in the Default User policy will be merged into the current user portion of the Registry.

Computer policy is the last group of settings to be merged into the Registry. This is because computer policies merge into a different portion of the Registry. While user policies are added to the HKEY_CURRENT_USER section, computer policies are added to the HKEY_LOCAL_MACHINE section. As such, any previously added settings for users cannot be overwritten by the computer policy. If there is a policy for the computer the user is logging on to, then these settings will be merged into the Registry. If no policy exists for that particular computer, then the Default Computer policy is used, and its settings are merged into the local computer portion of the Registry.

Configuring User-Specific System Policies

System policies can be created or modified in the System Policy Editor. To create a new policy, you simply click the New Policy item on the File menu. When a new policy is created, you will see two default policies. One is Default User and the other is Default Computer. These are used if a specific computer policy hasn't been created for the machine being logged on to, or a user profile hasn't been created for the user logging on to the system.

Once you've created a new policy, you can then add users. To add a new user, select Add User on the Edit menu. A dialog box will appear, allowing you to enter the name of the user to create a policy for. A Browse button on this dialog box will open an Add Users dialog box, which lists the names of the user accounts currently on the system.

Once you've created a user profile, or decided to modify the default user profile, you simply need to double-click the icon for that user. This will open a dialog box, containing settings that can be configured (seen in Figure 4-10). After double-clicking the Default User, a properties dialog box is displayed. Contained in this dialog box are a number of nodes that can be expanded to view related settings.

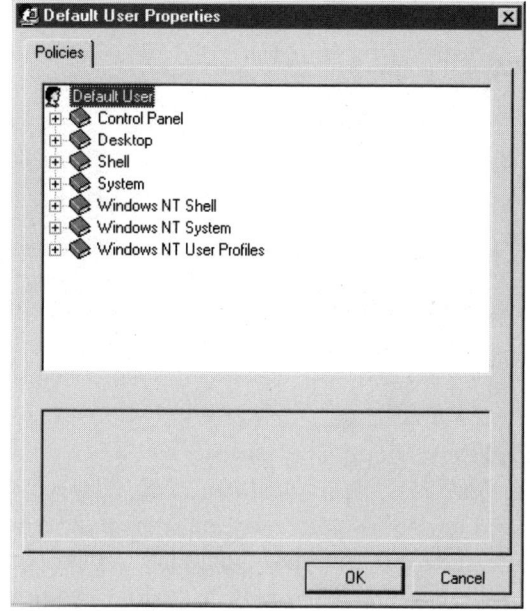

FIGURE 4-10

User
configuration
properties of the
System Policy
Editor

The first category is the Control Panel, which contains a Display node that can be
further expanded. This is used to restrict the display settings available through the
Control Panel. When this is selected, you can deny access to the display icon, hide
the Background tab, Screen Saver tab, Appearance tab, and/or Settings tab. This
prevents users from being able to change display settings on their computer.

The next category is the Desktop, which expands to show the Wallpaper and
Color Scheme settings. When Wallpaper is selected, you can specify the image to be
used as the background on this computer, and whether it is to be tiled or not. When
Color Scheme is selected, you can select a default color scheme from a drop-down
list, which is applied when the user logs on to the system. This category allows you
to force a uniform appearance on workstations, and prevents users from modifying
display settings that could keep them from properly viewing what's on the screen.

The Shell category expands to display a subcategory called Restrictions. In the
Restrictions subcategory, there are a number of options that control the user's
environment. These are:

- Remove Run command from Start menu
- Remove folders from Settings on Start menu
- Remove Taskbar from Settings on Start menu

- Remove Find command from Start menu
- Hide drives in My Computer
- Hide Network Neighborhood
- No Entire Network in Network Neighborhood
- No workgroup contents in Network Neighborhood
- Hide all items on Desktop
- Remove Shut Down command from Start menu
- Don't save settings on exit

The System category also has only one subcategory contained in it, which is called Restrictions. The settings here allow you to Disable Registry Editing Tools (i.e., REGEDIT.EXE), and Run Only Allowed Windows Applications. With this second setting, you can create a list of applications users may utilize, keeping them from accessing applications that may contain sensitive data, or ones they simply don't need to use. This option is useful for controlling licensing issues, where only a certain number of users are allowed to operate a particular program.

The Windows NT Shell category contains several subcategories, which allow you to control the NT environment in a number of ways. The Custom User Interface subcategory allows you to specify what shell program will be used in NT. By default, this is EXPLORER.EXE. The Custom Folders subcategory has a more lengthy list of settings. These include:

- Custom Programs Folder, which allows you to specify paths to program items
- Custom Desktop Icons, which allows you to specify the path to where custom desktop icons are stored
- Hide Start Menu Subfolders
- Custom Startup Folder, which allows you to specify the path to where items run at startup are stored
- Custom Network Neighborhood, which allows you to specify the path to where Network Neighborhood items are stored
- Custom Start Menu, which allows you to specify the location of Start menu items

The Restrictions subcategory in Windows NT Shell also contains a number of settings you can configure. Many of these apply specifically to NT Explorer, and the options found within this program. The settings consist of:

- Only use approved shell extensions
- Remove View->Options menu from Explorer
- Remove Tools->GoTo menu from Explorer
- Remove File menu from Explorer
- Remove common program groups from Start menu
- Disable context menus for the taskbar
- Disable Explorer's default context menu
- Remove the "Map Network Drive" and "Disconnect Network Drive" options
- Disable link file tracking

The Windows NT System category contains settings that allow you to control how the computer starts up, and what a user can do. When the Parse Autoexec.bat setting is enabled, environment variables in the autoexec.bat are included in the user's environment. When the Run Logon Scripts Synchronously is set, then all scripts must finish running before the user's shell is started. Each of the other settings in this category is self-explanatory:

- Disable Logoff
- Disable Task Manager
- Disable Lock Workstation
- Disable Change Password
- Show welcome tips at logon

The final category is Windows NT User Profiles, which allows you to control settings dealing with user profiles. The Limit Profile Size setting allows you to control how large the profile can be in kilobytes, notify the user when storage space has been exceeded, and remind them of this every so-many-minutes. You can also specify a custom message to display to the user. The other setting under Windows NT User Profiles is the Exclude Directories In Roaming Profiles which allows you to specify what directories a user with a roaming profile cannot access.

EXERCISE 4-3

CertCam 4-3

Configuring User Policy

This exercise shows how to specify what a user's wallpaper will be when the user logs on to his or her computer.

1. Open the System Policy Editor by clicking the Start menu and selecting Programs | Administrative Tools (Common), then clicking the System Policy Editor item.

2. From the File menu, select Open Registry.

3. Double-click the Default User icon.

4. Expand the Desktop category and select the Wallpaper setting.

5. Enter the path to a bitmap file (.bmp) on your hard disk.

6. Click OK.

Configuring Computer Policies

Computer policies are also created and modified using the System Policy Editor. When a new policy has been created (by clicking New Policy item on the File menu), you will see the Default User and Default Computer sections. Specific computer policies can then be added by clicking the Edit menu, followed by the Add Computer item. A dialog box will appear, where you can enter the name of the computer to create a policy for. A Browse button on this dialog box will open a Browse For Computer dialog box, which allows you to browse the computers on your network.

Once you've created a user profile, or decided to modify the default user profile, you can open a dialog box containing configuration settings by double-clicking the icon for that computer. This dialog box is shown in Figure 4-11. Like the User Properties dialog box, this dialog box provides a number of nodes that can be expanded to view related settings.

The Network category contains a subcategory called System Policy Updates, which allows you to do a remote update of a system policy. When the Remote setting is selected, a number of options become available to you. The Update mode allows you to select Automatic and use the default path to the system policy, or Manual. If

FIGURE 4-11

Computer
configuration
properties of the
System Policy
Editor

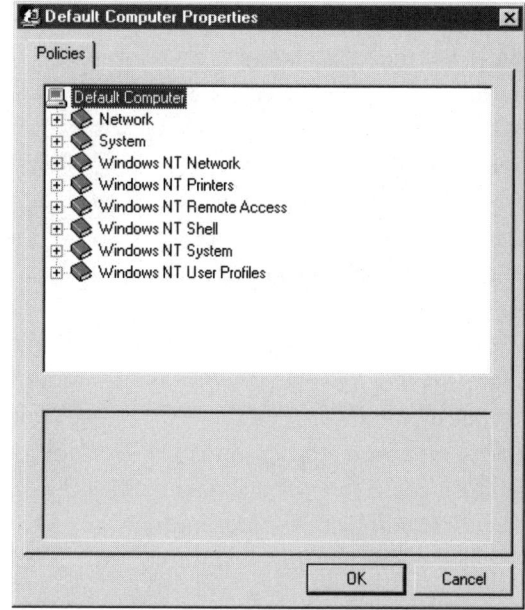

Manual is selected, then you can specify a path to the file. In addition, this setting allows you to enable a check box to display error messages if the policy file can't be found, and load balancing (used by computers running Windows 9*x*).

The System category provides subcategories called SNMP and Run. SNMP is the Simple Network Management Protocol (SNMP). The Run subcategory, on the other hand, allows you to specify which programs run at startup.

The Windows NT Network category contains a single subcategory called Sharing. The settings here allow you to specify whether hidden shares are created for each drive letter when the system starts.

The Windows NT Printers category contains three settings that can be configured. The Disable Browse Thread On This Computer setting configures the print spooler so it doesn't send shared printer information to other print servers. The Scheduler Priority setting allows you to set the priority of print jobs. Finally, the Beep For Error Enabled option configures the computer to beep every 10 seconds if an error occurs on a print job on a remote server.

The Windows NT Remote Access category is used to configure what will occur when the computer attempts to connect to a remote access server. The Max Number Of Unsuccessful Authentication Retries setting determines how many unsuccessful attempts to be authenticated may occur before the client must give up. The Max Time Limit For Authentication setting allows you to set the number of seconds the computer will wait to be authenticated. The Wait Interval To Callback setting lets you set the number of seconds the client will wait before dialing back into the remote access server. Finally, the Auto Disconnect setting allows you to control how long the client will remain connected to the server without activity before disconnecting.

The Windows NT Shell category allows you to configure the locations of custom shared folders. This allows you to set the path to where shared Programs items, Desktop icons, Start menu items, and items to launch at system startup are located.

The Windows NT System category contains two subcategories: Logon and File System. The Logon subcategory contains options that allow you to create a banner that appears when users log on to the network. In the Logon Banner setting, you can specify a caption to appear in the title bar when users log on, as well as the text that should appear in the message box window. The Enable Shutdown From Authentication Dialog Box setting allows you to shut down the computer from the dialog box where you log on to the system. The Do Not Display Last Logged On User Name setting will leave the username field blank when you log on. This keeps users from knowing the username of the last user of the computer, which would provide hackers a better shot at getting into the system (as only the password would need to be guessed now). Finally, the Run Logon Scripts Synchronously is used to ensure that all logon scripts run completely before the user's shell is displayed. You will remember that this setting also appeared when we discussed user policy in the previous section. If Run Logon Scripts Synchronously is set in this section, then that value takes precedence over what is set in the user section.

The File System subcategory has options dealing with how the file system is dealt with. The Do Not Create 8.3 File Names For Long File Names setting will allow long filenames to be used with the system, rather than replacing these filenames with names consisting of eight characters and a three character file extension. The Allow Extended Characters In 8.3 File Names allows short filenames with extended characters to be used. These may not be viewable on some computers that don't have the same code page, however. Finally, the Do Not Update Last Access Time setting is useful for system performance. When enabled, files that are read-only will not have their last access time updated.

The final category is Windows NT User Profiles, which is useful for performance issues. The Delete Cached Copies Of Roaming Profiles setting in this category is useful for saving disk space. When a user with a roaming profile logs off, the profile is deleted from the hard disk. The Automatically Detect Slow Network Connections allows a computer to automatically detect a slow connection during log on. The next two settings also allow you to configure how to deal with slow connections. The Slow Network Connection Timeout lets you specify how many milliseconds to wait, while the Slow Network Default Profile Operation lets you specify whether a profile should be downloaded or the local profile be used. The Choose Profile Default Operation is a setting that allows you to select whether profiles will be downloaded by default, or if local user profiles are used by default. Finally, Timeout For Dialog Boxes allows you to specify the number of seconds Windows NT should wait for dialog boxes before timing out.

EXERCISE 4-4

CertCam 4-4

Configuring Computer Policy

This exercise will create a warning box that will appear when users log on to the computer. This can be used to notify users of legal issues or warnings about using this computer.

1. Start the System Policy Editor. From the File menu, click Open Registry.

2. Double-click the Local Computer icon.

3. Expand the node called Windows NT System.

4. Expand the Logon node.

5. Click the option labeled Logon Banner.

6. In the Caption field, type the text that will appear in the title bar of the logon banner.

7. In the Text field, enter the text that will appear in the window of the logon banner.

8. Click OK.

Group Policies

Groups are collections of users who have identical requirements. These may be members of a team, coworkers in a department, and so forth. Because of their similarities, the user accounts of these users are put into a group. By creating the group, and then adding users to it, you can set policies for this single group rather than creating policies for each individual user, making administration of your network much easier to manage.

Group policies apply to groups in your domain. Because they are a collection of users, the settings of a group policy are identical to that of a user policy. To learn about the settings available, you should go back and review the Settings Available To User policies.

From the Edit menu, select the Add Group item, then wait for the Add Group dialog box to appear. This dialog box has a field in which you can enter the name of the group the profile will apply to. If you're unsure of the group, or want to save yourself the trouble of typing, then click the Browse button to display a list of available groups. To add a group from the listing on the subsequent dialog box, select the group you want to use, then click Add. Once you've finished adding groups, click the OK button to confirm your choices, then click OK again to create the group policy.

SCENARIO & SOLUTION

I am planning to lock down a user's computer so they are limited as to what changes they can make to system settings. Is there anything I need take into consideration before starting this?	Remember to have an ADMIN account created on each computer you're changing, so you aren't restricted by policy settings as well. If you lock down a user's computer with policies, and don't have an account set up on the computer that has full access, then you may be unable to change settings afterwards.
What program should I use to create and modify system policies?	The System Policy Editor (i.e., POLEDIT.EXE) is a tool used to create and modify policy settings.
Why would I want to use group policies, when I could simply set each user's account?	It is easier to manage groups than it is to manage large numbers of user accounts. By adding users to a group, you only have to change policy settings for that one group. This saves considerable time, and makes the network easier to administrate.

CERTIFICATION SUMMARY

Trust relationships provide a secure channel between two or more domains. These relationships are one-way and nontransitive, and always involve two parties: the trusted domain and the trusting domain. In using trust relationships, you can allow users to access resources in other domains, and design your network based on these trusts.

Account policies are used to control security settings dealing with users' passwords. By creating an effective account policy, you can control how long a password must be, its uniqueness, the length of time it is valid, and what occurs when invalid passwords are entered. By using account policies, you can ensure that passwords don't become a major security vulnerability on your network.

System policies are used to control the environment and actions of users, and are managed through the System Policy Editor. Using policies, you can control what settings users are allowed to view and modify. This allows you to secure a computer, restrict display settings, and adjust other elements that determine how the computer will function.

✓ TWO-MINUTE DRILL

Configuring and Troubleshooting Trust Relationships

❏ Trust relationships provide a secure communication channel between domains, allowing one domain access to the resources of another domain.

❏ Trust relationships in Windows NT are one-way and nontransitive.

❏ There are four different models that can be used in Windows NT networks: single domain, single master domain, multiple master domain, and complete trust.

❏ Windows NT domains are limited to fewer than 40,000 accounts. Because user accounts reside in one domain in the single domain model and single master domain model, these should only be used for small and mid-sized enterprises. If more than 40,000 accounts exist, then either the multiple master domain model or complete trust model should be used.

❏ Client Services for NetWare (CSNW) allows Windows NT 4.0 workstations to connect directly to NetWare servers. Gateway Services for NetWare (GSNW) allows clients and the Windows NT Server to access resources on a NetWare network. CSNW is only available on Windows NT 4.0 workstations, while GSNW only runs on Windows NT 4.0 Server.

Configuring and Troubleshooting Account Policy

❏ Account policies are set using the Account Policy dialog box that's available through User Manager For Domains.

❏ Password uniqueness determines how many unique passwords a user must employ before being able to call upon a previously used password.

❏ Minimum password length is put in place to keep users from implementing passwords that are short and easy to guess. This option can be set to a value of 1–14, preventing users from using passwords with less than this number of characters.

❏ Maximum password age allows you to set the maximum number of days a user can retain the same password before changing it.

❑ Minimum password age allows you to set the minimum number of days a user must keep a new password before changing it.

❑ Account lockout allows you to configure what the system will do when a number of failed logon attempts occur.

Configuring and Troubleshooting System Policies

❑ System policies are used to control the user's environment and actions. These policies allow you to modify settings in the Registry that dictate the availability of various features and how they will operate.

❑ System policies are created and modified using the System Policy Editor.

❑ There are different system policies that can be created. These include user policy, computer policy, group policy, default user policy, default computer policy, and domain-wide system policy.

❑ Domain-wide system policies will affect all users and/or computers who log on to a domain containing their user account.

❑ User policies will affect settings under the HKEY_LOCAL_USER subtree of the Registry, while computer policies will affect settings under the HKEY_LOCAL_MACHINE subtree of the Registry.

SELF TEST

The following questions will help you measure your understanding of the material presented in this chapter. Read all of the choices carefully, as there may be more than one correct answer. Choose all correct answers for each question.

Configuring and Troubleshooting Trust Relationships

1. Your network consists of three domains, with Windows NT Server running on servers in each of the domains. Domain A has a trust relationship with Domain B. In this relationship, Domain A is the trusted domain, and Domain B is the trusting domain. Domain B has a trust relationship with Domain C. In this relationship, Domain C is the trusting domain, and Domain B is the trusted domain. Which of the following is true? (Choose all that apply.)

    A. Domain A will be able to access resources in Domain C.

    B. Domain C will be able to access resources in Domain B.

    C. Domain B will be able to access resources in Domain C.

    D. Domain A will be able to access resources in Domain B.

2. You have taken over administration of a network running Windows NT servers, with Windows 2000 Professional running on each of the workstations. All resources reside in a single domain, which also contains the user accounts and groups used on the network. Users are able to access all resources on the network. What domain model is being used?

    A. Single domain

    B. Single master domain

    C. Multiple master domain

    D. Complete trust

3. Your network has Windows NT servers running in two domains. One domain is called ADMIN, while the other domain is called DATA. The DATA domain has a SQL Server used by members of the Finance and Sales departments. No other departments have the need to use databases on this server. What steps will you perform to allow users from these departments to access databases on the SQL Server?

    A. Create two local groups called Finance and Sales in the Master domain. Add users from the Sales and Finance departments to the appropriate group, and assign permissions to the SQL Server.

    B. Create a local group in the Master domain, and assign users from the Sales and Finance departments to it. Create a global group on the SQL Server, and assign permissions to this group, so they can properly access the databases they need. Add the global group to the local group.

C. Create a global group in the Master domain, and assign users from the Sales and Finance departments to it. Create a local group on the SQL Server, and assign permissions to this group so they can properly access the databases they need. Add the local group to the global group.

D. Create a global group in the Master domain, and assign users from the Sales and Finance departments to it. Create a local group on the SQL Server, then assign permissions to this group so they can properly access the databases they need. Add the global group to the local group.

4. A company has hired you to design and implement a new network. The only criteria they have stressed is that Windows NT is used on all servers, while Windows 2000 Professional is used on each of the workstations in the company. Due to the limited number of IT staff, you want to keep trust relationships to a minimum, as this will make management of the trusts easier. You also want centralized management of user accounts.

After analyzing the number of user accounts necessary for the company, you find that there will be 75,000 users. Users are primarily located in the main building of the company, but other offices are located in other buildings elsewhere in the city. These offices have various resources that users in other locations will need to use. Which domain model will you use for the network?

A. Single domain

B. Single master domain

C. Multiple master domain

D. Complete trust

5. A network uses the multiple master domain model. This network has three master domains, and ten resource domains. How many trust relationships are used?

A. 36

B. 42

C. 13

D. 26

6. A network uses the complete trust model. It has five domains. How many trust relationships are used?

A. 45

B. 5

C. 20

D. 25

7. You want to install GSNW on a Windows NT 4.0 Server. This server is currently running TCP/IP as the only protocol. What will happen when you attempt to install GSNW?

    A. IPX/SPX will automatically be installed.

    B. NWLink will automatically be installed.

    C. Because current versions of NetWare use TCP/IP as the default protocol, GSNW will be able to run properly using the TCP/IP protocol that's currently installed.

    D. The installation will fail.

Configuring and Troubleshooting Account Policy

8. You have decided to set the account policies on your network, which is running Windows NT 4.0 servers. Which program will you use to set account policies?

    A. User Manager For Domains

    B. Password Manager

    C. Local Users And Groups In Computer Management

    D. System Policy Editor

9. Jennifer is a user on your network. A few months ago, you implemented account policies to control password usage on your Windows NT network. She calls you and says she logged on to the network and tried changing her password, but that it failed. The last time she changed her password, she had no problem. Why is she probably having difficulty now?

    A. Because her maximum password age has been exceeded.

    B. Because of conflicts involving password uniqueness.

    C. Her account has been deleted.

    D. Only administrators can change passwords.

10. You are setting account policy on the Windows NT 4.0 Server that acts as the PDC on your network. You want to set a minimum password length, so users are required to have a minimal number of characters in their password. What is the maximum number of characters you can specify for the minimal password length?

    A. 1

    B. 14

    C. 25

    D. 127

11. You have just taken over administration of a Windows NT 4.0 network, and have learned that users have never changed their passwords. For this reason, a number of employees know one another's passwords, and commonly use each other's accounts. You decide to force users to change their passwords once every 60 days. Which of the following will you set to force this change?

    A. Minimum password age

    B. Maximum password age

    C. Password uniqueness

    D. None. Windows NT automatically forces users to change their passwords once every 60 days.

12. After setting an account policy for passwords on a Windows NT 4.0 PDC, you find that users are changing their passwords, and then changing their passwords again so they can continue using their old password. This activity is making your previous account policy pointless, and causing a security vulnerability. What setting can you apply to prevent users from immediately changing a password back to their old password?

    A. Minimum Password Age

    B. Maximum Password Age

    C. Password Uniqueness

    D. None. There is no setting that prevents a user from immediately changing their password back to the old password.

13. You come across a user who is repeatedly entering his username and password to log on to the network. Upon asking, you find he has been trying to log on numerous times, because he forgot his password. You are concerned you may have incorrectly set account policy, because the user wasn't locked out after the numerous failed logons. Which of the following may be set incorrectly? (Choose all that apply.)

    A. The No Account Lockout option has been selected.

    B. The Lockout After…Bad Logon Attempts option has been set too low.

    C. The Lockout Duration has been set to Forever (Until Admin Unlocks).

    D. The Lockout After…Bad Logon Attempts option has been set too high.

Configuring and Troubleshooting System Policies

14. Which of the following tools will you use to create a system policy for clients running Windows 95 on a single domain NT 4.0 network? (Choose all that apply.)

    A.   User Manager For Domains

    B.   The System Policy Editor

    C.   EDIT.EXE

    D.   Poledit

15. You have created a user policy, and want to check whether the policy is actually being applied. To determine this, you decide to check Registry settings. Which of the following keys would you check under to confirm the policy has actually changed certain settings?

    A.   HKEY_CURRENT_USER

    B.   HKEY_USERS

    C.   HKEY_LOCAL_MACHINE

    D.   HKEY_SYSTEM_POLICY

16. Which of the following templates would you use to create a system policy for Windows 95 clients? (Choose all that apply.)

    A.   WINDOWS.ADM

    B.   WINNT.ADM

    C.   COMMON.ADM

    D.   WIN95.ADM

17. You have created a system policy that will be applied to all Windows NT clients on your network. To ensure that clients can download this file, and have the settings applied to their computer, what name will you give to this file, and where will you save it?

    A.   Save the file as Config.pol on the local machine.

    B.   Save the file as Config.pol on the Netlogon$ directory, which is located on the PDC.

    C.   Save the file as NTConfig.pol on the Logon$ directory, which is located on the PDC and all BDCs.

    D.   Save the file as NTConfig.pol on the Netlogon$ directory, which is located on the PDC.

18. Your network consists of two domains, with a complete trust relationship between them. You have created domain-wide policies for each of these domains. Julie is a user from DOMAIN1, and when she logs on to a computer in DOMAIN2, she experiences a number of problems. The first occurs when she logs on to the computer, and sees a message welcoming her to DOMAIN1. She knows the computer is part of DOMAIN2. What is causing these problems?

A. The system policy for DOMAIN1 is being used, because this user's account is in that domain.

B. The system policy for DOMAIN2 is being used, because this user's account is in that domain.

C. The system policy for DOMAIN2 is being merged with the system policy for DOMAIN1, and conflicts are being experienced.

D. The trust relationship is preventing this user from logging on to DOMAIN2.

19. Your network runs Windows NT 4.0 servers and workstations, and doesn't use domain-wide system policies. User and group policies are used. Joe is a new user, and isn't a member of any groups. Because he is new, you haven't created a user policy for him, but the computer he uses does have a policy associated with it. Based on this information, what policies will apply to him? (Choose all that apply.)

A. Computer policies for the computer being used

B. User policy

C. Group policy

D. Default computer policy

E. None of the above

20. You want to ensure all logon scripts run completely before the user's shell appears. To do this, you check the Default User section of a system policy, and find that the Run Logon Scripts Synchronously setting is enabled. When checking the Default Computer section, you find this same option is disabled there. What will happen when a user logs on and the Default User and Default Computer settings are applied to them?

A. The Default Computer setting will take precedence over the Default User setting.

B. The Default User setting will take precedence over the Default Computer setting.

C. The settings will merge and both will be applied.

D. The settings will conflict with one another, and neither will apply.

LAB QUESTION

You are planning a network for a mid-sized company with 10,000 users with each user having his or her own workstation. As a number of programs required by the company will only run on Windows NT 4.0 servers, you will not install Windows 2000 Server on any of the servers. Once the server software is available for Windows 2000 Server, you will later upgrade the network to Windows 2000. As most of the computers used in the company are already running Windows NT on their workstations, you will only install Windows 2000 Professional on new workstations.

Because departments in this company have different resources that are needed by users in other departments, you have decided to break the network into different domains. A minimum number of domains will be used for user accounts, while five departments will become resource domains. This will allow departments to control access to their resources. The five departments will be Sales, Finance, Advertising, Shipping, and Warehouse. Each of these will have their own server, containing applications and databases that other departments may have need to use.

1. Which is the best model to use for this network, and how many trust relationships will be required for it?

2. The Sales manager states that his sales representatives have occasional need to access an Accounting server application that will be located in the Finance department. How can users in the Sales department access the server application located in the Finance department?

3. You want to control bad logon attempts, and keep users from attempting to log on to the network repeatedly. When an account is locked out, you want users to contact you, so you can train them on properly logging on to the network, as well as monitor and deter hacking attempts. What setting will you enable?

4. You decide to create a policy that will apply to all members of each of the different departments. What type of system policy should you create?

5. You decide to create a policy that will apply to all members of the domain. Using the System Policy Editor, what mode will you use to create the policy?

6. You decide to create system policies that are specific to clients running on your network. What templates will you use with the System Policy Editor to create the policy?

SELF TEST ANSWERS

Configuring and Troubleshooting Trust Relationships

1. ☑ **C and D.** Domain B will be able to access resources in Domain C, and Domain A will be able to access resources in Domain B. This is because Domain A and Domain B have a trust relationship, and Domain B and Domain C have another trust relationship. In the first trust relationship, Domain B is the trusted domain, and Domain C is the trusting domain. In the second relationship, Domain A is the trusted domain, and Domain B is the trusting domain. This relationship allows users in Domain A to access resources in Domain B, and Domain B to access resources in Domain C.

   ☒ **A** is incorrect, because Windows NT trust relationships are nontransitive. Although Domain B trusts Domain A, and Domain C trusts Domain B, there is no trust relationship between Domain A and Domain C. **B** is incorrect, because Domain B is the trusted domain, and Domain C is the trusting domain. In this relationship, Domain B will be able to access the resources in Domain C, but not vice versa. This is because NT trust relationships are one-way.

2. ☑ **A.** A single domain model is being used here. With this model, user accounts and resources reside in a single domain. Because only one domain exists, no trust relationships are necessary.

   ☒ **B, C, and D** are incorrect, because each of these use trust relationships, with user accounts and resources residing in different domains.

3. ☑ **D.** Create a global group in the Master domain, and assign users from the Sales and Finance departments to it. The global group will be visible across the trust. Create a local group on the SQL Server, then assign permissions to this group so they can properly access the databases they need. Add the global group to the local group. Any additional users can then be added to the global group in the master domain, and changes to access can be controlled from the resource domain.

   ☒ **A, B, and C** are incorrect, because local groups aren't available across a trust relationship. Only global groups are visible across a trust. For this reason, it would be impossible to add the users to a local group and make it available across the trust.

4. ☑ **C.** Multiple master domain. This model uses two or more master domains containing user accounts, which are connected with two one-way trusts. Resource domains are used to store resources, and these are connected to the master domains with one-way trusts. This allows you to keep user accounts centralized and have a network that is highly scalable.

   ☒ **A and B** are incorrect, because the single domain model and single master domain model are limited to 40,000 user accounts. **D** is incorrect, because the complete trust model makes extensive use of trust relationships, and the question states that you want to keep the number of trusts to a minimum, and management of user accounts centralized.

5. ☑ **A. 36.** The network has three master domains and ten resource domains. Therefore, the formula $M\times(M-1)+(R\times M)$ becomes $3\times(3-1)+(10\times3)$. When breaking this down further, it becomes $3\times2+30$, which equals 36. Therefore, 36 trust relationships are used by this network.
   ☒ **B, C,** and **D** are incorrect, because a network with three master domains and ten resource domains requires 36 trust relationships.

6. ☑ **C. 20.** A network using the complete trust model uses two one-way trusts between each domain. Using the formula $n\times(n-1)$, this means that 5 domains would need $5\times(5-1)$ or 20 trust relationships. Therefore, 20 one-way trusts would need to be established for this network.
   ☒ **A, B,** and **D** are incorrect, because a network with 5 domains using the complete trust model would need 20 trust relationships.

7. ☑ **B.** NWLink will automatically be installed. Gateway Services for NetWare requires the NWLink protocol be running on the server on which GSNW is being installed. If NWLink isn't present, it will be auto-installed with GSNW.
   ☒ **A** is incorrect, because IPX/SPX isn't available for installation on a Windows NT 4.0 Server. NWLink is Microsoft's implementation of this protocol. It was developed by Microsoft to avoid paying royalties on IPX/SPX, and provides many of the same features as IPX/SPX. **C** is incorrect, because NWLink is required by GSNW. Although current versions of NetWare use TCP/IP as the default protocol, at the time Windows NT 4.0 was released, the default protocol for NetWare was IPX/SPX. Therefore, the Microsoft implementation of IPX/SPX is required. **D** is incorrect, because GSNW will auto-install NWLink if it isn't present during installation.

Configuring and Troubleshooting Account Policy

8. ☑ **A.** User Manager For Domains. To set account policies, you would use the User Manager for Domains tool. Once User Manager For Domains has started, open the Policies menu and click the Accounts item. This will display the Account Policy dialog box, where account policies are set.
   ☒ **B** is incorrect, because there is no tool in Windows NT called Password Manager. **C** is incorrect, because Local Users And Groups In Computer Management is used to set account policies on Windows 2000 machines. **D** is incorrect, because the System Policy Editor is used to set system policies, not account policies.

9. ☑ **B.** Because of conflicts involving password uniqueness. Based on the circumstances outlined in the scenario, this is the only setting in an account policy that would affect Jennifer's

ability to change her password. If password uniqueness is set, and a user attempts to invoke a previously used password, they will be unable to change their password.

☒   **A** is incorrect, because Maximum Password Age is a setting that determines how long a user can use a password before they must change it. **C** is incorrect, because the question states that the user logged on and attempted changing her password. If her account were deleted, she would have been unable to log on. **D** is incorrect, because (although administrators can change passwords), users are able to change their own passwords.

10. ☑   **B.** 14. The maximum number of characters you can set as the minimal password length is 14 characters. Windows NT passwords can be a maximum of 14 characters in length.

☒   **A** is incorrect, because (outside of allowing blank passwords), the minimum number of characters you can set for the minimal password length is 1 character. **C** is incorrect, because the maximum number of characters you can use in an NT password is 14 characters. **D** is incorrect, because this is the maximum number of characters that can be used on a Windows 2000 system.

11. ☑   **B.** Maximum password age. This setting determines the maximum amount of time a user's password can remain the same before it must be changed.

☒   **A** is incorrect, because the Minimum Password Age setting determines how long a user must keep a changed password before being able to change it again. **C** is incorrect, because Password Uniqueness prevents a user from using previously used passwords. **D** is incorrect, because Windows NT doesn't automatically force users to change passwords every 60 days.

12. ☑   **A.** Minimum Password Age. This setting allows you to set the minimum amount of time a user must keep a password before changing it. It keeps users from changing their password, and then immediately changing it back to the old password.

☒   **B** is incorrect, because the Maximum Password Age setting determines the maximum amount of time a user's password can remain the same before it must be changed. **C** is incorrect, because Password Uniqueness prevents a user from employing previously used passwords. **D** is incorrect, because the Minimum Password Age setting prevents users from immediately changing their passwords back to the previous password.

13. ☑   **A** and **D.** If the No Account Lockout option has been selected, then users will be able to attempt logging on indefinitely. If the Lockout After…Bad Logon Attempts has been set too high, then users will be able to attempt failed logons a considerable number of times.

☒   **B** is incorrect, because if the Lockout After…Bad Logon Attempts is set too low, then the user would have been locked out after a few logon attempts. **C** is incorrect, because the Forever (Until Admin Unlocks) in the Lockout Duration section will set accounts to be permanently locked out after failed logon attempts, until the administrator releases the account.

Configuring and Troubleshooting System Policies

14. ☑ **B and D.** The System Policy Editor and Poledit. System Policy Editor is a program that exposes Registry settings, allowing you to enable, disable, and set specific settings. It is an executable called POLEDIT.EXE, making each of these choices correct.
    ☒ **A** is incorrect, because User Manager For Domains is used to create system accounts and account policies. It is not used to create and modify system policies. **C** is incorrect, because EDIT.EXE is a text editor program that is DOS-based. It isn't used to create policies.

15. ☑ **A.** HKEY_CURRENT_USER. User policies allow you to control the environment of the user who is currently logged on. Changes to a user policy will modify the HKEY_CURRENT_USER subtree of the Registry.
    ☒ **B** is incorrect, because system policies do not affect the HKEY_USERS subtree of the Registry. **C** is incorrect, because HKEY_LOCAL_MACHINE is the key where computer policy settings are applied. User policy settings are not applied to this subtree. **D** is incorrect, because there are no keys in the Registry called HKEY_SYSTEM_POLICY.

16. ☑ **A and C.** WINDOWS.ADM and COMMON.ADM. WINDOWS.ADM contains settings specific to the Windows 9*x* Registry, while COMMON.ADM contains settings common to Windows NT and Windows 9*x* machines.
    ☒ **B** is incorrect, because WINNT.ADM is the template used to create system policies for clients running Windows NT. **D** is incorrect, because there is no template called WIN95.ADM that's installed with the System Policy Editor.

17. ☑ **D.** Save the file as NTConfig.pol on the Netlogon$ directory, which is located on the PDC. This is a shared directory on the PDC, and NT clients logging on to the PDC will look for this file in this directory. The Netlogon$ directory is the \System32\Repl\Import\Scripts folder in the root directory of Windows NT, on the boot partition of the Primary Domain Controller.
    ☒ **A and B** are incorrect, because Config.pol is the file used by Windows 95 clients to acquire domain-wide system policy settings. **C** is incorrect, because there is no Logon$ directory on PDCs and BDCs used to store the NTConfig.pol file.

18. ☑ **A.** The system policy for DOMAIN1 is being used, because this user's account is in that domain. In all cases, the system policy will be taken from the domain containing the user's account. This user's account is located in DOMAIN1, so the NTConfig.pol file located on the DOMAIN1 PDC is being used. It doesn't matter which domain the computer is in, only which domain the user account is located.

☒ **B** is incorrect, because the user is experiencing problems, which indicate that the system policy from DOMAIN1 is being applied. The indicator of this is that a banner message displays welcoming her to DOMAIN1 (where her user account resides). C is incorrect, because only one domain-wide system policy is applied. When the user logs on, the NTConfig.pol file will not be applied from each domain, only the one where the user account resides. D is incorrect, because the trust relationship wouldn't affect being able to access the domain in which the computer resides. Also, the complete trust appears to be functioning properly as it is allowing the user to access her account in DOMAIN1.

19. ☑ **A and C.** The default user policy will be used, as will the computer policy for the computer being used. Because there is no domain-wide policy, he doesn't have his own user policy, and he isn't a member of any groups, the default user policy is the only one that would apply to him. As the computer he is logging on to has a policy associated with it, this will also be used.

☒ **B** is incorrect, because the question states that this user doesn't have a user policy associated with him. D is incorrect, because the computer being used has a policy associated with it. E is incorrect, because there are policies that apply to this user and computer.

20. ☑ **A.** The Default Computer setting will take precedence over the Default User setting.

☒ **B, C,** and **D** are incorrect, because Run Logon Scripts Synchronously is set in the Default Computer, then that value takes precedence over what is set in the user section. One must take precedence over the other to avoid conflicts.

LAB ANSWER

1. A single master domain model should be used for this network. Because there are less than 40,000 users, multiple master domains aren't needed. Because control of user accounts isn't to be distributed, a complete trust model wouldn't apply here. As the question states that there will be five departments made into resource domains, this means a one-way trust would be established between each of these resource domains and the master domain. Therefore, only five trust relationships would be required.

2. In the master domain, create a global group containing the user accounts needing access to the server application. In the resource domain, create a local group with permissions to the server application. Add the global group to the local group.

3. Select the Forever (Until Admin Unlocks) option under the Lockout Duration section of the Account Policy dialog. This will prevent the system from releasing locked out accounts, and force users to contact you to have their locked out accounts released.

4. Group policy. Group policies apply settings to users who are members of specific groups.

5. You will need to use Policy File mode to save settings to a separate file. This will allow you to create an NTConfig.pol file that will be downloaded by users who log on. Once downloaded, these settings will be applied.

6. As clients are running Windows NT, you will need to create an NTConfig.pol file with the necessary templates. WINNT.ADM allows you to change settings specific to Windows NT, while COMMON.ADM contains settings common to both Windows NT and Windows 9x.

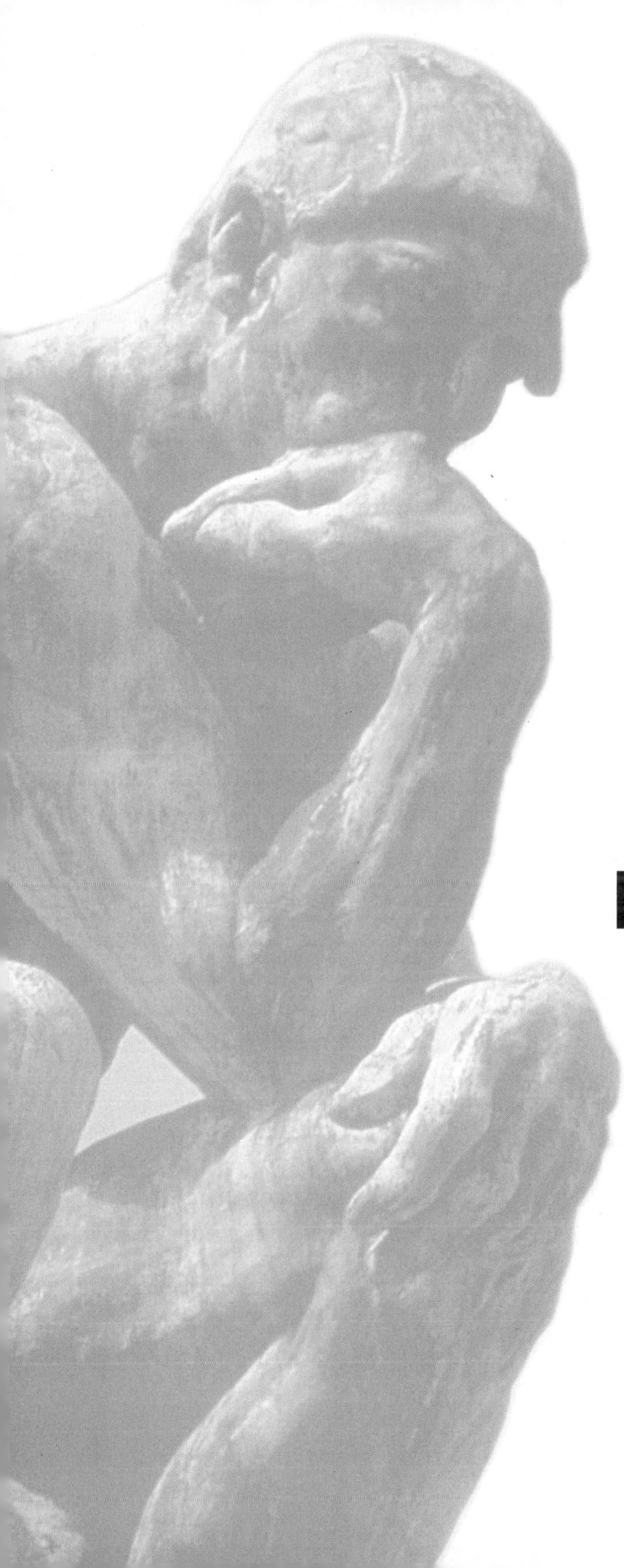

MCSE
MICROSOFT CERTIFIED SYSTEMS ENGINEER

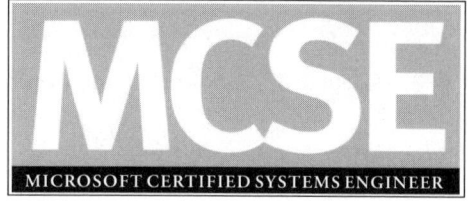

5

Configuring and Troubleshooting User Accounts, Profiles, and Logon Scripts

CERTIFICATION OBJECTIVES

5.01	Configuring and Troubleshooting User Accounts, Profiles, and Logon Scripts
5.02	Configuring and Troubleshooting Groups
✓	Two-Minute Drill
Q&A	Self Test

I n this chapter, we will learn how to efficiently set up user and group accounts, and manage the default desktop environment for your users. Planning and foresight are essential skills with this topic. To be certified you must know how to configure these components, but to be a good network administrator you must know when to use profiles and logon scripts and combine them to make both your job, and your users' jobs, easier.

We focus on creating user accounts and managing their desktop and resource access with profiles, logon scripts, and groups, but it will become evident that the most important and time-consuming portion of these topics lies in the planning stage. Effectively planned user accounts and user environments will provide happier users and administrators, because less time will be spent fixing configuration errors.

CERTIFICATION OBJECTIVE 5.01

Configuring and Troubleshooting User Accounts, Profiles, and Logon Scripts

Microsoft requires that you understand how to configure and troubleshoot user accounts, user profiles, and logon scripts. User accounts provide a way to manage network resources based on the person working. For example, User McKay logs on to the network and needs to access secure documents meant only for a select few. By having a user account, you have a means by which you can control the access permissions.

User Profiles are made up of the components you see on your screen when no application window is open. It is called the Desktop. There are usually shortcuts to commonly used applications, such as Internet Explorer, My Computer, and Network Neighborhood (called My Network Places in Windows 2000).

Logon scripts give an administrator the ability to customize user's desktops and shortcuts. They are designed to run every time a user logs on to the network. This gives you central administrative control. The following sections discuss these topics and their corresponding subtopics.

Creating and Renaming User Accounts

Windows NT requires users to log on with a valid username and password. NT compares the username and password entered with those in the user accounts database. If the names and passwords match, NT lets the user log on. This database, called a SAM (Security Accounts Manager), exists on every Windows NT box, be it a workstation, server, or domain controller. If the SAM is on a domain controller, then it uses NTDS (NT Directory Services) and is a centrally located and administered database.

On nondomain controllers (i.e., member servers and workstations), the SAM is still important because the permissions assigned to the local groups must be granted at that local computer. This relationship is described in the Groups section later in this chapter. It can be a bit bewildering and more than one student has found themselves confusing the local SAM with the Domain SAM, so be sure you know which is which. In the domain model, the accounts are called domain accounts, and users log on to the domain or PDC, while the local SAMs are used for their local groups only.

Creating a domain user account is a fairly simple task. You must use the appropriate tool by choosing Start | Programs | Administrative Tools | User Manager For Domains | Select New User and then filling in the blanks. Simple, right? Sort of. To fill in the actual information and fields does require a bit of planning first.

Figure 5-1 shows the New User dialog box. Table 5-1, on the other hand, describes the fields and buttons to choose from.

FIGURE 5-1

A blank New
User dialog box

TABLE 5-1	Field	Value
User Account Properties	Username	REQUIRED. Limit of 20 characters, both uppercase and lowercase letters and numbers (except " / \ [ ] : ; | = , + * ? < >). Is not case-sensitive. Each username must be unique within the domain.
	Full Name	OPTIONAL. Full name of user: Joe Willie Namath
	Description	OPTIONAL. Possibly put user's job title or physical location here.
	Password	OPTIONAL, depending on Account policy. Blank passwords are allowed by default, but not recommended. Up to 14 characters and case-sensitive. This field displays asterisks for security. Once Add or OK is selected after typing in a password, the field will display 14 asterisks, again for security reasons.
	Confirm Password	Retype password here to avoid a typo in your password. This field, of course, also displays asterisks.
	User Must Change Password At Next Logon	Selecting this check box forces the user to change his password the next time he logs on. Be careful not to use this field in conjunction with User Cannot Change Password, since the user would be unable to change the password as required.
	User Cannot Change Password	This check box field makes it impossible for a user to change their password. Use this if you have a scenario where an account is shared, like the Guest account, or for a kiosk type user account.
	Password Never Expires	Checking this box will override both the Account Policy setting and the User Must Change Password At Next Logon. Normally this option is used by applications that require a user account. You wouldn't want the password to expire every 90 days and cause your backup program to fail, right?
	Account Disabled	Prevents users from logging on to the network. Useful for temporarily taking an account out of service.
	Account Locked Out	Grayed out unless the Account policy Lockout threshold of failed logons is reached. Clear this to restore the account for use again.

	Field	Value
TABLE 5-1 User Account Properties *(continued)*	Groups button	Assigns group membership.
	Profile button	Define roaming profile, logon scripts and home directory paths
	Hours button	Specify what hours a user can log on to the network. Default is 24x7.
	Logon To button	Configure which computers a user is allowed to log on to the network from. Default is any computer.
	Account button	Specify an expiration date and account type. Default is never expire and global account.
	Dialin button	Configure dial-in permissions and call-back settings. Default is no dial-in allowed.

As mentioned before, the tasks to create a user are simple, but naming these accounts is only simple if you have a naming convention to follow. A naming convention is a plan that outlines how users will be identified on the network and includes rules to follow when duplicate names occur. Many popular naming conventions follow one of the following formulas:

- First Initial + Last Name: JNamath
- First Name + First Initial of Last Name: JoeN

Sometimes companies like to avoid long usernames and thus will specify a maximum number of characters like 8, which would shorten a name from, FTarkenton to FTarkant. It is more important to have a convention than what that convention is. However, take into account the number of users you will create and the possible duplicates that could occur. For example, how many users named JoeN might there be compared to the less likely JNamath? I personally like the First Initial Last + Name convention for that reason.

When a duplicate name does occur, what will you do? Again, it is more important to have a rule than what that rule necessarily is. A suggestion might be to add a number at the end of a name such as JNamath1, or to use the middle initial of the user such as JWNamath.

FROM THE CLASSROOM

Troubleshooting

When troubleshooting, it is important to know for sure what username you are logged on as. You can verify who you are logged on as (on the domain or computer) by pressing CTRL-ALT-DEL. This opens the Windows NT Security dialog box. The first section is labeled Logon Information. There is a line that reads, "You are logged on as DOMAIN\Username." This indicates who you are logged on as.

Note that when working with users, don't ask, "Who are you logged on as?" Instead ask, "Press CTRL-ALT-DEL and read to me what it says after, 'You are logged on as'." I have solved many support calls by asking that rather than assuming that the user knows.

—M. Troy Hudson MCSE, MCT, MCP+I, Master CNE, Master CNI

EXERCISE 5-1

CertCam 5-1

Creating a User Account

In this exercise, you learn how to create a user.

1. Verify you are logged on to your domain as Administrator. Press CTRL-ALT-DEL and you should see the Windows NT Security dialog box. The first section is labeled, Logon Information. There is a line that reads, "You are logged on as DOMAIN\Username." This is who you are to the network.

2. Open User Manager For Domains.

3. Click the User menu and select New User…

4. Type in your First Initial+Last Name with no spaces.

5. Type in the word **password** in the Password field, press TAB and type in **password** again. Click the Add button.

6. Notice that the fields are cleared and you are ready to add another user. Click the Close button.

7. Verify that you can see your new user. Close User Manager For Domains.

8. Log off as the administrator and log back on as your new user.

9. Did you have to change your password? Why or why not?

CertCam 5-2

EXERCISE 5-2

Testing User Accounts from a Domain Controller

Do this exercise if you are working from a domain controller but need to test your user accounts. If this is the case right now, and you attempted Exercise 5-1, you probably got an error message that the local policy does not allow you to log on. This is because the default setting for domain controllers is to deny "normal" or non-administrator users to log on at the domain controller. Follow these steps to modify this. (Note that this is only for your personal lab, do not do this in a real-world production environment.)

1. Verify that you are logged on as Administrator. (CTRL-ALT-DEL... remember?)

2. Open User Manager For Domains (as seen in Figure 5-2).

3. Click the Policies menu and select User Rights. This opens the User Rights Policy dialog box.

4. From the drop-down menu, scroll down and select Log on locally.

5. Click the Add button and choose the local group, Users.

6. Click the OK button and close User Manager For Domains.

You should now be able to log on as any valid domain user from the domain controller.

Template Accounts

Template accounts are used when you have a user environment that requires many usernames with similar user properties. For example, a technical support department typically has high turnover and new users are quite common. The new users require

FIGURE 5-2

User Manager
For Domains

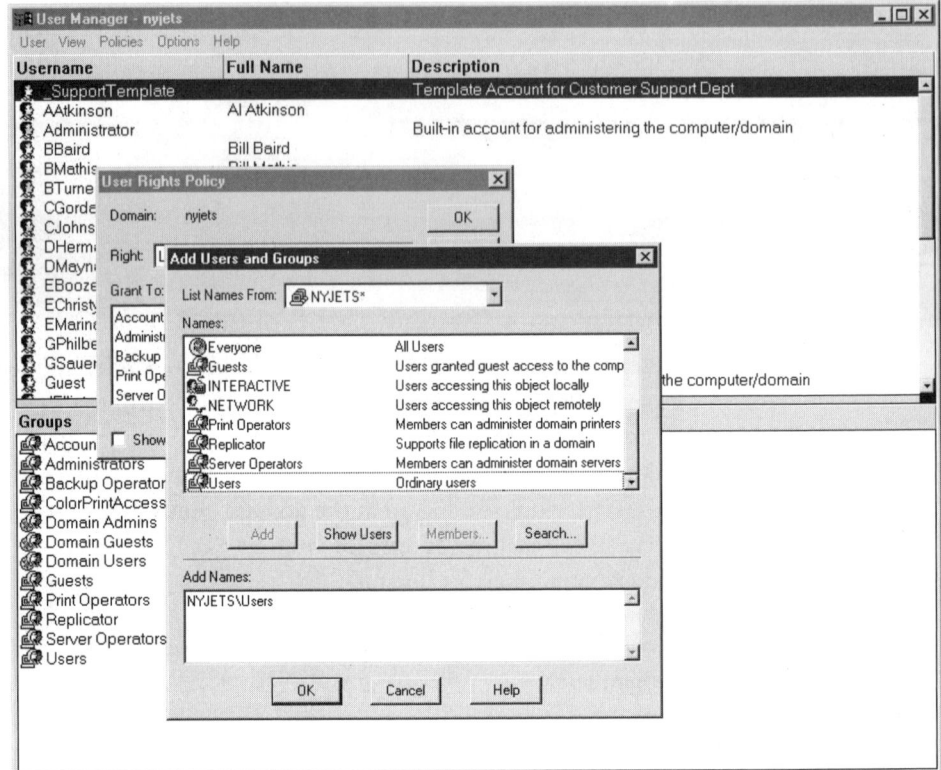

access to all the same resources, such as the client database and support data. You could create a template that has all the appropriate groups, logon hours, and dial-in permissions, save it as a template-user account, and name it _SupportTemplate. Create template accounts for all of your departments where there are common "default" user settings. Obviously a user account, like the manager of Support, would not need a template, because that user is not typical and requires more access than the employees she manages.

To create a new user from a template, select the _SupportTemplate, Click User menu, and select Copy. A new user account is created containing all the settings of the template user except the Username, Password, and Account Disabled. You should disable template accounts to ensure there are no unnecessary accounts for malicious crackers to exploit.

on the job *Name your template accounts with an underscore to group them together at the top of the user list in User Manager For Domains.*

Deleting Versus Renaming Accounts

User accounts are seen and accessed by users according to the friendly name we assign them; however, Windows NT authentication actually occurs at the SID (security identifier) level. Each new user account is assigned a unique SID to ensure the security and integrity of the directory services. A SID looks like this:

S-1-5-21-299502267-813497703-839522115-500

The username is simply a property of the SID. The SID is the "true" identity of the users on an NT network.

The implication of this newfound knowledge is that there is a huge difference between deleting a user account and renaming it. Deleting an account deletes the SID, rendering the account unrecoverable. Renaming an account retains the SID and simply changes the friendly username property of the SID.

This means you could have a user named SFergusan who is the manager of technical support and has certain permissions defined. She leaves the company and is replaced by DWales. Instead of deleting SFergusan, you could rename the account to DWales and all the previously defined permissions remain intact for the new manager in one "gesture"! Once a user account is deleted, you cannot just re-create it with the same name, because a new SID is generated. For this reason, it is recommended you disable user accounts instead of deleting them.

on the job *Rename accounts that have been disabled with a zUserName to group them at the bottom of the user list.*

Configuring and Troubleshooting User Profiles

User profiles are generally seen as the items on your desktop called shortcuts. This is only a piece of the actual profile, which is a combination of folders and registry settings. Table 5-2 lists the folders in a Windows NT profile and describes what is in each folder. Please note that there is no need to memorize these for a test. This is simply here for reference.

TABLE 5-2	Profile Folder	What Is in the Folder
Profile Folder Organization	Application Data	Application-specific data for some Windows applications, such as user preferences for Microsoft Word.
	Desktop	Nonsystem icons defined on the user's desktop, including shortcuts.
	Favorites	Shortcuts to favorite programs and locations, such as Favorites defined in Internet Explorer (used by some applications).
	NetHood	Shortcuts defined in the user's Network Neighborhood.
	Personal	Shortcuts to personal program items (used by some applications).
	PrintHood	Shortcuts defined in the user's Printers folder.
	Recent	Shortcuts to documents that have been accessed most recently. These are what show up under Start	Documents.
	SendTo	Destinations available in the Send To option appearing in the context menus for files; entries are defined by some applications.
	Start Menu	Entries in the user's personal areas of the Start Menu.
	Templates	Shortcuts to templates for some applications.

Local User Profiles

The first time a user logs on to a computer, the default profile is copied onto the hard drive and a hive is created in the Registry using the user's SID to name and track the profile. This copy is now "owned" by that user and any changes to the desktop are saved there. This allows multiple users to use the same computer yet maintain personal desktops with custom shortcuts and backgrounds.

A profile consists of a file called NTUSER.DAT, which is a Registry hive, and several folders. In Windows NT, these are stored in %systemroot%\profiles\<username> folders, as in Figure 5-3. In Windows 2000 Professional, the profiles are stored in the boot partition under \documents and settings\<username> folders (as seen in Figure 5-4).

on the job

Windows 2000 has added the now popular My Documents folder on a user's desktop, and the contents are included in the user's profile. This can make a profile very large, so be sure to plan appropriately for this. Alternatively, you may want to redirect the location of My Documents to the user's home directory to make sure their files are backed up and secure on the network, and eliminate large profiles.

FIGURE 5-3

Profile files and
folders in
Windows N

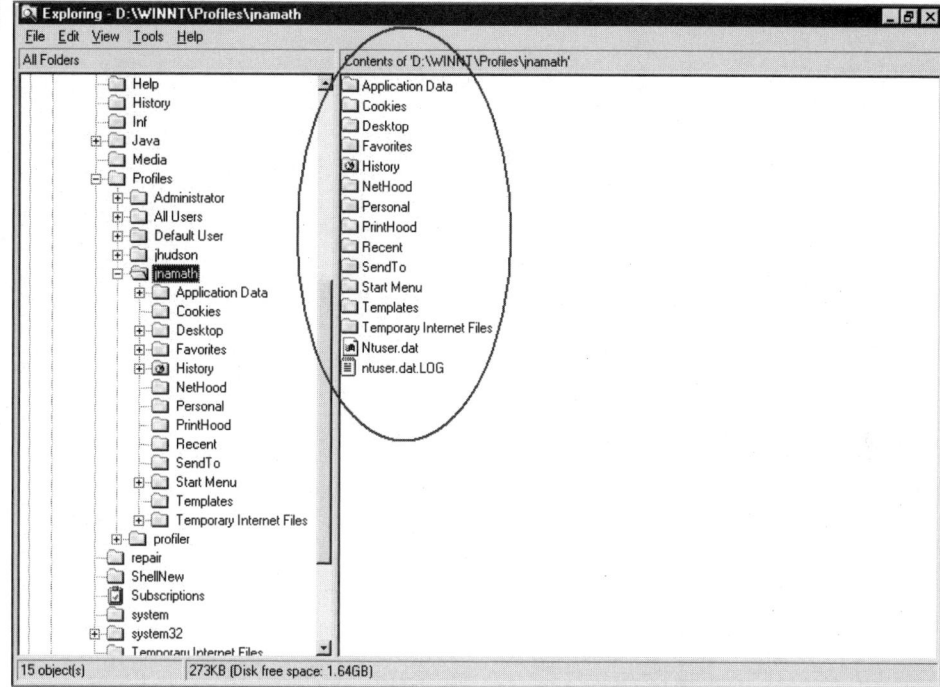

FIGURE 5-3

Profile files and folders in Windows N

Roaming User Profiles

Since the profile is created on the local machine—if a user goes to a different computer—the process just described starts all over again and our poor user must re-create their custom desktop again. This problem is addressed through roaming profiles.

A roaming profile is simply a profile from the local computer copied to a server and then accessed remotely from whatever computer our user logs on. To create this, you must first specify that the user account look for the profile somewhere else. This is accomplished in the properties of the user account in User Manager For Domains. Select the user account and choose File | Properties. This opens the dialog User Properties. Click the button on the bottom, titled Profile. Type in the UNC (Universal Naming Convention) path to your server that will host the roaming profiles. Figure 5-5 shows the screen that displays this. Notice that the environment variable %username% is used here. You must manually create the folders and permissions for each user to store their profile.

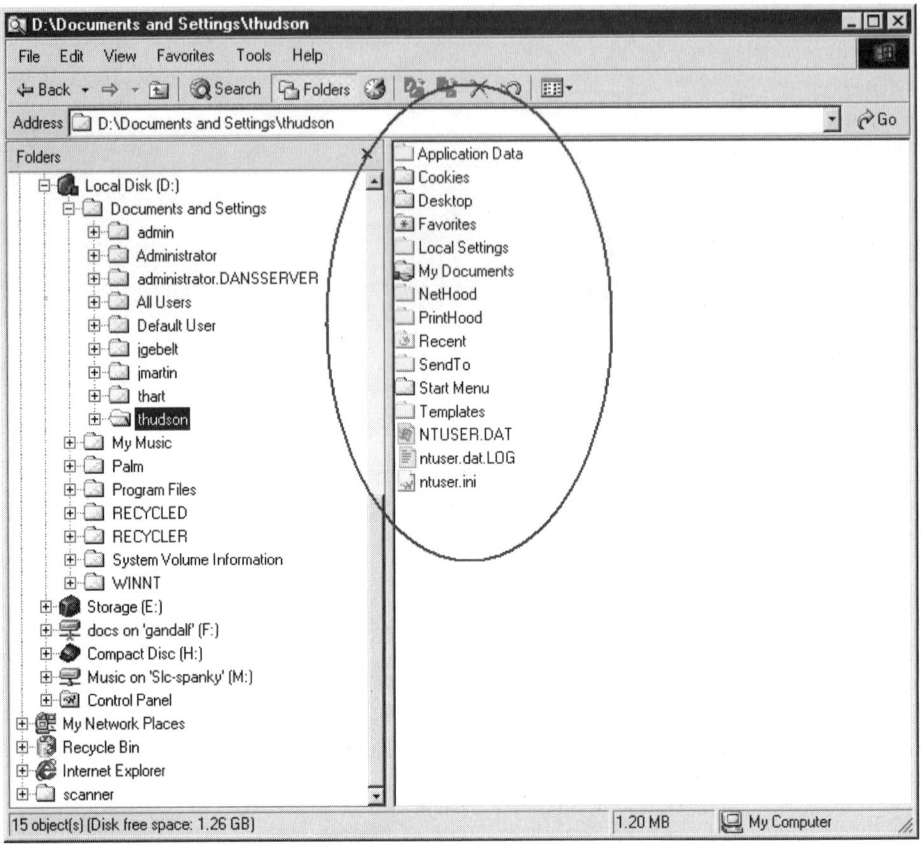

FIGURE 5-4

Profiles files and
folders in
Windows 2000

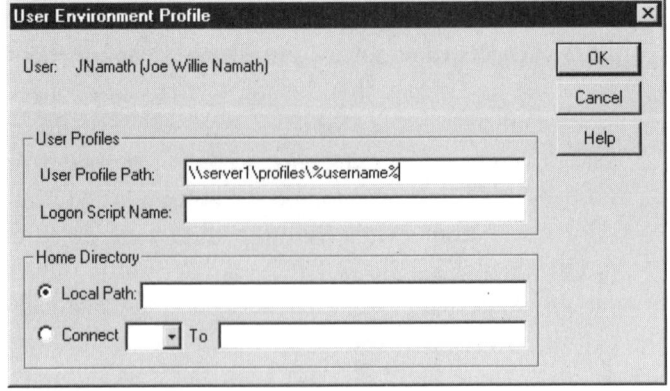

FIGURE 5-5

User Profile Path
using the
%username%
environment
variable

FROM THE CLASSROOM

Teaching Windows Networking

When teaching Windows networking, the %username% is taught as an efficient tool to ease administration. %username% is "an environment variable that expands to become the user account ID for the current logged on user. This identifies the user account in Windows NT (Microsoft Knowledge Base: Article ID: Q161334). Not only does it replace the variable with an account ID, but in some cases it will create the directory and apply permissions as well. Use this variable whenever you can. Two examples follow:

1. Let's say you have 100 user accounts already and now want to implement roaming profiles. As explained in this chapter you must specify all the individual directory locations for each user account. This proves to be quite tedious. The %username% solution is to select all the accounts in User Manager for Domains that you need to change. Select File | Properties | Select the Profile button. Now type in the User Profile Path using the %username% variable as shown in Figure 5-6. This will populate all 100 accounts that you selected with the appropriate path including the individual username folders.

2. The %username% is especially beneficial when used to specify home directories. In the same Profile tab in the user account properties there is the lower section entitled Home Directory. Choose the Connect radio button and type in the path to your Home Directory server, which typically hosts both the home directories and profiles. Use the %username% variable here as well. If the shared Users folder resides on an NTFS partition, the system will not only create the subfolder for each user, but will also apply specific permissions to each user, removing the default permissions of Everyone with Full Control.

This is the way we teach administrators to use the variable, which makes their jobs easier and more efficient.

—*M. Troy Hudson, MCSE, MCT, MCP+I, Master CNE, Master CNI*

If you are dealing with many users, I suggest you create one generic profile and place the same one in each user's directory, then let the users make changes themselves. The goal is not security or administration here, but merely a way for users to log on from any computer and retain their desktop.

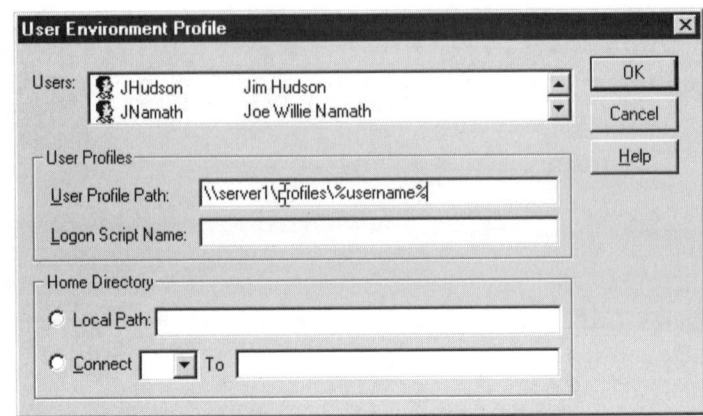

Create a generic profile by setting up a desktop environment for a user. Log on to a computer as a "test" user and define the backgrounds and shortcuts the user needs. Next, copy the user profile to a shared folder on a file server. The best way to copy the profile is to use the Copy To feature in Windows NT or Windows 2000 Professional (as shown in Figure 5-7).

This is the same in Windows 2000 as it is in Windows NT.

Access the System Properties by right-clicking My Computer and selecting properties. Click the User Profiles tab, select the profile you want to copy, click Copy To, and type in, or browse to, the server, profiles share, and user's folder. Since this is automatically assigned to your test user, you will need to assign permissions to a group the user belongs to. Going with my earlier suggestion to create one generic default profile, you should assign this to the Everyone group so all users can access it initially.

The Copy To feature will copy the ntuser.dat file as well as all folders and subfolders within the profile, ensuring that all the pertinent files and folders are copied. You can do this for each user, or once the files and folders have been copied, manually copy them to each user's profile folder, which gives them their default profile.

The ntuser.dat file is a Registry hive and can be edited in the Registry editor. (See Microsoft Knowledge Base Article 146050 for details.)

FIGURE 5-7

The Copy To dialog box for copying a user profile to the network

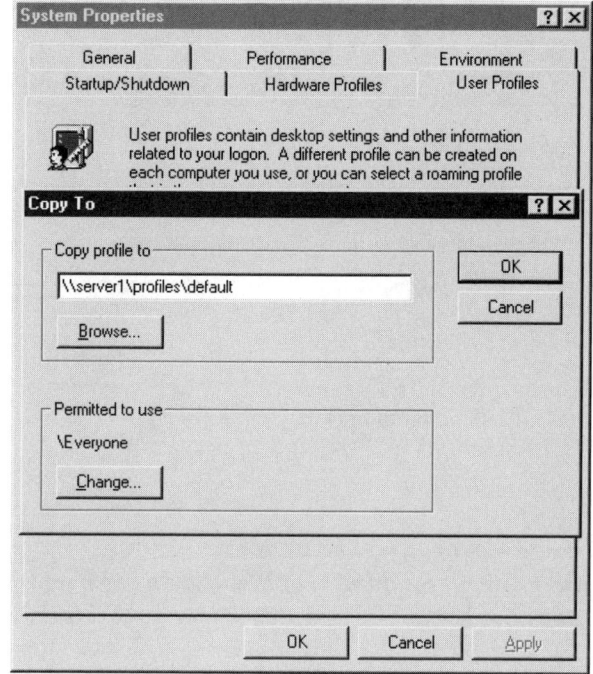

Mandatory User Profiles

Roaming profiles are changeable by the user, and only one user can be assigned to one profile. Mandatory profiles are not changeable and can be assigned to many users. What are they for? With mandatory profiles we are concerned with security *and* a consistent user desktop. One that will be the same at every workstation for every user. A real-world example is a bank teller. Each person may work at a different workstation, but the settings and shortcuts would always be the same.

To configure a mandatory profile, you follow a plan similar to that used with roaming profiles. Create the default profile with the test profile account; copy the profile as before to a server share. Be sure to assign the Everyone group permissions. Now simply rename the ntuser.dat file to ntuser.man. It is that simple! Of course, you must still assign the user accounts to this mandatory profile. Select all the users and go into the properties dialog box, then choose the Profile button. Type in the UNC path to the server and share name. Do NOT use %username% in this case, since all users are using the same profile. Instead point all users to the same folder. Users will be able to make changes while logged on, but those changes will not be saved when the user logs off. They will have the original profile you created again the next time they log on.

SCENARIO & SOLUTION

A user is assigned to one computer which no one else uses.	Do nothing. Allow the default local profile to be copied and then used by the user.
Four users share one computer at different times of the day and do not log on from any other computer.	Do nothing. Allow the default local profile to be copied and then used by each user.
Users work at a front desk but can be assigned different workstations at any time. They need all the same shortcuts and access to network resources.	Use mandatory profiles to fill this need.
Users log on from many different workstations and need custom desktops to suit each individual.	Use roaming user profiles and let each user modify the profile as they see fit.

exam
ⓌatcH

Users dialing in will be unhappy with the delayed performance at logon, if they have a roaming profile assigned to them. Remember that the profile is downloaded to the client at logon, so disable this feature for remote users.

Configuring and Troubleshooting User Accounts

Once user accounts are created, they must be maintained. What should you do when a user leaves the company? Delete the account? What are the consequences of doing that? Can you restrict the user from logging on based on time of day? Location? Or anything else? The answers are all right ahead of you… Read on!

Disabled User Accounts

Disabled user accounts are user accounts that were once valid for logging on to the network, but have now been invalidated or "put on hold." A disabled user account will be rejected logon privileges if used by someone to log on.

Why is this done? Earlier in the chapter, template accounts were mentioned, and it is suggested that these types of accounts should be disabled. That is one reason. Another reason (also mentioned earlier) is that it is better to disable an account instead of (or at least before) deleting a user account.

exam
ⓌatcH

Remember! Deleting a user account is permanent, so instead, always disable accounts no longer in use.

To disable or reenable a user account, simply check or uncheck the Account Disabled box in user properties (shown in Figure 5-8).

Logon Restrictions

Logon restrictions are ways to control when, where, and how, users log on to your network domain. These settings are located in the user account properties. There are three buttons for this.

The Account Button Clicking the Account button opens the dialog box in Figure 5-9. There are two settings here: Account Expires and Account Type.

The Account Type is set to Global Account by default and is used most of the time. A global account is what we have talked about and primarily used. It is assigned within a domain and can be given to global groups. Global accounts can be assigned to other local groups in different domains with trusts properly configured.

The Local Account has a limited scope and appears only on the computers it was created on. Since domain controllers replicate their SAM, it will appear on all domain controllers. A local user account does not support interactive logon (also called logging on locally). This account type is rarely used, except in cases where access from a non-Windows NT network is required. Local user accounts enable

FIGURE 5-8

The User Account Disabled check box

FIGURE 5-9

The Account
Information
dialog box in user
properties

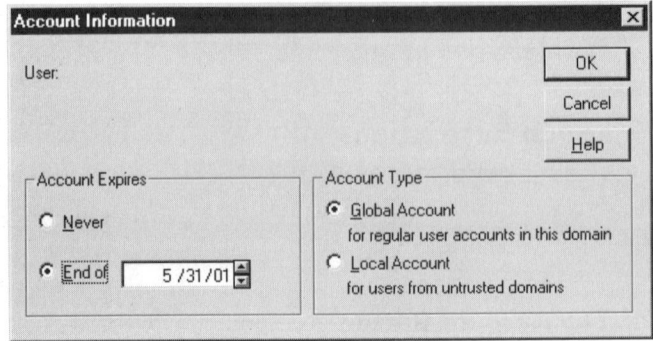

users from LAN Manager, IBM LAN Server, or NetWare environments to participate in Windows NT server domains.

Account Expires is set to never by default, but can be useful for scenarios in which you have a temporary worker such as an intern at your company. Since you know the date that the employee will leave, you can adjust this setting to that day so that without administrative interference the account expires and is no longer valid. The effect is the same as placing an account on hold by disabling it. Should it be required, you can go back into this dialog box and extend the expiration time or set it to never, where all rights and permissions are retained.

The Hours Button   When you select this, the Hours dialog opens. Here you can specify what time and what days a user is allowed to log on to the network. The default is to access the network 24 hours a day, seven days a week. You may wish to increase security by restricting logon times to scheduled work hours. Figure 5-10 shows the logon hours available Monday through Friday, 6:00 A.M. to 6:00 P.M.

on the !job

Use the Hours restriction cautiously. If security requires it, then ok; however, think about whom a user or manager will call on Saturday morning at 7:00 A.M. when they can't get access and legitimately needs it? In case you're unsure...the call would come to you. Remember that both security and the necessity of users getting the job done must be balanced and carefully planned!

The Logon To Button   The next restriction is the Logon To button. The default is that any user can log on from any computer—no restrictions. With the Logon To option, you can specify which computers a user is allowed to log on to the

The Logon Hours dialog box in user properties

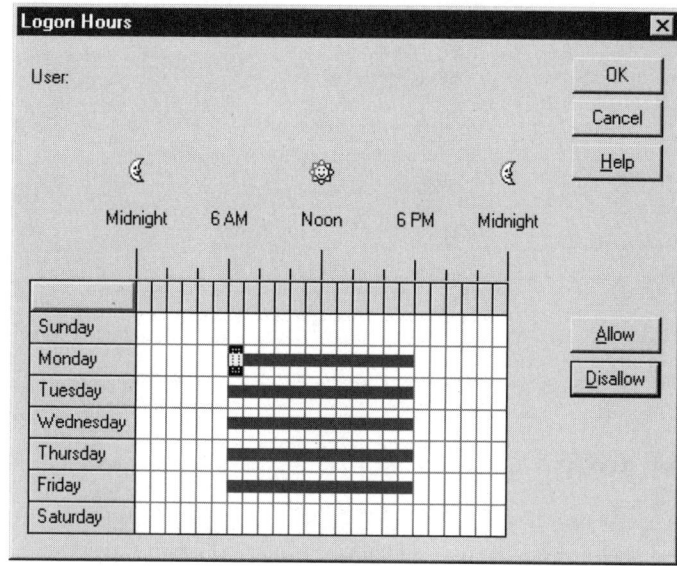

network from. Up to eight workstations can be specified. For example, you work for a manufacturing company and have four computers on the manufacturing floor used by many different employees. Since these are the only computers they should ever use, make sure to restrict their accounts so they can log on only from those computers. Now, if a user tries to log on using, say, one of the administrative employees' computers, they won't be able to. Figure 5-11 shows the dialog box with a restriction of two computers. The computer's names are WORKSTATION1 and WORKSTATION2.

Dial-in Permissions

The Dialin button opens a dialog box, shown in Figure 5-12, where you can specify two options about a user's ability to dial in to the network from a remote location. The default is to disallow users to dial in. Select Allow and you get more options regarding the user dialing in.

Call-back settings allow the Remote Access Server to call the user back after they have been authenticated. There are two reasons for this: first, the long distance bill gets charged to the RAS phone number and thus the company; and second, for security reasons, you can set the call-back number to dial the user back at their house, or some other predetermined location, only. This restricts the user to dialing in from that location, and nowhere else.

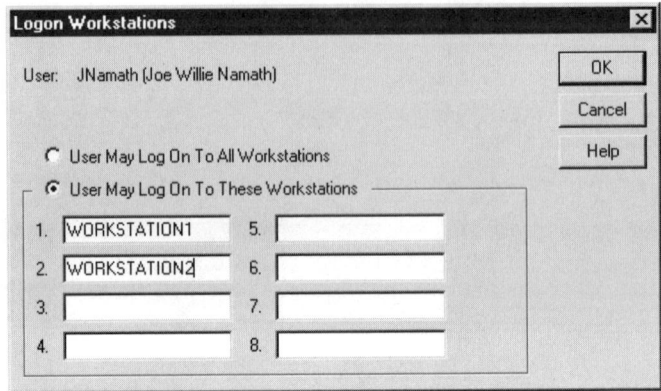

FIGURE 5-11

The Logon To
dialog box in user
properties

Troubleshooting Logon Scripts

As the network administrator, it is your job to make sure users are connected to the data they need to get their job done. Logon scripts will provide this, thereby making the life of a user much easier. The logon script actually executes on the client workstation and is in the form of a batch program, such as .bat or .cmd, or even an executable program with .exe. With logon scripts, you can create an "ignorant" environment. The user does not have to know the name of a file server or share, they just know that drive U: is their home directory and drive S: is where they save company files. After all, users don't care how things are done, as long as the system works. When it comes to the technical details, they prefer to be ignorant.

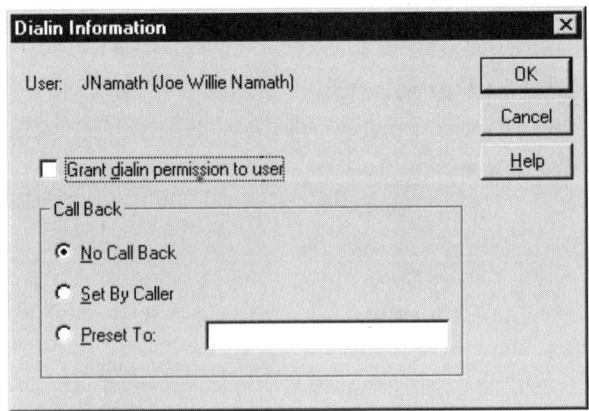

FIGURE 5-12

The Dialin
Information
dialog box in user
properties

SCENARIO & SOLUTION

I need to create drive mappings for my users in a logon script.	Automatic drive mappings are set with the NET USE command.
I need to add directories to the user's PATH statement.	Environment variables can be defined with a logon script, including the PATH variable.
I want all my computers to be on at the same time and updated with each logon.	The NET TIME command will set a computer's logon time and can be placed in a logon script.

To troubleshoot logon scripts, you need to know a few things about how the scripts are created, replicated, and processed. Three conditions must be met to implement logon scripts. First, you must have a domain environment. Logon scripts will not work properly in a workgroup. Second, the script must be in the NETLOGON share of whatever domain controller authenticated the user. And third, the logon script must be specified in the user account's properties.

Script Location

Windows clients automatically look for the logon scripts during logon authentication, and will download the script from the same server that authenticated them. In a domain, a client searches for a logon server, which is either a PDC (Primary Domain Controller) or a BDC (Backup Domain Controller). Whichever server responds first will authenticate the user. The Microsoft redirector on the client will determine if there is a logon script, and, if so, download and process it by looking on the logon server's NETLOGON share. The actual path is %systemroot%\system32\Repl\ Import\Scripts, and it is automatically created and shared on every Windows NT Server (as seen in Figure 5-13).

on the
Job *Windows clients that support logon scripts include Windows 2000, Windows NT (Server and Workstation), Windows 9x, Windows for Workgroups, and MS-DOS. Notice that Macintosh and Unix clients do not use these logon scripts.*

exam
Watch *If you plan to use multiple logon scripts and you begin to see erratic errors or conflicts occurring, you may need to enable the logon scripts to run synchronously instead of the default asynchronous way. This is a Registry change and can be applied to either a computer or a user.*

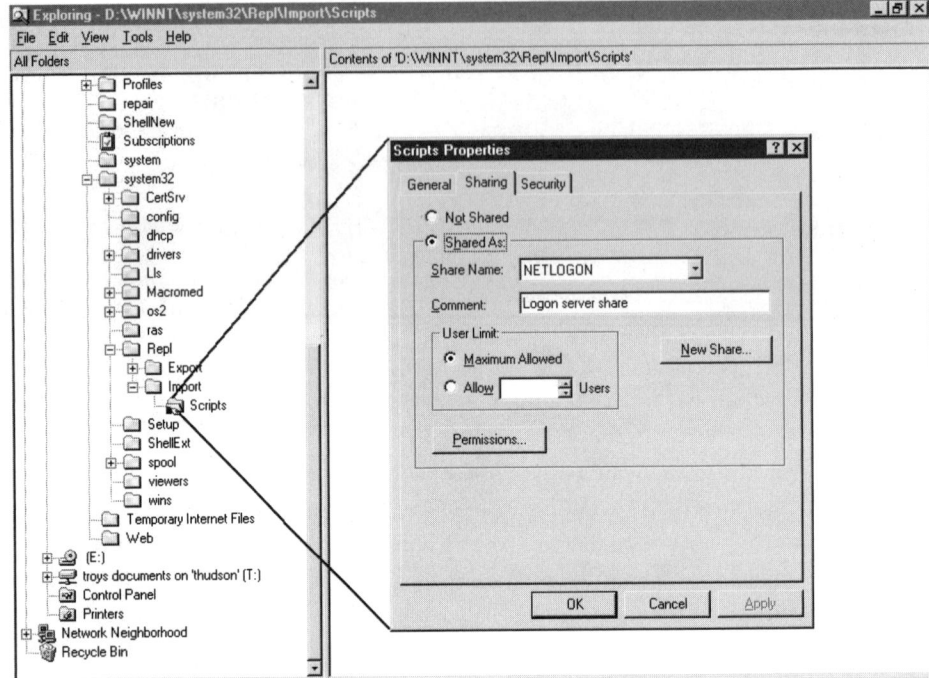

FIGURE 5-13

The NETLOGON Share actual location and folder properties

User Account Configuration

The user account needs to know that it should look for a logon script. You tell the client to do this by specifying the logon script name in the user account properties in User Manager For Domains. Remember that the Profile button is where logon scripts are configured. Type in the name of the logon script this user account will use (see Figure 5-14).

Replication of the NETLOGON Shared Folder

As mentioned previously, the logon script is downloaded to the client from the domain controller that authenticated the user account. The logon script, therefore, must reside on every domain controller and be kept current. To do this manually would prove tedious and prone to errors, so luckily there is a solution. It is called Directory Replication.

The Logon Script
Name in the
Profile dialog box
in user properties

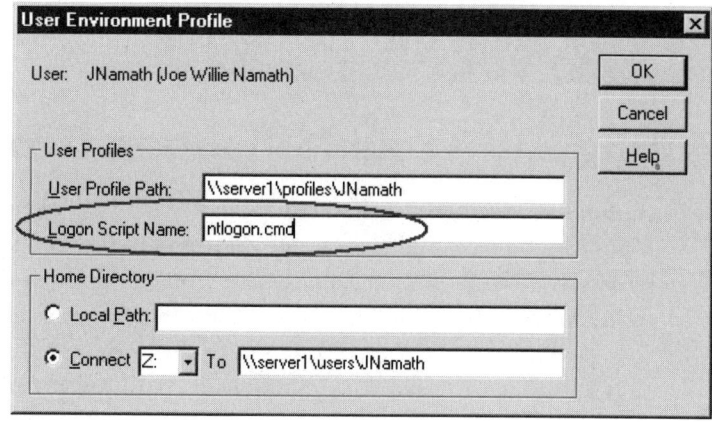

The default is for any subfolder under the %systemroot%\system32\repl\export folder to be replicated to another server's %systemroot%\system32\repl\import. Please note that the import folder is the same location as the subfolder "scripts" shared as NETLOGON. What a sweet coincidence! And one we must surely take advantage of! In both cases, there is a subfolder called Scripts, and it is here that you should put your logon scripts. Specifically, put them in the PDC's %systemroot%\system32\repl\export\scripts folder, then make all your BDCs import servers and your PDC the export server. This will ensure all the logon scripts are the same in every domain controller.

In Windows 2000, sysvol replaces the Netlogon share that was just mentioned. In the Windows 2000 world of replication anything placed in this volume is replicated to all other domain controllers, so this is the folder where you should place your logon scripts. When you do upgrade your Windows NT domain controllers to Windows 2000, you need to import the files and folders from the %systemroot%\system32\repl\import to %systemroot%\system32\sysvol.

When using logon scripts, the logon process will take a little longer, because the script must be downloaded to the workstation. If users are authenticating across a WAN link this can become even worse, so you should make sure a BDC is at each geographic location and that directory replication is in place.

CERTIFICATION OBJECTIVE 5.02

Configuring and Troubleshooting Groups

Groups allow you to use less administrative effort to control access to resources. Suppose you have 120 users in the information services department who all need access to the same printers and folders. You could assign the appropriate permissions to each user account individually… 120 times… Yikes! Or you can assign all 120 users to a single group and assign the permissions once.

Groups make Access Control Lists (ACLs) simpler. An ACL is simply the list of users or groups and their permissions that are a property of any given resource. In the previous example, there would be 120 Access Control Entries (ACEs) in the printer's properties which is much more complex and harder to understand and follow. One ACE in the printer's ACL is much simpler. The system itself also becomes more efficient by decreasing the size of an ACL (as shown in Figure 5-15).

Groups also make management of users simpler. Combining users based on their function and location makes life easier for an administrator. Suppose a new user has just been hired in the accounting department. Being the savvy and efficient administrator you are, you simply copy the _AccountingTemplate you previously created, employing it to create the user, and voilà!, the user is now a member of the appropriate groups, thereby granted access to his required resources.

FIGURE 5-15

The Printer Permissions dialog box showing ACEs and ACLs

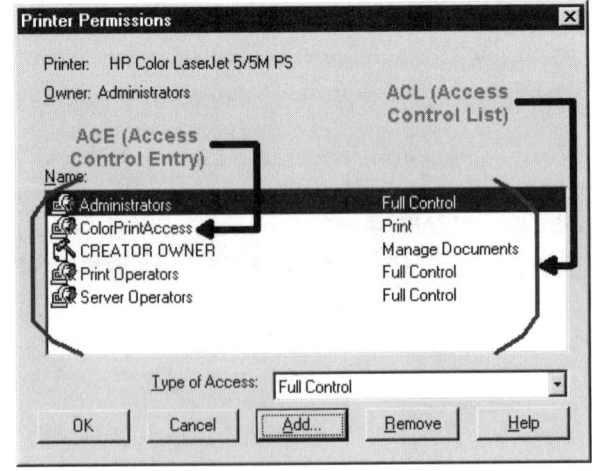

Group Membership

Groups are very important for administration, and Microsoft has recommended a method for group implementation called AGLP. AGLP stands for <u>A</u>ccounts (users) are placed into <u>G</u>lobal Groups, which are placed in <u>L</u>ocal groups to which <u>P</u>ermissions are assigned. This is a pattern that appears tedious and drawn out, but in the end makes life as the administrator easier.

Consider this scenario. You have a color printer for your marketing department and need to keep a tight rein on the users allowed to print to it. The steps to set this up using AGLP are as follows:

1. Create a local group on the print server called ColorPrintAccess.

2. Assign the Print permission to the ColorPrintAccess local group. Be sure to remove the Everyone group that is there by default. (See Figure 5-15.)

3. Place the global group Marketing in the local group ColorPrintAccess.

4. Place the users from the marketing department in the global group Marketing.

As you know, users or groups within a group inherit the permissions assigned to that group. Once this relationship is established, you only need to determine who should be in the Marketing global group. Removing a user from the Marketing group removes the permission to print to the color printer. Placing a user in the Marketing group grants permission to the color printer.

e x a m
🅦 a t c h

The Windows 2000 curriculum teaches the same method, but uses a different acronym. UGLR, pronounced "uglier", is defined as <u>U</u>ser accounts which are placed in <u>G</u>lobal groups, which are placed in <u>L</u>ocal groups, which are then assigned permissions to <u>R</u>esources. Why they chose to use a new acronym is a mystery, but you must be aware of it. The methodology is still the same.

Default Groups

Microsoft has created some built-in or default groups to aid in minimizing administration and delegating privileges. The terms "built-in" and "default" seem to be used interchangeably in many books—even within Microsoft's own documentation—so we will also interchange them here.

A computer will have different built-in groups depending on the role it plays in a network. Windows NT domain controllers include the following default local groups. (This is just a quick list. Detailed descriptions follow.)

- Account Operators
- Administrators
- Backup Operators
- Guests
- Print Operators
- Replicator
- Server Operators
- Users

In addition to the preceding groups, Windows NT domain controllers have the following global groups:

- Domain Admins
- Domain Guests
- Domain Users

Windows NT member servers and Windows NT Workstations include the following built-in groups:

- Administrators
- Backup Operators
- Guests
- Power Users
- Replicator
- Users

exam
Ⓦatch   *Domain controllers have Account, Printer, and Server Operators, while member servers and workstations do not. Instead, there is a group called Power Users that has the same rights as all three of the Operator groups on a domain controller.*

Microsoft Windows NT creates the AGLP relationship already by placing some of the built-in global groups in some of these built-in local groups. Be aware of these groups and their relationship to better manage security and minimize administrative overhead (see Table 5-3).

In addition to this relationship, on a domain controller any computer, server, or workstation that joins a domain and thereby has a computer account, has the following default global groups added to the workstation or member server's local groups.

Administrators (local)	Domain Admins (global)
Guests (local)	Domain Guests (global)
Users (local)	Domain Users (global)

By doing this, it enables the administrator to have admin privileges on every workstation and simplify any permissions that need to be assigned to all authenticated users.

Windows NT comes with these built-in local groups to make administration easier. This is done by assigning default rights to the local groups, so when you place a user or global group in that built-in local group, the users inherit these rights as well. Rights are system privileges that determine whether the logged on user is allowed to shut down the computer, log on at all, change the system time, perform the backup and restoration of files and many other rights. These rights are defined in what is called a User Rights Policy.

You can access these rights to view or modify them by opening User Manager For Domains, selecting the Policies menu, and then choosing User Rights…, which opens the User Rights Policy dialog box. Use the Rights drop-down menu to select which

TABLE 5-3	Group	Default Members
AGLP Relationships	Administrators (local)	Domain Admins (global)
	Domain Admins (global)	Administrator (default user)
	Domain Guests (global)	Guest (default user)
	Domain Users (global)	Administrator (default user) plus any new users you create are automatically added
	Guests (local)	Domain Guests (global)
	Users (local)	Domain Users (global)

right you want to view or modify. Use the Add and Remove buttons accordingly to add or remove local groups to these rights. Note that you can grant these system rights to individual users as well, but it is always better to use local groups. See Table 5-4 to get an overview of what groups have what rights, by default.

To ensure a better understanding of the roles built-in local groups have, the following sections explore the groups built in to Windows NT by default.

TABLE 5-4   Default User Rights

User Rights	Comments	Granted to Domain Controllers	Granted to Workstations and Member Servers
Manage auditing and security log	Specify what types of file and object access are to be audited. View and clear the security log.	Administrators	Administrators
Back up files and directories	Have Read access to all files and folders, regardless of what groups they are a member of.	Administrators, Server Operators, Backup Operators	Administrators, Backup Operators
Restore files and directories	A user with the Restore right can, when performing a restore, overwrite files for which he or she has no permissions.	Administrators, Server Operators, Backup Operators	Administrators, Backup Operators
Change system time		Administrators, Server Operators	Administrators, Power Users
Access this computer from the network	Access the computer from another workstation on the network. Called Remote logon.	Administrators, Everyone	Administrators, Power Users, Everyone
Log on locally	Ability to log on the computer itself using the computer's keyboard. Called interactive logon.	Administrators, Server Operators, Account Operators, Print Operators, Backup Operators	Administrators, Backup Operators, Power Users, Users, Guests

| TABLE 5-4 | Default User Rights *(continued)* |

User Rights	Comments	Granted to Domain Controllers	Granted to Workstations and Member Servers
Shut down the system		Administrators, Server Operators, Account Operators, Print Operators, Backup Operators	Administrators, Backup Operators, Power Users, Users, Guests
Add workstations and member servers to domain	Allows a user who is not a member of the domain's Administrators group to add computers running Windows NT Workstation or computers running Windows NT Server as member servers to the domain.	None[1]	N/A
Take ownership of files and other objects	Take ownership of files and directories on the computer.	Administrators	Administrators
Load and unload device drivers		Administrators	Administrators
Force shutdown from a remote system	No application in Windows NT. Will be supported in future upgrades of the operating system.	Administrators, Server Operators	Administrators, Power Users

[1] Members of the domain's Administrators and Account Operators groups can always add workstations to a domain, whether or not they have this right assigned to them. This right is needed only to enable users who are not members of these groups to add workstations to the domain. With this right, Windows NT Server does not have to check that the user is a member of the Administrators or Account Operators group.

exam
ⓦatch

Microsoft expects you to know what rights the built-in groups have and what impact those rights have on your network.

Account Operators   Members of the Account Operators local group can use User Manager For Domains to create user accounts and groups for the domain and to modify or delete most user accounts and groups of the domain. Account Operators can also log on to domain servers, can shut down domain servers, and use Server Manager to add computers to a domain.

However, an account operator cannot modify or delete the Domain Admins global group, nor the Administrators, Account Operators, Backup Operators, Print Operators, or Server Operators local groups, or any global groups belonging to these local groups. Account operators cannot modify the accounts of members of any of these groups and cannot administer security policies.

Use this group to disseminate administrative duties to others. For instance, it would be helpful to have someone else do the typing when a new user is created, especially if there are a lot of user accounts to add. So, deputize your administrative assistant by putting their account in the Account Operators group.

Administrators   The Administrators local group in a domain, on a computer running Windows NT Workstation, or on a member server has full control over its computer. The Administrators local group is the only group automatically granted every built-in right and ability. Administrators manage the overall configuration of the domain and the domain's controllers.

Backup Operators   Members of the Backup Operators local group can back up and restore files on the domain's primary and backup domain controllers. They can also log on to these servers and shut them down.

on the **!** **ⓘob**   *A security risk exists if the same user can back up and restore the files since he or she can restore the files to any location with any permission. In high security environments, it is recommended that another group be created called Restore Operators, and then granted the Restore files and directories right, and remove the Backup Operators from the Restore files and directories right. This provides a checks-and-balances solution to a security risk.*

Guests   The Guests local group allows occasional or one-time users to log on to a workstation's built-in Guest account interactively (local guest logon) or to a domain's built-in Guest account remotely (network guest logon), and be granted limited abilities. Users logged on as members of the Guests local group have no rights at domain servers. However, they do have certain rights at their individual workstations. By default, the domain Guests global group is a member of the Guests local group, but it can be removed.

Print Operators　Members of the Print Operators local group can create, delete, and manage printer shares on the domain's primary and backup domain controllers. They can also log on at these servers, and shut them down.

Replicator　The Replicator local group supports directory replication functions. The only member of the domain's Replicator local group should be a domain user account used to log on the Replicator services of the primary domain controller and the backup domain controllers in the domain. Do not add the user accounts of actual users to this group.

Server Operators　Members of the Server Operators local group can manage the domain's primary and backup domain controllers. For example, server operators can create, delete, and manage printer shares at these servers; create, delete, and manage network shares; back up and restore files; lock and unlock these servers; format a server's hard disk; and change the system time. They can also log on from servers and shut down servers.

These users typically manage the hardware of the servers.

Users　Users logged on as members of the Users local group *cannot* log on locally at servers running Windows NT Server. However, they do possess certain rights at their local workstations and can perform most necessary tasks.

exam
ⓦatch

The Domain Users global group is a member of the Users local group, but it can be removed.

Workstations and member servers have the same built-in local groups except that instead of separating the Account, Print, and Server Operators individually for more granular delegation, a group was created, called the Power Users, that encompasses all those rights together.

SCENARIO & SOLUTION

100 new users have been hired and require logon user accounts	Assign this task to your assistant administrator and put his user account in the Account Operators local group
New servers have come in and require some hardware management and application installation	Create a global group called AsstAdmins and place it in the Server Operators local group. Place the user account of an assistant admin in the AsstAdmins group.
You have three branch offices with two printers each	Create global groups for each branch office. Maybe call them Branch1Admins, Branch2Admins, etc. On the print servers at each location, place the corresponding global group, Branch#Admins, in the Print Operators local group.
You need to determine who has been printing to the color printer in the marketing department	Set up auditing of the Everyone group on the printer assigned to the color printer.

EXERCISE 5-3

CertCam 5-3

Setting up Assistant Administrator Groups

In this exercise, we will create a global group called AsstAdmins and place your username in it.

1. Verify you are logged on to the domain as Administrator. (CTRL-ALT-DEL!)

2. Open User Manager For Domains.

3. Highlight your username.

Click the User menu and select New Global Group. This opens the New Global Group dialog box.

Notice that the user you highlighted is automatically added as a member of this group. Although this seems convenient, it can actually be irritating if you forget this and accidentally add a user you did not intend to add.

1. In the Group Name field, type **AsstAdmins** and press TAB.

2. In the Description field, type **Assistant Administrators**. This is an optional field.

If you have other users you would like to add, select them from the right-hand side of the dialog box in the Not Members list. (TIP: You can select multiple users at once using CTRL-click and SHIFT-click.)

3. Click the OK button to accept the settings.

With this global group, you can assign various administrative duties by placing it in one of the built-in groups we just discussed.

Special Groups

In addition to the built-in groups mentioned, there are groups created by the system, which are used for special purposes. Membership to these groups cannot be altered, and the groups are not listed in User Manager For Domains. However, when you administer a computer, and Windows NT presents lists of groups to be added to an ACL, these special groups sometimes appear in the list. For example, they can show up when assigning permissions to directories, files, shared network directories, or printers. Figure 5-16 has hands pointing to some of the available special groups. Table 5-5, meanwhile, lists the special groups and what they refer to.

The Everyone Group   The Everyone group requires separate and additional recognition here. Microsoft approaches administration with the idea that it should be very easy. By doing so, they have captured a fair amount of market share, so you can't fault them there. What this means for you as the administrator, however, is that there are security issues existing right from the start of installation.

With the creation of any Share or NTFS permission, the Everyone group is granted Full Control by default. Who is Everyone? In Windows NT, Everyone is any and all connections on the network irregardless of authentication. This means a user such as the anonymous account on a Web server is included. By default, Read permission is granted to the Registry for the Everyone group.

on the
job

It is recommended that when creating shares and assigning NTFS permissions, you should remove the Everyone group and add the local group Users. The Users group contains the global group, Domain Users, which only holds valid and authenticated user accounts.

FIGURE 5-16

Special groups in
the Add Users
And Groups
dialog box

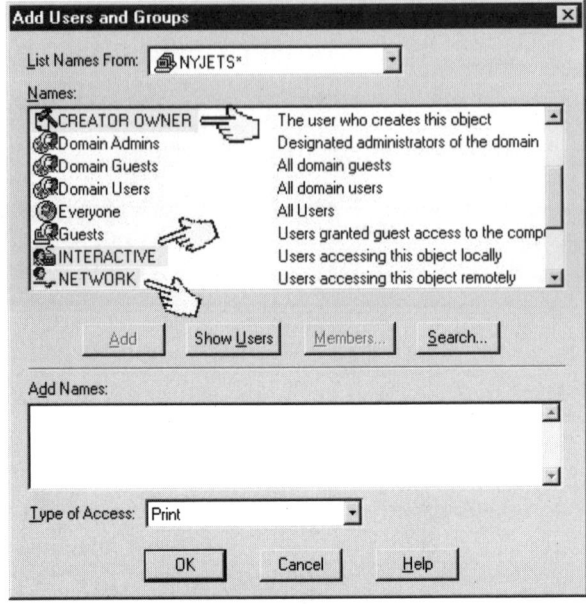

TABLE 5-5	Group	Refers to
Special Groups	Everyone	Anyone using the computer. This includes all local and remote users (that is, the Interactive and Network groups combined). In a domain, members of Everyone can, by default, access the network, connect to a server's shared network directories, and print to a server's printers.
	Interactive	Anyone using the computer locally.
	Network	All users connected over the network to the computer.
	System	The operating system.
	Creator Owner	Transfer of permissions to creators of subdirectories, files, and print jobs. For a directory, if permissions are granted to the Creator Owner group, the creator of a subdirectory or file will be granted those permissions for that subdirectory or file. For a printer, if permissions are granted to the Creator Owner group, the creator of a print job will be granted those permissions for that print job.

Global Groups

Global groups contain a list of user accounts from within a single domain and are used to combine users logically together. A global group can include accounts only from the domain in which the global group was created and cannot contain other global groups.

A global group created in one domain can be granted permissions in another domain provided the domain trusts are in place. Global groups are commonly referenced by the domain name\group name (see Figure 5-17) when working in a multidomain environment to distinguish which domain the group resides in. You would see this in domain management utilities such as the ACL.

The following is a list of global group characteristics to remember:

- Can contain users from the domain in which the group was created

- Cannot contain users from other domains

- Cannot contain other groups

Global groups
are commonly
referenced by
the domain name\
group name

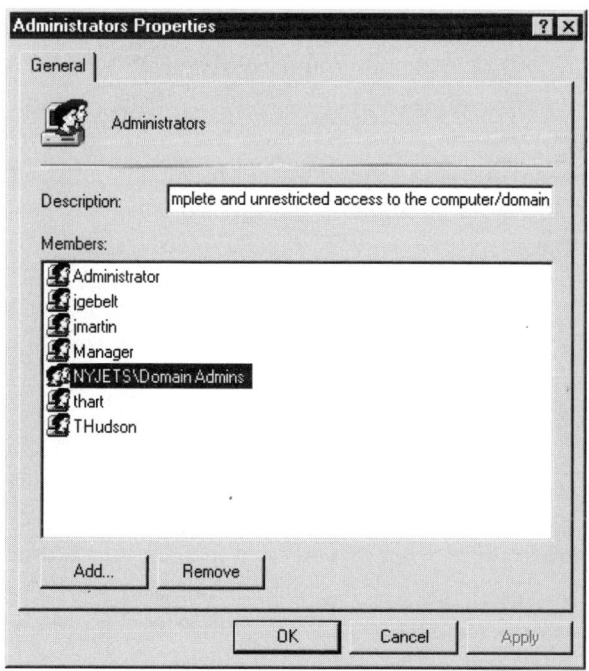

- Can be assigned privileges in the domain in which the group was created
- Can be assigned privileges in the domain that trusts the domain in which the group was created

Local Groups

Local groups can only be assigned privileges to resources on the same local computer that the local group was created in. Since domain controllers share a Security Accounts Manager (SAM), a local group created on a domain controller can be seen, and privileges can be granted on any domain controller.

Local groups can contain both users and global groups from within its own domain, as well as other domains that trust its domain. This capability allows a local group to accept and hold entities from many domains, and have the privileges assigned to it just once. When you assign privileges to a local group, all of the groups and users within it inherit those same privileges.

Universal Groups

Universal groups are a new concept in Windows 2000, used to combine users from multiple domains in order to assign "cross-domain" privileges. For example, there is a new default group in Windows 2000 called Enterprise Admins. Membership in this group grants administrator privileges within all domains of the tree.

This information is to notify you of coming changes as you begin mixing Windows 2000 and NT together. Universal groups, however, cannot be used until you run Windows 2000 in native mode, which means all your NT domain controllers have been upgraded to Windows 2000.

CERTIFICATION SUMMARY

In this chapter, you learned how to plan and create user accounts. Use a naming convention and stick to it. Likewise, make allowances for duplicate names. There are many properties to modify and manage user accounts, including group membership, profiles, logon scripts and home directory paths, logon times, types of accounts, where to log on from, and whether the user can dial-in remotely.

You also learned that a user's desktop can be maintained with profiles. You can allow free reign of what a user is allowed to do on their own desktop environment with local profiles and allow that profile to "roam" to wherever the user logs on from by copying the profile to a network server. With mandatory profiles, you can create a permanent desktop that is always the same and cannot be modified.

Next, you learned that a user's environment can be further manipulated through logon scripts. Use logon scripts to set up drive mappings and run startup programs for the users. Make sure to set up directory replication on all your domain controllers to keep the logon scripts synchronized across your entire network.

Lastly, you learned about groups. AGLP is the preferred and recommended method to create an administrative relationship that eases the task of assigning permissions to users. Remember: Accounts go into global groups. Global groups, meanwhile, go into local groups, to which permissions are assigned. In addition to the groups you create for your users, there are default built-in groups that already have certain system rights assigned to them. Use these groups first before creating new ones yourself. You will find that the built-in local groups are fairly well designed to accommodate most of your administrative needs.

✓ TWO-MINUTE DRILL

Configuring and Troubleshooting User Accounts, Profiles, and Logon Scripts

❑ You must have administrative privileges to modify and create user accounts.

❑ Planning user accounts through a naming convention eases the creative process of coming up with usernames.

❑ Instead of deleting user accounts, rename and/or disable them. Deleting the accounts removes the SID, making the act unrecoverable.

❑ Use template accounts to define default-common user properties and copy the templates to create new users.

❑ The location of profiles on Windows NT exists here: [system_drive:]\%systemroot%\profiles\<username>

❑ Profiles on Windows 2000 exist here: [system_drive:]\documents and settings\<username>

❑ Create roaming profiles for users who log on to more than one workstation.

❑ You can create mandatory profiles by renaming ntuser.dat to ntuser.man.

❑ Utilize the %username% environment variable when creating home directories.

❑ Balance logon restrictions with usability. Don't over-restrict. You will only cause yourself more work.

❑ Logon scripts are used to set up network drive mappings.

❑ Logon scripts should be stored in the NETLOGON share: [system_drive:]\%systemroot%\system32\repl\imports\scripts, which is located on each domain controller.

❑ Set up directory replication with the PDC as the Export server and all the BDCs as import servers.

Configuring and Troubleshooting Groups

❑ Use AGLP! User accounts go into global groups. Global groups go into local groups. Assign permissions to local groups.

❑ Default local groups have predefined system rights.

❑ System rights are defined in the User Rights policy.

❑ Special groups exist for network connectivity and cannot be seen in User Manager For Domains.

❑ Security issues exist by default because of Microsoft's use of the Everyone group and assigning Full Control permissions to it.

❑ Account Operators are used to delegate rights to someone besides the administrator in order to let them create and manage the general user population without granting full administrative privileges.

❑ Print Operators are used to delegate rights to an assistant administrator in order to allow printer management without granting full administrative privileges.

❑ Server Operators are used to delegate rights to an assistant administrator in order to allow hardware and application management without granting full administrative rights.

SELF TEST

The following questions will help you measure your understanding of the material presented in this chapter. Read all the choices carefully, as there may be more than one correct answer. Choose all correct answers for each question.

Configuring and Troubleshooting User Accounts, Profiles, and Logon Scripts

1. You have just created a new share for the accounting department. The default permissions are in effect. Select which group has permissions to this share.

   A. Accounting

   B. Server Operators

   C. Administrators

   D. Everyone

   E. Domain Users

2. After creating a template user account for the customer support department, you begin copying it to create new users. Which fields in the user properties do NOT transfer or copy to the new users? (Select all that apply.)

   A. Password

   B. Description

   C. Group Membership

   D. Username

   E. User Must Change Password At Next Logon

   F. Account Disabled

3. If the system dive is C: and the domain controller is named DC1, what is the default location for User Michelle's profile in Windows NT? Windows 2000? (Select two.)

   A. \\DC1\profiles\michelle

   B. \\DC1\profiles\default

   C. c:\winnt\profiles\michelle

   D. c:\winnt\profiles\default

   E. \\DC1\documents and settings\michelle

   F. c:\documents and settings\michelle

4. To create a mandatory profile what must you do?

    A. Rename ntuser.dat to ntman.dat

    B. Rename ntuser.dat to ntuser.man

    C. Rename the default profiles folder to \mandatory

    D. Rename the user's profile folder to \mandatory

    E. Copy the user's profile to network share, and type the profile path into user properties

    F. Create a logon script that points users to the same profile folder

5. The user, JettH, was deleted last week. Afterward, it was determined the user never left the company and is still an employee. He works in the Customer Support department and has no extra permissions than the original ones created by the template account, _CustSuptTemplate. Which procedures would restore this user and reestablish all their permissions? (Select all that apply.)

    A. Create a user account and name it JettH. Give the user a temporary password and have him re-create his drive mappings and connect to his shares to reestablish his permissions.

    B. Copy the _CustSuptTemplate and name the new user JettH.

    C. All that's needed is to create a new user named JettH. Since all the groups already know about user JettH, this takes care of the problem.

    D. The user account, JettH, is lost and cannot be re-created, because you cannot use the name JettH again.

    E. Create the user with a different username and reassign the user to the same groups they had before their account was deleted.

6. Upper management has recently charged you with solving the following problem for 70 users. These users have had their own unique desktop environments and wish to retain those same desktops, along with the freedom to modify them. Their job, however, sends them to many locations, requiring they log on from various computers. All users already have their home directory stored on a member server named ALTA, in a share called USERS, where the BDC that authenticates these users is named DC5. What is the most efficient solution? (Select all that apply.)

    A. Create a new generic profile and copy it to each user's home directory on ALTA.

    B. Create a new generic profile and copy it to the NETLOGON share on DC5.

    C. Create a share on ALTA named Profiles, and create a subfolder for each of the 70 users with the same name as their usernames.

D. Using the Copy To feature on each of the user's local workstations, copy each profile to the NETLOGON share on DC5.

E. Using the Copy To feature on each of the user's local workstations, copy each profile to \\ALTA\users\<username>.

F. Using the Copy To feature on each of the user's local workstations, copy each profile to \\ALTA\profiles\<username>.

G. In User Manager For Domains, add a path to the User Profile Path: field.

H. In User Manager For Domains, select each of the 70 users using CTRL-click and press ENTER. Add a path to the User Profile Path: field, using %username% variable, instead of the actual username.

7. Which of the following are considered logon restrictions? (Select all that apply.)

A. Account Disabled

B. Password Never Expires

C. Logon Hours

D. Logon To

E. Group Membership

F. Local Account Type

G. Dialin Permission

H. Logon Script Name

8. You need to configure directory replication to keep your logon scripts synchronized. What directory path on the PDC should you put the logon script that is scheduled to be exported to the BDCs? (Assume that C: is the system drive and the PDC is named DC1.)

A. c:\winnt\system32\config

B. c:\winnt\profiles\default user

C. c:\winnt\system32\repl\import\scripts

D. c:\winnt\system32\repl\export\scripts

9. You have recently added the Remote Access Service to your network and have set up a group of ten users to test the efficiency of your configuration. They are all using 56K modems. Six of these users report good connectivity and logon speed. The other four complain that the logon is very slow. What may be causing this?

A. Four users do not have dial-in permission.

B. Six users have multilink set up.

C. Four users have roaming profiles, while the other six do not.

D. Six users have logon scripts, while the other four do not.

Configuring and Troubleshooting Groups

10. You need to delegate to an assistant administrator the rights to create 50 new user accounts and associated groups, assign them to those groups, and create computer accounts for all involved. You create a global group called AsstAdmins and put the assistant administrator's user account in that group. What do you do next?

A. Create a local group called UserMngmt and place the global group AsstAdmins in it.

B. Add the Account Operators local group to the global group, AsstAdmins.

C. Add the global group, AsstAdmins, to the local group, Server Operators.

D. Add the global group, AsstAdmins, to the local group, Account Operators.

11. What is the Microsoft preferred method of assigning permissions to users through groups in Windows NT?

A. MADCAP

B. ICMP

C. AGLP

D. TCP/IP

E. UGLR

F. SMTP

12. You have a need for increased security on your network. One issue is that, currently, the same person can back up and restore files, which gives him the ability to see any file that gets backed up. You decide to create separate local groups, one that has the right to back up files but not restore, and one that can restore files but not back up. You also want only these two local groups and the administrators group to have this ability. What steps are required to do this? (Select all that apply.)

A. Create a local group called Restore Operators.

B. Delete the local group Backup Operators.

C. In the User Rights policy, remove Backup Operators from the Back Up Files And Directories right.

    D. In the User Rights policy, remove Backup Operators from the Restore Files And Directories right.

    E. Add the local group, Restore Operators, to the Restore Files And Directories right.

    F. Add the local group, Restore Operators, to the Back Up Files And Directories right.

    G. Remove the Server Operators local group from both the Back Up Files And Directories right, and the Restore Files And Directories right.

    H. Remove the Account Operators local group from both the Back Up Files And Directories right, and the Restore Files And Directories right.

13. What default rights does the Printer Operators local group have? (Select all that apply.)

    A. Log on locally

    B. Manage printer shares on any server

    C. Manage printer shares on domain controllers only

    D. Shut down the system

    E. Install device drivers

14. What default user rights does the Server Operators local group have? (Select all that apply.)

    A. Install device drivers

    B. Create, delete, and manage printer shares

    C. Create, delete, and manage network shares

    D. Manage auditing and security logs

    E. Back up and restore files

    F. Format a server's hard disk

    G. Shut down servers

15. You have a two-domain network with one-way trusts to each other. One domain is in Dallas and the other is in Salt Lake City (SLC). You need to delegate the responsibility to manage all printers to Becca, who is a user in SLC. Your printer servers reside on a mixture of domain controllers and member servers. What steps should you take to configure this? (Select all that apply.)

    A. Create a global group called PrinterAdmins in SLC and make Becca a member of it.

    B. Create a global group called PrinterAdmins in Dallas and make Becca a member of it.

    C. Create a local group called PrinterMngmt on all print servers.

    D. Make SLC\PrinterAdmins a member of each PrinterMangmt local group.

E. Make Dallas\PrinterAdmins a member of each PrinterMangmt local group.

F. Make Dallas\PrinterAdmins a member of each Printer Operators group in both domains.

G. Make SLC\PrinterAdmins a member of each Printer Operators group in both domains.

H. Make SLC\PrinterAdmins a member of the PowerUsers on every member server that is a print server.

I. Make Dallas\PrinterAdmins a member of the PowerUsers on every member server that is a print server.

16. In the same domain environment as the last question, you have a help desk group that requires the right to reset passwords in either domain. Users assigned this responsibility are in both domains. What is the minimum number of new global groups and new local groups that must be created to set this up?

A. One global group, two local groups

B. Two global groups, one local group

C. One global group, no local groups

D. Two global groups, no local groups

E. No global groups, one local group

F. No global groups, two local groups

17. User Ryan has just created a file in a folder on a remote server named SERVER1. What special groups on SERVER1 is Ryan a member of? (Select all that apply.)

A. Everyone

B. Domain Users

C. Users

D. Creator Owner

E. Interactive

F. Network

G. System

H. Replicator

18. Company Zed has three domains in a complete trust configuration. The domains are New York, Berlin, and Moscow. The Berlin domain contains five Web servers managed by three users from each domain. You must give these users full administrator rights to the Web servers but not to anything else. What must you do to accomplish this using Microsoft's preferred method? (Select all that apply.)

A. Create a global group called WebAdmins in all three domains.

B. Create a global group called WebAdmins in Berlin only.

C. Place all nine users in the Berlin\WebAdmins.

D. Place the three users from each domain in their respective WebAdmins group.

E. Place New York\WebAdmins, Berlin\WebAdmins, and Moscow\WebAdmins in each of the local Administrators groups on each Web server in BERLIN.

F. Create local groups called Webmasters on each Web server and assign administrator rights to them.

G. Place the Berlin\WebAdmins group in the local groups Webmasters.

19. Your company requires higher security than the default permissions for shares and NTFS provide. Which is the more secure way to grant all users permissions than the provided default?

A. Remove the Everyone group and add the Domain Users group. Grant Domain Users Full Control.

B. Add Server Operators, Account Operators, and Server Operators, then grant them Full Control.

C. Add the Administrators group and grant it Full Control. Remove the Everyone group. Add the local Users group and grant it the appropriate permissions.

D. Nothing. The default permissions are sufficient for high security environments.

LAB QUESTION

You are the IT manager for ZEDCO. There are 248 employees, all in one Windows NT domain and one geographical location. You have ten servers and everyone is running Windows 2000 Professional or Windows NT Workstation. Five of your servers are Windows 2000, while the rest are Windows NT Server. You have been charged with the task of setting up home directories for all users with only the assigned user having access to their files and no one else. You must also provide a place for file sharing that all users can copy files to and manage the documents they create there, but that no one else can modify. You will do this on server ZEDUSERS. Describe how you would set up such an environment.

SELF TEST ANSWERS

Configuring and Troubleshooting User Accounts, Profiles, and Logon Scripts

1. ☑ **D,** Everyone, is the correct answer. The key term in this question is "default." Windows NT default permissions on shares and NTFS are used to grant the special group, Everyone, Full Control.

   ☒ **A, B, C,** and **E** are incorrect because the groups can only be added after a shared or NTFS folder is created, and are not there by default.

2. ☑ **A, D,** and **F.** The purpose of a template account is to create new users. New users require a unique username and password, of course. The template account is disabled for security. However, since we are trying to make things easier, we do not want to have to remember to "un-disable" each new account, right? Remember, the purpose of a template account is to create a user account that has user properties and group memberships common to the department.

   ☒ **B** is incorrect because this field is used to give a general explanation, which is usually the same for each user in the department where we created the template account (e.g., "Customer Support Representative"). **C,** Group Membership, is incorrect because the user created by the template needs to inherit these groups and is the primary reason for having a template account. **E,** User Must Change Password At Next Logon, is the check box that forces a password change the next time the user logs on. The reason this is incorrect is because we want this to copy to the new user account so they change their password right away.

3. ☑ **C** and **F.** In Windows NT, user profiles are saved on the system drive (C:) under the system root (WINNT), and then under the folder named Profiles. Each user has a subfolder named after their username; as in the questioned case, which would be: c:\winnt\profiles\michelle. In Windows 2000, user profiles are saved on the C: drive as well, but here there is a "documents and settings" folder with subfolders named for each user: c:\documents and settings\michelle.

   ☒ **A, B,** and **E** are incorrect because they are not the default location. The default location of profiles is on the local hard drive. They would, however, be a good candidate for a roaming profile. **D** is incorrect because it points to the computer's default location and not the user's. The folders and files in c:\winnt\profiles\default are copied to the user's folder the first time they log on to that local computer.

4. ☑ **B.** The only requirement to creating a mandatory profile is renaming the profile's Registry hive from ntuser.dat to ntuser.man. Although it is common to put this type of profile on a server and let users access it from anywhere, it is not required you do so. You can have a mandatory profile that is local to the user's hard drive.

☒   **A, C,** and **D** are incorrect because they do nothing that relates to profiles. **E** contains steps necessary to creating a roaming profile, but not a mandatory profile. **F** is incorrect because a logon script is not used to specify a profile location.

5. ☑   **B** and **E.** Because the username is actually a property of the SID (security identifier), when a user account is deleted, so is the SID. If the error was caught right away, one solution might be to restore the SAM to the PDC from the last backup, but since a week has passed, it's likely information in the SAM has changed. So, the only option is to create a brand new user, thereby creating a new SID. Give it the username, JettH, so they can use the same logon name. Since JettH did not have any special setting beyond what was in the template, you can create the user using that template. This will place the new SID in all the appropriate groups and get JettH back to work again. You can, likewise, manually add JettH (with a new SID) to all the groups they were in before.

☒   **A** is incorrect because re-creating drive mappings and connecting to shares does NOT reestablish permissions. Instead, the user account must be put back in the global groups JettH was in before. **C** is incorrect because the SID the groups know about is no longer there, so the groups really DON'T know about JettH SID #1, and need to know about JettH SID #2. **D** is incorrect because although usernames must be unique within the domain, if one is deleted it can be used again. There is no conflict.

6. ☑   **C, F,** and **H.** To create a roaming profile, the files must be stored on a file server in individual locations for each user. A path must exist in the user properties pointing the user account logon process to the profile location. Since the users already have a profile, you should use the Copy To feature on each of their computers to copy the profile to the \\ALTA\profiles\ <username> folder. To be more efficient, however, you can select all 70 users at once and add the profile path \\ALTA\profiles\%username% and this way have all 70 entries taken care of in one step.

☒   **A** and **B** are incorrect since each user wishes to maintain their currently created profile. A generic profile would not meet this requirement. In addition, the NETLOGON share is used for logon scripts, not profiles, thus **D** is incorrect as well. **E** copies the profiles to the users' home directories which will cause confusion and possibly delete portions of the profile. Finally, **G** is incorrect because **H** is more efficient!

7. ☑   **C, D, F,** and **G.** Admittedly, this question may lend itself to some interpretation as to what a restriction is, but Logon Hours restricts the user to a time and day that allows logon; Logon To restricts the user to certain workstations to log on from; Local Account Type restricts a user to one domain and remote logon only; and Dialin Permission restricts users from dialing in to your network.

☒   **A,** Account Disabled, is one that could be argued, but a disabled account is essentially no account. **B,** Password Never Expires, exempts the user from having to change a password and is permissive not restrictive. The same is true of **E,** Group Membership, which grants permissions not restrictions. **H,** Logon Script Name, is just a property that neither restricts nor permits the account directly; instead, the account may have certain settings granted or denied based on the script contents.

8. ☑ **D.** Directory replication copies all subfolders under the c:\winnt\system32\repl\export\. Therefore, if you want your logon script to be replicated, it must be in this subfolder.

☒   **C** is the NETLOGON share that clients look for to download the script itself, and is where directory replication imports to. **A** is where the Registry hives are stored. **B** is where the default profiles for each workstation are stored.

9. ☑ **C.** A RAS logon is similar to the user logging on locally to your LAN; so, if a roaming profile exists, it will be downloaded. Across a dial-in connection, this slows down the entire logon process. You should, therefore, eliminate roaming profiles and logon scripts for dial-in users.

☒   **A** is incorrect because, without dial-in permissions, the users would not have a slow logon, or rather they would have *no* logon. **B** is incorrect because, although overall connectivity would be better, there is not enough information to warrant this answer. **D** is also incorrect. Logon scripts would increase logon times, not decrease them. Since the six users are not complaining, we should assume this is not an issue to them.

Configuring and Troubleshooting Groups

10. ☑ **D.** Global groups go into local groups (AGLP). The Account Operators local group already has the rights needed to accommodate the scenario of an assistant administrator, so there is no need to create a new one.

☒   **A** is incorrect because there is a local group already there by default that grants these rights: Account Operators. **B** is incorrect because placing local groups into a global group would not grant rights to that global group. **C** puts the global group into a local group, but the Server Operators do not have the rights to create and modify user accounts as required. Therefore, **C** is incorrect as well.

11. ☑ **C.** AGLP stands for user <u>A</u>ccounts are placed in <u>G</u>lobal groups, which are placed in <u>L</u>ocal groups, which are assigned <u>P</u>ermissions. This is the preferred method for associating user accounts and groups for permission assignment.

☒   **A, B, D, E,** and **F** are incorrect. **A,** MADCAP, means Multicast Address Dynamic Client Allocation Protocol, a service in Windows 2000. **B,** ICMP, stands for Internet Control

Message Protocol, used in TCP/IP connectivity. **D**, TCP/IP, translates as Transmission Control Protocol/Internet Protocol, which is the reference to a suite of protocols used to route and connect packets to hosts on an internetwork. **E**, UGLR, stands for <u>U</u>ser accounts placed in <u>G</u>lobal groups, which are placed in <u>L</u>ocal groups, which are then assigned permissions to <u>R</u>esources. This is just like AGLP, but is used in Windows 2000 reference material not Windows NT. **F**, SMTP, stands for Simple Mail Transfer Protocol, which is used for Internet mail.

12. ☑ **A, D, E,** and **G.** This question requires that you know the default rights for several built-in groups and what rights grant backup and restore privileges. The rights are 1) Back Up Files And Directories, and 2) Restore Files And Directories. In both cases, the default built-in groups are Administrators, Account Operators, and Server Operators. So, to meet the scenario requirements, the Server Operators (G) must be removed from both rights; the Backup Operators must be removed from the Restore Files And Directories right (D); a new local group must be created since there is no built-in group to accommodate this (A); and then that new group must be added to the Restore Files And Directories right.

    ☒ **B** is incorrect because you still need the Backup Operators group for backups, plus you are not allowed to delete these groups anyway. **C** and **F** are incorrect because they are doing the opposite of what is needed. Backup Operators should have backup rights and Restore Operators should have restore rights. **H** is incorrect because Account Operators do not have these rights anyway, so there is no need to remove them.

13. ☑ **A, C,** and **D.** This is a memorization of user rights. Printer Operators are local groups on the domain controllers, so rights only apply on domain controllers and not any other servers (B). Printer Operators can shut down and log on locally to these domain controllers as well. Only Administrators can install device drivers (E).

    ☒ **B** and **E** are incorrect because Printer Operators are local groups on the domain controllers, so rights only apply on domain controllers and not any other servers. Printer Operators can shut down and log on locally to these domain controllers as well. Only Administrators can install device drivers.

14. ☑ **B, C, E, F,** and **G.** Again, we must memorize the User Rights assignments associated with the built-in groups. In this question, Server Operators is the group to look at. Server Operators can manage printer and network shares, back up and restore files, shut down servers, and format hard disks.

    ☒ **A** and **D** are incorrect because only the Administrators local group can install device drivers and manage auditing and security logs.

15. ☑ **A, G,** and **H.** First, you need a global group in the SLC domain because that is where Becca resides. Users can only be added to global groups within their same domain. Following

the AGLP methodology, you must put SLC\PrinterAdmins into the local groups that have the necessary privileges or rights to manage printers. Windows NT includes built-in local groups with these rights: Printer Operators on domain controllers and Power Users on member servers and workstations. Place SLC\PrinterAdmins in the Printer Operators local group on the PDC, and in the Power Users local group on each print server that is not a domain controller.

☒ **B, F,** and **I** are incorrect because the user Becca is in the SLC domain and therefore cannot be made a member of the Dallas\PrinterAdmins global group. **C, D,** and **E** are incorrect because there is no need to create any other groups if your needs can be met with the existing built-in local groups. It could be argued that the Power Users group is granting too many privileges and that a separate PrinterMangmt local group on member servers and workstations is warranted. However, these answers would still be incorrect because there is no step mentioning the assigning of rights to the new local group.

16. ☑ **D.** One global group is required in each domain making a total of two, while the Account Operators built-in local group already exists and grants the reset password privilege.

☒ **A, B, E,** and **F** are incorrect because a new local group is not required. Account Operators already exist to give this right. **C** is incorrect because the users requiring the right to reset passwords exist in two different domains. Users can only exist inside of global groups that were created in their own domain.

17. ☑ **A, D,** and **F.** Any connection on the network is made a member of the Everyone group. Since the file was created remotely, Ryan is also a member of the Network group on SERVER1; and since Ryan created the file, he is made the Creator Owner of that file.

☒ **B** and **C** are incorrect because they are not Special Groups. Domain Users is a global group containing all users that are not the default or built-in type, and Users is a built-in local group that usually contains the global group Domain Users. **E** is incorrect because an Interactive group is anyone logged on locally. Ryan is a member of the Interactive group on his workstation, but not on SERVER1. **G** is incorrect because the System group is used by the operating system, and users are not typically made members of these groups. Instead, these groups are designed for general network connectivity between computers and applications. **H** is incorrect because the Replicator group is used in Directory Replication, and membership is added manually.

18. ☑ **A, D,** and **E.** Global groups must be created in each respective domain, and the three users from each domain should be placed in those same global groups. Next, following AGLP, all three global groups are placed in the local Administrators local groups on each Web server. The key here is that administrator rights are already granted to the local Administrators groups, and global groups are the only type of groups that can traverse domains.

☒ **B** and **C** are incorrect because the nine users requiring administrator privileges are in three different domains. There must be a global group in each of the three domains to put the users in. Users from one domain cannot be members of a global group in another domain. **F** and **G** are incorrect because an Administrators local group already exists to grant administrative rights, so making a new group is redundant. Also, it is much more difficult to make sure all user rights are granted to this new group. You can grant Full Control *permissions* to resources, but that does not give the users rights to shut down the server, install device drivers, and so on.

19. ☑ **C.** The accepted higher security configuration is to remove the Everyone group from the shares and NTFS permissions. Everyone is a special group that contains any network connection, including users that have not been authenticated, like anonymous Internet accounts. Membership is controlled completely by network attachments and not by the administrator. You should always make sure someone has Full Control permissions to manage the access of any resource, so grant the Administrators local group this permission. Now, add the local group, Users, to the Access Control List and grant the appropriate permissions. Users contains the global group, Domain Users, which is made up of users that have been created by the administrator and are accessing the network only after they have been properly and securely authenticated.

☒ **A** is incorrect because although you should remove the Everyone group, Domain Users is a global group and you should avoid assigning permissions to global groups. Remember AGLP! **B** is incorrect because the built-in local groups, Server, Account, and Printer Operators are used to delegate administration, not to give Full Control of resources. **D** is incorrect because the default permissions grant Full Control to the Everyone group, which is completely UN-restrictive and has NO security.

LAB ANSWER

The first step is to assess the actual tasks, along with the pertinent information, then disregard the rest. Two tasks exist:

1. Set up home directories for each user.

2. Set up shared folders for all users.

The fact that ZEDCO is on a Windows NT domain is important, but the workstation and other server operating systems do not affect our tasks.

Step two is to determine the server for theses files, which is stated in the scenario: ZEDUSERS. Create a share on ZEDUSERS called USERS, grant the share permission Full Control to the Users group. (Remove the Everyone group.) Make sure the file system is NTFS.

Next, go to User Manager For Domains. Select all 248 users with SHIFT-click or CTRL-click. Press ENTER to get to the User Properties dialog box. Click the Profile button and click the Home

Directory field. Type **\\ZEDUSERS\users\%username%**, click OK, and then Add. This will automatically create the subfolders under Users for each username, and grant the Full control permissions to the user, removing the Everyone group. This is the most efficient way to establish home directories and is quite easy!

Our second task can be resolved in many ways, but I suggest the following: Create a subfolder under Users on ZEDUSERS and share it as ALL. Give the Users group Full Control, then set up the following Access Control List entries.

- **Users**   Read

- **Creator Owner**   Full Control

As you can see, setting up the permissions like this allows users to read and copy any file in the ALL folder. Keep in mind, however, that each file created or copied into this folder is only controlled by the user that created it.

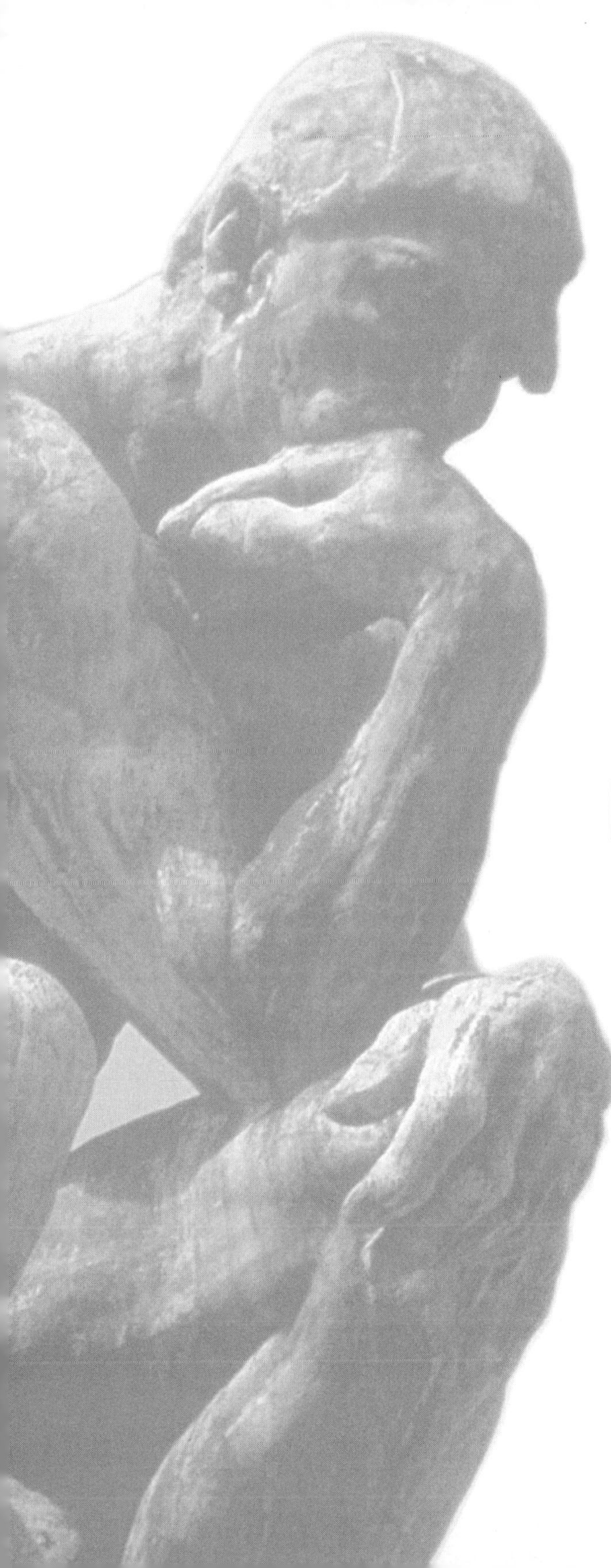

6

Analyzing, Configuring, and Monitoring Security

CERTIFICATION OBJECTIVES

A lot has changed since Microsoft released Windows NT 4.0 in 1996. The exam objectives for the now-retired NT 4.0 core exams reflected the importance of network security in 1996. The security objectives for the 70-244 exam, on the other hand, reflect the security concerns for today's networks. Many ideas and concepts have carried over from the original NT 4.0 exams. However, with the release of Windows 2000, Microsoft has back-ported some utilities from its newest enterprise-class operating system to reinforce Windows NT 4.0. This chapter reflects the changes in Windows NT 4.0 since its release. The first exam objective introduces a new product launched with Windows 2000—the Security Configuration Manager (SCM). The Security Configuration Manager has been adapted to work with Windows NT 4.0 to ease security configuration and administration.

The second exam objective reviews the methods and tools used to audit and monitor your Windows NT 4.0 network. If you are currently an administrator for an NT 4.0 network and/or an NT 4.0 MCSE, you will find the utilities in this section very familiar.

The third and final exam objective covered here introduces some advanced security configuration options released with the various service packs for Windows NT 4.0.

CERTIFICATION OBJECTIVE 6.01

Configuring the OS and User Environments by Using the Security Configuration Manager

Windows NT 4.0 supplies an administrator with a sufficient quantity of graphical security configuration tools. Before Service Pack 4, however, the only security monitoring tool built-in to NT 4.0 was the Event Viewer. With the release of Service Pack 4 (SP 4) for Windows NT 4.0, Microsoft introduced a new security configuration tool to ease administration of your Windows NT network. With the release of the Service Pack 4 CD, Microsoft introduced the Security Configuration Manager (SCM). The Security Configuration Manager is a product originally designed for Windows NT 5.0 (now known as Windows 2000). With the installation of SCM, an administrator is provided with the prime Windows 2000 management interface—the Microsoft Management Console (MMC). The MMC is a multiple document interface. If you have worked with any of the Microsoft Office line of applications, you are familiar with a multiple document interface. Let's take a look at what the SCM offers.

The SCM was designed to provide the following features:

- **Comprehensiveness** SCM allows the administrator to analyze several security aspects of the existing network. The SCM facilitates the analysis and configuration of the following:

    - **Account Policies** Local and domain password and lockout settings.

    - **Local Policies** Audit policies and user rights assignment.

    - **Restricted Groups** Manage group membership for built-in and specific groups.

    - **System Services** Audit and configure various system services.

    - **System Registry** Security configuration of Registry keys.

    - **System Store** Local file system security configuration.

- **Flexibility** Because the SCM is based on basic text files, configurations are easily distributed throughout your network.

- **Extendibility** The SCM has been designed to give administrators and third-party software vendors the ability to add new security parameters and configurations to the existing SCM structure.

- **Simplicity** The SCM uses a graphical user interface (GUI) to provide simplified administration of various security aspects of your network without forcing you to learn several new applications.

The following section walks you through acquiring and installing the Security Configuration Manager and consequently, the Microsoft Management Console.

The Microsoft Management Console and the Microsoft Security Configuration Manager

The Microsoft Security Configuration Manager is an application supplied with the Windows NT 4.0 Service Pack 4 CD. If you do not have the SP 4 CD, you can download the SCM application from Microsoft's Web site at http://www.microsoft .com/NTServer/nts/downloads/recommended/scm/default.asp. The application is a self-extracting zipped file.

The SCM eases administration and allows for more consistent security configurations in a Windows NT 4.0 network. Before SP 4, the security configuration of a Windows NT 4.0 network involved using User Manager or User Manager For Domains, Windows Explorer, the System Policy Editor, and the Windows NT Registry Editor. With the introduction of the Windows NT Security Configuration Manager, security configuration of a Windows NT 4.0 network can now be configured from one convenient tool. Now, let's take a look at the installation process.

Installing the Microsoft Security Configuration Manager

Installing the SCM to your Windows NT 4.0 system will alter the structure of your Access Control List (ACL) interface. The new interface uses the same permissions a standard install of Windows NT 4.0 would use, however you now have the option to allow or deny the specific permissions. Before installing the SCM, the ACL interface only permitted administrators to allow the various permissions. Figure 6-1 displays the new permission structure for the ACL interface.

FIGURE 6-1 The new ACL interface after installation of the Security Configuration Manager

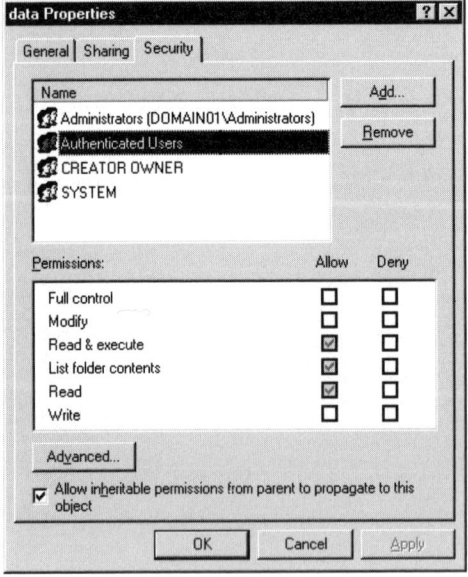

exam
ⓦatch

Become very familiar with the new permission structure implemented through the Security Configuration Manager installation. Windows 2000 administrators should be well acquainted with the new permission configuration since it has been back-ported from Windows 2000.

After downloading the scesp4i.exe file from Microsoft's site, running the application extracts the necessary files to a user-specified directory. Figure 6-2 is a listing of the extracted files and folders.

Running mssce.exe will begin the installation process for the Security Configuration Manager. You will be prompted with a dialog box confirming the installation of the Microsoft Windows NT Security Configuration Manager.

The next screen you encounter will be a dialog box confirming installation of the Microsoft Management Console. Again, select YES to continue the installation.

FIGURE 6-2

Files extracted from scesp4i.exe (your files may look different depending on screen and folder options settings)

Name	Size	Type	Modified	Attributes
symbols		File Folder	5/5/01 10:23 AM	
immc	1,188KB	Application	7/16/98 2:15 PM	A
mssce.cab	718KB	CAB File	10/15/98 11:04 AM	A
mssce	218KB	Application	10/15/98 11:04 AM	A
readme	12KB	Text Document	10/15/98 11:04 AM	A
regsvr32	37KB	Application	10/15/98 11:04 AM	A
scefiles	2KB	Setup Information	10/15/98 11:04 AM	A
scesetup	1KB	Setup Information	10/15/98 11:04 AM	A
setup	9KB	Setup Information	10/15/98 11:04 AM	A

9 object(s)   2.12MB

The Microsoft Management Console is a customizable multiple document interface. The MMC allows administrators to specify the availability of various administrative tools in one convenient interface. After the MMC installation dialog box, another dialog box warns that a system restart might be required.

on the *!*Job

When working in a production environment, it is highly recommended you schedule server maintenance and changes for nonbusiness hours to prevent loss of service for your users.

The next dialog box is the end user license agreement for the Microsoft Security Configuration Manager. From the End User License Agreement dialog box, continue with the installation by selecting YES.

The file copy process begins as soon as you agree to the end user license agreement. When the file copy process completes, a command prompt opens displaying the initialization screen. The installation of the Microsoft Security Configuration Manager is now complete. The next section of this chapter walks you through the process of customizing your Microsoft Management Console to include the Security Configuration Manager.

Microsoft Management Console Customization

One of the benefits of the Microsoft Management Console is that it facilitates customization of some of your administrative tools. To open the Microsoft Management Console, select Start | Run | and type **mmc** at the run prompt.

Upon running mmc.exe, a Microsoft Management Console splash screen opens where you are presented with a blank MMC, as seen in Figure 6-3.

The next step is to add the Security Configuration Manager snap-in to the MMC interface. To add the SCM snap-in, from the menu bar of the MMC, select Console | Add/Remove Snap-in, as seen in Figure 6-4.

Select the Add button from the Add/Remove Snap-in dialog box, as shown in Figure 6-5.

You will be prompted with a list of various MMC snap-ins. Select the Security Configuration Manager from the snap-in list. Once you have added the snap-in, you should save your newly configured MMC. For simplicity, we will save the MMC to the desktop as scm.msc, as seen in Figure 6-6.

Now, the Security Configuration Manager is ready for use. In the next section, we will look at the various preconfigured templates available in the SCM.

FIGURE 6-3

The blank
Microsoft
Management
Console

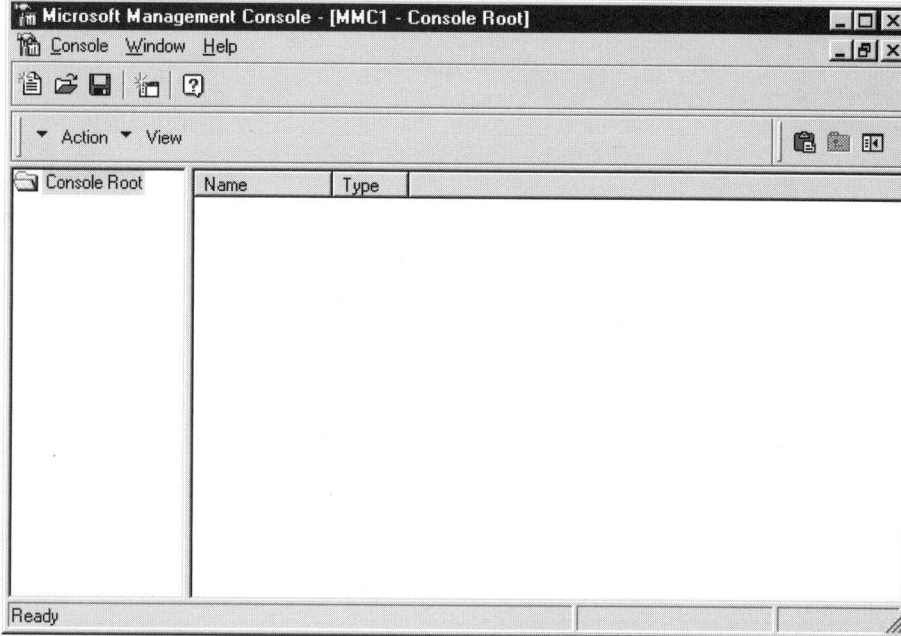

FIGURE 6-4

Adding the SCM
snap-in

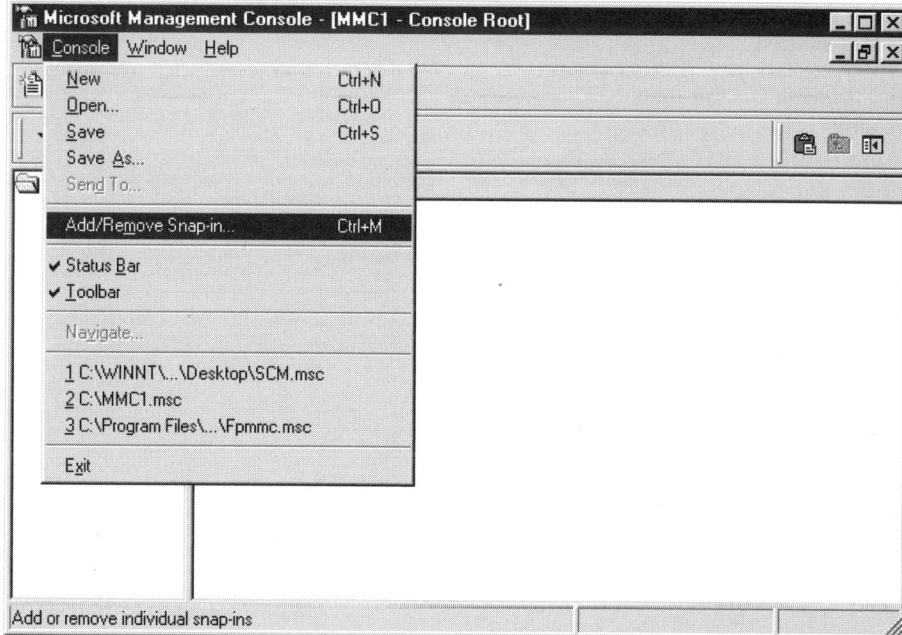

FIGURE 6-5

The Add/Remove
Snap-in dialog
box

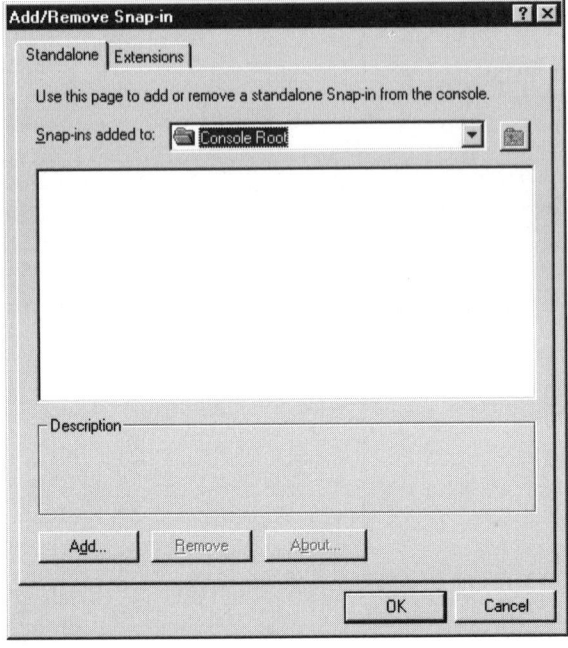

FIGURE 6-6

Saving the newly
configured
Microsoft
Management
Console

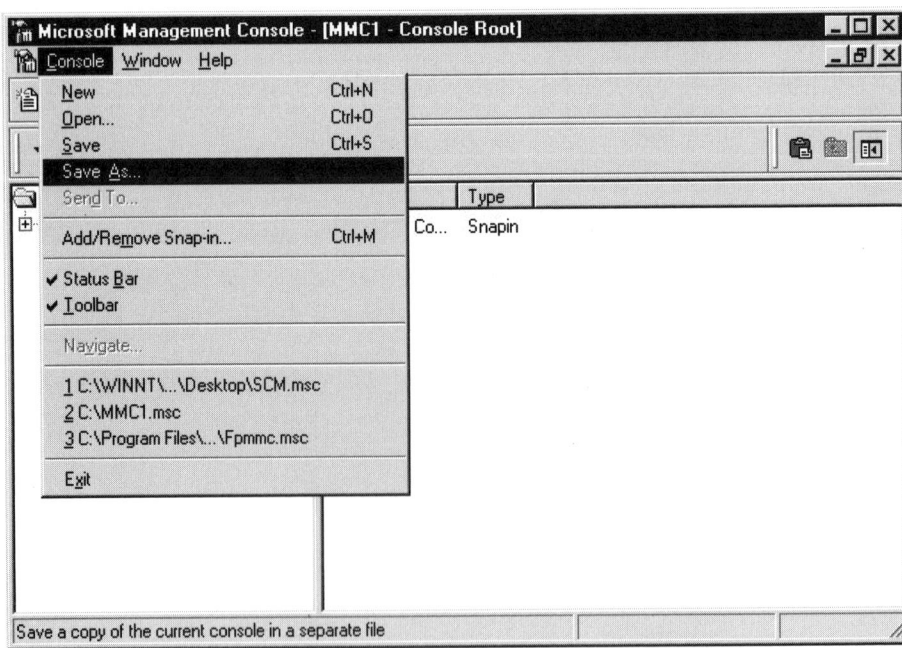

Applying the Appropriate Security Template Based on Server Function

One of the benefits of the SCM is its capability to provide a consistent security configuration for workstations, servers, and domain controllers. The SCM provides a graphical user interface (GUI) via the Microsoft Management Console, as well as a command line utility via the secedit.exe command. The secedit.exe command line utility provides the capability to apply templates through logon scripts as an option.

exam
ⓦatch

Because the command line options for the Security Configuration Manager may be applied through a logon script, be sure to familiarize yourself with the command line options. Take a look at the command line options for the SCM by typing secedit at a command prompt and following the options provided.

Because the SCM utilizes Microsoft's *.inf* file format to store security settings, it is very easy to import or export configurations from system to system. Microsoft provides the Windows NT 4.0 administrator with several preconfigured templates suited to several different security requirements. The preconfigured templates provide a baseline on which to build customized configurations. Figure 6-7 demonstrates the preconfigured templates available in the SCM.

FIGURE 6-7

The preconfigured templates for the SCM

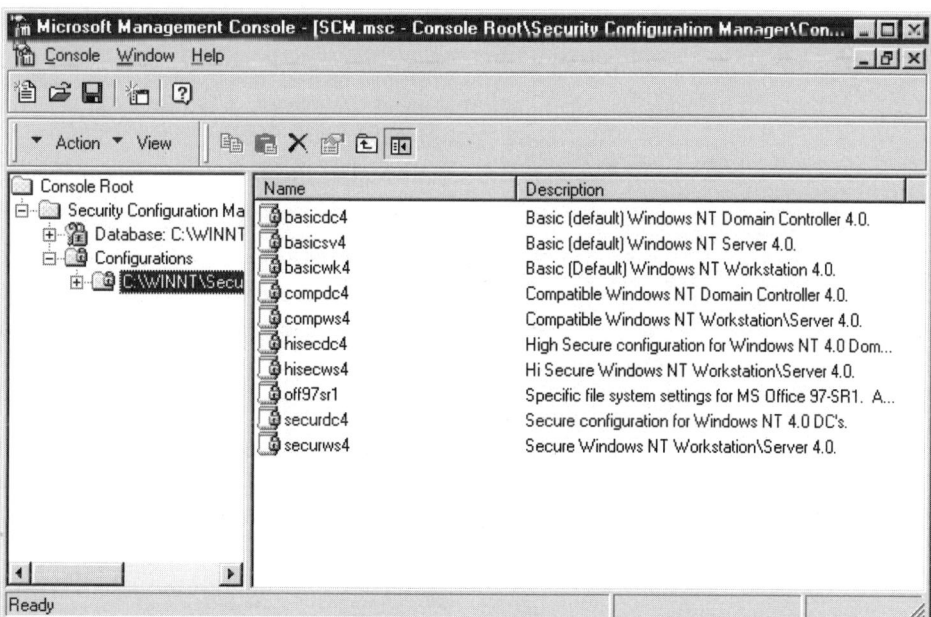

On the right side of the right pane, you see a basic description of each of the security templates. The following list describes the reason for using each of the preconfigured security templates:

- **Basicdc4** The purpose of this template is to reverse the effects of templates or configurations previously applied to an NT 4.0 domain controller.

- **Basicsv4** The purpose of this template is to reverse the effects of templates or configurations previously applied to an NT 4.0 member server.

- **Basicwk4** The purpose of this template is to reverse the effects of templates or configurations previously applied to an NT 4.0 workstation.

- **Compdc4** The purpose of this template is to loosen security to allow installation of software for your NT 4.0 domain controllers.

- **Compws4** The purpose of this template is to loosen security to allow installation of software for your NT 4.0 member servers or workstations.

- **Hisecdc4** The purpose of this template is to strengthen network security on your NT 4.0 domain controllers. Only NT 4.0 systems configured to run the high secure settings may communicate over the network.

- **Hisecws4** The purpose of this template is to strengthen network security on your NT 4.0 member servers or workstations. Only NT 4.0 systems configured to run the high secure settings may communicate over the network.

- **Off97sr1** The purpose of this template is to strengthen security on your NT 4.0 systems running Microsoft Office 97 with Service Pack 1. This template should be applied after the appropriate compatibility template (compdc4, compws4).

- **Securdc4** The purpose of this template is to execute Microsoft's recommended security settings for NT 4.0 domain controllers for all security areas except files, folders, and Registry keys. File system and Registry permissions are configured securely by default.

- **Securws4** The purpose of this template is to execute Microsoft's recommended security settings for NT 4.0 workstations and member servers for all security areas except files, folders, and Registry keys. File system and Registry permissions are configured securely by default.

To apply a preconfigured template to your system, highlight the database icon in the left pane and select action from the toolbar. Select Import Configuration to

FIGURE 6-8

Importing a
security template

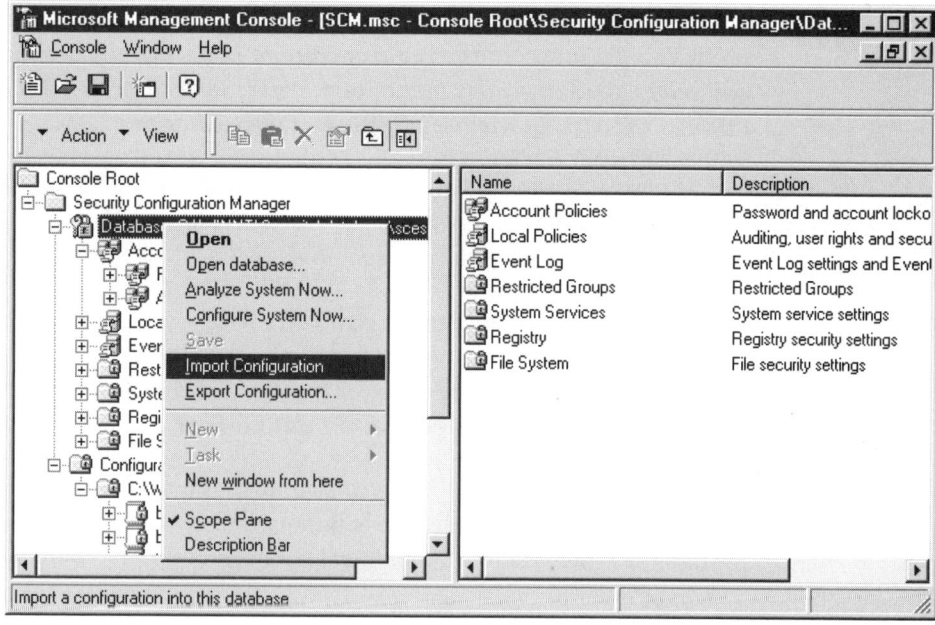

import the appropriate template based on the descriptions from the preceding list.
Figure 6-8 demonstrates the importing of a template.

FROM THE CLASSROOM

The Windows NT 4.0 Security Configuration Manager

The Windows NT 4.0 Security Configuration
Manager was designed for Windows 2000 and
altered to work with Windows NT 4.0. If you
have not worked with the Security Configuration
Manager in either environment, I highly
recommend you set up a lab to see this
application in a network environment. In the
classroom, we devote several labs to products
like the Security Configuration Manager

because the best way to learn this type of
utility is by working with it. Since Microsoft
deemed the Security Configuration Manager
important enough to add to Windows NT
4.0, after designing it for Windows 2000, you
can bet they will deem it important enough to
devote several test questions to this topic.

—*Hal Kurz, MCSE, MCP, MCT, CCNA*

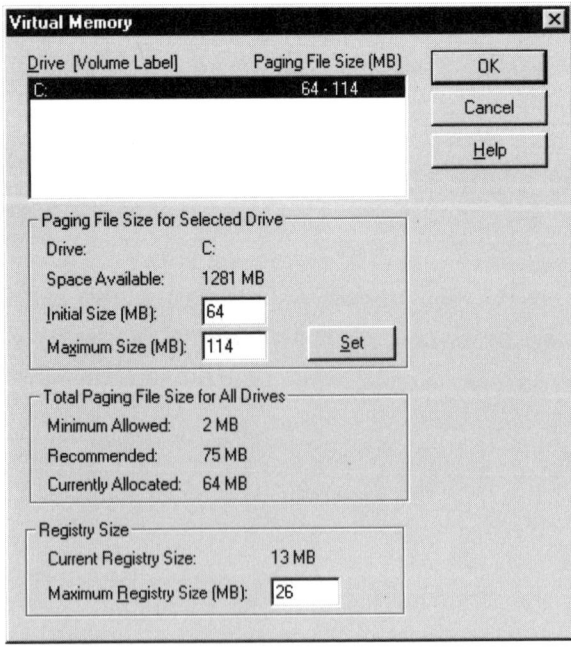

on the **Job** *On some systems, you may experience a registry error due to insufficient resources. To increase the registry storage capacity, right-click My Computer and select the Properties menu item. Next, select the Performance tab and through the Virtual Memory Settings, select Change.*

The next step is to extend the registry to a more adequate size. In Figure 6-9, I have increased the registry from the default setting of 13MB to a more sufficient 26MB to allow for security configurations.

on the **Job** *Be aware that modifying the registry size will require a system reboot. Rebooting a production server during normal operation can result in disconnecting users and a possible loss of data for the same. Reconfigure or alter your servers during nonbusiness hours to prevent data loss or production problems.*

Once a security template has been imported, the next step is to either analyze or configure the system with the newly imported template. The next section describes the difference between the Configure The System option and the Analyze The System option.

FIGURE 6-9

Increasing the maximum registry size to 26MB

Analyzing the Current Environment

Use the analyze option to see the settings of the existing system configuration compared to the configuration that the imported file would produce. Use the configure option to apply a specific configuration without displaying the specific security settings. To compare an imported configuration to the system's existing configuration, highlight the database icon in the left pane and select Action from the toolbar. From the Action menu, select Analyze System Now, as shown in Figure 6-10.

Once the system has been analyzed, you can compare the imported system settings to the current settings. You can browse the configuration settings in much the same way you would browse folders in Windows Explorer. Figure 6-11 is a comparison of the hisecdc4.inf configuration file compared against a basic system configuration (basicdc4.inf).

exam
ⓦatch

The 70-244 exam places a heavy emphasis on the analysis portion of the objectives. After running an analysis, be sure you understand which security settings increase or decrease security on your system.

To apply the configuration changes to a system, select the database icon in the left pane and select Action from the toolbar. From the Action menu, select Configure System Now, as seen in Figure 6-12.

The next section discusses the customization of existing security templates to meet specific security requirements of your organization.

Customizing Existing Security Templates to Meet the Organization's Security Requirements

The preconfigured security templates provide a basic framework to begin a specialized configuration of your network environment. The first step to customizing your network security is to determine the security requirements. Does your environment require passwords with a certain level of complexity? Should the passwords be changed more frequently than the default 42 days? Is a password history required? Should a certain number of failed logon attempts result in a locked account? Will a locked account unlock automatically after a predetermined time, or will it remain locked until an administrator unlocks it? These are some of the many questions an administrator should ask when configuring the security settings for a network environment.

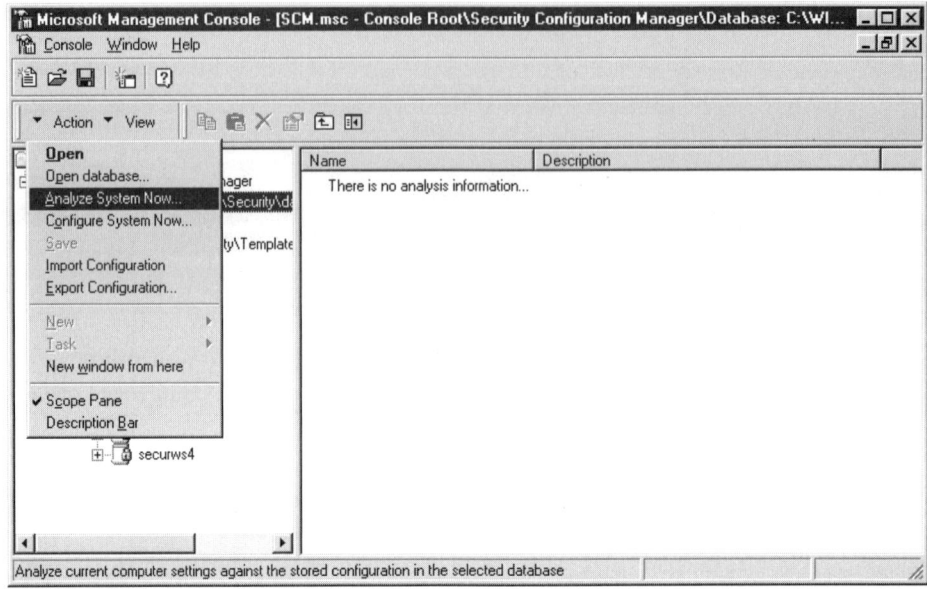

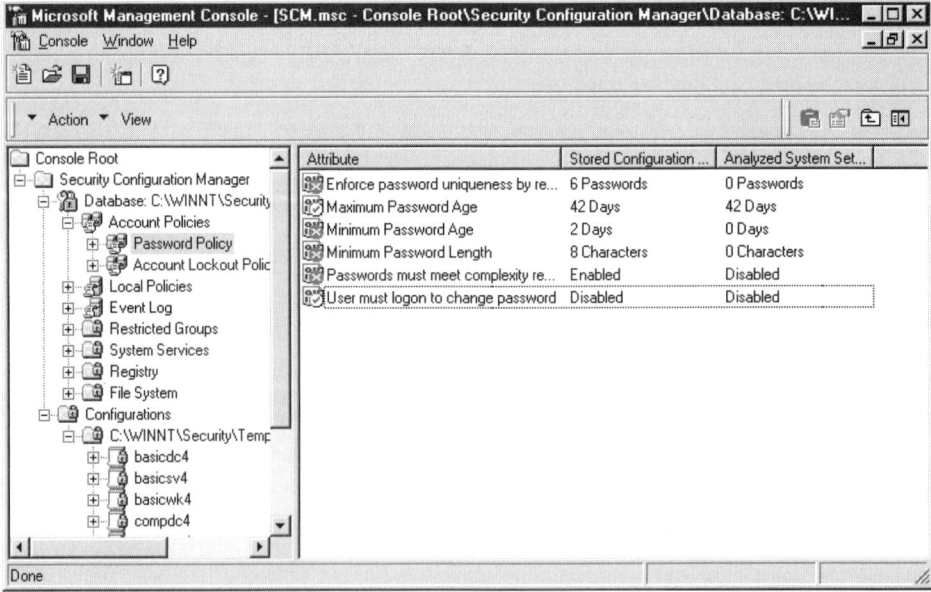

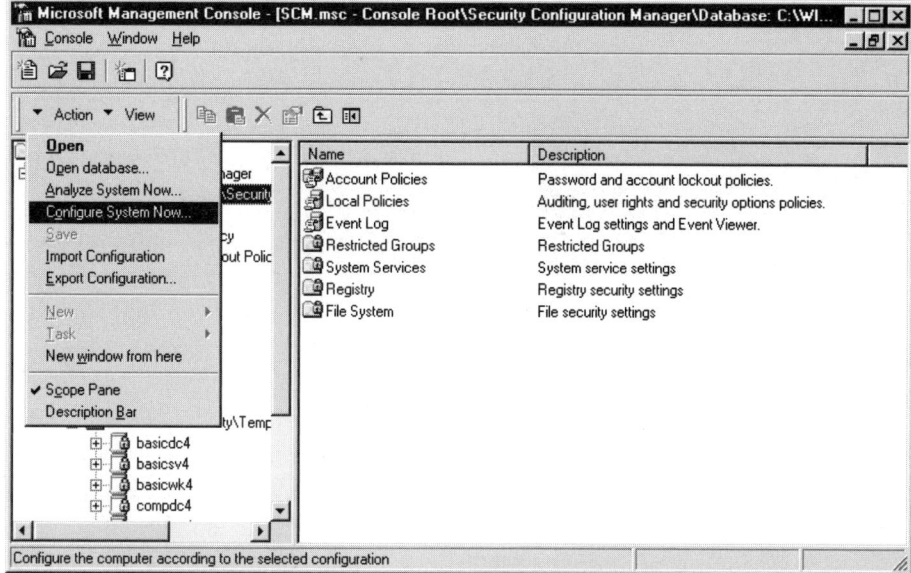

FIGURE 6-12

Configuring the system to use the imported security template

The SCM provides an administrator with several configuration options. Let's take a look at the configuration options for the SCM. The following list describes each of the basic configuration areas available in the SCM:

- **Account Policies**   Configure password and lockout settings
    - **Password Policy**   Password uniqueness, maximum password age, minimum password age, minimum password length, password complexity, logon to change password
    - **Lockout Policy**   Lockout count, lockout duration, count reset
- **Local Policies**   Configure auditing, user rights, special security options
    - **Audit Policy**   Account management, logon events, object access, policy change, privilege use, process tracking, system events
    - **User Rights Assignment**   Access this computer from the network, backup options, bypass traverse checking, change the system time, create a page file, create a token object, create permanent shared objects, debug programs, force shutdown from a remote system, generate security audits,

increase quotas, increase scheduling priority, load and unload device drivers, lock pages in memory, log on locally, manage auditing and security log, modify firmware environment values, profile single process, profile system performance, replace a process-level token, restore files and directories, shut down the system, take ownership of files or other objects

■ **Security Options** Task scheduling permission, shut down without logging on, system object access, audit use of user rights, auto disconnect of idle sessions, auto disconnect time limit, change administrator account name, change guest account name, clear virtual memory page file when system shuts down, always digitally sign client-side, digitally sign client-side when possible, always digitally sign server-side, digitally sign server-side when possible, disallow account enumeration by anonymous users, do not display last username in logon screen, forcibly log off when logon hours expire, logon message text, logon message title, number of cached logons, prevent print driver installation, restrict CD-ROM access to local logon, restrict floppy to local logon, restrict shared resource management, always digitally encrypt secure channel, encrypt secure channel when possible, digitally sign secure channel when possible, send downlevel LanMan-compatible password, send unencrypted password for third-party SMB servers, shut down system immediately if unable to log security audits

■ **Event Log** Configure Event Viewer properties

　　■ **Event Log Settings** Application log maximum size, security log maximum size, system log maximum size, restrict guest access to application log, restrict guest access to security log, restrict guest access to system log, retention method for application log, retention method for security log, retention method for system log, shut down system when security audit log becomes full

■ **Restricted Groups** Permanently configure account membership

■ **System Services** Configure startup options and security for system services

■ **Registry** Configure registry access permissions

■ **File System** Permanently configure specified file and folder permissions

In the next section, we will look at security auditing and monitoring.

SCENARIO & SOLUTION

Where is the current configuration of the machine? When I try to look it up, the database display says "not loaded."	You have to analyze the existing system to produce a viewable configuration.
The system produces a stop error, now that I have configured the system with a new template. What should I do?	Make sure the security audit log is not full. It is possible to configure the system to shut down if the security log becomes full.
The system requests I change the password, but when I type in a new one, a message box appears saying the password does not meet the complexity requirement. What has happened?	If you enabled a password complexity requirement, the password must be alphanumeric with a combination of capital and lowercase letters.
Why do some of the settings have a red X mark?	If the imported configuration differs from the current configuration, a red X will be displayed on the conflicting configuration settings.

EXERCISE 6-1

CertCam 6-1

Protecting Account Configuration with SCM's Restricted Groups

In this exercise, we will configure the Security Configuration Manager to protect the group membership of a user account.

1. Create a user account named user1 applying User Manager For Domains by selecting Start | Programs | Administrative Tools (Common) | User Manager For Domains.

2. Select User | New User. In the Username box, type **user1**.

3. Select Groups to determine the group membership for user1 (should be domain user).

4. Select the Add button, then choose Close to exit User Manager For Domains.

5. Open the Security Configuration Manager.

6. To ensure the configuration database is available for viewing, select the Database container, then choose Action from the toolbar, followed by Analyze System Now.

7. Once an analysis is loaded, select Database | Restricted Groups from the left pane of the SCM.

8. From the Restricted Groups container, select the Domain Administrators Attribute in the right pane of the SCM.

9. Now, select Action | Security… | Add from the toolbar and select user1 from the list. Select Add | OK | OK to complete the Restricted Group configuration.

10. Select Database from the left pane, then choose Action | Configure System Now.

11. Once system configuration is complete, navigate back to the Restricted Groups container to ensure it's marked with a green check mark.

12. Open User Manager For Domains and observe the new group membership of Domain Admins for user1.

CERTIFICATION OBJECTIVE 6.02

Implementing Auditing and Monitor Security

Once your security configurations are in place, you will want to ensure they work properly. One way to make certain your network security is doing its job is to monitor network events through an audit policy. Traditionally, setting up an audit policy would first require enabling auditing from User Manager For Domains and then second, setting the auditing of the particular object that requires monitoring. In the next section, we will explore two ways to configure auditing in a Windows NT 4.0 domain.

Configuring Audit Policy

Auditing in a domain environment requires enabling auditing on the domain controller. To enable auditing in a non-domain environment, enable auditing on the server that hosts the object that you wish to audit. In the next section, we will explore the traditional means for configuring auditing.

User Manager For Domains (the Traditional Approach)

To configure auditing in a Windows NT 4.0 domain, the first step is to enable auditing from the domain controller using User Manager For Domains. Open the Audit dialog box within User Manager For Domains by selecting Start | Programs | Administrative Tools (Common) | User Manager For Domains, and then selecting Policies | Audit from the menu bar.

From the Audit dialog box, enable the types of auditing our environment will require. To enable the various types of auditing, we configure the Auditing dialog box.

If you previously applied a template to your domain controller, you will notice that auditing is already configured. Before Service Pack 4, this was the way to configure auditing. In the next section, we will discuss another method for configuring an audit policy.

Using the Security Configuration Manager to Enable Auditing

As you may have noticed, applying security templates through the SCM is another way to configure auditing for a Windows NT 4.0 domain. Up to this point, we have reviewed options that will produce audit events for logon and logoff, but not for object access. Auditing object access is a two-step process.

e x a m

ⓦ a t c h

Take a close look at the configurable options for Event Logging through the SCM. Event Log configuration plays a large part in auditing a network environment and, consequently, will be emphasized on the exam.

To view the overall audit policy through the SCM, from the left pane of the SCM, select Database | Local Policies | Audit Policy. To make modifications to the policy for object access, from the domain controller open the Audit Object Access dialog box by selecting Audit Object Access from the right pane, selecting Action from the toolbar, and selecting Security (as seen in Figure 6-13).

From the Audit Object Access dialog box, select the event to audit (as seen in Figure 6-14).

As mentioned earlier, auditing file and object access is a two-step process. The next section outlines the second step.

FIGURE 6-13

Changing audit
policy using
the Security
Configuration
Manager

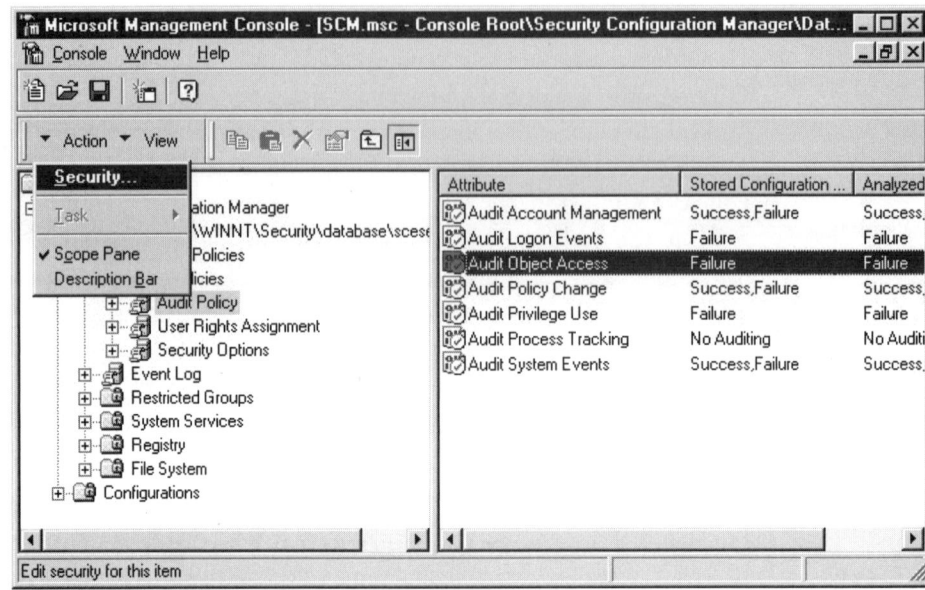

Enabling Auditing on Objects

The steps taken so far will produce audit events for logon and logoff events but not
for object access. To complete auditing of Object Access events, the first step is to
turn on auditing through one of two methods described in the previous section. The

FIGURE 6-14

Selecting the
audit event

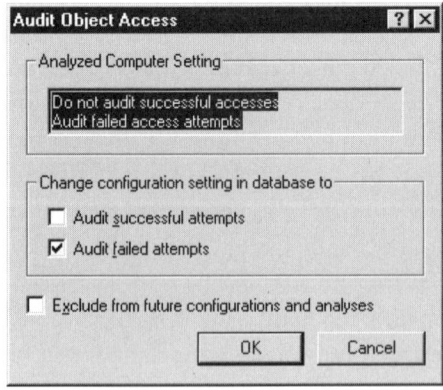

next step requires enabling auditing for the system hosting the resources through either User Manager or User Manager For Domains in the same fashion as described earlier in this chapter. The final step is to enable the specific types of events to audit on the resource itself. In order to audit attempted access to files or folders, the files or folders must be stored on an NTFS partition. To configure auditing of attempted access to files or folders hosted by Windows NT 4.0 systems that do not have the SCM installed, navigate to the file or folder through Windows Explorer or My Computer, choose the file or folder to audit, select File | Properties, then on the Security tab select the Auditing button. Now, add the user(s) and/or group(s) you wish to audit and select the types of events to audit. Specify whether existing audit settings shall be replaced on files or subfolders, then select OK and/or choose YES to the remaining dialog boxes to complete the audit configuration.

Because the Security Configuration Manager alters the security interface on a Windows NT 4.0 system, expect to see a Security tab identical to that of a Windows 2000 system. On a system running the SCM, to view specific audit policies for file and object access, navigate through the File System container in the file server's SCM to find the file or folder to audit. If the file or folder is not visible in the SCM's File System container, you can add it by selecting File System from the left pane, selecting Action from the toolbar, and selecting either Add Files or Add Folder from the Action menu. Once you find the file or folder to audit, open the Security Configuration Properties dialog box for the file or folder by first selecting the file or folder and then choosing Action | Security from the SCM toolbar. From the Security tab open the Auditing dialog box by selecting the Advanced button from the Security tab and selecting the Audit tab. Add the user(s) and/or group(s) you wish to audit, as seen in Figure 6-15.

After selecting a user or group to audit, the next step is to select the types of events to audit. Figure 6-16 shows the list of available events to audit.

Select the events you wish to audit and specify whether the subfolder shall also be audited by marking the Apply These Audit Entries To Objects And/Or Containers Within This Container Only check box. Selecting OK for the next two dialog boxes will cause audit policies to propagate downward to this folder. Select Remove to force the chosen audit properties to apply to this folder.

Now that we have set up auditing, it's time to look at the results. The next section discusses the use of the Event Viewer to view various audit events.

FIGURE 6-15

Selecting users
to audit

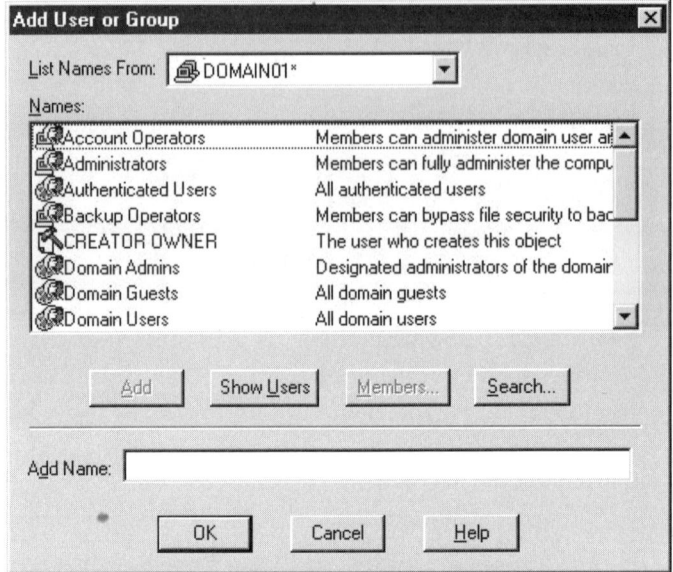

FIGURE 6-16

Selecting the
events to audit

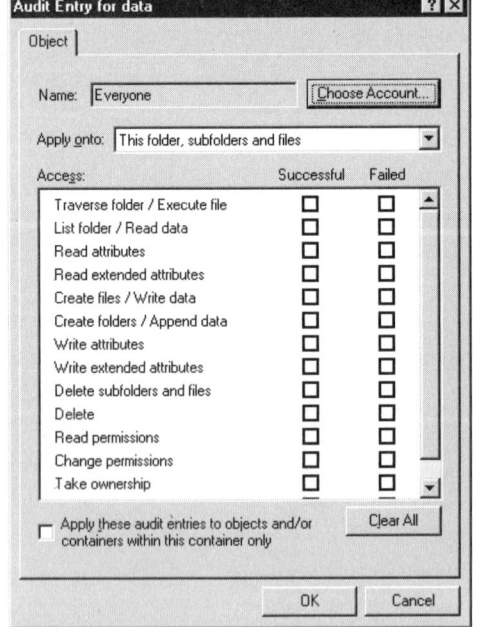

Analyzing Audit Logs

The tool used to analyze audit logs is the Windows NT 4.0 Event Viewer. In this section, we will look at the Event Viewer and its configuration for analyzing Windows NT 4.0 audit logs.

Audit logs are viewed using the Event Viewer. To open the Event Viewer, select Start | Programs | Administrative Tools (Common) | Event Viewer. Event Viewer logs are divided into three sources: System, Security, and Application. Audit events will display as Security sources. To view a complete list of all of the events audited, select Log | Security from the Event Viewer menu.

The Event Viewer allows for filtering of events. This capability eases administration. To take advantage of the filtering feature of the Event Viewer, select View | Filter Events from the Event Viewer menu bar. Figure 6-17 displays the Event Viewer filter options.

As mentioned earlier in this chapter, the Event Viewer's properties can be configured through the SCM. The SCM allows an administrator to not only set the size of the event log, it allows an administrator to configure the effects of filling the event logs.

FIGURE 6-17

The Event Viewer filter options dialog box

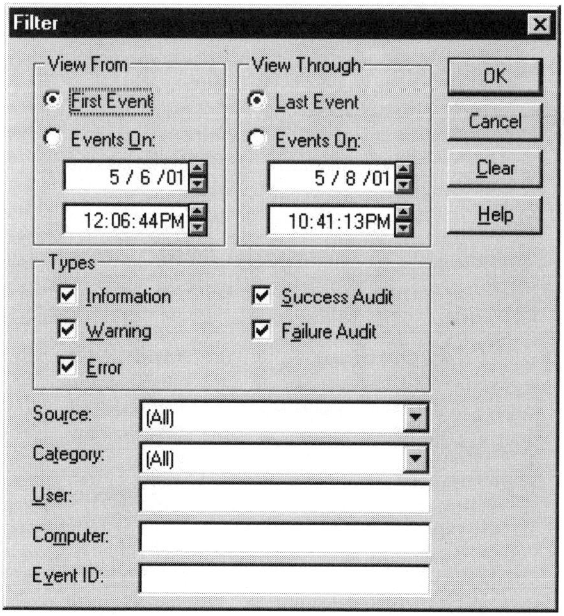

SCENARIO & SOLUTION

I have configured auditing of several different events, but there are no events displayed in the event log. What should I do?	Make sure that filtering of events is turned off.
Where do I set the log size?	The size of each event log (system, security, application, and so on) can be configured through the Event Viewer by selecting Log | Log Settings or through the Security Configuration Manager by choosing Event Log\Settings For Event Log\ Retention Method For…
I am unable to set auditing on the files or folders on my drive. How can I correct this?	Make sure the drive is formatted with the NTFS file system. Auditing is only available through NTFS.

SCM allows an administrator to force a system shutdown if the security log reaches its specified maximum size. As another option, the log can be configured to "wrap." Wrapping the event log causes it to overwrite previous entries. It is good security policy to configure your system to shut down when the security event log becomes full and for you or your coworkers to back up and clear the security event logs on a regular basis. The next section introduces the advanced security options added to Windows NT 4.0.

EXERCISE 6-2

CertCam 6-2

Configuring the Audit Log Settings

In this exercise, we will configure the audit log size as well as configure the system to shut down if the log becomes full.

1. Open the Security Configuration Manager.

2. To ensure the configuration database is available for viewing, select the Database container, then choose Action from the toolbar, and select Analyze System Now.

3. From the Database container in the left pane, select Event Log \| Settings For Event Logs.

4. Select Retention Method For Security Log from the right pane and choose Action \| Security.

5. From the Retention Method For Security Log dialog box, select Do Not Overwrite Events (Clean Log Manually) and click the OK button.

6. From the right pane, select Shutdown System When Security Audit Log Becomes Full.

7. Select Action | Security from the toolbar. Then from the dialog box, select Enabled within the Change Configuration Setting In Database section. (If Enabled and Disabled are grayed out, uncheck Exclude From Future Configurations And Analysis).

8. Select Maximum Log Size For Security Log from the right pane and select Action | Security from the SCM toolbar.

9. If the size is not configured to 512KB, adjust it accordingly and select OK.

10. Highlight the Database container and select Action from the SCM toolbar.

11. Select Configure System Now.

12. Upon completion, the system is now configured to shut down once the Security Log reaches 512KB.

13. Based on this configuration, the Event Viewer should be saved and cleared on a regular interval.

CERTIFICATION OBJECTIVE 6.03

Implementing Advanced Security Options

In this section, we will explore three security utilities built into later builds of Windows NT 4.0. The tools we will analyze here were added to Windows NT 4.0 during its lifecycle through various service packs. The next segment introduces the syskey.exe utility.

Syskey

The syskey.exe security tool was introduced with Windows NT 4.0 Service Pack 3. Windows NT 4.0 stores user account information (including a form of the user's password) in the Security Accounts Management database (SAM). This database is stored in a secure, encrypted portion of the registry. To increase the security of a Windows NT system, syskey.exe utilizes a system key to highly encrypt the information contained in the Security Accounts Management database (SAM).

Raising the level of encryption makes unauthorized access to the system and to system resources much more difficult than it would be without syskey enabled.

To enable system key encryption, select Start | Run | and type **syskey**. The next dialog box gives the administrator the option of enabling or disabling the system key. Selecting the Encryption Enabled option prompts the administrator with a confirmation dialog box warning the administrator to update the emergency repair disk (ERD) before continuing. Make sure you have an updated ERD before going any further. OK the confirmation dialog box to continue.

on the Job

If you lose your system key, you have the option of reinstalling NT 4.0 or repairing the registry with the pre-syskey ERD and consequently losing any system changes or updates that later ERDs would have backed up.

exam Watch

Recovering from a lost syskey floppy or forgotten syskey password is not a good position to be in. Remember your recovery options (ERD or reinstall) going into the exam.

The next dialog box presents the user with three options: password startup, store startup key on floppy disk, and store startup key locally.

The first of the three user options is the Password Startup option (mode two encryption). The Password Startup option presents the system's users with a Password dialog box during system startup.

The second option offered by the Account Database Key dialog box presents the administrator with the choice of storing the system-generated key to a floppy disk (mode three encryption). This option stores the system key on a floppy disk for easy removal. Once this encryption setting is selected, the system key floppy will be required to boot this system after syskey configuration is completed.

on the Job

Storing your system key to a floppy presents two concerns. The first is the single point of failure created by the system key. Back up your syskey disk and make updated ERDs to ensure you have alternatives if your syskey disk fails or becomes unavailable. The second concern is the security information stored on the syskey floppy. Protect the syskey floppy the same way you protect ERDs and backup tapes.

SCENARIO & SOLUTION

I get an error when I type syskey from the run prompt. How can I change this?	Make sure SP 3 or later is installed on your system. Windows NT 4.0 does not ship with syskey. Syskey was added with SP 3.
I lost my syskey floppy. How do I boot my system?	If you lose a syskey floppy or forget your syskey password, you have the option of reinstalling the operating system or running the repair process by booting from the CD or installation floppies and selecting the Repair option.
What level of encryption is used by syskey?	Syskey uses a 128-bit cryptographic random key.

EXERCISE 6-3

CertCam 6-3

Generating a System Key Floppy

This exercise will demonstrate the steps required to generate a system key floppy disk (mode three). This provides the most secure syskey configuration available.

1. First, create an updated repair disk by running the rdisk.exe utility. Select Start | Run, then type **rdisk /s**.

2. Upon completion of the repair disk, begin the syskey process by selecting Start | Run, and typing **syskey**.

3. Select the Encryption Enabled option, followed by OK.

4. Select System Generated Password and Store Startup Key On Floppy Disk, followed by OK.

5. From the Account Startup Key dialog box, select OK.

6. When prompted for a floppy disk, insert a blank formatted floppy disk and select OK.

The third selection presents the administrator with the option to locally store the system key without intervention (mode one). This option generates a system key and stores it to the local hard drive. On system startup, the syskey utility retrieves the stored system key to complete the boot process.

As mentioned, syskey provides three levels or modes of protection. Mode one, locally stored system key, provides convenience but affords the lowest level of security available through syskey. Mode one is only slightly more secure than a nonsyskey enabled system. Mode two, password protected syskey, provides the next highest level of security. Mode three, floppy-based system key encryption, provides the highest level of security available through syskey. The security provided by mode three syskey is only as good as the physical security provided for the syskey floppy. If the syskey floppy is readily available, mode three syskey is realistically only as good as the locally stored mode one syskey. The next section describes the reason for using Server Message Block (SMB) signing and illustrates the process used to enable SMB signing.

Server Message Block

Server Message Block (SMB) authentication protocol, also known as Common Internet File System (CIFS) file sharing protocol, is the protocol used to access shared resources in a Windows NT 4.0 network. Network communication involves two steps, authentication and authorization. Authentication is the process of verifying a user or computer's identity. Authorization is the process of allowing or disallowing access to network resources or services. Service Pack 4 (SP 4) updates the features of SMB on Windows NT 4.0 systems to allow for mutual authentication of client and server. Mutual authentication ensures that both of the communicating systems are not being spoofed or falsely represented by an outside party. This increased level of security makes certain network communication only occurs between the systems intended to communicate. Installing SP 4 on a Windows NT 4.0 server does not automatically update SMB authentication for that system. To take advantage of the SMB update on a Windows NT 4.0 Server, SMB signing must be enabled. SMB signing has three possible configurations for a Windows NT 4.0 Server.

SMB signing provides three options: disabled (default), enabled but not required, and required. Enabling SMB signing causes a server to attempt communication with clients using signed packets, but the server will not require signed SMB traffic. Enabling SMB signing on a server with the RequireSecuritySignature setting will require all SMB traffic to be mutually authenticated with signed packets. Enabling SMB signing on Windows NT 4.0 requires modifying the system registry.

on the **Job**

While enabling SMB signing increases network security for your Windows NT 4.0 network, be aware that by doing this, network performance can decrease by as much as 10 to 15 percent.

To enable SMB signing on a Windows NT 4.0 system, start the Registry Editor by selecting Start | Run, and then typing **Regedt32**. Navigate to the following registry key: HKEY_LOCAL_MACHINE\System\CurrentControlSet\Services\ LanManServer\Parameters, as seen in Figure 6-18.

If the registry keys for EnableSecuritySignature and RequireSecuritySignature already exist, please move to the SMB Signing Registry Key Values section later in this chapter. If the registry keys for EnableSecuritySignature and RequireSecuritySignature DO NOT exist, please move to the next section, labeled Creating the Required SMB Registry Keys.

FIGURE 6-18

Editing the registry to enable SMB signing

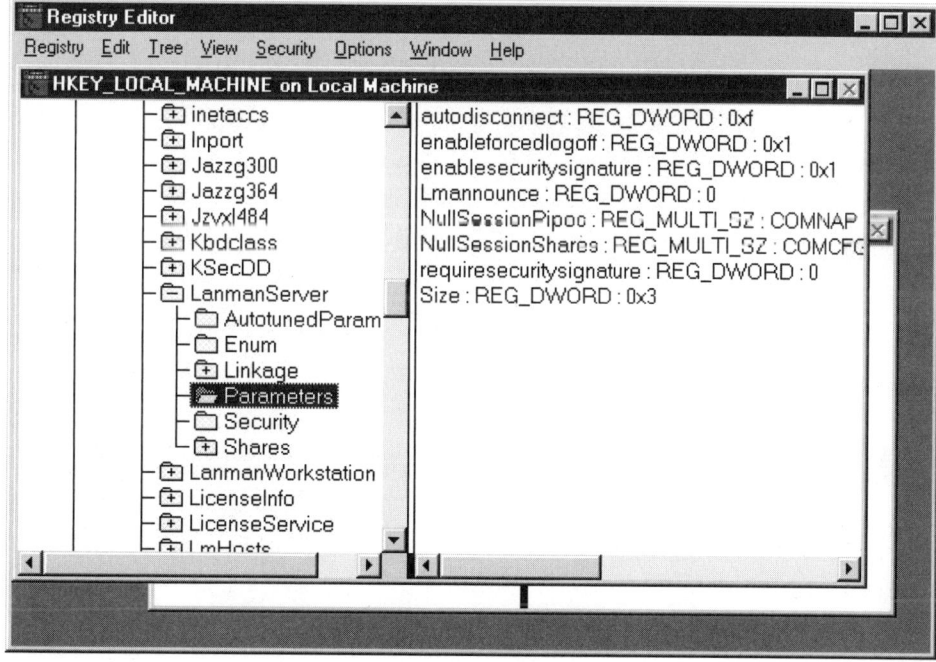

Creating the Required SMB Registry Keys

From the Edit menu, select Add Value. From the Add Value dialog box, select REG_DWORD for the data type. Two values must be added to complete the configuration of SMB signing. First, add the Value Name EnableSecuritySignature, as seen in Figure 6-19.

After selecting OK from the Add Value dialog box, a DWORD editor dialog box will be displayed. Set the Data value to 0 to disable (the default setting), or to 1 to enable SMB signing. Enabling EnableSecuritySignature means if the client also has SMB signing enabled, then that is the preferred communication method.

Next, add the Value Name RequireSecuritySignature, as seen in Figure 6-20.

Set the Data value to 0 to disable (the default setting), or to 1 to enable SMB signing. Enabling RequireSecuritySignature means SMB signing must be used, and consequently, if the client does not have SMB signing enabled, then communication will fail.

Now, close the Registry Editor, then shut down and restart Windows NT. SMB Signing configuration is complete. Please continue to the section "Enforcing Usage of the Appropriate Version on Windows NT LAN Manager."

FIGURE 6-20

Adding the
RequireSecurity
Signature Value
Name

Add Value
Value Name: RequireSecuritySignature
Data Type: REG_DWORD
OK Cancel Help

SMB Signing Registry Key Values

Installing the SCM updates the registry to include the required keys for SMB signing. If the registry keys already exist for EnableSecuritySignature and RequireSecuritySignature, the next step is to properly set the values. For the EnableSecuritySignature registry key, set the Data value to 0 to disable (the default setting), or to 1 to enable SMB signing. Enabling EnableSecuritySignature means that if the client also has SMB signing enabled, this is the preferred communication method.

Next, for the RequireSecuritySignature registry key, set the Data value to 0 to disable (the default setting), or to 1 to enable SMB signing. Enabling RequireSecuritySignature means SMB signing must be used and, consequently, if the client does not have SMB signing enabled, then communication will fail.

Now, close the Registry Editor and shut down and restart Windows NT. SMB Signing configuration is complete. The next section illustrates another registry modification that can be made to a Windows NT 4.0 system to increase network security.

Enforcing Usage of the Appropriate Version on Windows NT LAN Manager

Windows NT 4.0 evolved from the LAN Manager (NTLM) network operating system. For backward compatibility, Windows NT 4.0 uses a version of LAN Manager authentication known as LAN Manager challenge/response (LM), as well as a Windows NT challenge/response known as NTLM by more recent systems. NTLM authentication is significantly stronger than LM authentication. Whether Windows NT is communicating with LM-only systems or systems capable of NTLM authentication, Windows NT will use both authentication methods. SP 4 for Windows NT 4.0 introduced a new version of Windows NT challenge/response authentication known as NTLMv2. Forcing NT 4.0 systems to use NTLM or NTLMv2 significantly increases the difficulty involved in brute force or dictionary attacks against network password hashes. To take advantage of NTLMv2 authentication, or to just disable LM authentication, your Windows NT 4.0 system requires SP 4 be installed along with a registry modification.

To ensure the proper challenge/response method is used, edit the registry key located at HKEY_LOCAL_MACHINE\System\CurrentControlSet\control\LSA (as seen in Figure 6-21).

FIGURE 6-21

Changing the LM/
NTLM/NTLMv2
Challenge/
Response registry
setting

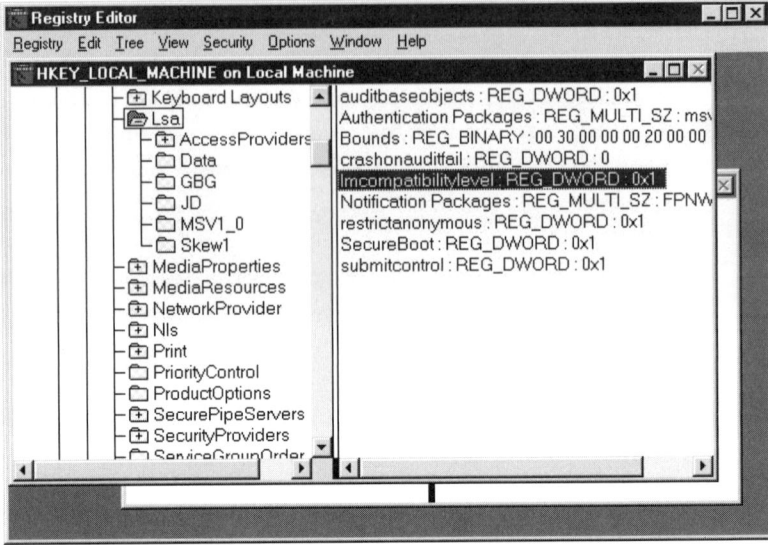

Adjusting the lmcompatibilitylevel registry key controls the type of challenge/response authentication that will be used. Table 6-1 lists the possible settings for the lmcompatibilitylevel registry key.

TABLE 6-1

Possible Registry
Settings for the
LMCompatibility
level Registry Key

Registry Key Value	Effect of Registry Setting
Level 0	Sends LM response and NTLM response; never uses NTLMv2 session security
Level 1	Uses NTLMv2 session security, if negotiated
Level 2	Sends NTLM authentication only
Level 3	Sends NTLMv2 authentication only
Level 4	DC refuses LM authentication
Level 5	DC refuses LM and NTLM authentication (accepts only NTLMv2)

CERTIFICATION SUMMARY

Windows NT 4.0 has acquired several new security options since its release in 1996, by way of several hotfixes and service packs. With Service Pack 4, Windows NT 4.0 acquired the Security Configuration Manager in conjunction with the Microsoft Management Console. Administrators benefit from the ability to configure most Windows NT 4.0 security settings from a single administrative tool. Administrators also benefit from more consistent security settings throughout their Windows NT 4.0 network through the use of security templates. Security templates provide an administrator with the ability to import, export, save, and compare Windows NT 4.0 security configurations. SCM also provides auditing capabilities previously available only through registry configuration. Today, audit logs can be sized, and systems can be configured, with various options in the event of a full audit log.

Because Windows NT 4.0 is most often used in a network environment, network security has increased throughout Windows NT 4.0's lifecycle. SMB signing provides for mutual authentication of systems communicating on a Windows NT 4.0 network. It also presents an increase in network security while granting users an additional 10 to 15 percent increase in network traffic. Mutual authentication ensures communication is only available to known systems, preventing third parties from retrieving network traffic not intended for their viewing. Installing the SCM or modifying the system registry provides for SMB signing on a Windows NT 4.0 network.

Another network security improvement in Windows NT 4.0 is the introduction of NTLMv2 and the capability to disable LAN Manager (LM) authentication. Because LM authentication operates with a lower encryption level compared to NTLM or NTLMv2, the option to disable LM authentication provides an increase in network security. The option to utilize only NTLMv2 authentication further increases network security by providing an even higher level of encryption.

 # TWO-MINUTE DRILL

Configuring the OS and User Environments by Using the Security Configuration Manager

❑ The Security Configuration Manager (SCM) provides security administration through a graphical user interface (GUI) via the Microsoft Management Console (MMC).

❑ Secedit.exe is the command line interface (CLI) of the Security Configuration Manager.

❑ Eleven preconfigured templates are provided with the SCM.

❑ Security templates are stored as *.inf files.

❑ Basic*.inf provides default settings to reverse previously applied security configurations.

❑ Secur*.inf provides an increased level of security when compared to nonconfigured systems.

❑ Hisec*.inf provides a level of security that will only allow Windows NT 4.0 systems configured with the hisec*.inf templates to communicate.

❑ The relaxed security settings of Comp*.inf allow installation of various software packages.

❑ Off97sr1.inf provides specific file system settings for Office 97 installation.

Implementing Auditing and Monitor Security

❑ Logon and logoff auditing is configured on domain controllers for a domain environment, and on local systems for a workgroup.

❑ File and Object Access is configured through User Manager For Domains on the domain controllers, then through User Manager on the system hosting the resources, and finally through Windows Explorer on the resource being audited.

❑ Audit log settings are configured through the Event Viewer, or through the Security Configuration Manager.

❑ The event log can be arranged with a maximum size in mind, while the system can be configured to overwrite the event log (wrapping) or shut down if the event log reaches its maximum size.

❑ File and Object Access auditing for files and folders requires the NTFS file system.

Implementing Advanced Security Options

❑ Syskey provides three modes of protection:

    ❑ Locally stored

    ❑ Password Startup

    ❑ Floppy Disk stored

❑ A lost syskey floppy or forgotten password requires reinstallation of the operating system, or a system repair using the emergency repair disk (ERD).

❑ SMB Signing provides mutual authentication at a cost of a 10 to 15 percent decrease in network performance.

❑ SMB Signing is configured using the Registry Editor, or through the Security Configuration Manager.

❑ LM, NTLM, and NTLMv2 are options configured through the Registry Editor.

SELF TEST

The following questions will help you measure your understanding of the material presented in this chapter. Read all the choices carefully, as there may be more than one correct answer. Choose all correct answers for each question.

Configuring the OS and User Environments by Using the Security Configuration Manager

1. Your company uses Office 97 for productivity. Which security template provides security settings specific to Office 97?

    A. Basicdc4.inf

    B. Basicwk4.inf

    C. Off97sr1.inf

    D. Compws.inf

2. A user in your environment is unable to install a required software package. What template loosens security to allow installations?

    A. Hisecdc4.inf

    B. Hisecws4.inf

    C. Off97sr1.inf

    D. Compws.inf

3. Which security template will reverse the configuration of a previously applied security template?

    A. Hisecdc4.inf

    B. Basicwk4.inf

    C. Off97sr1.inf

    D. Securdc4.inf

4. Which option will provide an increase in security?

    A. An increase in password uniqueness from 6 to 8

    B. An increase in the maximum password age from 42 days to 60 days

    C. A decrease in the minimum password age from 7 days to 2 days

    D. Disabling password complexity requirements

5. Joe grants users elevated permissions on occasion to complete certain administrative tasks. If all users are returned solely to Domain User group membership, how can you reconfigure the correct group memberships for your users?

   A. By using Event Log settings in SCM

   B. By using Local Policies settings in SCM

   C. By using System Services settings in SCM

   D. By using Restricted Groups settings in SCM

6. What options are provided in the event of a full event log?

   A. Overwrite Events By Days

   B. Overwrite Events As Needed

   C. Automatically Resize

   D. Do Not Overwrite Events

7. Tom must log on to the domain controller to perform a specific task. What setting allows him local access to the domain controller?

   A. \Local Policies\User Rights Assignment\Log On Locally

   B. \Security Options\User Rights Assignment\Log On Locally

   C. \Restricted Groups\Domain Users

   D. \Local Policies\User Rights Assignment\Access This Computer From Network

Implementing Auditing and Monitor Security

8. Your manager is concerned that an unauthorized user is logging in to your network. Where is Logon Auditing configured?

   A. Windows Explorer

   B. Internet Explorer

   C. User Manager For Domains

   D. Event Viewer

9. Someone is deleting important files in your network. What utilities are used to configure auditing for this event?

   A. User Manager For Domains

   B. Windows Explorer

   C. Disk Administrator

   D. The Security Configuration Manager

10. What utility will provide, through logon script, consistent audit settings on all member servers in your environment?

    A. mmc.exe

    B. regedit.exe

    C. The Security Configuration Manager MMC snap-in

    D. secedit.exe

11. What category of event will be logged after a file is deleted?

    A. Object Access

    B. Use of User Rights

    C. Logon and Logoff

    D. Privileged Use

12. To prevent folder audit settings from applying to a folder, select _____ from the Security dialog box while configuring auditing.

    A. Copy

    B. Remove

    C. Cancel

    D. Apply

13. To display only all Logon and Logoff events in the Event Viewer, you should filter _____ events.

    A. Source

    B. Category

    C. User

    D. Computer

14. What utility allows an administrator to configure the system to shut down once the event log is full?

    A. SCM

    B. USRMGR.EXE

    C. MMC.EXE

    D. SYSKEY.EXE

Implementing Advanced Security Options

15. Which syskey option provides the highest level of security?

    A. Syskey Floppy

    B. Password Enabled Syskey

    C. Local Syskey

    D. ERD

16. Joan is configuring her systems to run syskey. What command should Joan run before syskey?

    A. fdisk /mbr

    B. ipconfig /all

    C. secedit

    D. rdisk /s

17. Syskey is enabled on Windows NT 4.0 systems...

    A. By default

    B. Through the SCM

    C. Using the syskey utility

    D. By installing SP 4

18. You are concerned that sessions are being hijacked on your network. What utility decreases the likelihood of session hijacking?

    A. SYSKEY.EXE

    B. NTLM

    C. LM

    D. SMB signing

19. Matt wants to configure SMB signing on his Windows NT 4.0 network. What utilities will allow Matt to accomplish this task?

    A. SCM

    B. REGEDT32.EXE

    C. REGEDIT.EXE

    D. SECEDIT.EXE

20. To refuse LM authentication, and utilize either NTLM or NTLMv2, the lmcompatibilitylevel registry key should be configured with a setting of?

    A. 1

    B. 2

    C. 3

    D. 4

21. After configuring NTLMv2-only authentication on your workstations, you are unable to log on to the domain. What registry setting is required on the domain controllers to allow the workstations to log on to the domain?

    A. lmcompatibilitylevel key to 0

    B. lmcompatibilitylevel key to 1

    C. lmcompatibilitylevel key to 2

    D. lmcompatibilitylevel key to 3

LAB QUESTION

In this lab question, we will look at a common administrative scenario. Most companies today have a corporate office or corporate headquarters that dictate company policies or company standards. Oftentimes, regional or district offices that are lower on the chain of command will be required to adhere to certain company-wide policies. There are occasions where these company-wide policies will result in a weaker security strategy than your present local security strategy. Let's take a look at this scenario and determine the best approach to prevent a weakened security strategy.

    Scenario: You are an administrator for the regional office of a large enterprise. You have standardized the network security configurations for all the workstations in your environment. The corporate headquarters has e-mailed a new security template to you and requested you apply this template to all your workstations. What should be your approach for applying the template?

SELF TEST ANSWERS

Configuring the OS and User Environments by Using the Security Configuration Manager

1. ☑ **C.** Off97sr1.inf is the preconfigured template used for systems running Office 97. Install the compws.inf template first, then apply the off97sr1.inf template.
☒ **A** is incorrect because basicdc4.inf is used to reverse the effects of templates or configurations previously applied to an NT 4.0 domain controller. **B** is incorrect because basicwk4.inf is used to reverse the effects of templates or configurations previously applied to an NT 4.0 workstation. **D** is incorrect because compws.inf is used to loosen security to allow installation of software for your NT 4.0 member servers or workstations.

2. ☑ **D.** Compws.inf is used to loosen security to allow installation of software for your NT 4.0 member servers or workstations.
☒ **A** is incorrect because hisecdc4.inf is used to strengthen network security on your NT 4.0 domain controllers. Only NT 4.0 systems configured to run the high secure settings may communicate over the network. **B** is incorrect because hisecws4.inf is used to strengthen network security on your NT 4.0 member servers or workstations. Only NT 4.0 systems configured to run the high secure settings may communicate over the network. **C** is incorrect also, because off97sr1.inf is the preconfigured template used for systems running Office 97. Install the compws.inf template first, then apply the off97sr1.inf template.

3. ☑ **B.** Basicwk4.inf is used to reverse the effects of templates or configurations previously applied to an NT 4.0 workstation.
☒ **A** is incorrect because hisecdc4.inf is used to strengthen network security on your NT 4.0 domain controllers. Only NT 4.0 systems configured to run the high secure settings may communicate over the network. **C** is incorrect because off97sr1.inf is used for systems running Office 97. Install the compws.inf template first, then apply the off97sr1.inf template. **D** is incorrect because securdc4.inf is used to execute Microsoft's recommended security settings for NT 4.0 domain controllers for all security areas except files, folders, and registry keys. File system and registry permissions are configured securely by default.

4. ☑ **A.** Increasing the password uniqueness (password history) will force users to use more passwords, thereby making it harder for an unauthorized user to guess someone else's password.
☒ **B** is incorrect because an increase in the maximum password age means passwords are used for a longer period of time, thereby increasing the likelihood that an unauthorized user can guess someone else's password. **C** is incorrect because decreasing the minimum password age

means a user can change passwords more frequently, increasing the likelihood of using their preferred password. The increased frequency of using one password elevates the likelihood that an unauthorized user will gain access with that password. **D** is incorrect because password complexity forces users to create alphanumeric passwords, which are harder to dictionary attack and more difficult to guess, thereby increasing network security. Disabling this option will decrease network security.

5. ☑   **D.** The Restricted Groups settings in SCM allow an administrator to configure group membership through a security template.
☒   **A, B,** and **C** are incorrect. **A, B,** and **C** are SCM containers, but they provide different options. Event Log settings allow an administrator to configure properties and settings for the event log. Local Policies allow an administrator to configure audit policy, user rights, and specialized security options. System Services allow an administrator to configure the startup properties for the various services running on the system.

6. ☑   **A, B,** and **D.** When using the SCM to configure the audit log, the options are Overwrite Events By Days to set the log to overwrite based on the number of days of information stored, Overwrite Events As Needed to configure the audit log to "wrap," and Do Not Overwrite Events to cause the audit log to stop writing once the log reaches capacity.
☒   **C** is incorrect because Automatically Resize is not an available option.

7. ☑   **A.** In order for a domain user to log on to a domain controller, the user must be granted the right to Log on Locally. This is selected from the Local Policies | User Rights Assignment container.
☒   **B** is incorrect because Security Options does not provide for user rights assignment. **C** is not an option because Restricted Groups only provides for specific group memberships. Tom could be placed in a group that has the right to log on to the domain controller, but this would unnecessarily elevate Tom's permissions. **D** is incorrect because the Access This Computer From Network option provides for network access (remote access) to the domain controller, not local access.

Implementing Auditing and Monitor Security

8. ☑   **C.** Auditing is configured from the Policies menu option in User Manager For Domains or by configuring a security template using the Security Configuration Manager.
☒   **A** is incorrect because Windows Explorer only provides a way to configure File and Object Access auditing for the specific file or object that requires an audit. **B** is incorrect because although Internet Explorer provides a history of Web sites accessed, it does not provide for

auditing of Logon events. **D** is incorrect because Event Viewer is the utility used to view the audit log, not to configure it.

9. ☑ **A, B,** and **D.** User Manager For Domains is the utility used to enable auditing in a domain environment, Windows Explorer provides for auditing of specific files or folders on an NTFS volume, and the Security Configuration Manager provides a single interface to configure all of the available types of auditing.
☒ **C** is incorrect because although the Disk Administrator provides capabilities for generating NTFS volumes, its interface does not provide auditing.

10. ☑ **D.** Secedit.exe is the command line interface for security configuration and analysis. Secedit.exe is basically the command line version of the Security Configuration Manager.
☒ **A** is incorrect because the Microsoft Management Console (MMC) is a graphical user interface (GUI) that provides an environment for graphical tools like the SCM. **B** is incorrect because the Registry Editor Regedit.exe is a graphical interface for modifying the Windows registry. It does not provide for command line interaction. **C** is incorrect because the Security Configuration Manager snap-in for the MMC utilizes the GUI Microsoft Management Console to provide for system security configurations. Because the SCM is a graphical user interface, this is not a valid option for use in a logon script.

11. ☑ **A.** Deleting a file from an audited folder produces an Object Access event.
☒ **B** is incorrect because Use of User Rights involves events like local access to domain controllers, creation of workstation accounts, and so on. **C** is incorrect because Logon and Logoff events are a result of users being authenticated by a domain controller or a local system. **D** is incorrect because Privileged Use events result from system configuration changes that can only be accomplished by users with elevated permissions (i.e., Local or Domain Administrators).

12. ☑ **B.** Selecting Remove from the Security dialog box prevents settings from a parent folder from propagating to the child object.
☒ **A** is incorrect because selecting Copy will copy the parent folder setting to the child object. **C** is incorrect because selecting Cancel will end the audit configuration. **D** is incorrect because Apply is not an available option from the Security dialog box.

13. ☑ **B.** Logon and Logoff are both Category events.
☒ **A** is incorrect because Source events include those such as LSA, Security, and Spooler. **C** is incorrect because User Filtering only displays events pertaining to a specific user account. **D** is incorrect because Computer Filtering only displays events pertaining to a specific computer account.

14. ☑   **A.** The Security Configuration Manager (SCM) provides configuration options for the event log.

   ☒   **B** is incorrect because USRMGR.EXE (User Manager For Domains) provides capabilities to enable auditing, but does not facilitate configuration of the Event Viewer or its properties. **C** is incorrect because the Microsoft Management Console (MMC) provides a graphical user interface (GUI) that enables an administrator to customize the administrative environment with various MMC snap-ins or utilities. Although the MMC provides the GUI for the Security Configuration Manager, the MMC itself is not the utility for configuring security or event logs. **D** is incorrect because SYSKEY.EXE is a utility for encrypting account information stored on the system. SYSKEY.EXE does not provide configuration options for the event log.

Implementing Advanced Security Options

15. ☑   **A.** A floppy-based system key provides the highest level of security for a Windows NT 4.0 system.

   ☒   **B** is incorrect because a Password Enabled Syskey still maintains information on the local system. Although the syskey password will have to be broken before any other information becomes available, this option is still not considered as secure as the floppy-based syskey. **C** is incorrect because the Locally Stored Syskey maintains local encryption information on the protected system. Because local access to the system would provide an intruder with the syskey encryption information, this syskey option is considered the least secure of the three. **D** is incorrect because ERD is an emergency repair disk. It is recommended that an administrator update the ERD before and after generating the system key, but the ERD itself is not a syskey option.

16. ☑   **D.** It is recommended that Joan create an emergency repair disk (ERD) before enabling syskey on her system. rdisk /s generates an ERD and updates all system information.

   ☒   **A** is incorrect because fdisk /mbr will repair the master boot record on a hard drive. This command would only be used on a system experiencing problems with the hard disk. **B**, ipconfig /all, is incorrect because this command would only display TCP/IP information about the system. This would not have any bearing on the syskey. **C** is incorrect because secedit provides a command line interface for security configuration and analysis. Configuring or analyzing security would not be a benefit to syskey.

17. ☑   **C.** SYSKEY.EXE opens the syskey utility, which provides an administrator with syskey encryption options.

   ☒   **A** is incorrect because although syskey is enabled by default on Windows 2000 systems, it is not enabled by default on Windows NT 4.0 systems. **B** is incorrect because the Security

Configuration Manager provides various security configuration options, but it does not provide an administrator with syskey configuration options. **D** is incorrect because installing SP 4 does not configure syskey. SP 4 provides an administrator with the syskey utility, but in order to enable syskey, the SYSKEY.EXE utility has to be activated.

18. ☑ **D.** SMB signing provides for mutual authentication of communicating systems, and mutual authentication provides added session security.

☒ **A** is incorrect because syskey provides for local encryption of the SAM and its related registry keys. Syskey does not provide for session security. **B** and **C** are incorrect because NTLM and LM are authentication protocols used by Windows NT 4.0. NTLM and LM do not provide for session security.

19. ☑ **A, B,** and **D.** SCM provides for security configuration options through a graphical user interface. SCM provides for SMB signing as one of the security configuration options. The Windows NT Registry Editor (REGEDT32.EXE) provides for registry modifications. Although this is a more tedious approach, the Registry Editor does provide the options necessary to configure SMB signing. SECEDIT.EXE is the command line interface for security configuration. SECEDIT.EXE provides for the SMB signing configuration.

☒ **C** is incorrect because REGEDIT.EXE is another Registry Editor provided with Windows NT. The REGEDIT.EXE utility provides better search capabilities than the Windows NT Registry Editor (REGEDT32.EXE).

20. ☑ **D.** Configuring the lmcompatibilitylevel key to 4 will allow NTLM or NTLMv2 authentication, but will not allow LM authentication.

☒ **A** is incorrect because a level 1 setting requests the use of NTLMv2 if negotiated but does not exclude LM, or require NTLM or NTLMv2. **B** is incorrect because a level 2 setting requires NTLM authentication only. **C** is incorrect because a level 3 setting requires NTLMv2 authentication only.

21. ☑ **B** and **D.** A level 1 setting will use NTLMv2, if negotiated. Because the workstations require NTLMv2, that is what the server will negotiate. A level 3 setting will force NTLMv2 authentication.

☒ **A** is incorrect because a level 0 setting will never user NTLMv2. **C** is incorrect because a level 2 setting will only use NTLM authentication.

LAB ANSWER

Since the Security Configuration Manager provides for analysis, the best approach is to first analyze the new template to determine its effective security configuration. The first step should be to import the template to a workstation and analyze the configuration with the imported template.

Now that we have an analysis, it is time to compare the imported template settings to the current settings in the environment. Look for stored configurations that provide greater security than the analyzed configuration. When weaker security configurations are encountered in the template supplied by corporate, you will either have to modify the template to protect the current configuration or, based on the company policy, you might have to contact corporate to ensure the security configuration is sufficient for your environment. If it is decided that the template be modified, make the necessary modifications to the new template to ensure that applying this template does not reduce your network security. Save the template after making your changes. Finally, deploy the template to each of the workstations, either on a system-by-system basis, or by using the secedit.exe command as part of a logon script.

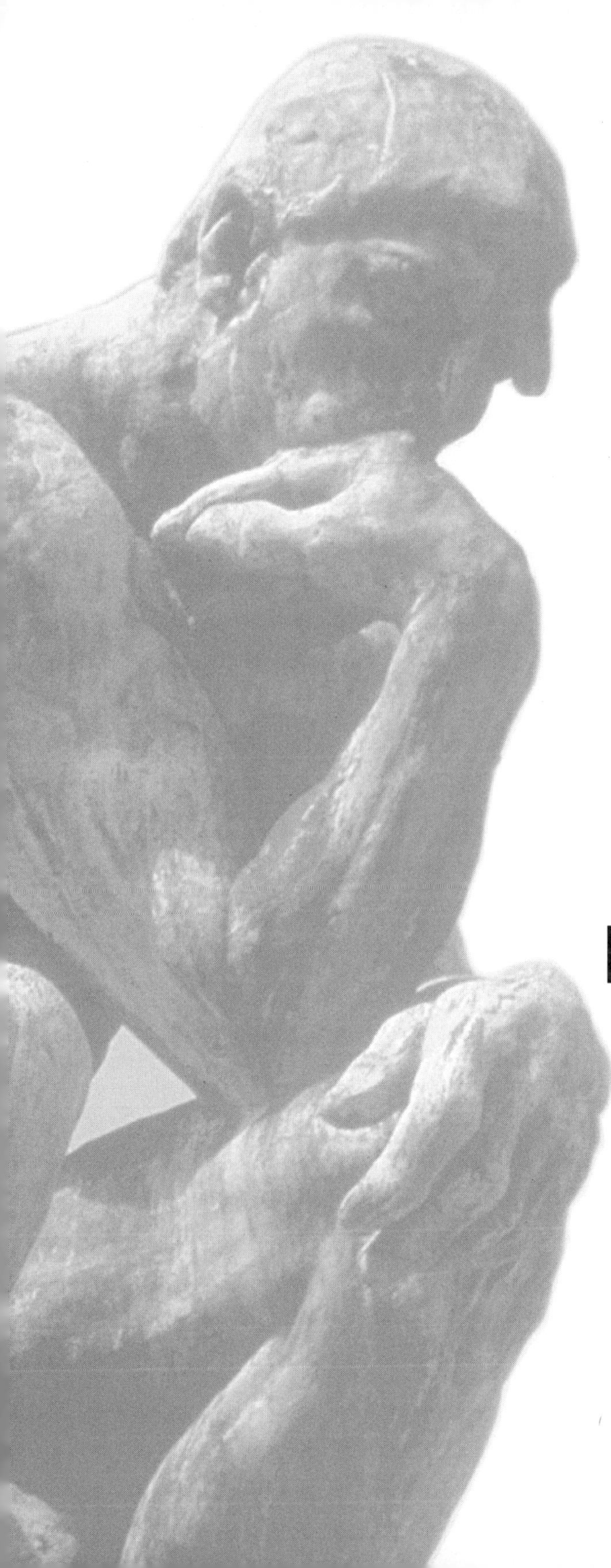

MCSE

MICROSOFT CERTIFIED SYSTEMS ENGINEER

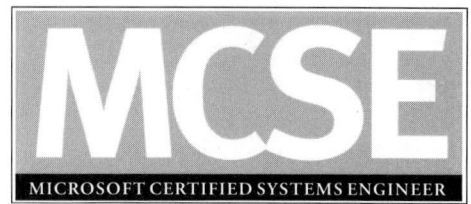

7

Configuring, Managing, and Troubleshooting Access to Permissions and Resources

CERTIFICATION OBJECT

7.01 Creating, Configuring, and Troubleshooting Permissions

7.02 Installing and Troubleshooting File-based Resource Access by Using Dfs on Multiple Servers

✓ Two-Minute Drill

Q&A Self Test

S haring files and printers is one of the most useful and important reasons to create a network. Windows NT 4.0 Server is extremely flexible in its ability to control access, but this flexibility can create confusion and security holes in the hands of an uncertain administrator. Share level access controls the ability to access information over a network, and file and directory access controls the ability to access information locally. The proper combination of share and file/directory level control can create a network environment that is extremely secure without hindering either an administrator's ability to control usage, or a user's ability to access this information.

CERTIFICATION OBJECTIVE 7.01

Creating, Configuring, and Troubleshooting Permissions

There are two types of access permissions in an NT environment: File & Folder level (NTFS) permissions and share level permissions. File & Folder level permissions are only possible on an NTFS formatted partition. They have the ability to secure a file locally, which means a user could be restricted from accessing a file on a computer the user has permission to log on to. Share level permissions are only relevant when accessing resources over a network. Folders are shared for network access—meaning that files in these folders have the potential to be used across a network.

exam
Watch

Remember that File & Folder level permissions can only be set on an NTFS formatted partition. If the question mentions that FAT or FAT32 permissions are not possible, the only protection available is share level.

File & Folder Permissions

File & Folder level (NTFS) permissions are set on the Security tab of the Properties dialog box. To access the Properties dialog box, right-click the file and select Properties from the pop-up menu. In the Properties dialog box, select the Security tab (Figure 7-1). If the Security tab is not present, the file system may not be NTFS. (If this is the case, run the CONVERT command and change the format to NTFS.) The Security tab has three options: Permissions, Auditing, and Ownership.

FIGURE 7-1

The file
Properties
dialog box

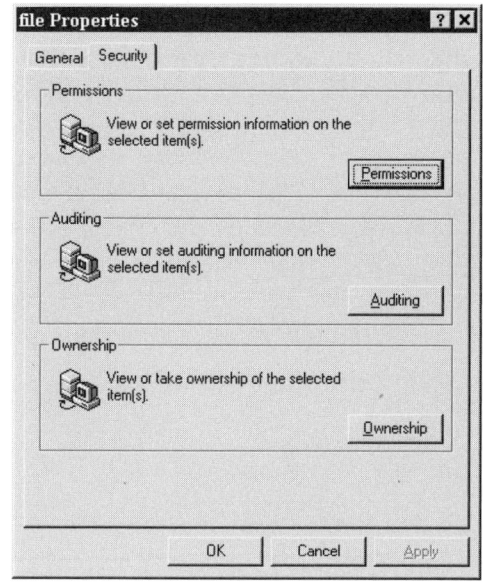

By selecting the Permissions tab, you access the NTFS File Permissions dialog box (shown in Figure 7-2).

File Level Permissions

File level permissions can be assigned on an NTFS partition by anyone with Owner or Administrator access. By default, each file and folder has the group Everyone assigned the Full Control permission. When assigning file level permissions on an

FIGURE 7-2

The File
Permissions
dialog box

NTFS partition, you have five choices: No Access, Read, Change, Full Control, and Special Access. These choices are combinations of the six special access levels: Read (R), Write (W), Execute (X), Delete (D), Change Permissions (P), and Take Ownership (O).

- **No Access**   This is exactly what it sounds like—the user can't access the file in any way. No Access overrides all other permissions. If a user has Full Control over a file through one group membership, and No Access permission to the same file through another group, the user won't be able to access the file. This is the only time NTFS permissions are not cumulative.

- **Read**   (RX) Read gives the user permissions to read and execute the file.

- **Change**   (RWXD) This gives the user the ability to create a new file or modify an existing one. They can even delete the original if they like. The user can also execute a file.

- **Full Control**   (RWXDPO) User has full control over all contents, including the ability to alter files, change permissions, and take ownership.

- **Special Access**   Allows user to make special customizations to Full Control (RWXDPO) access.

Folder/Directory Level Permissions

Folder level permissions utilize the same special access levels as file permissions: Read (R), Write (W), Execute (X), Delete (D), Change Permissions (P), and Take Ownership (O). These are combined into the same default choices as File level security—No Access, Read, Change, and Full Control, with the new additions of List, Add, and Add & Read. See Figure 7-3 for details.

Notice the two sets of permissions for Dan's account—Add & Read (RWX) (RX). The first set (RWX) is Dan's permission on the directory; the second (RX) is Dan's permission on the contents of the directory.

- **List**   (RX) Gives the user the ability to read and execute contents.

- **Add**   (WX) The user can write to the folder, execute contents, but not view the contents.

- **Add & Read**   (RWX) User can view contents, add to the folder, and execute the folder's contents.

FIGURE 7-3

The Directory
Permissions
dialog box

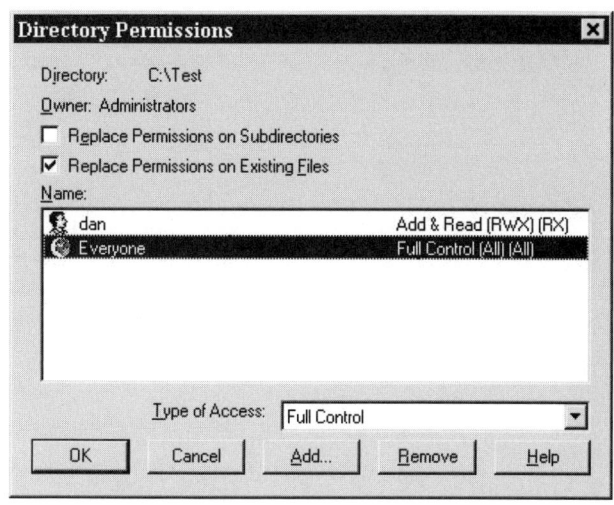

Table 7-1 shows the permission levels in detail.

TABLE 7-1

NTFS
Permissions

Permission	File Permissions	Directory Permissions
No Access	Prevents any access. Overrides all other permissions.	Prevents any access. Overrides all other permissions.
Read	Ability to read and execute a file.	Ability to view filenames and display file attributes.
Change	Ability to create a new file or modify an existing one. Includes ability to delete the original and execute a file.	Ability to rename the directory, as well as read, write, and execute its contents.
Execute	Ability to run a program and display attributes.	Ability to display attributes and manipulate subfolders.
Write	Ability to read, execute, and rewrite a file.	Ability to view filenames and display file attributes. Also allows creation of subdirectories.
Delete	Ability to delete files.	Ability to delete folders.
Change Permissions	Ability to change a file's permissions.	Ability to change a folder's permissions.

TABLE 7-1	Permission	File Permissions	Directory Permissions
NTFS Permissions (continued)	Take Ownership	Ability to take ownership of a file.	Ability to take ownership of a folder.
	List	N/A	Gives the user the ability to read and execute contents.
	Add	N/A	The user can write to the folder, execute contents, but not view contents.
	Add & Read	N/A	User can view contents, add to the folder, and execute the folder's contents.

Moving and Copying NTFS Permissions

NTFS permissions can be altered by the processes of moving and copying. Within the same partition (e.g., from anywhere on the C: drive to anywhere else on the C: drive), files that are moved retain their NTFS permissions, regardless of the permissions of the destination folder. Files copied in the same manner inherit the permissions of the target folder. The reason is simple if you stop and think about the process. When moving a file within the same partition, the physical bits of the file are not changed or moved, only the index pointer is changed in the directory structure. When copying a file, a new copy is physically written, making for two copies on the hard drive—the old one in its original location, and the new one in the target destination. The file is physically rewritten when copied. When moving or copying between partitions (e.g., from C: drive to D: drive), NTFS permissions are inherited from the target destination. Of course, if any NTFS protected file or folder is moved or copied to a destination that is not NTFS formatted, all permission settings are lost, as FAT and FAT32 do not support this type of protection. (Refer to Table 7-2.) The exercise at the end of the chapter will help reinforce this concept.

Share Permissions

Share level permissions are available on any machine running the server service by anyone in the Administrator or Server Operators group. These permissions control access to information over a network. Shared folders (shares) are created, and files are added to these shares. Files can't be shared over the network. They must be added to shared folders to enable access.

| | **TABLE 7-2** | | Various Permissions Situations When Moving and Copying Files | |

Situation	Original Format	Destination Format	Resulting Permissions
You move file from C:\shape\round\ball to C:\shape\round.	NTFS	NTFS	Permissions retained from original location.
You copy file from C:\shape\round\ball to C:\shape\round.	NTFS	NTFS	Permissions inherited from target location.
You move file from C:\shape\round\ball to D:\shape\round.	FAT32	NTFS	Permissions inherited from target location. There were no permissions to move because the original file was on a FAT partition.
You move file from C:\shape\round\ball to D:\shape\round.	NTFS	NTFS	Permissions inherited from target location. When a file is moved between partitions, the file inherits the permissions from the target location.
You move file from C:\shape\round\ball to D:\shape\round.	NTFS	FAT32	All permissions are lost; FAT and FAT32 don't support NTFS protection.
You copy file from C:\shape\round\ball to D:\shape\round.	NTFS	NTFS	Permissions inherited from target location. When a file is copied from one partition to another, the file inherits the permissions from the target location.

Creating Shares

Shares are created in NT File Explorer by right-clicking the folder and selecting either Sharing or Properties. On the Sharing tab (shown in Figure 7-4), the default Not Shared is selected. By clicking the Shared As option, the ability to control the share is enabled. The folder name is added by default, but you can name the share anything up to 12 characters. Hidden shares can be created by adding a dollar sign ($) to the end of the sharename. These hidden shares cannot be seen when browsing through the network, but they can be accessed by using the UNC pathname. By default, hidden admin shares are created. These include ADMIN$, which is a share of the systemroot directory (usually c:\WINNT), and a hidden share for each of the drive partition's root directories (C$, D$, and so on). Only administrators can access these shares, and the hidden shares can't be permanently deleted. However, the administrative shares can be removed through the use of system policies or by editing the registry.

The Sharing
tab in the Test
Properties
dialog box

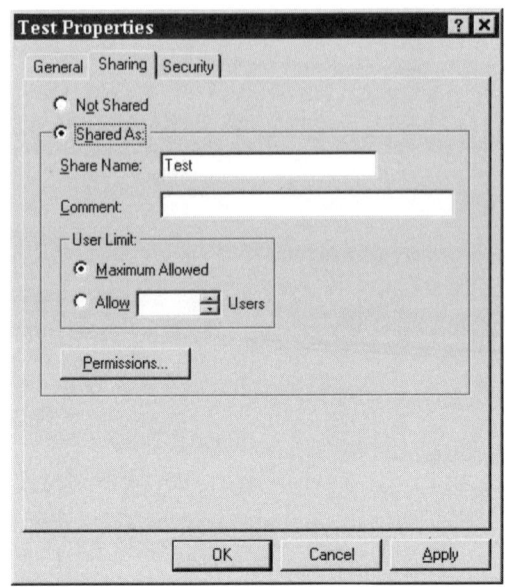

Share Settings

Once you name a share, you can set user access permissions, limit the total concurrent connections, and allow access for specific groups or users. By clicking the Permissions button, you can control access. By default, everyone will have Full Control of the share. The options for share level access are Full Control, Read, and Change. Share level security is only relevant when accessing the resource over a network connection. If you are local on the machine, they are not considered in overall permissions. You can access the share locally by making a UNC connection to your own machine by typing **\\computername\sharename** from the run prompt.

Combined NTFS and Share Permissions

While NTFS and share permissions each offer flexibility, true security comes with the combination of both types of access in an NT domain. While share level permissions have been around before NT, and provided a very effective method for accessing information over networks, they do nothing to protect access locally at the computer. A properly implemented NT network should contain both types of access control: share level, to protect network access; and NTFS, to protect local access.

In both NTFS and share level access control, permissions may be given directly to a user or through group membership. A user may be granted access through multiple group memberships. When a user is a member of multiple groups, they get the aggregate of the permissions of all of the groups, which gives them the most permissive access (unless one of the groups has the No Access permission, which then overrides all the others). This method holds true for both NTFS and share level permissions, but is restricted when combining the two types of permissions.

For example, Dan is a member of multiple groups, which have access to the file SQUARE in the shared folder CIRCLE. The groups have the share level permissions listed in Figure 7-5.

Assuming there were no specific file level permissions set, if Dan was a member of Accounting, Marketing, and Sales, his permissions to this share would be Read and Change, the cumulative tally of his group memberships. Assume the file SQUARE in the CIRCLE folder has the following NTFS permissions shown in Figure 7-6.

Dan's NTFS access would be Read permission. Therefore, if Dan accessed the file locally, he would have Read permission, which is the aggregate of his group permissions.

We have seen how each type of access control works—the user gets the most permissive permissions from the combination of his group memberships, unless No Access is given to the user at any level. When you are combining NTFS and share level security, this method is changed. The combination of permissions is taken from both the share level and NTFS level. In this situation, the most restrictive of

FIGURE 7-5

Access to the share CIRCLE

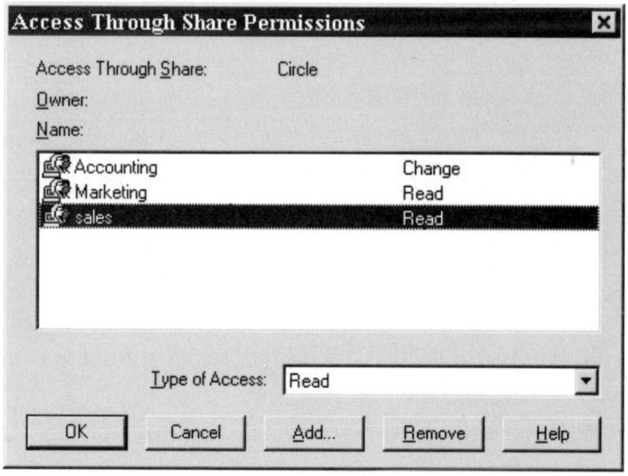

NTFS access to
the file SQUARE

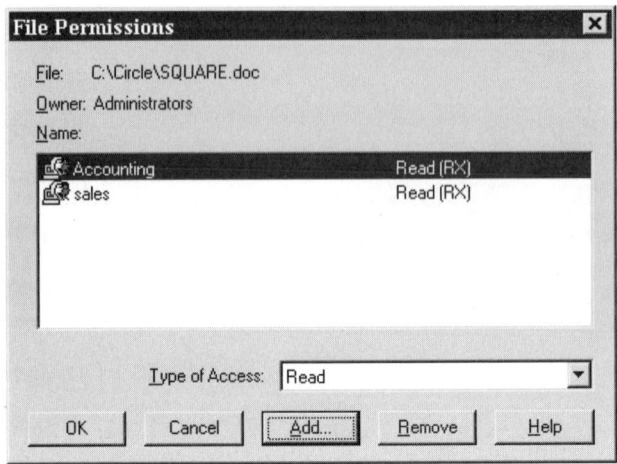

the two methods is the effective permission for the resource. In the examples used in Figures 7-5 and 7-6, the effective share permissions for Dan are Read and Change, whereas the NTFS permissions are Read. Therefore, accessing the NTFS file through the share would give Dan the most restrictive of the NTFS and share access permissions, which would be the Read permission.

Troubleshooting Permissions

Troubleshooting access permissions can be a bit of a mess if you have an unorganized group structure in your domain. Let's say we're trying to open the file SQUARE in the share CIRCLE located on a computer named SERVER with Dan's user account. A good method or path to take is from the source out. Start at the source of the resource being accessed. Is the file available? Can you access the resource with the Administrator's account from Dan's computer? First, look at the NTFS permissions on the file SQUARE. Does any group that Dan is a member of have access permissions? Does any group that Dan is a member of have the No Access permission?

Troubleshooting access permissions requires a full understanding of the effect of combining NTFS and share permissions. Remember, when combining NTFS and share permissions, you first find the least restrictive of each type of access. Find the least restrictive of the NTFS permissions, and write it down. Then find the least restrictive of the share permissions, and write it down. If the file is being accessed

TABLE 7-2	Type of Permissions	Access Locally or Through The Network	Resulting Permissions
NTFS and Share Permissions	NTFS file: Read, Change NTFS Folder: Read Share: Full Control	Network	Read and Change
	NTFS File: Read, Change NTFS Folder: Read Share: Full Control	Locally	Read and Change
	NTFS File: Not Specified NTFS Folder: Not Specified Share: Full Control	Network	Full Control
	NTFS File: Full Control NTFS Folder: Read Share: Full Control	Network	Full Control

over the network, take the most restrictive permission you wrote down for either the NTFS or share permissions. This would be your effective permission. If you are accessing the file from the local computer, the share permissions are irrelevant. Share permissions are only relevant if the file is accessed over the network. If No Access is listed anywhere, it overrides all other permissions and access is denied.

Table 7-3 shows NTFS permissions.

EXERCISE 7-1

Testing Share and NTFS Permissions

1. Log on with an account with administrative privileges.

2. Create a user account called Dan using the word "password" as your password; uncheck the box to have the user change the password at the next logon.

3. Create a folder on an NTFS partition called **Circle**.

4. Right-click the folder, choose Properties, select the Security tab, and click permissions. Remove the Everyone group, add Dan's account and mark it as Full Control. Click OK.

5. Select the Sharing tab, click Shared As; the default sharename Circle will appear in the Name box. Click Permissions, remove the Everyone group, click Add, and click the Show Users button. Add Dan's user account, click OK. Next to Type Of Access, click Read. Click OK twice to finish up.

6. Log off as administrator, then log on as Dan with the password of "password." Go to the folder you created, and double-click the folder Circle. Right-click in the Circle explorer window, pick New, choose Text Document, and press the ENTER key to accept the default name. Double-click the new document you just created. Type one line of text, click the file, then save it.

7. To test the share permissions, make a UNC connection by typing *servername*\circle (substitute your computer name as the servername).

8. Double-click the text document, add a line of text, and resave the document.

Printer Permissions

In order to understand printer permissions, you must first understand printer terminology. When we think of printers, we think of the physical printer we see connected to the back of a server. From the permissions perspective, the *printer* is only a logical reference to the icon for the printer definition in a computer's Printers Folder.

The *print device* is the actual printer you can see and touch. The print device is physically connected to the *print server*. The print server hosts the driver files used to translate instructions from the operating system to the print device. When you submit a print request, the instructions as well as your print data are submitted to the *print queue*. The print queue is nothing more than files located on the print server that have been given a place in line for the printer.

Table 7-4 shows a matrix of rights for each printer permission setting available. If you assign the permission No Access to *any* user or group, the user or group will have No Access. The Print permissions are for most users, and only gives users control of their own documents. The Manage Documents permissions are typically given to more experienced users in a department, and allows the users control over all the documents for the printer. This is useful in a situation where a user has submitted a very large job that is printing, and the user is not available to cancel the job. Other users need the print jobs that are in the queue waiting for the large job, but do not have rights to cancel other users' print jobs. The individual with Manage Documents permissions can delete the print job and allow others to print. Users with the Full Control permissions could send the print job to the end of the queue, allowing others to print their jobs first.

Another feature of print management is the ability to assign priorities and pool printers. Priorities are assigned to a printer definition and range from 1, which is the lowest priority, to 99, which is the highest. An administrator would create two printers for one print device, assign a low priority (1) to one printer and a high priority (99) to the other.

è x a m
ⓦ a t c h
Remember that priority level 99 is the highest level, which means it will be moved to the top of the list of print jobs. Many test takers forget that 99 is high and 1 is low when it comes to priorities.

Once the priorities are defined, regular users would be assigned Print permissions on the low priority printer and configured to use that as their printer. Executives would be assigned Print permissions on the high priority printer and be configured to use that printer. When an executive submits a print job, their job would move to the front of the queue, ahead of all the regular users and behind the last job

TABLE 7-4   Printing Permissions

Setting\Rights	No Access	Print	Manage Documents	Full Control
Print		Own	All	All
Pause		Own	All	All
Resume		Own	All	All
Delete		Own	All	All
Restart		Own	All	All
Change Document Settings			All	All
Change Print Order				All
Change Permissions				All
Change Properties				All

submitted with the same priority. An administrator can also configure times that a printer is available to print. This allows a user to submit a large job to a printer that will print after hours, and not cause unnecessary delays during normal working hours. The job will remain in the queue until the time the printer is active, then begin the job. The user is not required to take any additional steps in submitting the print job, other than selecting the after hours printer.

A *printer pool* is a *printer* that refers to more than one *print device* attached to the same *print server*. The jobs submitted to the printer are automatically sent to the next available print device. All print devices should be similar, and must use the same print driver. This promotes high availability of print resources and quicker print times.

exam
Watch

Printer pools must contain only the same type of print device. You can't mix the types of printers. In a printer pool, you cannot direct a print job to a specific printer.

When you share a printer on Windows NT 4.0 machines, it will prompt you to install the driver files for the selected operating systems. This does not actually install the drivers, but copies them to the print server. When a computer connects to the printer, it will check to see if a valid driver exists for its operating system, then automatically install the driver on the local machine. If you update the drivers on the server, Windows NT 4.0 or better computers will automatically update the driver as soon as the machine connects to the print server. Non-Windows NT computers may only install the drivers initially, and must be updated manually.

Troubleshooting Printers

Some printers require installation of special protocols in addition to the printer's drivers. For instance, some HP print devices require the DLC protocol in order to print correctly. If the DLC protocol is not installed on a workstation using an HP printer, it may not be able to connect to the correct port for that printer. If a print device becomes jammed, "Pause" the print job, correct the problem, and "Restart" the print job that was currently printing. On occasion, a print job can cause the print spooler service to hang. Simply restart the Spooler service to correct this problem. Although rebooting the server will correct this problem, it is not necessary, since rebooting corrects the problem by stopping and starting.

exam
ⓌＡtch

The DLC protocol in a question is a tip-off that the answer will be something that revolves around an HP laser printer.

Default Permissions

The default permissions on a newly created file, folder, or share is the Everyone group having Full Control. This can cause a security hole if you create a share or folder and forget to not only apply the appropriate settings, but remove the Everyone group having Full Control. Figure 7-7 shows the Directory Permissions dialog box.

If we just add Dan's account with the Add and Read permission without removing the Everyone group with Full Control, Dan's account would have Full Control permission because he is part of the Everyone group.

The Deny Permission

We have mentioned a couple of times that the No Access or Deny permission overrides all others. If Dan is a member of Marketing, he will not have access to the resource even if he has Full Control through another group or through share access. Troubleshooting can be hindered by having permissions denied to someone who has multiple group membership.

FIGURE 7-7

Folder
Permissions
on C:\Test

CERTIFICATION OBJECTIVE 7.02

Installing and Troubleshooting File-based Resource Access by Using Dfs on Multiple Servers

The Distributed File System (Dfs) is a network service that enables client computers to access shared file resources on many servers through a single share point on the server hosting Dfs. This is a valuable tool for network administrators on rapidly changing or growing networks. A client computer only needs to connect to one share point on the Dfs server, then the information regarding the specific location of the files is transparently resolved, and the client accesses the files directly on the server where the files actually exist. For instance, a network administrator purchases a new server. One of the servers on this network is the Microsoft Exchange server, and hosts public file shares for all the users on the network. The administrator decides to move 75 percent of the files to the new server. Once the files are moved, every client computer that has a drive mapped to that share must be reconnected to the new share, yet still remain connected to the old share. Using Dfs, the network administrator would only need to share the new files, and add a Dfs definition in the Dfs Administrator. When the client computers using the Dfs client connect to the same old share point, they would be redirected to the new file server without any change to the client computer. That is why Dfs is a truly powerful resource to a network Administrator.

Installing Dfs

The Distributed File System (Dfs) is a tool made available by Microsoft for sharing data over a network in a manner that is both efficient and secure. To install the Dfs service, work through the following exercise.

EXERCISE 7-2

Installing the Dfs Service

The Dfs service requires NT 4.0 Server with Service Pack 3 or later. Once the service pack is installed, the Dfs service must be downloaded from Microsoft's

Windows NT Server Web site: http://www.microsoft.com/ntserver/nts/downloads/winfeatures/NTSDistrFile/default.asp. This site also contains the links for the Windows 95 Dfs Client, which must be installed on the Windows 95 client workstations in order to connect to and use the Dfs service. Windows 98 and ME are able to connect to Dfs shares without any additional software. If you wish to share folders on Windows 95, 98, or ME, and "graft" them into a Dfs tree, then you can install the Dfs client from the Dfs root server directory: \\%systemroot%\system32\Dfs\Win95. This directory can also be used in lieu of downloading the Windows 95 client separately.

Once you have downloaded the file for the Dfs service, run the downloaded file (dfs_v41_i386.exe). You will be prompted with a license agreement which you must agree to in order to use the software. In the next dialog box, you will be given the option to continue, exit, or read the Help on Dfs. Click Continue to proceed. After clicking Continue, the necessary files will be copied as indicated to the %systemroot%\system32\Dfs folder. Once the operation is complete, click the Exit button to close setup. Verify the files and directories were created in the Dfs folder, as shown in Figure 7-8.

Now that the files are in place, we must install the service. Since Dfs runs as a network service, it is installed like any other network service:

FIGURE 7-8

The Dfs files

1. Right-click Network Neighborhood.

2. Select the Services tab (Figure 7-9).

3. Click Add.

   The Distributed File System may be listed in the directory of available services. Ignore it, however, and click Have Disk (Figure 7-10).

4. Type the path to the folder where the extracted files are located, and click OK. Type the path for the Dfs installation files in the Insert Disk dialog box.

5. The next step will ask you to create a Dfs root share (Figure 7-11). This will be the root Dfs server on your network, and will be the starting point for all of your Dfs requests.

6. Click the Create Share button to display the basic new share dialog box, as shown in Figure 7-12. Create a share and set the appropriate permissions for this share. You may also choose to limit the number of users that can connect to it. Once you are satisfied with your choices, click OK.

FIGURE 7-9

The Services tab of the Network dialog box

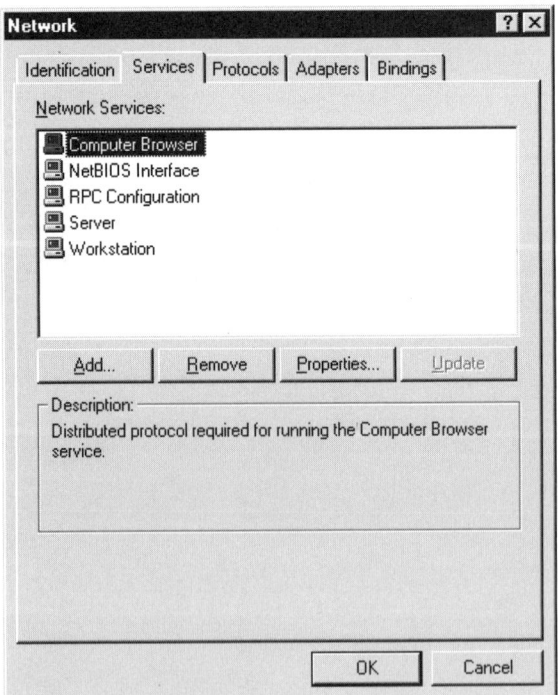

FIGURE 7-10

The Select
Network Service
dialog box

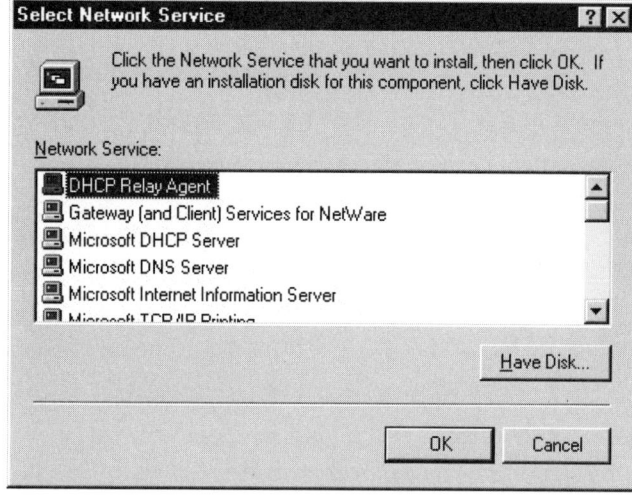

FIGURE 7-11

Create a Dfs
root share

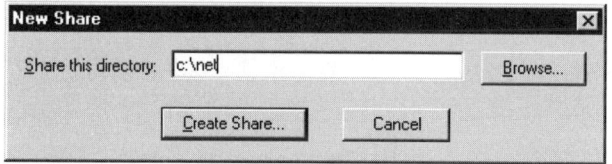

FIGURE 7-12

Create a
new share

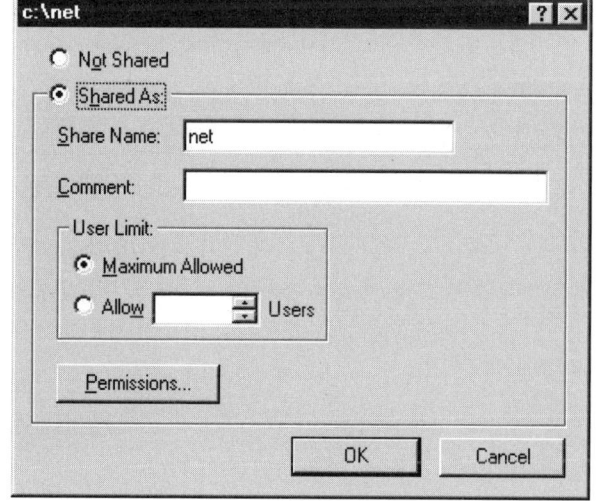

FIGURE 7-13

The Configure
Dfs dialog box

7. As indicated in Figure 7-13, check the Host A Dfs On Share: box and click OK to establish the Dfs root.

8. Once the Dfs root share is established, the Services tab of the Network dialogue box will be active, and the Distributed File System service will be listed among the other network services (as indicated in Figure 7-14). Click Close to continue.

9. You must restart your server in order to enable Dfs to operate properly. It is highly recommended that you reapply the current NT service pack after completing the installation of any network services. Run the service pack setup after you have restarted the server.

FIGURE 7-14

The Services tab
of the Network
dialog box with
Distributed File
System installed

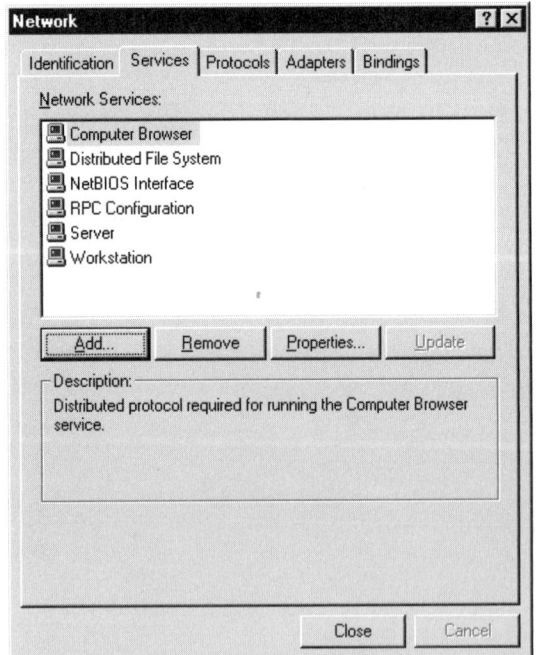

Administering Dfs

The tool used to administer Dfs is called Dfs Administrator (as shown in Figure 7-15). On the server that hosts the Dfs Root, a shortcut to the Dfs Administrator will be added to the Start menu under Programs\Administrative Tools. If you would like to use this application from another workstation or server, simply copy DfsAdmin.exe and DfsAdmin.hlp to the %systemroot%\system32 folder on the local machine. The files will be located in the %systemroot%\system32\Dfs folder. You must be a Domain Administrator on the domain you wish to administer. Another utility that can be used to administer Dfs is Dfscmd.exe. This tool is a command line application. Once you have a grasp of Dfs Administrator, the Dfscmd tool is easy to use. Just open a command prompt, run dfscmd, and follow the command line instructions.

The Distributed File System structure follows a tree analogy. The root of the tree is the Dfs root, of which there is only one. A Dfs tree is the point of connection in a Dfs structure. This tree has volumes that are merely share points (known as leaf volumes) on a network. Each tree can have up to two levels of volumes, with many volumes on each level. So, for example, the accounting department has four share points on different servers. We can create a tree called Accounting in the Dfs root. Then we

FIGURE 7-15

Dfs
Administrator

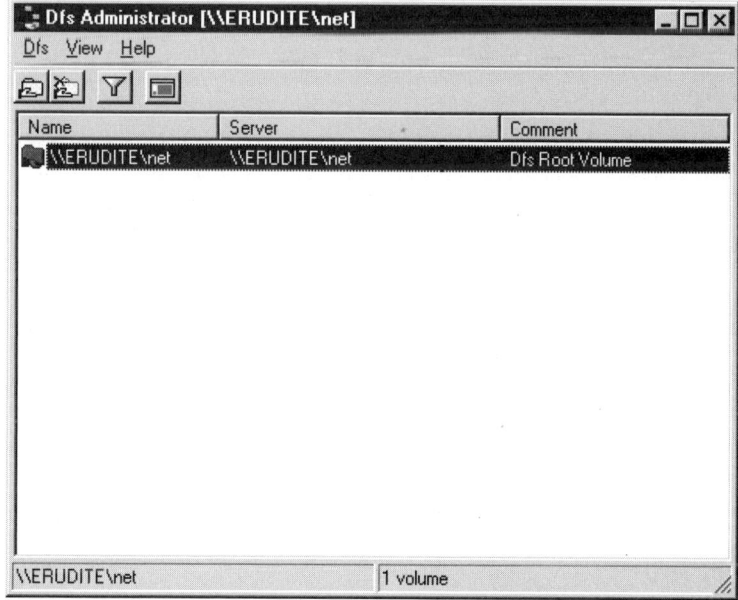

add the four leaf volumes to the Accounting Dfs tree. When a user browses the leaf, Dfs sends the network user to the location of the share point on the original server automatically, a process completely transparent to the user. With the new structure, an accountant need only map one drive to the Accounting tree and access all the necessary resources. These steps can be taken in turn for each department to allow users simplified network access. If a volume has more than one shared folder, it is said to have alternate paths. This is very beneficial on a Web server using Microsoft Internet Information Server. It is possible to direct a Web site to a volume with alternate paths to allow for load balancing and higher availability without adding any complexity to the Web application programming. It is also possible to move resources within a Dfs tree without rewriting code or updating hyperlinks.

To begin, we need to add a tree volume to the Dfs root. Click the Dfs menu and select Add To Dfs (as demonstrated in Figure 7-16). It is always a good idea to plan your directory structures before you actually begin.

In the Add To Dfs dialog box (Figure 7-17), type in the name of a local folder or click Browse to select the local Dfs path. Next, type in the UNC (Universal Naming Convention) path to the share (e.g., \\Junk\e) or click Browse (as in Figure 7-18) to select a share that the users will be redirected to when they access the Dfs path you have specified.

In this example, the file server Junk has a share point "e" that will be the access point (or leaf volume) for this Dfs tree.

Once you click OK, you should type in a comment for others who will administer Dfs or browse the Dfs trees through Explorer. This is shown in Figure 7-19.

FIGURE 7-16

Add a Dfs tree volume to the root

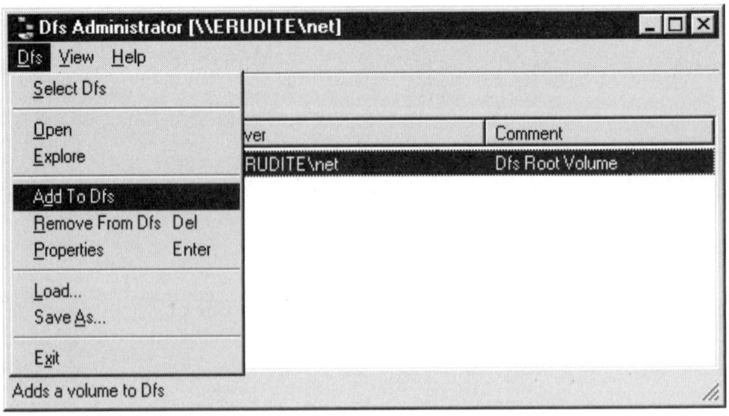

FIGURE 7-17

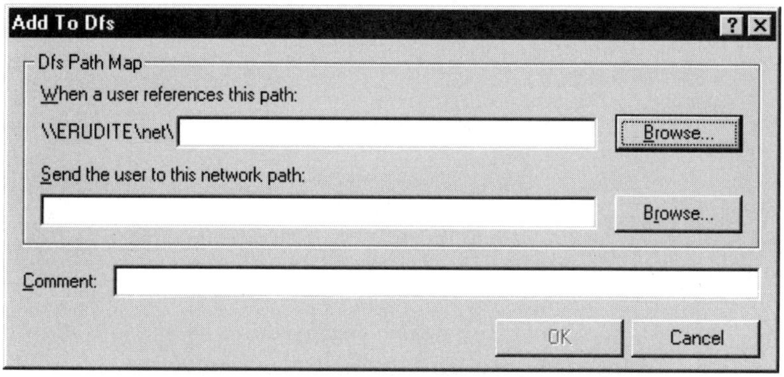

The Add To Dfs
dialog box

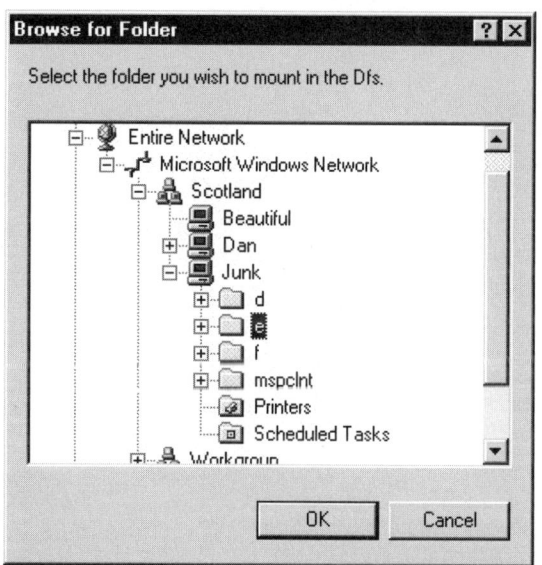

FIGURE 7-18

Select a network
share for the
leaf volume

FIGURE 7-19

Complete the
Dfs addition
with a concise
description

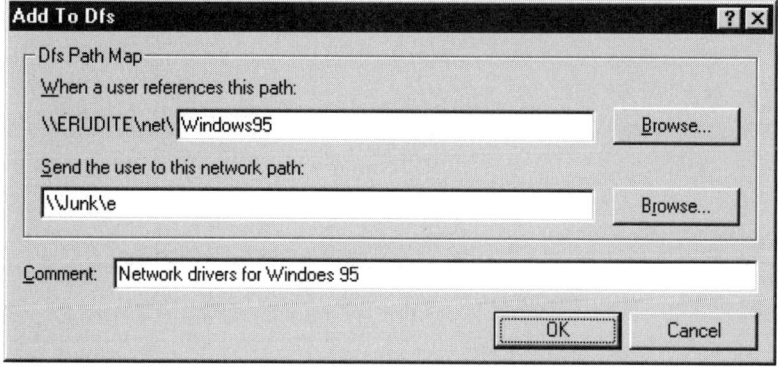

FIGURE 7-20

The list of Dfs volumes and the actual server\ share that the volumes refer to

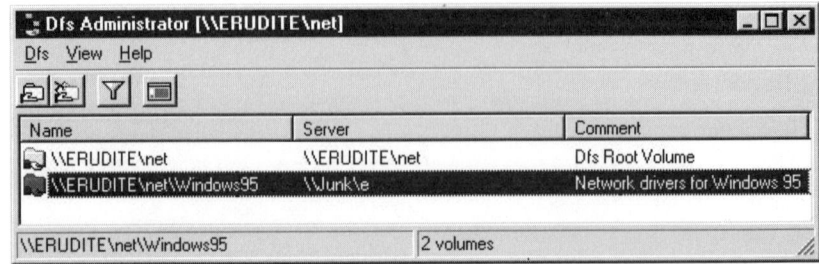

The new volume will be displayed in Dfs Administrator (as seen in Figure 7-20). A filter can be applied to reduce the number of volumes listed. Figure 7-21 displays Filter options for the list of Dfs paths in the Dfs Administrator tool.

Notice that in Figure 7-22, the folder Windows95 is an actual folder. You can copy files and folders in this directory and users accessing the \\Erudite\net\Windows95 volume will see them. When browsing the local machine, the Dfs service is bypassed and the only files accessible actually exist in the displayed folder.

FIGURE 7-21

Filter options for the list of Dfs paths in the Dfs Administrator tool

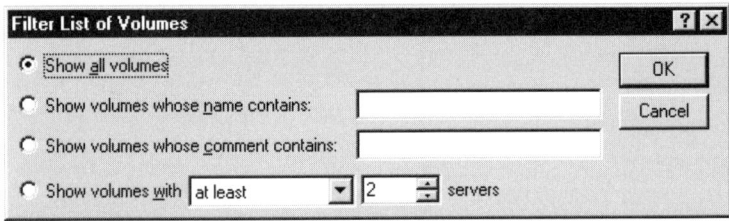

FIGURE 7-22

The view of the local folder in Windows Explorer

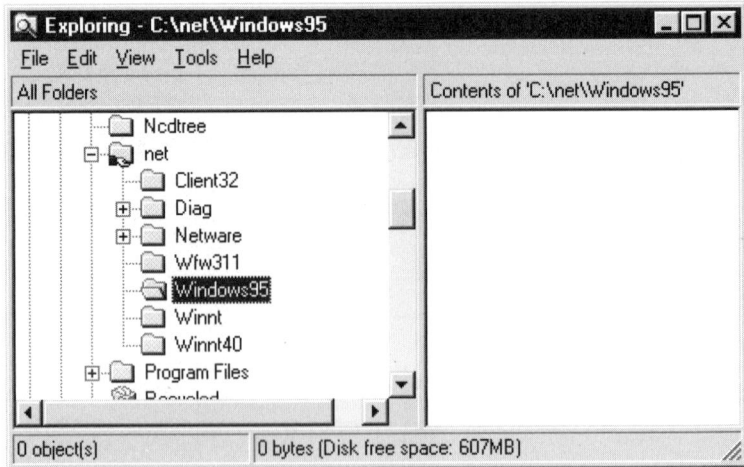

FIGURE 7-23

Files in the
remote folder
are displayed
while browsing
in Network
Neighborhood

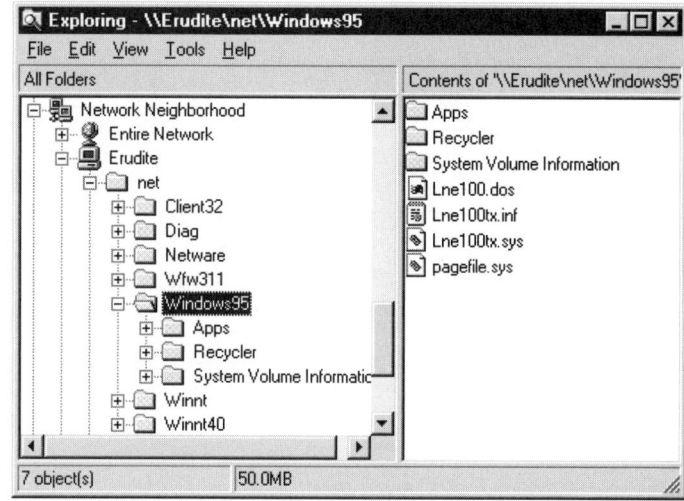

While browsing Network Neighborhood, you can see the files and folders that
exist in the shared folder on the remote server, as in Figure 7-23. When you browse
to the Windows95 volume, the Dfs service responds to the request by transparently
passing the UNC path \\Junk\e to the requesting application. The files and folders
displayed exist in \\Junk\e, but the user is not necessarily aware of them. This is why
it's so much easier for users to find the files they want—being they only need to
access one location for all their data.

Additional volumes may be added to a Dfs path, removed from a Dfs path, or
edited by accessing the properties of a Dfs tree. The properties are accessed from the
Dfs menu, and then the Properties menu item. (Refer to Figure 7-24.) Notice the
difference in the Send The User To This Network Path: data entry?

Once you have assigned one path, you can click Add. You will then be notified that
Dfs will automatically distribute client requests to each server (Figure 7-25). Note that
this requires the files and folders to be synchronized, which is not handled by Dfs.

After you have added the new volume to the same Dfs tree, you will be able to
access the properties for each volume by selecting it from the drop-down list (as
shown in Figure 7-26), making the necessary changes, and clicking OK or Apply.

After the second volume is added, Dfs Administrator will no longer display the
server\share information unless you access the properties of the Dfs tree. Instead,
you will see the number of servers that are hosting shares in that tree. In this case,
two servers will be displayed (as seen in Figure 7-27).

FIGURE 7-24

Dfs share
properties

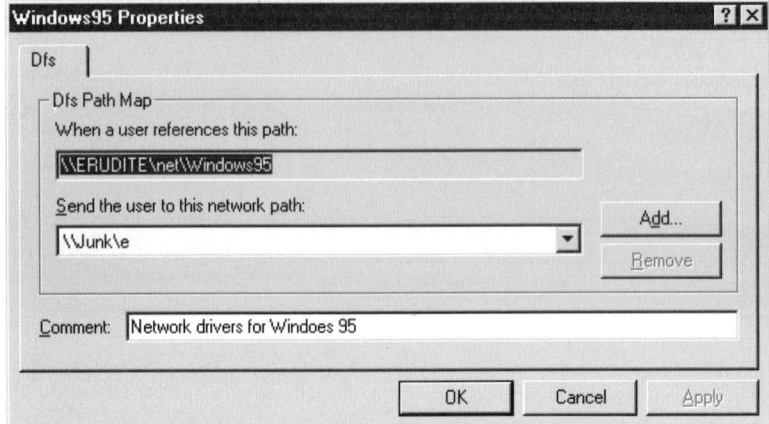

FIGURE 7-25

Notice for
multiple volumes
in a single tree

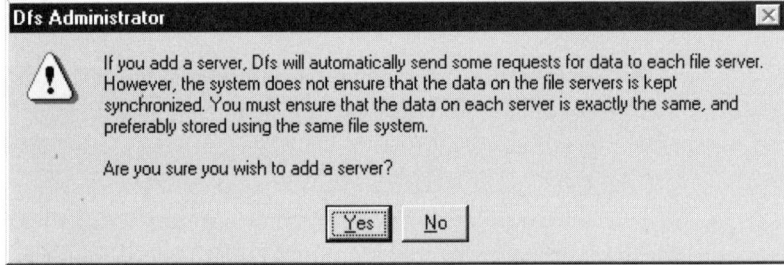

FIGURE 7-26

Multiple volumes
for one Dfs tree

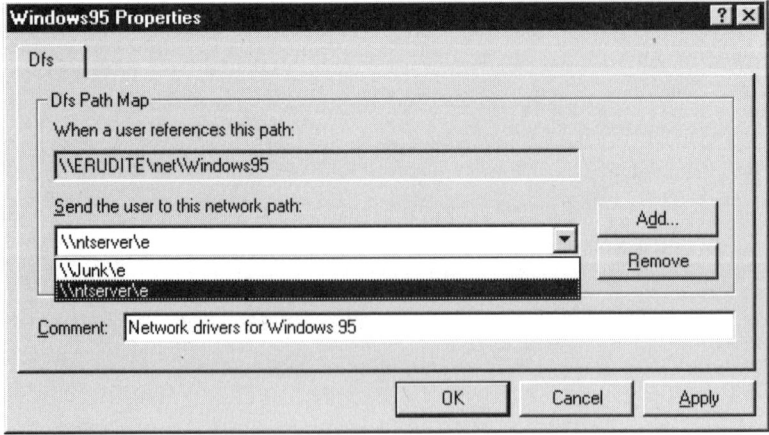

FIGURE 7-27

With two server's
shares added to
the same tree,
Dfs Administrator
only displays "2
Servers" and no
longer displays
the server\share
information

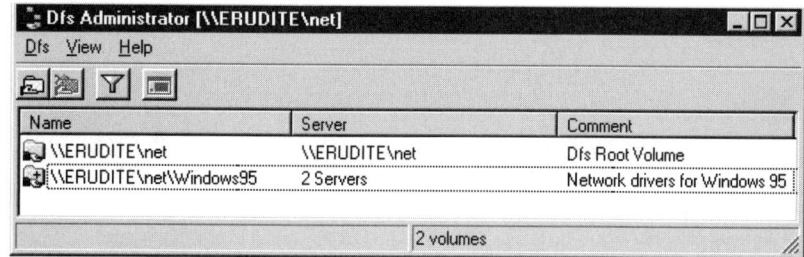

Since you can only have one Dfs root per server, you may wish to back up your settings, and maybe even build an identical server for redundancy. This can be accomplished by selecting Save As from the Dfs menu. This will display the Save As dialog box (shown in Figure 7-28) and save the information into a comma delimited (comma separated values or CSV) file.

If you want to reload or add Dfs volumes, select Load from the Dfs menu. You will be prompted for the file with the .csv extension, as in Figure 7-29.

Figure 7-30 shows the next prompt to be displayed. Pay careful attention to the question. If you answer Yes, all the current Dfs settings will be removed and the new settings loaded. This cannot be undone. If you answer No, then the information

FIGURE 7-28

Save the Dfs
configuration
to a file

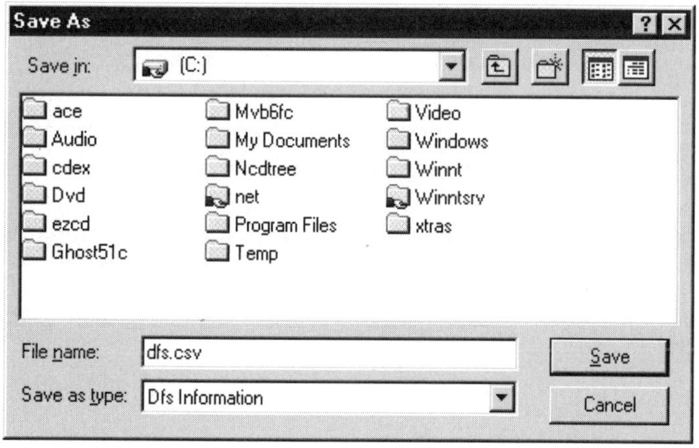

Select the Dfs
information
to load

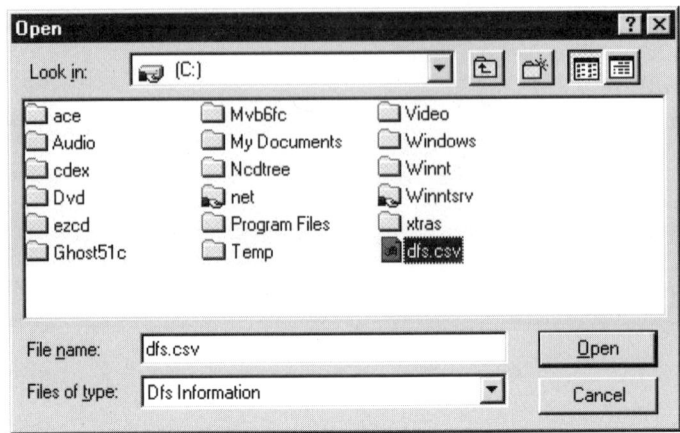

about the Dfs volumes that is in the file will be added to the current Dfs server. If
you are not sure, you may cancel as well.

It is always a good idea to back up your server configuration. When you load
the Dfs information file, Dfs Administrator can also verify the shares while restoring
the volumes.

Troubleshooting Dfs

Dfs security is the same as the shared folder and file permissions that exist on the
resource. If a user has permission to access a file or folder on a shared volume in a
Dfs tree, it is not required that the user have permissions granted on the Dfs root.
To simplify troubleshooting, remember that Dfs services only respond to user requests
with the actual UNC name of the resource that the Dfs path is mapped to. If a user
is having difficulty accessing a resource through a Dfs tree, simply determine the

Watch out! Pay
careful attention
to this question.
You could lose
all your Dfs
information

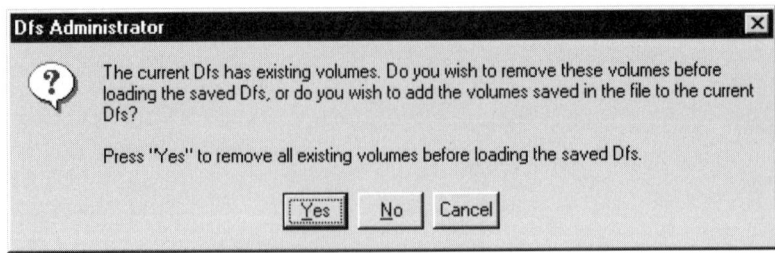

actual path and verify that the appropriate share and NTFS permissions have been granted to that user for that resource.

If you are able to access some of the resources in a Dfs tree, but other resources in the same tree are not available, then you should check the servers hosting the shares. It is possible that one or more of the shared volumes are accessible, while a share on another server is not available. The user will not be informed of the unavailable resource until they attempt to access a file or folder that is exclusively on that share.

If no resources are available for a given Dfs root, then verify that the server is available on the network. If the server is available, but you still cannot access resources in that Dfs Root, verify the Dfs service is running. It's also possible (unlikely, but possible) that Deny permissions have been applied at the root, or to all shared resources for that server.

CERTIFICATION SUMMARY

Creating, configuring, and troubleshooting permissions has always been a big item on Microsoft's certification tests. Understanding NTFS permissions, Share permissions, and Printing permissions is a key to understanding how NT works. Learning to troubleshoot permissions in various configurations is a necessity in today's IT world.

One of the mantras you'll learn is AGLP. The paths in which permissions are applied are important and help keep your network secure and running efficiently. One of the most common issues on a network is resolving printing problems. Print devices have a tendency to lock up, so you need to know how to work out printing difficulties.

The Distributed File System network service enables the sharing of file resources through a distributed model. Files can be on any Dfs server, but are accessed through a common share point. This type of model allows for failure of a server on the network. Should one occur, the share point can be redirected to a new point by way of a process transparent to the users. Dfs is stressed in the Windows 2000 Certification tests, so learn this model well.

✓ TWO-MINUTE DRILL

Creating, Configuring, and Troubleshooting Permissions

❑ File and folder permissions are only possible on NTFS formatted partitions.

❑ Sharing is only relevant through a network connection; shares offer no protection for resources accessed locally.

❑ The default permission for NTFS and shares is the Everyone group having Full Control. Remove this and issue the appropriate permissions to enable a secure environment.

❑ Special Access permissions allow flexibility in assigning access, but can evolve into security holes if not properly thought out.

❑ To print, all you need is the Print permission. The term *printer* refers to the combination of a print driver and a port, not the physical machine that puts ink on paper.

❑ Print pools allow multiple print devices of the same type to act as one. This allows for fault tolerance and additional speed when printing.

❑ Printers can be assigned priorities from 1 (the lowest) to 99 (the highest) to give some print jobs higher priority.

❑ When accessing NTFS protected resources through a share, both NTFS and share access is in effect. In such cases, you get the most restrictive access of either NTFS or share level permissions.

❑ NTFS permissions are inherited from the destination location if resources are copied to any other location or moved to a different partition.

❑ NTFS permissions are retained if resources are moved to a different location on the same partition, and are lost if resources are moved or copied to a FAT partition.

❑ If you have multiple group memberships with different NTFS permissions to a resource, you get the cumulative tally of all the permissions unless you have No Access specified in any group, in which case the No Access permission overrides all others.

❑ If you have multiple group memberships with different share permissions to a resource, you get the cumulative tally of all the permissions unless you have No Access specified in any group, in which case the No Access permission overrides all others.

Installing and Troubleshooting File-based Resource Access by Using Dfs on Multiple Servers

❑ Dfs allows clients to see resources across the whole network, as if the resources were on only one machine.

❑ Dfs allows for rapidly expanding networks to appear as if resources are not being moved.

❑ NT CD must be downloaded from Microsoft's Web site.

❑ Dfs is installed as a network service.

❑ Dfs Administrator is used to manage the Dfs service.

❑ Dfs utilizes share and NTFS permissions for access.

SELF TEST

The following questions will help you measure your understanding of the material presented in this chapter. Read all the choices carefully, as there may be more than one correct answer. Choose all correct answers for each question.

Creating, Configuring, and Troubleshooting Permissions

1. Ron is a salesman who needs read and write access to a new folder named Sales Reports on the server named Dallas. What is the best way to create the folder and give Ron access while keeping security as high as possible?

   A. Simply create the folder. Since Ron is part of the Sales group he will have access by default.

   B. Add Ron to the Administrators group for the shared folder named Sales Reports. Ron will be able to read and write to the new folder with the Administrator privileges.

   C. Put Ron in the global group Sales, put Sales in the local group Dallassales on the server Dallas, then give Dallassales the ability to read and write to the new folder Sales Reports.

   D. Create the folder Sales Reports, then share it out. Give Ron's user account read and write permissions to Sales Reports.

2. Permissions on a folder copied from an NTFS formatted C: partition to an NTFS formatted D: partition on the same physical drive will:

   A. Inherit the permissions of the destination

   B. Keep its current permissions

   C. Depend on the level of the user copying the folder

   D. Lose all NTFS permissions

3. Your manager is complaining because he has to stand at the printer and watch ten other print jobs emerge before his. He says he needs his information printed immediately. What can you do to make this possible?

   A. Create a printer, give only the manager print permissions, then give this printer a priority of 1.

   B. Create a printer, give only the manager print permissions, then give this printer a priority of 99.

   C. Create a print pool, allow only the manager to print to one of the printers.

4. A user on your network is using Windows NT 4.0 Workstation. The user launches the Add Printer Wizard to connect to a shared HP printer on a Windows NT 4.0 Server print server. The drivers download automatically and install with no error, but the user still cannot print. Why?

   A. The user is connected to the network.

   B. The DLC protocol is not installed.

   C. The NetBEUI protocol is not installed and is required for all Windows NT 4.0 printing.

   D. There is a paper jam and the printer is not available at this time.

5. What permissions are required to change the order of print jobs in a queue?

   A. No Access

   B. Manage Documents

   C. Print

   D. Full Control

   E. None

6. There are three printers in a printer pool, printer 1, printer 2, and printer 3. Printer 3 runs out of toner on page 56 of a 100-page job. What will happen to pages 57 - 100?

   A. They will automatically be routed to another printer in the pool where only pages 57 - 100 will print.

   B. They will automatically be routed to another printer in the pool where all 100 pages will print.

   C. Nothing will happen until the toner is replaced. The job will wait for the print device to come back online and then complete.

7. You attempt to add the No Access permissions for the Marketing group to a new folder called Round. You are unable to change the permissions, however, because the Security tab is not listed when you look at the folder's permissions. Why would the Security tab not be available. (Choose all that apply.)

   A. The partition is formatted with FAT.

   B. The partition is formatted with NTFS.

   C. You are logged on without Administrator rights.

   D. You are part of a group that has No Access.

8. Users are complaining that the Accounting department is tying up the printers with 200 page reports. The accounting department must run these reports each day, but does not need the data until the next day. What is the best way to keep these reports from tying up the printers while allowing the Accounting department to get their data in a timely fashion? (Choose all that apply.)

   A. Create a printer pool, give only the Accounting department access to the pool. Have the Accounting department print the large reports to this printer.

   B. Create a printer that is only available between the hours of 5 A.M. and 8 P.M. Give Accounting access to the printer, then have them print their large reports to this printer.

   C. Create a printer with the priority of 1, give only Accounting access to print to this printer. Have the Accounting department print the large reports to this printer.

   D. Create a printer with the priority of 99, give only Accounting access to print to this printer. Have the Accounting department print the large reports to this printer.

Installing and Troubleshooting File-based Resource Access by Using Dfs on Multiple Servers

9. You have completed the implementation of Dfs on your TCP/IP-based network. The Windows 98 clients are able to browse the Dfs trees and access all the files, while the Windows 95 clients are able to browse shares on all the servers, but are unable to browse the Dfs trees. What is the most likely reason for this?

   A. The Windows 95 computers do not have a TCP/IP address.

   B. The Windows 95 users do not have appropriate permissions.

   C. The Windows 98 computers have the Dfs client installed.

   D. The Windows 95 computers do not have the Dfs client installed.

10. Which tool(s) can be used to manage Dfs configuration? (Choose all that apply.)

    A. Dfscmd.exe

    B. Dfstools.exe

    C. DistFSA.exe

    D. DfsAdmin.exe

    E. Windows Explorer

    F. File Manager

LAB QUESTION

Your company (ABC) has just purchased a financial management company (Financial Co.). You are tasked with integrating Financial Company's computer data into the data structure of ABC. Much of the information from Financial Co. is extremely private, containing the financial records of customers throughout the world. You need to allow nine employees full access to the data, while two additional employees need to at least be able to view the data. How would you make this possible while allowing for further growth in the company (meaning more people may eventually need access to the files)?

SELF TEST ANSWERS

Creating, Configuring, and Troubleshooting Permissions

1. ☑ **C** is correct because it complies with the AGLP method of adding the account to a global group, adding the global group to a local group, and assigning permissions to the local group. It is a method that helps keep the permissions structure under control while allowing only that access which is needed.

   ☒ **A** is incorrect because it creates the folder, but the folder must be shared to allow network access. **B** is incorrect because it would give Ron access, but adding him to the Administrators group would not fit the requirement of a secure environment. **D** is incorrect because it would give Ron access but is not the best method of administration. The policy of AGLP helps control the directory and permissions structure.

2. ☑ **A** is correct because moving or copying a file or folder to a different NTFS partition will cause the file or folder to inherit the permissions of the target folder.

   ☒ **B** is incorrect because the physical drive doesn't matter. The partitions are the only determinate. **C** is incorrect because it concerns whether a folder *can* be copied, not what happens when the folder *is* copied. **D** is incorrect because this occurs when the destination drive is not formatted with NTFS.

3. ☑ **B** is correct. A priority of 1 is the lowest, while 99 is the highest. Creating a separate printer with a priority of 99 that only the manager can use will move his print jobs to the top of the print queue automatically.

   ☒ **A** is incorrect because priority 1 is the lowest possible. **C** is incorrect because you can't direct a job to a specific printer in a print pool.

4. ☑ **B.** The DLC protocol is not installed. Some HP printers require that the DLC protocol be installed in order for clients to print to the port correctly on the HP printer. Other printers may require special protocols in order to print properly and may include a driver disk with the appropriate files.

   ☒ **A** is incorrect because the user was able to connect to the print server to download the driver, and was able to see the printer to connect to it using the Add Printer Wizard. **C** is incorrect because the user was able to connect to the print server to download the driver, and was able to see the printer to connect to it using the Add Printer Wizard, so the appropriate network protocols were installed. NetBEUI would only be required if that was the only network protocol used on the print server. **D** is incorrect because an offline printer would not be available to connect to in order to install the printer.

5. ☑ **D. Full Control.** You must have Full Control in order to change the order of print jobs in the queue. (See Table 7-1).
   ☒ **A** is incorrect because if any user has No Access, that user has absolutely no access at all to that resource. **B** and **C** are incorrect because neither Print nor Manage Documents permissions have the right to reorder jobs in the cue. If you have not been assigned permissions to the printer, then you will not have any rights to that printer, therefore answer **E** is also incorrect.

6. ☑ **C.** Print jobs are routed to one of the operating devices in a print pool. Once the document is routed to a print device, it stays in the queue of that print device until completed.
   ☒ **A** and **B** are incorrect because jobs are not automatically rerouted to other devices in the pool if they fail to complete.

7. ☑ **A.** If the Security tab is not available, then the partition is formatted with the FAT file system.
   ☒ **B** is incorrect because the Security tab would show. **C** is incorrect because you do not have to be an administrator to see the tab. **D** is incorrect because even if you have no access you can still see the Security tab, you just cannot view the permissions from the tab.

8. ☑ **B** is correct because it would allow the large reports to print after hours.
   ☒ **A** is incorrect because it does not address the issues in the question. **C** is incorrect because it would allow all print jobs to have a higher priority than the large accounting reports, but would not prevent the reports from starting if the queue was empty during work hours. **D** is incorrect because it would give the reports the highest priority during work hours.

Installing and Troubleshooting File-based Resource Access by Using Dfs on Multiple Servers

9. ☑ **D.** The Windows 95 computers do not have the Dfs client installed. The Windows 95 computers cannot browse Dfs volumes without first installing the Dfs client, but they are able to browse shares directly, provided the users have been granted the appropriate permissions on those shares.
   ☒ **A** is incorrect because the Windows 95 clients are able to browse shares on the network, so they must have a valid TCP/IP address. Since the Windows 95 users were able to browse the share, they must have the appropriate permissions to the shares. Dfs does not add any security layers to the share points, so answer **B** is also incorrect. **C** is incorrect because Windows 98 computers do not require the Dfs client to browse Dfs volumes on a network.

10. ☑ **A and D.** Dfscmd.exe is the command line utility that allows you to manage Dfs from a command prompt. **D** is the Windows GUI-based utility used to administer, create, remove, and manage Dfs.

☒ B and C are incorrect because they are not actual applications. Answers E and F are incorrect because File Manager and Windows Explorer only allow you to modify share points and permissions, not configure Dfs specifically. Although you could stop sharing a resource in these tools, it would only stop providing those resources to all users, regardless of their access method. The other shared volumes available will still be accessible through Dfs.

LAB ANSWER

Start with a NTFS formatted partition. Use the AGLP method to design a structure to allow the needed access. Move the secure data into a separate folder on the NTFS partition called Finance Data. Assign the nine employees that need full access to the data to a global group called Finfull. Assign the two employees that need to only view the data into a group called Finread. Make two local groups on the server, call one group Finsecure and the other Finview. Add Finfull to Finsecure and Finread to Finview. Assign NTFS permissions on the Finance Data folder, remove the Everyone group, add Finsecure with Full Control permission and Finread with read access. Share the folder Finance Data with the sharename Findata$. Remove the Everyone group from the share permissions, add Finsecure with full access, and Finread with read access.

While many solutions would provide the same levels of access, this solution provides proper access, follows the AGLP method, and allows for further expansion for the ABC company.

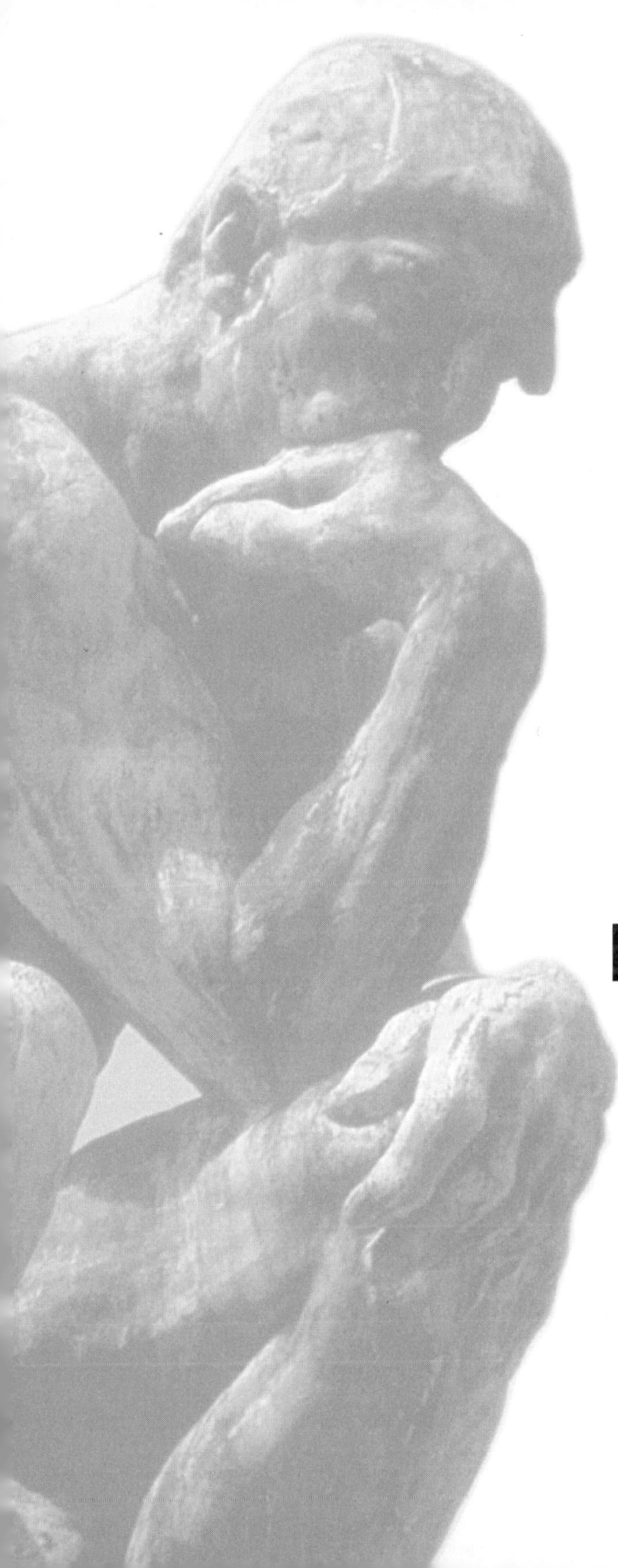

8

Configuring and Troubleshooting Access to Resources and Internet Protocols

I n this chapter, we will cover all aspects of managing printers on an internal network as well as over the Internet or an intranet using Internet protocols. First, we will examine printing terminology, because certain terms in Windows NT and 2000 have specific meanings. Then we will look at configuring and managing printers. This includes creating printers, installing drivers, managing queues and using priorities and permissions to control and secure access.

In the second part of the chapter, we will examine different types of Internet services, the use of domain names and Internet protocols (such as HTTP and FTP), and the use of the Internet Printing Protocol to connect to printers on Windows 2000 servers. We will then look at different ways of providing centralized access to the Internet.

CERTIFICATION OBJECTIVE 8.01

Configuring, Managing, and Troubleshooting Printers and Print Devices

Managing printing, which involves a number of tasks, is a routine part of almost every administrator's job and in this section we will examine how to deal with most of those tasks. Managing printing under Windows 2000 is not significantly different from NT 4.0, though as we shall see in the next section, the new Internet Printing Protocol promises to make connecting to printers even easier for users.

Terminology

In discussing printer configuration, it is important to learn the terminology used with Windows NT and Windows 2000 printing. Unfortunately, not everybody uses the same definitions.

- **Print Device**   The device that produces printed output is known as a print device (e.g., a laser or inkjet printer) rather than a printer. Think of the print device as a physical object, or as the hardware.

- **Printer**   The printer is the interface between the operating device and the actual device that does the printing. A printer may be regarded as a logical device. The reason for the distinction between a printer and a print device is that several printers (logical devices) may be associated with the same print device (hardware). It is unfortunate that the term "printer" has developed this specific meaning, as so many people use the word today to mean the physical device. A better definition might have been printer queue.

- **Print Job**   A print job is the result of a user request to print a document. The print job contains what is to be printed as well as the instructions for printing.

- **Print Spooler**   The print spooler is an operating system service that manages the printing of user documents. It will hold print jobs on disks until they can be printed and routes print jobs to the appropriate print device (be it a local or network print device).

- **Print Server (or File and Print Server)**   This is a server computer used to manage print jobs for printer devices. The print device will be connected directly to the print server using a serial or parallel port, or to the network.

Creating Printers

Printers are added using the Add Printer Wizard, which can be found in the Printers folder in the Control Panel. The wizard takes you through a series of dialog boxes where you specify information about the printer. The basic steps are to:

1. Choose a port (serial, parallel, or network) for the printer.

2. Choose a printer driver.

3. Choose a name for the printer.

4. Select whether the printer will be available to other computers over the network by sharing it. Choose a sharename.

The remaining sections for this objective will explore each of these steps in more detail and examine other configuration tasks.

Connectivity

How a printer is configured for use by client computers on a network depends on how the print device is connected to the network. If the print device has a serial or parallel connector only, then the print device should be connected to one of your file and print servers (running Windows NT 4.0 or Windows 2000 Server). The steps necessary for making the print device available to other computers on the network would be to install a printer on the server and to then share the printer. Each client computer would then connect to the printer using one of two methods. The first method would be to use the Add Printer Wizard and select a network printer server. The second, and probably faster method, is to browse to the printer, right-click it, and choose either Install or Connect, depending on the client computer's operating system.

Many modern print devices also have network connections, allowing the print device to be connected directly to a LAN via a hub. If you have such a print device, then you can choose how to configure the print device for network access. The first method is to install a local printer that connects directly to the network print device using a network print port on each client computer.

The second method is to install a local printer on a print server using a network print port and to share the printer. Clients would then connect to the print device on the print server.

The first method is more complicated to set up, and does not have any of the benefits of centralized queue management. However, it is slightly more efficient in that print jobs are sent directly from the client to the print device, not to the print server and then to the print device as in the second method (thus doubling network traffic as far as printing is concerned). However, the benefits of centralized management far outweigh the minor gain in network efficiency and a central print server should always be used.

FROM THE CLASSROOM

Local and Network Printers

Students often get confused between local and network printers, especially when adding networked printer devices. The way to get around this confusion is to pay close attention to the terminology. Remember that a printer is a logical device and might be created locally, or might be a connection to a printer that has already been shared on another server. A networked printer device, on the other hand, is a physical device and is connected directly to a LAN rather than a server. This means a networked printer device could be added as

FROM THE CLASSROOM

a local or network printer. Generally, a local printer is one managed by the server that the printer is defined on, while a network printer is one that is managed by another server. So a print device connected to the network should be installed as a local printer on the print server, and as a network printer on client

computers. The NT Add Printer Wizard is reasonably clear about this, but the Windows 2000 Add Printer Wizard is not and might make you choose the wrong option (refer to Figure 8-1).

—Feridun Kadir, MCP,
MCP+I, MCSE, MCT

Drivers

A print driver is needed for each print device installed on a computer. The print driver is used to convert a print job to the print commands specific to the selected

FIGURE 8-1

The Windows 2000 Add Printer Wizard

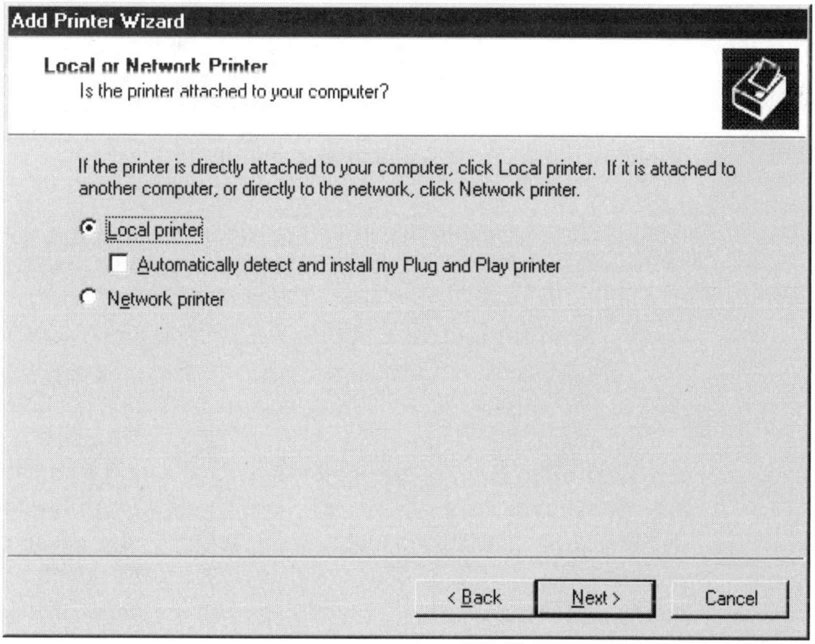

print device. For example, some print devices use the Postscript language, while most HP laser printers use PCL.

When installing a print device, you will need to select the appropriate print driver. Windows NT Server includes drivers for many printers on the installation CD, though of course very many new printers have been produced since Windows NT Server was released. If a driver is not listed for your printer, then you will need a driver from the manufacturer of the print device. You probably received a print driver with the print device when you bought it. However, nearly all printer manufacturers make print drivers available on their Web sites.

The print driver is also specific to the client operating system being used. So, when configuring a user's computer to use a print device, you will need to take into account the operating system on that computer. When configuring a printer for network use, you can install additional print drivers for other operating systems such as Windows NT 3.51 and Windows 95.

Printer Pools

A printer pool is useful when the print device becomes very busy and cannot print users' documents as quickly as desired. In this situation, you could buy another print device of the same make and connect it to the server using a free port. Instead of creating a new printer, modify the properties for the existing printer, select Enable Printer Pooling, and choose the new port you used to connect the print device to the server. Figure 8-2 shows an example of a printer using two ports; note the same printer name is shown against the two ports.

Whenever a user prints to this printer, which is now a pool, the print job will be sent to the first print device that is not busy. Note that the entire job is sent to one of the devices and is not split. For a printer pool to be useful, all the print devices should be identical, or very nearly identical, because the same print driver will be used for all the print devices in the pool. If the print devices print at different speeds, then connect the fastest one to the first port that appears in the ports list, because the ports are used in the order they are listed.

on the

Job

With a printer pool, a user cannot control which print device will print their job. This means that even an apparently small difference between the print devices, such as different amounts of RAM, could cause a job to fail. The print devices should also be located very close to each other. It would be very annoying for a user if you created a printer pool with one device on the first floor and the second device on another floor. How would the user know which print device to go to? They wouldn't.

FIGURE 8-2

Printer pooling

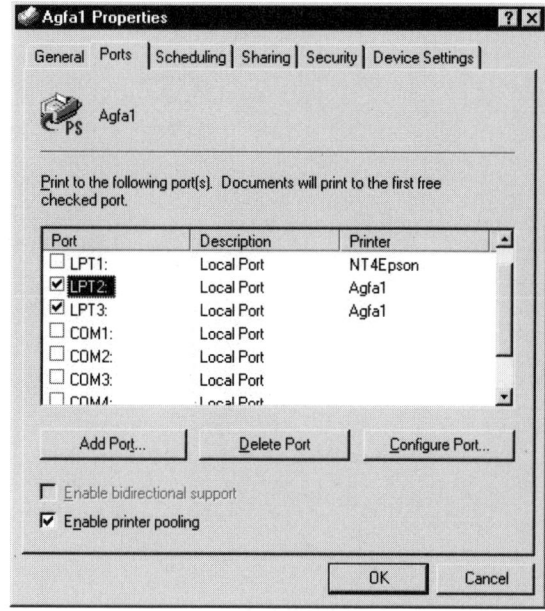

Printer Security

You need to plan the security configuration of printers on your network to control who has access, and whether you need to audit usage of a printer. The security configuration is managed via the Security tab in the Properties dialog box for a printer (as shown in Figure 8-3).

Printer Permissions

Printer permissions control who can use a printer and whether that user can modify the properties of the printer. There are four types of printer permissions (shown in Table 8-1). Permissions can be granted to users and groups.

on the *Job*

It is generally best to grant permissions to groups rather than users, because it requires less administration and is easier to manage. For example, instead of giving fifty sales users access to a printer individually, create a group called sales, make the users a member of the sales group and give the sales group permission to the printer. When there is a new sales user or someone leaves, all you need to do is change the membership of the group. It is likely you will be able to use the group to assign permissions for other resources as well.

Configuring
security for
a printer

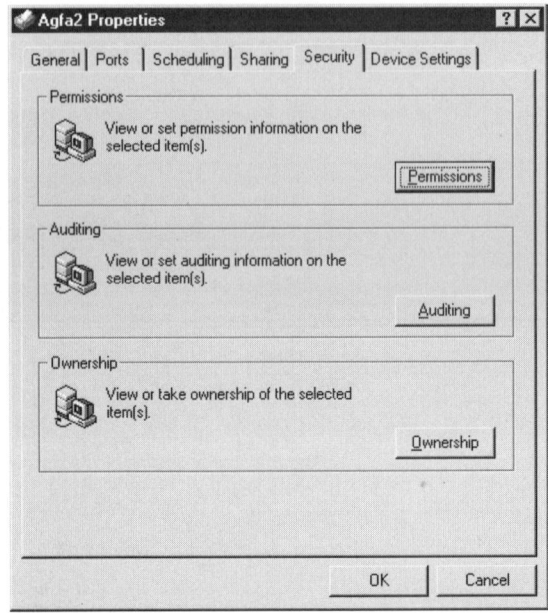

As with file system permissions, printer permissions are cumulative. So, if a user has Print permission and is a member of a group that has Manage Documents permission then the user will have both permissions. However, if a user or a group, of which the user is a member, has the No Access permission, then the user will have no access, regardless of any other permissions he might have.

e x a m

ⓦ a t c h

When restricting access to a printer, make sure you remove the default Print permission for the Everyone group.

TABLE 8-1

Windows NT
Printer
Permissions

Permission	Purpose
No Access	User or group cannot print to printer
Print	User may send print jobs to the printer and delete own jobs
Manage Documents	User may send print jobs and delete own jobs, as well as pause, resume, restart, and delete printing of all jobs
Full Control (Manage Printers in Windows 2000)	All of the above, plus the option to share a printer, change printer properties, delete a printer, and change printer permissions

Figure 8-4 shows the default permissions for a newly created printer on a Member Server, and Figure 8-5 shows the default permissions on a Domain Controller. All users can print to the printer and delete their own jobs. The Power Users and Administrators groups have full control. On a Domain Controller, the Power Users group does not exist; instead, the Print Operators and Server Operators groups are used to grant administrative privileges on printers to specific users.

To add permissions for a printer, right-click the printer, select Properties, select the Security tab, and click the Permissions button. In the Printer Permissions dialog box, select Add to open up the Add Users And Groups dialog box. Select the user or groups and the type of access required. Removing permissions is a similar process. In the Printer Permissions dialog box, highlight the user or group from which permission is to be removed, then click the Remove button.

on the
job

Don't be tempted to remove the Manage Documents permission from Creator Owner. This permission is added by default when you create a printer. Creator Owner is a special system group that contains the user that created or owns a print job, and it is this permission that allows users to delete their own jobs. If you remove this permission, then users will not be able to delete their print jobs.

Auditing Printers

Auditing is used to record whenever a user or group tries to exercise a permission (whether successfully or not) on a printer. You can choose which permission events

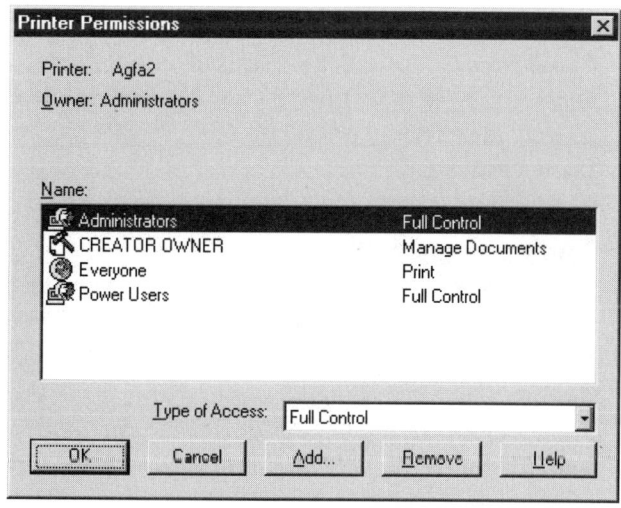

FIGURE 8-4

The default printer permissions on a Member Server

FIGURE 8-5

The default
printer
permissions
on a Domain
Controller

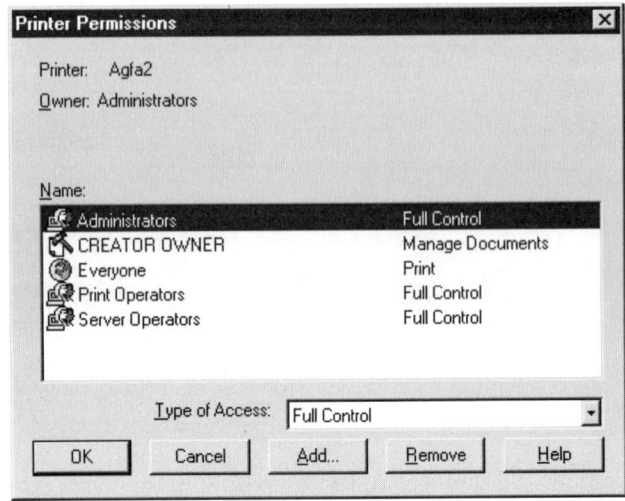

to audit, whether to audit success, failure, or both, and who to audit. To configure auditing, right-click the printer, select Properties, select the Security tab, and click the Auditing button. In the Printer Auditing dialog box, click the Add button to choose whom to audit, and then select the events you want to audit. Figure 8-6 shows the Printer Auditing dialog box.

Audit events are written to the security log of the NT Event Viewer. Be careful not to select too many events, otherwise the security log will become very large very quickly. Only use auditing if there is a specific need.

exam
🐶*atch*

Recall from Chapter 6 that File and Object Access auditing has to be enabled for the server using User Manager or User Manager for Domains, as well as individual printer auditing, before any events will be recorded in the security log.

Taking Ownership

A printer always has an owner who can change permissions even if they have the No Access permission. However, the owner of a printer cannot hand off ownership of that printer to someone else. Another user can become the owner of that printer by using the Take Ownership button on the Security tab in the Properties dialog box for the printer. However, only Administrators or users who have been granted the Take Ownership permission by the current owner can use the Take Ownership button.

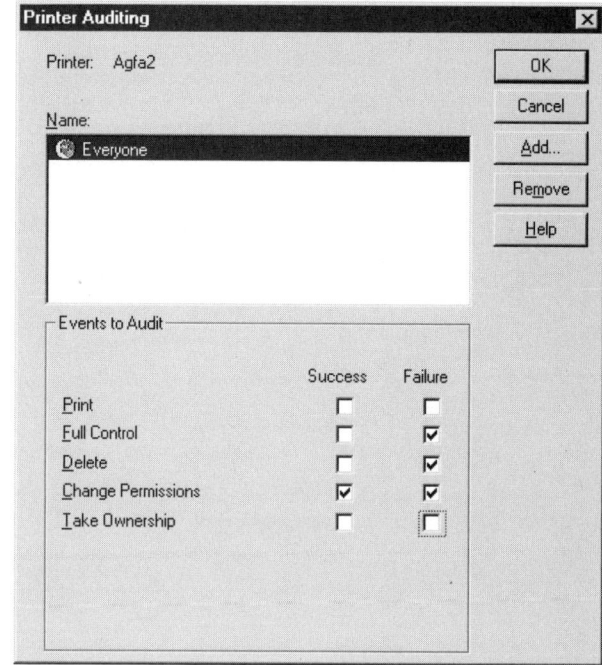

FIGURE 8-6

Configuring
auditing for
a printer

Scheduling Printers

It is possible to control when print jobs are sent to a print device. By setting a schedule on a printer, users can continue to submit print jobs at any time, but the jobs will not be printed until the scheduled availability time.

This may be useful for occasions where users have to print large documents that are not needed immediately, such as audit reports. Without scheduling, printing such a document may delay prints for other users. The solution in this case is to create a second printer that prints to the same print device, change the availability time to non-office hours and advise staff to use the second printer for the larger reports. Scheduling is configured on the Scheduling tab of the Properties dialog box for a printer. Figure 8-7 shows a printer whose availability time is set between 6:00 P.M. and 8:00 A.M.

Printer Priorities

All printers and print jobs have a priority setting that ranges from 1 to 99 with 99 being the highest. The default priority setting for a printer is 1. Any print job that

FIGURE 8-7

Printer scheduling
and priorities

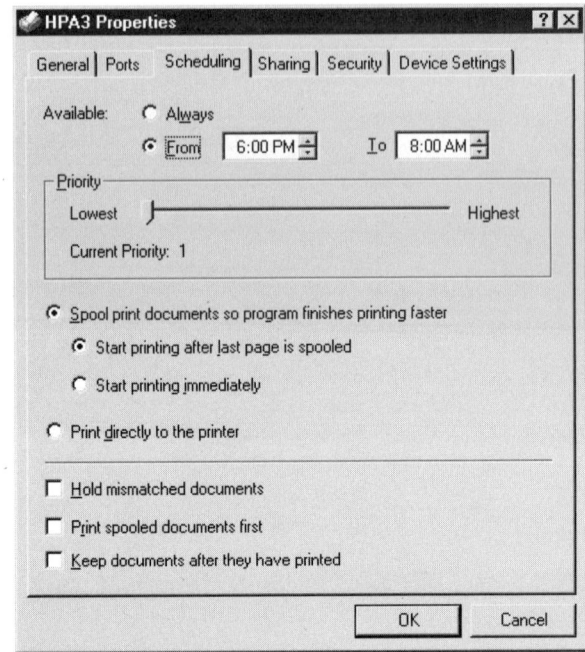

enters the queue has the same priority as the printer. If a user has a job that needs to be printed urgently, an administrator, or someone who has the Manage Documents permission to a printer, can change the properties for the job to upgrade the priority and prompt the job to print next, despite the print order.

Another use of printer priorities is to give preferential treatment to a particular group of users. For example, you may be asked to ensure that managers' jobs print before anybody else's on a particular print device. To set this up, follow this procedure:

1. Create two printers (with the names Laser and LaserMgrs, for example) so both queues print to the same print device.

2. Change the priority for the LaserMgrs printer to a value higher than 1 (this is done on the Scheduling tab; refer back to Figure 8-7).

3. Remove the Print permission for Everyone from the LaserMgrs printer.

4. Add the Print permission for managers (the best way to do this would be using a group) to the LaserMgrs printer.

As a result of this procedure, you will have two printers pointing to the same print device, one of which only managers can use and whose print jobs will be serviced first.

You may want to consider changing the priority for all printers to a value higher than 1. This means you have the option to reduce the priority of a job so it won't print until all the other jobs have done so.

TCP/IP Printing

Many print devices come with a network interface. This means you can connect the print device directly to your LAN rather than using a serial or parallel port. However, in order to do this, you will need to create a TCP/IP printer port during installation of the printer on your server. Exercise 8-1 takes you through the steps to create a TCP/IP printer. Management of a TCP/IP printer is no different from a printer that uses a parallel or serial port.

Some operating systems, such as Unix, use TCP/IP printing utilities to manage printing. Table 8-2 shows the utilities.

These utilities can be installed on an NT Server to provide the following gateway functions:

- Any non-Windows client can use lpr to submit print jobs to printers defined on the NT Server using lpd

- A Windows NT client can use lpr to send print jobs to any host (e.g., Unix) running lpd

To set up an NT Server to act as a gateway for TCP/IP printing, you need to install the Microsoft TCP/IP Printing service. This service provides access to print servers that use the lpd service (e.g., Unix hosts) for your NT client computers, and also enables your NT Server to act as an lpd server so that non-NT clients (such as Unix computers) can print to any printers defined on the NT Server. To enable the NT Server to act as an lpd server, you must ensure the TCP/IP Printer Server service is running. The service is set to start manually by default, so you should change it to start automatically.

TABLE 8-2	Command	Purpose
TCP/IP Printing Utilities	Lpd (line printer daemon)	Listens for print requests sent using TCP/IP
	Lpr	A command-line program used to submit print jobs to a printer or host that is running lpd
	Lpq	Used to examine a printer queue

EXERCISE 8-1

CertCam 8-1

Installing and Configuring a Networked Print Device Using TCP/IP and lpd

In this exercise, we will add an HP LaserJet 5Si print device to our print server using the following specification:

- The HP LaserJet is connected directly to the network and has an IP address of 10.50.1.15.

- The lpd name of the print device is hplj5.

- The printer queue and sharename should be HPA3.

- Only users in the Sales group should be allowed to print to the print device.

The steps to achieve this are as follows:

1. Ensure the TCP/IP protocol is installed on the print server.

2. Install Microsoft TCP/IP Printing from the Services tab of the Network icon in the Control Panel. This will require a reboot of the server.

3. Click on Add Printer in the Printers folder of the Control Panel.

4. In the Add Printer Wizard (Figure 8-8), select My Computer, then click Next.

5. On the next screen, select Add Port, rather than choosing from the available ports list (Figure 8-9).

6. In the Printer Ports dialog box (Figure 8-10) that appears, highlight LPR Port, then click New Port.

7. In the Add LPR Compatible Printer dialog box, enter 10.50.1.15 for the IP address and hplj5 for the name of the printer (Figure 8-11). Note that if there was an entry for the print device in a hosts file or a DNS server, we could use the host name instead of the IP address.

8. Click OK. If you are carrying out this procedure as an exercise, there may be a long delay, because at this point the Add Printer Wizard will attempt to communicate with the printer. If there is no printer at the IP address specified, the LPR Port Configuration Warning will appear (shown in Figure 8-12). You can safely ignore this error for the purposes of the exercise. Click OK, then click Close in the Printer Ports dialog box.

FIGURE 8-8

The Add Printer
Wizard screen

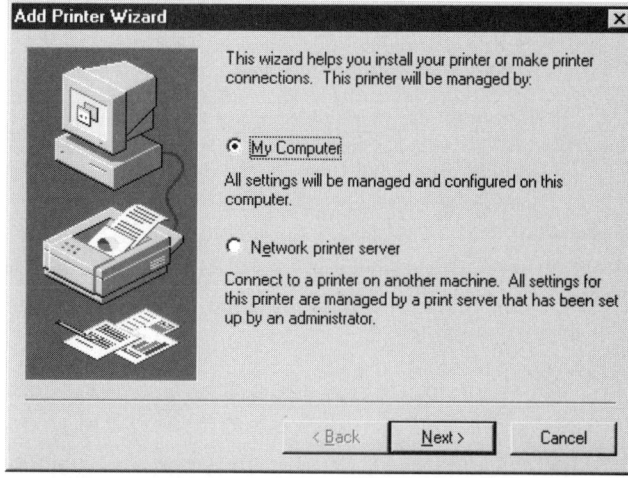

FIGURE 8-9

Select Add Port

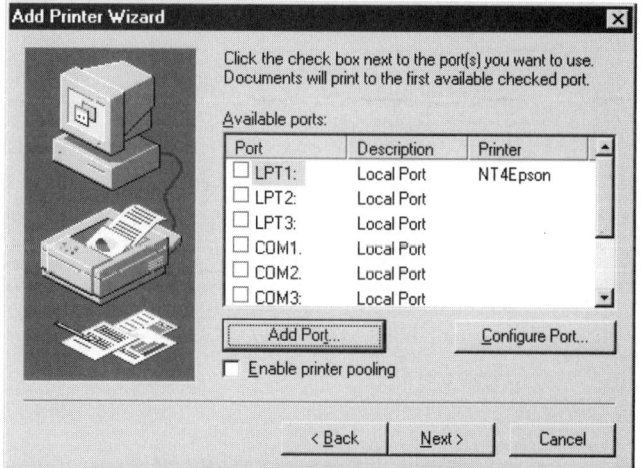

FIGURE 8-10

The Printer Ports
dialog box

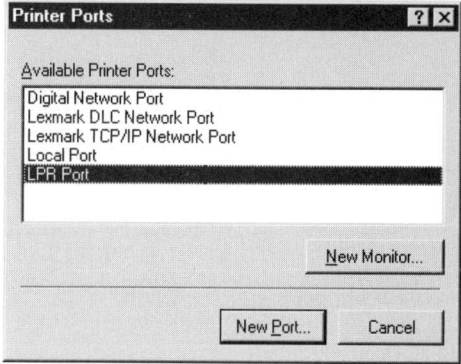

FIGURE 8-11

The Add LPR
Compatible
Printer dialog box

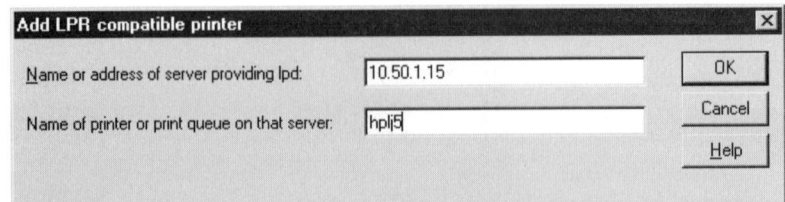

9. This will return you to the Available Ports page of the wizard (Figure 8-13). Note that a TCP/IP port has been added in the Available Ports list, and is checked. Click Next.

10. Scroll through the Manufacturers and Printers lists to select the appropriate driver and then click Next (Figure 8-14).

11. Enter HPA3 as the printer name and select whether the printer should be the default printer. Then click Next (Figure 8-15).

12. In the Sharing dialog box, select Shared (Figure 8-16) and enter HPA3 as the Share Name, then click Next.

13. In the next dialog box, you will be asked whether to print a test page or not. Since this is an exercise, select No. NT will then copy some files to the WINNT directory (you may need to provide your Windows NT 4.0 Server CD-ROM for this), and the printer will be created.

14. We now need to configure the permissions. In the Printers folder, right-click the HPA3 printer, select Properties, and click the Security tab (Figure 8-17).

FIGURE 8-12

The LPR Port
Configuration
Warning

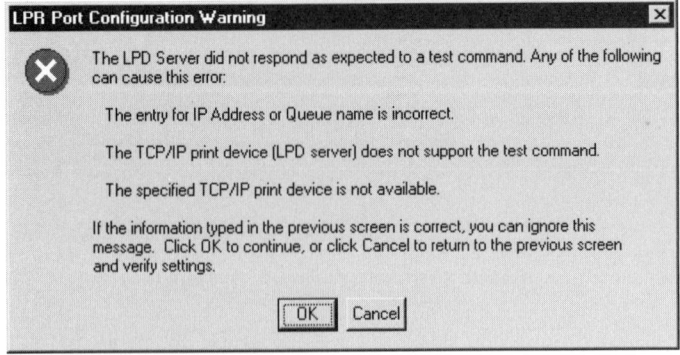

FIGURE 8-14

The Available
Ports page of the
Add Printer
Wizard

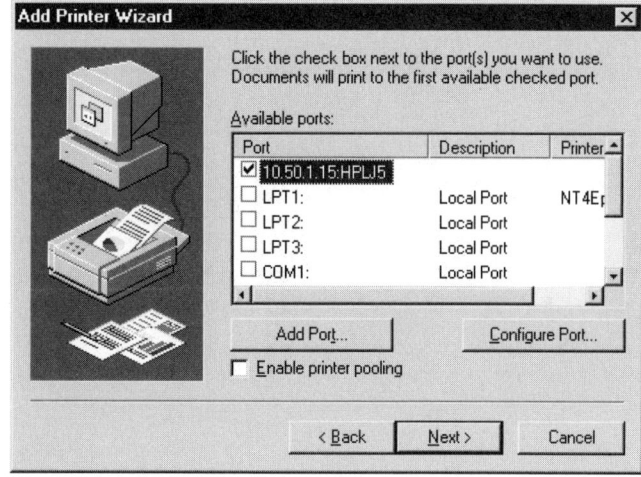

15. Click the Permissions button. The Printer Permissions dialog box will appear (Figure 8-18). Note that, by default, the Everyone group is allowed to use the printer.

16. Highlight the Everyone group, then click Remove to remove permissions for the group. Now click Add, and in the Add Users And Groups dialog box, scroll through the Names list, highlight Sales, and click Add (Figure 8-19). The Sales group appears in the Add Names box. Ensure the Type of Access

FIGURE 8-13

The Manufacturers
and Printers lists

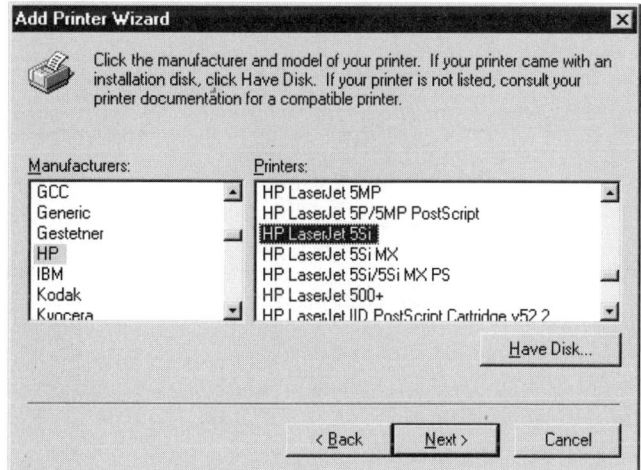

FIGURE 8-15

The Printer
Name screen

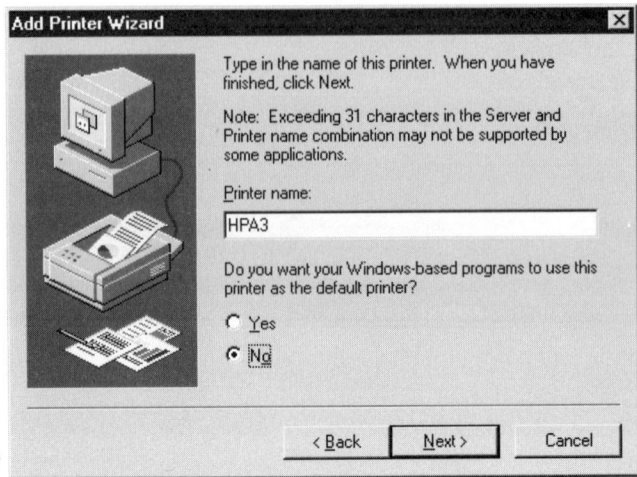

is set to Print since we don't want to give the group any additional rights to manage the queue, then click OK.

17. The Printer Permissions dialog box should now look like Figure 8-20.

18. Click on OK twice to close the remaining property sheets for the printer. The print device is now configured for use, as per the specification.

FIGURE 8-16

The Sharing
dialog box

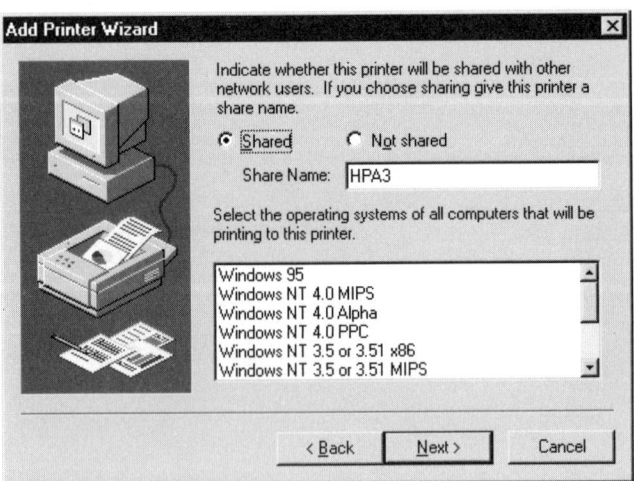

FIGURE 8-17

The Security tab

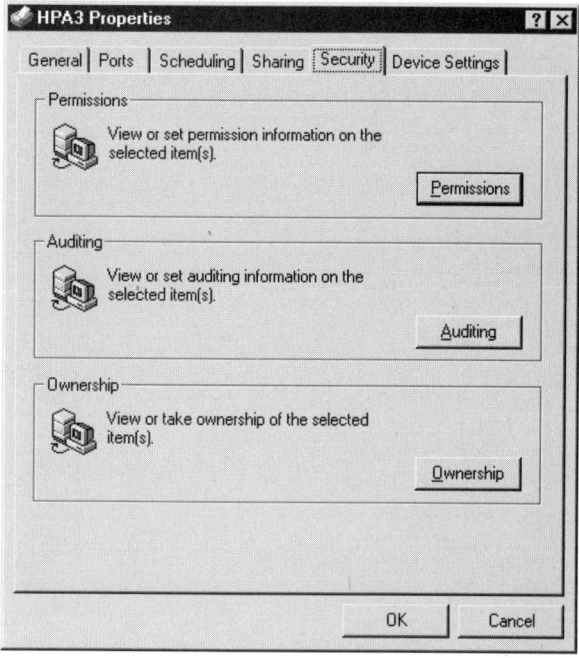

FIGURE 8-18

The Printer
Permissions
dialog box

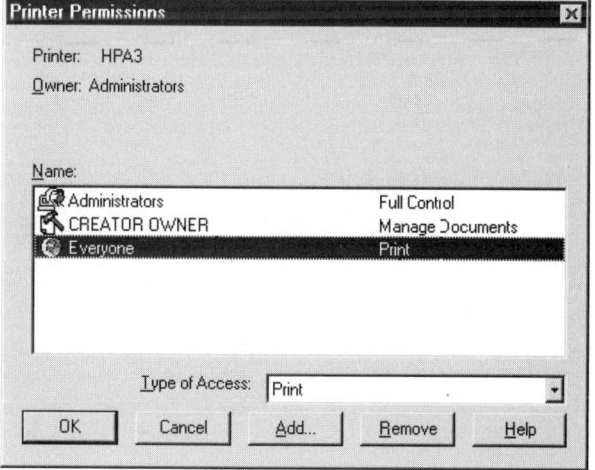

FIGURE 8-19

The Add Users
And Groups
dialog box

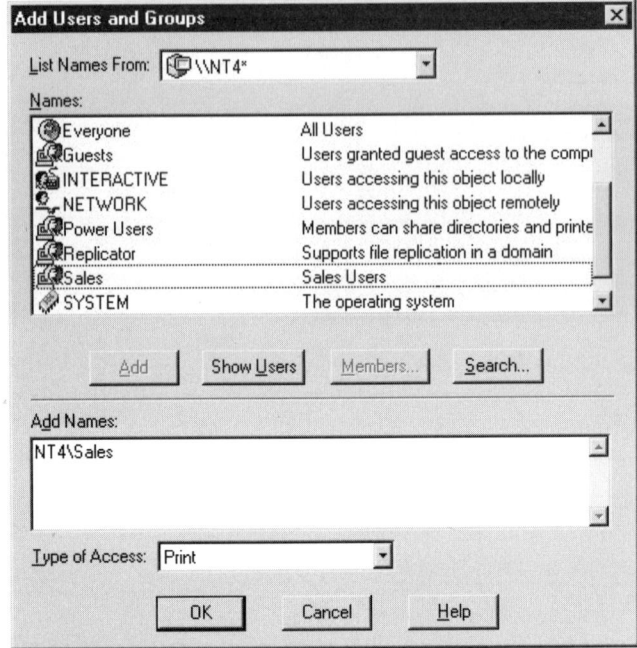

FIGURE 8-20

The Printer
Permissions
dialog box

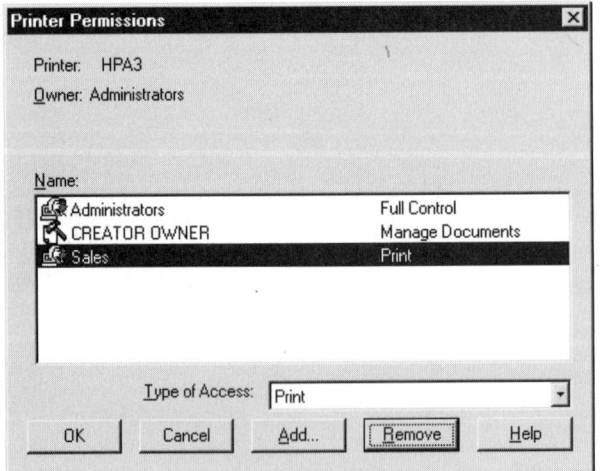

Other Network Protocols

On networks that use computers running non-Microsoft operating systems, you may have need to configure printers that use other network protocols. Windows NT 4.0 and Windows 2000 support such printers, but you have to make sure the appropriate network protocol is installed before attempting to configure the printer.

The Print Spooler Service

The print spooler, which runs as a service (called Spooler), manages print jobs and print devices. If the print spooler is not running, then users will not be able to print.

The print spooler has a number of configuration options. To access these options, open the Printers folder in the Control Panel, then click File and select Server Properties. The Print Server Properties dialog box opens containing three tabs, Forms, Ports, and Advanced.

The Forms Tab is used to define custom paper sizes and margins. Custom forms can then be used with individual printers to associate a particular tray with the form. This is configured using the Device Settings tab on the properties sheet for a printer.

The Ports tab is used to add, delete, or configure a printer port. This tab is also available in the properties sheet for each printer.

The Advanced tab is used for additional options and is shown in Figure 8-21.

SCENARIO & SOLUTION	
How do I connect an AppleTalk print device?	To support an AppleTalk print device, install Services for Macintosh on a Windows NT Server. When creating the printer, select AppleTalk Printing Devices from the Printer Ports dialog box, then select the appropriate print device in the AppleTalk Printing Devices dialog box.
How do I connect to a NetWare print queue?	To support printing to NetWare print queues, install the Gateway Service for NetWare on a Windows NT Server. Then create a printer using the Add Printer Wizard and select Network Printer. In the Connect To Printer dialog box, browse through the NetWare or Compatible Network entry to select the appropriate NetWare print queue.

FIGURE 8-21

Advanced Print
Server Properties

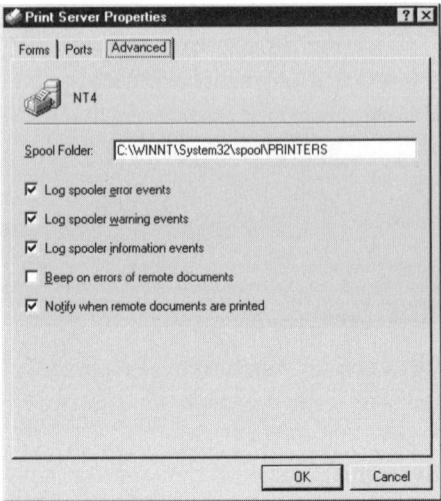

The spool folder is where print jobs are stored until a print device is ready to receive it. On large networks with many printers, the spool folder may get quite large.

e x a m
ⓦ a t c h

If you have a large amount of printing activity, it is a good idea to create a separate disk partition for the spool folder, and to change the location of the spool folder to the new partition. It is important to ensure that users have access to the spool folder. In particular, they require the NTFS Change permission to the folder.

SCENARIO & SOLUTION

Problem: Print jobs are shown in the queue, but none are printing.	The spooler may have locked up. Restart the spooler service (either by way of Control Panel | Services, or by using the NET STOP SPOOLER and NET START SPOOLER commands).
Problem: Users cannot see any printers on the print server.	Check that the printer has been shared.
Problem: Users cannot print to a shared printer.	Check that users have the Print permission.
Problem: Users can submit print jobs, but none come out of the print device.	This could be due to a variety of reasons. Items to check include the scheduling time of the printer, whether the printer is paused, the priority of the job, and seeing whether the print device has a paper jam.

Configuring and Troubleshooting Internet and Intranet Access to File and Printer Resources

More and more companies and individuals are using the Internet to publish and share information. Internet protocols, which can also be used on your own network to form an intranet, are based on the TCP/IP protocol suite. Throughout this chapter, whenever Internet is mentioned, the information is just as applicable to an intranet.

Internet services comprise many facilities. Some of these are:

■ **News**   A service that provides discussion groups for almost any topic. With the appropriate client software, users can contribute articles or simply browse.

■ **File Transfer Protocol (FTP)**   A service that allows users to transfer files from a server computer to a client computer.

■ **The World Wide Web (WWW)**   A term used to describe the enormous number of computers connected through the Internet. Web browsers are used to access these computers.

■ **Electronic Mail**   E-mail provides a facility by which people connected to the Internet can send messages to one another.

Domain Names

To connect to computers on the Internet, users normally use a domain name. A domain name consists of a series of words separated by dots (i.e., www.syngress.com). The domain name system is based on a hierarchical naming structure that includes top-level, second-level, and lower-level names. Some top-level names are shown in Table 8-3.

There are also top-level domains for each country such as .uk for the United Kingdom, .fr for France, and .au for Australia. There are some new top-level domains due to come into use towards the end of 2001. These include .info for organizations such as museums, and .name for individuals.

Domain names are purchased and registered through a Domain Name Registrar. For example, Syngress has purchased and registered the domain name syngress.com. A Web site is usually referred to as www followed by the domain name. So the name of the

TABLE 8-3	Top-level Name	Description
DNS Top-level Names	com	Commercial organizations
	gov	Government agencies
	net	Internet providers
	mil	Military organizations
	edu	Educational establishments

Web site for Syngress, whose domain name is syngress.com, is www.syngress.com. Note that the name of the actual computer hosting the Web site might be different from the Web site name. As long as the DNS records for the Web site name point to the correct computer, it doesn't matter what the computer is called on the internal network.

Although a user types in a domain name to communicate with a computer on the Internet, connectivity is established using IP addresses. There are a number of methods that can be used to resolve domain names to IP addresses. We will examine these in Chapter 9.

Internet Protocols

To provide the services described earlier, a variety of protocols are used. A protocol is an agreed standard for the transfer of information. Most Internet protocols work using a client/server model. This means that software runs on both server and client computers, with the server servicing client requests. Table 8-4 shows some of the more common protocols.

HTTP and HTTPS

These two protocols are used for the transfer of Web documents from server to client. The format of the documents is specified by other standards such as HTML and DHTML.

HTTP (which stands for HyperText Transfer Protocol) is a TCP/IP protocol and is the most common protocol used for transferring Web documents. When entering the name of a Web site in a browser, it is customary to put http:// at the beginning. This instructs the browser to use HTTP to connect to the Web site. However, many Web browsers assume that HTTP is to be used, so it can be left out.

TABLE 8-4	Protocol	Client	Server
Common Internet Protocols	HTTP (HyperText Transfer Protocol) and HTTPS (secure HTTP)	Web browser (e.g., Internet Explorer)	Web server (e.g., Internet Information Services)
	FTP (File Transfer Protocol)	FTP client	FTP server
	SMTP (Simple Mail Transfer Protocol)	Mail reader	Mail server (e.g., Microsoft Exchange)
	POP3 (Post Office Protocol)	Mail reader (e.g., Microsoft Outlook)	Mail server
	NNTP (Network News Transfer Protocol)	News reader (e.g., Outlook Express)	News server

The transfer of Web documents is normally carried out using clear text, in other words unencrypted. Now that the Internet is being increasingly used for financial transactions, it is important to provide a way for Web traffic to be encrypted. This can be achieved using HTTPS (Secure HyperText Transfer Protocol). HTTPS provides the same facilities as HTTP but ensures that all traffic between a Web server and browser is encrypted. Whether encryption is used is determined by the Web site. For such Web sites, you would connect by entering https:// in front of the Web site name. This instructs the browser to make a secure (i.e., encrypted connection). You may wonder why all Web traffic is not encrypted. The reason is simply one of performance. Encryption has a performance impact on a server and client and therefore is only used when necessary. Note that using a secure connection is not the same as requiring authentication. Most Web sites allow users to browse without requiring usernames and passwords. However, if access were to be restricted to certain users, then a Web site would require authentication (i.e., a username and password). A Web site can use encryption regardless of whether it uses authentication and vice versa.

FTP

FTP (File Transfer Protocol) is used to transfer files between computers. Clients can initiate FTP sessions with a server either from the command line using the FTP command or within a browser by typing **ftp://** in front of the FTP site name.

When you connect to an FTP site you have to provide a username and password. But most FTP sites allow anonymous connections, which means a separate username and password is not required to access the site. In this case, just enter "anonymous" as the username and anything as the password. Figure 8-22 shows an example of logging on to an FTP server from the command line.

When you connect to an FTP site in a Web browser, the browser automatically tries to connect you using the anonymous user. If you need to connect through another username and password, then the address format to use is as follows: ftp://username:password@ftp.syngress.com.

exam
ⓌatcH

Make sure you remember that different protocols can be specified as part of a URL within a browser, such as http://, https://, and ftp://.

Note that HTTP also allows the transfer of files, but is not as efficient as FTP. If a Web site offers you the choice of downloading a file using either HTTP or FTP, then select FTP.

Internet Printing Protocol

A new feature of Windows 2000 is the ability to print to printers on an intranet or the Internet. It doesn't matter whether the printer is located on an intranet or the Internet because the same protocols are used. Using the Internet Printer Protocol (IPP) you connect to a printer using its URL (Uniform Resource Locator). Of course, you still have to have the appropriate permissions to the printer. This can be very useful for sending print jobs to printers located at another geographical site, perhaps half-way around the world.

FIGURE 8-22

A command line
FTP session

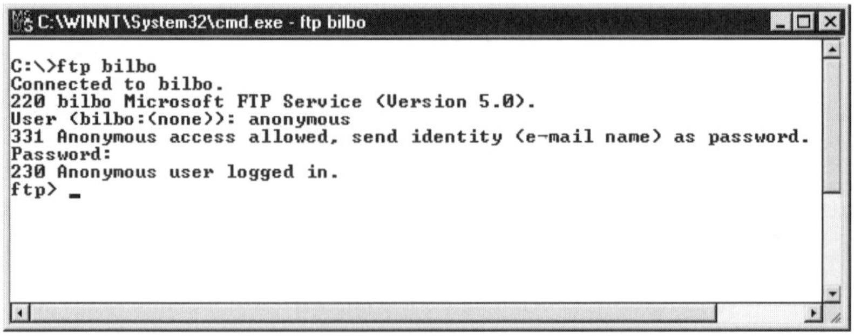

```
C:\>ftp bilbo
Connected to bilbo.
220 bilbo Microsoft FTP Service (Version 5.0).
User (bilbo:(none)): anonymous
331 Anonymous access allowed, send identity (e-mail name) as password.
Password:
230 Anonymous user logged in.
ftp> _
```

The ability to use the Internet Printing Protocol is also available for Windows 95 and 98 clients by installing the client software from the Windows 2000 Server CD-ROM. A Web browser can also be used to connect to Internet printers as well as manage them. The Internet Printing Protocol is based on Internet standards still being developed. For further information, refer to the IPP working group's Web site at www.ietf.org/html.charters/ipp-charter.html.

Requirements for Internet Printing

In order for users to be able to connect to printers on a Windows 2000 print server using Internet Printing, the following requirements must be met:

- The printer must be shared.
- The user must have permissions to the printer.
- The print server must be running Internet Information Services (IIS) for a Windows 2000 Server computer, or Peer Web Services (PWS) for a Windows 2000 Professional computer.
- The client must be running Internet Explorer 4.0 or later.

e x a m
ⓦatch
Remember that Internet Information Services must be running on the print server in order for clients to connect to a printer using a Web browser.

EXERCISE 8-2

Installing a Printer Using a Web Browser

In this exercise, we will configure a printer on a server, share it and then connect to it from a client computer in two ways: using a Web browser and using the Add Printer Wizard.

The steps to achieve this are as follows:

1. On a server running Windows 2000, choose Start | Settings | Printers and then click Add Printer.

2. Add a printer using the wizard.

3. Ensure the printer is shared.

4. On a client computer, open a Web browser and connect to http://server/printers where server is the name of the server used in Step 1. You should see something similar to the example in Figure 8-23. The Web page shows the printers available for sharing from this server.

5. Click on a printer to obtain more information (Figure 8-24). A Web page appears showing the printer queue and possible actions. Click Connect to install the printer on the client computer.

6. The printer can now be used by client applications. Note the other possibilities for managing the printer and individual documents.

7. An alternative way to connect to the printer from the client is to use the Add Printer Wizard. On the Local or Network Printer page, select Network Printer.

FIGURE 8-23	

The http://server/
printers Web page

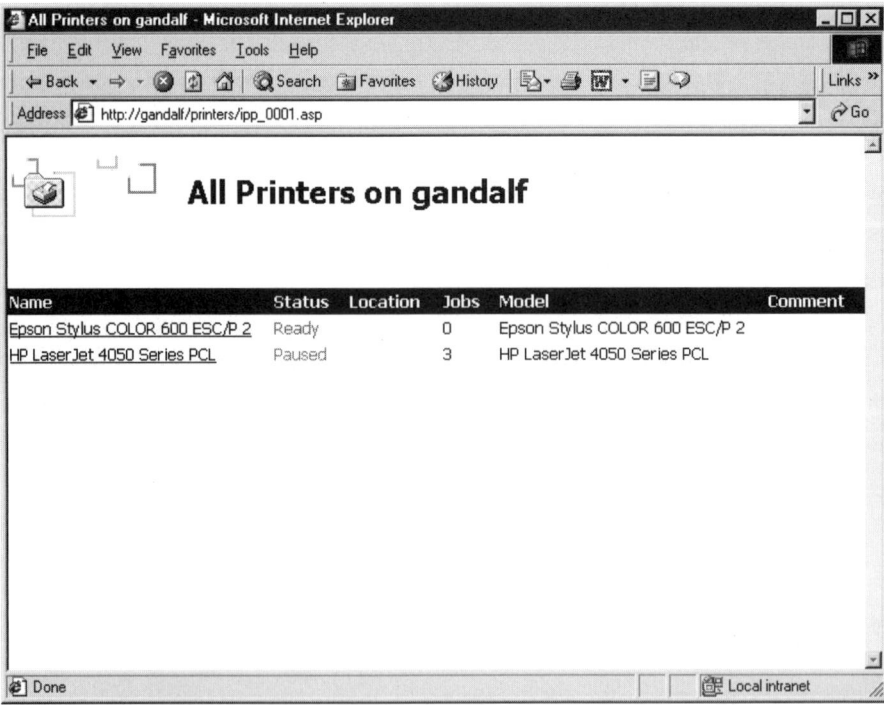

FIGURE 8-24

The Web page showing the printer queue and possible actions

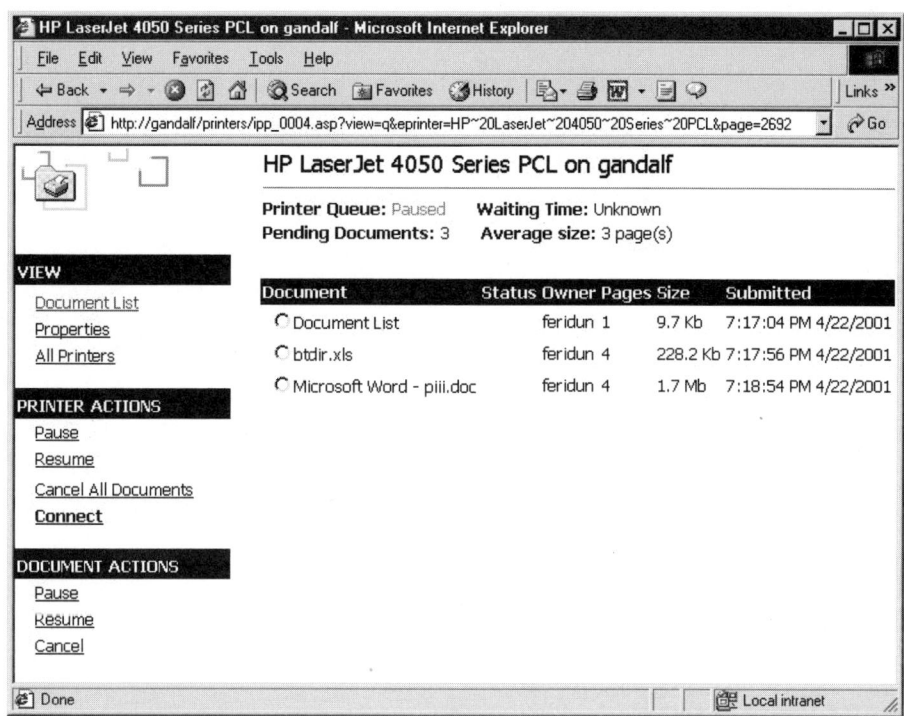

8. On the Locate Your Printer page, select Connect to a printer on the Internet or on your intranet and type in the URL for the printer. The format for Windows 2000 printers is http://*server*/printers/*sharename*/printer where *server* is the name of the print server and *sharename* is the shared name of the printer. An example is shown in Figure 8-25. The disadvantage of this technique is that you need to know the URL for the printer first.

You might like to create your own Web page that shows the printers available on your network using a floor plan or similar diagram. It would then be easy for users to recognize the printer nearest to them.

Configuring Internet Connectivity

There are a number of ways in which you can connect users to the Internet. In deciding which method to use, you should always bear in mind network security.

FIGURE 8-25

Locate Your
Printer Page

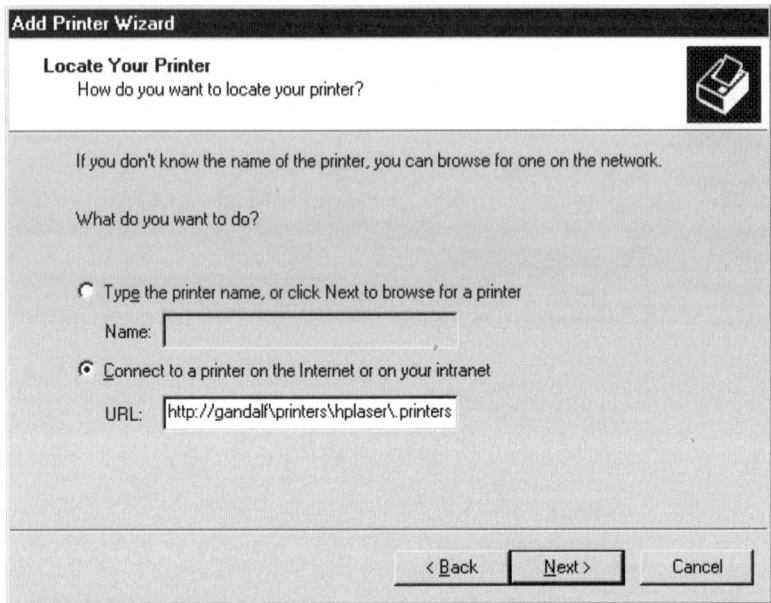

FIGURE 8-25

Locate Your
Printer Page

Once a user's computer is connected to the Internet there is a risk of hacking or
of unauthorized users accessing your network from outside your organization. By
choosing the appropriate networking components, you can minimize the risk.

The first decision on how to provide access is whether to provide centralized
access or to use dial-up modems on every computer that requires Internet access.
Unless your network is very small and there are only two or three computers that
need access, then you should always use centralized access. This will give you much
better control and make life easier for users since they don't have to be bothered
with configuring and using dial-up connections.

Network components used to control access typically include proxy servers,
network address translation, and firewalls. Network components used to connect
to the Internet include dial-up modems, ISDN, ADSL, routers, and leased lines.

We will review the access components. In order to connect to the Internet a
computer must have a public IP address. You could assign a public IP address to each
of the computers in your network. However, this approach is not recommended
because it exposes your network to the Internet. A better approach would be to
use private IP addresses and a network address translator. NAT acts like a router
between your network and the Internet. It translates private IP addresses of outgoing

traffic to public addresses, and public addresses into private IP addresses for incoming traffic. This maintains the security of your network by "hiding" its internal structure. You can implement NAT using Windows 2000 or use dedicated hardware.

A proxy server is similar to NAT in that it is also used to connect networks with private IP addresses to the Internet, but it offers additional features. A proxy server can improve the performance of Web access because it caches (i.e., saves) the results of requests made to external Web sites. So, if another user browsed a site whose pages were cached, then the proxy server would return the page rather than forward the request to the Web server and consume bandwidth on the Internet connection. This could save time and money, particularly on dial-up connections. Proxy servers can also be used to restrict access to specific Web sites on a per-user or per-computer basis. Exercise 8-3 shows how to configure Internet Explorer to use a proxy server.

EXERCISE 8-3

CertCam 8-3

Configuring Internet Explorer to Use a Proxy Server

1. Start Internet Explorer and select Internet Options from the Tools menu. Note that the location of this option may vary between versions of Internet Explorer.

2. Alternatively, right-click the Internet Explorer icon and select Properties. This will bring up the same dialog box as in Step 1, except it will be called Internet Explorer Properties instead of Internet Options.

3. Select the Connections tab (Figure 8-26).

4. Click the LAN Settings button and in the Proxy Server section click Use A Proxy Server and type in the address of the proxy server and the port that the proxy server is listening on. This is often 80 or 8080, however this depends on the proxy software you are using. Setting the Bypass Proxy Server For Local Addresses option means that the browser will not use the proxy server for addresses on the local network (Figure 8-27).

5. Press the Advanced button to reveal additional options (Figure 8-28). By clearing the Use The Same Proxy Server For All Protocols option on the Proxy Settings page, we can choose different servers for each type of Internet access. In the example shown, FTP requests will be sent to a different proxy server from the other protocols. Normally, you would use the same proxy server for everything.

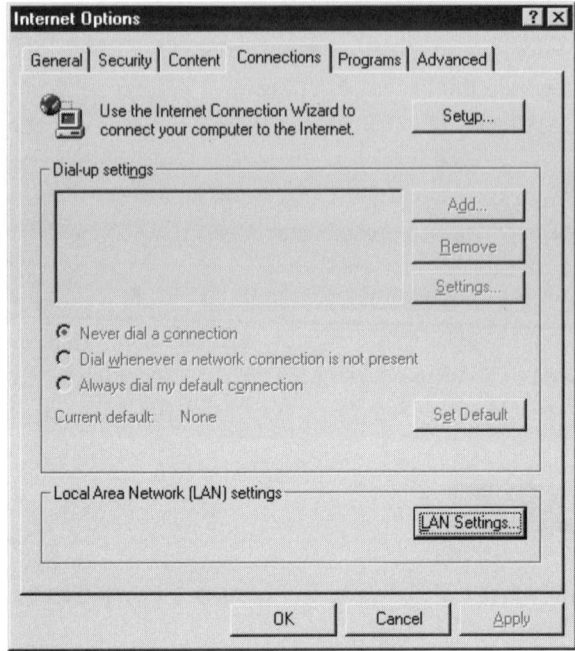

FIGURE 8-26

The Connections tab

6. Click OK three times to close all the dialog boxes. Internet Explorer is now configured to use a proxy server.

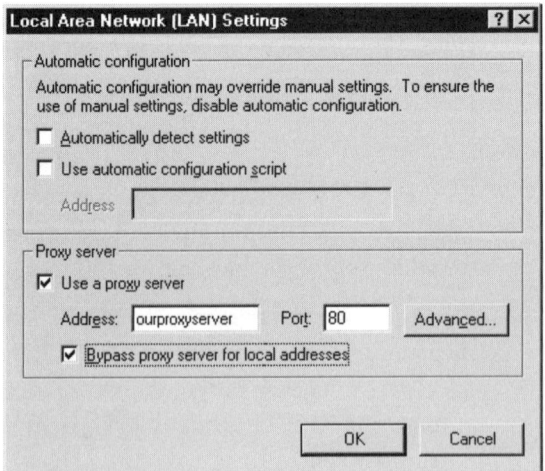

FIGURE 8-27

The Local Area Network (LAN) Settings

FIGURE 8-28

The Proxy
Settings
dialog box

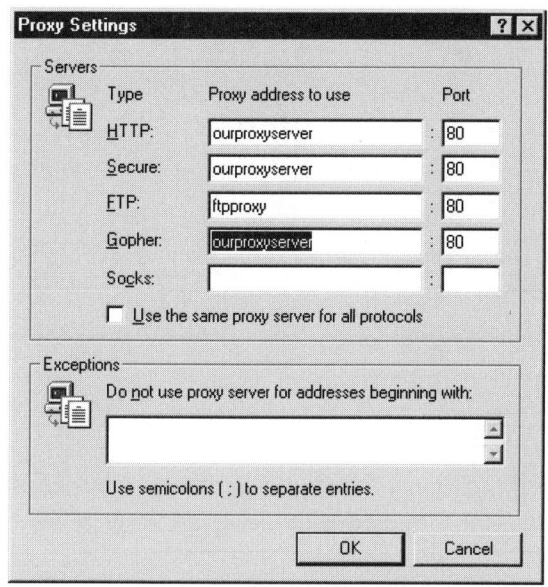

Although Internet Explorer can be configured to use a proxy server, this will not provide access to Internet services to other programs, such as FTP at the command line, or to other Internet protocols, such as NNTP (for news) or POP3 (for mail). In such cases, additional software, called a proxy client, has to be installed on the client computer. The proxy client redirects network access to remote sites (i.e., not on the local network) that use Internet protocols to a proxy server. If the proxy client is not installed then, even though Web access may work, other types of Internet access will fail.

A firewall is used to provide a high level of security for networks connected to the Internet. A firewall sits between the network and the Internet and therefore all traffic, in and out, must pass through the firewall. The firewall can examine the traffic and only allow it through if it meets pre-configured rules. For example, a firewall could be configured to allow Web and e-mail traffic through but nothing else. While a firewall can be very effective in ensuring only a particular type of traffic is allowed through, it does not examine the content of the data and so would not stop, for example, viruses being downloaded.

Most networks use a combination of a proxy server and a firewall, sometimes in a software product or sometimes using hardware (or sometimes using both).

SCENARIO & SOLUTION

Problem: User can't access any Web sites, but other users can.	Check the configuration of the user's Internet Options and the proxy settings.
Problem: User cannot connect to a printer using a Web browser.	Check that IIS is running on the print server.
Problem: User cannot use FTP to connect to an Internet site.	FTP access may have been disabled in the firewall.

CERTIFICATION SUMMARY

In this chapter, we covered printing on internal networks, intranets, and the Internet. We reviewed printing terminology and then covered the different aspects of configuring printers. This started with the fact that all print devices require a print driver used to convert print jobs to the appropriate print commands suitable for the print device.

We reviewed the different ways (local or networked) in which printers can be connected to a network and examined the use of printer pools to provide load balancing for busy queues. In printer security and auditing, we examined how access to printers can be controlled and also logged for providing an audit trail.

The use of TCP/IP printing was explained and we looked at the TCP/IP printing utilities. We then examined the print spooler service and its properties.

In the second section of the chapter, we examined the types of Internet services, the use of domain names and Internet protocols. The use of the Internet Printing Protocol to connect to printers on Windows 2000 servers was also covered. We then looked at different ways of providing centralized access to the Internet that included network address translators, proxy servers, and firewalls. This section ended with some troubleshooting tips.

TWO-MINUTE DRILL

Configuring, Managing, and Troubleshooting Printers and Print Devices

❑ Learn the printing terminology. In particular, note that a *printer* is a software interface (like a queue) and that a *print device* refers to the physical device that produces printed output.

❑ A print driver is required for a print device, and the print driver is specific for each operating system.

❑ A printer is created using the Add Printer Wizard. Printers can be either a local printer (i.e., locally managed) or a network printer (defined on another server). Remember that even a *networked* printer is created as a local printer when it is first defined.

❑ A printer pool is used to provide load balancing for one printer (queue) across several print devices.

❑ There are four permissions for use with printers. No Access (cannot access the printer), Print (may submit print jobs), Manage Documents (print, as well as pause, resume, restart, and delete the printing of all jobs), and Full Control (Manage Documents and share a printer, change printer properties, delete a printer and change printer permissions).

❑ Printer priorities and permissions can be used to give certain users and groups preferential access to a print device.

❑ Printer scheduling is used to prevent printing to the print device during specified times. Users can still submit print jobs.

❑ The print spooler (the Spooler service) manages print jobs and print devices. If the print spooler is not running, users will not be able to print.

❑ Many networked printers use the TCP/IP protocol though AppleTalk. NetWare protocols may also be used.

Configuring and Troubleshooting Internet and Intranet Access to File and Printer Resources

❑ A variety of services are available on the Internet, including: Newsgroups, File Transfers, the Web, and E-mail.

❑ To connect to a computer on the Internet, you normally use a domain name (though you could use an IP address).

❑ There are many Internet protocols used. Some of the more common ones include: HTTP, HTTPS, FTP, SMTP, and NNTP.

❑ HTTP and HTTPS are used for the transfer of Web pages. HTTPS is the secure version of HTTP.

❑ FTP is used to transfer files between computers, while SMTP is used to transfer mail, and news servers use NNTP.

❑ The Internet Printing Protocol allows users to connect to a printer using a Web browser.

❑ The requirements necessary for Internet printing to work on a Windows 2000 server are that the printer is shared, IIS is running on the print server, and that the client is running Internet Explorer 4 or later.

❑ There are several ways of providing a centralized connection to the Internet, including network address translation, proxy servers, and firewalls.

SELF TEST

The following questions will help you measure your understanding of the material presented in this chapter. Read all the choices carefully, as there may be more than one correct answer. Choose all correct answers for each question.

Configuring, Managing, and Troubleshooting Printers and Print Devices

1. You have made available two printers (that use the same hardware) to users over the network. Their computers have a mixture of Windows NT 4.0 Workstation, NT 4.0 Server, Windows 98, and Windows 2000 Professional operating systems. How many different print drivers will be required?

   A. Two

   B. Three

   C. Four

   D. Eight

2. Which of the following ports would be appropriate for a networked printer? (Choose all that apply.)

   A. COM1

   B. LPT1

   C. LPR Port

   D. AppleTalk Printing Device

3. Your network has one A4 laser print device that has become very busy. You decide to buy an additional print device of the same model to cope with the workload rather than replace the print device with a higher capacity model. The new print device will be connected to port LPT2 on the same server as the existing print device (which uses LPT1). How would you configure the print server to use the new print device while minimizing the configuration changes on client computers?

   A. Create a new printer on the print server using LPT2. Instruct half the users to use the new printer and the other half to use the existing printer.

   B. Modify the existing printer by enabling printer pooling, then configure it to use LPT2 as well as LPT1.

    C. Create a new printer on the print server using LPT2. Configure the current printer to use the new printer when it is busy, and the new printer to use the current printer when it is busy.

    D. Create a new printer on the print server using LPT2. Create a printer pool consisting of the current and new printers.

4. A user complains that the print queue is very long and that it is important her job be printed as soon as possible. How would you best achieve this?

    A. Delete all print jobs in the queue before the user's job.

    B. Delete the user's job and ask her to print it again using a higher priority.

    C. Increase the priority of the user's job in the queue.

    D. Open the printer queue, highlight the user's print job, and drag it to the top of the queue.

5. Your network has a color print device. Users print to this using a printer called A4Color. You've been asked to provide the Managers group with preferential access to this color printer. It is important all users can still use the print device as well. How would you best achieve this?

    A. Create a new printer called MgrsColor using the same port as A4Color, ensure that only the Managers group has permission to print to MgrsColor and change the default priority to a higher value than A4Color.

    B. Give the Managers group Manage Documents permission to the A4Color printer so they can change the priority of their jobs.

    C. Give the Managers group Print permission to the A4Color printer and change the default priority for Managers to a higher value than the Everyone group.

    D. Manually change the priority of any manager's job to a higher value as it is submitted.

6. What permission(s) does a user need for a printer in order to delete print jobs that have been submitted by any user and to be able to submit their own print jobs?

    A. Full Control

    B. Manage Documents

    C. Print

    D. Print and Manage Documents

7. A user called Jim has taken ownership of a printer and removed all permissions to the printer. As a result, no one can print to the printer. What would be the best way for you, the administrator, to correct the situation so all users can print to the printer?

    A. Log in as Jim, change the owner of the printer to Administrators and add the Print permission for the Everyone group.

    B. Log in as Administrator, delete the printer, create a new printer with the same name and ensure that the Everyone group has the Print permission.

    C. Log in as Administrator and add the Print permission for the Everyone group.

    D. Log in as Administrator, take ownership of the printer and add the Print permission for the Everyone group.

8. You have a new networked TCP/IP print device. How would you create a printer for this print device on a print server before sharing it with users?

    A. Add the printer as a local printer using an LPR Port.

    B. Add the printer as a network printer using an LPR Port.

    C. Add the printer as a local printer using an LPT Port.

    D. Add the printer as a network printer.

9. Which TCP/IP print command would be used to submit a print job on a Unix host?

    A. lpq

    B. print

    C. lpr

    D. lpd

10. Your network has five print devices. One print server manages the queues for the print devices. Your help desk has received many calls about printing. It seems users cannot print to any printers and that none of the print devices are printing. What is the most likely reason?

    A. Users do not have the appropriate permissions.

    B. The print devices are out of paper.

    C. The partition that contains the spool folder is full.

    D. The spooler has stopped.

Configuring and Troubleshooting Internet and Intranet Access to File and Printer Resources

11. Which Internet service provides discussion group facilities?

    A. FTP

    B. The World Wide Web

    C. News

    D. Electronic mail

12. The name www.syngress.com is an example of which of the following?

 A. A domain name

 B. An e-mail address

 C. An IP address

 D. A discussion group

13. A user is complaining that they cannot connect to a Web site. The error message is "The page must be viewed over a secure channel." How would you explain the error?

 A. The user requires a password to view the site.

 B. The user should connect to the Web site using HTTPS instead of HTTP.

 C. The proxy server settings are incorrect on the user's computer.

 D. The proxy server has been configured to deny the user access.

14. Several users have called the Help Desk complaining they cannot connect to printers using their Web browser on a particular server, but they can connect using the Add Printer Wizard by specifying the server and sharename. What is the most likely reason for this problem?

 A. The printers have not been shared.

 B. Users have not been given sufficient permissions for Web access.

 C. The Internet Printing Protocol has not been installed on users' computers.

 D. Internet Information Services is not running on the server.

15. Which protocols does a Web server use? (Choose all that apply.)

 A. HTML

 B. HTTP

 C. HTTPS

 D. WWW

16. How would you make an AppleTalk print device available to users via their Web browser?

 A. Install services for Macintosh (to provide the AppleTalk protocol) on a Windows 2000 print server running Internet Information Services, create a local printer on the print server that points to the print device, and share the printer.

 B. This is not possible because the AppleTalk print device does not run TCP/IP.

 C. Install TCP/IP and the Internet Printing Protocol on the AppleTalk print device and provide users with the appropriate URL for the print device.

D. Install services for Macintosh (to provide the AppleTalk protocol) on a Windows 2000 print server running Internet Information Services, and create a virtual directory in the default Web site that points to the print device.

17. A number of users have complained that their print jobs are coming out garbled. They all set up the printer via a Web browser. What is the most likely reason for the garbled output?

   A. IIS is not running on the print server.

   B. The print device is not compatible with the Internet Printing Protocol.

   C. The incorrect driver was installed on the client computer.

   D. The incorrect driver was installed on the print server.

18. Your network consists of a single segment. You are about to provide access to the Internet for Web browsing to your users. Some of your users also want to use FTP at the command line to download files from the Internet. Which of the following methods would you use to provide Internet access?

   A. Install a proxy server and configure it to allow Web and FTP access. Configure the Internet Options for each user's browser to use the proxy server for all Internet protocols.

   B. Install a firewall and configure it to allow Web and FTP access. Configure the Internet Options for each user's browser to use the firewall for all Internet protocols.

   C. Install a firewall and configure it to allow Web and FTP access. Set the default gateway on the client computer to the IP address of the firewall.

   D. Install a proxy server and configure it to allow Web access. Install a firewall and configure it to allow FTP access. Configure the Internet Options for each user's browser to use the proxy server for the HTTP protocol and the firewall for the FTP protocol.

19. Which network component caches Web requests for future use?

   A. A firewall

   B. A router

   C. A Web server

   D. A proxy server

20. Your network is connected to the Internet using a proxy server. Client computers have been configured to access Internet Web sites using the Internet Options in Internet Explorer. One of your users wants to access their personal e-mail account, which uses a POP3 mailbox, from their computer. They have configured Outlook with an appropriate Internet mail account, but

cannot connect to their mailbox. The error message is "The POP3 server name you specified cannot be found. Please check the name and try again." What are the most likely reasons this is happening? (Choose all that apply.)

A. The Internet Options in Internet Explorer has not been configured with a proxy server address for the POP3 protocol.

B. Proxy client software is not installed on the user's computer.

C. The proxy server has not been configured to allow POP3 traffic for the user.

D. The POP3 protocol has not been installed on the user's computer.

LAB QUESTION

You have been assigned the task of setting up a network at a new office for your company. The network is to consist of two servers, one running Windows 2000 Server and one running NT 4.0 Server, with 200 computers running Windows 2000 Professional. Five networked laser print devices are to be installed for use by all users, one high-quality color print device is to be installed for use by staff in the marketing department only, and one A3 print device is to be installed for use by all staff (except that the Accounts department is to have preferential access). The color and A3 print devices have parallel port connections only.

How will you configure the print devices and the printers to provide the required access?

SELF TEST ANSWERS

Configuring, Managing, and Troubleshooting Printers and Print Devices

1. ☑ **B.** There is only one type of print device. A print driver is required for each type of print device and each type of operating system; the same print driver is used for NT 4.0 Workstation and Server. Therefore, three drivers are required (one for NT 4.0, one for Windows 98, and one for Windows 2000 Professional) making **A**, **C**, and **D** incorrect.
   ☒ **A**, **C**, and **D** are incorrect because three drivers are required (one for NT 4.0, one for Windows 98, and one for Windows 2000 Professional).

2. ☑ **C and D.** The LPR Port is used to add a TCP/IP-based (networked) printer. The AppleTalk Printing Device uses the AppleTalk network protocol, and is therefore a networked printer.
   ☒ **A and B** are both incorrect because they are ports directly connected to a print server using the serial and parallel interfaces respectively.

3. ☑ **B.** A printer queue can send print jobs to more than one print device if printer pooling has been enabled and more than one port is selected. Print jobs will be submitted to either print device depending on which one is free. This option also means there is no configuration change required on users' computers.
   ☒ **A** is incorrect because it requires a configuration change on users' computers. **C** is incorrect because it is not possible to redirect print jobs to other printers in this way. **D** is incorrect because it is not possible to create a pool of printers. A printer pool can only be established by selecting multiple ports.

4. ☑ **C.** Every print job has a priority that controls when it is printed. Higher priority jobs will be printed first.
   ☒ **A** is incorrect because it is not necessary to delete other users' print jobs. **B** is incorrect because it is not necessary to get the user to resubmit the job. **D** is incorrect because it is not possible to drag print jobs to another place in a queue.

5. ☑ **A.** It is possible to create several printers that point to the same print device. Each printer can be configured separately and have different permissions.
   ☒ **B** is incorrect because it requires Managers to change the priority of their print jobs each time, and gives them the right to delete jobs for all users. **C** is incorrect because it is not possible to specify a priority for a group. **D** is incorrect because it is not the best solution.

6. ☑ **B.** The Manage Documents permission allows a user to delete jobs submitted by anyone and includes the Print permission.
☒ **A** is incorrect because it gives more rights than necessary. **C** is incorrect because it does not give the user the right to delete jobs. **D** is incorrect because it is not necessary to give both Print and Manage Documents permissions. The Manage Documents permission includes the Print permission.

7. ☑ **D.** This is the best way because it preserves all the settings of the printer.
☒ **A** is incorrect because it is not possible to hand off ownership of a printer to someone else; another user has to take ownership. **B** is incorrect because no one will be able to delete the printer apart from Jim, since all access has been removed. **C** is incorrect because the administrator will not have access to the printer until he takes ownership.

8. ☑ **A.** The printer server will manage the print device, and LPR Ports are used for TCP/IP print devices.
☒ **B** and **D** are incorrect because network printers are used to connect to an existing printer that has been shared. **C** is incorrect because an LPT Port is for print devices that are directly connected to a server and that do not use a network connection.

9. ☑ **C.** lpr is used to submit print jobs on Unix hosts.
☒ **A** is incorrect because lpq is used to check the status of a queue. **B** is incorrect because the print command is not used on Unix systems. **D** is incorrect because lpd is the name of the line printer daemon.

10. ☑ **D** is the most likely explanation, because the spooler manages printing for all printers on a print server. The cure would be to restart the spooler service.
☒ **A** is incorrect because, although possible, it is not very likely that permissions would have been removed from all five printers. **B** is incorrect for the same reason as **A**, possible but not likely. **C** is incorrect because although users might not be able to submit new print jobs, existing print jobs should continue to be processed if the spooler is running.

Configuring and Troubleshooting Internet and Intranet Access to File and Printer Resources

11. ☑ **C.** The News service provides discussion groups for almost any topic.
☒ **A** is incorrect because FTP is a file transfer service. **B** is incorrect because the World Wide Web is a collection of computers connected to the Internet. **D** is incorrect because electronic mail is used to send messages.

12. ☑ A, a domain name, is the correct answer.

☒ B, C, and D are incorrect because www.syngress.com is an example of a domain name.

13. ☑ B. HTTPS has told the browser to make a secure connection. In other words, all traffic is encrypted.

☒ A is incorrect because the error is not about authentication. C and D are incorrect because it is not a proxy server configuration problem.

14. ☑ D. Internet Printing is not available unless IIS is running on the server. Since the problem affects all printers this is the most likely answer.

☒ A is incorrect because users can connect by using the server and share name. B is incorrect because no additional permissions are necessary for access over the Web and because they can connect using the share name. C is incorrect because the Internet Printing Protocol does not need to be installed. It is automatically available via the users' browsers.

15. ☑ B and C. HTTP (HyperText Transfer Protocol) and HTTPS (secure HTTP) are used by Web servers.

☒ A is incorrect because HTML is the format of Web documents. D is incorrect because WWW (the World Wide Web) is the name of the Web service and not the protocol.

16. ☑ A. By creating a local printer on a Windows 2000 Server and sharing it, the printer will be accessible to users at the URL http://server/printers where server is the name of the server as long as the server is running Internet Information Services.

☒ B is incorrect because it is possible to make the print device available via a Web browser. C is incorrect because it is not possible to install TCP/IP on an AppleTalk printer. D is incorrect because virtual directories are not used to connect to printers. They are used to make another directory available within a Web site.

17. ☑ D. When a printer is created on a print server, the administrator has to choose the print driver. If the incorrect one is chosen, then the client that connects to the printer will download the incorrect driver.

☒ A is incorrect because IIS is not relevant to the format of printed output. If IIS was not running, then users would not be able to connect to the printer using their Web browser. B is incorrect because a print device does not have to run the Internet Printing Protocol. In a Windows 2000 environment, it is a print server that runs the Internet Printing Protocol. As long as a print device can be made available using a network share, then provided certain conditions are met, it can be accessed via a Web browser. C is incorrect because users do not need to choose which driver to install when connecting to a network printer share or Internet printer.

18. ☑ C. A firewall can be used to control exactly what type of traffic is allowed through. Setting the default gateway on the client computer to the IP address of the firewall ensures the computer can communicate with the Internet.

    ☒ A and B are incorrect because, although they would provide Web access, they would not provide FTP access from the command line. The Internet Options settings for the browser do not apply to other programs. D is incorrect because, again, the Internet Options settings for the browser do not apply to other programs.

19. ☑ D. A proxy server caches Web requests for reuse if other users browse to the same Web site and page.

    ☒ A, B, and C are incorrect because they do not provide caching of Web requests. A controls what type of traffic can pass through a network. B is used to connect networks together. C is used to host Web sites.

20. ☑ B and C. To provide access to sites on a remote network for the POP3 protocol, proxy client software is required on a client computer. Furthermore, the proxy server must also be configured to allow POP3 traffic through for the user.

    ☒ A is incorrect because the Internet Options in Internet Explorer are not relevant. D is incorrect because the POP3 protocol is not a separately installable protocol.

LAB ANSWER

There are a total of seven print devices to configure. Local printers could be created for the networked print devices on either the client or server computers. However, for ease of administration and management, printers should be created on a server. There are two servers available, either one may be used. If the server running Windows 2000 Server is used, then users will be able to connect to the printers using their Web browser. You could produce a Web page that shows floor plans for the office and the location of each print device, making choosing the appropriate print device very easy for users. If the server running NT 4.0 is used, then users will have to choose a printer based on the sharename, though the comment and location fields could be used to assist them.

Check that you have the latest printer driver for all the print devices and that there are two free LPT ports on the server. Different servers could be used for some of the print devices, but this would require users to know which server managed which printer. It is easier for users to have all the printers defined in one place. However, the use of several servers to manage printers should be considered when printing throughput is very high.

Regardless of which server is used, the steps to create printers for each of the five networked print devices are as follows:

1. Configure the print device with an IP address appropriate for the network.

2. On the server, create a local printer.

3. Create a TCP/IP port with the appropriate IP address.

4. Select the appropriate driver.

5. Share the printer with an appropriate name.

6. Leave the permissions at the default setting (the Everyone group can print).

The steps to create a printer for the color print device are as follows:

1. Create a local printer using a free LPT port.

2. Select the appropriate driver.

3. Share the printer with an appropriate name.

4. Remove the print permission for Everyone and add the print permission for marketing users. Use an appropriate security group if one exists, otherwise, create one.

The steps to set up the A3 print device are as follows:

1. Create a local printer using a free LPT Port.

2. Select the appropriate driver.

3. Share the printer with an appropriate name (for example, A3Laser).

4. Leave the permissions at the default setting (the Everyone group can print).

5. Create another local printer using the same LPT Port as in Step 1 and with the same driver as in Step 2.

6. Share the printer with an appropriate name (for example, A3Accounts).

7. Remove the print permission for Everyone and add the print permission for accounts users. Use an appropriate security group if one exists, otherwise, create one.

8. Increase the default priority for the printer.

All users can use the A3Laser but only Accounts department users can use the A3Accounts printer. Also, any print jobs submitted to the A3Accounts printer will print ahead of those submitted to the A3Laser printer.

MCSE

MICROSOFT CERTIFIED SYSTEMS ENGINEER

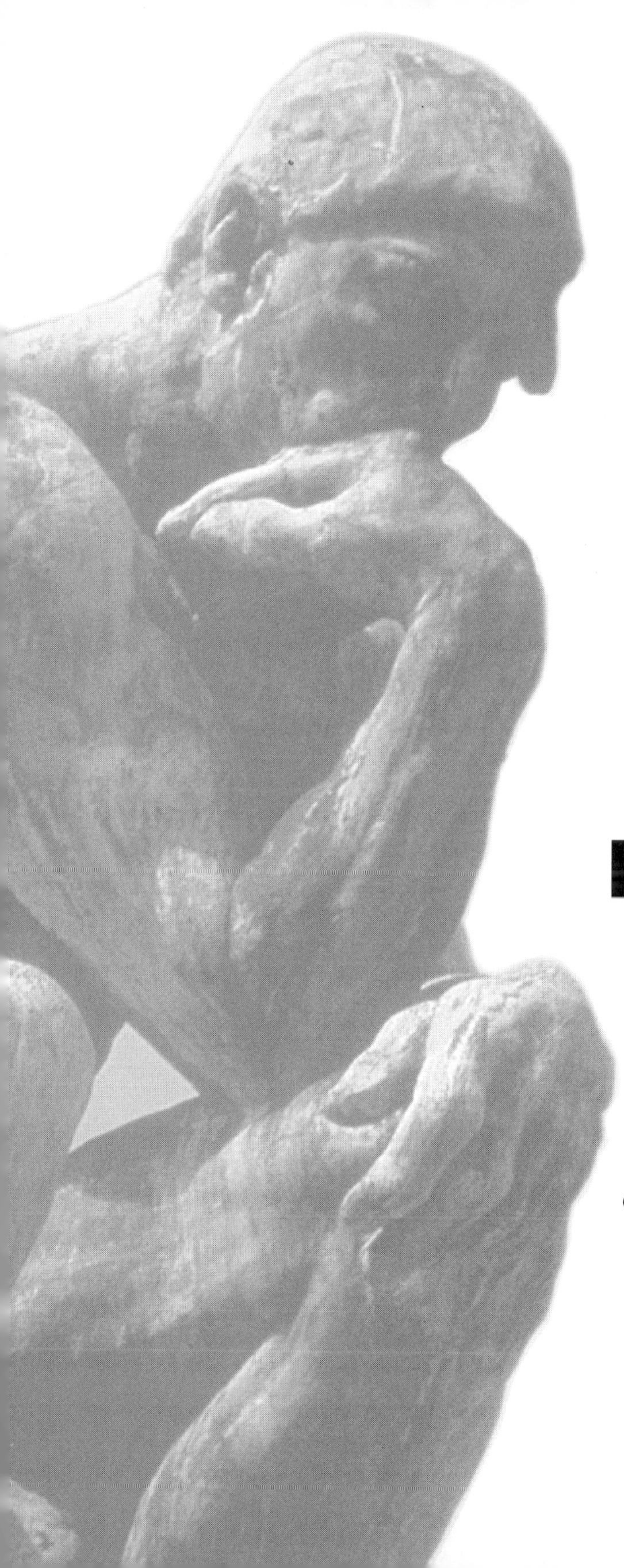

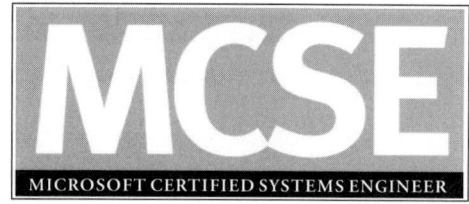

9

Configuring, Managing, Troubleshooting, and Optimizing Network Services

CERTIFICATION OBJECTIVES

9.01	Configuring and Troubleshooting Network Connectivity
9.02	Monitoring, Maintaining, and Troubleshooting Name Resolution
9.03	Troubleshooting and Optimizing Network Performance
✓	Two-Minute Drill
Q&A	Self Test

I n this chapter, we will cover important topics related to configuring, managing, troubleshooting, and optimizing network services. First we will examine network connectivity which includes the types of computer names, the different ways names are resolved to IP addresses and how IP addresses can be allocated automatically.

In the next section, we will further examine name resolution, including the order in which name resolution techniques are used and how the ability to browse a network using Explorer is provided. Finally, we will examine some of the tools that can be used to troubleshoot network performance.

CERTIFICATION OBJECTIVE 9.01

Configuring and Troubleshooting Network Connectivity

Many problems with connectivity are due to an incorrect network configuration and usually involve computer names, IP addresses, or the inability to determine an IP address. Therefore, being an effective troubleshooter requires a good understanding in this area.

In this section, we will review how a computer is known by both a NetBIOS name and a host name. We will then examine the ways in which a computer name can be resolved to an IP address. This process, called name resolution, is often the cause of network connectivity problems.

Finally, we will examine how TCP/IP parameters can be configured using DHCP, and how they can be checked using the ipconfig utility.

Computer Names

Windows NT 4.0 and Windows 2000 use two types of computer names: NetBIOS names and host names.

NetBIOS Names

NetBIOS stands for *Network Basic Input/Output System* and is used to provide file and printer sharing between computers. NetBIOS is a session layer protocol rather than a network protocol and therefore relies on the presence of network protocols such as TCP/IP or NWLink to function. Within Windows NT 4.0, NetBIOS is an essential component because many network services use it. However, in a network that consists entirely of Windows 2000 computers, NetBIOS is not required.

NetBIOS calls for all computers in a network to have a unique name. A NetBIOS name is 16 characters (i.e., bytes) long. Only the first 15 bytes are used for the name of the computer, the sixteenth byte is used to identify a particular service that is running on a computer. The sixteenth byte is often expressed in hexadecimal, so its value can range from 0 to FF. For example, a value of 0 refers to the Workstation service and a value of 20 (in hexadecimal, 32 in decimal) refers to the Server service.

Host Names

A host name is used to identify a computer to TCP/IP applications. A host name can be up to 255 characters long and can contain alphanumeric characters and hyphens. A host name can either be a single word (or alias) or use the Domain Name System; for example, www (an alias) or www.syngress.com (using DNS).

Within any network all computers must have unique host names, so it would not be possible to have two computers called www, unless, for example, one was called www.syngress.com and the other was called www.microsoft.com.

Both Windows NT 4.0 and Windows 2000 maintain a separate host name and NetBIOS name. However, Windows NT 4.0 allows an administrator to set the host name and NetBIOS name to different values. In Windows 2000, the NetBIOS name is the same as the first part of the host name (subject to a limit of 15 characters). For example, the NetBIOS name for a Windows 2000 computer called thisisaverylongname.example.com would be THISISAVERYLONG.

SCENARIO & SOLUTION

What type of name does … use?	Type of Name
PING	Host name
FTP	Host name
A Web browser	Host Name
Net use	NetBIOS
Browsing to a Windows NT 4.0 Server	NetBIOS

Name Resolution Methods

Despite the fact that computers have names, they communicate with each other using IP addresses. It is obviously much easier for users to remember names than IP addresses, and most programs such as Internet Explorer and FTP, allow users to enter a name for the destination computer (in fact, many programs allow the use of computer names or IP addresses). However, before the client computer can begin communicating with the destination computer, a name must be converted to an IP address. This process is called name resolution.

Name resolution uses databases to find out an IP address. There are four places where computer name to IP address mappings are stored. Two of these are referred to as static mappings, because an administrator has to manually update them, and two are referred to as dynamic mappings, because they are automatically updated with no administrator intervention.

Static Mapping

The two static mapping methods are the HOSTS file and the LMHOSTS file. Both are stored in %systemroot%\SYSTEM32\DRIVERS\ETC (where %systemroot% is the location of the Windows directory, usually C:\WINNT).

LMHOSTS The LMHOSTS file is a text file that contains name to IP address mappings and is used by NetBIOS applications. A sample LMHOSTS file called LMHOSTS.SAM is provided in %systemroot%\SYSTEM32\DRIVERS\ETC. To create an LMHOSTS file, either copy the LMHOSTS.SAM to LMHOSTS or use an editor such as Notepad (make sure the file is called LMHOSTS, with no extension). If you copy the LMHOSTS.SAM, remove all the comments, as these will slow down reading of the file. The LMHOSTS.SAM file includes details on using keywords to control the name resolution process.

HOSTS The HOSTS file is a text file that contains name to IP address mappings and is used by TCP/IP applications (as opposed to NetBIOS applications). An example is shown in Figure 9-1. Note that an IP address might have several names.

The disadvantage of LMHOSTS and HOSTS files is that every computer has its own copy, which makes maintenance a laborious process.

TABLE 9-1

Example of a
HOSTS file

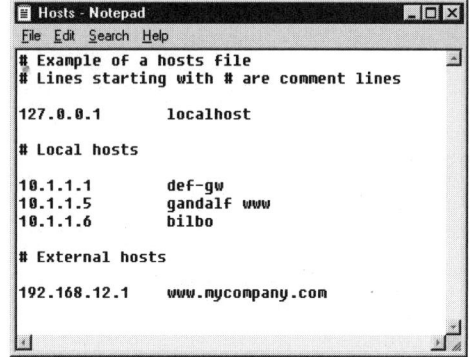

```
Hosts - Notepad
File  Edit  Search  Help
# Example of a hosts file
# Lines starting with # are comment lines

127.0.0.1        localhost

# Local hosts

10.1.1.1         def-gw
10.1.1.5         gandalf www
10.1.1.6         bilbo

# External hosts

192.168.12.1     www.mycompany.com
```

Dynamic Mapping

To overcome the need to manually maintain LMHOSTS and HOSTS files, two automatic mapping services are available. These are the Windows Internet Name Service (WINS) and the Domain Name System (DNS).

Windows Internet Name Service (WINS)   WINS provides a central database for registering NetBIOS names. When a computer that uses NetBIOS starts up, it can be configured to register its name with a WINS server. Other computers can then query the WINS server to look up the IP address for a NetBIOS name.

The WINS service can be installed on servers running Windows NT 4.0 Server or Windows 2000 Server. The server must have TCP/IP installed. Only one WINS server is required in a network, even if it consists of several subnets, because clients are configured with the IP addresses of a WINS server. This means that they are using unicast packets that will pass through routers. However, consider using two WINS servers for fault tolerance. The two WINS servers must be configured to share their databases with each other. Additional WINS servers may be used to improve performance; an approximate guideline is two WINS servers for every 10,000 client computers, though this would depend on the number of subnets and routers in the network.

An additional benefit of WINS is that it can reduce the number of network broadcasts used to resolve NetBIOS names.

Domain Name System (DNS)   DNS uses a hierarchical naming structure (as opposed to the flat name system of NetBIOS) that consists of domains and subdomains as described in Chapter 8. The Internet is probably the largest example of a network that uses DNS.

A significant advantage of DNS is that no one server maintains records for the entire namespace. The responsibility for resolving names is shared between DNS servers, and on the Internet many hundreds of DNS servers are used. At a minimum, the records for a single domain must be hosted on one DNS server, but the records for a subdomain could be hosted on another DNS server. For example, DNS server A might contain records for the syngress.com domain but DNS server B contains records for the sales.syngress.com subdomain. On the other hand, DNS server A could host records for both the syngress.com domain and the sales.syngress.com subdomain. The term *zone of authority* is used to describe the portion of the namespace for which a DNS server holds records.

DNS originally only allowed manual updates, which meant that records had to be manually added or changed by administrators. However, recent updates to the DNS standards have added the dynamic update facility allowing records to be added or changed automatically. The DNS service included with Windows NT 4.0 does not support dynamic updates, whereas the DNS service included with Windows 2000 does.

Default Gateway

Many networks consist of several subnets connected together by routers, which forward packets from one subnet to another. Part of the TCP/IP configuration for all computers includes a default gateway setting which is used when packets need to be delivered to another subnet. The default gateway is the IP address of a router that a computer will use to deliver packets for subnets. A network with several subnets is often called an internetwork. On a large network, every computer would normally be configured with the address of a default gateway.

on the **job**

The term default gateway is a bit of a misnomer, considering that to some people the word gateway means a device that translates between different network protocols or applications. A better term might have been default router.

When a program on a client computer needs to communicate with a program or service on another computer, the IP addresses of the computers are used to determine how to establish the connection.

The TCP/IP software on the client computer needs to determine whether the destination computer can be contacted directly (i.e., it is located on the same subnet) or a router has to be used (i.e., it is located on another subnet). This is done by comparing the network IDs of the client and destination computers. If the network IDs are the same, then the client and destination computers are on the same subnet. If not, then they are on different subnets.

The network ID is determined by carrying out a logical AND between the IP address and the subnet mask. For example, the network address for a computer whose IP address is 172.16.56.5 and whose subnet mask is 255.255.0.0 is 172.16.0.0.

If the network IDs are different, then the TPC/IP software on the client computer discovers it cannot directly contact the destination (because it is on another subnet) and therefore must communicate with the destination via a router.

Note that use of the correct subnet mask is very important. If an administrator chose the wrong mask, this could lead the TCP/IP software to make incorrect decisions as to whether a destination computer was on the local network or a remote one. This type of error can be very difficult to trace.

Consider the network in Figure 9-2. Computer A is not configured with a default gateway, but needs to communicate with computer B. For example, suppose a user on computer A enters the command:

```
C:\ ping 141.13.10.1
```

First, computer A will resolve the name B to an IP address. The TCP/IP software on computer A will then determine that computer B is on another network and that the packet needs to be forwarded to the default gateway. Because the default gateway is not configured, the TCP/IP software will return an error message, "Destination host unreachable." So, it is important where connectivity is required between networks that the default gateway is configured to an appropriate setting. Exercise 9-1 shows how to configure the default gateway.

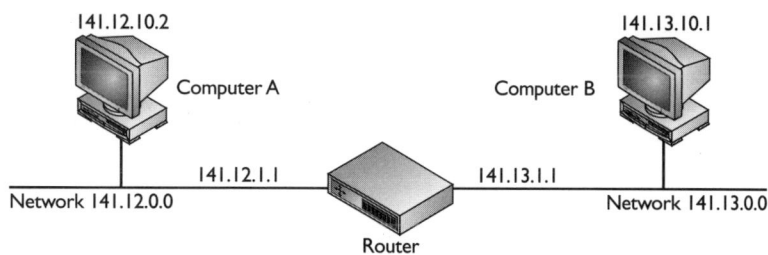

FIGURE 9-1

Communication via a router

EXERCISE 9-1

CertCam 9-1

Configuring a Default Gateway on Windows NT 4.0

1. Select the Protocols tab of the Network icon in the Control Panel.

2. Highlight TCP/IP Protocol and then click Properties.

3. In the Microsoft TCP/IP Properties dialog box, ensure that the IP address tab is selected and enter the IP address of the default gateway in the Default Gateway box (see Figure 9-3).

4. Click OK twice to close the dialog boxes.

5. Note that the IP addresses of the default gateway and the computer must have the same network ID, otherwise the client computer won't be able to communicate with the default gateway.

FIGURE 9-3

The Microsoft
TCP/IP
Properties box

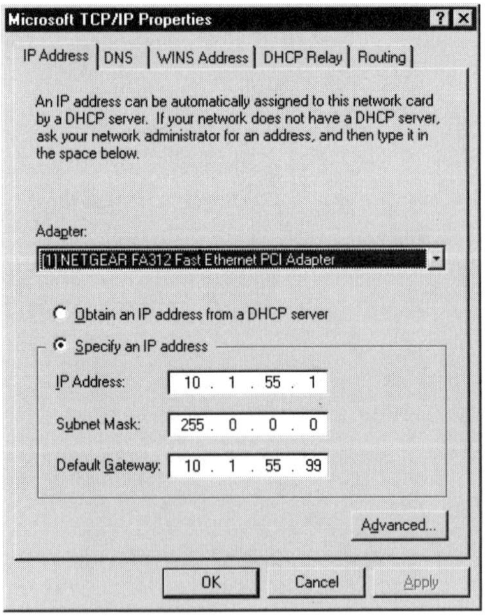

> **Microsoft TCP/IP Properties**
>
> IP Address | DNS | WINS Address | DHCP Relay | Routing
>
> An IP address can be automatically assigned to this network card by a DHCP server. If your network does not have a DHCP server, ask your network administrator for an address, and then type it in the space below.
>
> Adapter:
>
> [1] NETGEAR FA312 Fast Ethernet PCI Adapter
>
> ○ Obtain an IP address from a DHCP server
>
> ● Specify an IP address
>
> IP Address: 10 . 1 . 55 . 1
>
> Subnet Mask: 255 . 0 . 0 . 0
>
> Default Gateway: 10 . 1 . 55 . 99
>
> Advanced...
>
> OK | Cancel | Apply

DHCP

The Dynamic Host Configuration Protocol (DHCP) is used to set IP addresses for computers automatically. DHCP evolved from an earlier protocol, BOOTP, that was used to set IP configuration information for diskless workstations. Without DHCP, administrators would have to set IP addresses manually by visiting every computer on a network. For larger networks, this is time-consuming, can lead to the use of duplicate IP addresses if proper records are not kept, and is prone to errors.

DHCP is not used just to set the IP address for a computer; it can also set other TCP/IP parameters. A DHCP server will always set, as a minimum, the IP address and subnet mask for a computer. Other items that can be set (called options) include the default gateway, DNS servers, WINS servers, and domain name. Note that although the standards (which are RFCs) that define DHCP list a large number of options, they are not all necessarily used by DHCP clients.

IP addresses that are set using DHCP are not usually permanent, they are leased. This means that the client can use the address for a period of time set by the server, then attempt to renew the lease. This ensures that the DHCP server does not run out of IP addresses and that they are reused when clients are removed from the network. The administrator sets the lease time on the DHCP server. A longer lease time reduces network traffic (since there are fewer DHCP renewal packets), but changes to options (such as the default gateway) will take longer to take effect. A shorter lease time, on the other hand, increases network traffic, but allows changes to options to take effect more quickly.

DHCP Process

You should be familiar with the DHCP process in order to troubleshoot potential problems. The allocation of IP address information using DHCP is a four-stage process as shown in Figure 9-4.

When the DHCP client boots up, it sends out a DHCPDISCOVER packet. This packet is a request for an IP lease and is addressed as a broadcast packet. If a DHCP server receives this packet and is configured with addresses for the client it will respond with a DHCPOFFER packet that contains the offer of an IP address. The client may receive several offers if there is more than one DHCP server on the network. In the third stage, the client chooses which IP address it will use and sends a DHCPREQUEST packet requesting the offered address. In the fourth stage, the DHCP server confirms the IP address that has been allocated with a DHCPACK

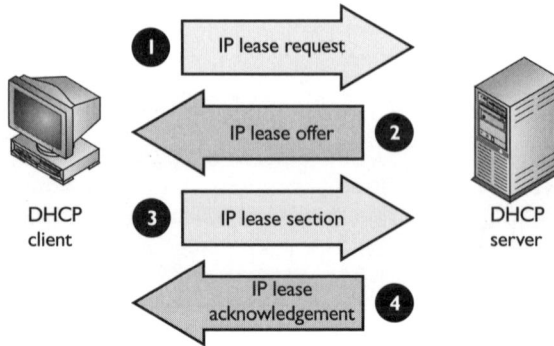

FIGURE 9-4

DHCP process

packet. This packet also contains any options that have been set. The client is now configured with an IP address and can begin communicating normally on the network.

Note the use of broadcast addresses as the destination. For the first and third stages this is because the client does not know the IP address of the DHCP server. In fact it wouldn't make sense to have to specify the IP address of a DHCP server on the client, as this would defeat the advantage of no administration. For the second and fourth stages, the DHCP server uses a broadcast address, because the client does not yet have a valid IP address. A consequence of using broadcast addresses is that for networks with several subnets connected by routers, additional configuration is required for DHCP to work properly. We will discuss this further in a later section.

Lease Renewal

A client will attempt to renew its IP address when 50 percent of the lease time has expired. The renewal uses a DHCPREQUEST packet that is sent to the DHCP server that allocated the IP address. If that DHCP server is running, then it will renew the lease with a DHCPACK packet that includes any updated configuration parameters. If renewal fails, then the client retries renewal when 87.5 percent of the lease time has expired. However, this time a broadcast DHCPREQUEST packet is used so that any DHCP server may respond. If there is still no response, the client can continue to use the IP address until the lease expires, at which time the client must stop using the IP address, and network operations must stop as well. The client will then enter the first stage of the DHCP process, as previously described.

DHCP Server

The DHCP Server service can be installed on servers running Windows NT 4.0 Server or Windows 2000 Server. The server must have TCP/IP installed and must be configured with a static IP address. Exercise 9-2 shows how to install and configure the DHCP service.

It is possible to install several DHCP servers on a network to provide fault tolerance and to cope with networks that have several subnets. It is very important to ensure that the DHCP servers do not have overlapping address scopes, otherwise duplicate IP addresses might be issued.

DHCP Client

To configure a computer to use DHCP, use the TCP/IP Properties dialog box. Figures 9-5 and 9-6 show the dialog boxes for Windows 2000 and Windows NT 4.0 computers, respectively, that have been configured to use DHCP. Note the slight difference in wording.

The same dialog box is used to set a static IP address. As a minimum, the IP address and subnet mask must be specified.

FIGURE 9-5

Configuring a
Windows 2000
computer to
use DHCP

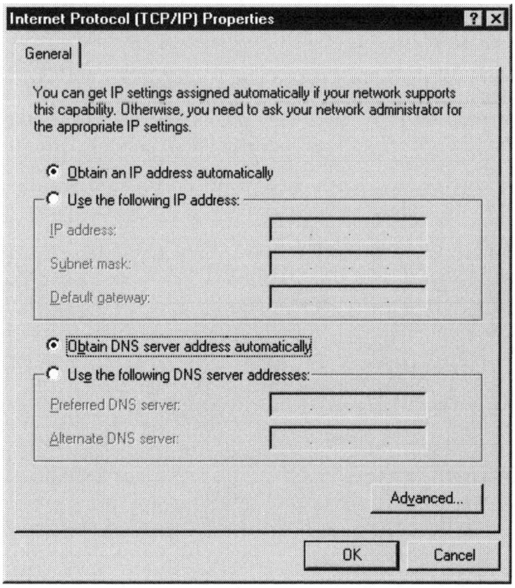

Configuring a
Windows NT 4.0
computer to
use DHCP

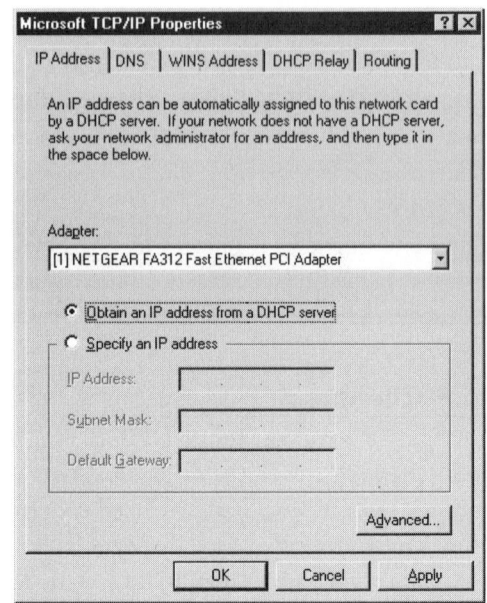

DHCP Relay Agent

Recall that the DHCP process uses broadcast packets and that routers do not forward broadcast packets. This means that on a network with several subnets some extra effort is needed to get DHCP working properly.

There are two options for such a scenario:

- Install a separate DHCP server configured with an appropriate scope on each subnet.
- Use a relay agent.

Some routers have the ability to recognize DHCP broadcast packets, and can be configured to allow them through. This facility is called a DHCP relay agent and is defined in RFC1542. However, the router does not simply pass through DHCP broadcast packets unaltered, instead it forwards them as unicast packets to a named DHCP server rather than transmit them as a broadcast packet.

The DHCP relay agent service can be installed on any computer running Windows NT 4.0 Server or Windows 2000 Server. The IP addresses of the DHCP servers to which DHCP broadcast packets are to be forwarded must be added (there must be at least one for the relay agent service to operate). The DHCP relay agent service should be installed on subnets that do not have a DHCP server. Note that you should not configure the relay agent on both a Windows computer and on the router.

On a network with multiple subnets, several DHCP servers can be used in conjunction with a relay agent to provide fault tolerance. Each DHCP server would then be configured with a scope for its own subnet, but also with ranges for other subnets (ensuring that none of the ranges overlap). If the local DHCP server failed, then a DHCP server on another subnet would be contactable via the relay agent and IP addresses could still be issued.

You may be wondering how many DHCP, DNS, or WINS servers to have on your network. Table 9-1 should help you decide.

TABLE 9-1 Number of DHCP, DNS, or WINS Servers to Have on Your Network	How many ... should I have in my multiple subnet network?	Required Number and Explanation
	DNS Servers (in a Windows NT 4.0 domain)	*None.* There is no requirement to use DNS in an NT 4.0 domain. If there are non-Windows resources on the network, such as UNIX servers, then using DNS servers could simplify name resolution. An alternative would be to update the HOSTS file on all computers. If DNS is to be used, then only one server is required, but consider using two for fault-tolerance. Use additional DNS servers on subnets that are on slow WAN links to reduce query times and WAN traffic.
	DNS Servers (in a Windows 2000 domain)	*One.* At least one DNS server is required to host domain controller resource records. As in the previous entry, consider using additional servers for fault tolerance and to reduce query times.
	WINS Servers	*None.* WINS is not a requirement on a Windows NT 4.0 or Windows 2000 network. However, consider using WINS to enable browsing across subnets and to reduce the amount of broadcast traffic. Only one WINS server is needed, but as with DNS, consider additional servers for fault tolerance and to reduce query times.
	DHCP Servers	*None.* A DHCP server is only required if IP addresses are to be allocated automatically. On a network with multiple subnets, at least one DHCP server will be required, with additional servers or DHCP relay agents on other subnets.

EXERCISE 9-2

CertCam 9-2

Installing and Configuring the DHCP Server Service

In this exercise, we will install DHCP on a server running Windows NT 4.0 Server and configure a scope with the following specification:

- The scope range is 10.0.0.1 to 10.0.0.100.

- IP address 10.0.0.99 is reserved for a Web server whose MAC address is 08-00-36-0d-de-00.

- The subnet mask for the scope is 255.255.255.0.

- Addresses 10.0.0.50 to 10.0.0.59 should be excluded as they are used as static addresses by other computers.

- Clients should be configured with DNS server addresses of 12.1.5.1 and 13.1.5.1.

The steps to achieve this are as follows:

1. Ensure that the TCP/IP protocol is installed on the server and that a fixed IP address is in use.

2. Install DHCP server from the Services tab of the Network icon in the Control Panel. This will require a reboot of the server.

   The DHCP server service will now be running. To configure DHCP, run DHCP Manager by clicking the Start button and choosing Programs | Administrative Tools | DHCP Manager. You should see a screen similar to Figure 9-7. This shows that there are no scopes configured.

3. To configure a scope, double-click Local Machine, then select Create from the Scope menu. This brings up the Create Scope – (Local) dialog box as seen in Figure 9-8.

4. Enter **10.0.0.1** as the start address, **10.0.0.100** as the end address and **255.255.255.0** as the subnet mask.

5. Enter **10.0.0.50** in the Exclusion Range Start Address and **10.0.0.59** in the Exclusion Range End Address, then click Add. Click OK. This will bring up another dialog box. Click Yes to activate the scope.

FIGURE 9-7

DHCP Manager

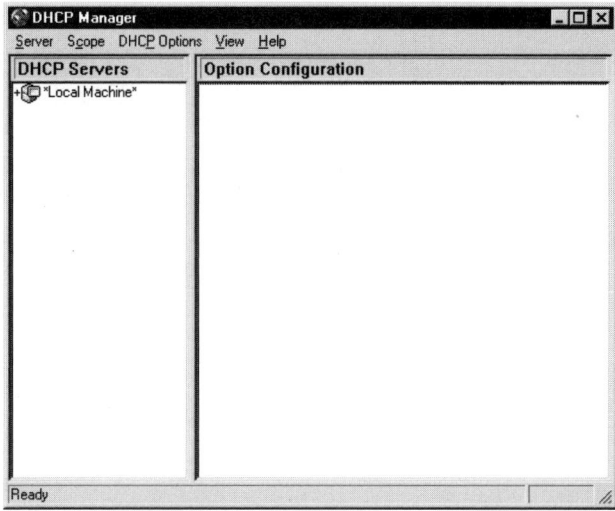

6. In the left-hand pane of DHCP Manager, ensure that 10.0.0.0 is highlighted and select Properties from the Scope menu. The Scope Properties – (Local) dialog box should look like Figure 9-9.

7. To add the reservation for the Web server, close the Scope Properties – (Local) dialog box and select Add Reservations from the Scope menu.

FIGURE 9-8

The Create
Scope – (Local)
dialog box

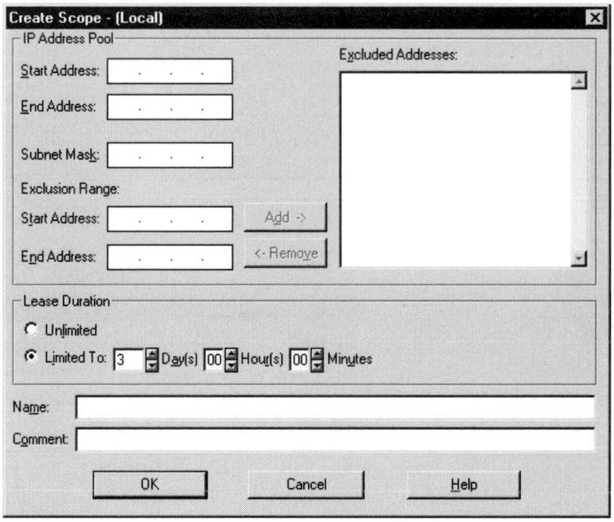

FIGURE 9-9

The Scope
Properties –
(Local) dialog box

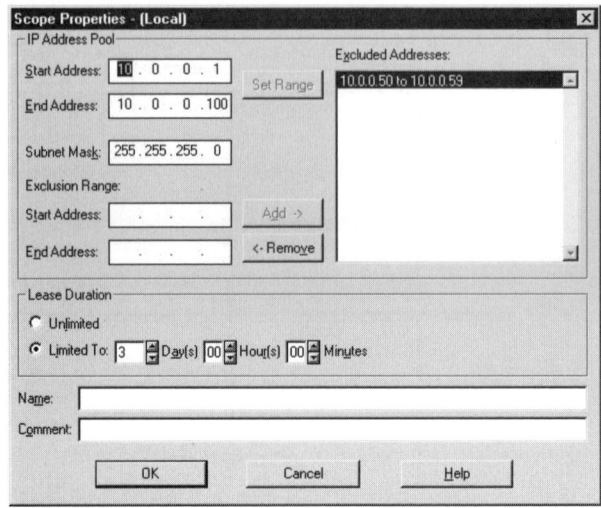

8. In the Add Reserved Clients dialog box, enter **0.0.99** in the IP Address field. Note that 10 has already been entered.

9. Enter **0800360dde00** in the Unique Identifier field. Note that hyphens should not be used.

10. Enter **Web Server** in the Client Name field.

11. Enter an optional comment in the Comment field.

12. The Add Reserved Clients dialog box should look like Figure 9-10.

13. Click Add and then Close. The reservation has been added. To confirm this, select Active Leases from the Scope Menu. The Active Leases – [10.0.0.0] dialog box should look like Figure 9-11.

14. Click OK to close the Active Leases – [10.0.0.0] dialog box.

FIGURE 9-10

The Add
Reserved Clients
dialog box

Add Reserved Clients	
IP Address:	10 . 0 . 0 . 99
Unique Identifier:	0800360dde00
Client Name:	Web Server
Client Comment:	

[Add] [Close] [Help] [Options...]

FIGURE 9-11

The Active
Leases – [10.0.0.0]
dialog box

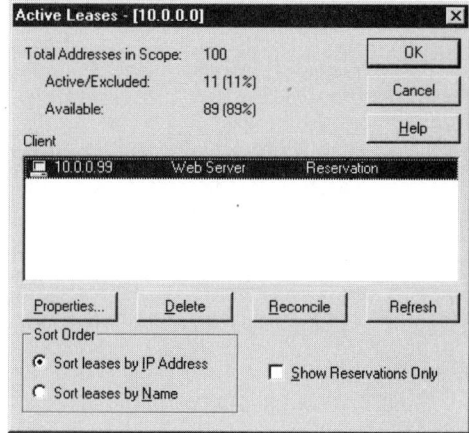

15. We now need to configure the DNS server IP addresses. Ensure that 10.0.0.0 is highlighted and select Scope from the DHCP Options in the Scope menu.

16. In the Unused Options box of the DHCP Options: Scope dialog box, highlight 006 DNS Servers, then click Add. 006 DNS Servers should move over to the Active Options box as shown in Figure 9-12.

17. Click Value. The dialog box should expand. Now click Edit Array.

18. In the IP Address Array Editor box, enter 12.1.5.1 in the New IP Address box and click Add. Enter the second DNS server address 13.1.5.1 in the New IP Address box, then click Add.

19. Click OK to close the IP Address Array Editor box.

20. Click OK to close the DHCP Options: Scope dialog box.

21. Close the DHCP Manager dialog box. This completes configuration of the DHCP server.

FIGURE 9-12

The unused
Options box of
the DHCP
Options: Scope
dialog box

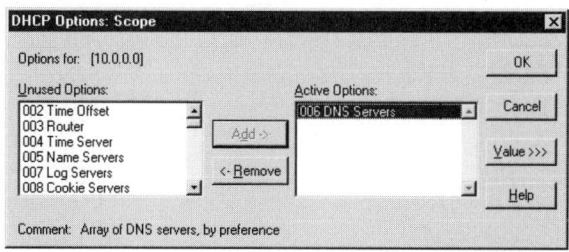

exam
⍟atch

It is very important when configuring several DHCP servers on a network that you do not use overlapping scopes, otherwise duplicate IP addresses might be issued.

Automatic Private IP Addressing (APIPA)

If a Windows 2000 client has been configured to obtain an IP address automatically and it does not get a response from a DHCP server, then the client will allocate itself an address. The addresses used for self-allocation are in the range 169.254.0.1 to 169.254.255.254. This process is called Automatic Private IP Addressing (APIPA). Note that Windows NT 4.0 does not offer this facility; TCP/IP on Windows NT 4.0 DHCP clients remains unconfigured in the absence of a response from a DHCP server.

FROM THE CLASSROOM

How a DHCP Server Chooses Which Scope to Use when Allocating Addresses

Students often ask how a DHCP server chooses which scope to use when allocating addresses. A DHCP server might be configured with several scopes, particularly if there are several subnets and relay agents in use for fault tolerance purposes. When a DHCP server receives a DHCPDISCOVER packet requesting an IP address, it examines the packet to see if it has been relayed. If it has not been relayed, then the DHCP server knows that the DHCPDISCOVER packet came from the local subnet and will look for a scope whose network address matches that of the local subnet. Now imagine we have a computer on a subnet with no DHCP server or that the local DHCP server has failed but a DHCP relay agent has been configured.

When the computer boots up, it sends out a DHCPDISCOVER packet to obtain an IP address. There are no DHCP servers on the local subnet, but the relay agent will see the packet and forward it to the configured DHCP servers. Before it forwards the packet, the relay agent sets a field in the DHCPDISCOVER packet (called the gateway address) to the IP address of the relay agent. When the DHCP server receives the packet, it notes that the gateway address has been set and uses the IP address of the gateway to determine which scope to use when allocating the IP address for the client computer. If the DHCP server is not defined with an appropriate scope, then it will not be able to respond to the DHCPDISCOVER packet.

—Feridun Kadir, MCP, MCP+I, MCSE, MCT

APIPA allows clients on a single subnet to communicate with each other. The DHCP client software will continue to try and contact a DHCP server while the APIPA address is used.

APIPA is enabled automatically and is mainly of use on very small or home networks where the overhead of a DHCP server is not necessary. On large networks that consist of multiple subnets, APIPA is not so useful. This is because computers have an incorrect IP address and so they will not be able to contact their default gateway and hence resources on other subnets. By editing the Registry, the use of APIPA can be disabled for the whole computer or only on particular network interfaces (should the computer have more than one network interface).

The ipconfig/all command (see the next section for more details on ipconfig) can be used to check whether APIPA has been used. If it has, the word "Autoconfiguration" appears before the IP address, as shown in Figure 9-13.

exam
Watch

Remember that on Windows 2000 computers if an IP address starts with 169.254 then it has probably been set using APIPA. This means that the DHCP process has failed to provide a valid IP configuration. This could be due to a number of reasons, for instance, there may not be a DHCP server on the network, the DHCP server may be down, or the DHCP server may not be configured with an appropriate scope.

FIGURE 9-13

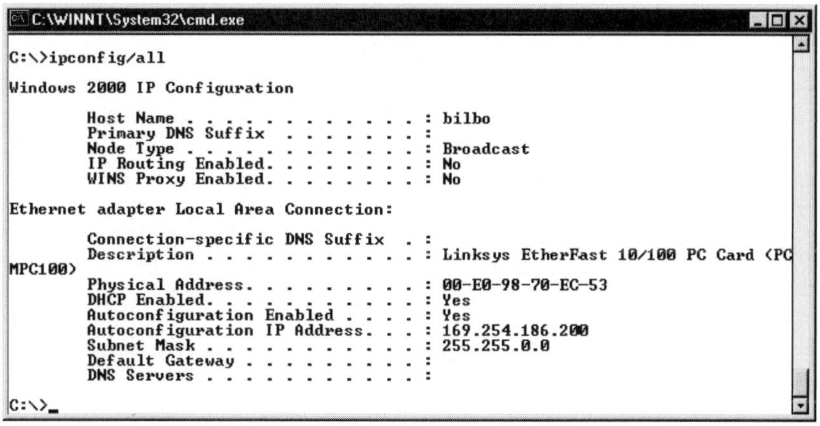

Output of
ipconfig/all
command
showing
automatic IP
addressing

```
C:\WINNT\System32\cmd.exe                                          _ □ ×

C:\>ipconfig/all

Windows 2000 IP Configuration

        Host Name . . . . . . . . . . . . : bilbo
        Primary DNS Suffix . . . . . . . :
        Node Type . . . . . . . . . . . . : Broadcast
        IP Routing Enabled. . . . . . . . : No
        WINS Proxy Enabled. . . . . . . . : No

Ethernet adapter Local Area Connection:

        Connection-specific DNS Suffix  . :
        Description . . . . . . . . . . . : Linksys EtherFast 10/100 PC Card (PC
MPC100)
        Physical Address. . . . . . . . . : 00-E0-98-70-EC-53
        DHCP Enabled. . . . . . . . . . . : Yes
        Autoconfiguration Enabled . . . . : Yes
        Autoconfiguration IP Address. . . : 169.254.186.200
        Subnet Mask . . . . . . . . . . . : 255.255.0.0
        Default Gateway . . . . . . . . . :
        DNS Servers . . . . . . . . . . . :

C:\>_
```

The Ipconfig Utility

The ipconfig utility is used to check the TCP/IP configuration of a computer. Figure 9-14 shows the output of the ipconfig command. Three configuration parameters are shown for each network adapter in the computer, these are the IP address, subnet mask, and default gateway.

The ipconfig utility cannot be used to set TCP/IP parameters. This must be done via the Control Panel. More detailed information can be obtained using the /all option as shown in Figure 9-15. The output of ipconfig/all varies slightly between the Windows NT 4.0 and Windows 2000 systems.

If an IP address was obtained from a DHCP server, then additional information about when the lease was obtained and when the lease is due to expire would be provided with the ipconfig/all command.

Ipconfig can also be used to manually renew or release an IP address obtained from a DHCP server. Ipconfig/release will give up use of a DHCP assigned address. This might be used if a computer was to be permanently removed from the network, freeing up the IP address immediately rather than when the lease expires. Ipconfig/renew is used to renew a DHCP assigned IP address. This would be used if the DHCP scope options had been updated (for example, a new DNS server was added). Rather than waiting for the lease to be renewed normally for the option change to take effect, an administrator could use ipconfig/renew.

FIGURE 9-14

Output of ipconfig

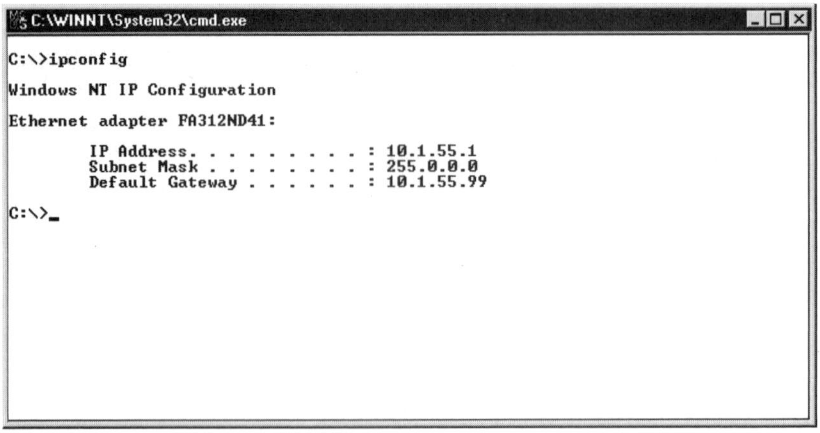

```
C:\WINNT\System32\cmd.exe                                    _ □ X

C:\>ipconfig

Windows NT IP Configuration

Ethernet adapter FA312ND41:

        IP Address. . . . . . . . . : 10.1.55.1
        Subnet Mask . . . . . . . . : 255.0.0.0
        Default Gateway . . . . . . : 10.1.55.99

C:\>_
```

FIGURE 9-15

Output of
ipconfig/all on a
Windows NT 4.0
server

```
C:\WINNT\System32\cmd.exe                                              _ □ ×

C:\>ipconfig/all

Windows NT IP Configuration

        Host Name . . . . . . . . . : nt4
        DNS Servers . . . . . . . . :
        Node Type . . . . . . . . . : Broadcast
        NetBIOS Scope ID. . . . . . :
        IP Routing Enabled. . . . . : No
        WINS Proxy Enabled. . . . . : No
        NetBIOS Resolution Uses DNS : No

Ethernet adapter FA312ND41:

        Description . . . . . . . . : NETGEAR FA312 Fast Ethernet PCI Adapter
        Physical Address. . . . . . : 00-A0-CC-A1-3A-43
        DHCP Enabled. . . . . . . . : No
        IP Address. . . . . . . . . : 10.1.55.1
        Subnet Mask . . . . . . . . : 255.0.0.0
        Default Gateway . . . . . . : 10.1.55.99

C:\>_
```

Ipconfig under Windows NT 4.0 only supports the options already described (/all, /renew, and /release). Under Windows 2000, additional options have been added. Three of these options are relevant to the use of DNS.

- **Ipconfig/flushdns** is used to clear the computer's local DNS resolver cache. DNS lookups are cached locally. If you are sure that names are being resolved incorrectly, it may be that a DNS record has been updated on a DNS server but the local computer is resolving the name from the local cache. Clearing the cache will force the computer to query the DNS server.

- **Ipconfig/registerdns** renews DHCP leases for all network adapters and reregisters the DNS names for the computer with a DNS server. This option would be used if the DNS registration information went missing for some reason.

- **Ipconfig/displaydns** displays the current DNS resolver cache contents. Information is held in the cache for a set amount of time, which is determined by the DNS server that hosts the record. This option may be useful in troubleshooting whether a DNS name is being resolved to the correct IP address.

- **Ipconfig/showclassid** and **Ipconfig/setclassid** are used to show and set the class ID for the adapter. Class options are set on a DHCP server to provide different options for specific clients; class options only apply to clients belonging to a particular class.

CERTIFICATION OBJECTIVE 9.02

Monitoring, Maintaining, and Troubleshooting Name Resolution

Earlier in this chapter, the different methods used to resolve computer names to IP addresses were described. There is a set order (which can be changed to some extent) in which the various name resolution methods are used, depending on whether a NetBIOS or host name is being resolved.

In this section, we will examine the order in which the name resolution methods are tried. We will then explore how computers are able to view resources on other subnets using the browser service.

NetBIOS Name Resolution

Recall from the previous section that NetBIOS names are resolved using LMHOSTS or a WINS server. There are four additional methods for resolving NetBIOS names.

NetBIOS Name Cache

The cache holds recently resolved names for a short period of time. This improves resolution response time for frequently accessed resources. The cache can be viewed and managed using the nbtstat command, which has a number of options. To view the cache, use nbtstat –c.

Broadcast

Broadcast packets can be employed to see if a computer on the local subnet is using a particular NetBIOS name. A computer sends out a name query broadcast packet containing the NetBIOS name for which it wants an IP address. If a computer that is using the queried name received the packet, it replies with a name query response. Note that NetBIOS name resolution broadcast packets will not work across subnets because routers block broadcast traffic.

HOSTS and DNS

The HOSTS file and DNS servers can also be used to try and resolve a NetBIOS name.

The order in which NetBIOS resolution is carried out is as follows:

1. **NetBIOS name cache.** The cache is always consulted first.

2. **NetBIOS name server, such as WINS.** If the cache does not have the name then a WINS server will be contacted. The computer has to be configured to use WINS and can be configured with the IP addresses of more than one WINS server (two in Windows NT 4.0 and twelve in Windows 2000). A client will try each WINS server listed until it finds one, then it is up and running. If that WINS server does not know the IP address the client will *not* contact any other WINS servers.

3. **Broadcast packet.** Up to three broadcasts packets are sent querying if any computer on the subnet is using the NetBIOS name that needs to be resolved.

4. **LMHOSTS.** If a broadcast fails to resolve the name, then the LMHOSTS file will be examined.

5. **HOSTS.** At this point the NetBIOS name resolution methods have failed to resolve the name and now TCP/IP host name resolution methods will be used. The HOSTS file is consulted first.

6. **DNS.** Finally, DNS servers, if configured, are used. If a DNS server does not reply, additional attempts are made. This can lead to long delays in resolving a name.

Exercise 9-3 shows how to configure a computer to use the various NetBIOS name resolution methods.

The default order in which the NetBIOS name resolution methods are tried can be altered and configured further by changing the resolution node type of the computer by changing a Registry setting. However, the cache is always consulted first. Table 9-2 shows the node types.

TABLE 9-2	**Node Type**	**Behavior**
NetBIOS Node Types	B-Node	Use broadcast only.
	P-Node	Use a NetBIOS Name Server (WINS) only.
	M-Node	Use broadcast, then WINS (B-Node then P-Node).
	H-Node	Use WINS, then broadcast (P-Node then B-Node).
	Enhanced B-Node	Use broadcast, then LMHOSTS.

Be sure to learn the name resolution orders, as well as how to alter the sequence of NetBIOS name resolution by changing the resolution node type of a computer. Consider using a mnemonic such as Can We Buy Large Hard Drives. The first letter of each word gives you the default order of NetBIOS name resolution (Cache, WINS, Broadcast, LMHOSTS, HOSTS, DNS).

EXERCISE 9-3

CertCam 9-3

Configuring Name Resolution on a Computer

In this exercise, we will configure a computer running Windows NT 4.0 to use two WINS servers whose addresses are 10.5.1.1 and 11.5.1.1, to use DNS servers whose addresses are 10.5.2.1 and 11.5.2.1, and not to use LMHOSTS.

The steps to achieve this are as follows:

1. Open the properties page for TCP/IP from the Protocols tab of the Network icon in the Control Panel.

2. Click the WINS Address tab and enter **10.5.1.1** in the Primary WINS Server box and **11.5.1.1** in the Secondary WINS Server box.

3. Ensure that the Enable DNS For Windows Resolution box is checked.

4. Ensure that the Enable LMHOSTS Lookup box is cleared. The properties page should look like Figure 9-16.

5. Click the DNS tab.

6. Under the DNS Service Search Order box, click Add.

7. In the TCP/IP DNS Server dialog box, enter **10.5.2.1** and click Add.

8. Under the DNS Service Search Order box, click Add.

9. In the TCP/IP DNS Server dialog box, enter **11.5.2.1** and click Add.

10. The DNS sheet should look like Figure 9-17.

11. Click OK twice to close the properties and network page dialog boxes. This completes the configuration.

FIGURE 9-16

Microsoft TCP/IP
Properties
dialog box

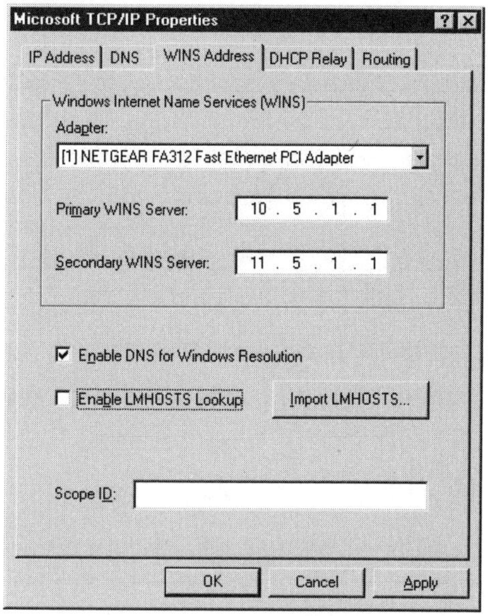

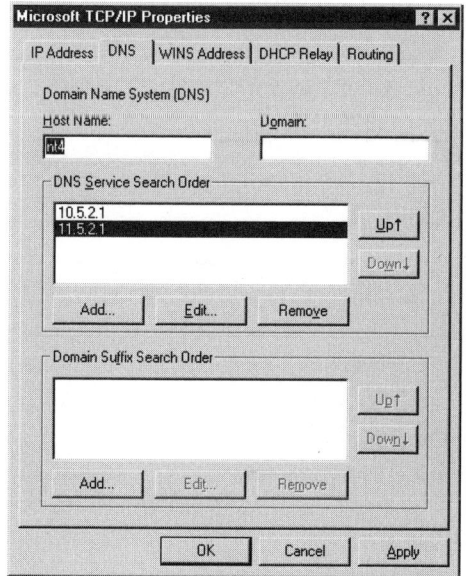

FIGURE 9-17

The DNS sheet

Host Name Resolution

Host name resolution uses either HOSTS or DNS. However, just as NetBIOS name resolution can use host name resolution, host name resolution can also use NetBIOS name resolution techniques.

The order in which host name resolution is carried out is as follows:

1. **Local host name.** The local host name is checked to see if it is the same as the host name that needs to be resolved.

2. **HOSTS.** If the names are different, then the HOSTS file is checked.

3. **DNS.** The next step is to use DNS servers, if configured.

4. **NetBIOS name cache.** If DNS fails to resolve the name, or is not used, then NetBIOS name resolution methods are tried starting with the name cache.

5. **NetBIOS name server, such as WINS.** If the cache does not have the name, then a WINS server will be contacted.

6. **Broadcast packet.** Up to three broadcasts packets are sent querying if any computer on the subnet is using the NetBIOS name that needs to be resolved.

7. **LMHOSTS.** If a broadcast fails to resolve the name, then the LMHOSTS file will be examined.

There is very little that can be configured for host name resolution, since the local host name and HOSTS file are always consulted. Whether DNS is used can be controlled by the presence (or absence) of DNS server addresses. NetBIOS name resolution will always be used if host name resolution fails.

Note that many networks do not use HOSTS, LMHOSTS, DNS, or WINS. This means that all name resolution is achieved using broadcasts. This is acceptable for a smaller network, but for larger networks and certainly where several subnets are involved, the use of WINS or DNS should be considered. A DNS server is required for Windows 2000 domains, though it doesn't have to be on a Windows server, as long as the DNS server meets certain requirements, DNS on a UNIX server could be used.

The nslookup command-line utility can be used to check DNS name resolution. Nslookup can be used interactively or directly from the command line. The following query tries to resolve an address for a Web site.

```
C:\>nslookup www.syngress.com
Server: cache-2.ns.demon.net
Address: 158.152.1.43
```

```
Name: syngress.com
Address: 205.181.158.215
Aliases: www.syngress.com
```

Errors reported by nslookup could indicate a wrongly configured DNS server address or that a name could not be resolved.

Computer Browser Service

In order to access resources, users need to be able to determine what resources (for example, shared folders) are available. This is usually done using Explorer and browsing Network Neighborhood (or My Network Places in Windows 2000) to see what servers are available. The information shown in Network Neighborhood is collected by a service called the Computer Browser.

The Computer Browser service is responsible for the collection and distribution of shared resource information, as well as the servicing of client requests for information. This responsibility is shared across some of the computers in a network. If the Computer Browser service is not running, then the computer will not be able to display available network resources in Explorer.

There is no configuration required for browsing to work on a network that consists of a single subnet, but for a network that consists of several subnets, some configuration is needed.

SCENARIO & SOLUTION

Problem: Users can't see resources on other subnets in Network Neighborhood.	Configure browsing using LMHOSTS or WINS.
Problem: Users can't connect to resources on other subnets.	A default gateway is not configured.
Problem: Users can't browse to the company's intranet site, which is hosted on a UNIX server.	Make sure there is an entry for the UNIX server in the HOSTS file on each computer, or add a record to the appropriate zone if DNS is being used. UNIX servers do not generally respond to NetBIOS name resolution query packets.

Browser Roles

The Computer Browser service uses a number of roles to provide the browsing facility. Each computer will have one of the roles. The decision as to which computers will fulfill certain roles is decided by browser elections and does not normally require manual intervention.

Master Browser   A master browser collects and maintains a list of available servers within its domain (or workgroup) and a list of other domains on the local subnet. It also distributes this browse list to backup browsers. Note, there is only one master browser per domain per subnet.

Backup Browser   The backup browser does not collect its own information; instead it receives the browse list from the master browser and services requests from clients for browsing information. A domain controller, if not a master browser, is always a backup browser. There is one backup browser for every 32 computers on a subnet.

Domain Master Browser   The domain master browser receives lists from every master browser in a network that consists of several subnets. The lists are used to produce a single list of all resources on the network. This single list is then copied back to the master browsers. There is only one domain master browser on a network.

Potential Browser   A potential browser is a computer that could be a master or backup browser, but is not currently fulfilling that role. Most computers can be potential browsers.

Non-Browser   A non-browser is a computer that will not become a backup or master browser and therefore will not keep lists of resources.

Client Browsing

When a client needs a browse list, it contacts the master browser of the relevant domain. The master browser will reply with a list of backup browsers. The client will then contact the backup browsers for a list of the available resources in the domain. The client can then select a particular server to see what resources have been shared. Note that the master browser does not service client requests directly.

Browsing Across Subnets

The browsing process uses broadcasts packets. This means that on a network consisting of several subnets separated by routers, some configuration will be needed to make browsing work.

An easy solution is to configure routers to allow broadcast traffic, but this is not recommended because of the increased network traffic on every subnet. A better solution is to use LMHOSTS or WINS.

Browsing Using LMHOSTS   On the domain master browser, add an entry to the LMHOSTS file that contains the name and IP address of every master browser in the entire network.

On the master browser for each subnet, add an entry to the LMHOSTS file that contains the name and IP address of the domain master browser with the #PRE and #DOM tags.

This ensures that directed packets are used in communication between the domain master browser and the master browsers. It is probably a good idea to have an entry for every master browser in LMHOSTS on every master browser in case one of them becomes the domain master browser.

Browsing Using WINS   Using WINS solves all browsing problems, as no further configuration is needed. If all computers are configured to use WINS, then all NetBIOS names are registered with WINS servers and the Computer Browser service will use it.

on the
Job

If you are using several WINS servers, ensure they are configured to replicate with each other. Otherwise, each one will have incomplete information and this will impact a user's ability to browse the network and connect to resources.

exam
Watch

Learn the various browser roles and, in particular, make sure you know how to configure browsing across subnets.

Monitoring Browser Activity

In order to monitor browser activity, two utilities are available from the Windows NT Server Resource Kit. These are called browmon.exe and browstat.exe. Browmon.exe is a graphical tool that provides statistical information about browser activity and can be used to display the master browser for a domain. Browstat.exe, which runs from the command line, can force elections and provide statistics. Figure 9-18 shows the options available with browstat.exe.

FIGURE 9-18

Browstat.exe
options

```
 C:\WINNT\System32\cmd.exe                                              _ □ ×

C:\ntreskit>browstat
Usage: BROWSTAT Command [Options | /HELP]
Where <Command> is one of:

    ELECT         ( EL) - Force election on remote domain
    GETBLIST      ( GB) - Get backup list for domain
    GETMASTER     ( GM) - Get remote Master Browser name (using NetBIOS)
    GETPDC        ( GP) - Get PDC name (using NetBIOS)
    LISTWFW       (WFW) - List WFW servers that are actually running browser
    STATS         (STS) - Dump browser statistics
    STATUS        (STA) - Display status about a domain
    TICKLE        (TIC) - Force remote master to stop
    VIEW          ( VW) - Remote NetServerEnum to a server or domain on transport

In server (or domain) list displays, the following flags are used:
    W=Workstation, S=Server, SQL=SQLServer, PDC=PrimaryDomainController,
    BDC=BackupDomainController, TS=TimeSource, AFP=AFPServer, NV=Novell,
    MBC=MemberServer, PQ=PrintServer, DL=DialinServer, XN=Xenix,
    NT=Windows NT, WFW=WindowsForWorkgroups, MFPN=MS Netware,
    SS=StandardServer, PBR=PotentialBrowser, BBR=BackupBrowser,
    MBR=MasterBrowser, DMB=DomainMasterBrowser, OSF=OSFServer, VMS=VMSServer,
    W95=Windows95, DFS=DistributedFileSystem

C:\ntreskit>_
```

CERTIFICATION OBJECTIVE 9.03

Troubleshooting and Optimizing Network Performance

As an administrator, it is important to know how to resolve performance issues. Windows provides a number of tools that can be helpful, but the skill is knowing when to use each one. Some of the tools described in this section are useful for troubleshooting connectivity and name resolution problems as well as performance issues.

Event Viewer

The Event Viewer is a very important tool for troubleshooting problems. Computers running Windows NT 4.0 and Windows 2000 record events in three logs that can be viewed using the event viewer.

Events are recorded as one of four types:

- **Information** events indicate a successful action such as a service starting.
- **Warning** events highlight a situation that is not a problem at present but could have an impact later on; these should be monitored.
- **Error** events show a failure of a service, an action that has not completed, or some other condition that will prevent proper computer operation.
- **Auditing** events are used to record access to resources that have been configured to be audited.

	Log	Purpose
TABLE 9-3 Event Logs and Their Purpose	System log	Records information, warning, and error events generated by operating system components such as the printer spooler, DHCP, or DNS.
	Security log	Records audit events such as failed logons, accessing a file and so on.
	Application log	Records information, warning, and error events generated by applications such as SQL Server, rather than the operating system.

Table 9-3 shows the three logs and the purpose of each one.

It should be part of an administrator's routine work to regularly review the event logs and take corrective action where appropriate. To run Event Viewer on a Windows NT 4.0 computer, select Start | Programs | Administrative Tools | Event Viewer. Figure 9-19 shows an example of the system log. Double-clicking an event reveals more details about it (as shown in Figure 9-20). It is quite common for many error events to be listed one after the other. In such cases, look at the oldest event in the sequence first. Usually, the subsequent errors are a result of this first error, and when this error is fixed, the subsequent errors are resolved, too.

The size of the logs can be individually configured. It is possible to restrict a log to a set size and to control whether events are overwritten. It is very important to ensure the security log does not fill up, otherwise the computer will stop. Figure 9-21 shows the configuration settings for controlling the size of a log.

FIGURE 9-19

Example of the system log

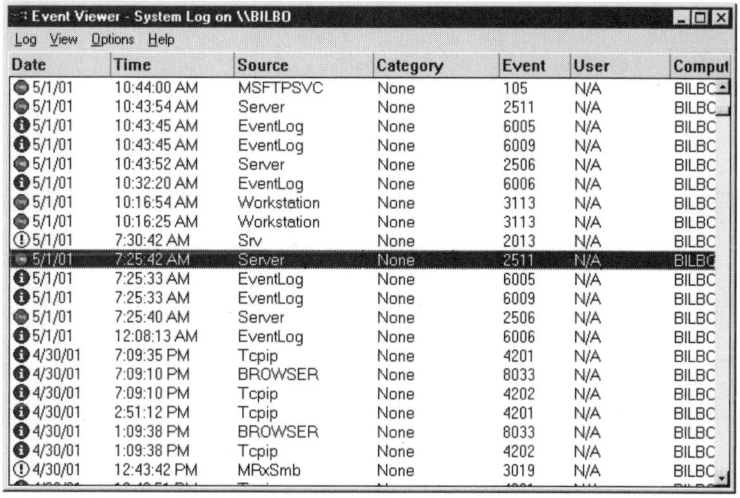

Example
of detailed
information
for an event

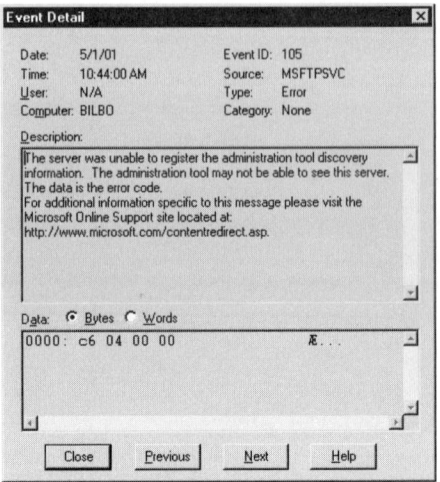

If there are a very large number of events in the log, use the filtering options to restrict what is shown. For example, you may be looking for errors during a certain time period. Figure 9-22 shows the filtering options.

exam
ⓦatch

Make sure that you know the three types of logs shown in Event Viewer and the purpose of each one.

Performance Monitor

Performance Monitor is used to monitor the performance of Windows NT 4.0 workstations and servers in considerable detail. A similar tool, called System Monitor, is provided for computers running Windows 2000. Both tools assist in diagnosing the cause of processing bottlenecks and which parts of a computer would benefit from upgrades.

Configuring the
size of an
event log

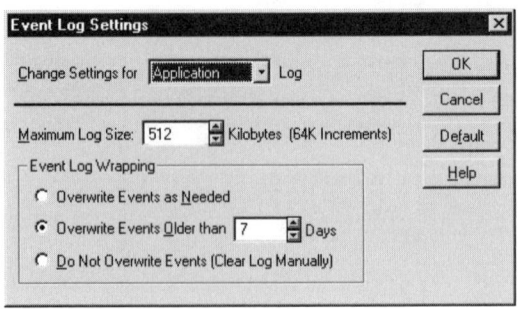

FIGURE 9-22

Filtering events
displayed in
Event Viewer

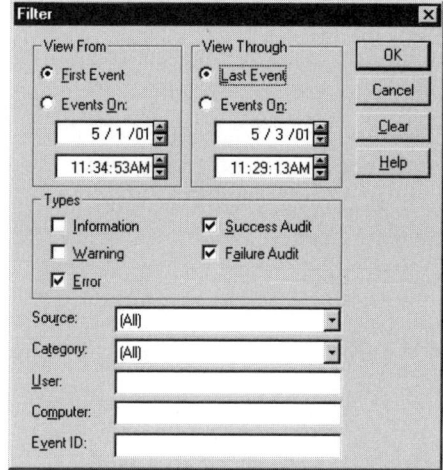

It is generally accepted practice that performance monitoring and tuning starts with establishing a baseline. The baseline records how a computer performs under a normal load (i.e., when it is running the usual programs and has the usual number of users connected to it). Because Performance and System Monitor can measure so many things it can be difficult to know whether a particular value for an item is good or bad, hence the use of the baseline. Measured values under the problem situation can be compared with the baseline to help determine where the problem is occurring and what remedial action should be taken.

Although the rest of this section describes Performance Monitor, it is equally applicable to System Monitor.

Objects, Counters, and Instances

Performance Monitor divides the different aspects of a computer that can be measured into objects. An object is a hardware or software component of the computer, such as a processor, disk, or TCP.

Some objects appear several times in a computer. For example, a computer might have two processors, in which case there is said to be two instances of the processor object. Each instance can be monitored separately, or all instances can be monitored together.

An object will have a number of items that can be measured, called counters. Each object will have a different list of counters. For example, one of the counters for the processor object is "%User Time". This represents the percentage of time that the processor is executing tasks. So, when using Performance Monitor, you will have to specify which counters are to be monitored.

Using Performance Monitor

To run Performance Monitor, select Start | Programs | Administrative Tools | Performance Monitor. This will bring up a dialog box that is remarkably empty. This is because no counters are monitored on startup.

Performance Monitor has four views: Chart, Alert, Log, and Report that can be selected from the View menu as shown in Figure 9-23. Performance Monitor starts in Chart View. System Monitor also provides the same views, but they are accessed slightly differently.

Chart View Chart View shows counter data as a graph that is updated on a regular basis. There will be no data until a counter has been added, which can be done using the + button or selecting Add To Chart from the Edit menu. This brings up the Add To Chart dialog box shown in Figure 9-24. Using this dialog box, you can select which counters to add and for which instance. You can also control how the graph will look for the counter using the color, scale, width, and style pull-down menus. Clicking the Explain button provides more detailed information about what the counter is measuring.

Note that it is possible to add counters from a variety of computers on to the same dialog box.

FIGURE 9-23

Views available with Performance Monitor

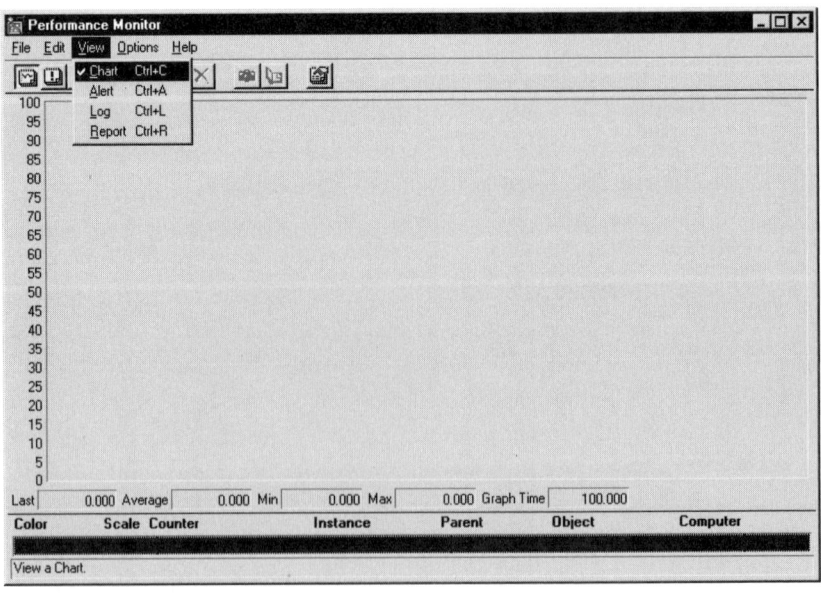

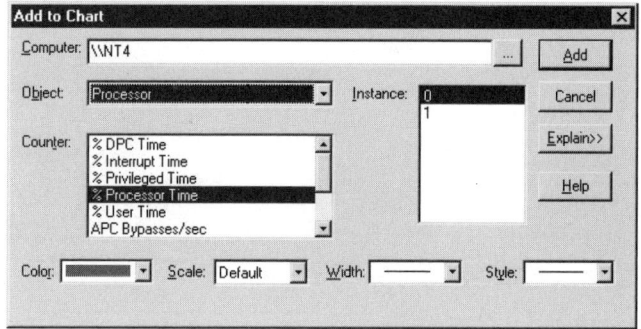

Once the view has been configured, the settings can be saved to a file for future use. This saves having to add the counters again, but note this does not save historical values for the counters, only the counters that are being monitored.

Figure 9-25 shows Performance Monitor in Chart View with two counters, each one added from a different computer.

Alert View   Alert View is used to monitor counters based on a threshold value rather than showing a continuous display of the value of the counter. Each counter to be monitored is added in a similar way to Chart View, but this time an Alert if Over or

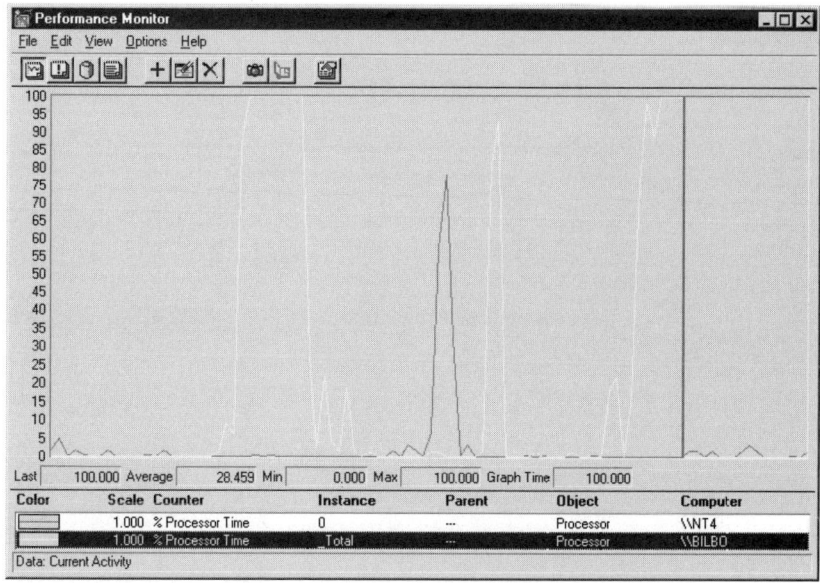

FIGURE 9-26

Choosing a
counter to add
to Alert View

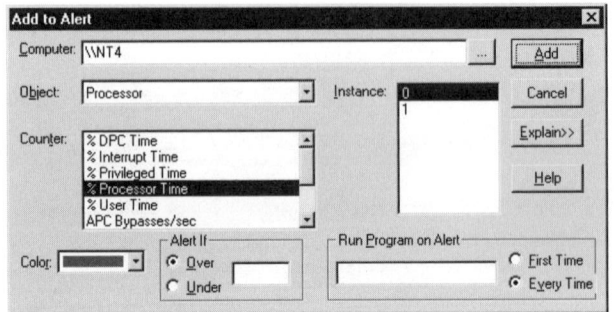

Under value is specified. If the value for the counter exceeds or drops below the value, then an entry will appear in the Alert Log section of Alert View. Figure 9-26 shows the Add To Alert dialog box and Figure 9-27 shows an example of Alert View. Note that the Add To Alert dialog box is very similar to the Add To Chart dialog box.

Log View   Log View is used to save measured counters to a log file, which can be viewed at a later time. To configure a log file, you will need to specify which objects are to be monitored. All of the available counters for the object will be recorded. Under Options | Log, you can configure where the log file is to be stored and how frequently data is to be sampled. This file can then be opened using Performance

FIGURE 9-27

Performance
Monitor in
Alert View

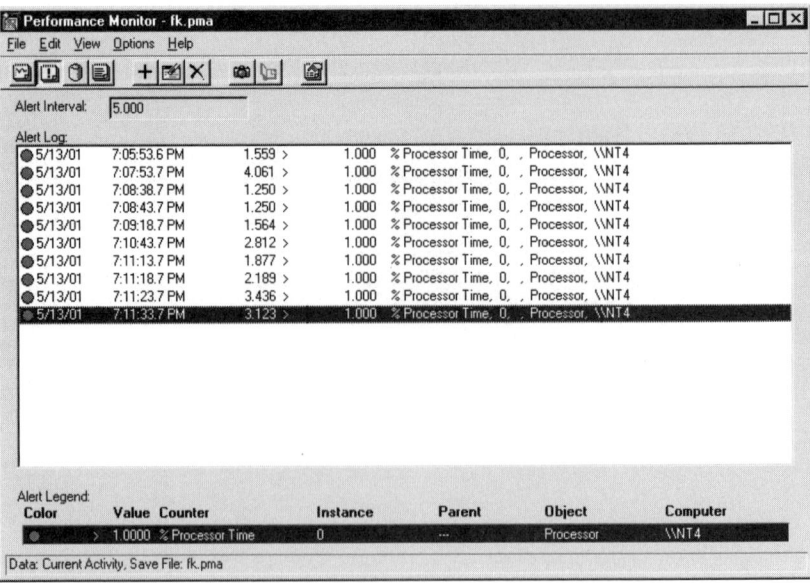

Monitor to review system performance. Consider using Log View to record a baseline for a computer.

Report View   Report View is used to display the current value of counter data as text in a report format. The report can be written to a file, but note that Report View does not maintain a history of data measured, only the last measured value is recorded. As with Chart and Alert Views, you will need to include the counters to be added. Figure 9-28 shows an example of Report View.

Network Monitor

Network Monitor is used to monitor network performance by capturing and viewing network packets. Network Monitor is also used to provide a variety of network statistics. There are two versions of Network Monitor, one that comes with Windows NT 4.0 Server and one that ships with Systems Management Server. The version included with Windows NT 4.0 Server is a reduced functionality version and will only capture packets addressed to or from the computer on which Network Monitor is installed. The Systems Management Server version can capture all packets on the local subnet.

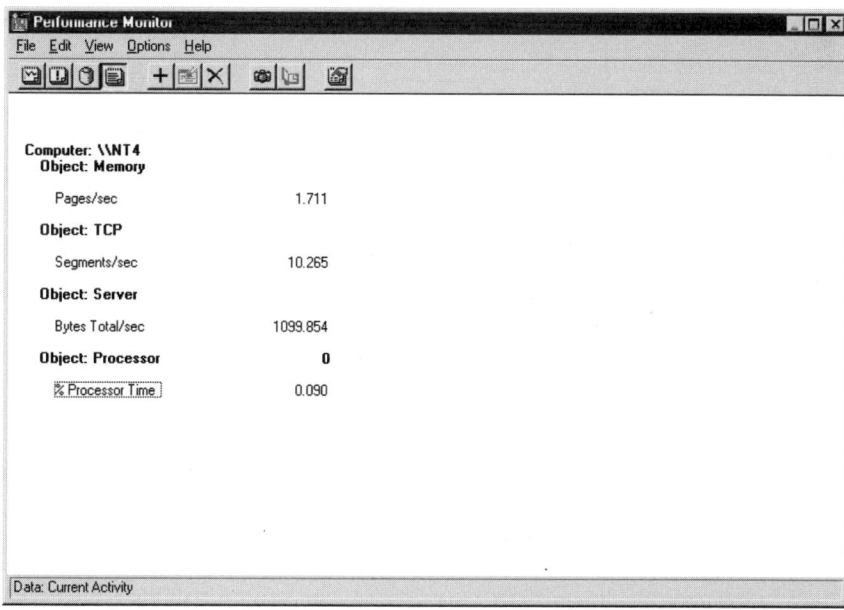

FIGURE 9-28

Performance
Monitor in
Report View

Running Network Monitor

Network Monitor is not installed by default. Exercise 9-4 shows how to install Network Monitor. Once installed, to run Network Monitor, select Start | Programs | Administrative Tools | Network Monitor. This will bring up the Capture Windows dialog box that initially has no information in it. The dialog box consists of four panes called Graph, Total Statistics, Sessions Statistics, and Station Statistics. Figure 9-29 shows the Capture Window dialog box after some packets have been captured.

The Graph pane (top left) is a scrolling box and shows how busy the network is with a number of measurements: % Network Utilization, Frames Per Second, Bytes Per Second, Broadcasts Per Second, and Multicasts Per Second. A persistently high % Network Utilization could indicate a heavily loaded subnet that requires some remedial action.

The Total Statistics pane (top right) is also a scrolling box and shows a variety of statistics. These are Network Statistics, Captured Statistics, Per Second Statistics, Network Card (MAC) Statistics, and Network Card (MAC) Error Statistics. The Per Second Statistics provides the same information as the Graph pane.

FIGURE 9-29

The Capture
Window of
Network
Monitor

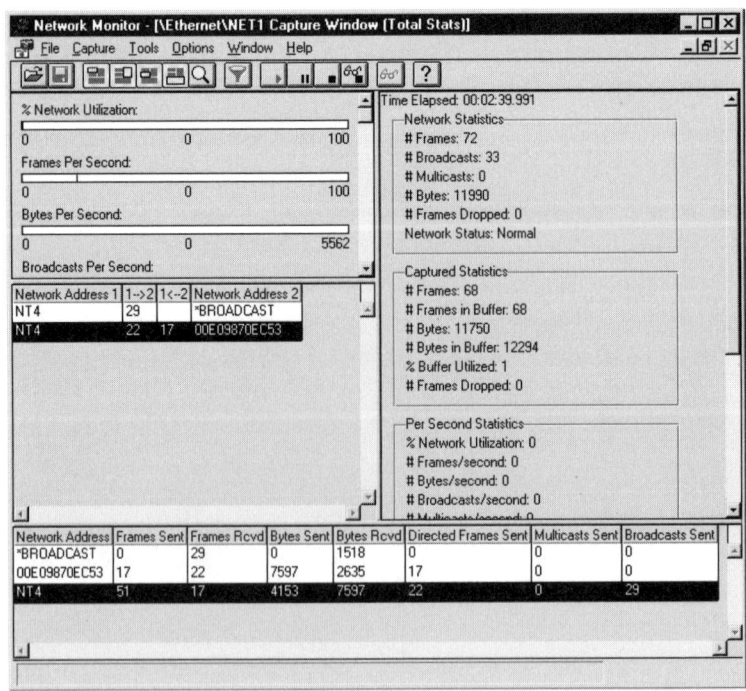

The Session Statistics pane (middle left) is also a scrolling box and shows the computers that have been involved in network conversations and the numbers of packets that have been sent from one computer to the other.

The Station Statistics pane (bottom) is also a scrolling box and shows a summary of the number of packets sent and received for each computer that Network Monitor has captured data. This pane can be used to identify the computers that generate the highest amount of network traffic.

Capturing Data

Network Monitor won't display any statistics or information until network packets have been captured. A capture is started by selecting Capture | Start from the pull-down menu or pressing the Play button on the toolbar. Network Monitor will then capture network packets and update statistics in the various panes until the capture is stopped. This is done by selecting Capture | Stop from the pull-down menu, or pressing the Stop button on the toolbar.

Once a capture is complete, the Capture Window will show various statistics in the four panes just described. These four panes can be used to analyze network usage, to see which computers are generating the most traffic, and to see the type of packets being sent. For example, the Station Statistics pane can be used to see the amount of broadcast traffic on the network.

The Capture Summary window shows details for every packet that was captured. To display this window, select Capture | Display Captured Data once a capture has been completed. Figure 9-30 shows an example of a Capture Summary dialog box.

By double-clicking a particular packet (or frame as it is called in the Capture Summary window) the Capture Summary window changes to detailed information about the packet. Figure 9-31 shows an example of the detailed information for an arp packet. The middle pane shows information about the packet in terms of the network protocols. The level of information displayed can be controlled by clicking on the + and – icons. The lower pane shows the packet information in hexadecimal. Captured packets can be saved to a file for later analysis.

The Capture Summary window is more useful for troubleshooting particular network issues rather than measuring overall network performance. For example, Capture Summary could be used to investigate problems with the DHCP process.

Network Monitor is a very powerful tool and you should not normally allow your users access to it. For example, Network Monitor could be used to discover passwords if there are applications that transmit passwords in an unencrypted format. Before

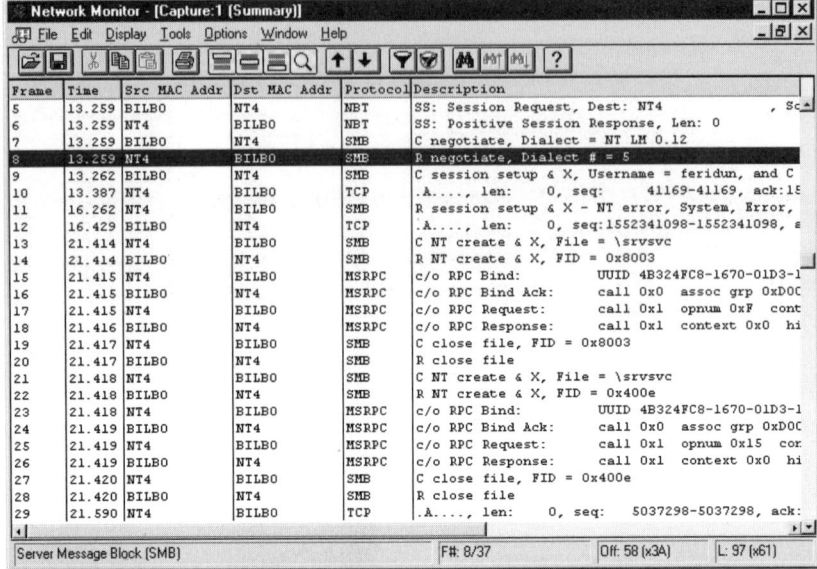

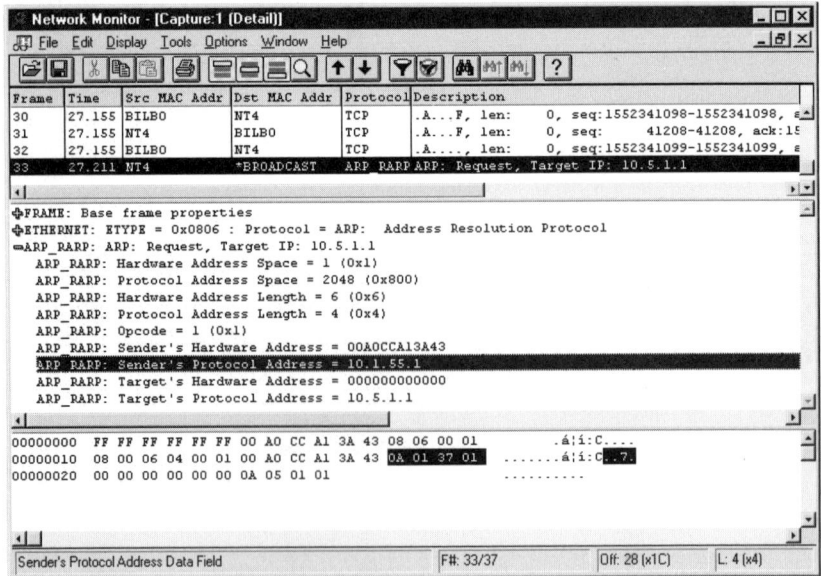

using Network Monitor, make sure you have a good idea of what you are looking for. A capture taken on a network of a reasonable size for even a short period of time will yield a very large amount of information, and without some idea of the problem, searching through the results could be like searching for a needle in a haystack. Some of the features of Network Monitor, such as the ability to filter what is displayed to show only particular types of packets, may assist in making it easier to find what you are looking for.

EXERCISE 9-4

CertCam 9-4

Installing Network Monitor

In this exercise, we will install Network Monitor on a Windows NT 4.0 Server computer.

1. Double-click the Network icon in the Control Panel.

2. Click the Services tab.

3. Click the Add button.

4. In the Select Network Service dialog box, select Network Monitor Tools And Agent.

5. In the Windows NT Setup dialog box, ensure the correct path to the NT Server files is entered. Click the Continue button.

6. A number of files will be copied to the computer. The Network dialog box reappears showing that Network Monitor Tools And Agent has been installed (as shown in Figure 9-32).

7. Click the Close button. Various binding operations are carried out and a Network Settings Change dialog box appears saying the computer must be restarted.

8. Click Yes to restart the computer.

9. Network Monitor Tools And Agent is now ready for use.

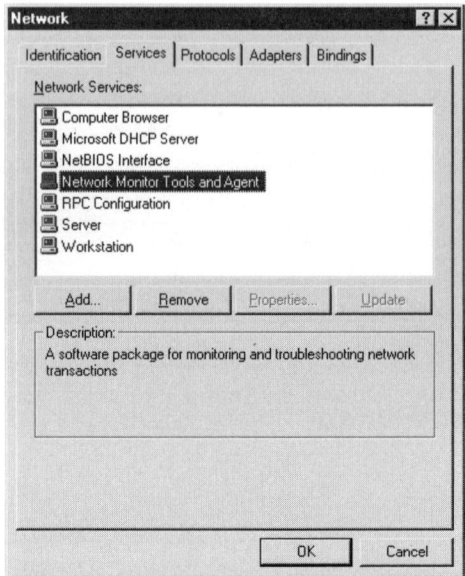

FIGURE 9-32

The Network
dialog box

---

on the
job

Don't get carried away with using every possible troubleshooting tool in sight as soon as you hit a problem. Sometimes thinking about how to resolve a problem can present an unexpected answer. For example, one time I was faced with correcting slow network performance. Before I started using Network Monitor, it occurred to me that each user's computer had virus-scanning software. I checked the settings for the virus-scanning software and sure enough, it had been configured to scan all network files as well as local files. Turning this setting off vastly improved network performance (this didn't present a risk, because all files on the servers are scanned anyway).

CERTIFICATION SUMMARY

This chapter examined issues related to network connectivity, name resolution, and network performance.

In the first section, the use of NetBIOS names and host names for computers was explained and the different methods for resolving computer names to IP addresses was examined. The importance of setting the default gateway for connectivity to other subnets on larger networks was discussed. The use of the Dynamic Host Control Protocol to automate the allocation of TCP/IP configuration information was then explained, as well as the use of Automatic Private IP Addressing for Windows 2000 computers. The first section concluded with a description of the ipconfig utility, which is used to check the TCP/IP configuration of a computer.

In the second section, name resolution was explored further and the order in which the different name resolution methods are tried was described. The order depends on whether a NetBIOS name or host name is being resolved. The computer browser service was then described, which provides shared resource information to client computers.

The final section of this chapter described some of the tools that can be used to troubleshoot network performance. These included Event Viewer, Performance Monitor, and Network Monitor.

✓ TWO-MINUTE DRILL

Configuring and Troubleshooting Network Connectivity

❑ There are two types of computer names: NetBIOS and host names.

❑ Name resolution can use static (HOSTS or LMHOSTS files) or dynamic mappings (DNS or WINS).

❑ The default gateway must be configured on a computer in order to allow communications with other subnets.

❑ A DHCP server allocates IP addresses automatically.

❑ The ipconfig utility is used to check the TCP/IP configuration on a computer.

Monitoring, Maintaining, and Troubleshooting Name Resolution

❑ The default order for NetBIOS name resolution is Cache, WINS Server, Broadcast, LMHOSTS, HOSTS, then DNS.

❑ The default order for host name resolution is HOSTS, DNS, Cache, WINS Server, Broadcast, then LMHOSTS.

❑ The Computer Browser service enables users to search for network resources using Explorer.

❑ There are three browser roles: domain master browser, master browser, and backup browser.

❑ On a network with several subnets, use LMHOSTS or WINS to ensure browsing works properly.

Troubleshooting and Optimizing Network Performance

❑ Event Viewer is used to review events in the system, security, or application logs.

❑ Performance Monitor (System Monitor on Windows 2000 computers) is used to check system performance using counters.

❑ Performance Monitor has four views: Chart, Alert, Log, and Report. Chart View provides a graphical view of counter date. Alert View displays alerts when a counter exceeds or drops below a preconfigured value. Log View is used to save measured counters to a file. Report View is used to display the current value of counter data as text.

❑ Network Monitor is used to capture and analyze network traffic.

❑ There are two versions of Network Monitor. The standard version, available on all Windows NT 4.0 and Windows 2000 Server computers, only captures network traffic to or from the computer on which Network Monitor is running. The full version, included with Systems Management Server, can capture all traffic on the local segment.

SELF TEST

The following questions will help you measure your understanding of the material presented in this chapter. Read all the choices carefully, as there may be more than one correct answer. Choose all correct answers for each question.

Configuring and Troubleshooting Network Connectivity

1. Which of the following databases contain host names and could be used to resolve the address of a Web site, such as www.syngress.com, to an IP address? (Choose two.)

   A. HOSTS

   B. LMHOSTS

   C. WINS

   D. DNS

2. A user complains that, although she can access resources on the local subnet, she cannot browse to any Web sites either by name or IP address. Which of the following TCP/IP parameters' items on the user's computer should you check first?

   A. DNS servers

   B. Default gateway

   C. WINS servers

   D. Subnet mask

3. Your network consists of one subnet and you have configured two DHCP servers (DHCPA and DHCPB) for fault tolerance. However, duplicate IP addresses are being allocated. How should you resolve the problem?

   A. Configure half the clients to use DHCPA and the other half to use DHCPB.

   B. Remove one of the DHCP servers, because there can only be one DHCP server on a subnet.

   C. Configure DHCPA and DHCPB as partners to share their databases of active leases.

   D. Configure the scopes on each server, ensuring they do not overlap.

4. Your network consists of two subnets (A and B) connected by a router. A DHCP server has been installed on subnet A and configured with scopes for both subnets, while all computers

have been configured to use the DHCP server. However, computers on subnet B are not getting an IP address. Which of the following will allow computers on subnet B to obtain their IP address automatically? (Choose all that apply.)

A. Install a DHCP relay agent on subnet A.

B. Install a DHCP relay agent on subnet B.

C. Set the default gateway on computers on subnet B.

D. Install another DHCP server on subnet B.

5. Your network consists of several servers with static IP addresses and a large number of client computers. How would you configure the client computers to use a DHCP server to obtain their IP configuration?

A. Configure each computer to obtain an IP address automatically.

B. Configure each computer to use Automatic Private IP Addressing.

C. Install the DHCP client on each computer.

D. Configure each client computer with the IP address of a DHCP server.

6. Which of the following would you use to set a static IP address for a network card on a computer running Windows NT 4.0?

A. Winipcfg

B. Ipconfig

C. Control Panel | Networks

D. Ipconfig/registerip

7. The DNS service has been moved to different computers on your network. DHCP is being used, so you update the DNS server options for the scope to reflect the IP addresses of the new DNS servers. Which command would you use to get client computers to update their TCP/IP configuration immediately?

A. Ipconfig/updateoptions

B. Ipconfig/renew

C. Ipconfig/release

D. Ipconfig/flushdns

Monitoring, Maintaining, and Troubleshooting Name Resolution

8. In which order are the following name resolution techniques used to resolve a NetBIOS name?

   A. DNS

   B. WINS

   C. NetBIOS cache

   D. LMHOSTS

9. Which utility would you use to look up the IP address of a host name?

   A. Ipconfig

   B. Dnscheck

   C. Network Monitor

   D. Nslookup

10. A user reports that from his computer he can view the resources on a server that is on a different subnet using the NET VIEW command, but cannot connect to that server using FTP. The error message is "connection timed out." The user's computer is not using WINS or DNS, though WINS and DNS servers are running on the network. How would you fix the problem?

   A. Check that the HOSTS file has the correct IP address for the server.

   B. Check that the LMHOSTS file has the correct IP address for the server.

   C. Configure the user's computer to use WINS.

   D. Configure the user's computer to use DNS.

11. Your Windows NT 4.0 network consists of two subnets connected by a single router with a WINS server on each subnet. What would be the best way to configure use of the WINS servers to keep resolution time and administration to a minimum?

   A. Configure computers on each subnet to use the WINS server on their own subnet and the WINS servers to replicate with each other.

   B. Configure half of the computers on each subnet to use their local WINS server, and the other half to use the WINS server on the remote subnet.

C. Configure computers on each subnet to use the WINS server on the remote subnet and the WINS servers to replicate with each other.

D. Remove one of the WINS servers and configure all computers to use the remaining WINS server.

12. Because the Computer Browser service is not running on a user's computer, which of the following will not be possible? (Choose all that apply.)

A. Connecting to shared resources on the local subnet

B. Browsing the local subnet

C. Browsing remote subnets

D. Connecting to shared resources on remote subnets

13. Which browser role services client requests for resource lists?

A. Domain master browser

B. Backup browser

C. Potential browser

D. Master browser

14. Your Windows NT 4.0 network consists of several subnets connected by routers. How would you ensure that browsing in Explorer worked properly?

A. Do nothing, the browser service will configure itself.

B. Configure one DNS server on the network and configure all computers to use it.

C. Configure one WINS server on the network and configure all computers to use it.

D. Ensure all computers have the correct default gateway.

Troubleshooting and Optimizing Network Performance

15. Which tool is used to measure performance on a Windows 2000 computer?

A. Performance Monitor

B. System Viewer

C. Network Performance Monitor

D. System Monitor

16. You have recently taken responsibility for a Windows NT 4.0 server and have decided to measure its performance to provide a baseline for future comparisons. Which of the following would be the best way to do this?

    A. Start Performance Monitor and leave it in Chart View. Add appropriate objects to be measured and allow Performance Monitor to run for a while and then take a screen dump of the Performance Monitor dialog box.

    B. Start Performance Monitor and change to Log View. Add appropriate objects to be measured and allow Performance Monitor to run for a while, then save the log file.

    C. Start Performance Monitor and change to Report View. Add appropriate objects to be measured and allow Performance Monitor to run for a while, then save the results to a file.

    D. Start Performance Monitor and leave it in Chart View. Add appropriate objects to be measured and allow Performance Monitor to run for a while, then save the Performance Monitor settings.

17. You suspect that one of the subnets on your network has a large number of broadcast packets. What would be the best way to verify this?

    A. Use Network Monitor on every computer on the subnet.

    B. Check the system log in Event Viewer.

    C. Use Network Monitor on one computer on the subnet.

    D. Configure an alert in Performance Monitor that logs every broadcast packet.

18. Users are reporting that they are getting a slow response when accessing a server. Which of the following actions should you take to help resolve the problem? (Choose all that apply.)

    A. Use Performance Monitor to check system performance on the server.

    B. Check Event Viewer on each user's computer.

    C. Check Event Viewer on the server.

    D. Use Performance Monitor to check system performance on each user's computer.

19. Which tool would you use to check for application errors?

    A. Performance Monitor

    B. System Monitor

    C. Event Viewer

    D. Network Monitor

20. Your network consists of one hundred computers on three subnets, and you are investigating a problem on a particular subnet. You have used Network Monitor on a computer to capture packets, but are puzzled as to why only packets to and from the computer have been captured, and not all packets on the subnet. What is the most likely reason?

A. Network Monitor is being used on a Windows NT 4.0 workstation.

B. Network Monitor is being used on a Windows NT 4.0 server.

C. There is no other traffic on the subnet.

D. The computer running Network Monitor is on the incorrect subnet.

LAB QUESTION

You have a large network of multiple subnets that consists of several hundred computers running a mixture of Windows 2000 Professional, Windows NT 4.0 Workstation, and Windows NT 4.0 Server. There are also a few UNIX hosts.

How would you configure IP addressing, name resolution, and browsing so as to automate as much as possible and minimize the amount of manual administration?

SELF TEST ANSWERS

Configuring and Troubleshooting Network Connectivity

1. ☑ **A** and **D.** HOSTS and DNS are used to resolve host names. HOSTS is a file, whereas DNS is a central service that might be a dynamically updated database depending on the version.

   ☒ **B** and **C** are incorrect because they are used to resolve NetBIOS names.

2. ☑ **B.** The default gateway specifies the IP address of the router to use for computers on other subnets.

   ☒ **A** is incorrect because DNS is used to resolve names to IP addresses. Browsing by IP address does not work, so name resolution is not the issue. **C** is incorrect because WINS is not used for resolving Web site names. **D** is incorrect because if the subnet mask were incorrect, then the user wouldn't be able to connect to resources on the local subnet.

3. ☑ **D.** DHCP servers do not communicate with each other, so it is most likely that DHCPA and DHCPB have been configured with overlapping scopes.

   ☒ **A** is incorrect because the address of a DHCP server cannot be specified when configuring a computer as a DHCP client. **B** is incorrect because it is possible to have more than one DHCP server on a network. **C** is incorrect because DHCP servers cannot be configured to share their databases.

4. ☑ **B** or **D.** The problem is due to the router not forwarding DHCP broadcast packets. A DHCP relay agent is designed to get around this problem, but needs to be installed on the subnet without a DHCP server. Installing a DHCP server would also work, but a DHCP relay agent would not be needed.

   ☒ **A** is incorrect because the relay agent needs to be installed on a subnet without a DHCP server. **C** is incorrect because it is not relevant and because it is not possible to set the default gateway if DHCP is being used.

5. ☑ **A.** This option is used to specify that a DHCP server is to be used on computers running Windows 2000. On Windows NT 4.0 computers the wording is: "Obtain an IP address from a DHCP Server."

   ☒ **B** is incorrect because Automatic Private IP Addressing is used by a computer to allocate itself an address when a DHCP server cannot be contacted. **C** is incorrect because the DHCP client does not need to be installed. **D** is incorrect because the address of a DHCP server is not specified when configuring a computer as a DHCP client.

6. ☑ **C.** A static IP address has to be set on the TCP/IP properties sheet within the Networks icon in the Control Panel.

☒ **A** is incorrect because winipcfg is used on Windows 9x computers. **B** and **D** are incorrect because ipconfig can only be used to view TCP/IP settings. **D** is also incorrect because /registerip is not a valid option for the ipconfig command.

7. ☑ **B.** The renew option will update TCP/IP parameters that have been changed in the scope as well as in renewing the lease.

☒ **A** is incorrect because there is no such option. **C** is incorrect because it is used to give up a lease. **D** is incorrect because it is used to clear the local DNS resolver cache.

Monitoring, Maintaining, and Troubleshooting Name Resolution

8. ☑ **C, B, D,** and then **A.** The cache is always examined first. DNS is a host name resolution technique and is used after NetBIOS name resolution techniques.

9. ☑ **D.** Nslookup is used to run name resolution queries. It can also be used to test that a DNS server is working as expected.

☒ **A** is incorrect because ipconfig is used to check the TCP/IP settings on a computer. **B** is incorrect because there is no such utility. **C** is incorrect because Network Monitor is used to examine network traffic.

10. ☑ **A.** The connection timed out error message suggests that name resolution has occurred because an attempt to make a connection has been made. The explanation for the error is that the entry for the server in the user's HOSTS file has the incorrect IP address.

☒ **B** is incorrect because the NET VIEW command is working. This means that there must be a correct entry in LMHOSTS. Broadcasts will not resolve the name, because the server is on a different network, and WINS is not in use. **C** and **D** are incorrect because WINS and DNS are consulted after HOSTS. The name is being resolved incorrectly and this can only be because there is an incorrect entry in HOSTS.

11. ☑ **A.** The most efficient system would be to use the local WINS server. This keeps resolution time at a minimum. The WINS servers, however, must be configured to replicate their databases with each other, otherwise they will not know about the computers on the subnet that is remote to them.

☒ **B** is incorrect because replication between the WINS servers is needed, and because it requires more administration. **C** is incorrect because, although it will work, it means that all name resolution queries have to go through the router, increasing resolution time. **D** is incorrect for a similar reason to **C**. It will work, but for computers on the subnet without the WINS server, queries will have to go through the router.

12. ☑ **B** and **C**. If the Browser service is not running, then browsing is not available at all.
    ☒ **A** and **D** are incorrect because the user can still connect to shared resources if he knows the name of the server.

13. ☑ **B**. The Backup browser sends resource lists to clients.
    ☒ **A** and **D** are incorrect because they do not provide resource lists to clients. The master browser sends a list of backup browsers to a client. The client then requests a resource list from one of the backup browsers. **C** is incorrect because it is not a browser role. A potential browser is a computer that might become a browser.

14. ☑ **C**. The browsing service uses broadcast packets which means that additional configuration is required in a routed network. The simplest method is to use WINS.
    ☒ **A** is incorrect because users will not be able to browse to resources on other subnets. **B** is incorrect because DNS does not play a role in the browser service. **D** is incorrect because, although having the correct default gateway is a requirement, it is not sufficient to ensure that browsing will work across subnets.

Troubleshooting and Optimizing Network Performance

15. ☑ **D**. System Monitor is used to measure performance on a Windows 2000 computer.
    ☒ **A** is incorrect because Performance Monitor is used on Windows NT 4.0 computers and not Windows 2000 computers. **B** and **C** are incorrect because there are no such utilities.

16. ☑ **B**. Performance Monitor has several views. The Log View is the best one to use for producing a baseline, because the log file can be opened in chart view, counters can be added from the log file, and the way the data is presented can be changed as if it were live data.
    ☒ **A** is incorrect because a screen dump wouldn't allow modifications to how the historical data was presented, and it may be difficult to check the precise value of a counter. There may also be too many counters to view each one clearly. **C** is incorrect because Report View only shows the last measured value of a counter, and does not record historical data. **D** is incorrect because saving Performance Monitor settings only saves the counters that were being monitored, not the recorded values.

17. ☑ **C**. Network Monitor is used to monitor network traffic and can be used to view the amount of broadcast packets being used. It is only necessary to run Network Monitor on one computer, because broadcast packets will be received and processed by every computer on the subnet.
    ☒ **B** is incorrect because the incidence of broadcast packets is not recorded in Event Viewer. **A** is incorrect because it is not necessary to run Network Monitor on every computer. The required information can be gathered from just one computer. **D** is incorrect because it is not possible to configure an alert in Performance Monitor to record the amount of broadcast packets used.

18. ☑ **A** and **C.** Performance Monitor is used to check system performance, and Event Viewer is used to view events. Since all users are experiencing a problem, then the server is the computer to check out.

☒ **B** and **D** are incorrect because the problem is more likely to be on the server since all users are experiencing the problem.

19. ☑ **C.** The application log in Event Viewer is used to check for application error events.

☒ **A** is incorrect because Performance Monitor is used on NT systems to view system performance data, not error events. **B** is incorrect because System Monitor is the Windows 2000 equivalent of Performance Monitor. **D** is incorrect because Network Monitor is used to capture network activity.

20. ☑ **B.** The version of Network Monitor included with Windows NT 4.0 Server will only capture packets addressed to or from the computer on which Network Monitor is installed. Systems Management Server includes a full version of Network Monitor that will capture all packets on a subnet.

☒ **A** is incorrect because Network Monitor is not available for Windows NT 4.0 Workstation. **C** is incorrect because, although it is possible, it is highly unlikely on a network with so many computers. **D** is incorrect because whatever subnet the computer is on, Network Monitor would be able to capture all packets on the subnet if the full version of Network Monitor is being used.

LAB ANSWER

The question's emphasis is on minimizing the amount of administration required. To configure IP addressing, DHCP should be used. Because there are several subnets, the use of several DHCP servers should be considered. It may be possible to use only one DHCP server on one subnet and DHCP relay agents on every other subnet, but it would be wise to have at least two DHCP servers for fault tolerance. Make sure that each DHCP server has appropriate scopes for each subnet and that none of the scopes overlap. The DHCP servers must have a static IP address. Configure all the client computers (including the UNIX hosts) to obtain an IP address from a DHCP server.

To enable name resolution to work successfully, and with the minimum of administration, install one or more WINS servers. Each client computer must be configured with the IP addresses of the WINS servers, but this can be set by using options in the DHCP scope, preventing the need to manually configure each client. By using WINS servers, the problem of resolving names for computers on other subnets is solved. Use more than one WINS server to provide fault tolerance and to reduce query times, but every WINS server must be configured to replicate with each other so they all have complete information about every computer on the network.

The UNIX hosts present a small problem in that they will not register their names with a WINS server. In order to resolve the UNIX names, the best approach would be to install a DNS server and configure each client computer with the IP address of the DNS server. As with WINS, this can be done automatically by using options in the DHCP scope. A domain name should be established for the network, and the DNS server configured to host zone records for the domain name. Address records for each of the UNIX servers should be added to the zone on the DNS server. An alternative approach would be to manually configure the HOSTS file on every computer. This would prevent the need to use DNS, but doesn't fulfill the requirement to minimize the amount of manual administration. Use more than one DNS server to provide fault tolerance and reduce query times.

Because WINS has been used, browsing will present no further problems and all users will be able to browse to Windows resources without any further configuration.

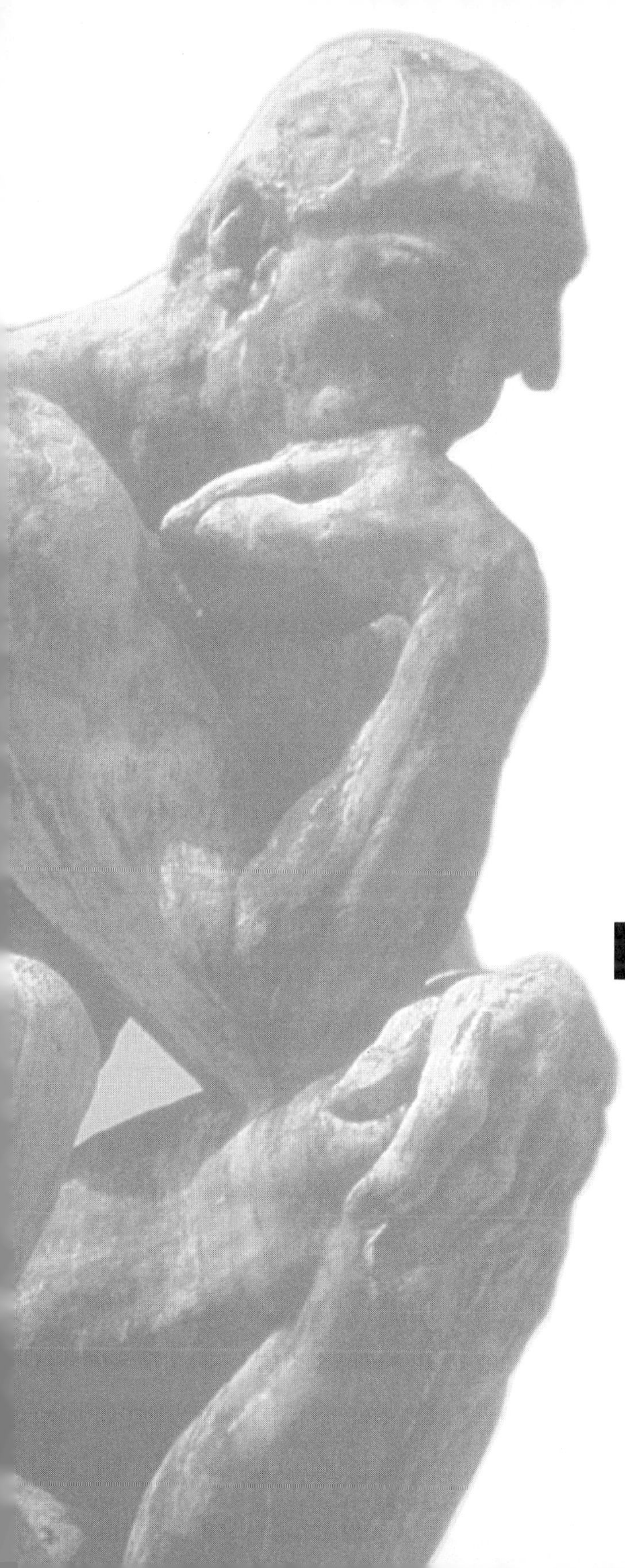

10

Configuring and Troubleshooting IIS Web Servers, RAS, and Performance Tuning

CERTIFICATION OBJECTIVES

M

aintaining an IIS 4.0 Web server in a Windows NT environment is no easy task for Administrators. This chapter is intended for either current IIS 4.0 Administrators who may need a refresher course, or new IIS Administrators who are learning how to implement IIS 4.0 in their environment. It will show you the proper steps of installing IIS and how to do performance tuning on the Web server, how to set up RAS and the Routing and Remote Access Service, as well as how to install VPN on the server and client machines. The Internet Authentication Service (RADIUS) is also briefly covered at the end of this chapter.

CERTIFICATION OBJECTIVE 10.01

Configuring, Managing, and Troubleshooting Microsoft IIS on the Server

This section gives IIS Administrators an overview on how to configure, manage, and troubleshoot Microsoft IIS 4.0. IIS 4.0 may be found on the NT Option Pack or downloaded from the Microsoft Web site. If you subscribe to the Microsoft TechNet Subscription, it is included on the Option Pack CD-ROM. Check that your server meets the minimum requirements for installation and make sure you know what the site will be running as far as applications before you begin the installation process. To take full advantage of the security that IIS 4.0 offers, it must be installed on a drive formatted with NTFS. The minimum requirements, as well as the proper installation steps for IIS 4.0, are listed in the following:

- Install Windows NT 4.0 if it is not already installed.

- At minimum, installing Windows NT SP3 is required for IIS 4.0 installation.

- Install Internet Explorer 4.01 Service Pack 2 without the Active Desktop. Internet Explorer 4.01 SP1 is included with the NT Option Pack, but Microsoft recommends that Internet Explorer SP2 be installed instead of the version with the Option Pack. I.E. 4.01 creates protective storage on IIS 4.0, which is necessary for IIS to run properly.

- Install the Windows NT 4.0 Option Pack, which includes the IIS 4.0 software. This can be purchased on a CD-ROM or downloaded from the Microsoft site. For minimum hassle, do a Typical install. Once IIS is running properly, go back and add any additional features.

- Reapply the latest NT 4.0 Service Pack. This would be Windows NT SP6a. Remember to reapply the latest NT SP even if it was previously installed when you installed software to a server.

- Install MDAC 2.1 SP2 to upgrade your MDAC to the latest version.

After IIS 4.0 has been installed, it needs to be configured based on the types of applications it will be running. Depending on which type of setup you selected during the installation, you will have various options to configure. There are three types of setup in IIS 4.0. They are as follows:

- **Minimum**   Installs only components needed to run ASP pages.

- **Typical**   Loads same as minimum, but includes FTP Service, HTML version of ISM, and online documentation.

- **Custom**   Allows Administrator to decide which components to install. Allows you to choose the destination of installation files, as well as how much disk space each option may consume.

NTFS and Security in IIS 4.0

The NT File System, or NTFS, is the front line of protection for an IIS 4.0 Web server. IIS 4.0 is intended for use with Windows NT 4.0's security system. NTFS offers customizable security where its predecessor, the file allocation table (FAT) system, did not. An important point to remember is that Web server security settings apply to all users accessing your Web site. NTFS security, on the other hand, can be used to grant a variety of access permissions to different users and groups on a folder or even a single file. Whenever both Web server and NTFS permissions are set, the more restrictive of the two applies. In other words, the permissions that explicitly deny access always take precedence over the permissions that grant access.

Using IIS 4.0 and NTFS

NTFS allows you to control who has access to files on the Web server. For instance, you can give a department, such as Human Resources, full access to information they post on the Web site and give all other users read-only access. This means that the Human Resources department has complete control over the content, and users not belonging to this group can only read the content.

Keep this fact in mind when you set up IIS 4.0 for the first time. Always check permissions on the Inetpub and wwwroot folder. Control your permissions from there at the very beginning. Remove the Everyone group and put the proper groups in these folders.

on the **job**

When you install IIS 4.0 on an NTFS partition, NTFS security is set by default to Full Control for the Everyone group.

NTFS Rules

You can grant NTFS permissions to a group of users or individual users. If you have a user who belongs to more than one group, that user could have different permission levels granted to them on the same folder. If this occurs, then the least restrictive set of rules are applied to the folder. There is only one exception to this rule and that is that the NO ACCESS right will override any other access right regardless of the level of the other right. For example:

No Access Permission Settings   Mary belongs to the SALES group, and the SALES group is granted Full Access to the Sales Reports folder. Mary also belongs to the ACCTG group and the ACCTG group is granted the No Access permission to the Sales report folder. Since the NO ACCESS right overrides all other rights Mary will not have access to the Sales Reports folder.

Least Restrictive Rule   Mary belongs to the SALES group, and the SALES group is granted Change access to the Sales report folder. Mary also belongs to the ACCTG group and the ACCTG group is granted read-only permission to the Sales report folder. Using the least restrictive rule set by Windows NT, Mary is granted Change access to the Sales Reports folder.

NTFS Permissions and Drive Partitions

Table 10-1 shows File Tasks and permission results. It details the results of copying and moving files from one folder to another on other partitions.

Accessing Your IIS 4.0 Security Settings

IIS 4.0 has its own built-in security system that can be accessed through the Internet Service Manager (ISM). To access the security settings on your Web sites, open ISM

TABLE 10-1	File Task	From	Target	Permission Results
File Tasks and Permission Results	Copied	One folder to another	Same NTFS partition	Permissions are inherited from the target folder.
	Copied	One folder to another	Between folders on different NTFS partitions	Permissions are inherited from the target folder.
	Moved	One folder to another	Same NTFS partition	Permissions are retained from the original folder.
	Moved	One folder to another	Between folders on different NTFS partitions	Permissions are inherited from the target folder.
	Moved	One folder to another	From NTFS partition to FAT partition	Permissions are lost.

by clicking Start | Programs | Administrative Tools | Windows NT Option pack | Internet Services Manager. After the MMC opens up, click on the server and expand the contents beneath. Right-click the default Web site, select properties, then select the Home Directory tab. Your Web site security settings should now be shown. In the middle of the Properties dialog box, you will see permissions assigned to this Web site. Read, Write, Directory Browsing, and Script are permissions that pertain to the site in general. To control permissions regarding the content of the Web site, it is necessary to go to the source of the content. Open Windows Explorer and browse to the wwwroot folder. Click the wwwroot folder in the left pane, then look at the list of files in the right pane. Here is where we set the NTFS permissions regarding the content of the Web site. Table 10-2 reviews the NTFS file permissions.

on the job *If you are using FrontPage for content editing and publishing, the FrontPage server extensions must be installed on the IIS server. Make sure you set all your folder and file permissions first. Then install the server extensions and from that point on let FrontPage handle all the security. You can develop problems by changing file and folder permissions after the server extensions are installed.*

The standard permissions that can be applied to files are greater than the permissions that can be applied to folders. Table 10-3 shows permissions for folders in IIS 4.0.

TABLE 10-2	File Permission	Description
Permissions for Files in IIS 4.0	No Access	Denies access to either a user or a group of users. A user can see the directory or filename, but cannot access it to read or edit information. Caution: If this is applied to the Everyone group, all users would be denied access, as doing so would deny access to everyone.
	List	Users can see the filenames in the folder, but cannot view or execute any files.
	Read	Users can read and execute files, but no changes may be made.
	Add	Users can add files to the folder, but cannot view or execute the files.
	Add & Read	Users can add files to the folder and view and execute files.
	Change	Users can read, execute, write, and delete files or folders. Users have no access to change any directory permissions for the files or directory itself. Change access also gives users the ability in the folder to delete other folders within the folder they have created, but not the folder they have been granted Change access to.
	Full Control	Users can read, execute, write, and delete files or folders within the directory to which they have been granted Full Control. They can also change permissions for the directory and files contained in the directory. Users with this permission can also take ownership of files and folders.

If you give users conflicting security settings to a folder or file, the least restrictive wins again, unless it is the NO ACCESS right. The NO ACCESS right always wins out over the other security settings in NTFS and IIS 4.0.

TABLE 10-3	File Permission	Description
Permissions for Folders in IIS 4.0	No Access	Denies access to a user or a group of users. A user can see the filename, but cannot access it.
	Read	Users can read and execute files, but cannot make changes to the files.
	Change	Users can read, execute, write, and delete the file, but cannot change the permissions for files they don't own.
	Full Control	Users can read, execute, write, and delete the file. They can also change permissions for the file, and take ownership of the file.

on the

●**o b**

It is not necessary to share any folders on an IIS server. This is a common misconception. As a matter of fact, if you create a share on a Web server, you are opening a potential security hole. Make it a practice to never create shares on a Web server.

The "What if" Tool

Microsoft has created a utility named the "What If" tool. This is an IIS Security-related utility designed to assist administrators with troubleshooting security issues in IIS 4.0. The tool requires a DHTML-enabled browser and Microsoft has tested this tool with Internet Explorer versions 4.0 and 5.0. You can download and find out more information regarding this tool by using the Knowledge Base Article Number Q229694 at Microsoft's Web site: http://support.microsoft.com/support/kb/articles/Q229/6/94.asp).

exam

ⓦ**a t c h**

Remember this simple equation: moving from NTFS to NTFS = permissions are retained. Copying from NTFS to NTFS = permissions are inherited. Moving or copying from NTFS to FAT = lost permissions.

Groups in IIS 4.0

Usually, Administrators find it easier to add users to groups, then give the group the right to the specific folder. If you use this strategy, do not overlook the Guest group in IIS 4.0. If you allow anonymous access to your Web site, then IIS 4.0 will add the IUSR_computername account. The computername is the name of the server or computer that your site is running IIS 4.0 on. Do not give the Guest group or the IUSR_computername account too many permissions. This could cause undesirable consequences on your Web site. The IUSR_computername account is the account used by anonymous users to authenticate to the Web server. Do not add the IUSR_computername to another group that has higher permissions than read or execute, or they will have more control over the Web site than needed. The other guest account created by IIS 4.0 is the IWAM_Computername account. This account is used to start out-of-process Web applications in IIS 4.0. Use the same caution with the IWAM_Computername account as you would with the IUSR_computername account.

Configuring Microsoft Internet Information Services 4.0

Now that NTFS and security settings have been discussed, let's look at configuring IIS 4.0. During setup, the \Inetpub directory is created as well as two subdirectories named \wwwroot and \scripts. The \wwwroot is the default home directory, while the \scripts subdirectory is used for CGI, ISAPI, and ASP. If you installed the HTML version of the IIS Internet Service Manager, it automatically installs two directories named default and administration. The default site handles HTTP browser requests through port 80 and the administration site handles browser requests through a port number configured at random during installation. The Administration site provides IIS 4.0 administrators with the opportunity to remotely administer their Web sites using a browser and connecting over the Internet. Figure 10-1 shows the HTTP version of the Internet Service Manager. To publish additional content to your IIS 4.0 server, you can create virtual directories or publish to the default structure. The

FIGURE 10-1   Using your Internet browser to administer your IIS 4.0 Web server; notice the port number in the Address bar

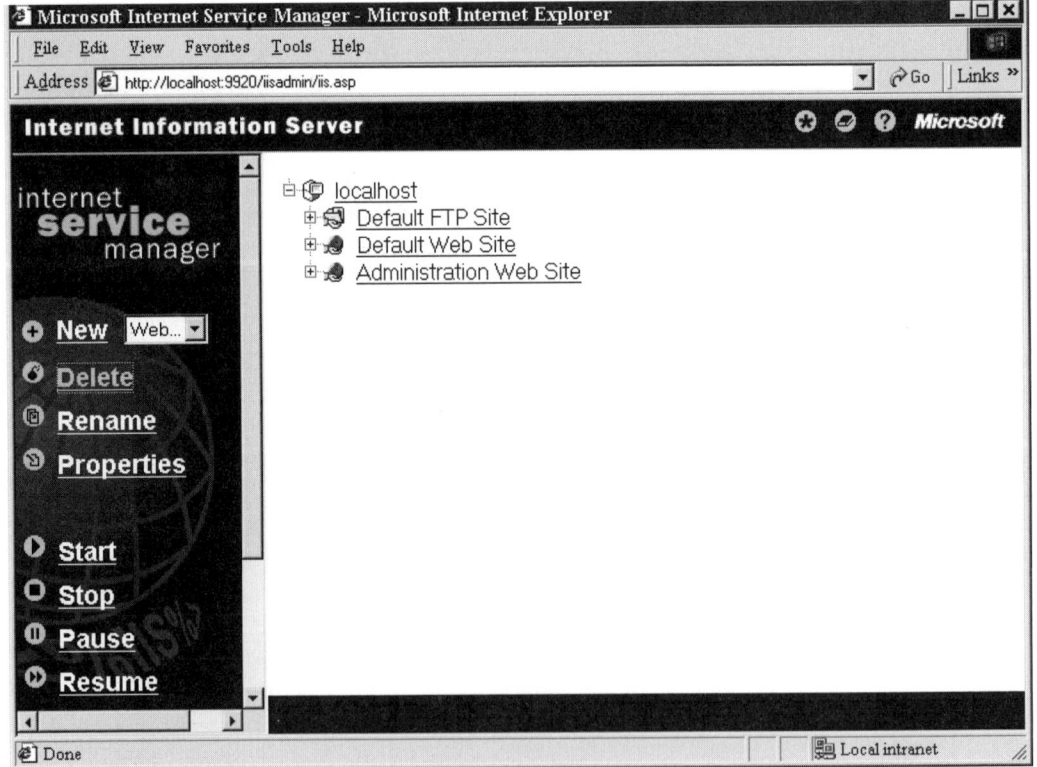

default target of inetpub is c:\inetpub and the default content is c:\inetpub\wwwroot. It is important for these two paths to be consistent. Many programs you may install later look to these two directory paths for installation. If you chose a different directory path during installation, you could be asking for trouble in the future.

Virtual Directories

If information needs to be referenced on the Web server, it can be placed in what are called virtual directories. Virtual directories can be considered publishing directories on a Web server, another hard disk, or even another computer on the network, pointing to information that can be accessed by the IUSR. An alias is associated with the virtual directory when it is created in the Internet Services Manager (ISM). Clients use the alias to access information in the virtual directory. If the Administrator does not give an alias name, it is generated by the ISM. You can create a virtual directory by clicking Start | Programs | Administrative Tools | Windows NT Option Pack | Microsoft Internet Service Manager. After the MMC opens, expand your computername, then right-click the default Web site, select New, then choose Virtual Directory from the menu. The New Virtual Directory Wizard will appear, its first screen displaying security permissions. If you are using ASP, check the box Allow Script Access, or select Allow Execute Access for scripts to run on the Web server. Figure 10-2 shows the welcome screen of the New Virtual Directory Wizard.

This allows read access and gives clients the ability to read the contents of the script files.

FIGURE 10-2

Check the Allow Execute Access box if you are running ASP on your Web

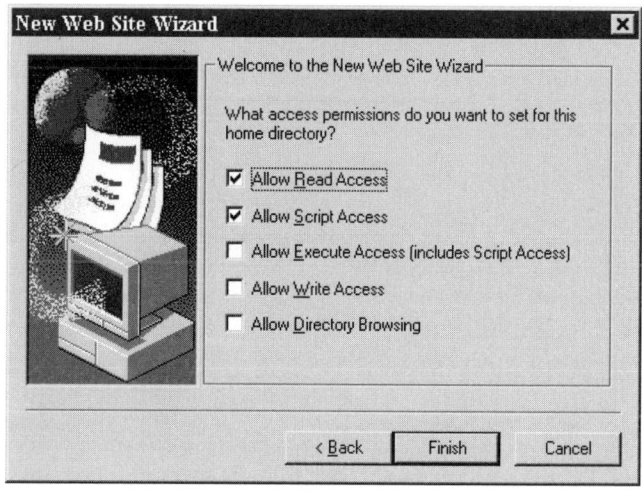

Configuration of IIS 4.0

You can use the Master Properties settings (shown in Figure 10-3) to configure the master properties of your IIS server and any sites that have already been made. These are the master properties, not the individual properties. Each individual Web site will have its own individual properties that you can configure after the master properties are set. Open the ISM and right-click the computer icon, then choose properties. In the Master Properties dialog box, under the Master Properties section, WWW Service, click Edit. A tabbed properties page should appear where you can configure the master properties. The Web Site tab allows you to change the description of the site, set the connection timeout, enable HTTP Keep-Alives and configure the Active log format.

The Operators section allows you to control who will administer the Web Site. The page is straightforward. Just click the Add button to give administrative access to users of the Web site. Normally, you will leave this page alone and leave the Administrators in control. The Operators property page is shown in Figure 10-4.

Figure 10-5 shows the Performance page. This page is used to set the performance level on the Web site. You can throttle Web site bandwidth and tune performance

FIGURE 10-3

The Web Site properties tab

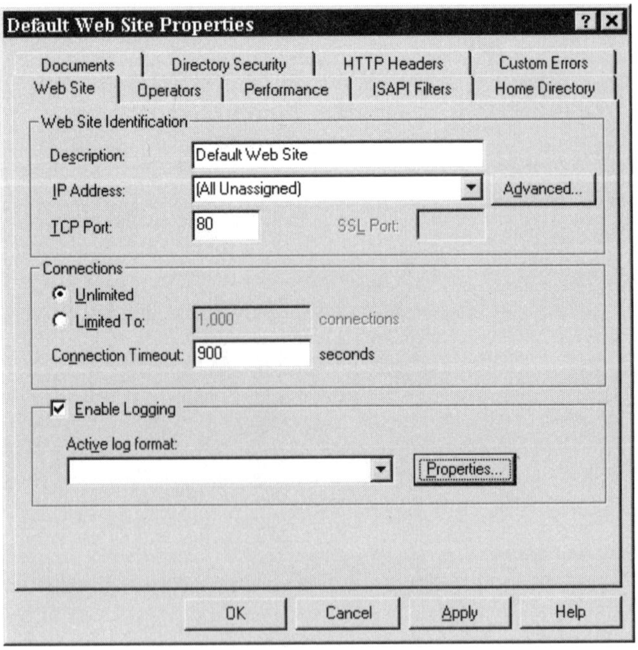

FIGURE 10-4

Use this page to give access to operators for this Web site

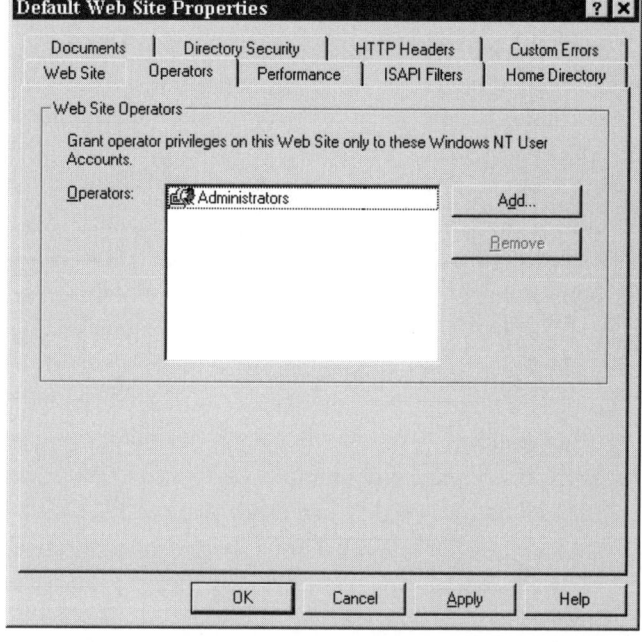

FIGURE 10-5

Configure the performance settings on the Web site using this screen

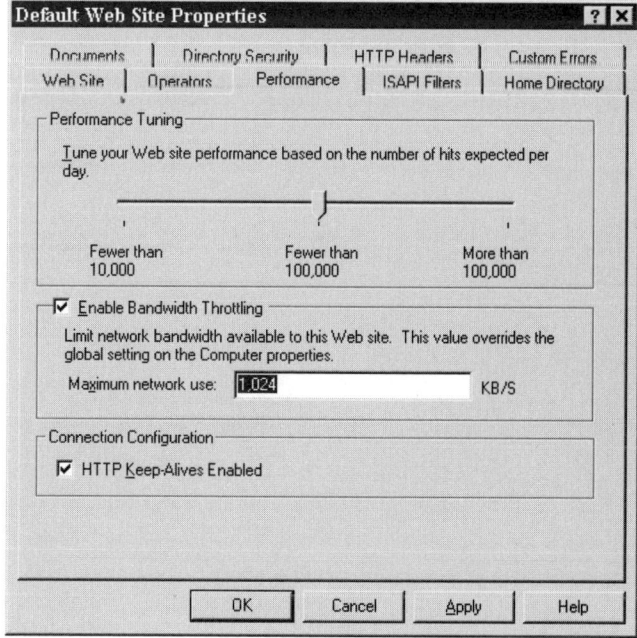

based on the number of expected hits on the Web site. You can also configure the HTTP Keep-Alives on this screen. Keep-Alives are HTTP connections that are not closed after the user makes a request from the Web site. Without Keep-Alives enabled, the server performance would be affected, because client browsers would continually make connection requests for a page with multiple elements, such as graphics. Sometimes more than one connection would need to be made from the client browser to pages with multiple elements. If you have other services running on your IIS 4.0 Server, such as e-mail or news, you may want to limit the amount of bandwidth your server is using so other services run more efficiently.

The ISAPI Filters tab (Figure 10-6) is used for configuring special DLLs that the Web server loads, as well as those requested by the server at particular points. ISAPI filter programs respond when the Web Server receives an HTTP request. They are different from applications because they do not respond to client requests. They are driven by Web server events. For example, each time a read or write request event occurs, the ISAPI filter is notified. When more than one filter has been registered for the same event, they are called in sequential order. Higher priority filters will run before lower priority filters. If they have the same priority, they are run according to the order they were loaded. You can allow specific filters to be called in a higher order than others.

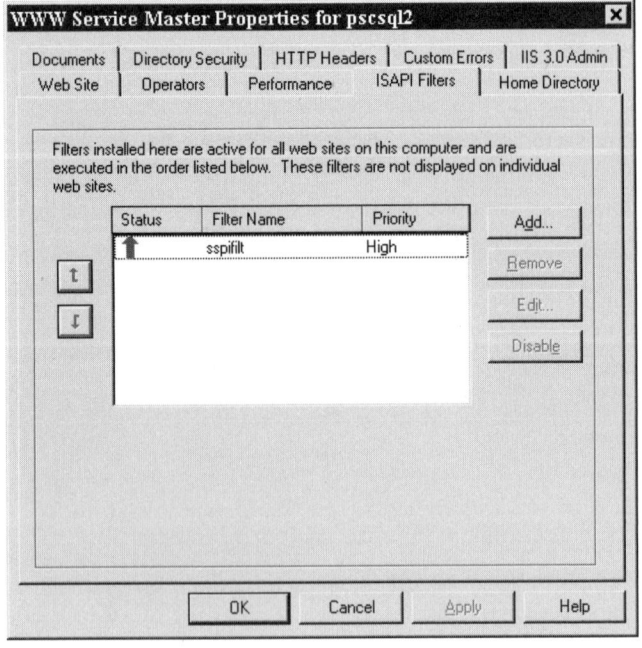

FIGURE 10-6

Configure specific ISAPI filters to be set at a higher priority than others

Home Directory Property Tab

The Home Directory property tab is used to change the home directory for your Web site, or modify the properties of your home directory. The default home directory is called wwwroot, and was created automatically when IIS 4.0 installed the WWW service. Since this constitutes the master properties of the server, you cannot change the home directory path here. It must be set on the properties of each individual Web site. The information that follows is taken from the Home Directory tab of the default Web site, and would pertain to any Web sites created under the *computername*.

Access Permissions

The Access Permissions properties appear when you are working with a local directory or a network share. Use these settings to determine the type of access allowed to a directory.

Content Control   The Content Control properties appear when you are working with a local directory or a network share.

Log Access   If you need to record visits to this directory, you would place a check in this box. Visits are recorded only if logging is enabled for this Web site. Logging is enabled by default.

Directory Browsing Allowed   Choose this check box to show a listing in hypertext of the files and subdirectories in the virtual directory, so the user can navigate through the directory structure. If a browser makes a request and does not include a specific filename, or a default document has not been named, a hypertext directory listing is automatically sent to the user. Most Administrators may decide to leave this option disabled because directory browsing will reveal your Web site structure to users.

Index This Directory   Choose this option to instruct the Microsoft Index Server to include this directory in a full-text index of your Web site. This will allow users to quickly search for words or phrases contained in documents on your site. This feature is only available in Windows NT Server.

FrontPage Web   If the FrontPage server extensions are installed on this server, this box will be active. Checking it allows the Web site to interact with the extensions.

Application Settings This setting is used to make a directory an application starting point. If your home site is set to be used as an application starting point, then every virtual directory and physical directory within your site can take part in the application. To make this directory an application starting point, click the Create button, type the name of the application in the Name text box, click the Configuration button to set the properties for the application, then click the OK button.

Run in Separate Memory Space You can use this option to run an application separately from the Web server. For instance, if an application that is currently running fails, select this check box to run the application in a process separate from the Web server process. Running in a separate memory space allows the Web to remain unaffected by the failure of the problem application.

Permissions Permissions were covered briefly at the beginning of this chapter. What follows is another brief overview of the proper security settings. The application permissions properties control whether applications can be run in this directory.

- **None** No programs or scripts can run in this directory.
- **Script** Allows applications mapped to a script engine to run in this directory without having to give the execute permission setting to applications. Use this setting for directories that contain ASP scripts, or other scripts.
- **Execute** This permission will grant any application to run in this directory, including applications mapped to script engines.

Mappings Property Sheet The Exact URL Entered Above redirects a virtual directory to the destination URL without adding any other portions of the original URL. You can use this option to redirect an entire virtual directory to one file.

A Directory Below This One This option will redirect a parent directory to a child directory. To redirect your home directory to a subdirectory named /mynewdir, type **/mynewdir** in the Redirect To text box and select this option. Without this option checked, the Web server would map the parent directory to itself.

A Permanent Redirection For This option will send the message "301 Permanent Redirect." to the client. Redirects are considered temporary. Figure 10-7 shows the Default Web Site Properties page.

FIGURE 10-7

This screen is
used to configure
a number of
options on the
Web server

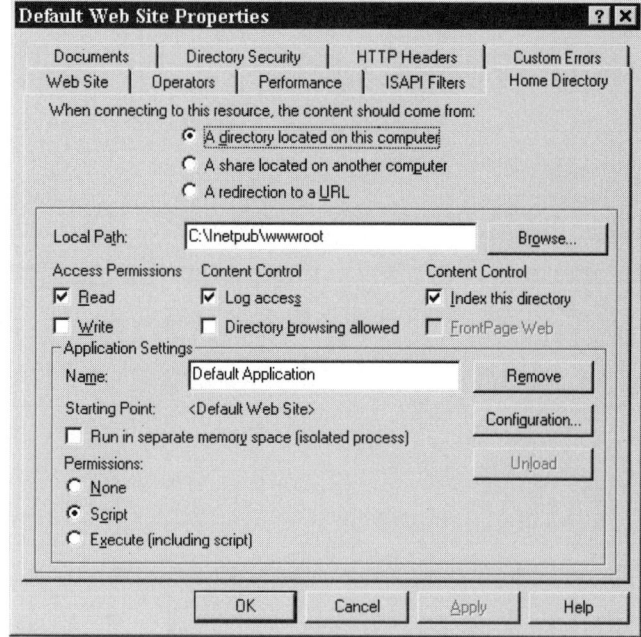

Figure 10-8 shows the properties page used to set the default document for your Web server. For example, if your default home page is named index.htm, you can add that as the default home page for your server. Clients accessing your site could type in www.mysite.com to access the site instead of www.mysite.com/index.htm. Default.htm and Default.asp are files installed during installation to give the default Web site a starting point. When browsing your default Web site, these pages should show up in your browser, testing and verifying that IIS is running properly.

The Directory Security page is used to allow anonymous access to your site, allow basic authentication, or use the Windows Challenge Response for authentication to the Web site. Also, you may restrict or grant access to your site by entering a specific IP address or domain name. You can also configure the Key Manager to create a Certificate Request. Figure 10-9 shows this property page.

By clicking the Edit button at the top of the dialog box, you can access the IUSR_Computername account and, if absolutely necessary, change the IUSR_Computername password. Do this only if you have read the 12-step paper issued by Microsoft that walks you through the process of changing the password. The IUSR_Computername password is originally set and encrypted by IIS on installation and should not be messed with.

FIGURE 10-8

Set your Home
directory page as
the default for
your Web server

FIGURE 10-8

Set your Home
directory page as
the default for
your Web server

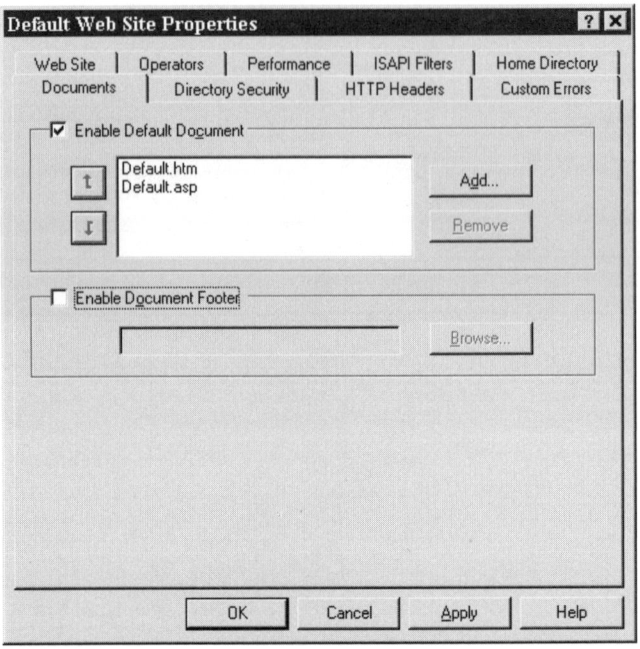

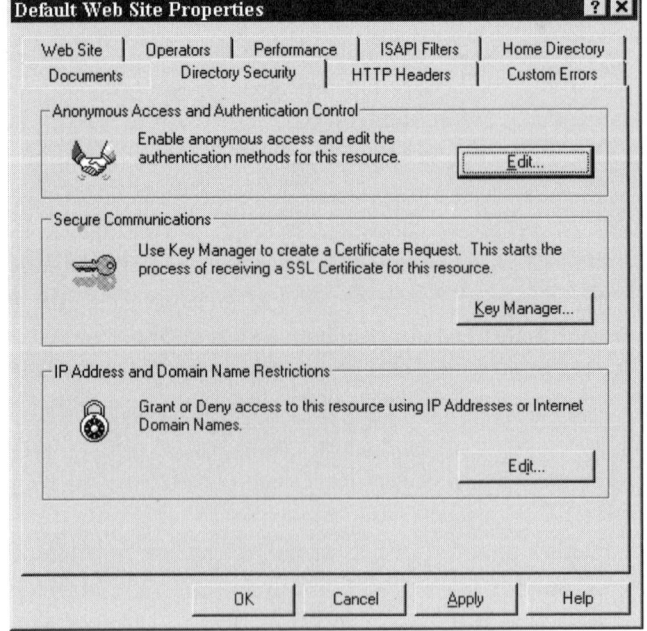

FIGURE 10-9

Set up your Web
site security using
this properties
page

The HTTP Headers properties page is used to set content expiration, add HTTP custom headers, edit content ratings, and configure additional Multipurpose Internet Mail Extensions (MIME) types for your Web server. MIME types are used by the Web server to map the filename extension to the file type. For example, to start Microsoft Excel in the browser, the browser would need to recognize the application vnd.ms-excel MIME type. Figure 10-10 shows this property page.

If you have time-sensitive information on the Web site, you can use the content expiration setting to set an expiration date on the page. When content expiration is enabled, the Web browser will compare the current date to that set on the content expiration page.

Figure 10-11 details the Custom Error page that allows Administrators to add custom errors to their Web site. The IIS 4.0 server comes with installed basic error messages for clients to use if they receive an error message while accessing your Web site. Administrators may want to create different error messages for clients accessing their Web server.

FIGURE 10-10

Use this page to configure ratings, content expiration, and HTTP headers

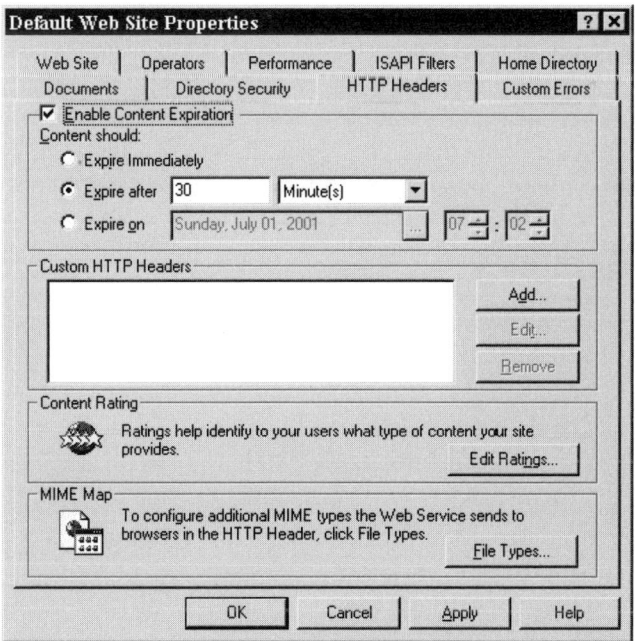

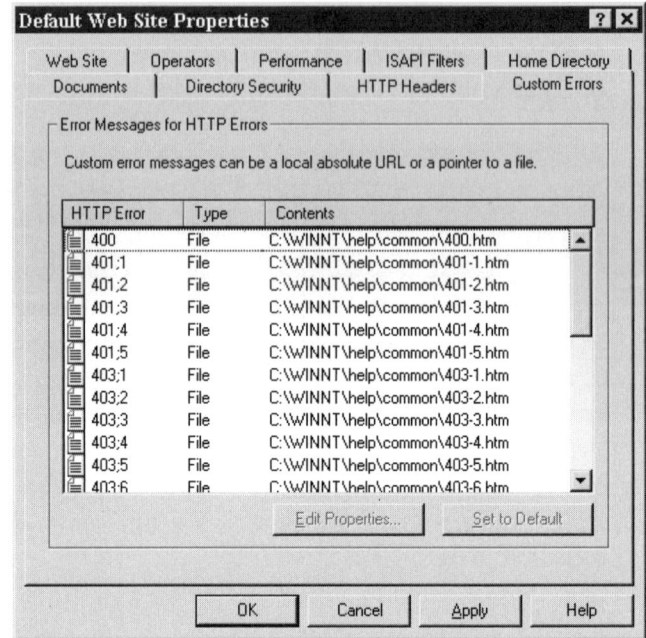

This section covered the basic configuration information for your Web site. Most of the property pages shown here also apply to tuning your virtual directories on the Web server. Remember that settings changed on the Master Properties page will affect settings in all current Web sites. To fine-tune individual sites, use the Property settings on each of the individual Web sites.

Hosting Multiple Web Sites

IIS 4.0 allows administrators to configure the hosting of multiple Web sites in three different ways. This section covers each in detail.

Unique IP Addressing

Using multiple IP addresses to host more than one Web site is called a Virtual Server. To bind an additional IP address to your network card, do the following: click Start | Settings | Control Panel | Network. Select the Protocols tab, choose TCP/IP, then click Properties. From the IP Address tab, click the Advanced button. In the IP Address section, click Add. Enter the additional IP address and subnet mask you want the machine to respond to, then click Add. Finish out the rest of the screens by clicking OK three times, then reboot the Web server. Next, you need to configure the DNS server to respond to the new hostname.com with the new IP address.

exam
ⓦatch

When using this setting, remember that All Unassigned refers to the IP addresses assigned to a server but not a specific site. The default Web site in IIS 4.0 uses all IP addresses not assigned to other sites. Only one site per server may be set up to use the unassigned option.

Using Host Headers

This method allows you to host multiple Web sites on a single IP address. Not all browsers can support the use of host header names. Please note that host headers only work with Web sites, not FTP sites. You must make certain you have your DNS properly set up to point to the IP address on the server. Host headers may not be employed while the Secure Sockets Layer (SSL) is being used, because HTTP requests using SSL are encrypted. Host Headers are part of the encrypted request and cannot be translated to the correct Web site.

Using TCP Port Numbers

By default, Web sites will use port 80. If you're using only one IP address, but need to host multiple sites, you can configure different ports on the sites. Your site would only need one IP address. Unless users know the port number you have set up for the Web site, they will not be able to access the site. To configure this setting, open ISM, expand the Web server name, right-click, then choose the Properties tab on the Web site you wish to change the port settings on. Under the Web Site tab, there is a setting for TCP Port. Enter the port information here. Click Apply, then click OK. The TCP port settings are now changed. Do not forget, however, that this setting does not support host names.

Performance Tuning

If you are using IIS 4.0 to run your Web site, you may want to follow the guidelines in this section to begin performance tuning on your Web server. Look at the following sections closely regarding monitoring the use of performance counters and how to tune your Web server and Web site.

Performance Monitoring

Performance Monitor or (Perfmon) is a tool that allows administrators to use counters to monitor their Web site. Performance Monitor can be started by choosing Start | Run, and then typing **Perfmon** in the Run box, or by choosing Start | Programs | Administrative Tools | Performance Monitor. To monitor the server for performance issues, you need to know which counters to add and what you need to monitor. Since we are working with IIS 4.0, we need to use specific monitoring counters to check for accuracy. See Table 10-4 to view the counters and values they should measure for good performance.

Make note that Table 10-4 does not give an exhaustive list of all resource counters available to Performance Monitor in your IIS 4.0 server. Now that you have the counters chosen for your baseline performance reading on the Web server, you need to add them to Performance Monitor (Perfmon). Once you open Perfmon, you may add counters by selecting View | Log | Edit | Add To Log. Select all the objects by simultaneously clicking the mouse and pressing the SHIFT key, then click Add | Done. To start the logging session, select Options | Log, then enter the name of your log file, specify an interval, and click Start.

Watch the site counters during peak hit-times while it is running. Do not run the Perfmon counter for an extended period, because it will create overhead on your Web server. After you have a good idea of the performance on your IIS 4.0, you

TABLE 10-4	Counter	Preferred Value
IIS 4.0 Performance Counters and Their Preferred Values	Memory Available: Bytes	Minimum of 5% of total memory.
	Memory: Page Faults/sec	If the number is consistently over 0, you need to add memory.
	Memory: Page Reads/sec	If you have high numbers, this indicates reads are going to the disk rather than cache.
	Physical: % Disk Time	If the number is consistently over 80%, you may have a memory leak.
	System: % Total Processor Time	A number consistently over 85% indicates a possible processor bottleneck.
	System: Processor Queue Length	If the queue consistently contains more than two orders, you may have a processor bottleneck.
	Web Service: Connections refused	Lower is better. If you're seeing high numbers, check your NIC or processor.
	Web Service: Maximum connections	If the number grows during testing, this could be a sign of congestion.

should be ready to tune the Web server for enhanced operation. A baseline is simply a snapshot of your system performance. When you are finished viewing the information and need to save it, click the Performance Logs And Alerts button, and either export the list to a .txt file or view the information using the New Taskpad view.

Load Testing Your IIS Server with the Web Capacity Analysis Tool

The Web Capacity Analysis Tool (WCAT) is used to measure capacity on a Web server. The tool may be found in the Windows Internet Information Resource Kit. WCAT is used to test the Web server under various stress tests. It enables you to get an idea of how your server will perform when running HTML or ASP. Several components make up the WCAT utility.

- **WCAT Controller**   The test controller for the software.
- **WCAT Server**   The Web server being tested.
- **WCAT Client**   The WCAT software installed on each client in the test (Wclient.exe is the executable to install on client machines).

Each WCAT client generates a load of approximately 200 users on the Web server. To configure WCAT, you need to place the WCAT controller on a separate server. When the test is run on the Web server, WCAT creates one or two files. They are named either .prf for performance results, or .log for a log file. You can execute WCAT with a -p switch to get performance results. WCAT creates the .prf files by running Perfmon on the counters you selected for testing.

on the
job

If Developers are creating applications, test them for performance using the WCAT tool. It's free and can place a decent load on the server to detect how a program will function.

Metabase Backup and Restore

IIS 4.0 does not use the registry, but some of the performance issues that occur when using IIS 4.0 can be fine-tuned through the registry. Instead of the IIS 4.0 settings being controlled by the registry, IIS uses what is called a metabase. The metabase is a database that contains all the IIS 4.0 properties. It can be backed up and restored using the IIS snap-in. To back up IIS 4.0 in the console, choose Console | Save. Then give the console a name, using the extension .msc. To restore a console that has been backed up, click Console | Open, then go to the path with the saved .msc file.

Tuning for ASP

If you are using Active Server Pages (ASP) on your Web server, you can enhance performance by making a couple of registry tweaks on the server. Remember, before you make any adjustments to the Web server registry, make sure you have a good backup of the server, the metabase, an ERD, and a backup copy of your registry in the event of an emergency. You can tune the ASP request pool and the thread pool to increase your IIS 4.0 performance. If you have a congested site, a large amount of queuing can occur because of the ASP Server CreateObject requests. Translated loosely, this means a component is getting requests at a faster rate than it can handle. The requests are placed in the IIS ASP queue, then processed in the order received. If the queuing lasts a long time, 20 to 25 seconds or more, the queue builds and the registry value RequestQueueMax hits its limit of 500 queues. Client number 499 will see an hourglass while waiting for his request to be serviced. However, if the client is number 500, then the RequestQueueMax will return the HTTP error "Server Too Busy" notification to client 500. You can tune the RequestQueueMax to a larger size by using the Regedt32 or Regedit tool. Click Start | Run | Regedt32, then go to the following registry key:

```
HKLM\SYSTEM\CurrentControlSet\Services\W3SVC\ASP\Parameters
```

Set this to a larger size. Monitor the performance after changing the setting, altering the setting until the performance has improved. If the queue is too small, the "Server Too Busy" error will appear to clients. If you set the RequestQueueMax value too high, then the page that clients are accessing will appear to hang up and be unreachable. To calculate the queue, use the Perfmon utility to see just where the queue spikes and goes down. For best performance, it should stay near the zero mark.

Tuning ProcessorThreadMax for Performance

The goal of tuning this counter is to get at least a 50% processor utilization rate on the Web server processor. Use the following counters with Performance Monitor to monitor processor performance:

- **ASP**   Requests/Second, Requests Rejected, Total Queue Length.
- **HttpService**   Connections/Second, Current anonymous users.
- **Processor**   %ProcessorTime (for each processor).

Any changes made to the registry will require a reboot. If you notice the queue going up and down, you may want to increase your threads. Change the ProcessorThreadMax to 20 from the default 10. After the reboot, view the Perfmon processors again and you should see an increase in performance. On the down side, if you do not see an improvement, it usually means there are additional problems that you haven't been aware of till now. If you're having difficulty with your home page, for example, you may want to have the page redesigned for better optimization. The goal when tuning this registry entry is for CPU utilization to stay below 70 percent, and the ProcessorThreadMax to stay below 100. Table 10-5 shows the effects on performance when a parameter is changed.

Tuning Memory on the Server

You can also adjust how your server handles memory. This is especially helpful if you are running an application server instead of a file server. Click Start | Settings | Control Panel | Network | Services. Right-click the Server service. Select Maximize Throughput For Network Applications. This prevents the NT Server from paging a portion of IIS 4.0 to the disk drive. Simply put, it will slow down the request handling on your server. Figure 10-12 shows this setting.

TABLE 10-5	Parameter	Settings	Performance Effect
Server Performance Tuning in IIS 4.0	Make NT Server an application server.	Right-click Network Neighborhood. Then click Properties	Services Tab, double-click Server service, then Select Network Services.	Tells Windows NT to cut down the file cache in a more aggressive manner.
	Disable logging when not needed.	Open ISM. Navigate to the Web site. Right-click the Web site. Choose Properties, then uncheck the Enable Logging box. Click OK.	Eases system strain, so performance improves on the Web server.
	If you use logging, write the log files to a striped partition attached to a controller that allows write-back caching.	Open ISM. Navigate to the Web site. Right-click the Web site. Choose Properties, then check the path to the striped partition. Click OK.	Log files in IIS 4.0 can become a source of bottlenecks. By placing them on a separate drive, you are isolating them from the server and improving disk drive performance.

FIGURE 10-12

Optimization on
a Windows NT
Server

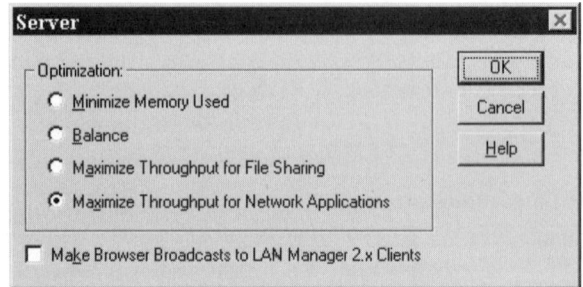

The other settings are Minimize Memory Used, Balance, and Maximize Throughput For File Sharing. The Minimize Memory Used should be selected when you have 10 or fewer connections, and need to minimize the memory used. The Balance option should be used if you have NetBEUI as the default software, or if you have up to 64 client connections concurrently. The Maximize Throughput For File Sharing setting will allocate the maximum amount of memory for file sharing applications. Use this setting if you have NT servers installed on a large network. The Make Browser Broadcasts To LAN Manager 2.x Clients option should only be used when you have LAN Manager 2.x clients on your network and you need that server to browse share resources located on this server.

EXERCISE 10-1

CertCam 10-1

Configuring a Virtual Directory for the Default Web Site

1. Open the Internet Services Manager.

2. Expand _computername to see the Default Web site.

3. Right-click the Default Web site, and from the pop-up menu, choose New | Virtual Directory.

4. In the Virtual Directory Wizard, choose Next.

5. A Virtual Directory needs an alias to identify it, so in the dialog box, type **Test**.

6. Choose Next to continue.

7. The Virtual Directory now needs a place to "live."

8. Choose the Browse button to point to the C:\Inetpub\wwwroot folder.

9. Select Next to continue.

10. Now set the permissions for the Virtual Directory. The default is Read and Scripts. Continue with the default permissions. Choose Next.

11. The Virtual Directory is now created. Click Finish.

12. Look in the ISM MMC and you will see the Test Virtual Directory under the Default Web Site.

The Windows NT Load Balancing Service

The Windows Load Balancing Service (WLBS) combines two or more Windows NT servers into a single virtual server called a cluster. To use the Windows Load Balancing Service you will need two or more Windows NT servers, 1.2MB of available disk space, a network interface card on each server, a dedicated IP address on each server, and an Ethernet or FDDI LAN connected by a switch or a hub. A copy of the application should also be installed on each server. The WLBS supports services such as:

- IIS 4.0 VPN
- Proxy
- Streaming Media

The Windows NT Load Balancing Service (WLBS) provides enhanced scalability, fault tolerance, controllability, and ease of use. WLBS supports multihomed servers as well as SSL and scaled performance of up to 32 nodes.

Fault Tolerance

The Windows NT Load Balancing Service automatically detects and recovers from a node failover. It will then rebalance the network load when the cluster set changes. The cluster workload automatically redistributes itself within ten seconds of the failure.

Manageability

When using the WLBS, you can block network access to certain ports. Optional single-host rules let you direct all client requests to a single host to further refine load balancing among different applications. If you need to monitor the WLBS, you can check the event log in Windows NT for any events. The NT event log monitors the WLBS for any cluster changes or issues that may arise. In the event you need to remotely administer the WLBS, it can be stopped, started, and controlled by any Windows NT Server on the network by using either the command prompt or scripts.

WLBS or MSCS

The WLBS allows clustering of up to 32 nodes, while the Microsoft Cluster Service (MSCS) allows clustering of 2 nodes. The WLBS should be used when you need high availability and scalability of TCP/IP services such as Web servers, streaming media, VPN, and proxy services. MSCS is a solution made for the availability of services such as SQL Server, Microsoft Exchange Server, and file and print services. If you have a high volume of data that is constantly changing, MSCS would be the best choice for fault tolerance.

Affinity Settings

The affinity setting when using the WLBS is simply a method specifying how client requests should be distributed to cluster members. The three affinity level settings are as follows:

- **None**   This method distributes client requests across cluster members based on the client's IP address and port. All client requests using this method are balanced across members, regardless of the source of the request.

- **Single**   Using this method directs multiple incoming client requests from the same IP address to the same cluster member.

- **Class C**   Using this method directs multiple incoming client requests from the same TCP/IP Class C address range to the same cluster member.

Table 10-6 shows the applications, affinity settings, and ports.
Take note of this table and use it for the port settings on your firewall.

Installation

The WLBS is installed as the standard Windows NT networking driver component. WLBS requires no hardware changes to install and run. It enables the clients to access the cluster with a single IP address, and WLBS continues to retain individual

	Application	Affinity Setting	Port
TABLE 10-6 Application Port Numbers and Affinity Settings	HTTP	80	None.
	HTTPS	443	Single or Class C.
	FTP	21 for control connection, 20 for data return connection	Single or Class C. Create two port rules to cover ports 20-21 and 1024-65, 535.
	TFTP	69	None. Create port rule covering port 69.
	SMTP	25	None.
	NetBIOS over TCP/IP	139	Single is preferred for maximum compatibility with server applications.

computer names on each node. Server applications do not need to be modified to run in a WLBS cluster. All operations, including recovery, require no human intervention. Computers can be taken offline for preventive maintenance without disturbing cluster operations. Installing the WLBS on a server is done by downloading the file from the Microsoft NT Download site. Once the file downloads, you will need to double-click the executable and extract it to a folder. Afterward, click Start | Settings | Control Panel. Choose Network | Adapters | Add | Have Disk, then navigate to the folder where you placed the extracted files. Check Yes to accept the EULA. Finish the installation procedure. Click Bindings | Reboot. Now, open up the WLBS from the Network Icon in the Control Panel and choose Properties. Figure 10-13 shows the Windows NT Load Balancing Setup properties page.

Failover with Windows Load Balancing Service

To configure WLBS for failover, do not add any port rules. Whichever host was set in the WLBS setup screen with the highest priority, which would be 1, will handle all incoming requests. If a node fails, then the node with the second highest priority will pick up and handle all connections.

Windows Load Balancing for TCP/IP

Select the WLBS Virtual NIC from the directory of adapters in the drop-down list. Enter the cluster IP address in the space for the IP address. This address corresponds to the primary cluster IP address you entered in the WLBS Setup dialog box. Enter

FIGURE 10-13

The Windows
NT Load
Balancing Setup
properties page

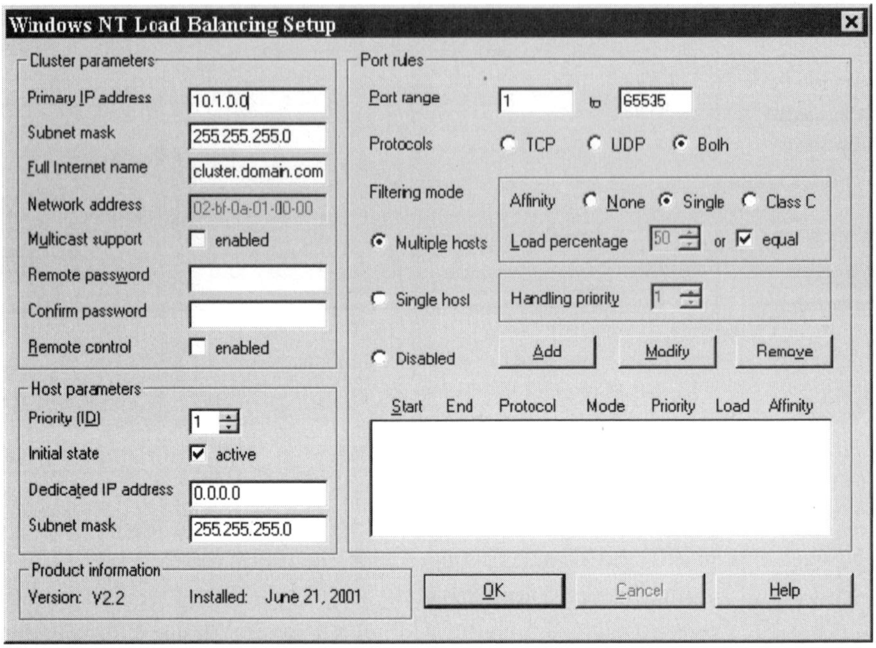

Windows NT Load Balancing Setup

Cluster parameters

Primary IP address: 10.1.0.0
Subnet mask: 255.255.255.0
Full Internet name: cluster.domain.com
Network address: 02-bf-0a-01-00-00
Multicast support: ☐ enabled
Remote password:
Confirm password:
Remote control: ☐ enabled

Host parameters
Priority (ID): 1
Initial state: ☑ active
Dedicated IP address: 0.0.0.0
Subnet mask: 255.255.255.0

Port rules
Port range: 1 to 65535
Protocols: ○ TCP ○ UDP ● Both
Filtering mode:
  Affinity: ○ None ● Single ○ Class C
  ● Multiple hosts Load percentage 50 or ☑ equal
  ○ Single host Handling priority 1
  ○ Disabled [Add] [Modify] [Remove]

Start End Protocol Mode Priority Load Affinity

Product information
Version: V2.2   Installed: June 21, 2001

[OK] [Cancel] [Help]

the subnet mask and leave the default gateway blank. The default gateway should only be assigned to the dedicated adapter so that it handles the responses to requests accepted by the virtual adapter. When running a multihomed server, you may want to add additional IP addresses by clicking the advanced button, then adding additional IP addresses. Select the WINS Address tab and fill in the information. Click the OK button. Allow the components to rebind, then reboot the server.

The Windows Load Balancing Service and PPTP

You can configure the WLBS to provide load balancing and/or failover for PPTP servers. Each Windows Load Balancing Service must have two network interface cards for this to perform correctly. Set one of the network cards to respond to the WLBS IP address, and the other to respond to the dedicated IP address on each server. You may want to disable the Multicast support, because one card is set to handle cluster loads. This will enhance the performance of the WLBS.

exam
Watch

Before implementing this, remember that because of a VPN limitation, each adapter IP address must belong in a different Class C address.

The WLBS bindings need to be set for use with multiple network cards. Click Start | Settings | Control Panel, then double-click Network, choose Bindings, then click Show Bindings For, and Select All Protocols. Figure 10-14 shows the bindings for the Network Service.

Click the plus sign by each protocol to see the adapters to which it is bound. Enable the adapter binding from the WLBS Driver to the WLBS Virtual NIC adapter. Do this by selecting the adapter and clicking the Enable button. Enable the binding from the WLBS Driver to the network adapter that will handle cluster traffic. Next, you need to disable the binding from the WLBS Driver to any other adapters installed on the server. You can disable the binding on other adapters by selecting the disable button. Enable the binding from the TCP/IP Protocol to the WLBS Virtual Network card. Enable the binding from the TCP/IP Protocol to the network adapter or adapters that will handle network traffic other than the cluster traffic. Disable the binding from the TCP/IP Protocol to the cluster adapter. Move the WLBS Virtual Network Card down so it is below the dedicated adapter in the TCP/IP list of adapters. Enable the binding from the WINS Client to the WLBS Virtual Network Card. Enable the binding from the WINS Client to the dedicated

FIGURE 10-14

Binding settings
for the Windows
Load Balancing
Service

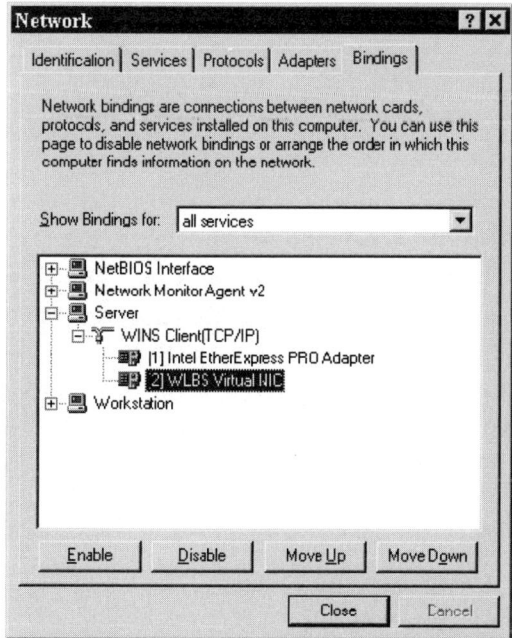

adapter or adapters. Disable the binding from the WINS Client to the cluster adapter. Move the WLBS Virtual Network Card adapter down so it is below the dedicated adapter in the WINS Client list of adapters. Disable the bindings from all other protocols to the cluster adapter. Click the close button and allow the components to rebind. The system will need to reboot if this process completes successfully. If the process does not complete successfully, correct any binding problems that occurred. Otherwise, you may not be able to log in to the network after rebooting.

CERTIFICATION OBJECTIVE 10.02

Configuring and Troubleshooting Remote Access Service and Routing and Remote Access Service

Remote Access Service (RAS) gives clients the ability to connect remotely to an NT Server by either VPN or dial-in. Once you have connected to the network via the VPN or dial-in connection, you can do anything on the network that could be done if you were physically at the site, short of inserting a floppy disk. If you are an NT Administrator and need to access the server remotely to perform administrative tasks, this is a helpful tool.

Installing Remote Access Service

You must have a modem installed and configured on the server before beginning the installation of RAS. Also, you should have, at minimum, SP4 installed on the NT 4.0 Server. After installing your modem, go to the Control Panel and choose Open Network | Services. Click Add. When the Select Network Service box opens, choose Remote Access Service from the Network Service window and click OK. Have your Windows NT CD available because you will be prompted to load the CD into the drive unless you have your installation files on a folder on the hard drive. Browse to the installation folder path and click OK. After the files have been installed, you should see the Add RAS device.

After the RAS device has been added, the Remote Access Setup screen should appear (as shown in Figure 10-15).

FIGURE 10-15

The Remote
Access Setup
screen

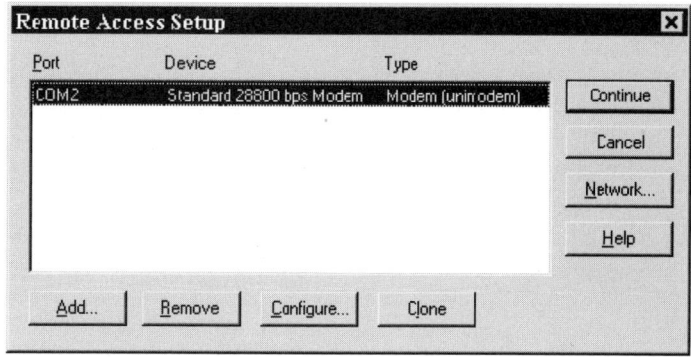

Configuring the RAS Server

Use the Remote Access Setup screen and click the Configure button. The Configure Port Usage dialog box should appear, like that shown in Figure 10-16. This window allows you to choose how your RAS will be used. By default, it is set to Receive Calls Only. Unless you intend to use RAS for other types of services, leave it set to the default, Receive Calls Only. Click the OK button to close the window.

Now it is time to choose how RAS will work with your Network. Click the Network button to see the Network Configuration window (shown in Figure 10-17).

For this example, we will leave the setting to the TCP/IP default. Next, click the Configure button. You should now see the box shown in Figure 10-18

The Allow Remote TCP/IP Clients To Access section of this window controls what you are allowing remote clients to access on the network. A client has access to the entire network, by default. As long as you have the user account for the client security settings in check, you should be all right. You can limit the client to have access to only the server they are connecting to by selecting the setting This Computer Only.

FIGURE 10-16

Configuring the
port usage in RAS

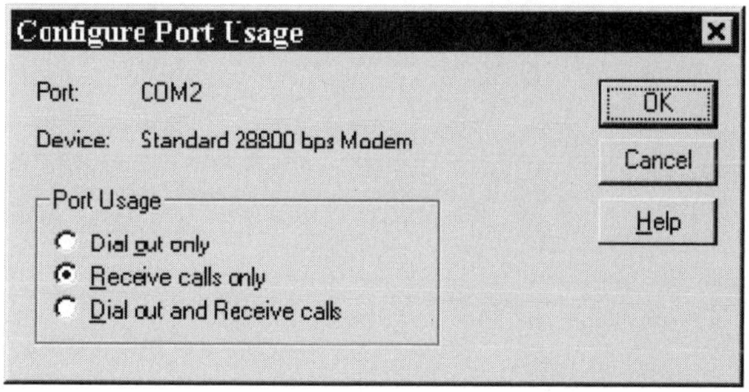

FIGURE 10-17

Configuring RAS
to work with
your network

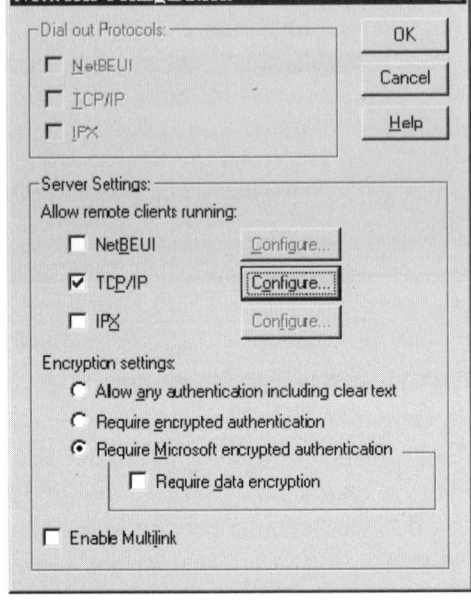

FIGURE 10-18

Configuration
Properties for
TCP/IP in
Remote Access
Service

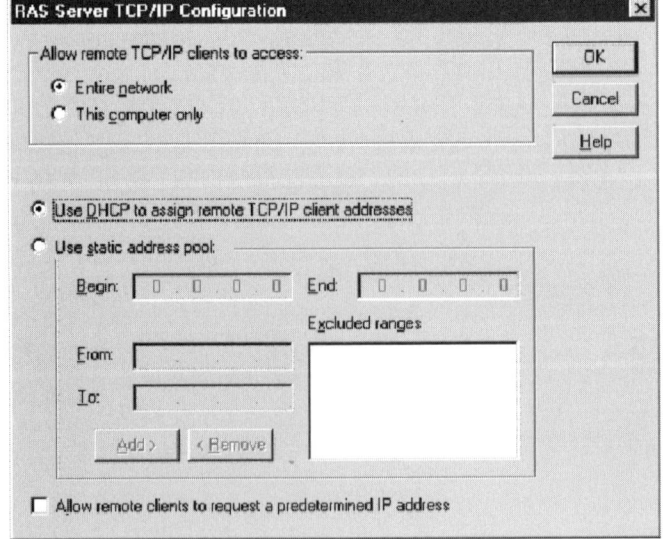

Notice in the Network Configuration window that the Dial Out Protocols section is unavailable. This is because you have chosen the default setting and not enabled the dial out option on the configuration menu. If you later wish to enable dial out sessions, you will need to return to the Network Configuration windows and reconfigure this section.

Next, set up an IP address to be used by inbound clients. By default, inbound RAS clients look for an available RAS server on the network to obtain IP addresses. If this default setting is correct for your configuration, do not change the option for inbound clients to This Computer Only, unless DHCP is also running on the RAS Server. You may, however, want to establish a pool of static IP addresses instead of using DHCP. The upside of this is that you can monitor static IP addresses closely for security purposes. To configure this setting, select the Use Static Address Pool option and enter a beginning and ending address. Click OK when you are finished, and the Network Configuration windows will appear. If you plan to use security with RAS, you can choose an Encryption method. By default, the option chosen is Require Microsoft Encrypted Authentication. Make note that if this option is chosen and you are using Unix, Linux, or a MAC to access this server, you will not be able to connect via RAS. Only Microsoft operating systems are capable of logging on with this setting. Instead, if you are using a non-Microsoft machine to access the server, choose the Allow Any Authentication Including Clear Text option. Click OK when you are finished, and the Network Properties sheet will appear. You can close this window by clicking the Close button. Make sure you allow Windows NT to update the bindings, and that you reboot the server before testing the connection.

Troubleshooting Remote Access Service

This section briefly explains some troubleshooting techniques when dealing with RAS. If you are having problems, such as clients being disconnected or not being able to connect to the RAS server and so on, see the following Scenario & Solution for some common fixes.

SCENARIO & SOLUTION

RAS Error	Fix
Error 633: Port is already in use or not configured for Remote Access dial out.	This occurs if you installed RAS on a Windows NT 3.51 server before Windows NT 4.0. Remove the unimodem driver and reinstall with a current Windows NT 4.0 driver.
Error 640: A NetBIOS error has occurred.	The modem cannot negotiate a connection at a higher speed. Set the modem speed lower on the client computer.
Error 692: Hardware failure in port or attached device.	If a client receives this message, it means the modem is not working properly. Check the modem and make certain it is functioning.
Event ID 20091 Error in event log when client tries to access RAS.	Either you are using DHCP and have not created an active scope with the same subnet address as the RAS client, or you have no DHCP server on your network. The two fixes include correcting the scope properties or installing DHCP on the server.
RAS clients cannot browse the server with IPX only.	This is by design. To resolve this, install NetBEUI on the client machine.

The next Scenario & Solution shows the most frequent error notices received when using RAS. Be sure to carry out the most common tasks first. For instance: Does the modem have a dial tone? Are the drivers installed correctly? Are the clients using the proper steps to connect via RAS? If necessary, you can review more information regarding troubleshooting RAS at the Microsoft Web site.

SCENARIO & SOLUTION

Event Viewer error 7022 when using RAS on Server with Exchange 5.5 installed.	Reenable the incoming and outgoing dial access by selecting RAS | Network | Control Applet. In the Control Panel, choose Services, select RAS Connection Manager, setting it to start up as automatic, and RAS Access Server, also setting it to start up as automatic.
Your modem is not supported by RAS.	Supports unimodem settings.

Routing and Remote Access Service

The Routing and Remote Access Service enables routing over IP and IPX networks by connecting local area and wide area networks. It connects LANs or WANs without the use of other hardware. Internet Protocol (IP) communicates across any type of interconnected network. NT Administrators may use the RRAS Admin tool to administer both RRAS and RAS services. This type of routing is suited for smaller offices, not for larger more robust organizations. Before installing Routing and Remote Access Service in Windows NT, you need to make certain you have the minimum requirements.

- Windows NT 4.0 plus Service Pack 4 or greater
- A 486 50MHz or higher CPU, or a RISC-based CPU, such as the Digital Alpha Systems
- One or more network adapter cards, WAN cards, or modems
- VGA, or higher resolution, monitor
- One or more hard disks with 40MB minimum free disk space on the partition that will contain the Routing and Remote Access Service system files
- 16MB RAM minimum

Before you begin to set up Routing and Remote Access Service, you must install RAS on your server. Once this has been completed, you are ready to configure the service. To install RRAS, you can download it from the Microsoft Web site. After installing the RRAS service, you can open the RRAS Admin program by choosing Start | Programs | Administrative Tools | Router And Remote Admin. We will discuss how to set up demand dial routing next. For this to function properly, you must select the demand dial routing option during setup. You will need to either reinstall RRAS or open the Control Panel, select Services, choose the Routing And Remote Access Service, and select Update.

exam
Ⓦatch

You may need to go to the Control Panel, choose the Services option, select the Routing And Remote Access Service, and select the Automatic button to have the service start automatically in the future.

Protocols Supported in RRAS

RIP and OSPF are IP routing protocols included with Routing and Remote Access Service. RRAS also supports third-party protocols, such as Border Gateway Protocol (BGP). Table 10-7 provides a description of the protocols supported by RRAS.

Check to make certain whatever device you're using to set up demand dial connections is configured for the demand dial service. Go to the Control Panel, choose Network | Services | Routing And Remote Access Service. Click Properties. In the Remote Access Setup dialog box, select the device that will be used for demand dial connections. Click Configure. Make certain the Ensure Dial Out And Receive Calls As A Demand Dial Router has been selected.

Creating a RAS Pool of IP Addresses

A RRAS server that is using demand dial routing must have its own address pool it uses to pull and assign IP addresses from. You can create a static pool or configure the service to obtain a range of addresses from DHCP. The addresses to be assigned should all be unique and not used by any other resource.

Troubleshooting Checklist

See Table 10-8 for some basic router configuration issues that may arise when using RRAS.

This section gave you an overview of RAS and RRAS in Windows NT 4.0. The Remote Access Service is extremely useful for accessing the network from a client machine, while the Routing and Remote Access Service is handy for enabling Windows NT to act as a router. Though RRAS is not intended for large networks, it is a useful tool for connecting smaller WANS or LANS to each other.

TABLE 10-7	Supported by RRAS	Description
RRAS Supported Protocols	RIP	Routing Internet Protocol. IGP supplied with Unix BSD systems. Uses a hop count for a routing metric.
	OSPF	Open Shortest Path First. IGP Protocol RIP's successor. Uses least cost routing, load balancing, and multipath routing.
	BGP	Border Gateway Protocol. Supports CIDR (classless interdomain routing), and uses route aggregation to reduce the routing table sizes.

TABLE 10-8	Question	Answer
Basic Router Configuration Issues	Is the RRAS service running?	If it is stopped and will not start, check the Event Viewer for error messages.
	Is the router receiving routes?	In the RRAS Admin tool, choose the Static Routes option under IP or IPX routing protocol. Click view routing table on the tool menu.
	Are the protocols in use enabled on each interface?	Use the RRAS Admin tool, expand IP or IPX routing, select the protocol and see which interfaces are using the protocol.
	Are you running OSPF?	If yes, use the RRAS Admin tool, expand IP or IPX routing, select the OSPF protocol, right-click, choose configure interface, select the General tab, confirm the Enable OSPF On This Interface box is checked.
	Is the default gateway configured correctly?	Use the ipconfig command at the prompt to ensure the default gateway is a router on a subnet that the computer running Windows NT is connected to.
	More than one default gateway?	You can only use one default gateway per computer.

EXERCISE 10-2

CertCam 10-2

Troubleshooting RAS

When you try and dial out using RAS, you get an Error 720: Cannot connect the phonebook entry. To correct this known problem, do the following:

1. Go to the Network Icon in the Control Panel (Start | Settings | Control Panel), and double-click the Network Icon.

2. Under the Installed Network Software, click Remote Access Service.

3. Next, click Configure, then select Configure again.

4. Under Port Usage, click either Dial Out Only, or Dial Out And Receive Calls.

5. Next, click OK, click Continue, then click OK again.

6. Click Restart Now to restart the computer so the settings can take effect.

This problem can occur if RAS is configured to receive calls only. To use RAS to dial out and use a phone book entry, it must be configured to either dial out, or dial out and receive calls.

Backing up and Restoring the RRAS Configuration

After the RRAS has been configured, you should back it up in the event you have a problem. The Routing and Remote Access Server Administrator allows you to back up and restore the configuration. The RRAS Admin tool may be found under Administrative Tools in Windows NT Server. Click Start | Programs | Administrative Tools | Routing And Remote Access Server Admin. The RRAS Admin utility can be seen in Figure 10-19.

This tool is straightforward. It can be used to back up and restore RRAS as well as connect to the domain. Under the Tools menu there is an option to telnet into a server.

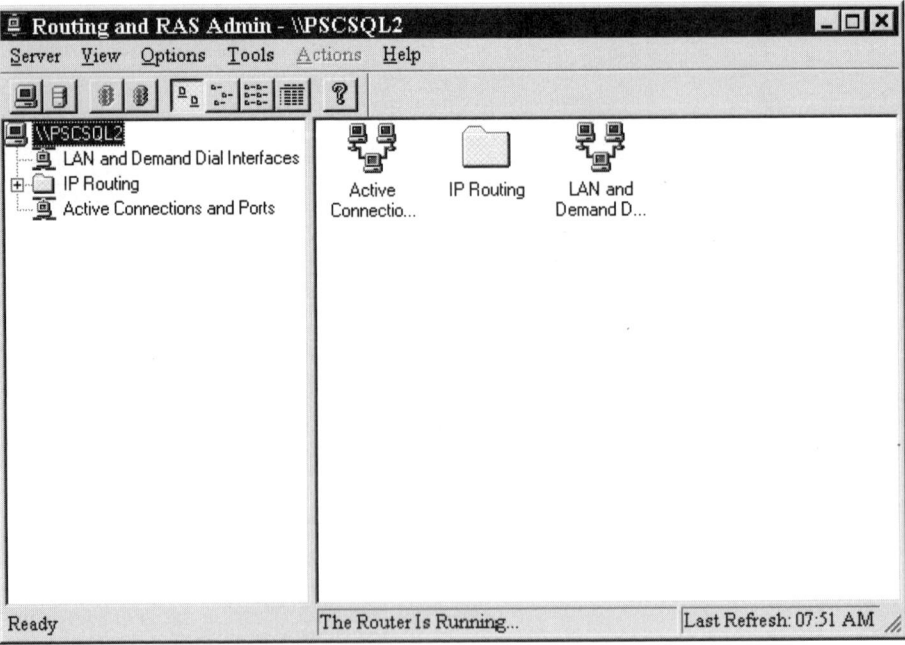

FIGURE 10-19

The Routing and Remote Access Administration tool

Backing up the Routing and Remote Access Service

To use the RRAS Admin utility to back up the RRAS configuration, just select the server and save the configuration. The option will become available for you to save the configuration file in a folder on the hard disk or you may save it to a floppy disk for further safekeeping. Be sure not to forget to update the saved configuration file if you make configuration changes. The utility may also be used to restore the RRAS service.

Restoring the Routing and Remote Access Service

The RRAS Admin utility also restores configuration files. Depending on where you saved the configuration file, you can browse and open the .mpr file. One has been created on this server named "test" (as shown in Figure 10-20). Choose the file and click open. This should open the saved file and restore the RRAS configuration.

This section covered using the RRAS Administration utility. Next, we'll learn how to install and configure the Internet Authentication Service.

Internet Authentication Service

The Internet Authentication Service (IAS) is an authentication and registration service that is integrated into Windows NT security when it's installed. IAS works by checking the user's identity when they log in to the system against a user account database. Because IAS is integrated into the Microsoft NT 4.0 security system, it permits NT Administrators to control which parts of the network the clients will access based on their existing NT account permissions. IAS allows NT administrators to track usage time for authenticated users by employing the Remote Authentication Dial-In User Server protocol, also known as RADIUS. IAS provides authentication,

FIGURE 10-20

Restoring the RRAS configuration file

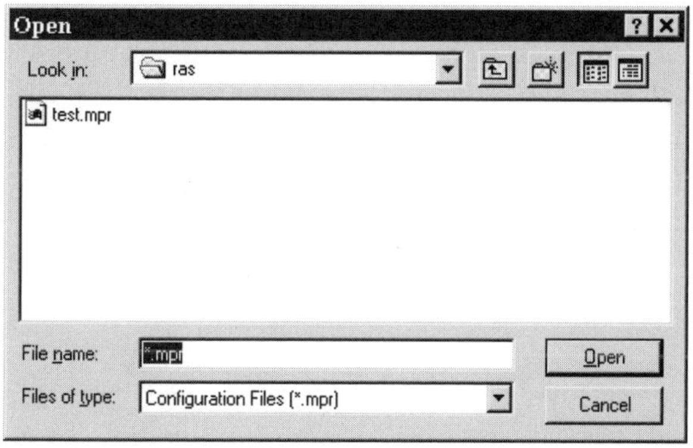

checks authorization, and provides accounting for clients attempting to connect to the domain. RADIUS supports three authentication methods. These methods and their descriptions are listed in Table 10-9.

RADIUS authentication identifies a remote user by checking the clients' credentials against a client account database. RADIUS authorization can be configured to restrict authenticated clients access to predetermined network services for added network security. The accounting method that RADIUS uses records the amount of network resources a remote client uses during a connected session. This information may be used in a corporate environment to bill different departments for usage. RADIUS may be used without accounting. Point-to-Point Tunneling Protocol (PPTP) encapsulates PPP protocol packets by using the MS-CHAP and Microsoft Point-to-Point Protocol.

Shared Secrets

A shared secret is a text string shared between an IAS RADIUS server and either clients or other servers that are connected to it. These servers include the Network access server (NAS), other RADIUS servers and proxies, and the authentication providers, which are often the corporate clients themselves. It is characterized as clear text in the IAS Clients file.

TABLE 10-9	Authentication Method	Description
Authentication Methods and Descriptions	Password Authentication Protocol (PAP)	Uses the two-way handshake method. Because passwords are being sent in clear, unencrypted text this is not a very secure method.
	Challenge Handshake Authentication Protocol (CHAP)	The server sends a randomly generated challenge string to the client, along with the host name. The client takes the host name to look up an appropriate key, encrypts the key information with the challenge, and sends it back to the server. The server performs the same steps, and if all the information matches, authentication is permitted.
	Microsoft(MS-CHAP)	The three-way handshake method is used. Does not require a plain text password. This is the most secure encryption algorithm supported by Windows NT. MS-CHAP corresponds to the Require Microsoft Encrypted Authentication encryption setting for the RAS server.

SCENARIO & SOLUTION

What type of security should I use with RADIUS?	
Need strong security?	MS-CHAP
Tough security not needed?	PPP
Medium security needed?	CHAP

Checklist for Installing Internet Authentication Service

To install the Internet Authentication Service, you need to meet the following requirements:

- Windows NT SP3, Pentium processor or higher
- 32MB of RAM or higher
- 27MB of hard disk space for installation
- 10MB of hard disk space for runtime at minimum
- Make certain the IAS server is either a member of, or in a trust relationship with, the Windows NT domain that will be authenticating the dial-in for clients.

Installing Internet Authentication Services

Now you can run the Windows NT 4.0 Option Pack, including the IAS components. The IAS components consist of the following tools:

- **Authentication Service**   This service is used to establish a connection for dial-in user authentication.
- **Microsoft Management Console (MMC) Extension**   The Microsoft Management Console (MMC) lets you manage the Internet Information Server and authentication service from the MMC window.

on the job   *If for some reason you have to reinstall the Internet Authentication Service, back up the _Adminui.mdb before installing a new copy.*

Start the NT Option Pack CD. If you do not have the CD, you may download the option pack from the Microsoft Web site. Choose the custom installation. If you already have the NT Option Pack installed, click the Add/Remove button. Choose the Select components box, click Internet Connection Services for RAS, click Show subcomponents, select the Microsoft Internet Authentication Services, click OK, then restart the server when the setup has been completed.

Configuring Internet Authentication Services

To view the Internet Authentication Service properties, click Start | Programs | Windows NT 4.0 Option Pack. Choose Internet Information Server | Internet Service Manager. Double-click Console Root on the left, double-click IIS, and double-click your computer name. The tree expands and shows RADIUS or IAS. Right-click RADIUS, select Properties, click the Service tab, then use the Maximum threads box to enter the maximum number of authentication requests that will be processed concurrently. The value must be between 1 and 63. If the RADIUS UDP ports are different from the default, enter the port settings in the Authentication and Accounting boxes. Select one or more check boxes under Capture To NT Event Log to capture packet traffic processed by IAS. If you need to capture packets that are causing trouble, click Malformed Or Invalid Packets. You must be logged on as a user with administrative privileges to administer IAS using this method.

Registering Clients to Use the Internet Authentication Service   The Clients tab allows administrators to add, remove, or edit the Internet addresses, DNS names, and shared secrets of the clients using this IAS server. To register clients on this server, select the Clients tab, then click Add. Click IP Address or DNS Name and enter the information. Next, enter the shared secret for the client in the Password (shared secret) box.

exam
ⓦatch

Remember, shared secrets (a.k.a. passwords) are case-sensitive.

Using the Logging Service   Use the Logging tab to turn off logging on RADIUS accounting packets. You may also specify how often you need to use logging and where you will store the log files. To configure the logging service, click the Logging tab, select the Enable accounting log box, select the Automatically Open New Log check box, and click the interval you wish to use. If you expect a small amount of activity, select Weekly or Monthly. If the server will experience heavy usage, choose the Daily option.

Troubleshooting IAS Internet Authentication Services Error Messages   Table 10-10 shows some common error messages and their meaning when using IAS. For more documentation, please see the Microsoft Web site at www.microsoft.com.

TABLE 10-10	Error Message	Definition	Solution
Common IAS Error Messages and Their Solutions	A password is required... Please enter a password... for the servers that will communicate with IAS.	The shared secret (passwords) from the client must match the RADIUS.	Check the passwords.
	The log file directory is invalid. Please enter a valid log file directory.	IAS does not create a log file directory if you specify a nonexistent directory.	Browse to an existing directory.
	Service property changes have been applied and will take effect the next time the authentication service is started.	The configuration changes to the IAS database have been saved, but the files that the IAS reads are not yet updated.	Stop and restart the IAS service in the Control Panel under services.

Use Table 10-10 to assist you with any IAS error messages and their solutions. If you need additional information, visit the Microsoft Web site at http://www .microsoft.com.

VPN Access

You have to install PPTP before your RAS server can accept incoming traffic. To install PPTP go to the Control Panel, choose Network | Protocols, then click Add. Choose Point-to-Point Tunneling Protocol, as shown in Figure 10-21. Use the PPTP Configuration box and enter the number of VPN connections you want to support. RAS can support up to 256 connections. You can enter more afterward if you need to.

Next, you will be prompted by the PPTP installation to enter your VPN devices to your RAS server. Select the devices from the RAS Capable Devices list and click OK to add the device to the RAS configuration. Configure each device for dial-in only since they will be handling inbound PPTP connections only.

If you are using security encryption, you need to configure this next. In the Remote Access Setup dialog box, click Network and select Require Microsoft encrypted authentication, and require data encryption.

on the job

Whatever you change here affects all connections to the RAS server, including dial-up.

You can enable PPTP filtering on the RAS Server to block non-PPTP packets from the server if your connection to the Internet is not that secure. Go to the

Installing PPTP
protocol for
VPN access

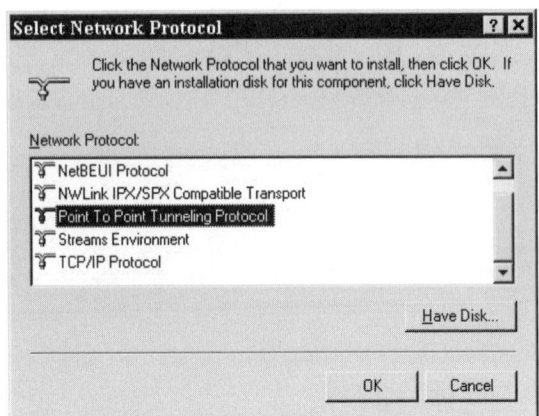

Control Panel, select Network | Protocols | TCP/IP | Advanced and select the check
box Enable PPTP Filtering for the network adapter connected to the Internet. You
need PPTP filtering only for direct connections to the Internet; filtering non-PPTP
packets does not work with dial-up adapters. PING and Tracert will not work on
the RAS Server either if this is enabled. If you are using IPX or NetBEUI, you have
completed the setup. If you are using TCP/IP, you need to do one more thing:
enable IP forwarding on the RAS Server. Open the Control Panel, select Network |
TCP/IP | Properties. Choose the Routing tab, and select Enable IP Forwarding.

Installing VPN to Windows NT Workstation

Once the Windows NT server has been configured with PPTP, you can add the
VPN client on an NT workstation. Click Start | Settings | Control Panel | Network |
Protocols | Add. Choose the Point-to-Point Tunneling Protocol, click OK, and
insert the Windows NT Workstation CD, if prompted. Select the number of virtual
private networks and click OK. The RAS Setup dialog box will be shown. Click
Add, select "VPN1 – RASPPTPM", and click OK. Click Continue on the RAS
dialog box, click the Close button, and reboot the computer. After the server has
been rebooted, start the Dial-Up Networking software and double-click New.
Under the device listing, select the Microsoft VPN Adapter, enter the IP address or
host name of the VPN server under the Phone Number box. To make a connection,
dial into the Internet, then select the VPN connection and enter a username,
password, and you should be connected.

on the
job

Use the User Manager in Windows NT to give clients dial-in rights to the server.

SCENARIO & SOLUTION

Can a Windows 98 client participate in a VPN connection?	Yes. Windows 98 allows for VPN connections through properties added in the Network Configuration dialog box.
Can you enable PPTP filtering on a RAS Server to block non-PPTP packets?	Yes, select the check box Enable PPTP Filtering for the network adapter that is connected to the Internet.
IAS is giving you logging errors. How can you correct this problem?	Reconfigure the path to the directory where the log files are stored.

Installing VPN on a Windows 98 Client

To install the VPN client on Windows 98, choose Start | Settings | Control Panel. Select the Configuration tab, click Add, select Adapter, click Add. Under Manufacturers, select Microsoft and choose Microsoft Virtual Private Networking Adapter in the Network Adapters box. Click OK. Insert the Windows 98 CD if asked, then reboot the machine. The last step is to create a new dial-up connection using the dial-up connection under My Computer. Click My Computer on the desktop, choose Dial Up Networking, select the Microsoft VPN Adapter, click Next, and enter the host name or IP address of the VPN server. To make a connection, dial into the Internet, then double-click the VPN connection, enter a username and password.

CERTIFICATION SUMMARY

This chapter covered the basics for troubleshooting and configuring IIS 4.0, Remote Access Service, Routing and Remote Access Service, and the Internet Authentication Service. It also explained how to use the Performance Counter to monitor Web server performance on the site. The WCAT tool should allow you to stress test your site before it is deployed.

RAS and RRAS are important concepts to understand in today's Laptop world. More and more companies are using Remote Access to retrieve information remotely. Read everything you can find on RAS and RRAS, and review the details presented in this chapter.

IAS, VPN connections are fast becoming the way we interact and communicate over today's networks. Understand the different types of connections available to you in NT Server, IIS, and IAS.

✓ TWO-MINUTE DRILL

Configuring, Managing, and Troubleshooting Microsoft IIS on the Server

❏ The NT File System, or NTFS, is the front line of protection for an IIS 4.0 Web server. IIS 4.0 is intended for use with Windows NT 4.0's security system. NTFS offers customizable security, whereas its predecessor, the File Allocation Table (FAT) system, did not.

❏ You can use the Master Properties settings to configure the master properties of your IIS server and any sites that have already been made. These are the master properties, not the individual properties. Each individual Web site will have its own individual properties that you can configure after the master properties are set in place.

❏ The Windows Load Balancing Service (WLBS) combines two or more Windows NT servers into a single virtual server called a cluster.

❏ To use the Windows Load Balancing Service you will need two or more Windows NT Servers, 1.2MB of available disk space, a network interface card on each server, a dedicated IP address on each server, and an Ethernet or FDDI LAN connected by a switch or a hub.

❏ The WLBS allows clustering of up to 32 nodes, while Microsoft Cluster Service (MSCS) allows clustering of 2 nodes.

❏ The WLBS should be used when you need high availability and scalability of TCP/IP services, such as Web servers, streaming media, VPN, and proxy services. MSCS is a solution made for the availability of services, such as SQL Server, Microsoft Exchange Server, and file and print services.

Configuring and Troubleshooting Remote Access Service and Routing and Remote Access Service

❑ Remote Access Service (RAS) lets clients connect remotely to an NT Server by either VPN or dial-in.

❑ The Routing and Remote Access Service (RRAS) enables routing over IP and IPX networks by connecting local area or wide area networks. It connects LANs and WANs without the use of other hardware.

❑ RIP and OSPF are IP routing protocols included with Routing and Remote Access Service. RRAS also supports third-party protocols such as Border Gateway Protocol (BGP).

❑ The Routing and Remote Access Server Administrator will allow you to back up and restore your configuration using the RRAS Admin tool.

❑ The Internet Authentication Service (IAS) is an authentication and registration service integrated into Windows NT security when it's installed. IAS works by checking the user's identity when they log in to the system against a user account database.

SELF TEST

The following questions will help you measure your understanding of the material presented in this chapter. Read all the choices carefully, as there may be more than one correct answer. Choose all correct answers for each question.

Configuring, Managing, and Troubleshooting Microsoft IIS on the Server

1. Your company needs to host several Web sites on a single IIS 4.0 Web server. How can this be done? (Choose all that apply.)

   A. By using Host Headers

   B. By using various TCP ports

   C. By using multiple IP addresses

   D. By installing numerous copies of IIS 4.0 on other servers

2. You need to enable bandwidth throttling on a virtual directory. How can this be accomplished?

   A. Open ISM and right-click the Web site. Select the Performance tab, click the Enable Bandwidth Throttling button, choose Apply, and click OK.

   B. Open ISM and right-click the Web site. Select the Performance tab. Tune your Web site performance based on the number of hits expected per day, choose Apply, then click OK.

   C. Open ISM and expand the Web site. Right-click the virtual directory that needs tuning. Select the Performance tab, click the Enable Bandwidth Throttling button, choose Apply, and click OK.

   D. Open ISM and expand the Web site. Right-click the virtual directory that needs tuning. Select the Performance tab, tune your Web site performance based on the number of hits expected per day, choose Apply, and click OK.

3. If you are running ASP pages and FTP on your IIS 4.0 Web server, which setup option should you select? (Choose all that apply.)

   A. Custom

   B. Maximum

   C. Minimum

   D. Typical

4. What option can you use to tune your IIS 4.0 server for enhanced memory when it comes to application performance?

   A. Maximize Throughput For File Sharing

   B. Minimize Memory

   C. Make Browser Broadcasts To LAN Manager 2.x Clients

   D. Maximize Throughput For Network Applications

5. To configure failover with the Windows NT Load Balancing Service, what should you do?

   A. Install Virtual Load Balancing Adapters.

   B. Do not add any port rules.

   C. Install Additional Network Cards.

   D. Add additional port rules.

6. Clients are receiving a "Server Too Busy" error when they try to access your Web site. What is the name of the registry setting that allows you to tune for increased performance? And where is it located? (Choose all that apply.)

   A. RequestQueueTotal

   B. RequestQueueMax

   C. HKLM\SYSTEM\Software\Services\W3SVC\ASP\Parameters

   D. HKLM\SYSTEM\CurrentControlSet\Services\W3SVC\ASP\Parameters

7. If you want to load-balance traffic on your Web server, what ports must you open? (Choose all that apply.)

   A. 80

   B. 21

   C. 442

   D. 443

8. What should your affinity setting be for TFTP service using the WLBS?

   A. Port 139

   B. Port 25

   C. Port 69

   D. Port 21

9. What services does the WLBS support? (Choose all that apply.)

   A. SQL Server

   B. VPN

   C. IIS 4.0 servers

   D. Exchange 5.5

10. How many users does each WCAT client generate on a server when it is run?

    A. 50

    B. 100

    C. 200

    D. 500

Configuring and Troubleshooting Remote Access Service and Routing and Remote Access Service

11. If you receive the error message "A password is required. Please enter a password" when using the Internet Authentication Service, what should you do?

    A. Reboot the service.

    B. Reset the NT user password.

    C. Start and restart the IAS service.

    D. Check that the shared secret and client passwords match.

12. What must be loaded and configured correctly for the Remote Access Service to install? (Choose all that apply.)

    A. The modem

    B. Windows NT SP6a

    C. Windows NT SP4

    D. Windows NT SP3

13. What are the protocols supported in Routing and Remote Access? (Choose all that apply.)

    A. BGP

    B. RIP

    C. OSPF

    D. NetBEUI

14. Your RAS clients are not able to browse the server. You have checked their configuration and they have IPX/SPX installed. What could be the problem?

   A. Install TCP/IP on the client machine

   B. Install NetBEUI on the client machine

   C. Change the bindings on the Server adapter

   D. Change the bindings on the client adapter

15. What are the minimum requirements for installing Internet Authentication Service? (Choose all that apply.)

   A. Windows NT SP3 or higher

   B. 32MB of RAM

   C. 37MB of total available hard disk space

   D. The IAS server is a member of, or in a trust relationship with, the Windows NT domain that is authenticating the dial-in for clients.

16. You need to reinstall the Internet Authentication Service because you are reinstalling Windows NT on the server. What file should you back up first?

   A. _Adminias.mdb

   B. _Adminras.mdb

   C. _Adminis.mdb

   D. _Adminrras.mdb

17. What should you use after you install the VPN adapter on a Windows 98 client machine to connect to a VPN server?

   A. Dial-up Networking

   B. The modem

   C. TCP/IP

   D. NetBEUI

18. What does the acronym RADIUS stand for?

   A. Remote Authentication Dial Up Server

   B. Remote Authentication Dial-In User Server

   C. Remote Authorization Dial-In User Server

   D. Remote Authorization Dial-Up User Server

19. What is a shared secret?

   A. A folder will Full Access to users

   B. A password

   C. An Administrator password

   D. A client password

20. What is the default setting for RAS regarding port usage?

   A. Dial Out Only

   B. Receive Calls Only

   C. Dial Out And Receive Calls

   D. There is no default.

LAB QUESTION

You are an Administrator for a small company. You need to set up a demand dial connection on your WAN for two separate cities: San Francisco and Miami. Due to budget cuts, it should be done without purchasing any additional hardware. How can this task be completed with the Routing and Remote Access Services? Both cities are running Windows NT 4.0 with Service Pack 6a. The Administrators in both cities have modems and RAS already installed on their servers. Both Administrators will install RRAS, which has already been downloaded from the Microsoft site. As RRAS is being set up, the Administrators choose the demand dial routing option. Both Administrators will now use the RRAS Admin program to configure the Dial On Demand settings. This can be done by clicking Start | Programs | Administrative Tools | Router and Remote Admin. Miami and San Francisco will perform the rest of the steps that follow to complete the connection between the two cities.

SELF TEST ANSWERS

Configuring, Managing, and Troubleshooting Microsoft IIS on the Server

1. ☑ **A, B,** and **C** are correct because there are three ways you can host multiple Web sites on your IIS 4.0 server.
   ☒ **D** is incorrect because this would not be a valid solution for this scenario.

2. ☑ **C.** To tune a virtual directory you need to select it from under the Web site. The Enable Bandwidth Throttling option needs to be chosen for this scenario.
   ☒ **A** is incorrect because the question asked to have the virtual directory throttled down, not the entire site. **B** is incorrect because to enable bandwidth throttling you would not tune the Web site based on the number of hits that are expected. **D** is incorrect because you do not need to tune the Web site, and you would not tune the Web site based on the number of hits expected.

3. ☑ **A** and **D. D,** Typical, is the correct answer because installing IIS 4.0 using this configuration installs components that will run ASP as well as FTP. **A** is also correct because by selecting the custom option you can choose to install the services that run ASP and FTP.
   ☒ **C** is incorrect because simply installing the minimum requirements will not install the FTP service. **B** is incorrect because Maximum is not a setup option when installing IIS 4.0.

4. ☑ **A** is correct because the Maximize Throughput For File Sharing setting will allocate the maximum amount of memory for file sharing applications.
   ☒ **B** is incorrect because Minimize Memory should be selected when you only have ten or fewer connections and you need to minimize the memory used. **C** is incorrect because the Make Browser Broadcasts To LAN Manager 2.x Clients option should only be used when you have LAN Manager 2.x clients on your network and you need that server to browse share resources located on this server. **D** is incorrect because Maximize Throughput For Network Applications should be used to tune memory performance.

5. ☑ **B** is the correct answer. To configure WLBS for failover, do not add any port rules. Whichever host was set in the WLBS setup screen with the highest priority will handle all incoming requests. If a node fails, then the node with the second highest priority will take over and handle all connections.
   ☒ **A** is incorrect because this is not the correct way to configure WLBS for failover. **C** is incorrect because this is not the way to configure WLBS for failover. **D** is incorrect because you would not add any additional port rules to configure WLBS with failover.

6. ☑ **B** and **D** are the correct answers. The RequestQueueMax is set to 500 by default. If a large number of clients (500) try to access the ASP at the same time, they will receive the "Server Too Busy" error. This can be changed at the registry setting located at HKLM\SYSTEM\ CurrentControlSet\Services\W3SVC\ASP\Parameters. Set this to a larger size.

   ☒ **A** is incorrect because the RequestQueueTotal setting does not exist in the registry, and **C** is incorrect because this setting does not exist in the registry either.

7. ☑ **A** and **D** are correct. To enable load balancing on your Web traffic, you need to configure port rules on port 80 and port 443. Configure one port rule on all cluster hosts for a port range of 80 to 80, and select both for protocols (TCP and UDP). Click to select Multiple Hosts. Affinity should be set to None, unless the Web server maintains client state in its memory, in which case Affinity must be set to either Single or Class C. If you want to load-balance HTTP over SSL (encrypted Web traffic), you need to configure a rule for this type of traffic; usually, the port is 443. Use the following steps: set up a rule for a port range of 443 to 443, both TCP and UDP. Affinity should be set to either Single or Class C to ensure that the server that has the SSL session established always handles the client connections.

   ☒ **B** is incorrect because port 21 is used for FTP. **C** is incorrect because it is not used for any HTTP services.

8. ☑ **C** is the correct answer. Create a port rule covering port 69 for the TFTP application in WLBS.

   ☒ **A** is incorrect because port 139 is used for NetBIOS over TCP/IP. **B** is incorrect for this scenario because it is not the default setting for TFTP, and is used for SMTP. **D** is incorrect because port 21 is for FTP services.

9. ☑ **B** and **C** are the correct answers. The WLBS allows clustering of up to 32 nodes. The WLBS should be used when you need high availability and scalability of TCP/IP services, such as Web servers, streaming media, VPN, and proxy services.

   ☒ **A** and **D** are incorrect because the Microsoft Cluster Service is a solution made for the availability of services such as SQL Server, Microsoft Exchange Server, and file and print services. Microsoft Cluster Service (MSCS) allows clustering of 2 nodes.

10. ☑ **C** is the correct answer. A load of approximately 200 users on the Web server is what the WCAT tool generates. To configure WCAT, you would need to place the WCAT controller on a separate server. When the test is run on the Web server, WCAT creates one or two files. They're named either .prf for performance results, or .log for a log file. You can execute WCAT with a -p switch to get performance results. WCAT creates the .prf files by running Perfmon on the counters you selected for testing.

   ☒ **A, B,** and **D** are incorrect because the load generation is 200 users.

Configuring and Troubleshooting Remote Access Service and Routing and Remote Access Service

11. ☑ **D** is the correct answer. The shared secret and client passwords must match, and they are case-sensitive.

☒ **A, B,** and **C** are incorrect because following these steps would have no bearing on this particular error message.

12. ☑ **A** and **C** are the correct answers. A modem must be installed and working properly, as well as Windows NT SP4.

☒ **B,** SP6a, is not a minimum requirement for installation of RAS, although it would be a preferable choice. **D,** SP3, does not meet the minimum requirement for installation of Remote Access Services on Windows NT 4.0.

13. ☑ **A, B,** and **C** are protocols RRAS supports. BGP is a third-party protocol called Border Gateway Patrol. RIP and OSPF, on the other hand, are IP-based protocols included with RRAS.

☒ **D** is incorrect because NetBEUI is not a routable protocol.

14. ☑ **B.** Install NetBEUI on the client machine. This is by design.

☒ **A** is incorrect because you can browse the network by having IPX/SPX installed and not TCP/IP, as long as you have NetBEUI installed as well. **C** and **D** are incorrect, because this would not prevent your RAS clients from browsing the server.

15. ☑ **A, B, C,** and **D** are all correct. All are minimum requirements for installing the Internet Authentication Service. You must have at least a Pentium processor on your server as well.

☒ There are no incorrect answer choices.

16. ☑ **C** is the correct answer. Before you reinstall the Internet Authentication Service, back up the _Adminis.mdb file. This will save you the tedious chore of having to reconfigure the Internet Authentication Service on the server.

☒ **A, B,** and **D** are incorrect because these files do not exist.

17. ☑ **A** is the correct answer. Dial-up networking should be used to configure the Windows 98 client to use a VPN connection.

☒ **B, C,** and **D** are all incorrect for this scenario. A modem is not necessarily used for VPN connections. TCP/IP is already installed on the client machine the last item you need to use is the Dial up networking software to create a connection.

18. ☑ **B** is the correct answer. RADIUS stands for Remote Authentication Dial-In User Server. RADIUS authentication identifies a remote user by checking the clients' credentials against a client account database. RADIUS authorization can be configured to restrict authenticated clients access to predetermined network services for added network security. The accounting method that RADIUS uses records the amount of network resources that a remote client uses during a connected session.

☒   A, C, and D are incorrect because these are not valid names for RADIUS.

19.   ☑   B. A shared secret is a text string shared between an IAS RADIUS server that either clients or other servers are connected to. These servers include the Network access server (NAS), other RADIUS servers and proxies, and the authentication providers, which are often the corporate clients themselves.

☒   A, C, and D are not the definitions of a shared secret.

20.   ☑   B is the correct answer. By default, RAS is set to Receive Calls Only. Unless you intend to use RAS for other types of services, leave it set to the default: Receive Calls Only.

☒   A, C, and D are not the default settings for RAS ports. Dial Out Only is used when it's necessary to configure the server to dial out and not receive any incoming connections. The Dial Out And Receive Calls option is used for the server to dial out and receive calls. D is incorrect because the default setting is Receive Calls Only.

LAB ANSWER

To make a connection from San Francisco to Miami, and Miami to San Francisco:

■   On Router 1, add an Interface with the name Miami.

■   On Router 2, add an Interface with the name San Francisco.

■   On Router 1, set the credentials to be used when dialing into Router 2.

■   On Router 2, create a user and give the username and password credentials as set in the Credentials dialog box on Router 1.

■   On Router 2, set the credentials to be used when dialing to Router 1.

■   On Router 1, create a new user and give the username and password credentials as set in the Credentials dialog box on Router 2. (See Figure 10-22.)

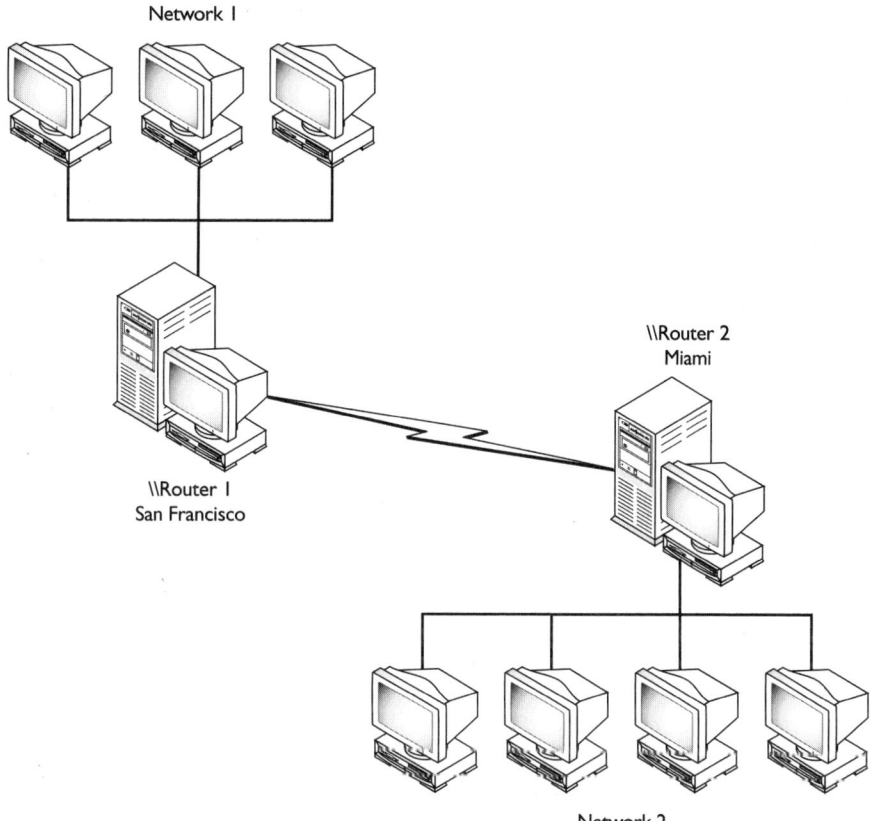

FIGURE 10-22

Lab Answer

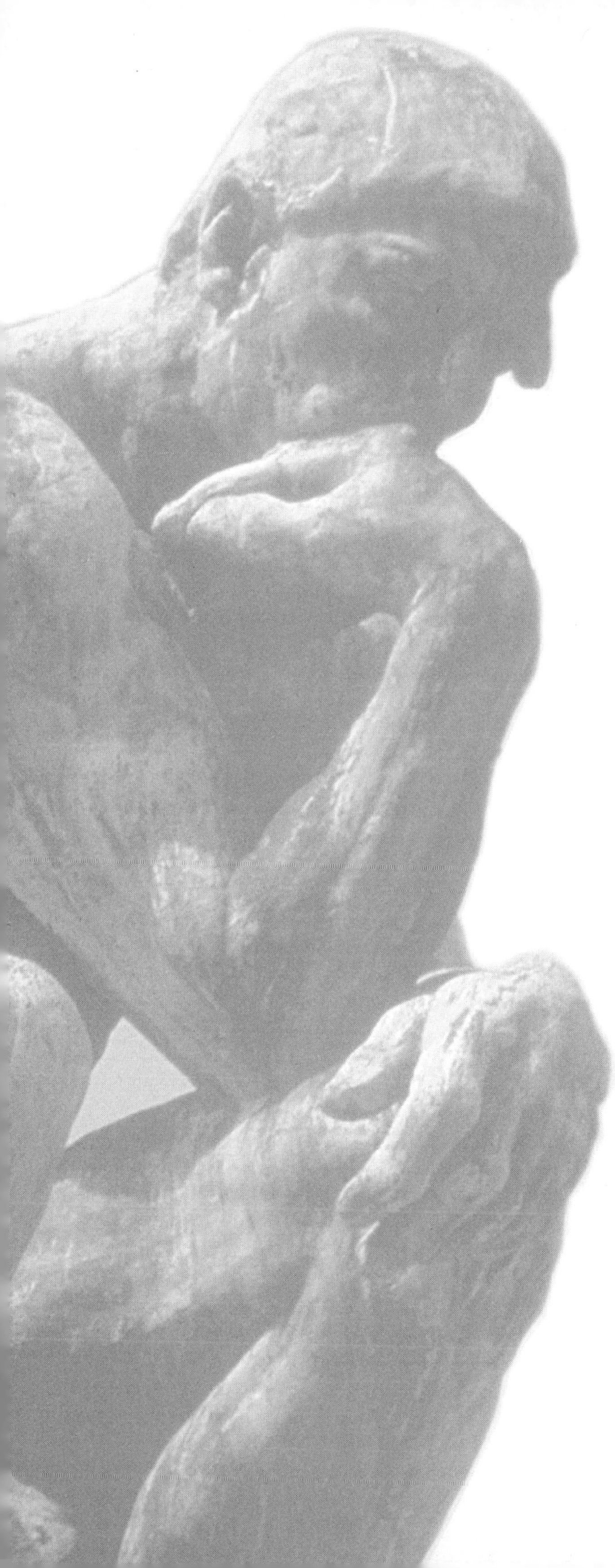

MCSE

MICROSOFT CERTIFIED SYSTEMS ENGINEER

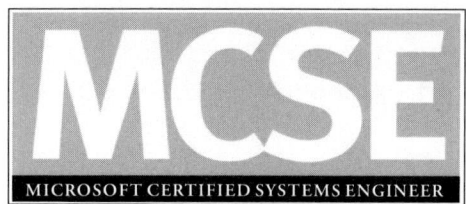

A

About the CD

This CD-ROM contains the CertTrainer software. CertTrainer comes complete with ExamSim, Skill Assessment tests, CertCam movie clips, the e-book (electronic version of the book), and Drive Time. CertTrainer is easy to install on any Windows 98/NT/2000 computer and must be installed to access these features. You may, however, browse the e-book directly from the CD without installation.

Installing CertTrainer

If your computer CD-ROM drive is configured to autorun, the CD-ROM will automatically start up upon inserting the disk. From the opening screen you may either browse the e-book or install CertTrainer by pressing the *Install Now* button. This will begin the installation process and create a program group named "CertTrainer." To run CertTrainer use START | PROGRAMS | CERTTRAINER.

System Requirements

CertTrainer requires Windows 98 or higher and Internet Explorer 4.0 or above and 600MB of hard disk space for full installation.

CertTrainer

CertTrainer provides a complete review of each exam objective, organized by chapter. You should read each objective summary and make certain that you understand it before proceeding to the SkillAssessor. If you still need more practice on the concepts of any objective, use the "In Depth" button to link to the corresponding section from the Study Guide or use the CertCam button to view a short .AVI clip illustrating various exercises from within the chapter.

Once you have completed the review(s) and feel comfortable with the material, launch the SkillAssessor quiz to test your grasp of each objective. Once you complete the quiz, you will be presented with your score for that chapter.

ExamSim

As its name implies, ExamSim provides you with a simulation of the actual exam. The number of questions, the type of questions, and the time allowed are intended to be an accurate representation of the exam environment. You will see the following screen when you are ready to begin ExamSim:

When you launch ExamSim, a digital clock display will appear in the upper left-hand corner of your screen. The clock will continue to count down to zero unless you choose to end the exam before the time expires.

There are three types of questions on the exam:

■ **Multiple Choice** These questions have a single correct answer that you indicate by selecting the appropriate check box.

■ **Multiple-Multiple Choice** These questions require more than one correct answer. Indicate each correct answer by selecting the appropriate check boxes.

■ **Simulations** These questions simulate actual Windows 2000 menus and dialog boxes. After reading the question, you are required to select the appropriate settings to most accurately meet the objectives for that question.

Saving Scores as Cookies

Your ExamSim score is stored as a browser cookie. If you've configured your browser to accept cookies, your score will be stored in a file named *History*. If your browser is not configured to accept cookies, you cannot permanently save your scores. If you delete this History cookie, the scores will be deleted permanently.

E-Book

The entire contents of the Study Guide are provided in HTML form, as shown in the following screen. Although the files are optimized for Internet Explorer, they can also be viewed with other browsers including Netscape.

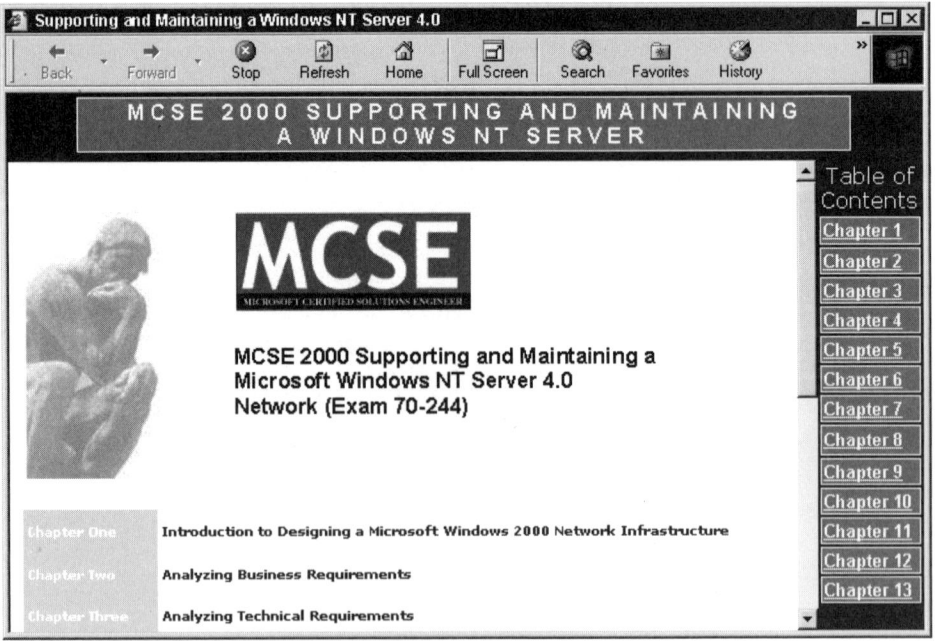

CertCam

CertCam .AVI clips provide detailed examples of key certification objectives. These clips walk you step-by-step through various system configuration. You can access the clips directly from the CertCam table of contents (shown in the following screen) or through the CertTrainer objectives.

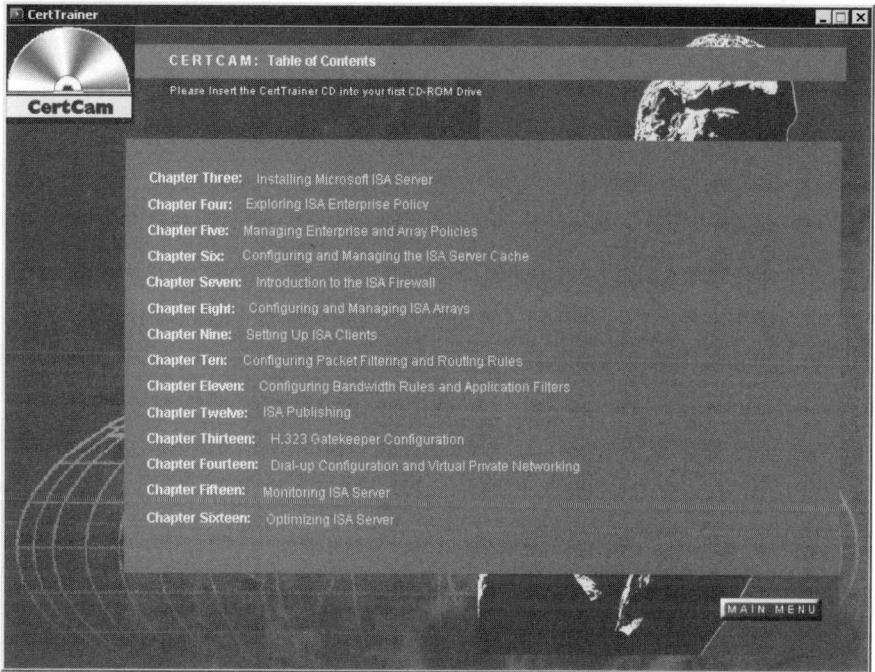

The CertCam .AVI clips are recorded and produced using TechSmith's Camtasia Producer. Since .AVI clips can be very large, ExamSim uses TechSmith's special AVI Codec to compress the clips. The file named **tsccvid.dll** is copied to your Windows\ System folder when you install CertTrainer. If the .AVI clip runs with audio but no video, you may need to reinstall the file from the CD-ROM. Browse to the "bin" folder, and run TSCC.EXE.

DriveTime

DriveTime audio tracks will automatically play when you insert the CD-ROM into a standard CD-ROM player, such as the one in you car or stereo. There is one track for each chapter. These tracks provide you with certification summaries for each chapter and are the perfect way to study while commuting.

Help

A help file is provided through a help button on the main CertTrainer screen in the lower right-hand corner.

Upgrading

A button is provided on the main ExamSim screen for upgrades. This button will take you to www.syngress.com where you can download any available upgrades.

MCSE
MICROSOFT CERTIFIED SYSTEMS ENGINEER

B

About the Web Site

A t Access.Globalknowledge, the premier online information source for IT professionals (http://access.globalknowledge.com), you'll enter a Global Knowledge information portal designed to inform, educate, and update visitors on issues regarding IT and IT education.

Get *What* You Want *When* You Want It

At the Access.Globalknowledge site, you can:

- Choose personalized technology articles related to your interests. Access a news article, a review, or a tutorial, customized to what you want to see, regularly throughout the week.

- Continue your education, in between Global courses, by taking advantage of chat sessions with other users or instructors. Get the tips, tricks, and advice that you need today!

- Make your point in the Access.Globalknowledge community by participating in threaded discussion groups related to technologies and certification.

- Get instant course information at your fingertips. Customized course calendars show you the courses you want, and when and where you want them.

- Obtain the resources you need with online tools, trivia, skills assessment, and more!

All this and more is available now on the Web at http://access.globalknowledge.com. Visit today!

Glossary

Access Control List (ACL)   The part of a security descriptor that allows or disallows access to the object based on permissions the owner of the object has set.

Access token (or security token)   An object that uniquely identifies the user who has logged on to the network.

Account lockout   A security feature that locks a user account if the number of failed logon attempts exceeds those specified in the account lockout policy. Locked accounts cannot log on to the network.

Account policy   The account policy controls the way passwords work on all user accounts in a domain or on an individual computer. The policy defines minimum length of password, frequency of password change, and reuse of old passwords.

Address Resolution Protocol (ARP)   A protocol that maps IP addresses dynamically to the actual addresses on a LAN.

Administrator privilege   One of three privilege levels you can assign to a Windows NT user account. Guest and User are the other two privilege levels available.

Alert View   Alert View is used to monitor counters based on a threshold value rather than showing a continuous display of the value of the counter.

ARP   *See* Address Resolution Protocol.

Array   *See* Redundant Array of Inexpensive Disks.

Array controller   An array controller is an interface card that connects to hard disks using a SCSI cable and stores and maintains the configuration information on the logical disk that is created.

Auditing   Auditing tracks the activities of users by recording selected events in the security log.

Audit policy   The audit policy defines the types of security events that will be logged for servers of a domain, or for an individual computer.

Authentication   The process of validating the identity of a user for the purpose of accessing network resources.

Automatic Private IP Addressing (APIPA)   A self-allocation process wherein a Windows 2000 client, which has been configured to obtain an IP address automatically and does not get a response from a DHCP server, allocates itself an address.

Backup browser   The backup browser does not collect its own information; instead, it receives the browse list from the master browser and services requests from clients for browsing information. A domain controller, if not a master browser, is always a backup browser. There is one backup browser for every 32 computers on a subnet.

Backup Domain Controller (BDC)   In a Windows NT Server domain, a server that receives a copy of the domain's directory database. The database is synchronized periodically and BDCs can authenticate users during the logon process.

Backup types   The Windows NT Backup program can create backups in the following formats: copy, daily, differential, incremental, and normal.

Basic Input/Output System (BIOS)   The BIOS is a small chip inside the computer responsible for informing the processor(s) which devices are present in the system and how to communicate with those devices.

BIOS   *See* Basic Input/Output System *and* NetBEUI.

Boot partition   The volume that contains the Windows NT operating system and supporting files. The boot partition can be the same as the system partition (but does not have to be the same).

Bottleneck   A condition that limits one part of the system from performing optimally.

Broadcast packets   Broadcast packets can be employed to see if a computer on the local subnet is using a particular NetBIOS name. A computer sends out a name query broadcast packet containing the NetBIOS name for which it wants an IP address. If a computer using the queried name receives the packet, it replies with a name query response.

Built-in groups   Default groups provided with Windows NT Server that have been granted a set of commonly used rights and capabilities for a particular group of users.

Cache memory   Memory that stores frequently accessed random access memory (RAM) locations and the addresses of where this data is stored.

Central Processing Unit (CPU)   A CPU is a chip with a number of transistors and is used to move and calculate data within the personal computer (PC).

Chart View   Chart View shows counter data as a graph that is updated on a regular basis.

Component Object Model (COM)   Microsoft's component architecture software. It creates a structure to aid in constructing routines to be retrieved and executed.

Computer Browser   Maintains a current list of computers and provides the list to applications when requested.

Copy backup   Copies all selected files, but does not mark files as having been backed up.

CPU   *See* Central Processing Unit.

Daily backup   Copies all selected files that have been modified the day of the backup.

Data backup   Data backups are copies of data written to a tape or other storage device. Using a backup program, files are archived to a medium that can be stored in another location.

Device driver   A program designed to enable a specific hardware device to communicate with the operating system.

Default gateway   The intermediate device on the network that has knowledge of other networks. Packets destined for remote networks are passed through the default gateway.

Default groups   Groups provided with Windows NT Server that have been granted a set of commonly used rights and capabilities for a particular group of users.

DDS   *See* Digital Data Storage.

DHCP   *See* Dynamic Host Configuration Protocol.

Diagnostic tools   Diagnostic tools are used to troubleshoot your computer and detect possible problems. Such tools may be included with the computer itself, available through the operating system installed on it, or added separately as utilities and software packages.

Differential backup   Copies those files created or changed since the last normal or incremental backup.

Digital audio tape (DAT)   The DAT drive was created by Sony and Philips for recording music in a digital format, but was found to be useful for recording data in backups. With this method, data is stored on 4 mm tapes. DAT is not as fast as DLT, and doesn't provide as large a storage capacity. However, it is less expensive than DLT, which makes DAT a popular method of tape backup.

Digital Data Storage (DDS)   The DDS format uses a process similar to that used in VCRs to store data on the DAT tape. It uses a helical scan, in which read/write heads spin diagonally across a DAT tape. Two read heads and two write heads are used. When data is written, the read heads verify that data has been written correctly to the tape. If it detects any errors, the data is rewritten.

Directory database   The database of security information containing user account names, passwords, and security settings. Also called the *Security Accounts Manager* (*SAM*).

Disk striping with parity   Disk striping (with parity), also known as RAID5, provides the performance of RAID0, but with fault tolerance. Disk striping consists of data being written in stripes across a volume that has been created from areas of free space. These areas are all the same size and spread over an array of 3 to 32 disks. The primary benefit of striping is that disk I/O is split between disks, improving performance, although improvements do not exceed the I/O capabilities of the disk controllers. Fault tolerance functionality is added to disk striping with the addition of parity information in one of the stripes. The parity stripe is the exclusive OR (XOR) of all the data values for the data stripes in the stripe. If no disks in the stripe set with parity have failed, the new parity for a write can be calculated without having to read the corresponding stripes from the other data disks.

Distributed file system (Dfs)   A network server component that allows files to span multiple file servers in order to better manage enterprise data and storage resources.

DNS   *See* Domain Name System.

DNS name servers   The servers containing information about a portion of the DNS database, providing name resolution across the Internet.

Domain   A collection of computers that share a common directory database.

Domain master browser   The domain master browser receives lists from every master browser in a network that consists of several subnets. The lists are used to produce a single list of all resources on the network. This single list is then copied back to the master browsers. There is only one domain master browser on a network.

Domain Name System (DNS)   The service that provides domain name resolution for TCP/IP hosts.

Duplexing   Of all the types of RAID, RAID1 (or mirroring) and RAID5 are the most often implemented. When configuring RAID1, two disks are installed, along with one or two controllers. When two controllers are used, it is called *duplexing*. Duplexing ensures fault tolerance not just with data, but also with the disk controller. With traditional mirroring, there is one disk controller. If the controller fails, the server is down until that component is replaced. Duplexing allows the use of a second controller.

Dynamic Host Configuration Protocol (DHCP)   A protocol used to automatically assign IP addresses to computers on a network.

Electronically erasable programmable read-only memory
Electronically erasable programmable read-only memory (EEPROM) is a programmable memory chip that can be erased by exposing it to an electrical charge.

Encryption   The process of making data indecipherable to protect it from unauthorized access and viewing.

Erasable programmable read-only memory   An erasable programmable read-only memory (EPROM) chip is one that can both be programmed and erased. To erase an EPROM, it must be exposed to ultraviolet light.

Ethernet   A networking protocol in which data is carried at rates of up to 10 megabits per second.

Event log   Most event logs are simply files of text written to the hard disk. Almost always, an event log is saved in the partition that is most easily available if the network operating system didn't boot. This is usually the system partition for the server. In the case of NetWare, you can find log information stored on the DOS partition.

Event Viewer   Tool provided in Windows NT that can be used to monitor, troubleshoot, and optimize the system. Essentially contains three logs available for viewing: system, security, and application. Event Viewer can also be used to view logs on other computers.

Extended Industry Standard Architecture   The Extended Industry Standard Architecture (EISA) bus is an updated version of the ISA bus, originally designed for use with the 80386, 80486, and Pentium processors. EISA buses, like PCI buses, are 32 bits wide and support multiprocessing.

Fast Ethernet   A LAN access method that runs at 100 Mbps. Ethernet runs at 10 Mbps, and Gigabit Ethernet runs at 1,000 Mbps.

Fault tolerance   Fault tolerance is the ability of a component, or an entire system, to continue normal operations even in the event of a hardware or software failure. Usually, fault tolerance is implemented through redundant components.

Thus, the disaster is prevented even though a failure has taken place. In Windows NT, fault tolerance is provided by the Ftdisk.sys driver and is implemented via mirror and stripe sets.

File allocation table (FAT)   A list maintained by some operating systems to track segments of the disk. Both FAT and NTFS are supported in Windows NT.

File level permissions   These can be assigned on an NTFS partition by anyone with Owner or Administrator access. By default, each file and folder has the group Everyone assigned the full control permission. When assigning file permissions, there are five levels to choose from: No Access, Read, Change, Full Control, and Special Access.

File Transfer Protocol (FTP)   Supports transferring files between local and remote computers. FTP is implemented as part of the Internet Information Service (IIS) in Windows NT.

Firewall   A system that protects the boundary between two or more networks, and keeps intruders out of private networks.

Full backup   Full backups are used to back up all directories and files on a volume, or all the volumes on a server. Depending on the amount of data being saved to a server, a full backup should be performed on a weekly or monthly basis. If tapes are filling quickly and important data is changing rapidly, then a full backup should be performed at least once a week. When a full backup is performed, the file is changed to indicate it has been backed up.

Gateway   Translates different protocols for heterogeneous networks. Translates transport protocols or data formats.

Gateway Services for NetWare (GSNW)   A service in Windows NT that allows Windows-based clients to access resources on a NetWare server through the gateway.

Global group   A group that can be used in its own domain and in trusting domains that contain only user accounts from its own domain. Global groups can be added to local groups.

Groups   Collections of users that have the same requirements for resource access, such as members of the Print Operators group or the Backup Operators group.

Guest privilege   One of three privilege levels you can assign to a Windows NT user account. Administrator and User are the other two levels available.

Hard page fault   A fault that occurs when a program needs data that is neither in its working set in the main memory nor anywhere else in physical memory, and yet data must be retrieved from the disk.

Hardware Compatibility List (HCL)   An HCL states what hardware at what firmware revision is compatible with the operating system (OS). For instance, the HCL lists what types of RAM is compatible. Hardware Compatibility Lists should be referenced to ensure your computer has hardware that will function correctly with any software that is installed.

HCL   *See* Hardware Compatibility List.

Host name   A host name is used to identify a computer to TCP/IP applications. It can be up to 255 characters long and can contain alphanumeric characters and hyphens. It can also be either a single word (or alias) or use the Domain Naming System; for example, www (an alias) or www.syngress.com (using DNS).

HOSTS   The HOSTS file is a text file containing name to IP address mappings and is used by TCP/IP applications.

Hotfix   Also called Quick Fix Engineering (QFE), hotfixes are fixes for mission-critical problems discovered within the operating system.

Hot Swap   Replacement of a device while the computer is still functional.

Hypertext Markup Language (HTML)   A markup language using ASCII text files with embedded codes denoting formatting and hypertext links.

Hypertext Transfer Protocol (HTTP)   The protocol by which clients and servers communicate on the World Wide Web (WWW). It is an application level protocol.

Incremental backup   Copies only those files created or changed since the last normal or incremental backup.

Industry Standard Architecture   The Industry Standard Architecture, or ISA, bus is found in virtually all computers. Based on older IBM XT computer architecture, today it is being replaced by the PCI bus. Many computer systems, however, still use the ISA bus for slower peripherals that do not require the fast throughput the PCI bus provides.

Input/Output (I/O) address   One type of computer resource is the I/O address. When the computer is started, the BIOS loads into RAM device-specific information about the existing devices, including their drivers and other rules of communication. Whenever the processor needs to communicate with a device in the computer, it first checks RAM for the entries pertaining to that device. Without an I/O address, components would appear nonexistent to the processor.

Internet Authentication Service (IAS)   The Internet Authentication Service (IAS) is an authentication and registration service integrated with Windows NT security when installed. IAS works by checking the user's identity (when they log in to the system) against a user account database.

Internet Control Message Protocol (ICMP)   A protocol employed to send error and control messages within TCP/IP.

Internet Information Server (IIS)   A file and application server that supports multiple Internet-related protocols including HTML and HTTP.

Internet Protocol (IP)   The messenger protocol that is part of the TCP/IP suite of protocols, responsible for addressing and sending TCP packets over the network.

Internet service provider (ISP)   A company or institution that provides Internet access to remote users via dial-up or leased lines.

Intranet   A TCP/IP network using Internet technology that is typically internal to a company and not connected directly to the Internet.

I/O address   *See* Input/Output address.

IP *See* Internet Protocol.

IP address An address used to identify each device on a network and to specify routing information. Each IP address on a network must be unique.

IPConfig An IP utility used to check the TCP/IP configuration of a computer.

IP router A component connected to two or more physical TCP/IP networks that can deliver IP packets between networks.

IPX/SPX A set of protocols used by Novell NetWare networks. IPX is a network-layer protocol and SPX is a transport-layer protocol.

LAN *See* Local area network.

Linux An Open Source implementation of Unix, which can run on many different hardware platforms. *See* Unix.

LMHOSTS The LMHOSTS file is a text file containing name to IP address mappings and is used by NetBIOS applications.

Local area network (LAN) A system using high-speed connections over high-performance cables to communicate among computers within a few miles of each other.

Local group For a Windows NT Server, a group that can be granted permissions only for the domain controllers in its own domain. Can contain user accounts and global groups from its own domain, and from trusted domains.

Local user profiles Profiles that are automatically created the first time a user logs on to a computer running Windows NT.

Logon script A file that runs automatically each time a user logs on. It can establish various environment settings for the logon session.

Log View Log View is used to save measured counters to a log file, which can be viewed at a later time.

Mandatory user profile   A profile downloaded to the user's desktop at each logon. It cannot be changed by the user.

Master boot record (MBR)   The MBR is an area on the hard disk. It contains the partition table for the disk and a small amount of executable code to begin the boot process.

Master browser   A master browser collects and maintains a list of available servers within its domain (or workgroup) and a list of other domains on the local subnet. It also distributes this browse list to backup browsers. Note, there is only one master browser per domain per subnet.

Member server   A computer running Windows NT Server that is not a PDC or BDC. Also called *a stand-alone server.*

Memory   Considered the primary storage area on a computer. *See also* Cache memory.

Micro Channel Architecture   Micro Channel Architecture (MCA) was designed by IBM to replace the older AT bus. It competed with the EISA bus, but was a proprietary architecture. For a variety of reasons, it never became popular in the industry and is now seen only in older machines.

Microsoft Management Console (MMC)   The MMC provides a standardized interface for using administrative tools and utilities. The management applications contained in an MMC are called Snap-ins, and custom MMCs hold the Snap-ins required to perform specific tasks. Custom consoles can be saved as files with the .msc file extension. The MMC was first introduced with NT Option Pack. Using the MMC leverages the familiarity you have with the other snap-ins available within MMC, such as SQL Server 7 and Internet Information Server 4. With the MMC, all your administrative tasks can be done in one place.

Mirroring   One of the more common ways to back up your data is to create a mirrored copy of the data on another disk. The mirroring system utilizes a code that duplicates everything written on one hard disk to another hard disk, making them identical. The best way to incorporate disk mirroring is at the hardware level with what is known as an array controller.

Mirror set   For the selected disk, an identical copy of the data is written to a second disk called a shadow disk, providing fault tolerance.

MMC   *See* Microsoft Management Console.

Modem   *See* Modulator/demodulator.

Modulator/demodulator (modem)   Modems are responsible for transmitting data to and from the computer.

Motherboard   The main component in computers, holding the processor as well as a host of other chips. These boards have many functions built into them, including parallel and serial ports, USB ports, memory, cache, power management, and BIOS (Basic Input/Output System).

Name resolution   Before the client computer can begin communicating with the destination computer, a name must be converted to an IP address. This process is called name resolution.

NetBEUI   A network protocol used in small networks. NetBEUI cannot be routed. *See* NetBIOS Extended User Interface.

NetBIOS   NetBIOS (Network Basic Input/Output System) is used to provide file and printer sharing between computers. It is a session protocol rather than a network protocol and therefore relies on the presence of network protocols such as TCP/IP or NWLink to function. Within Windows NT 4.0, NetBIOS is an essential component because many network services use it. However, in a network that consists entirely of Windows 2000 computers, NetBIOS is not required.

NetBIOS Extended User Interface (NetBEUI)   The transport layer for NetBIOS.

NETSTAT   A TCP/IP utility, NETSTAT provides information about each of a computer's active network connections, including the protocol, local address/port, foreign address and state, if applicable.

Network adapter *See* Network Interface Card.

Network administrator Person responsible for establishing and maintaining a network. Tasks include: software installation, assigning passwords, making backups, system security, and restores when the system goes down.

Network Fault Tolerance (NFT) NFT occurs when you install two NICs; one is the active NIC, while the other only becomes active upon failure of the first NIC.

Network Interface Card (NIC) A network adapter is also referred to as a Network Interface Card (NIC). You can configure multiple NICs in a single server to access the same local area network if the hardware and the network operating system support it.

Network Load Balancing (NLB) NLB occurs when you install two or more NICs, all of which are active on the same LAN, simultaneously sharing the network traffic load.

Network Monitor A tool, available with Windows NT Server and Windows 2000 Server, that analyzes network traffic and can determine why certain computers are unable to communicate. The versions that come with these operating systems are limited to only analyzing activity on the local network segment.

NFT *See* Network Fault Tolerance.

NIC *See* Network Interface Card.

NLB *See* Network Load Balancing.

Normal backup Copies all selected files and marks each as having been backed up.

NT File System (NTFS) A file system supported only in Windows NT that allows for greater management and control of file resources. All files are treated as objects with user-defined and system-defined attributes.

One-way Trust One domain "trusts" the domain controllers in a second domain to properly authenticate users to provide access to its resources. If the second domain does not "trust" the first domain, it does not allow users from the first domain to access its resources.

Open Systems Interconnection model (OSI)   Each layer of the TCP/IP model corresponds to one or more layers in the International Standards Organization (ISO) seven-layer OSI model. The OSI layers are Application, Presentation, Session, Transport, Network, Data Link, and Physical.

Owner   Every file and directory on an NTFS volume has an owner. By default, the owner is the one who creates the object and can control access through setting permissions.

Packet Internet Groper (PING)   *See* PING.

Page fault   A page fault occurs in the processor when a process refers to a virtual page in memory that is not in its working set in main memory.

Password Age (Maximum)   This sets the maximum amount of time a user can retain the same password without being forced to change it.

Password Age (Minimum)   This sets the minimum amount of time a user can utilize a password before they are able to change it. This is the result of a common problem wherein some users would change their password, then immediately change it back again—to their old password—making it seem as if they had never changed their password in the first place.

Password Length   The Minimum Password Length option allows you to set the minimum number of characters a password must contain. By setting this option, you can prevent users from using short passwords that will be easy to guess. This will make it harder for hackers to obtain the passwords of user accounts, and ensure simple passwords aren't being used on your network.

Password uniqueness   The requirement that when users change passwords, they use new, unique passwords for a period of time defined in the domain's policies.

Performance Monitor (PERFMON)   PERFMON is a tool used for monitoring performance issues on a Windows NT Server. It provides four methods of monitoring various components of NT: Report View, Chart View, Alert View, and Log View.

Peripheral Component Interconnect   The Peripheral Component Interconnect, or PCI, is a bus type found in most computers today. Though the PCI bus is a 64-bit bus, it is often implemented as a 32-bit bus, and runs at a clock speed of 33MHz or 66MHz. Being a fairly fast bus type, many peripheral controllers utilize the PCI bus for faster throughput. As a result, PCI has become increasingly popular, making it the *de facto* standard today.

PING (Packet Internet Groper)   A command used to verify connections to one or more remote hosts (computers).

Point-to-Point Protocol (PPP)   A standard for dial-up telephone connections of computers to the Internet.

Point-to-Point Tunneling Protocol (PPTP)   A secure networking technology that supports multiprotocol virtual private networks (VPNs).

Pop-up message   Pop-up messages are messages that will pop up on a user's screen. Such messages may appear on every workstation, or be directed to a specific user. If you can designate where the pop-up message will appear, you may have the ability to direct the message to a specific IP address or user account.

Potential browser   A potential browser is a computer that could be a master or backup browser, but is not currently fulfilling that role. Most computers can be potential browsers.

Primary Domain Controller (PDC)   In a Windows NT Server domain, a server that authenticates domain logons and maintains the directory database for a domain. This database is replicated to BDCs.

Print device   The device that produces printed output is known as a print device (e.g., a laser or inkjet printer) rather than a printer. Think of the print device as a physical object, or as the hardware.

Print driver   The print driver is used to convert a print job to the print commands specific to the selected print device. A print driver is needed for each print device installed on a computer.

Printer   The printer is the interface between the operating device and the actual device that does the printing. A printer may be regarded as a logical device. The reason for the distinction between a printer and a print device is that several printers (logical devices) may be associated with the same print device (hardware).

Printing pool   Two or more identical print devices associated with one printer.

Print server (or file and print server)   This is a server computer used to manage print jobs for printer devices. The print device will be connected directly to the print server using a serial or parallel port, or to the network.

Print spooler   A set of dynamic link libraries (DLLs) that receive, process, schedule, and distribute documents for printing.

Programmable read-only memory   A programmable read-only memory (PROM) chip can be programmed with particular data. It is similar in concept to a writeable CD-ROM, being that it is a blank formatted in a particular way. Once the blank is recorded (or programmed, in the case of PROM), it cannot be erased or rewritten. In other words, once the data is programmed onto a PROM chip, it is permanent.

Proxy server   Provides access to files from other servers by pulling them from either its local cache or from the remote server.

Public key cryptography   A method of securing data between servers.

QFE   *See* Hotfix.

Quick Fix Engineering   *See* Hotfix.

RAID   *See* Redundant Array of Inexpensive Disks.

RAID controller   A RAID controller handles the creation and regeneration of redundant information for the array.

Random access memory (RAM)   The memory of a computer that is used while running applications or working on system files. Random access means various files and memory portions can be accessed instantly and directly, instead of having to search for the data's location, as is the case with other media such as magnetic tapes, for example, which have to be wound to the spot where the data resides. If not saved to the disk before computer shutdown, all information in RAM will be lost.

Read-only memory   Read-only memory (ROM) typically resides on the motherboard and is used to execute instructions necessary to boot the computer.

Redundant Array of Inexpensive Disks (RAID)   A method of using disk drives in an array to provide fault tolerance and performance improvements. Windows NT supports three levels of RAID: 0, 1, and 5.

Remote Access Service (RAS)   A service that provides remote network access to file and print services, e-mail, scheduling, and other network-based tasks.

Remote troubleshooting   Remote troubleshooting refers to the ability to troubleshoot and resolve computer problems without having to sit at that computer. In many cases, one server on a network can be used to troubleshoot another server on the network. There are a number of services available for remote troubleshooting, such as Windows Remote Access Service (RAS) or third-party applications. These types of services provide the interface and tools for managing, configuring, and troubleshooting remote computers.

Report View   Used to display the current value of counter data as text in a report format.

Roaming user profile   A user profile that is enabled by an administrator when creating a path to a profile on a server. Whenever the user logs on, the path to the profile is established, allowing the user to have the same computing environment, regardless of the physical location of logon.

Routing and Remote Access Service (RRAS)   The Routing and Remote Access Service enables routing over IP and IPX networks by connecting local area or wide area networks. It connects LANs or WANs without the use of other hardware.

SCSI   *See* Small Computer System Interface.

Secure Sockets Layer (SSL)   A protocol used to provide secure data communications through data encryption and decryption. It utilizes public key cryptography and bulk data encryption.

Security Accounts Manager (SAM)   A directory database that stores user account names, passwords, and security settings.

Security identifier (SID)   A unique number that the OS uses to track users and objects.

Security policy   In Windows NT Server, security policies consist of Account, User Rights, Audit, and Trust Relationship policies. They are managed via User Manager For Domains.

Server Message Block (SMB)   A file-sharing protocol that allows access to files on remote computer systems.

Service pack   Industry-issued fix designed to correct unanticipated problems at the time of release, such as incompatibility with popular applications, prior to the next upgrade. Each service pack includes instructions explaining what the service pack fixes, and what previous service pack level is required.

Shadow disk   The second disk in a mirror set that contains an exact copy of data on the primary disk, providing fault tolerance.

Share permissions   Share level permissions are available on any machine running the server service by anyone in the Administrator or Server Operators group. These permissions control access to information over a network.

Simple Mail Transfer Protocol (SMTP)   Part of the TCP/IP suite of protocols that controls the exchange of e-mail.

Simple Network Management Protocol (SNMP)   A protocol used to get and set status information about computers (hosts) on a TCP/IP network.

Small Computer System Interface (SCSI)   SCSI is the most prevalent (and preferred) interface in servers. SCSI is superior to other interfaces because it manages its own power, freeing the CPU from that type of overhead. SCSI also has its own Basic Input/Output System (BIOS).

Smart cards   Yet another method of providing some security to your network, smart cards are small plastic cards that have a microchip and/or a memory module embedded in it, which can store a significant amount of information. The cards are generally inserted into a special reader that reads information on the card, although some readers can scan the cards from a distance. They come in both disposable and reprogrammable formats.

Snap-in   A snap-in is a module added to the MMC, allowing you to perform various functions through a central console program.

Software RAID   Software RAIDs are implemented in the OS and take a larger toll on OS performance. They usually do not allow for Hot Swap functionality, so, if a drive fails, the server must be taken offline to replace it.

Stripe set   A method of writing data across several physical disk drives to improve access times.

Stripe set with parity   A method of writing data across several physical disk drives using parity. Parity is an algorithm used to regenerate data if any of the other data is lost.

Striping   The striping of data is a way to spread the data across the disks. This can improve performance. To do striping properly, a minimum of three hard disks is needed. Three or more different hard disks all acting to get a piece of the data will make the Input/Output (I/O) faster. Striping also gives you the option of adding parity to the drive set. *See also* Disk striping with parity.

Subnet   A portion of a network that shares a network address with other parts of the network, but has a distinct subnet number.

Subsystem   Subsystems hold multiple disks, which can be configured as separate disk drives, or as a single RAID array, or some combination of these. *See also* Redundant Array of Inexpensive Disks.

Syskey utility   This security tool utilizes a system key to highly encrypt the information contained in the Security Accounts Manager (SAM) database.

System default profile   The user profile that is loaded when Windows NT is running but no user is logged on.

System Monitor   System Monitor allows you to monitor resource utilization and network throughput. It provides a visual representation of the counters being watched, and allows viewing of real-time and previously logged data about areas of its system and network.

System partition   The location of the hardware-specific files needed to load Windows NT.

System policy   A policy created using the System Policy Editor to control the user work environment.

Tape backup   Tape backups are the most common method of backing up data. With this method, magnetic tapes are used to store data sequentially. These tapes are similar to those used in micro-cassette recorders, which require you to fast-forward and reverse the tape to find what you want. This sequential access to archived data makes it slow to restore data, as the device must cue up the tape to where the data is located. However, the cost to purchase such tapes is minimal, with each tape costing a few dollars. This makes tapes a popular method of data recovery.

Task Manager   A tool provided in Windows NT to help monitor and optimize performance. It can be used to view applications, processes, and performance.

TCP/IP   *See* Transmission Control Protocol/Internet Protocol.

Telnet   A virtual terminal protocol that interfaces terminal devices with terminal-oriented processes.

Transmission Control Protocol/Internet Protocol (TCP/IP)   A suite of networking protocols that allow communication across interconnected networks.

Trust relationship   A link between two or more domains enabling users from one domain to access resources on another domain.

Two-way Trust   A relationship between two domains in which the users of each domain are allowed access to resources on the other domain.

Uninterruptible Power Supply (UPS)   A UPS is a large battery. In the event of a power failure, the UPS kicks in and supplies power to the server.

Universal Serial Bus (USB)   USB technology allows the user to add multiple external peripherals (e.g., printers, hard disks, modems, scanners, and so on) to a single port, without the conflicts associated with serial and parallel connections of the past.

Unix   Originally designed for minicomputers, then revised for use on mainframes and personal computers, Unix is a multiuser, multitask operating system compatible with several computer platforms.

Updates   One of the things necessary to do after installing a server is to update the drivers to the latest available from the manufacturer. By doing this, all the features of the hardware components will be available for use by the server.

User default profile   The user profile that is loaded by a server when a user's specific profile cannot be loaded.

User Manager For Domains   A Windows NT Server tool used to manage security for the domain, including user accounts, groups, and security policies.

User privilege   One of three privilege levels you can assign to a Windows NT user account. Administrator and Guest are the other two privilege levels available.

Video Electronics Standards Association   The Video Electronics Standards Association, or VESA, is a consortium of video adapter and monitor manufacturers that developed various standards for video in computer systems.

Virtual private network (VPN)   A virtual network created using the Point-to-Point Tunneling Protocol (PPTP) that provides for secure network connectivity from a remote location.

WAN   *See* Wide area network.

Wide area network (WAN)   A network using high-speed long-distance common-carrier circuits or satellites to cover a large geographic area.

Windows Internet Name Service (WINS)   A name resolution service that translates Windows computer names to IP addresses. A WINS server manages these services.

Windows Load Balancing Service   In Microsoft's Windows Load Balancing Service (WLBS), two or more servers work together to service the network traffic from the Internet. It is now called Network Load Balancing (NLB) by Microsoft.

WINS   *See* Windows Internet Name Service.

WLBS   *See* Windows Load Balancing Service.

INDEX

L

Q

T

U

Z

INTERNATIONAL CONTACT INFORMATION

AUSTRALIA
McGraw-Hill Book Company Australia Pty. Ltd.
TEL +61-2-9417-9899
FAX +61-2-9417-5687
http://www.mcgraw-hill.com.au
books-it_sydney@mcgraw-hill.com

CANADA
McGraw-Hill Ryerson Ltd.
TEL +905-430-5000
FAX +905-430-5020
http://www.mcgrawhill.ca

GREECE, MIDDLE EAST,
NORTHERN AFRICA
McGraw-Hill Hellas
TEL +30-1-656-0990-3-4
FAX +30-1-654-5525

MEXICO (Also serving Latin America)
McGraw-Hill Interamericana Editores S.A. de C.V.
TEL +525-117-1583
FAX +525-117-1589
http://www.mcgraw-hill.com.mx
fernando_castellanos@mcgraw-hill.com

SINGAPORE (Serving Asia)
McGraw-Hill Book Company
TEL +65-863-1580
FAX +65-862-3354
http://www.mcgraw-hill.com.sg
mghasia@mcgraw-hill.com

SOUTH AFRICA
McGraw-Hill South Africa
TEL +27-11-622-7512
FAX +27-11-622-9045
robyn_swanepoel@mcgraw-hill.com

UNITED KINGDOM & EUROPE
(Excluding Southern Europe)
McGraw-Hill Education Europe
TEL +44-1-628-502500
FAX +44-1-628-770224
http://www.mcgraw-hill.co.uk
computing_neurope@mcgraw-hill.com

ALL OTHER INQUIRIES Contact:
Osborne/McGraw-Hill
TEL +1-510-549-6600
FAX +1-510-883-7600
http://www.osborne.com
omg_international@mcgraw-hill.com

Custom Corporate Network Training

Train on Cutting Edge Technology
We can bring the best in skill-based training to your facility to create a real-world hands-on training experience. Global Knowledge has invested millions of dollars in network hardware and software to train our students on the same equipment they will work with on the job. Our relationships with vendors allow us to incorporate the latest equipment and platforms into your on-site labs.

Maximize Your Training Budget
Global Knowledge provides experienced instructors, comprehensive course materials, and all the networking equipment needed to deliver high quality training. You provide the students; we provide the knowledge.

Avoid Travel Expenses
On-site courses allow you to schedule technical training at your convenience, saving time, expense, and the opportunity cost of travel away from the workplace.

Discuss Confidential Topics
Private on-site training permits the open discussion of sensitive issues such as security, access, and network design. We can work with your existing network's proprietary files while demonstrating the latest technologies.

Customize Course Content
Global Knowledge can tailor your courses to include the technologies and the topics which have the greatest impact on your business. We can complement your internal training efforts or provide a total solution to your training needs.

Corporate Pass
The Corporate Pass Discount Program rewards our best network training customers with preferred pricing on public courses, discounts on multimedia training packages, and an array of career planning services.

Global Knowledge Training Lifecycle
Supporting the Dynamic and Specialized Training Requirements of Information Technology Professionals

- Define Profile
- Assess Skills
- Design Training
- Deliver Training
- Test Knowledge
- Update Profile
- Use New Skills

College Credit Recommendation Program
The American Council on Education's CREDIT program recommends 53 Global Knowledge courses for college credit. Now our network training can help you earn your college degree while you learn the technical skills needed for your job. When you attend an ACE-certified Global Knowledge course and pass the associated exam, you earn college credit recommendations for that course. Global Knowledge can establish a transcript record for you with ACE, which you can use to gain credit at a college or as a written record of your professional training that you can attach to your resume.

Registration Information

COURSE FEE: The fee covers course tuition, refreshments, and all course materials. Any parking expenses that may be incurred are not included. Payment or government training form must be received six business days prior to the course date. We will also accept Visa/ MasterCard and American Express. For non-U.S. credit card users, charges will be in U.S. funds and will be converted by your credit card company. Checks drawn on Canadian banks in Canadian funds are acceptable.

COURSE SCHEDULE: Registration is at 8:00 a.m. on the first day. The program begins at 8:30 a.m. and concludes at 4:30 p.m. each day.

CANCELLATION POLICY: Cancellation and full refund will be allowed if written cancellation is received in our office at least six business days prior to the course start date. Registrants who do not attend the course or do not cancel more than six business days in advance are responsible for the full registration fee; you may transfer to a later date provided the course fee has been paid in full. Substitutions may be made at any time. If Global Knowledge must cancel a course for any reason, liability is limited to the registration fee only.

GLOBAL KNOWLEDGE: Global Knowledge programs are developed and presented by industry professionals with "real-world" experience. Designed to help professionals meet today's interconnectivity and interoperability challenges, most of our programs feature hands-on labs that incorporate state-of-the-art communication components and equipment.

ON-SITE TEAM TRAINING: Bring Global Knowledge's powerful training programs to your company. At Global Knowledge, we will custom design courses to meet your specific network requirements. Call 1 (919) 461-8686 for more information.

YOUR GUARANTEE: Global Knowledge believes its courses offer the best possible training in this field. If during the first day you are not satisfied and wish to withdraw from the course, simply notify the instructor, return all course materials, and receive a 100% refund.

In the US:

CALL: 1 (888) 762-4442

FAX: 1 (919) 469-7070

VISIT OUR WEBSITE:

www.globalknowledge.com

MAIL CHECK AND THIS FORM TO:

Global Knowledge

Suite 200

114 Edinburgh South

P.O. Box 1187

Cary, NC 27512

In Canada:

CALL: 1 (800) 465-2226

FAX: 1 (613) 567-3899

VISIT OUR WEBSITE:

www.globalknowledge.com.ca

MAIL CHECK AND THIS FORM TO:

Global Knowledge

Suite 1601

393 University Ave.

Toronto, ON M5G 1E6

REGISTRATION INFORMATION:

Course title ——————————————————————————————

Course location —————————————————————————— Course date ——————————

Name/title ———————————————————————————— Company———————————

Name/title ———————————————————————————— Company———————————

Name/title ———————————————————————————— Company———————————

Address ————————————— Telephone ————————— Fax ————————————

City ————————————————— State/Province ————— Zip/Postal Code—————

Credit card ————————— Card # ———————————————— Expiration date —————————

Signature ———————————————————————————————

A COMPLETE STUDY PROGRAM BUILT UPON PROVEN INSTRUCTIONAL METHODS

Self-study features include:

Expert advice on how to take and pass the test:

"The exam tests your understanding of Windows NT Server 4.0 features as well as your understanding of how these features interact in a network environment."

Step-by-step Certification Exercises focus on the specific skills most likely to be on the exam. The **CertCam** icon guides you to the instructional video animation that demonstrates this skill set on CD-ROM.

Special warnings prepare you for tricky exam topics:

"You will likely get at least one question that requires that you discern the difference between the multi() and the scsi() syntax or that requires that you fully understand ARC path naming conventions. The most likely question will ask you the right ARC pathname given a set of criteria. Be sure to understand ARC path names both for the exam and for recovering from disk failures on the job".

MCSE **On The Job Notes** present important lessons that help you work more efficiently:

"Don't be tempted to remove the Manage Documents permission from Creator Owner. This permission is added by default when you create a printer. Creator Owner is a special system group that contains the user that created or owns a print job, and it is this permission that allows users to delete their own jobs. If you remove this permission, then users will not be able to delete their print jobs."

Two-Minute Drills at the end of every chapter quickly reinforce your knowledge and ensure better retention of key concepts:

"Maximum password age allows you to set the maximum number of days a user can retain the same password before changing it."

Scenario & Solution sections lay out problems and solutions in a quick-read format. For example:

Problem: User cannot connect to a printer using a Web browser.

Check that IIS is running on the print server.

More than 250 realistic practice questions with answers help prepare you for the real test.

You have recently taken responsibility for a Windows NT 4.0 server and have decided to measure its performance to provide a baseline for future comparisons. Which of the following would be the best way to do this?

A. Start Performance Monitor and leave it in Chart View. Add appropriate objects to be measured and allow Performance Monitor to run for a while and then take a screen dump of the Performance Monitor dialog box.

B. Start Performance Monitor and change to Log View. Add appropriate objects to be measured and allow Performance Monitor to run for a while, then save the log file.

C. Start Performance Monitor and change to Report View. Add appropriate objects to be measured and allow Performance Monitor to run for a while, then save the results to a file.

D. Start Performance Monitor and leave it in Chart View. Add appropriate objects to be measured and allow Performance Monitor to run for a while, then save the Performance Monitor settings.

☑ **B.** Performance Monitor has several views. The Log View is the best one to use for producing a baseline, because the log file can be opened in Chart View, counters can be added from the log file, and the way the data is presented can be changed as if it were live data.

☒ **A** *is incorrect because a screen dump wouldn't allow modifications to how the historical data was presented, and it may be difficult to check the precise value of a counter. There may also be too many counters to view each one clearly.* **C** *is incorrect because Report View only shows the last measured value of a counter and does not record historical data.* **D** *is incorrect because saving Performance Monitor settings only saves the counters that were being monitored, not the recorded values.*